DATE DUE

JUL 1 0 1995		

Demco

AFRICA: MOTHER OF WESTERN CIVILIZATION

Published 1988 by:
BLACK CLASSIC PRESS
P.O. BOX 13414
BALTIMORE, MD 21203

Published with the permission of the author. We are indebted to Malik Azeez of the Moorland-Spingarn Research Center, Howard University, for preparing the Select Bibliography, and Ms. Nonie Ford for preparing the Index for the B.C.P. edition of this work.

© 1971 Yosef ben-Jochannan
All rights reserved
Originally published by Alkebu-lan Books Associates

Library of Congress Catalog Card Number 88-72105
ISBN: 0-933-12125-3

Founded in 1978, Black Classic Press specializes in bringing to light obscure and significant works by and about people of African descent. If our books are not available in your area, ask your local bookseller to order them. Our current list of titles can be obtained by writing:

BLACK CLASSIC PRESS
c/o List
P.O. Box 13414
Baltimore, MD 21203

AFRICA

**MOTHER
OF
WESTERN
CIVILIZATION**

By Dr. Yosef A.A. ben-Jochannan

AFRICA: MOTHER OF "WESTERN CIVILIZATION"
───────────────────────────────────────

by: Yosef ben-Jochannan

Instructor of History: Marymount College, Tarrytown, N.Y.
Adj. Assoc. Prof. of History: Pace College, N.Y., N.Y.
Adj. Assoc. Prof. of History: Pace College, Westchester, N.Y.
Adj. Prof. of History: University of the City of New York,
    Manhattan Community College of New York.

Formerly
────────

Visiting Prof. of History: State University College at New Paltz,
    New Paltz, N.Y.
Chairman - African, African-American and African-Caribbean
    Studies Department, Harlem Preparatory School of New
    York, N.Y., N.Y.
Consultant in African History and Culture: African Diplomatic
    Missions Permanently Assigned to the United Nations
    Organization, N.Y., N.Y.
President: African Nationals In America, Inc., N.Y., N.Y.

AFRICAN-AMERICAN HERITAGE SERIES

<u>student's and researcher's edition</u>

ALKEBU-LAN BOOKS ASSOCIATES
New York, New York.

Copyright © by Yosef ben-Jochannan. All rights reserved. This book nor any part thereof may not be reprinted or copied without the express written permission of the author or his authorized representatives. All requests or communications should be directed to Alkebu-lan Books Assoc.

DEDICATED TO THE AFRICAN NATIONALIST "STREET-CORNER SPEAKERS" (deceased and surviving) WHO, IN THEIR OWN INIMITABLE SIMPLICITY, HAVE, FROM THE ADVENT OF THE LATE MARCUS MOZIAH GARVEY AND THE FOUNDING OF HIS UNIVERSAL NEGRO IMPROVEMENT ASSOCIATION (UNIA) IN 1918 C.E., KEPT THE FLAME OF AFRICA'S HISTORY AND CULTURE EVER PRESENT IN THE MIND OF AFRICAN PEOPLES EVERYWHERE IN THE "WESTERN HEMISPHERE."

OTHER WORKS BY THE AUTHOR

WE THE BLACK JEWS, Spain, 1949 (A Pamphlet in Spanish).

THE RAPE OF AFRICA AND THE CRISIS IN ANGOLA, Ghana, 1958.

AN AFRICAN NATIONALIST VIEW OF BLACK POWER, New York CORE
       MAGAZINE (Winter Issue), 1966.

AFRICA: THE LAND, THE PEOPLE, THE CULTURE, (co-authors,
           Yosef ben-Jochannan, Ph.D.; Kempton Webb,
           Ph.D.; Hugh Brooks, Ph.D.), W.H. Sadlier,
           Co., N.Y., N.Y., 1969.

SOUTHERN LANDS, (co-authors),W.H. Sadlier, Co. New York, N.Y., 1969.

SOUTHERN NEIGHBORS, (co-authors),W.H. Sadlier, Co. New York, N.Y.
       1969.

ARAB WORLD NEW AFRICA, (consultant to author),W.H. Sadlier, Co.,
       New York, N.Y., 1968.

BLACK MAN OF THE NILE, Alkebu-lan Books Associates, New York,
       N.Y., 1970.

AFRICAN ORIGINS OF THE MAJOR "WESTERN RELIGIONS," Alkebu-lan Books
       Associates, New York, N.Y., 1970.

African-American Heritage Series Publications
   (currently being edited for future release)
AFRICA AND HER EVER CHANGING MAP
ANOTHER ASPECT OF PAN-AFRICANISM
AFRICA (Alkebu-lan) IN HISTORY: A Chronology; 1,750,000 BCE –
       1966 CE.; Seven Volumes.

CONTENT

Prelude....vii-viii

THE NILE VALLEYS AND GREAT LAKES...ix

Preface...x-xvi

Introduction...xvii-xviii

Illustrations...xix-xxiv

The Dawn of Civilization; and, The Value of a Name...1-30

I) PreHistoric Homosapiens or Ancient African Man...31-56

II) Who Were/Are the Africans of Ancient Alkebu-lan (Africa)...57-167

III) Historic Quotations and Comments About, and of, the Africans...168-198

People Who Made Nile Valley History Yesterday and Today...199-227

Racism, Historians, and Ethiopians...228-252

The Return of Kimit, Zimbabwe, and Nubia to the Contient of Alkebu-lan (Africa)...253-291

Nubia - "Mother of Kimit" - Gateway to the North...292-303

IV) PreDynastic and Dynastic Kimit, Nubia, and Kush...304-313

The Egyptian Dynasties and Comments by High-Priest Manetho...314-347

Notes on Egyptology, etc...348-374

V) African Origin of "Greek Philosophy"...375-410

Arguments and Answers Relative to the African Origins of "Greek Philosophy"...411-452

Who Were the Indigenous Africans of Kimit (Egypt)...453-473

VI) Reflections on Ancient Kimit (Sais or Egypt)...474-498

VII) Chronology of Egyptian Rule Over Kush and Nubia...499-504

"Cleopatra's Needle": A Stolen African Treasure In America...505-521

VIII) The Rise and Fall of the Africans of Khart Haddas (Carthage)...522-548

The Black Man of Antiquity...549-566

What "Black Is Beautiful" Is Not Ready To Hear...567-583

Judaism, the "Black Jew" or "Israelite"...584-597

Roots of Biblical "anti-Negroism," etc.: A Cause for Black "anti-Semitism"...598-627

A Lecture on the Beginnings of the Christian Church in North and East Africa...628-655

The Africans Right to be Wrong is Sacred...656-677

Conclusion...676

Maps...679-714

Acknowledgements...715

Front Cover Design Description...716

Author's Statement on African (Black) History and Culture...717

Note: All titles prefixed with Roman numerals are Chapter; others are Lecture-Essays.

PRELUDE

When the vast majority of mankind in the "Western world" refer to a SLAVE it is the African-American or his African ancestor is meant. This image has been perpetuated by every branch of "Western" education and religion, both Christian (Roman Catholic and Protestant) and Jewish (all branches of Judaism); and presented in a manner that would suggest an origin dating back to a time of PURITY in ancient Europe amongst the Greeks and Romans; an origin that insinuate the beginning of WORLD CIVILIZATION, thus the terms:

"GREEK PHILOSOPHY" and "WESTERN CIVILIZATION."

On the otherhand "THE GREEKS WERE NOT THE ORIGINATORS OF GREEK PHILOSOPHY...," etc., as stated by professor George G.M. James in his major work, STOLEN LEGACY, of which will be detailed very much more later on in this volume. But, added to this declaration should be the fact that the Greeks and Romans did not create the "COLOR-BAR" that is so prevalent in every aspect of "Western" life today and for the past two-hundred (200) years. The closest to this was Aristotle's (one of the so-called "Greek Philosophers") reference to the "BARBARIANS" in his remarks justifying SLAVERY in Greece on the basis of the slaves "INNATE DIFFERENCE" (race) and "ABILITY" to others (Greeks). Yet, Aristotle was refering to the "BARBARIANS," of whom a large amount were in fact the antecedents of European-Americans today called such names as "CAUCASIAN" and "SEMITE," also "HAMITE." The "BARBARIANS" were of a special economic and social class, not of any particular COLOR or PHYSICAL TYPE (race).

With respect to all that have been stated so far, one finds Philemon (another Greek of ancient fame) saying in ANTIPHON, Frag. 44 in Diels, VORSOKR II, pp. 352-353:

> Even though a man is a slave, he is made of the same flesh. For no one was ever made a slave by nature...but chance has enslaved a man's body.

The above statement, or declaration, by Philemon was substantiated by the following writers and their works of a much more contemporary period (some of the present 20th century C.E.):James Jackson, AN INTRODUCTION TO AFRICAN HISTORY; T.J. Haarhoff, ANTHROPOLOGY AND THE CLASSICS; A. Zimmern, THE GREEK COMMONWEALTH; W.L. Westermann,SLAVERY AND THE ELEMENT OF FREEDOM (in: Quarterly Bulletin of the Polish Institute of Arts and Sciences I, 1943); Count C.F. Volney, RUINS OF EMPIRES; and Eva M. Sandford, MEDITERRANEAN WORLD. All of these works are mentioned in different instances throughout the Chapters and Lecture-Essays following in this volume.

This work's presentation, on the otherhand, will not take the position of Philemon above, in so far as slavery being but a "...CHANCE...." It will show that SLAVERY was in fact created as a result of a philosophic concept created by religious and secular bigots and racists for the purpose of their own enrichment at the expense of the vast majority of the "BARBARIANS" spoken of by Aristotle and other Greeks and Romans of his era; the same being true for those who wrote what is today called the HOLY TORAH, HOLY BIBLE, HOLY QU'RAN and many other names relating to the "GOD-GIVEN" myths in them directed at the enslavement of the mind for the benifit of the few at the expense of the many; this concept being the basis for the outgrowth of the COLOR-LINE and COLOR-BAR that found their origin in the dastardly SLAVE TRADE from Africa to the so-called "NEW WORLD" by the so-called "CAUCASIAN."

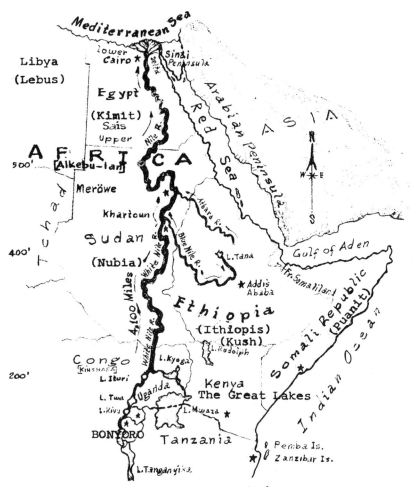

THE NILE VALLEYS & GREAT LAKES

This map shows the areas of Alkebu-lan (Africa) which Europeans and European-Americans for the last two-hundred (200) years have been trying to claim as the original home of the "CAUCASIANS" and "SEMITES"; a theory which is in total disagreement of their former claim of the so-called "GARDEN OF EDEN" around the Tigris and Euphrates rivers and their valleys. Note the location of the major nations of the Nile and Great Lakes where "CAUCASIANS, NEGROES, SEMITES, HAMITES," etc., allegedly were created independently of each other; thus the RACIST and RELIGIOUS BIGOTRY of today's "CAUCASIAN RACE" and "GOD'S CHOOSEN-PEOPLE" myth.

PREFACE

The following extract taken from Sir Harry H. Johnston, THE NILE QUEST: A RECORD OF THE EXPLORATION OF THE NILE AND ITS BASIN, Frederick A. Stokes Company, New York, 1903 (University Press -- John Wilson and Son - Cambridge, U.S.A.). explains fully the reason why this series of writings have been directed against racial prejudice and religious bigotry affecting the African peoples and their descendants adversely; at the same instance presenting a geo-political and socio-anthropological background of the history of the African continent and people. Sir Harry H. Johnston comments were written under the heading of PREFATORY NOTE. He wrote:

> When the author of this book was composing his recent work on the Uganda Protectorate, he was led through the history of its discovery into the general consideration of Nile exploration, since it was in the search for the Nile sources that the territories now forming the Uganda Protectorate were laid bare to the gaze of the civilized world. But as anything like a detailed review of the exploration of the Nile basin by the Caucasian race would have unduly extended a book dealing more particularly with Uganda, he gladly took advantage of the suggestion made by Dr. Scott Keltie (Editor of the series) that these studies should be applied to the present volume, which is one of a series on the history of great geographical discoveries.
>
> It is not for the author to say that this book on the Nile Quest will prove interesting; but he has striven to make it as accurate as possible, and he hopes it may be permanently useful as a faithful record of the names and achievements of those who solved the greatest geographical secret, after the discovery of America, which remained for the Caucasian's consideration.
>
> H.H. Johnston.

London, 1903

But, it is works such as that which you have just read, full to the point of refusal with their "Caucasian, civilized world", "exploration" and "discovery" myths, which cause the type of presentation in this volume.

The "Caucasian, Semitic" and "Hamitic" syndrome that skyrocketed into full bloom during the middle of the nineteenth century C.E. (A.D.) also fashioned this presentation of a socio-geopolitical nature of African history and High-Culture of the heritage of the African-American ("Black") Experience. Nevertheless previous writings, such as the following extract from the PREFACE of E. W. Bovill, THE GOLDEN TRADE OF THE MOORS, Oxford University Press, London, 1958, suffice me to recall that I do not stand alone in the presentation of my stance on this area of African history and High-Culture. Yet, I seem to stand apart from most who take the position that some peculiar phenomena called "academic discipline" must be maintained at the expense of direct confrontation and criticism of certain heretofore "established authorities" who have desecrated African history, solely on the basis that they are fellow historians - a sort of 'gentlemen's agreement." Bovill wrote:

> There seemed to me a need for a book showing how the Sahara enriched the Carthaginian and bewildered the Roman; how in the later times the great caravan routes, linking the sophisticated cities of the north with the great markets and modest seats of learning of the south, not only influenced the course of events in Barbary and even beyond but sometimes determined it; how, all down the centuries, Berbers and Arabs, Jews and Christians, never ceased to draw on the wealth and industry of the Sudanese.

If Bovill's understanding of African High-Culture and history was common among most European and European-American ("Caucasion") historians and European-style Christian missionaries, books like his and this would not have been necessary; but it is those of the type by Sir Harry H. Johnston that dominate the field of <u>African Studies</u> and <u>Black Studies</u> under the control of the same "CAUCASIANS" mentioned by him.

This work completes the three volumes combination -- <u>student, researcher and general reader</u> -- series on the indigenous peoples of the northern half of the continent of Alkebu-lan, otherwise called "<u>Africans</u>", from the Romans and Greeks "<u>Africa</u>;" following with the sub-groupings they labeled<u>"Egyptians, Ethiopians, Carthaginians, Libyans" and "Numidians</u>," etc.

This volume exceeds an extension of the documentary evidence presented in BLACK MAN OF THE NILE and AFRICAN ORIGINS OF THE MAJOR "WESTERN RELIGIONS" (both published in 1970) with respect to the oneness of the indigenous peoples of north, south, east, west and central Alkebu-lan. It's a critical citation and condemnation of the people and works that attempted to bismirch and destroy the image of the African-Americans as part of the true inheritors of Alkebu-lan's history and High-Culture — the "BLACK EXPERIENCE."

As such, I have purposefully traversed the once most holy grounds of the tabooed, and removed the cover of secrecy surrounding the myth of a "<u>Semitic, Hamitic</u>" or "<u>Caucasian</u>" east or north Africa; thereby, showing that behind these terms are the <u>seeds of racism and religious bigotry</u>, all of which had their origin as far back as the <u>Book Of Genesis</u> in the Hebrew (Jewish) <u>Torah</u> or Christian <u>Old Testament</u> of the Holy Bible (any version). For this, I am willing to pay the price that befalls anyone who dares to tread into the <u>Holy of Holies</u> of Judaeo-Christian Greek-Centric

Anglo-Saxon Indo-European Aryan mythological racism and religious bigotry.

Further examination of E.W. Bovill's THE GOLDEN TRADE OF THE MOORS (Second Edition, as well as the First Edition) reveals that he too sucumbed to the same type of racist interpretations of African history common among his fellow European historians and their European-American counterparts in the United States of America's institutions of learning - religious and secular. Thus, we find him saying on page 69 of the Second Edition:

> According to as-Sadi the kingdom of Ghana was of considerable age, having had twenty-two kings before the Hijra and as many after. <u>The ruling dynasty was white, but the people were black Mandingo.</u>

The underscored words have been so marked by me for emphasis on the major point of racism in the statement by Bovill; for in no way or fashion can anyone truthfully say that <u>"as-Sadi"</u> wrote about any "...<u>ruling dynasty was white</u>," with respect to any west African kingdom or empire during his lifetime (or before). This bit of racism was thrown in out of context as is the common practice by so-called "well-meaning" and "liberal" European and European-American historians and other educators who have set up themselves as the "authority" on everything people of African origin have ever done, whether bad or good; the same people who have pretended to deal with "Africa" and their so-called "Negroes" in their true historical perspective, nevertheless continually placing them in the position of "inferiority" to the position of their fellow Europeans and European-Americans - the so-called <u>"Caucasians"</u> or <u>"Semites,"</u> also <u>"Indo-European Aryans."</u>

Lastly: <u>Interpretations</u> are not the only area in which Africa's indigenous people and their descendants have been consistently maligned by "Western" writers and scholars; <u>translations</u> also present another most-precarious area in which such behaviour is evident. For example: The 15th through 17th century C.E. Portuguese and Spanish mariners and cartographers called an area of west Africa they met with hundreds of thousands of Africans:

"Tierra de los negros."

English-speaking Europeans, primarily Britishers and European-Americans of the United States of America, have translated this to read:

"NEGROLAND," and, "LAND OF THE NEGROES;"

both being completely and deliberately wrong. The word "<u>negro</u>" (which is never capitalized unless at the beginning of a sentence) in Spanish or Portuguese designates a COLOR, not a RACE. The correct literary translation to English is:

LAND OF THE BLACKS;

the word "<u>negro</u>" in Portuguese and Spanish having only one meaning -- BLACK -- and nothing else whatsoever. The other words the Portuguse and Spaniards used in describing these Africans were:

"AFRICANOS" and "MORROS;"

literally in English:

"AFRICANS" and "MOORS."

The last name, "MOORS," is adequately detailed further along in the general texts of this work in order to remove the confusion about whether -or -not "<u>the MOORS were in fact Negroes</u>;" all of which was created by the racist slant of history by so-called "modern" historians and educators.

One should readily understand why I have decided to write

my last three (3) works in the area of RACE RELATIONS and HISTOGRAPHY with a definite emphasis on AFRICAN GEO-POLITICAL ANTHROPOLOGY. There are, of course, many other reasons apparent in this volume, as in the other two volumes, all of which students, researchers and the general reading public will very easily recognize in the text, which I consider to be an honest and open presentation of a constructive revelation of the African and African-American (Caribbean Blacks included) heritage from their ancient ancestors' experiences and contributions to the World's High-Culture (civilization); most of which have been made to appear of "Caucasian" or "Semitic origin."

I have no apologies to make to anyone or institution for any of the citations or indictments and hypothesis in this work; for I have carefully examined each and everyone of them before they were finally printed. Nevertheless, I must say that <u>this work is not intended to purposefully attack any person or institution, religious or secular, vindictively; but, only to cite and correct the erroneous myths about the "inferiority" and "primitiveness" of the indigenous African peoples and their descendants who are today, in the late 20th century, still being maligned by the archaic terms</u> -- "NEGROES, BANTUS, PYGMIES, HOTTENTOTS, BUSHMEN" <u>and the likes of the same misnomers, none of which the Africans created</u>. In presenting my position, succinctly as it is, I am nevertheless aware of the fact that I have subjected myself to many kinds of attacks from those whose private sanctuary as "authority on Africa and "African peoples" I have invaded; particularly Europeans and European-Americans that dominate "AFRICAN STUDIES" and "BLACK STUDIES" departments in institutions of public and private education (religious and secular). This, of course, includes certain "Negro leaders of responsible integrated organizations" and even "Negro educators," who may find it necessary to do what they believe is their obligation to their benefactors and their particular alma mater's image or their own personal protection from appearing to have been totally mis-educated by their European-American paternal and maternal protectors. Yet such "Negro leaderships" outcry would be nothing new; they having so acted many times in the past, and particularly a choice selected few who became overtly involved during their attempt to stop the teaching of KiSwahili as an African language for credit in the City of New York public school system, but remained quiet as bedbugs when other area-studies languages are being taught to African-Americans by their European-American benefactors.

In order to make AFRICAN STUDIES and BLACK STUDIES truly relevant, I am certain, very strongly so, African and African-American (Caribbean peoples included) educators, historians, and other writers dealing with the BLACK EXPERIENCE, must first attack and ferret-out the root-cause of the cancer of "anti-Africanism" found in such abundance in the existing holdings in libraries, museums, and other literary depositories of the United States of America's private and public educational institutions. For herein, to me, lies the first cause for my last three volumes -- BLACK MAN OF THE NILE, AFRICAN ORIGINS OF THE MAJOR "WESTERN RELIGIONS," and this.

yosef ben-jochannan

May 1971

INTRODUCTION

The uniqueness of this book is not an accident. It was purposefully structured to create a balance between academic presentation of the data contained and a level of socio-political and histo-anthropological reading for the benefit of the student and the general reading public. The LECTURE-ESSAYS placed before and at the end of TEXTS are so arranged to allow everyone to have the benefit of being able to relate the historical findings of antiquity to present-day happenings that resulted therefrom.

In keeping with the tradition established in my former books (with respect to not being concerned with just who or what may be offended as long as TRUTH is maintained at all cost) I have cited many so-called "AUTHORITIES" on Africa and their works; pointing out all the time the RACISM and RELIGIOUS BIGOTRY they have applied to the detriment of the African peoples all over the world.

Every effort have been taken to assure everyone of the authenticity of the information. Where-ever possible I have included direct quotation from the person whom I have discussed. More often than not, I have tried to secure the original document or book, rather than use a revised version or a facsimile of the same.

References are constantly made with respect to the abundance of bibliographical materials available for back-checks by the reader. In this behalf, I have made certain that each and every major point I have raised is mentioned and the source identified in order that the reader may check the source for his or her self.

I have touched many sore spots with my analysis on SEMITISM; this I have done being of Hebrew religious background myself, also being very much aware of the possible consequences to follow.

The LECTURE-ESSAYS[1] are carefully arranged before and after certain Chapters. Each Chapter has its own documentary notes at the rear of the book; whereas, all Lecture-Essay notes are placed at the bottom of the page in which the references occur. Both methods allow for the free flowing of the reading matter without the usual interference in academically prepared works.

The AFRICAN ORIGINS OF WORLD CIVILIZATION being referred to in this work predates the Hebrews "ADAM AND EVE" and their "GARDEN OF EDEN" spoken of in the FIRST BOOK OF MOSES (Exodus). It shows the distinction between MYTH and HISTORICAL FACT; and heavily documents "Western"(European and European-American) civilization's earliest philosophical experiences from the beginning of its origin in Alkebu-lan (Africa). In so doing the entire basis for "Western philosophical thought", called erroneously "GREEK PHILOSOPHY," has been demonstrated to be in fact African and Asian heritage adopted by the Europeans; the same being true for so-called "JUDAEO-CHRISTIAN RELIGION" and "ISLAMIC CULTURE AND RELIGION" out of the philosophical teachings of the indigenous Africans of the African Great Lakes region and the Nile Valleys MYSTERIES SYSTEM. Even the origin of the so-called "CHRISTIAN CROSS" and the HEBREW MOGEN DAVID" (Star of David) are shown to have existed in central-east Africa thousands of years before the birth of JESUS CHRIST and KING DAVID of Palestine and/or Israel.

The student should use BLACK MAN OF THE NILE and AFRICAN ORIGINS OF THE MAJOR "WESTERN RELIGIONS" along with this work.

---

1. Lectures given over the last three years and condensed into written essays for use in classroom situations.

ILLUSTRATIONS

The Nile Valleys and Great Lakes Region...ix

The Face of African Peoples Everywhere...xx-xxiv
Prehistoric African and his art - 40,000± years ago...33
Key To Fossil Field Main Sites...34-35

Characteristics of Zinjanthropus Boisie...49

Reconstruction of Fossil-Man...50

Early Man of the Nile Valley (c1,750,000 BCE?)...51

43,000 - Year-Old Mine Discovered in Swaziland...56

Who Were/Are the Africans of Ancient Alkebu-lan (Africa)?...57

Map - Ethnography of Africa: Before 3000 BC, by Dr. Donald Wiedner...71

Map - PreHistoric Africa, by Dr. Albert Churchward, M.D....72

Map - PreHistoric Africans Migration In and Out of Africa...73

Le Grand Roy Monomotapa...177

The Comparative Works: King Solomon and Pharoah Amen-em-Ope...179
The Sphinx of Gizeh as seen in 1798 and 1970 C.E....195
The Nile Quest Preamble...199

Map of the Nile's Source, by D'Anville in 1772 C.E....215

Map of the Nile's Source, by Burton in 1864 C.E....216

Map of the Nile's Source, by Ptolemy V...217

African Peoples Along the Niles (Blue & White) and Great Lakes Region...218

"Conquering Lion of Judaeh" - Haile Selassie I...250

Queen of Punt (Puanit)...262

Inscriptions From the Tomb of Pharoah Huy...263

Dedication and Endowment Scene Inscription of the Queen of Napata...293

Ruins of the Temple of Tirhakah at Gebel Barkal...295

Chronology: Classification & Dates of Egyptian History...306-313

"The Oath" of Hippocrates...316

Imhotep and His Step Pyramid - "The God Of Medicine"...317

ILLUSTRATIONS (con'td.)

Sample Of Romiti (Egyptians) writing - HIEROGLYPH.....355

Diagram Of The Principle Of Opposites...384

Plagiarized Version Of Cleopatra VIII, Daugther Of Pharoah Ptolemy XIII...511

A Reconstruction of Carthage...547

(Map) Africa - 1868 C.E. Showing names of the continent...679

" Africa - 1729 C.E. (Showing area called "Negroland")...680

" Africa - 1878 C.E. (Showing Ethiopian Ocean)...681

" The Nile Valleys (Showing location of ancient nations and new political boundaries established in BERLIN ACT...682

" Origin of the Nile. The Major Lakes and Falls...683

" Archaeological Sites of Egypt: 3,100 BCE-30 BCE...684

" Africa: Egypt and the Beginning of World Trade - 1,400 BCE & Phoenician Trade Routes to Europe, Asia, Africa...685

" The Empire of Ethiopia and the Ethiopians in Europe - c700-650 BCE.; and The Egyptian Empire - 1400-1050 BCE...686

" Hyksos Invasion : Occupation of Egypt and Libya - 1700-1600 BCE...687

" The Empire of Carthage - 1000-150 BCE...688

" The Ethiopian Empire - 750-760 BCE; and, The Ethiopian Empire - 850 BCE...689

" Empire of the Moors - 750-1500 CE; The Roman and/or Byzantine Empire - 150-700 CE...690

" West Africa Empires: Ghana, Mali, Songhay - 100 BCE-1591 CE...691

" Photograph and Statement of the Author...717

IDENTIFY THE "NEGRO, SEMITE, CAUCASIAN" and/or "HAMITE" BELOW
(Use United States of America's Racial Standards)

1. Queen Charlotte Sophia, Consort of King George III of Great Britain, grandmother of Queen Victoria, great-great-grandmother of the present Queen of England, Elizabeth, descendant of Alessanro di Medici - Duke of Florence, Italy, a German Princess (from a portrait by Thomas Frye, 1719-1762 C.E.); 2 General of the Russian Army, Abraham Hannibal, Ethiopian by birth, great-grandfather of Alexandre Pushkin - father of Russian poets;3 Samuel Francis, father of Phoebe Francis who saved General George Washington (later America's first President) from being poisoned by his chief bodyguard - a British spy, Thomas Hickey; 4 Lidj Yasu - deposed Emperor of Ethiopia, East Africa, in a plot by the present Emperor, Haile Selassie I, and the British colonial and imperialist forces and other "Western" national groups; 5 Pedro I, Emperor of Brazil and King of Portugal, son of John VI (King of Portugal); 6 Don Juan de Pareja of Spain, an African (Moor) of Spanish royalty; 7 Father Louis Molina, Jesuit Priest and Roman Catholic Reformer of Castile, Spain (from a picture in Bibliotheque Nationale, Paris, France). P.S. No. 3 is the only "NEGRO."!!!

IDENTIFY THE "NEGRO, SEMITE, CAUCASIAN" and/or "HAMITE" BELOW
(Use United States of America's Racial Standards)

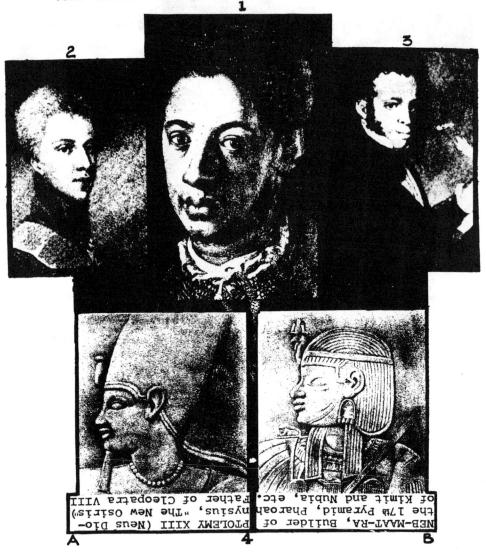

A. PTOLEMY XIII (Neus Dio-nysius), "The New Osiris") Father of Cleopatra VIII

B. NEB-MAAT-RA, Builder of the 17th Pyramid, Pharoah of Kimit and Nubia, etc.

1. Alessandro di Medici, Duke of Florence, Italy, son of the "Italian Cleopatra" – an African woman from Ethiopia – and a Roman Catholic Cardinal, grandfather of Charlotte Sopia – Consort of George III of Great Britain (portrait from the Medici Palace, Italy); 2 Gustavus IV, Adulphus, King of Sweden; 3 Alexander Pushkin, dean of Russian poets, great-grandson of Abraham Hannibal of Ethiopia, East Africa; 4 a so-called "Semite" or "Hamite" of the Nile Valley area? P.S. No. 4-B is the only "NEGRO."??

xxii

THE ONLY "NEGRO" ON THIS PAGE, ACCORDING TO UNITED STATES OF AMERICA'S RACIAL STANDARD. LOOK FOR THEM IN AMERICA'S HARLEMS.

THE ONLY "NEGROES" ARE THE TWO GABONESE DELEGATES IN THE CENTER PICTURE, ACCORDING TO UNITED STATES OF AMERICA'S RACIAL STANDARDS.

Economic leaders of New Africa gather for a conference in the Ethiopian capital city of Addis Ababa.

Lecture-Essay
by
Adjunct Assoc. Professor
Yosef ben-Jochannan
at
Pace College

"THE DAWN OF CIVILIZATION"

Introductory Remarks:

Among the most publicized of the published volumes on ancient history are those bearing the name or titles THE DAWN OF CIVILIZATION. For centuries The Dawn of Civilization was considered by European and European-American "educators" to have first occured around the Tigris and Euphrates valleys of southern Asia. Within the first one hundred (100) years, or more, The Dawn of Civilization theorists had taken their "Garden of Eden" to the end of the "Nile River Civilization." But they discovered very soon after, it had actually taken place around what is today called "central-east Africa." However, in removing the "Dawn" from both Persia (Iran) and Kimit (Egypt) to Tanganyika (Tanzania)[1] and other parts of central-east Africa, it became necessary to remove the origin of the so-called "Indo-European Aryan" and "Semitic Peoples" along with it. Why was this necessary? To facilitate the myth of the superiority of "Caucasian" over all other human beings who do not fit into this classification.

To accomplish said philosophical ideal, it also became necessary to develop entire departments of new studies under brand new titles with equally new explanations and terminologies designed to support the new declarations. In order to further accomplish these ends it was equally impelling that they had to ignore the traditions of many areas that existed for thou-

1

sands of years before the advent of writing in terms of alphabet and script -- ala-Western style -- and treated them as if they were never in existence.

This brings us to a major phase in the first of our lecture series, this afternoon, and that is the issue of NAMES. Names given to people, places and things indiscriminately without regards to the traditions or cultures involved; that is providing the name-changer or name-giver is not the one whose culture and history are not part of the heritage being destroyed.

There is a much greater purpose this lecture series serve, and that is, my tribute to the unclaimed heroes who stood on the Harlem street corners on their ladder day and night, almost every day and every night of each and every year, preaching "the Black man's heritage" to countless African-Americans who once passed them by as if they had leprosy. Such "street corner speakers," who mounted their ladder with the United States of America's Stars and Stripes posted at the top of the right wrung, as required by law, and the Tri-Colors of Africa (the Red, Black and Green flag introduced by the late Honourable Marcus Moziah Garvey, founder and President-General of the Universal Negro Improvement Association, UNIA, in 1917 C.E.) posted on the left; they "told it like it was." Even Stokely Carmichael, Roy Innis, Leroi Jones (Immamu Baraka), Adam C. Powell, Malcom X (al hajji Malik Shabaz), and countless others that made the limelight, received much of their cultural and history lessons in the "Black and Beautiful", "Back to Africa," and "Buy Black, Think Black, Look Black " African Nationalist impetus from these unsung heroes, most of whom will never make "Black Studies" courses biographical sketches of great Black men and women of the past and present.

These stalwart heroes, who followed in the footsteps of their departed <u>Provisional President-General of Africa</u>,[3] included such men and women as follows:

DECEASED

Hubert Harrison, professor of history and lecturer ; Sister Bessie Philips, lecturer and organizer; Arthur Reed, lecturer and businessman; Ira Kempt, lecturer and labor organizer; Ras the Killer, lecturer and labor organizer; Abdul Soufee, labor leader and lecturer; Carlos Cook, lecturer and political leader;

LIVING

James Thornhill, lecturer and labor organizer; Edward Mills (Pork Chop) Davis, lecturer; James Lawson, lecturer and public relations man; Lewis H. Michaux, lecturer, former minister, and book dealer specializing in African and African-American history and culture; George Simmonds, lecturer, teacher, political leader; Charles Peaker, lecturer, political leader, writer; Monroe Bales, educator, political leader, lecturer; and Jomo Logan, political leader and arranger for the annual "Ambassadors Ball for African and Caribbean delegates at the United Nations Organization. I too joined these lecturers from time to time in their ceaseless efforts to bring the African-American knowledge of his and her history and heritage.

The above is only a mere handful of the hundreds that mounted street ladders; but, to me, they are the people who made the greatest impact on the so-called "<u>average Black man</u>" on the streets of Harlem who were not aware of their African history and great heritage, most of whom clamoured to be called "Negro, coloured, mixed," and anything other than "Black" or "African", before their contact with "<u>street-ladder speakers</u>." I pay tribute to these "<u>little folks</u>" who stood in all kind of weather to listen to their much more informed brother and sister African Nationalists; not "Black Nationalists."

---

1. This standard has been co-opted by the so-called "New Left" under the misnomer -- "LIBERATION FLAG."
2. Marcus Moziah Garvey objected to the word "Negro," but he was obliged to use it to satisfy his fellow African-Americans who at the time knew no better.

THE VALUE OF A NAME. A NAME IS NOT JUST ANY NAME.

What is in a name? This is the proverbial question African-Americans are constantly asked by European-Americans who find it very inconvenient to say "<u>Black man</u>" instead of their favorite "<u>Coloured person</u>" or "<u>Negro</u>," and sometimes even "<u>Nigger</u>." Of course <u>die-hard</u> "Negroes,"(those who have adopted their slave-masters' assigned nomenclature for themselves and their home-land -- "Negro" and "Negroland") , quotes the English writer's, William Shakespare, works for refuge; thus they quote:

A ROSE BY ANY NAME SMELLS JUST THE SAME.

But , they have failed to note that a NEGRO BY ANY OTHER NAME HAS NO HISTORY BEFORE THE PORTUGUESE GAVE HIM OR HER THAT NAME DURING THEIR ENSLAVEMENT AROUND THE EARLY PART OF THE 17th century C.E. And, that, the name "<u>Negro</u>" identify them as common personal property then in the 17th century and now in the 20th century. For the same reason there is so much confusion in the history of the ancient Africans of Kimit, whom the Haribus called "Egyptians," and their land -- Egypt. The Greeks followed by renaming the pharoahs --Djoser to "Zozer" or Zoser;" Khufu to "Cheops" or "Kheops;" Men-Kau-Ra to "Mycerinus;" and Khaf-Ra to "Chephren;" etc. All of these are names the Greeks used in their plagiarization of the contributions by the indigenous Africans of the Nile Valleys who created and developed the greatest High-Culture of antiquity -- the Romiti of Kimit ("Egyptians of Egypt" according to the Haribus and Greeks).

The question which necessary follows the above analysis is: "Why so much fuss about the name Negro"? The anwer is simply one, and only one; that is, MAN NAMES HIMSELF FOR OTHERS TO ADDRESS

HIM ACCORDINGLY; in so doing he also NAMED THINGS HE ORIGINATED OR INHERITED accordingly. However, this answer is historically discribed and detailed in Richard B. Moore's book, THE WORD NEGRO, ITS ORIGIN AND EVIL USE, New York, 1964?; a most timely and provacutive work on the subject. Mr. Moore traced "THE WORD NEGRO" back to the colonialist Portuguese and other European slave traders of the late 16th and early 17th century C.E. He looked into the possibility of a "Latin origin" in ancient Rome, which was suggested by many "Western educators"(or mis-educators),but found no justification whatsoever for such a conclusion.

The main purpose for the examination into the tern "<u>Negro</u>," in this specific case, is primarily to clear the way for the presentation of early African history of antiquity, as history belonging to all Africans; just as European history of all times belong to all Europeans. It is in keeping in line of this perspective that I am now examining the many factors of the High-Cultures of the Nile Valley that reached their zenith at the end of the Nile River and its tributaries (or "DELTA") at the shores of the Mediterranean Sea. For the same reason, I shall use only African names wherever possible in these lectures. Words of which their Greek, Latin, English, French and other European language derivatives are commonly used, such shall be shown in brackets next to the correct African word; this shall be the same for Hebrew words of biblical mythology relating to Alkebu-lan (Africa). For example: <u>Kimit</u> will take prescedence over the Hebrew "Egypt;" equally <u>Romiti</u> over "Egyptians", and <u>Romitu</u> over "Egyptian." If these steps are not taken, then the history of this area of northern Alkebu-lan will continue, from my point of view, to appear as if it was of Greek, Roman or Hebrew origin, thefore justifying the mythological use of the terms "Semitic" and "Caucasian," or even "Hamitic North Africa," when in fact the history and culture of northern Africa, as all other parts of Africa -- Alkebu-lan, was solely of indigenous African creation and development up until the arrival of the first of the foreigners and invaders from Asia, the Hyksos, in Kimit (Egypt) around the year c1675 B.C.E. (Before the Christian Era).

As we enter into the history of Kimit, we find that two (2) names remain constantly dominant in almost every European and European-American Egyptologist, and other educators in various disciplines, mind with repect to the indigenous Africans who developed this area of northern Alkebu-lan. Thus, they are: Manetho and Jean F. Champollion. The former with regards to the first "Western-type" systematic chronological dating and division of Kimit's history into "DYNASTIES" and other periods; the latter with regards to the so-called "ROSETTA STONE" and its inscription translated by him into French from the original Greek and Hieroglyph; all of which made the Europeans and European-Americans involved with the stolen "Stone" from Kimit knowledgeable of its contents. It must be remembered that the stolen "Stone" was the illegal work of Emperor Napoleon Boneparte and his lieutenants in the latter part of the 18th century C.E.; and of course those stolen centuries earlier by other Europeans were primarily by the Greeks and Romans -- such as Aristotle; all of which began around the year 332 B.C.E. when the Greeks, under the barbarous leadership of Alexander ("the great") II of Macedonia, led his onslaught on Kimit; followed by the Romans with Caesar in 47 B.C.E.

Speaking of Napoleon Boneparte, whose soldiers it was that "<u>blew assunder the nose and lips of the Sphinx of Ghizeh with repeated blasts of cannon fire</u>...,"etc.(according to the writings of Baron Viviant Denon, who witnessed it),we will notice that he was "<u>white-washed</u>" from his role as the culprit of it all by the late professor Gaston Maspero in his book, THE DAWN OF CIVILIZATION (as edited by A. H. Sayce and translated by M. L. McClure, 4th ed., Society For Promoting Christian Knowledge, London, 1901), Chapter IV, Page 247; as follows:

> The cannon-shot of the fanatical Mamelukes has injured both the nose and beard, and the red colouring which gave animation to his features has now almost entirely disappeared.

Why should Baron Denon, who made the first known on-site sketch (hand drawn) of the <u>Sphinx of Ghizeh</u> before its face was marred by Napoleon and his men, say that the vandalism was done by his own Frenchmen; whereas professor Maspero , also a Frenchman, who was not present when either of the cases happened, held that it was done by the Mamelukes? The answer, as seen by your professor of this course, your lecturer, can be found in the attempt in most of the works written by European and European-American educators with respect to their countrymen's imperialist and colonialist roles throughout the world appear to have been angelic and messianic; all for the good of their victims, many of their victims having been blame for same in following accounts of history written by the victors' descendants. Yet their role of plundering for treasures, or "<u>trophies</u>," everywhere, including even their own continent, Europe. Such invasions included the use of cannon-fire, enslavement of entire nations, raping of young and aged females, the use of many forms of tactic today called "genocide;" and finally, claiming their victims contributions to the world's High-Culture (civilization) as their own; strangely enough such practices continue to the present day.

It is to be also noted; professor Maspero's information was second-hand information and hearsay evidence he received from Boudier's book, La DESCRIPTION de l'EGYPTE, Vol. 4. On plate No. 7 of the same book Boudier showed the same drawing of the <u>Sphinx of Ghizeh</u> and the three major background pyramids (copied by himself from Baron Denon's painting)[1]. But one must remember that the Mamelukes[2] who were already the mixture of indigenous Africans and foreigners, most of them invading conquerors and rulers of Kimit before the French arrival with Boneparte, had no logical reason to destroy one of their most treasured booty from their own conquest of the Africans of Kimit -- the <u>Sphinx of Ghizeh</u> and the <u>Major Pyramid Field of Ghizeh</u> -- the Pyramids of Khufu, Menaka-ere and Khafra. On the other hand the frustrations suffered by Napoleon Boneparte and his subordinate officers in their vain attempts to conquer and rule all of Kimit and her peoples, created amongst them the type of perversion that brought about the racial hatred and jealousy that caused them to strike-out in such lunatic rage against the helpless "<u>Wonder of the World</u>" --the <u>Sphinz of Ghizeh</u>. There should be no supprise of this racist action on the part of the French army in Alkebu-lan, its earlier history of ravaging European countries and peoples being none-the-less brutal; for all that were not French were barbarian and

---

1. See Baron Viviant Denon, TRAVEL IN EGYPT and SYRIA, London, 1800; and Yosef ben-Jochannan, BLACK MAN OF THE NILE, Chapt. III, p. 92 for pictures of the Sphinx of Ghizeh by Denon.

2. The Mamelukes were a mixture of Turks and other Europeans that sucessfully invaded and ruled Kimit before the full domination of the area by Juda Pasha or Mohammed Ali.

frightening abundance of materials on this area of the "African Experience" and "African-American heritage," and produce a quality of academic "TRUTH" out of them which so-called "modern scholars" have so far failed to accomplish by virtue of their own personal involvement in the protection of existing "racial theories" and "religious myths" originated from the Hebrew, Christian and Moslem "Holy Scriptures."

As we have observed in the "Hunting Scene" in the marsh and pool from the PAPYRUS OF ANI, and from professor G. Maspero's work, Le TOMBEAU de NAKHTI (in the <u>Memoires publies par les Membres de la Mission francaise du Caire</u>, vol. V), p. 480, from a drawing by Gayet and reproduced by Faucher-Gudin, that, even the "<u>boomerang</u>", which is only associated with the indigenous Alkebulan-Australian (the so-called "Aboriginies", by European and European-American educators and historians), had been commonly used among the Romiti of Kimit for centuries before the "dawn" of the Christian era -- the birth of the Christians' God --Jesus Christ of Nazzareth (also known as the "Nazzarine"). We have also read the various accounts of the many pharaohs (kings) of Kimit with respect to the type of voyages to Puanit, the most noted of which was that of Pharaoh (Queen) Hatshep-sut shown on page 160 of my book, BLACK MAN OF THE NILE, one of your texts.

In context of the above, it is unfortunate that the Museum of Natural History of the City of New York, New York, "educators" found it necessary to perpetuate the old worn-out racist myth on one of their main map at the entrance of the <u>African Wing</u> on the second floor of a 100% "Caucasian" north African, also East African, population that was supposed to be exclusive of people whom they still continue to designate as "NEGROES, BANTUS," and even "NILOTES," during the period shown as 7,000 B.C. This display of racism is headed, quite amusingly, under the caption:

THE FAMILY OF MAN.

The maps and graphs which go along with the description of the "Family OF Man," from a "Caucasian" point of view that is, are alleged to be 'true presentations.' But as one passes through these portals (created by "authorities" on theis subject disciplines), one is further to notice and be amused by the removal of Kimit (Egypt) from Alkebu-lan (Africa), and the very little of Cush (Ethiopia) they have managed to allow the public to see, is still perpetuated as part of "Black Africa Collections;" all of which, to the trained and experienced African historian, is better not shown. It would worth your while to know that Egyptian artifacts are displayed at, and in, the Museum of Art on Fifth Avenue and treated by the guides there as not being a part of the contributions of the Africans to world culture; and that "Egyptian culture and history are not African." The few artifacts on Ethiopia only relate back to the Christian Era; and of course to European influence in such, which they supposedly uderwent. As one leaves this racist display, which in many respects is worthy of viewing, one is constantly reminded by the next-to-last window that the Virgin Mary and Child concept was of "foreign influence" on the art-form used by the Ethiopians in this carving. Such benign stupidity, if not plain old ranked racism and religious bigotry, is still the official dogma being perpetuated by the entire educational system that supports said institution which even little African-American children are compelled to visit and have their mind totally "Caucasianized." These, unfortunately, are some of the various areas where so-called "BLACK STUDIES COURSES" should address students in the field of history, especially; but they, for the most part, have become convenient cells of "Third World" rhetoric of a "revolution" of young African-Americans who are not even aware of the nature of the historical foundations needed in order to prepare for said revolution; for if they realy knew this aspect of the "Black Experience" most of their "Third World" movers would be seen to be as dangerous as those to the "Right."

What logical explanation is there left that could be used for the creation of a "Caucasian north Africa" that was totally void of so-called "Negroes" other than from the mind of racially bigotted human beings? Is it not like saying that 'all of southern Europe was inhabited by Negroes from 7,000 B.C.'? What proof have these "authorities" submitted to show that their "Caucasian North African " left the Caucas Mountains of Eur-Asia and migrated to north Africa and found no indigenous peoples, the so-called "Negroes," there; equally in east Africa? Is this story not the same as that being presently used by the Europeans called "Boers" or "Afrikaaners" in the so-called "Republic of South Africa" in order to gain international support for their institution of genocide against the indigenous Africans of the Empire of Monomotapa which they met there upon their arrival in the 17th century C.E.? And, how did they ignore and bypass Herodotus, Diodorus, Diogenes Laterius, and other ancient writers, description that the ancient "...Egyptians, Colchians and Ethiopians..." were exactly the same in their physical appearance and color; and in their own respective works attributed "...thick lips, broad nose, wooly hair and burnt skin...," to all equally; as well as the first people to practice "...circumcision...." One must wonder what purpose is Black Studies to serve within the framework and context of White Studies institutions of "higher-learning" as long as such racism continues under the guise of "academic scholarship" on the part of European-Americans who have established themselves as "authorities" on Africa and everything relating to the African continent and its peoples. I am not one who can endorse such action by default; as such, I will continue to expose such racist teachings wherever and whenever the opportunity presents itself; and I shall make such opportunity be frequent. Of course there is a price to pay, and a very big one at that. My colleagues, academicians all I should suspect, many of whom have already began to exact of me certain retraction for this type and method of exposure, have also indicated that my work is in itself "racism in reverse." But, they have not been able to detail my racist contributions; it is, they feel, the mere fact that I have pointed out that the indigenous people of Alkebu-lan, all of it, were, and still are, "the original occupants of that continent," of which I concur. Yet, I find the price very minimal by comparison to the penalty I would have had to pay for silence.

The Cushites (Kushites) and Nubians of antiquity, not the present Arabs and their Arab-African offsprings who came to the Sudan in 640 C.E. or 18 A.H. and later, are depicted in the BOOK OF THE DEAD, and particualrly in the PAPYRUS OF ANI, as being equally the "...people of the Gods..." and "...rulers of the dwelling house of the Gods...," the same as those of Puanit and Kimit. Then how is it that these too have not become "Caucasians" in the process of the Caucasianization and Semiticization by the current "educators" and other "authorities" in-charge of racial certification for north and east Africa? And, How did the "Caucasian" and the "Semite" get to north and east Africa before the naturally African inhabitants, who today are still called "Negroes" and such other names of degrading characteristics? They too must not have been in north and east Africa by 7,000 B.C.E. and at the same time be at the Caucus Mountain, or not born from Noah -- the mythical character in the Hebrew story about the "End of the World;" this being so according to the Museum of Natural History "fellows" and "scholars."

The Semitic and Hamitic myth perpetuated by current racists masquerading as "authorities" on "Black" and "African studies," who also flood the reading market with tons of what they have decided is the true history of the Africans, from a reference of the "Caucasian" and "Indo-European Aryan" Hitlerism, is best understood if one realizes that it began with the story of Noah in the Hebrew Torah -- the FIVE BOOKS OF MOSES. There in the First Book of Moses, Genesis, "...the children of Ham,...," the mythical son of Noah, was supposedly "...cursed..." by the Hebrew God -- Jehovah; a curse which many Hebrew or Jewish writers of the 6th century in Europe were to translate into a racist piece of diatribe that shows the indigenous peoples of Africa as the "cursed children of Canaan," the grandchildren of Ham. And that the mark of the curse was that Jehovah "turned the children of Canaan Black." Why were they so turned by Jehovah? Their grandfather Ham, dared to look at his father, their great-grandfathers', "nakedness" one day while he was laying down in a fit of drunkedness; for this

Noah is supposedly to have gotten Jehovah to place a "<u>curse</u>"on Ham's"<u>children</u>"- otherwise called "<u>Canaanites</u>." All of this allegedly took place while Noah and his family were the only people in an Ark which Jehovah helped them make to save all of the species of every living thing in the world before He had <u>destroyed it by a flood</u>. The best detailed presentation on these myths, so far as I know, is to be seen in Robert Graves and Raphael Patai, HEBREW MYTHS, New York, 1964. But, is it not true that the Cushites and Egyptians' culture were not developed at the same time in history; the truth being that the former existed for thousands of years before the latter? Is it not equally true that the High-Culture (civilization) in Kimit (Egypt) reached its zenith with the help of other indigenous peoples from all over Alkebu-lan (Africa) before the beginning of the first pharonic dynasty, which was thousands of years before the birth of Moses, therefore before the <u>First Book of Moses</u>, Genesis, in which the story about the "<u>Cursed be Canaan</u>."...,appears? Also, is it not true that the High-Culture that existed in Zimbabwe and other parts of the Monomotapa Empire equalled that of Kimit before the dawn of the so-called "<u>Dynastic Period of Egypt</u> " as articulated by the High-Priest Manetho during the reign of the Macedonian general - Soter - who later on adopted the name "<u>Ptolemy I</u>," declaring himself -- "<u>Pharaoh of All Egypt</u>" subsequent to the death of Alexander II in about 320 B.C.E.; Alexander, his leader, having conquered the Lower Nile valley around c332 B.C.E.?

    The "<u>myrrh, lions, sweet incense</u>" and other produce Queen Hatshep-sut and other royalties of Kimit came to Puanit and Cush to secure were only a mere sampling of the comercial trade the

Romiti had with the Puanits and Cushites; the Puanits being the people the Romiti said occupied "...the lands where the Gods dwell" (according to the PAPYRUS OF ANI and the BOOK OF THE DEAD). At one time in history these two lands, Cush and Puanit, were the same as Kimit (or Egypt). The geo-political boundaries we, today, call "Egypt" or the "United Arab Republic" (UAR) did not exist until said area was demarcated by European and European-American imperialists and colonialists at the Berlin and Brussels conferences and their resulting "Acts" of 1884-85 (Berlin) and 1886-96 (Brussels); all of which were held in Berlin, Germany, and Brussels, Belgium, for the express purpose of further legalizing the enslavement of the African peoples and the robberies that were perpetuated against them for a period of more than four-hundred (400) years, much of which still goes on today.

Palaeontologist and medical doctor, Albert Churchward, author of many distinguished works that formed the basis for many palaeontological departments and research centers both in Europe and European-America (the Caribbean Islands included), in one of his most noted, SIGNS AND SYMBOLS OF PRIMORDIAL MAN, attributed the origin of all that became the zenith of the "Nile Valley Civilizations" (High-Cultures) to the so-called "Pygmies of Central Africa" (the Twa people -- their correct nomenclature). With respect for these fellow African people, I am reminded of the following teaching:

> The name of the Worm-God is sacred to Worms as is the name Jehovah to the Jews, Jesus Christ to the Christians, Al'lah to the Muslims..., etc.[1]

---

1. The "Worm God" is found in West Africa's Brew Anancee' Stories.

The "HYMN OF THE NILE" cited in the PAPYRUS OF ANI, which can be found in the prayers of adoration to the Nile-God that "...dwell in Nubia beyond the second Cataract..." was in all truth a God along the entire more than 4,100 miles long Nile River that begins in Uganda and ends at the Mediterranean Sea.[1] There were also two Goddesses for the Nile-God, both comparable to the two Hâpis -- Mirit Qimâit -- of the Upper Nile, Nubia; and Mirit Mihit for the Lower Nile, Kimit. It must be also noted that the Nile River was itself a God. This the Romiti believed, since most of their food and other physical needs were associated with the water of the Nile River. It is for this reason the God Hathâpi or Nûit-Hâpi (called "Nilopolis" by the Greeks),[2] was created. There was also a Shrine of the Nile built for this God, as shown on the bas-relief in the Temple of Philae. This Temple was built by the Pharoah Trajan and his successors.(See Jean Champollion, MONUMENTS, pl. xciii, 1; Dumichen, GEOGRAPHIE INS., vol. ii, pl. lxxix; and Rosellini, MONUMENTI del CULTO, pl. xxvii, 3). The festivals to the God of the Nile was the "most solem and joyous throughout the land of Egypt ever witnessed" - according to Heliodorus, AETHIOPICA, Book ix, Chap. 9, which he copied from writings dated back to the Ptolemies . Professor Brugsch in his work, MATERIAUX POUR SERVIR a la RECONSTRUCTION du CALENDRIER des ANCIENS EGYPTIENS, p. 37, et seq., also spoke of these great festivities;

---

1. The Blue Nile begins at Lake Tana in Cush; the White Nile begins at Mwanza (lake) Nyanza, which the European colonialists renamed "Lake Victoria" for the British queen of like name who caused millions of Africans throughout the continent to be murdered in order that she could enrich herself and her empire-builders who equally lived on the African peoples. The present royal family of England are the inheritors of Victoria's stolen trophies still to be found in England and the British treasury.
2. Stephanus of Byzantium's quotation from Hecatacus of Miletus

also E. DeRouge in his, SUR le NOUVEAU SYSTEME PROPOSE par M. BRUGSCH pour L'INTERPRETATION du CALENDRIER EGYPTIEN, in Zeitschrift, 1866, pp. 3-7. The major text of the HYMN OF THE NILE-GOD is preserved in two papyrus in the British Museum, London, England --the <u>second Sallier Papyrus</u> (Select Papyrus, vol. i, pl. xxi, 1, 6, and pl. xxiii) and the <u>Seventh Anastasi Papyrus</u> (ibid., pl. cxxxiv. ancienne des peuples de l'Orient, 4th edit., pp. 13-13 ; and Guieysse, RECUEIL de TRAVAUX, vol. xiii, pp. 1-26).

The ancients of Kimit <u>diet</u> also reflected the influence their neighbors at the the south held on them, even to the height of their glory -- the <u>Great Pyramid Age</u>. The use of the <u>Durrah</u> that came from as far south as the eastern Kongo (Congo) and Bonyoro Empire (today's Uganda region) was also influential. It is called <u>Holcus Sorghum, L.</u>, in modern terms. Even in the tombs of many of the pharoahs this plant was taken, an indication of the value placed upon its worth. E. DeCandolle's, ORIGINE des PLANTES CULTIVEES, pp. 305-307, states that "...<u>only the seeds were taken into the pyramids</u>..." (tombs); but, on the otherhand Loret's, La FLORE PHARAONIQUE, p. 12, No. 20, held that it was "...<u>the entire plant</u>...". It was even given the name -- "...GRAIN OF THE SOUTH."[1]

In the many scenes dipicted in most <u>papyrus</u> and <u>bas-relief works</u> of the Romiti they were always certain to describe Asian peoples quite differently to themselves; yet, this was very rarely done in the case of other fellow Alkebu-lan. In most cases the

---

the (fragment 277 in Muller-Didot's "FRAGMENT HISTORY, Grace, vol. i, p 19).

1. Whenever the ancients Romiti referred to the "South" they were solely dealing with points beyond the second cataract primarily. They called southern Kimit -- "Upper Kimit."

Asians were shown as slaves, or as royal members paying homage. "Westerners" say the Nubians and Puanits were "Negroid peoples;" whereas, the Ethiopians were supposed to have been "Hamites." In order to set this deep into the mind the history of a certain Pharoah of very black color was made to be a "Negro" of the Black Belt." This type of plagiarization is best seen in their interpretations dealing with the Pharoah, Amenemhait II (also known as Usirtasen II or Usertsen II), stele relating to the defeat of the Nubians by the Romiti. But nowhere in his writings did Pharoah Amenemhait referred to the Nubians other than as a seperate political entity. Never once did he used the term "race". (See Birch, TABLETS OF THE XIIth DYNASTY, in the Zeitschrift, 1874, p. 112; Brugsch, DIE BIBLISCHEM SIEBEN JAHRE der HUNGERSMOTH, pp. 106, 107; Naville, BUBASTIS, pl. xxxiv. A, and pp. 9-10; E. DeRouge, NOTICE des MONUMENTS, 1849, pp. 4-5; Wiedmann, AEGYPTISCHE GESCHICHTE, pp. 294-295; Lepsuis, DENKM., ii. 123d dealing with the stele of Pharoah Monthotpâ at Aswan; and Birch, HISTORICAL MONUMENT OF AMENOPHIS III in the Louvre, Paris, France, in the ARCHAEOLOGIA, vol. xxiv. pp. 489-491). In these works most of the authors placed Puanit near the district of Hûâ, which was always associated with Rameses III. (See Lepsius, DENKM., III. 209); others felt it was at the end of the Atbara River in the highlands of Cush (Ethiopia). The truth is that too many "modern" educators try to change the whole meaning of ancient history that deals with Alkebu-lan and Europe to avoid any kind of integration or amalgamation between both groups unless they are shown as "Caucasians" or "Caucasoids," even "Semites" or "Hamites" as a last-ditch effort to avoid them being "Negroes." Thus, we are now being introduced to a new group of people -- the "dark-skinned Caucasians" invented for north and east Africa by European-American historians and social anthropologists. This new people allow the racist co-optation of Zinjanthropus boise, Boskop man, Broken Hill man, and other noted fossil-men to become "Caucasian fossil remains" in the center of Alkebu-lan; all of which existed for hundreds of thousands of years before the first "Caucasian" left the Caucus Mountains of Russia to migrate into Europe; and none of these claims existed before Drs. L.S.B. & M. Leakey uncovered their find in Tanganyika, East Africa. Before the oldest known fossil-men were uncovered in Alkebu-lan all of this area was always treated by "Western" educators as strictly and solely "Negro" and "Bantu" territories.

The traffic between Kimit and Puanit included stopping-points at Elephantine and Nekhabit or the "Head of Nekhabit" (also called "Bernice" by the ancient Greeks). The road from Nekhabit to Koptos was travelled by the German Egyptologist -- Golenischeff, who wrote the most noted works on the area in an article entitled "Une Excursion a Bernice," published in RECUEILDE TRAVAUX, vol. xiii. pp 75-96. Another major work on this area is Dr. Brugsch's, DIE AEGYPTISCHE VOLKERTAFEL, in the VER HANDLUNGEN des v^{ten} ORIENTALISTEN-CONGRESSES, vol. ii., Afrikanische Sektion, p. 62. Dr. Brugsch was certain that Tap-Nekhabit, also known as the "HEAD" or "CAPE OF NEKHABIT", is the Greek "Bernice." The fact is that the Greeks were not very familiar with the geography of Alkebu-lan, even of the nation of Kimit beyond the first Cataract until Herodotus reached the second Cataract about 450-457 B.C.E. The total extent of their knowledge about Alkebu-lan dealt with northern "Africa" along the Lebus or Kimit Sea (Lebus being the ancient name of today's Libya; Kimit being today's Egypt);the Sea in question thus becomes the modern "Mediterranean Sea." But the lack of such knowledge to the Greeks caused much of the confusion they have passed on to other Europeans and European-Americans to this very day in history; for thousands upon thousands of their descendants bearing the titles "educator " and "historian " used the same errors made by the Greeks with repect to Alkebu-lan's ancient geography as the basis for most of their own fundamental treatise and hypothesis on the continent and its peoples. Unfortunately, this trend shows very little hope in the way of changing, even with the compelling force being generated by "<u>Black Studies</u>" and "<u>African Studies</u>" courses and scholars that have brought forward the ancient documents proving the ancient Greeks were in error with respect to the geography and much of the geopolitics of northern and north-eastern Alkebu-lan. The end result must then be <u>a direct confrontation with those who continue perpetuating Greek mythological concepts about Alkebu-lan</u> (Ethiopia, Libya or Africa, all of them being names which the ancient Greeks called this continent. See page 266 of BLACK MAN OF THE NILE for more) with no respect or feelings for the indigenous people and their descendants everywhere.

As I have already stated at the outset of this <u>lecture-essay</u> relative to"names," the terms "BUSHMAN" and "HOTTENTOT," or even "BANTU," only adds to prohibit the African peoples fron connecting the history of the different cultural groups, and that is the only difference of major importance between Alkebu-lan peoples of the various geo-political areas and nations of Alkebu-lan in a meaningful manner that would threaten continued European and European-American imperialim, colonialisn, neo-colonialism, and slavery on the continent. It is the old "DIVIDE AND CONQUER" tactic of the Napoleonic era in the 20th century C.E. And, one must admit that it has worked very effectively for the forces of slavery and genocide in Africa up until this present day. In too many ways and cases the trend is to disassociate the indigenous people of this continent's culture under the rediculous proposition that they are of different "ethnic" or "racial" origin and development. We can best observed this in the typical remark on this area, common among European and European-American "educators", use with respect to the nation of Kimit...:

"EGYPT AND AFRICA" or "BLACK AFRICA."

It is in this same regards that the painting of the people of the nation of Monomotapa, (at the southernmost tip of Alkebu-lan)-the Khoisans or Kalaharis whom the European and European-American imperialist and colonialist settlers renamed "Bushmen" and "Hottentots,") were said to be "non-Africans;" this being consistent with their racist theory that anyone who does not have a combination of "thick lips, broad nose, wooly hair and black skin" is not a "Negro" or "Bantu." Not to long ago, before the unearthing of the world's most ancient fossil-men and the declaration of central Africa as "the original Garden of Eden," these people were even declared "non-Africans" who migrated from Asia to the southernmost tip of the continent of Alkebu-lan. Yet, this criteria on "race" or "ethnic grouping" does not hold true with respect to their fellow Europeans and European-Americans who differ from each other with respect to the same points of the human anatomy;

this being true of Swedes against Greeks or Irish against Italians, Spaniards and Portugese against Germans, etc.,etc.,etc. The best example of this contention is seen in the 35,000 years old painting by a Khoisan artist of the Kalahari Desert shown on page 60 of my BLACK MAN OF THE NILE. This drawing, which is similarly duplicated elsewhere in Alkebu-lan, is used by many Europeans and European-Americans to prove the difference of the racial development theory they have concocted for the African peoples to satisfy their own bigotry.

For example: The double-reed double-pipe used by the people of central, west and east Alkebu-lan as early as 3,500 B.C.E., which only arrived in Kimit and Libus around 1,500 B.C.E., is purposefully not mentioned as such by so-called "modern" educators on the history of Kimit and other parts of northern Alkebu-lan. The same holds true in the case of architectural concepts of Alkebu-lan's people. In this area the word "primitive" has been applied by "modern educators" in one of its most vicious and destructive usage with respect to the peoples "South of the Sahara," the so-called "Black Africans," but hardly ever applied to people "North of the Sahara" or in the "Sahara," though the vast majority of those in the "Sahara" are thousands of years old. For the same reason the great cone structure of Zimbabwe (shown on page 162 of BLACK MAN OF THE NILE), which the "modern educators" prefer to call "Mecropolis of Rhodesia, was once held by them to have been "...constructed by shipwrecked Greek mariners..." on the sole basis that it did not "...look like the type of primitive architecture of which the Negroes are capable...,"etc. They also felt that the complexity of the engineering fete so obviously appearent in these structures could not have been calculated by the "Negroes;"neither could such mathematical genius be indigenous to the area; thus, they had completely overlooked, or purposefully forgotten, the "GREAT WALLS OF BENIN" West Africa and the "GREAT MOSQUE OF TOMBUT" (Timbuktu, Tibuctoo, etc.)[1] were totally designed, engineered and constructed by the so-called "primitive Negroes" of western Alkebu-lan. Never-the-less, the so-called "modern educators" of the "Western world", both of the United States of America and Europe (Britain included), constantly looked for "Egyptians influence" in all other parts of Alkebu-lan, never realizing that much of what "Westerners" call "Egyptian Civilization" today had their origin in the deep south and other areas of Alkebu-lan; of course the vast majority of them are not aware that there is documentary material of this nature of the history and culture of the continent of Alkebu-lan, most of them having become instant "authorities" on Africa and the African peoples within the last few years, five at the most, since "Black Studies" courses became the latest fad in "White Studies" institutions of "higher-learning."

I, personally, endorse the following extract taken from the "Editors Preface To The First Edition" of professor Gaston Maspero's book, THE DAWN OF CIVILIZATION: EGYPT and CHALDEA, p. iv.. He wrote:

> Naturally, in progressive studies like those of Egyptology and Assyriology, a good many theories and conclusions must be tentative and provisional only. Discovery crowds so quickly on dis-

---

1. There are many "Western" derivatives of the spelling of this word, all of which had to have been taken from the original African word..."TOMBUT."

> covery, that the truth of to-day is often apt to
> be modified or amplified by the truth of to-
> morrow. A single fresh fact may throw a wholly
> new and unexpected light upon the results we
> have already gained, and cause them to assume a
> somewhat changed aspect.

This "truth" should be, particularly, applied to most so-called "modern works" written about the continent and people of Alkebu-lan (Africa) by the current vintage of instant European and European-American "authorities," all of which must relate back to each and every volume published since the beginning of the planting of European-style "Christianity" and the expansion of imperialism by the late Henry Morton Stanley and King Leopold II of Belgium in Alkebu-lan. For ever so much have been written about Alkebu-lan and its indigenous sons and daughters, but so very little had been investigated as to truth in producing all of said writings by the imperialist, colonialist, and Christian mission class that raped both the land and the people after enslaving them, genocide having proven impossible against them. Therefore, until "Western man" is able to write about Alkebu-lan and its indigenous people from a distinctly different perspective than wishful racist hypothesis and bigoted beliefs of their messianic mission, there will be no truth in substance in their writings, which is certainly the case at present with very, very, very few exception, if any at all.

In closing this <u>lecture-essay</u>, I must take great pains in reminding everyone of you, my students, that it was virtually impossible for any place in northern Alkebu-lan not to have had total contact with the people of Asia and Europe- the so-called "<u>Indo-European Aryan Caucasian</u>," and at the same time not having more intimate contact with their fellow indigenous brothers and at the south of them solely on the basis that they were of a different "race" or "ethnic origin," and worse yet, "religious background." As such, the ignorance exhibited by most so-called "Western educators" with respect to their "Negroes, Bantus, Hottentots, Pygmies, Bushmen, Africans South of the Sahara, Black African" (what others are they?), and others manufactured by them for Alkebu-lan, including much more sophisticatedly racist terminologies, can only meet with heads-on confrontation of a nature that could only lead to physical ugliness which in the long run must end in victory for the peoples of African origin for whom this history and heritage -- the "BLACK EXPERIENCE -- solely belong. We must remember that there was, and still is, no insurmountable physical or mental barrier to had prevented the integration and/or amalgamation between the peoples of nothern and southern Alkebu-lan no more than between the people of northen and southern Europe, or northern and southern Asia, and those of North America and South America; even between those of different continents where oceans seperated them from each other ,(we should only examine the late collection of anthropological and archaeological data for proof of these facts). But, when we are tempted to believe that there may have been such existing, due to the propaganda of certain "racist" and "religiously bigoted" academicians and their writings in support of such hypotheses, ask yourself; Why did the Mediterranean Sea not present much more of a barrier to the ancients of Europe making contact with the ancients of Alkebu-lan than the Sahara sand and the flowing rivers of the Blue and White Nile? And; Why would the "black-skinned Egyptians," whom even "Westerners" agree were for the most part black in their color (even those who contended they were "Caucasians" or "Semites"), never-the-less, not feel happy with their fellow "Black" brothers and sisters to the south, but elated over their much"<u>White-skinned"</u> brothers and sisters from as far off as the Caucaus Mountains range between India and Russia(in Asia), and later on those from Greece and Rome across the Kimit Sea? If we take time out to look into this aspect of history, and the racist manner in which it has been presented to us over the last two to three-hundred (200 to 300) years, it may be possible for us to see TRUTH beyond BLACK AND WHITE, or even beyond CHRISTIANS, JEWS AND MUSLIMS against PAGANS and the UNCIVILIZED or PRIMITIVES. But, should we fail to assume this posture in Black Studies or African Studies courses, and continue the racism and religious bigotry that have permeated White Studies for the last few hundred years, maybe one day we will all discover that TRUTH has outlasted what we now prefer to call ... "CIVILIZATION."

The following works are suggested for further reading in this area of African and African-American history and culture. This does not mean that European and Asian High-Cultures, particularly of ancient times, are not to be found in them also, to the contrary. In these works much of the beginnings of what we call today "CIVILIZATION" can be seen to have taken place among all types of mankind on the planet Earth; not one contributing more than the other, but each contributing according to his possibility defferently at given times in world history. Thus, they are: Prof. George G.M. James, STOLEN LEGACY; Rudolph Windsor, FROM BABYLON TO TIMBUKTU; John Jackson, INTRODUCTION TO AFRICAN CIVILIZATION; Sir Ernest Wallis Budge, BOOK OF THE DEAD; OSIRIS;

PAPYRUS OF ANI; Albert Churchward, M.D., SIGNS AND SYMBOLS OF PRIMORDIAL MAN; THE ORIGIN AND EVOLUTION OF RELIGION; ARCANA OF FREEMASONRY; THE ORIGIN AND EVOLUTION OF THE HUMAN RACE; Sir Godfrey Higgins, ANACALYPSIS (2 vols.); Sir Charles Darwin, Jr., THE NEXT MILLION YEARS; Dr. Gertrude Caton-Thompson, THE ZIMBABWE CULTURE; H. Labourete, AFRICA BEFORE THE WHITEMAN; Yosef ben-Jochannan, AFRICAN ORIGINS OF THE MAJOR "WESTERN RELIGIONS;" also BLACK MAN OF THE NILE (both texts materials); Stanley Lane-Poole, THE MOORS IN SPAIN; Mrs. Steuart Erskine, VANQUISHED CIVILIZATIONS OF NORTHERN AFRICA; Jane Soaames, COAST OF THE BARBARY; Eva B. Sandford, THE MEDITERRANEAN WORLD; Dr. J. B. Danquah, AKAN CULTURE; J.J. Williams, HEBREWISM IN WEST AFRICA; Prof. J.C. deGraft-Johnson, AFRICAN GLORY; Jomo Kenyatta, FACING MOUNT KENYA; J. Jahn, MUNTU; Sir E. A. Wallis Budge, THE HISTORY OF EGYPT; Prof. Gaston Maspero, A HISTORY OF EGYPT: ASSYRIA AND CHALDEA; and others already surveyed by this class.

I end this series with Christopher Dawson's timely book, THE MAKING OF EUROPE, The World Publishing Company, Cleveland and New York, 1956 (originally published in 1932), Part One...<u>The Foundations</u>, under the subtitle ---"THE ROMAN EMPIRE," page 25; in which he wrote the following:

> We are so accustomed to base our view of the world and our whole conception of history on the idea of Europe that it is hard for us to realize what the nature of that idea is. Europe is not a natural unity, like Australia or Africa; it is the result of a long process of historical evolution and spiritual development. From the geographical point of view Europe is simply the north-western promolgation of Asia, and possesses less physical unity than India or China or Siberia; anthropologically it is a medley of races, and the European type of man represents a social rather than a racial identity. And even in cul-

ture the unity of Europe is not of the foundation and starting-point of European history, but the ultimate and unattained goal, towards which it has striven for more than a thousand years.

Although each and every one of you, my students, may disagree with the points raised by Mr. Dawson, I do hope he has given you enough reasons to reconsider the present form of relating everything in the world from a European and European-American perspective; wherein everything or everyone is good or bad, civilized or uncivilized, religious or heathen, using Europe and European-America as the point or points of reference where purity begins. If you are able to bear this fact in mind, and act positively on it, maybe there will be some meaningful change in the very near future in the manner of how WORLD HISTORY will be taught to everyone of us. Then, and only then, can the age-old indigenous African saying common among the ancients of the Nile Valley High-Cultures, which states:-

"AND THE TRUTH SHALL SET YOU FREE,"

have practical application to mankind (as we know ourselves).

Submitted for critical analysis and a 5,000 words documented essay --by Yosef ben-Jochannan; Adj. Assoc. Prof. of History, Pace College(Westchester Campus). Course: THE BALCK EXPERIENCE. History 272 D...Nov. 19, 1970.

CHAPTER II

PREHISTORIC HOMOSAPIENS or <u>Ancient African Man</u>?

"IN THE BEGINNING GOD CREATED MAN FROM THE EARTH AND CALLED HIM ADAM...," etc., is the manner in which the Hebrew and all of the other religious philosophies based upon this MYTH start. This of course will bring MAN back to the TIGRIS and EUPHRATES valleys of Asia. But MAN, the most ancient of MAN, has been found to have existed in the continent of ALKEBU-LAN hundreds of thousands of years before the birth or creation of the Hebrews' ADAM. This, then, places MAN IN AFRICA BEFORE HE WAS ANYWHERE ELSE ON THE PLANET EARTH. This too is the most important reason why the Africans and their ancestors must be denied their indigenous heritage and history of the areas on both sides of the Niles and all of North Africa, or all other places in that greatest of land masses called AFRICA by the Greeks and Romans. It is with all these cardinal points in mind that this chapter begins. For in these earliest of human or human-like fossils are the end to the racist premise of the "SUPERIORITY OF THE CAUCASIAN RACE OVER ALL OTHER RACES" which one has become so accustomed to hearing within the last two-hundred (200) or more years in these United States of America and Europe and all other areas of European and European-American colonial, neo-colonial, and/or political spheres of influence. African historians and others within the varied disciplines of education sat idly by while European and European-American counterparts reached into Africa and laid claim to the ancient FOSSILS being unearthed in the heart of the continent the Africans named ALKEBU-LAN, among many other names.

It is in this vein that this chapter also present the introduction of many of the African fossils which otherwise would not have been available to the average student or reader. It is also in this same realm that the anthropological terminologies normally applied are given, yet the general language used is not in a sense the type written solely for a strict academic audience that would be interested in the scientific technology of the subjects presented. For these reasons, and many others, the author of this volume desires to reach a much broader audience, as well as his students, in order to bring to the average reader just what lies behind the identification of the indigenous Africans and that which tries to deny them this heritage. This will be seen in the mere fact that it was only as a last resort that the earliest of the European and European-Americans began their excavation in Africa for the purpose of finding "THE MISSING LINK BETWEEN MAN AS HE APPEARS TODAY AND AS HE WAS AT THE BEGINNING OF TIME." Since this inquiry concentrates more so in the center of Alkebu-lan, this is a greater reason to deny the Africans their indigenous birthright. Thus one sees the Jeffreys, Junods, Wiedners, Sir Harry H. Johnstons and others like them that much better in retrospect, understanding why they must go to the extreme they have already gone in their feeble attempt to remove every trace of the Africans as the first of the ORIGINAL MEN to have inhabited the TRUE GARDEN OF EDEN - the OLDUVAI GORGE, Tanganyika (Alkebu-lan).

The fossils submitted for presentation are only a few of the hundreds found all over the continent of Alkebu-lan (Africa).

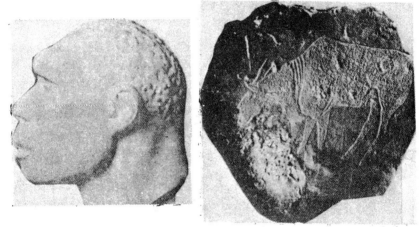

Left: The elegance of prehistoric African ART unearthed in southern Africa (Monomotapa), presently located in the PRETORIA MUSEUM. It is dated to have been sculpted around 30,000 years ago. Cut from FLINT STONE tools by prehistoric indigenous Africans of the type found all over Africa (Black people; not "NEGROES").

Right: Reconstruction of STONE AGE indigenous African skulls, like this one, are part of the African-American heritage from their "Mother-Land" - ALKEBU-LAN (Africa). See J. A. Rogers' AFRICA'S GIFT TO AMERICA, p 7; also, SEX AND RACE, vol. I, pp 26, 35).

There is very strong evidence that the fossil-type called

AUSTRALOPITHECINES* evolved in the regions of the northeast

---

*Like most of the other disciplines in European and European-American educational system, with respect to Africa and things African, the names assigned African fossils by anthropologists, paleontologists, archaeologists and other educators very often bear no relationship to the African continent or peoples, all in keeping with the general racist orientation of "Western education", which allows no credit to be bestowed upon Africa without having such things overshadowed by some sort of Caucasian value.

KEY

A. Tropical Rain Forest
1. Mediterranean-type vegetation
2. Desert
3. Steppe & Semi-Desert
4. Highland Forest
5. Savanna (Savannah)
6. Woodland & Savanna
7. South vegetation

MAJOR VEGETATION ZONES

KEY

Diagonally crosshatched areas are highlands. (Locations "a" through "l" are the same as the map below).

HIGHLANDS MORE THAN 5,000 ft. ABOVE SEA LEVEL

KEY

* 1. Broken Hill
* 2. Diredawa
* 3. Singna
* 4. Springbak (Tulnplaats)
* 5. Boskop
* 6. Hopefield
* 7. Tulnplaats
* 8. Vaal River region
* 9. Asselar
* 10. Mechta-el-Arbi
* 11. Rabat
* 12. Hau Fteah
* 13. Ngorongoro Crater

FOSSIL FIELD MAIN SITES

KEY TO FOSSIL FIELD MAIN SITES

(a) Gamble's Cave; (b) Olduvai and Eyasi; (c) Kanam and Kanjera; (d) Cape Flats and Fish Hoek; (e) Matjes River and Tzitzikama; (f) Florisbad; (g) Taung; (h) Sterkfontein; (i) Makapansgat; (j) Sidi Abderrahman; (k) Ternifine; (l) Afalou-bou Rhummel.

The maps above are intended to give approximate locations of the sites and terrain. The highlands range from 5,000 to 19,000+ feet elevation. They are drawn to the scale of 3/4" = 1000 miles (one-quarter of an inch equal one-thousand miles; unless otherwise shown).

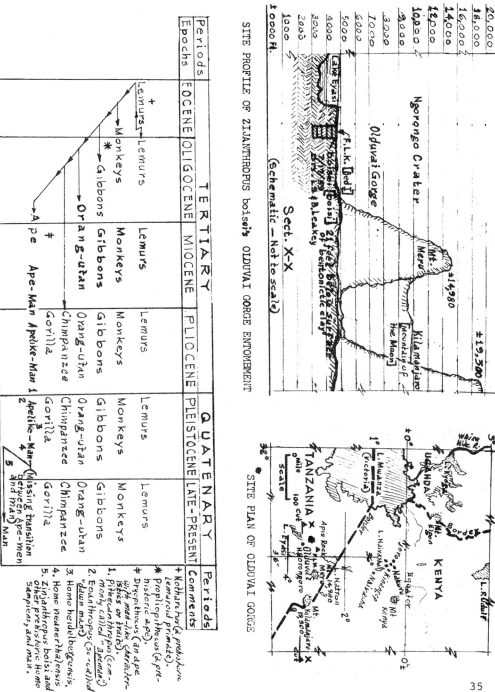

SITE PROFILE OF ZIJANTHROPUS boisei's OLDUVAI GORGE ENTOMBMENT

SITE PLAN OF OLDUVAI GORGE

ZINJANTHROPUS boisei & 20th CENTURY C.E. MAN's EVOLUTION

forest of Equatorial Africa. Also, they formerly spread from the
forest area into the wide open plaines. Their new environmental
conditions forced them to assume and adopt an <u>erect posture</u> and
to use <u>tools</u> as shown on pages 50 and 51 of this chapter.
Although it was not <u>tools</u> as man now know them; never the less
they served the same purpose - survival - the ability to hunt,
to make fire, to make clothing, and to make housing, and finally
to secure comfort and pleasure. It was also from this region
that they first migrated to southern Africa, Northern Africa,
Western Africa, Western Asia; and over the land masses of Europe.[3]

<u>A LIMITED GLOSSARY OF THE CLASSIFICATION OF MAN</u>

<u>First Or Prime Stage</u>:
AUSTRALOPITHECUS* (Paranthropus, Meganthropus, Zinjanthropus, and
possibly Homo havilis included). There are two species, Africanus
and Robustus, from approximately 1,750,000 years to 500,000 years
ago. Lower Pleistocene in North Africa (the Sahara region) and
the early Middle Pleistocene around the Kalahari Desert in Monomotapa (Union of South Africa), Palestine (Israel), and Java.

<u>Second Or Intermediate Stage</u>:
PITHECANTHROPUS (Homo erectus), Modjokertensis, and Erectus,
c500,000 years in Java. Germany (Heidelberg jaw); Peking (Pithecanthropus Pekinensis), Tanzania, East Africa (Olduvai Gorge Bed
II), and Algeria, North Africa (Atlanthropus), c450,000 years
(around the Middle Glaciation period). In Morocco, up to
c250,000 years.

<u>Third Or Final Stage</u>:
HOMO SAPIENS-NEANDERTHALOID dating to their ancestors in England
and Germany (Swanscombe and Steinheim), c250,000 years (during
the Second-Inter-glacial period).

HOMO NEANDERTHALENSIS generally found in most of Europe, very
few in Asia and Africa, c70,000 to 40,000 years.

---

*Not to be found anyplace in Europe.

ZIMBABNOIDS* Homo Soloensis and Homo Zimbabnoids found in Africa and Asia, c35,000 years.

HOMO SAPIENS, COMBE CAPELLE, exclusively in Europe, c30,000 to 35,000 years.

FLORISBAD, Monomotapa, South Africa, c40,000 years.

NIAH, c40,000, Kanjera, East Africa, unknown but generally given about c50,000 to 55,000 years.

A SHORT CHRONOLOGY OF THE HISTORY OF PALAEONTOLOGY
IN AFRICA

Date C.E.   Description and Event.

1863   During the 19th Century certain Europeans such as Boucher de Perthes became aware of the "MISSING LINK" between MAN and the so-called "LOWER PRIMATES".[4] Africa during this period was not considered to be of any importance as a possible source of such fossil deposits, since the Africans** were not considered HUMAN BEINGS.[5] As a result, only European and Asian fossils (Man) were sought out for the possible LINK between the so-called MODERN MAN and his original ancestors.***

For centuries before Boucher de Perthes found <u>one-half of a jawbone</u> and some <u>stone tools</u> of a Prehistoric Man, not very far

---

*The correct name of the area where this fossil was unearthed is correctly entitled ZIMBABWE. Why not call the fossil ZIMBABNOIDS rather than the name placed on them by Europeans of the colonial and slave trading periods - "RHODESTOIDS".
**At this period Africans now called "BANTUS, NEGROES, AFRICANS SOUTH OF THE SAHARA, BLACK AFRICANS," etc.; they were also called "HAMITES". This, of course, was before the first diggings.
***Note that Modern Man is used here in the same sense as Prof. Jeffreys' terminology, the term does not include all men, only Europeans and some Asians.

from a place called Abbeville in the Moulin-Quignon quarry of France; it was believed by Europeans and European-Americans that "ANCIENT MAN" stemmed (originated) from Southwestern Europe only. From this hypothesis each succeeding European and European-American anthropologist and archaeologist pursued his research with contempt with any suggestion that excavations for FOSSIL-MAN also should be conducted in Africa and Asia.

It was, however, in 1924 that Dart discovered a skull which he called "AUSTRALOPITHECUS", having found it in Australia.[6] Because of Dart's find some researchers in the field turned their attention outside Europe for the possible LINK between so-called "MODERN MAN" and his originators.

During the year 1937 in Java, then a colony of the Dutch Government in Europe, a Dutch geologist named Von Koenigswald found a fossil which he called "JAVA MAN". It was a complete skull, many thousands of years older than the fossil found by Boucher de Perthes in 1853.

The first skull (top half) that really caused alarm in European scientific circles was found in 1856 by workmen working in the Feldhofer Cave, between Dusseldorf and Elberfeld, Germany, at the side of a ravine called NEANDERTHAL. This discovery fell into the hands of one Dr. Fuhlrett who named it in honor of the place where it was unearthed - "NEANDERTHAL MAN". A description of this fossil was published in detail in a German scientific review under the authority of the world renowned scholar and palaeontologist - Dr. Schaffhausen.

By 1865 the mad rush for further discoveries of prehistoric man was in full force. The high point was reached when Sir Charles Darwin published his major treatise, THE ORIGIN OF MAN. Following Darwin was Huxley, Darwin's faithful follower who dared to claim that:

> "THE NEANDERTHAL SKULL IS THE TOP-HALF OF A HUMAN CRANIUM."

But Huxley also stated that it was:

> "MUCH MORE PRIMATE IN CHARACTER THAN CONTEMPORARY MAN"

of his era. He concluded, one should recall, with the type of damaging statement that brought forward the intemperate vituperations of one Bishop Wilberforce, an ultra-orthodox conservative type of ADAM AND EVE advocate of the Church of England type of European-style Christian. The good Bishop proclaimed that he:

> "...WOULD RATHER BE A PERFECTED APE THAN A DEGENERATE ADAM...," etc.[6a]

This comment seemed to have cowed Huxley to the point that, in later years, as the controversy increased between his followers and those of the Bishop, he was forced to declare that the same cranium was of...

> "A CREATURE CLEARLY INTERMEDIATE BETWEEN MAN:"

all of which he did without any new data or scientific theoretical reasoning given. Subsequently, Huxley reversed himself completely. He went so far as to question if the cranium had any possibility what so ever of being:

"THE INTERMEDIARY LINK BETWEEN MODERN MAN AND HIS MUCH MORE ANCIENT ANCESTORS."

Huxley's confusion is to be understood when one considers the social and political climate and pressures raised against him by Bishop Wilberforce and his fellow religious bigots who feared that their livelihood would be taken away - had it been proven, at that time, that the cranium was in fact:

"MAN'S INTERMEDIARY LINK TO AN APE-LIKE ANCESTOR."

At this juncture it must be noted that Sir Charles Darwin had used the term "APE-LIKE ANCESTORS", and not "AN APE"[7] as so many of his religious detractors have stated since his proclamation.

The confusion, as well as the persecution of all palaeontologists and their associates, <u>by members of the Clergy</u> of all three faiths labeled "WESTERN RELIGIONS" - Judaism, Christianity and Islam - continues to this very day. However, the collection of human fossils accumulated beyond imagination. A few are chronologically listed as follows, according to their date of discovery.[8]

PARTIAL CHRONOLOGICAL LISTING OF FOSSIL FINDS
ACCORDING TO DATES

1864   A fossil-head was discovered and displayed before the British Museum Association. It is also identical with that of the Neanderthal; yet, it was discovered in England.

1866   At LaNaulette, not very far from the City of Liege in Belgium, a lower jaw of much more ancient ("primitive") appearance than Neanderthal was discovered in an excavated cave.

1866   In a cave at Spy, very near to Namur, two Belgian geologists, dePuydt and Lohest, discovered the skeletal remains of three men. Two of these skulls were almost intact, including some of their limb bones. These human remains were also mixed with some animal bones of the Mousterian period, giving rise to the dating of the age of the remains.

1900   It was not until 1900 that Europeans and European-Americans engaged in the study of palaeontology decided to turn their attention towards Africa for possible discoveries of fossil man. As such, they decided to look in Egypt, since Egypt was always considered by the Modern European as a CAUCASIAN entity, and because of its proximity to Europe. And there was the possibility that they would have found further remains of fossils they could have identified with their own NEANDERTHAL MAN. They believed such men wandered into Africa from Europe thousands of years before the entrance of the Hyksos[9] (whom they also claimed) in 1675 B.C.E.*

1908   The discovery of a complete skeleton of the NEANDERTHAL MAN by three abbies in France, and its analytical explanation by the palaeontologist Marcellin Boule made "MODERN MAN" understand the true nature of man in scientific terms for the first time. However, this did not change the narrow predjudices of the Europeans to look for fossils in Africa as they were doing in Europe and Asia. For Asia had by this time became an acceptable area of research. A cranium with most of its jaw intact, similar to the Neanderthal Man, was also found in southern France.

1910   In 1910 the first two of more than forty different human-type skulls and limbs of fossil-man were discovered in Kimit (Egypt). They were named PARAPITHECUS FARDI and PROPLIOPITHESUS HAECKELLI. The latter being a chimpanzee-like skull with jaw. They also have teeth that are extremely similar to MODERN MAN, as observed at the turn of the twentieth century C.E.

1913   It was during the year 1913 that HOMO CAPENSES, otherwise called Boskop Man, was discovered through sheer accident in Monomotapa (presently called South Africa).[10] This discovery upset the entire racist and non-scientific approach of most European and European-American scientists of that period towards Africa and the indigenous African peoples. For it was then proven that ancient man, or man's LINK (Fossil man), was not exclusive to the regions of the shores along the Mediterranean Sea or Asia. That all over the Planet Earth there were fossils to be unearthed. From this juncture the drive for further fossil discoveries in Africa advanced beyond expectation. As a result the following incomplete, but most representative of available outstanding lists of fossil-human and proto-humans found in Alkebu-lan (Africa), is compiled according to date of find.[11]

---

*Note that up until this date the Europeans still believed that they originated in Europe and the Caucaus Mountain Range in Asia. They only expected to find "WANDERERS".

A PARTIAL CHRONOLOGICAL LISTING BY DATE OF FOSSIL-MAN UNEARTHED IN ALKEBU-LAN

1. PARAPITHECUS frasi, Egypt 1910, unearthed by Max Schlosser. An African ape of more than 35 million years.

2. PROPLIOPITHECUS haeckelli, Egypt 1910, unearthed by Max Schlosser. An African ape found at Fayoun, bigger than Parapithecus frasi and related.

3. HOMO capenses (Boskop Man), Monomotapa (colonial South Africa), 1913.

4. OLDOWAY skeleton, unearthed in Tanganyika, East Africa, 1914.

5. HOMO zambianiensis (misnamed "rhodesiensis"), unearthed in Zambia, East Africa (colonial Northern Rhodesia), in 1921.

6. AFRICANLOPITHECUS (misnamed "Australopitecus africanus"), unearthed in Botswana, Monomotapa (colonial Bechuanaland of South Africa), 1924.

7. WILLEY's KOPJE skeletons, unearthed in Kenya, East Africa, 1927.

8. ELMENTEITA skeletons, unearthed in Kenya, East Africa, 1927.

9. PARC EPIC skull remains, unearthed in Ethiopia, East Africa, 1928.

10. The ASSELAR skeleton, unearthed in Western Sudan (formerly a part of French colonial Soudan Sahara region), 1928.

11. The GAMBLE's CAVE skeletons, unearthed in Kenya, East Africa, 1928-1929.

12. PROCONSUL africanus skeletal remains, unearthed in Kenya, East Africa, 1931-48. An ape of about 20 million years, discovered by Dr. Mary Leakey, a British archaeologist - just as equally famous as her husband - Louis Leakey.[12] However, pro-consul africanus, like parapithecus, belongs to the most human-type apes found in Kenya. Linnopithecus molars are strikingly similar to those of present day humans.

---

*Cecil Rhodes (for whom this fossil is named) was similar to the African people as Adolph Hitler was to the Jewish people. Who would dare name a Jewish fossil in honor of Adolph Hitler? Why then name an African fossil in honor of Rhodes? The name of the area where this fossil was unearthed is Zambia. This fossil should be prefixed with its name.

13. HOMO KANMENSIA, unearthed in Kenya, East Africa, 1932.

14. The KANJERA skulls, unearthed in Kenya, East Africa, 1932.

15. The HOMO SHELL MOUND skeletons, unearthed in Kenya, East Africa, 1932.

16. The RABAT skull, unearthed in Morocco, North Africa, 1933.

17. AFRICANTHROPUS njarasensia, unearthed in Tanganyika (Tanzania), East Africa, 1936.

18. AFRICALOPITECUS* zululensis, unearthed in the Zulu Nation of what is today called "Transvaal", formerly part of the Monomotapa Empire (Southern Africa), 1936.

19. PLESIANTHROPUS zululensis, unearthed in the Zulu Nation of what is today called "Transvaal", formerly part of the Monomotapa Empire (Southern Africa), 1936.

20. PARANTHROPUS robustus, unearthed in the Zulu Nation, 1938.

21. TANGIER SKULL FRAGMENTS, unearthed in Morocco, North Africa, 1939.

22. MEGANTHROPUS africanus, unearthed in Tanganyika, East Africa, 1948.

23. PARANTHROPUS crassidens, unearthed in the Zulu Nation, 1948.

24. TELANTHROPUS capensis, unearthed in the Zulu Nation, 1949.

25. ATLANTHROPUS mauritanicus, unearthed in Algeria, North Africa, 1955-56.

26. ZINJANTHROPUS*, unearthed in Tanganyika, East Africa, on July 17, 1959 by Dr. Mary Leaky and Dr. Louis Leaky (husband and wife team) at Olduvai Gorge. Among the first of the TOOL-MAKING hominids. Man's most possible LINK with his prehistoric ancestors to date. Note that the suffix "<u>boisie</u>" is generally listed with this fossil's title. It is the name of the individual that aided the financial exploits of this find.

---

*Europeans and European-Americans have consistently renamed Africans and things African what they feel they should be named, always overlooking the Africans resentment at such tactics. This fossil is called "AUSTRALOPITHECUS transvaalensis" by the Europeans and European-Americans. It is neither from Australia nor Transvaal; these are European appendages, not African.

27. Pre-ZINJANTHROPUS (Homo habilus), same as Zinjanthropus. Unearthed in the lowest Bed of the Olduvai Gorge by Drs. Mary and Louis Leaky. Rated to be at least 1,750,000 (1.8 million) years old by the University of California new potassium-argon method test.[13]

28. CHELLEAN MAN, a skull unearthed in the Olduvai Gorge of Tanganyika, East Africa. It was named for the period in which it lived - from the earlier Chellean Stage of the Lower Palaeolithic Chelles-Acheul culture. It is considered to be a brain case of greater size than Pithecanthropus from Peking, China (Asia), but not larger than a Homo Sapien's. It is approximately 500,000 years old.

29. PITECANTHROPINE skull, unearthed at the Olduvai Gorge in Tanganyika, East Africa, during many different years since the first excavations started.

30. SKULL FRAGMENTS OF THE ACHEULIAN INDUSTRY FROM KAJERA, unearthed in Western Kenya, East Africa. Western Scientists are still puzzled as to their likeness to 20th century C.E. man. They are approximately 55,000 to 60,000 years old; and possibly the earliest of the "TRUE HOMO SAPIENS" in the world.

The PIONEERS and PREHISTORIANS of East African archaeological findings were men such as E.J. Weyland who used Uganda as the first East African area to gain attention. He was at the time Director of Uganda's Geological Survey soon after the first World War. He worked primarily on the cultural succession and past climatic changes of Africa; identifying the KAFUAN pebble culture (presently descredited as being of human workmanship). His SAN-GOAN and MAGOSIAN are names he selected from sites on the Kafu River, Sango Bay, on Mwanza Nyanza* shores, including a waterhole called MAGOSI - in Karamoja. See, ANNUAL REPORTS OF THE GEOLOGICAL

---

*Note that this area of Africa was under the colonia control of Britain. The British colonialists renamed this lake "VICTORIA" in honor of one of the world's most dangerous despotic monarchs in the history of modern man - QUEEN VICTORIA. To the Africans she represented their Adolph Hitler.

SURVEY OF UGANDA and other journals by T.P. O'Brien (1939) for discoveries by E.J. Weyland.

A South African Boer (Afrikaner), Professor C. Van Riet Lowe, in 1952, published the first known detailed account of Africa's cultural sequence. It was basically concerned with NSONGEZI on the Kagera River where most of the prehistoric sites are found in Uganda to date. But, the first of the Europeans to visit this same site was Weyland in 1930. Geologist W.W. Bishop and archaeologist M. Posnansky have also made very extensive interpretations of Uganda's archaeological past history in their studies of the entire region.

During the year 1926 Dr. Louis S.B. Leakey conducted the first systematic investigation of the STONE-AGE CULTURES of Kenya, East Africa.* His first archaeological expedition was in 1926 in the Nairraha-Nakura Lake Basin of the Rift Valley, where he noted the climatical changes and effects, as shown in many of his works on this subject matter. He was assisted by Weyland; and later on by the Swedish geologist E. Nilsson who was on his own investigation of Kenya's Rift Valley.

In 1893 a geologist named J.W. Gregory noted that a formation of a large lake in the Rift Valley must have been in existence for thousands of years, which he figured accounted for the vast

---

*Dr. Leakey was born in Kenya of English missionary parents. He was educated at Cambridge University, England. He became the Curator of the Coryndon Museum, Nairobi, Kenya. He held the position until 1961.

amount of deposits of diatomite accumulated in the Kamasian escarpment west of Lake Banngo and elsewhere in the general area. He also dated the Kamasian Lake to the Niocene period. However, Dr. Louis S.B. Leakey's hand axes were found imbedded in the lake deposit, thereby indicating its Pleistocene age.

In 1931 Dr. Leakey's book, THE STONE AGE CULTURES OF KENYA COLONY, was published. In this work the BLADE-AND-BURIN CULTURE, HAND-AXE CULTURE, FLAKE CULTURE, and the so-called MESOLITHIC and NEOLITHIC INDUSTRIES, were given full recognition. Within a period of five years Dr. Leakey had unearthed skeletal remains older than any other man had seen before. These remains were discovered at Kanam and Kanjera in Western Kenya. (See, L.S.B. Leakey, THE STONE AGE RACES OF KENYA, London, 1935.)

In 1913 the late Dr. Hans Reck, a German geologist, discovered a skeleton at Olduvai Gorge, which was to him contemporary with the Middle Pleistocene deposits. Later on he also found burial mounds in the Ngorongoro Crater which also contained skeletal remains, stone bowls and beads; but no Stone Age implements. In 1931 Dr. Leakey visited the Olduvai Gorge, and revisited it in 1932 - at which time he found his astonishing skeletal remains. This discovery is to date only surpassed by his later findings in Tanganyika (Tanzania).[14] From here on it was a field-day for archaeologists and anthropologists. In 1935 L. Kohl-Larsen found fragments of a highly humanized skull near the shores of Lake Eyasi, not very far from the Olduvai Gorge - from which H.Weinert created his new genus for AFRICANTHROPUS, a name which very soon after lost acknowledgement. The EYASI MAN, as the find was called, was regarded as a relative of "RHODESIA MAN"* - a fossil found at Broken Hill in 1921 by African and European miners in the area.

In 1929-31 Seton-Karr found the ACHEULIO-SEVALLVISIAN artifacts, which is the most ancient collection of its kind from the so-called "HORN" - approximately 90 miles southwest from Berhera, Somalia, at an area called ISSUTUGAN. Later on in the Somali Republic (formerly called BRITISH SOMALILAND by the British colonialists and slavers) C. Barrington found similar collections in the northeast during 1931. In the same year A.T. Curle found some artifacts on the Hageisa Plateau. (See, Sonia Cole, THE PRE-HISTORY OF EAST AFRICA; also Y. Gordon Childe, MAN MAKES HIMSELF).

With respect to all of the scientists mentioned, and those not mentioned, it is still the Leakeys - Drs. Mary and Louis -

---

*It is to be noted that the name RHODESIA MAN is a grave insult to the African peoples; for Cecil Rhodes, for whom it is named, derived its base from the colonial name RHODESIA which the British colonialist called both ZAMBIA and ZIMBABWE. And, as stated before, it is similar to giving the name Adolph Hitler or Adolph Eichmann to anything in honour of Jewish peoples. The correct name of the area is ZIMBABWE, the name the African peoples created. This find should have been called ZIMBABWE MAN. One will note that the Europeans and European-Americans who came to Africa in search of fossil-man were colonialist and imperialist in thinking and racist in practice. This was best seen in their attempt to make their fossil-finds everything from CAUCASIAN to HAMITIC and SEMITIC, etc.; the African peoples around being completely devoid of any past into antiquity of pre-history.

who made the greatest inroad on the <u>average man,</u> so far as PREHISTORIC MAN is concerned. Their unearthing of ZINJANTHROPUS BOISIE on July 17, 1959, on the slopes of Bed I of the Olduvai Gorge, Tanganyika (Tanzania),[14] eastern Africa, at a site known as F.L.K., has been to date the most outstanding find in the LINK between man, as we know him today, and his prehistoric ancestors dating thousands and millions of years ago before the origin of the myth of a "GARDEN OF EDEN" and the "CREATION OF ADAM". The prehistoric ancestors to which this analysis allude are those spoken of by Sir Charles Darwin, the Victorian scientist of Great Britain to whom reference has already been made in this chapter. With regards to the finds by the Leakeys, the following maps, graphs and charts on pages 34 and 35 should be closely examined for detailed information and geographic conditions of the sites.

It is in Bed I, which is full of VILLAFRANCHIAN FAUNA, as well as fossil remains of the type commonly called "AUSTRALOPITHECENES" by the European and European-Americans, with the PEBBLE CULTURE which they produced that the Leakeys (Mary the finder, and Louis) found their ZINJANTHROPUS and HOMO HABILIS entombed at its base. One can only imagine the extent of the work that was required in collecting the fragmented fossil remains and the subsequent reconstruction to their original form as shown on pages 49 and 50, considering the expansion and contraction caused by the

CHARACTERISTICS OF ZINJANTHROPUS BOISIE

Fossils Trace Man Back 600,000 Years In Gorge in Africa

LEOPOLDVILLE, Belgian Congo, Aug. 23 (Reuters)— Human fossils about 600,000 years old—possibly the earliest known trace of man—have been found in Tanganyika.

Dr. Louis S. B. Leakey, a prominent anthropologist, said that his wife, also an anthropologist, had found the fossils among animal remains in the Oldoway Gorge in Tanganyika, July 17.

Dr. Leakey, 56 years old, a British expert on East African anthropology, has searched for many years to prove his belief that man originated in Africa. He is curator of the Corydon Museum of Natural History in Nairobi, Kenya.

Dr. Leakey reported his wife's find to the Pan-African Congress of Prehistory here yesterday. Sixty delegates from fifteen countries, including the United States, are at the congress.

Crude tools were found with the fossils, suggesting some form of human culture, Dr. Leakey said. He said a reconstruction of the bones showed a skull that was estimated to date from the second half of the Pleistocene geological era 600.000 years ago.

N.Y.Times.Aug.24,1959

Palate and teeth of "boise" (below) compared with those of an Australian indiginous man (so-called "aborigine").

National Geographic Magazine, Sept. 1960, has a picture of one skull, and quotes Prof. Leakey as saying that it was that of the first tool-making human; and that the discoveries "strongly support Charles Darwin's prophecy that Africa would prove to have been the birthplace of mankind."

Prof. Leakey has since discovered a still older skull "considerably more than 600,000 years old." With it were other human relics, one of them a child. (New York Times, Feb. 25, 1961).

N. Y. Times, Aug. 24, 1959.

* * *

The age of the skulls is now set at 1,750,000 years. (*New York Times*, July 23, 1961.)

Side view of skull

External construction of skull and face.

Front view of skull

Left: Reconstruction of the Rhodesian Man with the original skull

The skull was found at Broken Hill, Rhodesia, almost in the heart of Africa with 160 feet of packed above it.

Note: Since the unearthing of Zinjanthropus beisie there has been many more fossil-men found in the same general area of East Africa, and in Ethiopia, some dated back to 5,000,000 years before "ADAM AND EVE IN THE GARDEN OF EDEN."

RECONSTRUCTION OF FOSSIL-MAN

(Top) Reconstruction of Zinjanthropus boisie (African fossil-man)

Full figure attempt by Maurice Wilson

(Top) A sculptured attempt at reconstructing Neanderthal man (European fossil-man).

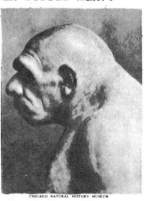

(Bottom) An attempt in paint. Both by Maurice Wilson.[1a]

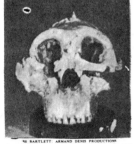

(Bottom) Skull of Zinjanthropus boisie unearthed in Bed I of Ol Olduvai Gorge, Tanganyika, by Dr's. L.S. & M. Leakey.[1a]

ACKNOWLEDGMENTS

British Museum (Natural History), Department of Anthropology

American Museum of Natural History, New York

Chicago Museum of Natural History

BBC School Publications

Leonard Grant of the National Geographic Society.

Note: Note the RACIST attempt to make the African fossil-man appear to be of "CAUCASIAN" or "SEMITIC" origin. Why was Zinjanthropus boisie not shown with the so-called "NEGROID" characteristics generally attributed to the so-called "BANTU", "NEGRO", or "AFRICAN SOUTH OF THE SAHARA" of Africa.

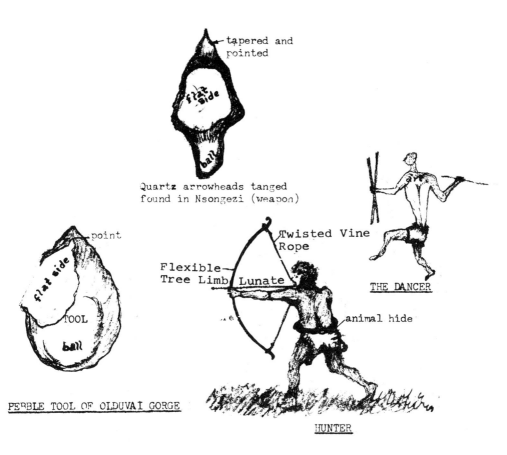

EARLY MAN of the NILE VALLEY
(c1,750,000 BCE - ?)

The above graphical demonstrations are projected for the student to grasp the earliest type of weapons mankind used in order to provide food, clothing and shelter; not for pleasure as so-called "modern man" who has all but exterminated certain animals.

BENTONITIC CLAY* in which these remains were trapped for so many hundreds of thousands of years at a level exceeding more than 21 feet below the top of Bed I. This substance, BENTONITIC CLAY, is approximately 40 to 42 feet thick at the point of first contact. Luckily the bones had not been distorted when they were covered thereby allowing for the successful removal of the most fragile pieces of the nasals in perfect condition.

At later periods the Leakeys also unearthed several fossil remains of the pre-Zijanthropus era, all of which may be studied in the many volumes of books and periodicals, also in the major papers presented before scientific societies of the world over, by both Louis and Mary Leakey. However, Zinjanthropus and his later descendants appear to have been very much more intellegent by far.[15] It is to be noted that the origin of the name ZINJAN-THROPUS BOISIE stems from the following words: ZENJ BAR, an early name which the Persian invaders and traders used to name the east coast of Africa. Thus: COAST OF THE BLACKS, MAN OF THE ZENJ, and BLACK COAST MAN. The BOISIE came from the name of the Englishman who was very influential in advancing the monies necessary for the project conducted by the Leakeys in which this fossil remain was unearthed.

---

*This is a mineral substance that is called "BENTONITE". It was so named because of its abundant quantity in the Fort Benton, Montana (U.S.A.) area. It is a special type of clay that is formed by decomposition of volcanic ash, having the ability to absorb very large quantities of water, thereby expanding to several times its normal volume.

Although the Leakeys' find is not the end to the LINK between man of the twentieth century C.E. (A.D.) and his most ancient ancestors, it is the best evidence, so far, that sets Alkebu-lan (Africa) as the apparently TRUE HOME OF THE ORIGINAL MAN ("Garden of Eden")[16]; our "Adam and Eve" not withstanding. Finds such as these are also the reason why men like the Jeffreys, Wiedners, Junods and Hitlers have to remove the indigenous Africans which they called "BANTUS, NEGROES", and the likes of same, from the PREHISTORY, ANCIENT HISTORY, and CONTEMPORARY HISTORY of Alkebulan. If this is not done the indigenous Africans to whom this land belong will appear as they should; thus the Africans whom "Western educators" call "AFRICANS SOUTH OF THE SAHARA", and all of their other insulting names of slavery and colonialism, would be the FATHERS AND MOTHERS of the LIGHT-SKINNED AND DARK-SKINNED CAUCASIAN, Modern Man, one hears so much about in the educational system of the Greek-centric Anglo-Saxon Judaeo-Christian racist and bigoted world otherwise called "WESTERN DEMOCRACY".

In conjunction with the above last paragraph it is of major importance that one's attention focus on the following article in the New York Times. This publication deals with the indigenous Africans' MINE where they smolted IRON thousands of years before there was the first European High-Culture - GREECE. It also contradicted those "Western educators" who have for generations maintained that:

"THE AFRICANS KNEW NOTHING OF IRON UNTIL THE EARLY

PART OF THE CHRISTIAN ERA, AT WHICH TIME IT WAS
INTRODUCED BY ASIAN INVADERS," etc.

(See page 56 for article entitled "43,000 - YEAR - OLD MINE DIS-
COVERED IN SWAZILAND." Specific attention should be also given
to the author's comment at the end of the article.)

BIBLIOGRAPHY FOR CHAPTER II

Hay, R.L.	STRATIGRAPHY OF BEDS I THROUGH IV, OLDUVAI GORGE, Tanganyika Science, 139, 1963.
Hooijer, D.A.	PALAEONTOLOGY OF HOMINID DEPOSITS IN ASIA, Advance Science, 18, 1962.
Montagu, M.F.A.	A CONSIDERATION OF THE CONCEPT OF RACE, Cold Spring Harbor Symposia on Quantitative Biology, 15, 1950.
Movius, T.H.L.	RADIOCARBON DATES AND UPPER PALAEOLITHIC ARCHAEOLOGY IN CENTRAL AND WESTERN EUROPE (ed. by A.L. Kroeber's, Anthropology Today, Chicago, 1953).
Seligman, G.G.	THE RACES OF AFRICA, New York, 1937.
Wieschoff, H.A.	THE ZIMBABWE-MONOMOTAPA CULTURE OF S.E. AFRICA, Uganda Journal, 14, 1950.
Wells, H.L.	THE FOSSIL HUMAN SKULL FROM SINGA (In: Pleistocene Fauna of Two Blue Nile Sites, British Museum of Natural History, London, 1951).
Coles, S.	THE PREHISTORY OF EAST AFRICA, New York, 1965.
O'Brien, T.P.	ANNUAL REPORTS OF THE GEOLOGICAL SURVEY OF UGANDA, 1939.
Leakey, L.S.B.	THE STONE AGE RACE OF KENYA, London, 1931.
-----	THE STONE AGE CULTURES OF KENYA COLONY, London, 1935.
-----	ANTIQUITY, STONE AGE CULTURES OF KENYA COLONY, London, 1951.

Bishop, W.W.　　　　　PLEISTOCENE ENVIRONMENTS AND EARLY MAN IN UGANDA, Uganda Journal. 24, 1960.

Clark, J.D.　　　　　THE STONE AGE CULTURES OF NORTHERN RHODESIA, 1950.

———————　　　　　THE PATTERN OF EVOLUTIONARY DEVELOPMENT OF THE GENUS HOMO (in: South African Journal of Medical Science, 23, 1958).

LeGross, Clark &　　THE NIOCENE HOMINOIDEA OF EAST AFRICA, British Museum of Natural History, London, 1951.
Leakey, Louis B.

Churchward, Dr. A.　ORIGIN AND EVOLUTION OF FREEMASONRY, London, 1920.
———————　　　　　ARCANA OF FREMASONRY, London, 1915.
———————　　　　　SIGNS AND SYMBOLS OF PRIMORDIAL MAN, London, 1925.

INSTITUTIONAL SOURCES:

The American Museum of Natural History of New York, N.Y., N.Y.

Chicago Natural History Museum, Chicago, Ill.

Peabody Museum Of Archaeology and Ethnology, Harvard University, Cambridge, Massachusettes.

Princeton University Museum of Natural History, Princeton, New Jersey.

University of Pennsylvania Museum, Philadelphia, Pennsylvania.

Cleveland Museun of Natural History, Cleveland, Ohio.

43,000 - YEAR-OLD MINE discovered in Swaziland

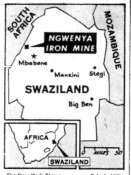

The New York Times — Feb. 8, 1970

Special to The New York Times

JOHANNESBURG, South Africa, Feb. 7—South African archeologists have reported discovering the world's oldest mine. The mine, in an iron-ore mountain in neighboring Swaziland, is 43,000 years old, according to radiocarbon dating.

It was discovered by Adrian Boshier, field research officer for the Museum of Man and Science in Johannesburg. Mr. Boshier made his discovery at Bomvu Ridge in the Ngwenya (Crocodile) mountain range in Swaziland.

He discovered caverns extending into the mountain and stone-age mining tools, indicating that, prehistoric man had been there mining hematite—a source of iron.

The early miners had excavated for hematite rich in specularite—one of the most prized pigments and cosmetics of ancient times, he said.

Mr. Boshier was joined by another young archeologist, Peter Beaumont, who excavated deeper. Mr. Beaumont' found samples of charcoal from old fires. The samples were sent to radio carbon dating laboratories at Yale and Groningen.

Note: One can only wonder how soon it will be before this mine will be claimed by the Jeffreys and Wiedners to be of CAUCASIAN or SEMITIC origin. It will be said that 'THE INDIGENOUS AFRICANS (the so-called "Bantus") HAD NOTHING TO DO WHATSOEVER WITH ITS OPERATION.' Of course no proof will be submitted to show how the CAUCASIANS or SEMITES got to Monomotapa (South Africa) and the INDIGENOUS AFRICANS did not. This will be no different than their former claims relative to the GRIMALDI SKULLS, BOSKOP MAN and ZINJANTHROPUS BOISIE.

CHAPTER I
WHO WERE/ARE THE AFRICANS OF ANCIENT ALKEBU-LAN (Africa)?

THESE TYPES IN THE HARLEMS OF THE UNITED STATES OF AMERICA

It is of very deep significance to commence the identification of the Africans by citing certain major quotations about them. In this sense there is no better way to start than with the following remarks by an Englishman named Thomas Hodgkin, former Secretary of the Oxford University Delegacy for Extra-Mural Studies and a Fellow of Balliol College, Oxford. The quotation from Mr. Hodgkin stems from an article that appeared in THE HIGHWAY, February, 1952, pp. 169-170, under the title - "<u>National Movements In West Africa.</u>" He wrote:

> It is no doubt flattering to our vanity to imagine that the peoples of Africa were 'primitive' and 'barbarous' before the penetration of the Europeans, and that it is we who have "civilized" them. But it is a theory that lacks historical foundation. The Empire of Ghana flourished in what is now French West Africa during the dark ages of Western Europe. By the fifteenth century there was a university at Timbuktu. The Ashantis of the Gold Coast* and the Yorubas of Nigeria possessed highly organized and complex civilizations** long before their territories were brought under British political control. The thesis that Africa is what Western European missionaries, traders, technicians and administrators have made it is comforting (to Western Europeans) but invalid. The eruption of Western European colonizers into Africa - with all the effects of their religion and their schools, their Gin and their cotton goods and their systems of administration is only an event, though a very important event, in the history of the African peoples.

---

*Gold Coast was the colonial name the British imperialists forced on peoples of an area in West Africa, which has since been renamed by the African inhabitants "<u>Ghana</u>" in honor of the ancient West African Empire bearing the same name.
**The use of this word is objectionable. It is a racist term that designed to indicate inferiority to Europeans.

> If, therefore, we wish to understand the
> national movements that have emerged in Africa -
> and have reached their most mature and advanced
> stage in West Africa - we have to begin by trying
> to rid our minds of the European preconceptions
> that influence our thinking on this subject.
> This is not easy, since, most of the available
> material on African affairs is presented from a
> European standpoint - either by imperial histor-
> ians (who are interested in the record of European
> penetration into Africa), or by colonial admin-
> istrators (who are interested in the pattern of
> instructions imposed by European governments upon
> African Societies), or by anthropologists (who
> are often though not always, mainly interested
> in the forms of social organizations surviving
> in the simplest African communities, considered
> in isolation from political developments in the
> world around them). We shall probably have to
> wait a little while for the real history of Africa
> to be written by African scholars for an African
> reading public.

Mr. Hodgkin's revelations were brought to light on somewhat of an official basis. His response was to certain allegations made by Sir Hugh Clifford, former Governor of Britain's West African colony which the British renamed "GOLD COAST CROWN COLONY"[1] (presently Republic of Ghana).*

Writing in BLACKWOOD'S MAGAZINE, January 1918, and having quite a bit to say about the Africans of the "Gold Coast" in a manner that was intended to be complimentary to the Africans, but in fact was very stereotyped in character, Sir Clifford stated:

> Much the most notable achievement that can be
> placed to his credit is his invention, without the
> assistance of extraneous influence, of the democratic
> system of government and State socialism, which

---

*First African composite political entity created by European imperialists at the Berlin Conference ("Act") as an "African nation" with its present geo-political boundary to gain "political independence". =1957 C.E. under Dr. Kwame Nkrumah, its liberator.

> are the basic principles upon which his tribal*
> policy is founded. Recent innovations, as I have
> indicated, tends seriously to undermine this system;
> and it is interesting to note that while European
> political theorists are apparently working their
> way back to a state of things closely resembling
> that which the TWI-speaking peoples long ago evolved
> for themselves, the latter are displaying an inclin-
> ation to discard them as an immediate and inevitable
> accomplishment of their first real and solid advance
> towards a higher standard of civilization.

The TWI people, who Sir Clifford referred to, are for the most part located around the Republic of Liberia, the Republic of Guinea, and the Republic of Ghana. These people are also found in other surrounding nations of this general area of West Africa. At one time they had one of the most flourishing cultures of the nations of West Africa. They used <u>their own language and alphabet</u> until their adoption of the <u>Islamic Faith</u> and the Islamic language - <u>Arabic</u>.

These are two most privileged firsthand accounts of great African "<u>civilizations</u>" on the part of two men who were in a position to know the "TRUTH" about Africa; West Africa in particular. But this work is dealing primarily with the Africans' cultural development. Therefore, there are those who, for various reasons, do not credit Africa's sons and daughters with being <u>human</u>, much less being able to produce human culture, civil traits and societies. This type of characterization has been

---

* This was true for African nations also. Most Europeans and European-Americans refused to deal with Africans from a point of nationhood, giving the impression that Africans had no national compacts that were subjugated by the European colonists.

perpetuated by certain "LEARNED" men such as Prof. M.D.W. Jeffreys. This "learned" (a holder of the highest academic degree) man's works (more specifically his personal views) were published in the September 1951 issue of the WEST AFRICAN REVIEW under the title - "The Negro Enigma". As a picture of racist propaganda, it revealed a profound disregard for documentation and it displayed an extraordinary gift for creating stereotypes. He wrote:

> The Negro is divided linguistically into two main groups. The Sudanic-speaking Negroes* of West Africa and the Bantu** speaking Negroes of the Congo, East and South Africa.*** All are of one race**** and are remarkably uniform in appearance.
>
> The Black Belt, anthropologically speaking, is that area on the earth's surface that comprises the dark-skinned races, excluding the American Negroes who were brought there by Europeans. The Black Belt extends from Africa, via India, to Melanesia and Australia. In this great arc the position of the Negro is the enigma.***** At the two ends, or horns, are the people who are Negroes, but in the centre there are none. The centre is occupied by a dark-

---

*This word is not African, it was placed on the Africans by the Portugese and other slavers around the 16th or 17th Century C.E.

**Of the host of racist terminologies used to label African peoples this one is the most stereotyped. Everyone is lumped into a linguistic setting that is also used as a "race".

***South Africa was originally called "MONOMOTAPA" by the indigenous Africans that inhabited that area for thousands of years before the first European (light-skinned Caucasian) arrived there in 1488 C.E. with Bartolome Dias (a Portugese). They lived there in their glorious High-Culture until it was destroyed by the British, Dutch, German, and French colonialists and masters of genocide against the African peoples.

****What makes Africans more uniform physically than Europeans?

*****This is a typical illness of most racists. Professors are no exception.

> skinned race, the Hindu, but he offers no difficulty. He belongs to the same race as the "European", namely the Caucasian, which is divided into the light-skinned Caucasians - the inhabitants of Europe - and the dark-skinned Caucasians, the inhabitants of North Africa, Asia Minor and India.

Though Professor Jeffreys, at this juncture, had established his racist hypotheses, he continued to expand his "LIGHT" and "DARK-SKINNED" Caucasianism theory to the point where he eliminated all of the indigenous Africans - the so-called "BANTUS" and "NEGROES" - from all of North and East Africa. Thus, he questioned:

> How comes it that east and west India is flanked by Negroes? That is the puzzle: i.e. that there are Oceanic and African Negroes separated from each other by Arabia, India and Malaya? Let us view the problem from another angle. The Caucasians come from an old human stock - a stock that is called today Modern Man. Modern Man goes back a long way in time. The Swanscombe skull found in Great Britain is dated 250,000 years and is our stock, not Negro. The skeletal remains dug up by the Leakeys in East Africa are us, not Negro. Boskop man, found in the Cape, is dated 50,000 years and falls into our group not that of the Negro.
>
> There are no Negro skulls of any antiquity - the oldest known is about 6000 B.C. The two Grimaldi skulls, one a woman and the other a boy, are not Negro skulls. They merely show Negro features.

Professor Jeffreys proved to be quite an expert at "hat tricks" as he jumped into North Africa and pulled out his "light-skinned Caucasians". At the Cape (the end of the Southern limits of Africa) he did the same with "BOSKOP MAN". Acting as a magician he hopped and skipped around looking for more "NEGROES" and "BANTUS" in the depths of Southern Africa, (Monomotapa, presently called the Republic of South Africa) and pulled out his Caucasianized "Grimaldi Skulls." At least the good professor pointed out that the "Grimaldi Skulls" have "Negro features." But, he, in no way whatsoever showed that the "skulls" have any "features" resembling his "Modern Man" or "Light-Skinned" and "Dark-Skinned" Caucasians; yet, he concluded..."THEY ARE OURS." He also failed to detail what "Negro features"? The Professor continued further in his admitted state of Negrophobia and enigmatic confusion:

> So the enigma deepens: all evidence points to the Negro being a comparitively recent race and here is the old Caucasian race in a continuous stretch from Britain to India and yet on either side of India are Negroes.

Still not satisfied with his enigmatic dilemma he continued on. Nevertheless the Professor's intemperate proclamations against his "BANTUS" and "NEGROES" reached their climax when he wrote:

> Now in Africa there is continuous evidence, unlike anywhere else on the globe, of man's uninterrupted occupation of the earth close to a million years.

The last sentence exposed the basis for the truly crucial "enigma" the Professor was suffering under. The fact that it is in the Africans' (the so-called "Negroes" and "Bantus") homeland-Alkebu-lan (Africa) that the true GARDEN OF EDEN is located, obviously upset the Professor. It was beyond his own ability to accept that "ADAM" was not a Light-Skinned Caucasian - "Modern Man". This fact he could not allow to remain unchallenged. However, the ground work for his challenge was most certainly established in his prior vituperations. But the tragedy is that his type of propaganda becomes FACT and TRUTH when applied to indigenous Africans, even though it lacks the most basic requirements of scientific or academic sensitivity. As the challenger, however, he knows very well that none of his professional colleagues would have openly condemnned his <u>Bantu-Negrophobia</u>. In like manner the Professor continued:

> Africa is thus today accepted by many scientists as the cradle of the human species. Thus, in Africa, from the Old Stone Age to modern time, Modern Man is the tool maker. Nowhere is the Negro, unlike the Bushman, associated with any of these Stone Age cultures.

One can readily understand why Professor Jeffreys had so many problems with his "<u>enigma</u>", and why most scientists would conclude that Africa, around the Great Lakes region, is the original home of mankind. And, that these earliest of men finally travelled north with the flow of the White and Blue Nile until they crossed into the continent now dominated by Professor's "<u>LIGHT-SKINNED CAUCASIANS</u>" who were once considered to be solely "ORIGINATED IN THE CAUCASUS MOUNTAIN RANGES OF ASIA." True, the Professor must claim the cradle of man's High-Cultures ("civilizations") and the oldest of men as "OURS" - "Modern Man" ("<u>Light-Skinned Caucasians</u>.") If he does not, then what would happen to his, and others' theory of THE SUPERIORITY OF THE WHITE RACE OVER THE DARKER RACES OF THE WORLD? What about Africans in particular? This is even more true when he failed to note that the Africans he selected to call

"Bantus" and "Negroes" were included on his side of the anthropological scale. For he included amongst his "LIGHT" and "DARK-SKINNED CAUCASIANS" such Africans as the Kushites (or Cushites, modern Ethiopians), Nubians (Sudanese), Agikuyu (Kenya), Libyans, Egyptians (Africans, Arabs, and Africanized-Arabs), Gandas (Ugandans), Masais (Tanzanians), and others along the more than 4,100 mile long Nile River Valley (from Uganda to the Mediterranean Sea).[3] Moreover, he also included the Rowzis - builders of the cone-shaped stone structures of Zimbabwe (once the capital of the Monomotapa Empire, presently called "RHODESIA" by European colonial slave masters), and he included the Swazis and Sethos (also of the former Monomotapa Empire, now called the "REPUBLIC OF SOUTH AFRICA" - an exclusively racist government controlled by the Professors' "Light-skinned Caucasians");[4] all of which is done in order to claim Tanzania's ZINJANTHROPUS BOISIE, also Monomotapa's BOSKOP MAN, and Monomotapa's GRIMALDI mother and son, for his superior race.

Other professors employ subtlety in academically camouflaged language not used by Professor Jeffreys, but the same conclusion is reached in their attempt to remove from Africa the Africans whom they too prefer to call "BANTU" and "NEGRO". But Professor Jeffreys was proving his point with respect to "LIGHT" and "DARK-SKINNED" Caucasians of antiquity. His obvious technique was to make a statement which was supposedly fact, knowing very well that it would have wide-range acceptance by millions who need such type of assurance of their racial superiority over others. He was also aware of the fact that researchers, historians, and scientists related to this field would ignore them, and they would never openly condemn him with some sort of an academic excuse to slap him on the hands. There would be no real reprimand. Why is all of this true? Because the Professor is only doing, (and to some extent going further than many), what the European-American system of education requires of him and others like him. As long as he remains in line of what is generally called "<u>academic responsibility</u>" he can continue in this manner, irrespective of the fact that he has not given the slightest evidence to justify any of his declarations. What is most important in this case is that his racism is excusable under the license of "HYPOTHESES." This dishonest term makes <u>lies</u> and <u>fictions</u> FACT. It even makes "NEGROES" and "BANTUS" become "LIGHT" and "DARK-SKINNED CAUCASIANS." But Professor Jeffreys was also proving that the so-called "<u>light</u>" and "<u>dark-skinned Caucasians</u>" were in fact <u>Africans</u> and not <u>Caucasians.</u> That all who call themselves <u>Caucasians</u> are in fact "NATIVES OF DARKEST AFRICA." And that all of the present textbooks dealing with "<u>race</u>" and "<u>ethnic studies</u>" in the United States of America and Europe are without foundation. This is true. For in most of the institutions of learning controlled by "<u>Westerners</u>", or "<u>Modern Man</u>", one of the first step in the humanities is to praise the **GREAT** WHITE CAUCASIAN RACE - of which the Nordic peoples are said to be the "<u>cream of the crop</u>." It is therefore regretable that one must assume that a professor of such note should have failed to read what the oldest of his "<u>Light-skinned Caucasians</u>" - the Greeks - had to say about his choice north Africans and east Africans (the EGYPTIANS and ETHIOPIANS.) The FATHER OF EUROPEAN HISTORY - a Greek* - wrote the following about them:

> THE COLCHIANS, EGYPTIANS, AND ETHIOPIANS HAVE THICK LIPS, BROAD NOSES, WOOLY HAIR, AND THEY ARE BURNT OF SKIN.[5]

Maybe Professor Jeffreys would also say that the above statement "<u>merely shows Negro features</u>" as in the case of his own comments on the "Grimaldi" Africans.** Is it also possible that this Greek, who was discribing the Africans that occupied Egypt, Colchis, and Ethiopia in the year 450 B.C.E., many of whom were his teachers, did not know enough to recognize them as "DARK-SKINNED CAUCASIANS?" He also failed to recognize that it was from these same people that the earliest "<u>Modern Man</u>" - the Greeks - patterned their ancient High-Culture, and all of Europe followed these one time "lowliest of the low"*** until now there is a European-America in which he could denounce their African teachers. All civil compacts today had their original basis of government in Africa, whether Northern, Southern, Eastern or Western.[6] And, from this same African background and origin his

---
*Herodutus in c. 450 B.C.E. For further details see Note No.
**See page 22A of this volume.
***Europeans were called the "lowliest of the low" by the African-Arab scholar Al-Jahiz. See Y-ben-Jochannan, AFRICAN ORIGINS OF THE "MAJOR WESTERN RELIGIONS."

Top: The elegance of prehistoric African art unearthed in southern Africa presently located in the <u>Pretoria Museum</u>, approximately 30,000 years old. Cut by Flint Stone tools by prehistoric indigenous Africans.

Bottom: Reconstruction of a <u>Stone Age</u> indigenous African skull. Such Africans lived during the same period as the artist who made the carving above. (See: J. A. Rogers, AFRICA'S GIFT TO AMERICA, p. 7; also, SEX AND RACE, vol. I, pp. 26, 35).

The prehistoric art of Africa was continuous, as one can readily see in the following statement:"<u>10,000 B.C.E. a Grimaldi</u>"(indigenous south African) sculptor in Monomotapa"(South Africa)"<u>carved the first known statue of a human body</u>."Europeans misnamed it "VENUS OF WILLENDORF." It was confiscated from Africa and placed in the <u>Museum of Vienna</u>, Austria (Europe).

Modern Man sprung.[7] This is recorded evidence, written by the Professor's own earliest "light-skinned Caucasians"' both Greeks and Romans. Maybe Professor Jeffreys would prefer to revise what these earliest of "Modern Men" wrote about their apprenticeship under the indigenous Africans - "NEGROES" and "BANTUS" - to suit his own apparent racism and prejudices. Or maybe he would just like to have his unscientific and irresponsible proclamations remain as they are.

One should understand, however, that the Professor should not totally bear the brunt of the criticism in this matter. Why? Because he also experienced this same line in institutions of higher learning here in these United States of America. And such still remain the basis upon which European-American education, with respect to the terms "RACE" and "ETHNOLOGY", is concerned. He is the basic product of an entire educational system that produces this type of racist history and stereotyped mythology. Not only is this type of racism educational in terms of public and private schools, it is inbeded in the religious institutions of each and every named religion that goes under the following labels: Judaism, Christianity, and Islam. Because, the first people to spread racism were those who advanced "THE CHOSEN PEOPLE" myth more than five thousand (5,000) years ago. This they backed up much later with another racist proclamation. Thus, we hear of the story about "Jehovah turning Cain BLACK because of his sin" - the murder of his brother ABEL. Of course

69

the Christians have it their own way. They maintain that "the BLACK MAN got his color because of his sin against God" - Jesus Christ (the SPIRIT, the FATHER, and the SON) when a fellow named HAM...

"STARED AT HIS FATHER'S (Noah) NAKEDNESS IN THE ARK." This type of mythology has been mentioned elsewhere in this volume, but at no time is it overstated, for it has caused so much bigotry on the part of racist teachings that it should be constantly exposed whenever or wherever possible.

The following two pages of this chapter are specially prepared with comments. They are about two hypotheses of Professor Jeffreys' "Modern Men" - Light Skinned Caucasians. They are both dealing with the origin of man in his respective ethnographical maps. One holds that the continent of Africa was originally settled by different kinds of "NEGROES." ("NILOTIC, TRUE, and MASABA.") The other notes that there was nothing else but "CAUCASIANS" in East-Central, East, and North Africa; and the "NEGRO" is placed in a tiny little streak across the West and West-Central portion of the continent. On the third page the author of this volume also adds his hypotheses (projected beliefs) as to just what the evidence, as seen by an African historian, points to in regards to the origin and travel of the original people of the continent. Note that the latter map has no CAUCASIANS, NEGROES, HOTTENTOTS, BUSHMEN or any of the other desparaging stereotypes reserved for peoples of African origin that resemble BLACK Americans (who are

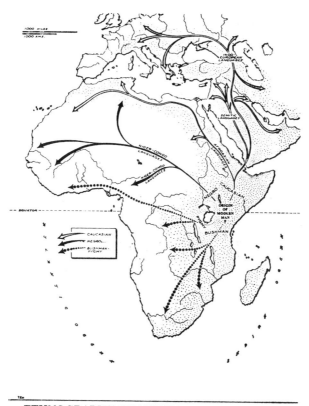

ETHNOGRAPHY OF AFRICA BEFORE 300 B.C. *(HYPOTHESIS)*

This map was taken from Dr. Donald L. Wiedner's, A HISTORY OF AFRICA SOUTH OF THE SAHARA...., etc., New York, 1962. Note the RACIST attempt to remove all so-called "NEGROES" from NORTH and EAST, also SOUTHEAST Africa. This so-called "AUTHORITY", one of Professor Jeffreys' "MODERN MAN" or "LIGHT-SKINNED CAUCASIAN", openly proclaimed that the indigenous Africans did not occupy the areas of North and East Africa he reserved for his "CAUCASIANS" and "AFRO-ASIANS", and ofcourse, his "SEMITIC" chosen people during antiquity; thus perpetuating the CAUCASIAN-SEMITE MYTH of the 19th century C.E.

PREHISTORIC AFRICA

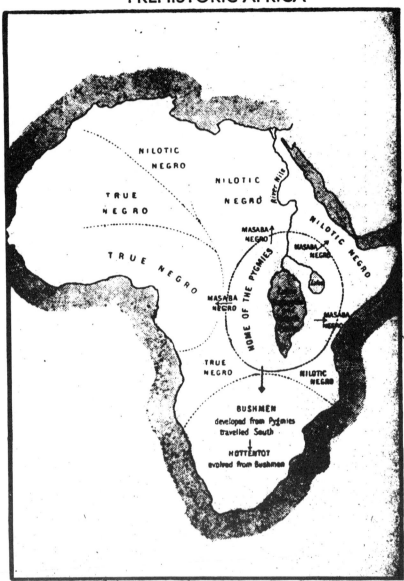

Map from Albert Churchward, M.D. (noted British archaeologist and palaeontologist) book, ORIGIN AND EVOLUTION OF **FREEMASONRY**. He stated that the area marked "HOME OF THE PYGMIES" was the original HOME OF MANKIND - Caucasians and Semites included. This refutes Dr. Donald Weidner's Negrophopic hypothesis on page 71. Strange it is that the so-called "Authorities" (modern man) are so far apart on whether or not the indigenous Africans (BLACKS) were the "INFERIOR NEGROES" or the "SUPERIOR CAUCASIANS".

PREHISTORIC AFRICAN MIGRATION IN AND OUT OF AFRICA

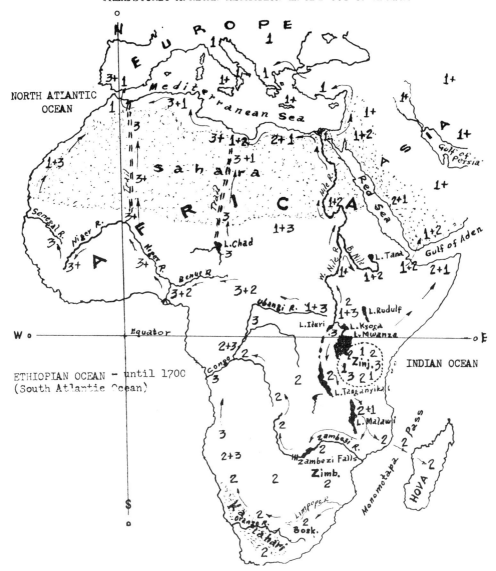

The author's non-RACIST hypothesis of the indigenous Africans migration from the approximate area around the Great Lakes region or Olduvai Gorge where mankind is believed to have originated. 1=Nile Bound Africans; 2=Monomotapa Bound Africans; 3=Congo River and Niger River Bound Africans. Original Home correspond with Dr. Churchward's on p. 72; the present "OLDUVAI GORGE" in Tanganyika, Republic of Tanzania-Home of <u>Zinjanthropus boisie</u>, a fossil-man of c1,750,000 years before the Hebrews' Holy Torah (Old Testament) "ADAM".

otherwise called BANTUS in Africa.)

The maps and hypotheses which have been presented for review and discussion are but a few of the thousands that fill volumes upon volumes of what is generally called "AUTHORITATIVE WORKS." Yet one will not find the type of conclusions Dr. Donald Wiedner reached in his hypotheses. This theory, which he follows, is nothing new - racist as it may be. But at one time in modern history, when it was still believed that the peoples of Africa would forever remain colonial subjects of Professor Jeffreys' Light-Skinned Caucasians, every "Modern" historian of note conceded that Africa was originally settled by the people they then called "NEGROES, HAMITES, ETHIOPIANS," etc. The term "BANTU" was not then used by any of the European and European-American educators. At that time it was also conceded that the only place where "CAUCASIANS ORIGINATED" was around the "CAUCUS MOUNTAINS." Also, that man "...ORIGINATED AROUND THE BANKS OF THE TIGRIS AND EUPHRATES VALLEY." Just a very few of the "AUTHORITIES" at that time held that Africa was the "PLACE WHERE MAN FIRST ORIGINATED." The most noted of these who held the latter position was Sir Charles Darwin of England, who stated that:

MAN ORIGINATED FROM AN APE-LIKE ANCESTOR..., etc.

Dr. Albert Churchward's works, such as his SIGNS AND SYMBOLS OF PRIMOIRDAL MAN, and ORIGIN AND EVOLUTION OF THE HUMAN RACE, were at that time also ignored and ridiculed; of course not as viciously as those by Sir Charles Darwin. Yet a few others continued bringing to light the true facts surrounding <u>the origin of man in Africa</u>. Another reason for this pathology was the fact that the people being dissected politically, historically, and culturally were all Africans - the so-called AFRICAN NATIVES, NEGROES, UNCIVILIZED PRIMITIVES, and a host of other such names - which also included HAMITES at that time. The "HAMITES" were not yet promoted to the rank of "DARK-SKINNED CAUCASIANS". There was no need at that time to embrace them, as very few of the "<u>Modern Men</u>" were knowledgeable of ZIMBABWE; and of course no one knew that <u>Zinjanthropus boisie</u> was under the earth of Tanzania. Even <u>Boskop man</u> in Zimbabwe (called Rhodesia by the imperialists) was unknown.

As one returns to the necessary research in the area of <u>the identification of the Africans</u> who originally, as now, were the first to inhabit the continent called AFRICA, it is very important that another point of view is examined. The recorder at this instance is one Sir Harry H. Johnston. The quotation is taken from his book entitled - A HISTORY OF THE COLONISATION OF AFRICA, p. 2. He wrote:

> There are certain anatomical differences between the existing Negroes of Asia and Oceania on the one hand and the Negroes of Modern Africa on the other. Whether the African Negro was the first human colonizer, or was preceded by more brutish* or generalized type, such as the Galley-Hill man, is not yet known to us.

---
*What made this racist believe that any "Negro" was (or is) "brutish" in the first place. One's action in 1,000,000 B.C.E. should not be equaled to 19th century C.E. morality.

Though Sir Harry avoided the direct denial of the Africans - the so-called "<u>Negroes, Bantus,</u>" etc., as did Professor Jeffreys, he never-the-less equated the "<u>Negroes of Modern Africa</u>" with...

> "MORE BRUTISH OR GENERALIZED TYPE, SUCH AS GALLEY-HILL MAN..."etc.

He continued on:

> ...But from the little we possess in the way of fossil human remains and other evidence it seems probable that every region of Africa, even Algeria and Egypt, once possessed a Negro population. In Mauretania (Morocco to Tripolitania) these ancient Negroes were partly driven out by prehistoric Caucasian invaders and partly absorbed by inter-marriage with the mixture resulting in the darkened complexions of so many of the North African people.[8] In Egypt a dwarfish type of Negro seems to have inhabited the Nile delta some 10,000 years ago; and big black Negroes formed the population of Upper Nubia and Dongola as late as about 4000 years ago.[9]

Why was it necessary to specify that the "<u>Negroes</u>" of Upper Nubia and Dongola were "...BIG BLACK..." and whatever else? Also, why did Sir Harry omit the fact that Egypt must have also had "BIG BLACK NEGROES." If one of the Nile Valleys High-Cultures had "BIG BLACK NEGROES" the others had them because all through the history of these nations there were periods when one group ruled the others.

Neither in Sir Harry H. Johnston's analysis nor in Professor M.D.W. Jeffreys' wide and sweeping non-scientific proclamations can one find the necessity for determining why proof of the Africans', which they called "<u>Negroes,</u>" origin in Africa is so utterly important, unless it is to justify certain prejudices which are apparently held by the overwhelming majority of <u>Modern Man</u>. One must be reminded of the fact that Sir Harry H. Johnston's conclusions were primarily based upon theories set forth by Sir Arthur Keith and W. L. H. Duckworth, much of which is apparent in the above quotation. Therefore, each compounded the others' misinformation. It seems that the compilation of errors was accomplished in too many instances in the writings of these two men (Sir Harry and Professor Jeffreys). However, as historian Professor Jeffreys must be separated from Sir Harry H. Johnston, all evidence points to the fact that Sir Harry based some of his conclusions upon certain stated scientific data and analysis that indicate historical evidence, and on actual examination of certain human remains (fossils). This cannot be said in the same context for the Professor. This does not, in any way or form, indicate that Sir Harry's proclamations are not racist in their orientation; such a conclusion could not be further from the truth. However, it does mean that Sir Harry's statement did have some of the basic ingredients which could have provided the necessary data for a non-biased presentation of the histography and anthropology of the Africans in his analysis. Never-the-less, Sir Harry, and other European and most European-American educators and writers, must maintain the superior status of his "RACE" in all cases, and at all costs. This Sir Harry did not originate, neither did Professor Jeffreys. It was designed long before their arrival in this world by their forefathers. They only inherited it. Yet, they have found comfort in its usage. They have reaped untold benefits from it. Because of the latter reason one should understand why his work is modified in terms of that of the Professor, yet it maintains its own subtle bias and racism. But, how can one dispel the Professor's apparently irrational statements about his "NEGROES" and other such stereotypes which he found to have very little existence on this earth? This must be accomplished by scientific and/or historical evidence to the contrary, using substantially varied sources of "AUTHORITATIVE" works by outstanding and respected "MODERN MAN" - Light-Skinned Caucasians - whom he also had to study in order to receive his doctorate, if such was not awarded on an honorary basis. Due to the overwhelming amount of such historical evidence on the part of the original occupants of Alkebu-lan (Africa) the task will not be difficult to accomplish.

Before referring to certain other universally recognized writers and scholars on African studies, one must again refer to Sir Harry H. Johnston - who earned the Honorable Science Doctorate of Cambridge University, England, for his extensive scientific and historical exploration and research on the subject of Africa and African things. He once wrote the following:

> The successor and supplanter of Homo primigenius in Western Europe was a generalized type of Homo sapiens, represented by the negroid strain, has never been completely eliminated in these lands.

Sir Harry H. Johnston's statement was supported by H.G. Wells in his book, A SHORT HISTORY OF THE WORLD, p. 59. Wells wrote:

> Three main regions and three main kinds of wandering and imperfectly settled people there were in those remote days of the first civilizations in Sumeria and early Egypt. Away in the forests of Europe were the blonde Nordic peoples, hunters and herdsmen, a lowly race. The primitive civilizations saw very little of this race before 1500 B.C.[10]

Somehow Wells and Jeffreys were not familiar with the same type of evidence in their respective research into the ancient and antiquity of mankind. It would seem, from the statement by Wells, that it is the fairest of the "LIGHT-SKINNED CAUCASIANS" - Nordic peoples (Swedes, Danes, Germans, etc.) who were the ones not in existence when the Stone-Age period was around. According to Wells, it seems that "AWAY IN THE FORESTS OF EUROPE WERE THE BLONDE NORDIC PEOPLES, HUNTERS AND HERDSMEN, A LOWLY RACE". This is a far cry from Professor Wiedner and Professor Jeffreys' CAUCASIAN North, East, Central-East, and South Africa. Is it more Logical for these Nordic people to have migrated from the center of Africa and passed around the Africans("NEGROES, etc.) of Nubia (Sudan) by way of the Red Sea, then spread all over North Africa; and from this point cross the Mediterranean Sea into Europe and end up in Sweden and other areas of the northernmost part of Europe than it was for the Africans of the Nubian High-Culture, or those from West Africa (Africa South of the Sahara), to have migrated into North Africa? This exposes the major problems faced by those who follow the baseless statements by the Jeffreys and Wiedners, those who would remove every trace of the indigenous Africans ("Negroes") but find it impossible to remove the pronounced "NEGROID (African) STRAIN"*from the <u>Light-skinned Caucasians,</u> especially of the Mediterranean region. Within this same line of reasoning, Sir Charles Darwin Jr., the grandson of Sir Charles Darwin - the world famous Victorian scientist, (and a scientist of great renown in his own right) wrote the following in an article entitled "THE NEXT MILLION YEARS":

> ...there is no scientific evidence of any difference of ability between the races.

Further on in the same article he stated that,

> ...the average skin color of the human race will get darker and, furthermore, economic and military power in Africa and Asia will wrestle the leadership from Europe...

C.P. Snow, in his comments on Sir Charles Darwin's statement, wrote the following in JOHN O'LONDON'S WEEKLY:

> ...it means, incidentally, that the racial discrimination which has been the least creditable feature of the period of White hegemony is not only wicked; it is worse than wicked, it is criminally foolish.

Since the above statements differ in such extremes to those of Professor Jeffreys, it is pertinent that reference to his positions already stated be closely re-examined. But, it must be also noted that even Sir Harry H. Johnston basically dis-

---

*Cited in Sir Harry H. Johnston's statement on page 78 of this volume.

agreed with practically every position taken by Professor Jeffreys with respect to the antiquity of the so-called "NEGROES." In contradiction to the good Professor Sir Harry's theory about the Indians (professor's "dark-skinned Caucasians") of Asia and with respect to their "NEGROID" characteristics, we note:

> There is a strong underlying Negroid element in the mass of the Indian population, and in the southernmost part of the great peninsula there are forest tribes of dark-skinned and strikingly Negro physiognomy, with frizzled or wooly hair. There is a negroid element in the gentle Burmese; and in the Andaman Islands - geologically little more than a depressed peninsula of Further India - the dwarfish people are absolute Negroes of the Asiatic type... In the more eastern among the Malay islands - especially in Burn, Jilolo, and Timor - the interior tribes are of obvious Negro stock. Still more marked is this in the case of New Guinea, and most of all in the Bismarch archipelago and northern Solomon Islands. In these last resemblance of the natives to the average Negro of Africa is most striking, although the distance is something like 8000 miles. Negro affinities extend east of the Solomon archipelago to Fiji and Hawaii, and south of New Caledonia, Ismania and New Zealand. On the other hand, Africa for many thousand years has been obviously the chief domain of the Negro.*[11]

Probably the above quotation should have been interrupted at certain points from an academic standpoint in line of what will follow. However, it is best to note that even Sir Harry cannot say with any certainty the true length of time (as he and all others of his fellow historians do in the case of the Europeans and Europe) just how long is "...FOR MANY THOUSAND YEARS..."

---

*West African Review, p. 3, September, 1951. One should also examine the following works by Sir H.H. Johnston: BRITISH ACROSS THE SEA-AFRICA; GEORGE GRENFELL AND THE CONGO, VOL. I & II, THE NILE QUEST; etc.

At least Jeffreys was quite definite. He said that:

> THERE ARE NO NEGRO SKULLS OF ANY ANTIQUITY – THE OLDEST KNOWN IS ABOUT 6000 B.C.

Of course Professor Jeffreys cannot agree with Sir Harry's facts. How could he agree that his "DARK-SKINNED CAUCASIANS" of India have...

> A STRONG UNDERLYING NEGROID ELEMENT IN THE MASS...,

and that...

> IN THE SOUTHERNMOST PART OF THE GREAT PENINSULA (of India)* THERE ARE FOREST TRIBES OF DARK-SKINNED AND STRIKINGLY NEGRO PHYSIOGNOMY, WITH FRIZZLED OR WOOLY HAIR.

This should not be true, for the professor said that these people are the ancestors of the...

> "HINDU, BUT HE OFFERS NO DIFFICULTY. HE BELONGS TO THE SAME RACE AS THE "EUROPEAN", NAMELY THE CAUCASIAN...," etc.**

Is it not strange that Sir Harry did not look into Europe to trace the same "...NEGROID STRAIN..." he found in Asia and other areas of the Pacific? Those who have had the privilege of traveling in the areas of the world in question, and in southern Europe also, know that Sir Harry's statement above is somewhat moderated. The truth of the matter is that no one can, with any certainty, deny that he or she is free of Sir Harry's stated:

---

*Words in brackets by the author for clarification.
**From Professor Jeffrey's own statement on page 62.

82

"NEGROID ELEMENT...,"* or his "...NEGRO AFFINITIES." These references, although made to show the differences between mankind, only help to magnify how closely related mankind really is in itself. The tone of one range in color is so varied, that one cannot tell at most times just who is Black and who is white. For example: All it needs is for someone to start a very good rumor that <u>President Nixon of the United States of America had ancestors who were Negroes.</u> When this is carried forward by the right underhanded personnel, so will the probability of his impeachment become important for forging his racial origin. Public gossip will do the rest. Because of this type of rumor mongering, WHITES in many southern states of the U.S.A. have been labeled BLACK, and BLACKS WHITE. In line with this type of reasoning, was it possible for the African-Moors, African-Carthaginians, African-Egyptians, African-Numidians, African-Ethiopians, and other BLACKS to enter Europe at various times throughout man's history and could Europe have remained completely WHITE? Was it possible for the African continent and the Asian continent to have been invaded by as many national armies of Europe (as they were) and their people remain purely whatever

---

*What in reality does the term "NEGROID ELEMENT" mean? Who determines what it is, and who has it? Is it not true that each and every group of people have some of the common characteristics that one group may have in much more uniformity than another? Is a straight nose and thin lips only to be found in the Nordic peoples and others indigenous to the continent of Europe? There are millions of Africans with every bit of so-called "NORDIC FEATURES" all over Africa, and they are indigenous to the African continent.

they were after the European soldier's occupation of hundreds of years?

History is quite clear on the role the Africans, "Negroes" or "Bantus", played in the cultural development of the Persians when they established their nation of ELAM.[12] This High-Culture (civilization) was established by the same Africans who also established their High-Cultures in Kimit (Egypt, Sais, etc.) Nubia (Sudan, Merowe, etc.), Kush (Ethiopia, Cush, Axum, etc.), Punt (Somaliland, Somali Republic, etc.), Zimbabwe (Rhodesia, Monomotapa, etc.), and all other areas of the entire African continent - including Ghana, Melle, Songhai, Trucolor, Benin, Ikjaw, Edoh, Mani-Kongo, and other West and West-Central African empires and nations and tribes - "ETHNIC GROUPS." It would seem that European and European-American historians have carefully forgotten that the GANGES RIVER in India got its beautiful name from the famous Ethiopian - General Ganges - who conquered much of India up to and beyond the limits of said body of water. That the thousands of Africans (Ethiopians) he carried in as soldiers became the fathers of millions of people who are only known as "INDIANS". These Ethiopians, all Africans, were of the same STOCK as those that entered Greece by way of Egypt. They were part and parcel of the ancient peoples who once ruled the UPPER, MIDDLE, and LOWER Nile Valley High-Cultures with Egypt (Kimit) included. If they were not "NEGROES" or "BANTUS" as the others are so labeled by most European and European-American educators, neither were the other Africans of the entire Nile Valley (from Uganda to the Mediterranean), and those of the Great Lakes regions. (See Joel A. Rogers, WORLD'S GREAT MEN OF COLOR, vols. I & II).

The "NEGROES" have become such an "ENIGMA" to the "LIGHT-SKINNED CAUCASIANS" of Professor Jeffreys, also to the North, East, and South African "CAUCASIANS" of Dr. Donald Wiedner, that now practically every major university and college in the United States of America and Europe have become over-indulgent in the areas of what they select to call - "BLACK STUDIES". Of course this trend would have been a blessing if the available materials dealing with the history and culture of the African peoples of the world were not of the type demonstrated in the works of the "AUTHORITIES" already cited in this volume. For as one can readily see, the most "LIBERAL" of the professors in control of AFRICAN STUDIES, who are Europeans and European-Americans of course, have to maintain the <u>paternalistic projection</u> which this subject has always received and this will continue as Mr. Thomas Hodgkin said:

> ...THE REAL HISTORY OF AFRICA (is) TO BE WRITTEN BY AFRICAN SCHOLARS FOR AN AFRICAN READING PUBLIC.

In order to accomplish anything better, the available documents of quality among the mass-produced history books that relates to racist colonial paternalism must be separated. But the replacements must be predominantly by African historians and other

educators in varied disciplines. In so doing, the African
Studies Department, as any other area of ETHNIC STUDIES, must be
under the control and administration of African, African-American,
and Africa-Caribbean scholars and administrators. This does not
in anyway conclude that Europeans and European-Americans cannot
teach African history; it does say, however, that the manner in
which it had been taught for the past few hundred years cannot
be tolerated any longer. For what is history, if it is not to
tell the world of the greatness and failures of a particular
High-Culture? Yet, only the failures in the African High-
Cultures have been highlighted by those who have controlled
African Studies department in Europe, the Americas - including
the Caribbean Islands, Africa, Asia and all other areas where
the colonial masters have dominated and still dominate. In this
same light only that which projects an image of European-type
Christian missionary paternalism and the Tarzan and Jane stereotype dominate the majority of the available material cover. Yet,
in reality, for peoples of African origin to have expected anything better from the sons and daughters of their former slavemasters of Europe and Europe-America, whether they are or were
capitalists, communists, socialists, feudalists, or others,
before the 19th Century C.E., is to expect that man is in reality
PEACE-LOVING and HONEST BY NATURE. The reason that there is a
major shift in emphasis with regards to what is being projected
as "BLACK STUDIES," is that the peoples of African origin

(young, middle age or old) have decided, finally, to take their own future in their own hands, which includes their own birthright HISTORY and HERITAGE. Of course this action is purposefully dubbed a "VIOLENT REVOLUTION." And, certainly most African-Americans have fallen for this title, not realizing that it was established for the purpose of creating a future excuse for their eventual liquidation if such should be ever needed. This CULTURAL REVOLUTION, and this is all it is at this stage in history, is never-the-less of major importance, for further tries at what was hypocritically called "INTERGRATION" and "AMALGAMATION OF THE RACES" are in fact exercises in fatalism and wishful thinking.[13] Why? Because there was never a time in the history of man where the slavemasters of one group ever voluntarily let the other group become its equal under the same government while the slavemasters still remained in control.

In keeping with the basic premises and ideals of the role in the past and present of those who allegedly came to Africa to stop <u>slavery, cannibalism, heathenism,</u> and of course <u>genocide</u> by fellow European imperialists and colonial settlers, another professor - C. P. Groves - in his book, THE PLANTING OF CHRISTIANITY IN AFRICA, Vol. I, p.1, wrote the following:

> "...it is the paradox of this vast continent (AFRICA)* that while sharing in the earliest history of the human race, it was yet not

---

*The word in brackets is for clarity. It was injected by the author of this volume.

opened up until the late nineteenth century."

Professor Groves' assertion that Africa "...YET WAS NOT OPEN-UP...," etc., is in no sense different to the remarks used by Professor Jeffreys and the racist hypotheses established on the ethnographical map by Dr. Donald Wiedner shown on page 7 of this volume. Yet, it contradicts the basic premises of Professor Jeffreys' "ENIGMA." For Professor Groves credited the indigenous Africans - Jeffreys' "BANTUS" and "NEGROES" - with "...SHARING IN THE EARLIEST HISTORY OF THE HUMAN RACE,"...etc. It is obvious that this is the complete reverse of the position held by the two other alleged "authorities on Africa and Africans."

In some circles, which, in particular, include Christian missionaries, Professor Groves is considered "ONE OF THE MOST LIBERAL CHRISTIAN EDUCATORS ON AFRICAN HISTORY." One can easily understand, from such liberalism, why more "modern" European and European-American "liberal" educators find it so difficult to speak and write about peoples of African origin, and of Africa, without first imposing upon such history their own feeling of superiority. If the works of men such as Professor Jeffreys, Dr. Donald Wiedner, Sir Harry H. Johnston, Professor C.P. Groves, and others who promulgate the same type of teachings, are to be the material which present day scholars must still use as "AUTHORITATIVE," and this is what is being done, then it should be very easy to comprehend why African-Americans and other peoples of African origin have rejected any control of the teaching of their heritage by anyone who is not of African origin.

Examining Professor Groves' hypothesis that Africa "...WAS NOT YET OPENED UP UNTIL THE LATE NINETEENTH CENTURY," one wonders why it was not "<u>opened up until</u>" Europeans arrived there? Of course AFRICA, to this professor, as to millions of other such professors of European and European-American institutions of higher-learning, is only that part of the continent that is geographically located below the imaginary line called "AFRICA SOUTH OF THE SAHARA." For one must assume that Professor Groves must have been aware, during the time he was writing his volumes, that the religion which he teaches about came to Europe by way of Africa. And that it was in Africa that the first martyrs of the Christian religion - FELICITA, NYMPHANO, and PERPETUA - were born, lived, and died. Also that it was in Africa that the most noted of the Christian educators, the FATHERS OF THE CHURCH - TERTULLIAN, St. CYPRIAN and St. AUGUSTINE - were also born, lived, and died. That it was in the same Africa that the foundation of all philosophic thoughts now called "WESTERN RELIGIONS" - Judaism, Christianity, and Islam - got their TEN COMMANDMENTS. These were taken from the Egyptian Mysteries System's "NEGATIVE CONFESSIONS" - all one-hundred and forty-seven (147) of them.* The truth is that there has never been a period in human history when Africa "...<u>was yet not opened-up</u>" to anyone who acted civilly. It

---

*See, Yosef ben-Jochannan, AFRICAN ORIGINS OF THE MAJOR "WESTERN RELIGIONS, Alkebu-lan Books Associates, New York, 1970.

seems that any place where a European or European-American has never been is always UNDISCOVERED, CLOSED, DANGEROUS, PRIMITIVE, UN GODLY, SAVAGE and all that goes with inferiority to things European and European-American - CAUCASIAN. However, when the first European or European-American sets foot on any such place, it immediately becomes SAFE, DISCOVERED, OPENED-UP, GODLY, and worthy of everything <u>the one and only true God</u> of Europeans and European-Americans alone reserved for His CHOSEN PEOPLE.

Not only was Africa "<u>opened-up</u>" to all of mankind, including Europeans, Africa carried her "<u>civilizing</u>" (High-Culture) influnces into Europe by way of her ancient and glorious sons and daughters of Egypt, Nubia, Kush,[14] Carthage and other lands before the dawn of Christianity and the birth of Judaism. Later on, she sent her sons (the Moors in 711 C.E.) from the northwest corner of North Africa, all over the Iberian Peninsula. They remained there as late as the 15th Century before they were finally driven out of Granada.* These Africans, "NEGROES, BANTUS," and whatever else, were "<u>civilizing</u>" the LIGHT-SKINNED CAUCASIANS of Europe before the first of the Europeans were able to establish their first system of education. The descendants of the most ancient Africans also added to the educational enlightenment of the Europeans through the efforts of "AFRICANS SOUTH OF THE SAHARAH" when Europeans journeyed to the institutions of higher <u>learning in West Africa, such as the University of SANKHORE</u> in

*The Moors entered Iberia in 711 C.E. (A.D.) and was finally defeated in 1485 C.E.

Tumbut.* In the first half of the 15th Century C.E., upon the arrival of the first Europeans (the Portuguese) in West Africa, the Africans were again the teachers and economic saviours to the Europeans who were at the time desperately in need of food and other basic necessities of life. It was this deplorable state of Europe, at the turn of the 15th Century C.E., that made her become the scourge of the earth. Europeans did not go to Asia, Africa, the Americas and the Caribbeans to carry "CIVILIZATION" and "CHRISTIANITY" as some would have everyone believe; they went to these lands for food, clothing and shelter.[15] When Pope Martin V of the Roman Catholic Church dared to separate the world between Spain and Portugal in 1441 C.E. it was over the dispute between both of these Roman Catholic nations as to which one of them would have the right to murder the peoples of Africa, Asia and the Americas - the Caribbeans included - and confiscate their real and personal property. Maybe "<u>Modern educators</u>" will also say in the future, as the Christian missionaries have maintained in the past, that CHATTEL SLAVERY was instituted by the Rt. Rev. Bishop Bartolome de LasCasas on the Island of Hispaniola (Hayte, Haiti) for the benefit of the wretched Africans who were brought there to slave in behalf of the Europeans and European-Americans.

---

*Tumbut is the correct name and spelling of this noted city of ancient Melle (Mali). There are many Western variants to this.

As for the Africans (the so-called "NEGROES") being indigenous to Kimit (otherwise misnamed EGYPT by the Haribus), is it not true that prehistoric anthropological and archaeological fossils and artifacts, plus historical records are in abundance, all of which prove that they inhabited said region of Africa before there were any nations in all of Europe? Don't they prove that the Africans who are now called "NEGROES" and "BANTUS," among many other names of inferiority, were there as creators during antiquity, and not as salves, as it is widely taught in Western institutions? Also, isn't it true that the first of the Pharaohs (Kings and Queens)[16] were all indigenous to Africa before the invasion of the first alien peoples - the HYKSOS or "SHEPHERD KINGS?" There could be no doubt that the BLACKS occupied Egypt long before the Stone-Age Culture. The Europeans that arrived there many thousands of years later met them there, according to the earliest records by European historians who were not at that time concious of color prejudice as "Modern Man" is today.[17] Sir Ernest Wallis Budge, former KEEPER OF EGYPTIAN AND ASSYRIAN ANTIQUITIES OF THE BRITISH MUSEUM, London, England, in his world renowned work entitled EGYPT, p. 42, wrote:

> There is no evidence that the Egyptians of the new Stone Age had invented the art of writing, but there is abundant proof that they could draw pictures of the symbols of their totems. These are found painted on pots at Makadah and are supported on standards fixed in the prehistoric period, and they form the oldest Egyptian hieroglyphs known. They are very important as showing that the earliest

attempts to write in Egypt was made by <u>native Africans</u>.*

Sir Wallis Budge's conclusion must be given very serious recognition as his works have been universally accepted by the most noted scholars of the world, many of whom are Africans and Asians. He is rated as "...ONE OF THE FOREMOST EGYPTOLOGISTS OF ALL TIME." The most noted of his works, entitled BOOK OF THE DEAD, is a compendium of extracts taken from the Africans of Egypt and other Nile Valley High-Cultures' PYRAMID and COFFIN TEXTS and translated into English from their original Hieroglyphs. It is also considered to be "...THE GREATEST MASTERPIECE ON EGYPTOLOGY AND HIEROGLPHICS..." by many <u>Western</u> Egyptologists.** Sir Wallis Budge's works, more specifically this one, shows that he was not suffering from any Negrophobia, acute "ENIGMA" or severe "CAUCASIANISM" as most of his more "<u>modern</u>" fellow professors and educators. He had no fear of Europeans and European-Americans reading that the original occupants[18] of Kimit (Sais, Egypt) were indigenous Africans whose descendants are today called "NEGROES" and other such names of inferiority. The fact that they were the first to inhabit the Nile Valleys[19] and Great Lakes regions, established the most ancient civil governments known to man, and set the standards

---

*Words underscored by the author of this volume are to draw attention to the origin of the ancient Egyptians who lived in Egypt before the arrival of the first Asians or Asian-Europeans - the Hyksos - about 1675 B.C.E. (or B.C.)
**One who specializes in the study of ancient Egypt.

for all religious philosophical principles, did not stop Sir Wallis Budge from saying that they did.

Since you are about to embark upon deeper insight into the reaches of African Studies, you must be extraordinarily clear on at least one major point from the outset. That is, NAMES. For example: HAMITE and SEMITE are names which Europeans and European-Americans (some are considered "scholars" and "educators") have adopted from Hebrew mythology (written and developed in Hellenic Greece) as written in the TORAH and Christian HOLY BIBLE. These words have no authoritative relationship to Africa, her indigenous peoples, cultures, or things Africa. They are racist in origin and bigoted in practice. Using these words as AFRICAN NAMES would be tantamount to calling the present occupants of North Africa "INDIGENOUS AFRICANS" on the basis that they invaded and captured this region of the African continent some 1327 years ago.[20] For nowhere in recorded history, written by Africans and other ancient peoples of the era in question, is there any mention of "HAMITES" or "SEMITES", before their appearance in their Jewish and Christian advocates' books by so-called "INSPIRED HOLY MEN OF GOD." It must not be forgotten that the Jews were at the time of the writing of their TORAH in Europe and Asia Minor; and that there were many TORAHS, many of which conflicted with each other. Also, the TORAH was mostly the historical records of the Haribu (Hebrews - today called Jewish peoples, in fact people of the TRIBE OF JUDAH) nation, mixed

with their national taboos and folk tales. Equally, before the
arrival of the Western Europeans in West Africa around the
middle of the 15th Century of the Christian Era (C.E.) they were
no words such as NEGRO and NEGROLAND. Yet, there is ample proof
that for more than 1,000,000 years the indigenous African, not
European or Asian, call him whatever else one may desire, has
occupied the entire continent of Alkebu-lan (Africa). And, at
no time during the entire length of this period did he once
named himself "HAMITE, SEMITE" or "NEGRO". The ancient Africans
of antiquity were like any other Africans one can see in the
so-called GHETTOES of the United States of America, with the type
of characteristics Herodotus described them of having during
450 years before the Christian Era (B.C.E. or B.C.) - "THICK LIPS,
BROAD NOSE, WOOLLY HAIR, AND THEY ARE BURNT OF SKIN." They were
this way when the first Haribu in the world, ABRAHAM (Avram),
arrived in Kimit (which Abraham's ancestors renamed EGYPT) to
avoid starving to death in the desert of Asia Minor.* They were
like that even before the birth of Abraham's parents, and before
the Hebrews made an ADAM and EVE for their mythological "CREATION
OF THE WORLD." The Africans needed no Hebrew mythological and/or
secular classification (the Biblical story about Ham and the
Flood with his father - or uncle Noah) to establish their own
African identity. Labels, or names, such as these - "NEGROES,

---

*See HEBREW TORAH (Christian HOLY BIBLE), Book of Genesis. Note
  that this work is also called "THE FIVE BOOKS OF MOSES."

HAMITES, SEMITES," etc., are only tools of subterfuge on the part of the racists and religious bigots of what is today called "WESTERN CIVILIZATION." This does not mean that said racist or bigots may be even conscious that these terms are in fact as dangerous to the peoples of Africa as they really are. Why is this so? Because those who are in authority over what everyone in "Western Society" learns in religious institutions, public and private schools, and other places of learning, have for the past few hundred years taught it that way, irrespective of the fact that Africans have always protested against such characterization and willful stereotyping. These words are also used as the basis for the removal of millions of Africans from sections of Africa in order to place others, in Africa who at one time claimed they were SEMITES, CAUCASIANS, and other such classifications, before it was known that Africa would prove to be the true GARDEN OF EDEN where the world's oldest MAN or MAN-LIKE fossil - ZINJANTHROPUS BOISIE - was to be found. This type of teaching is not only related to the Europeans and European-Americans in the United States of America, it is universal in schools in Africa and the Caribbean Islands that have been established and operated by the colonialists for their managing Africans, African-Americans and African-Caribbeans. No one should be surprised that this is the case. Most Africans and people of African origin who have had their Europeanization have accepted said brainwashing without reservations. Slavery makes people accept their own inferiority, even to the point of believing that as slaves they never produced any history. How long has this not been taught by Jews, Christians, Moslems, Communists, Capitalists, Feudalists, Anarchists, and all other sorts of Europeans and European-Americans about the peoples of Africa?

In light of the above, especially the last few sentences, an African by the name of J. C. deGraft-Johnson (an emminent professor of economics and history in his own right) has in his book, AFRICAN GLORY, [21] page 9, certain comments on the works of two noted egyptologists of world renown, E. Meyer and H.R. Hall, in which they cited the entrance of "...<u>the Negro into dynastic Egypt from about 5869 to 3315 B.C.</u>" He supported the position of these European writers and others who would remove the Africans (called "BANTUS" and "NEGROES") from the history of most of East Africa, and all of North Africa. In this regards Professor deGraft-Johnson wrote:

> All authorities, however, agree that the Dynastic Egyptians invaded Egypt during or before the fourth millennium B.C. They populated and ruled the narrow valley of the Desert Nile as far south as the First Cataract. They also ruled and populated the broad delta of the shores of the Mediterranean.

What Professor deGraft-Johnson seemed to have overlooked in his "ALL AUTHORITIES" hypothesis is the fact that "DYNASTIC EGYPTIANS INVADED EGYPT...," etc., from the southern half of the African continent. He also overlooked the fact that they had to pass or join others they met in Ethiopia and Nubia, if in fact these latter lands were not also the areas from whence the Egyptians began their invasion. That is, providing this theory is correct. One would assume that the professor is aware of the fact that <u>a theory is as good as the paper it is written on until proven correct</u>. But, the professor continued:

> To the south of the First Cataract were peoples of mixed origin - Egyptians, Hamites, and Negroes of the Nubian race. Beyond the Second Cataract the population of the Nile Valley, while Dynastic Egyptian rule lasted, was entirely Negro.

There are many basic questions one would have to ask this "<u>scholar.</u>" First: What is a "NUBIAN RACE?" Second: What group of people is PURE and not "<u>mixed</u>" with other human beings? Third: Is the professor saying that the "<u>Nubians</u>" (the so-called mixed people or "Negroes") and the "<u>Egyptians</u>" (whom one is asked to assume were different from all other Africans; maybe an EGYPTIAN RACE) never mated with each other and had offsprings? Or, is he saying that there was a imaginary barrier called <u>RACE</u> between Egypt and Nubia that prevented these two national groups of Africans from intra-sexual cohabition and other types of social intercourse? Probably it is that the professor was confused by the racist jargon of his European teachers, most of whom were Englishmen whose major interest in Egyptian history was the perpetuation of the "<u>Caucasian</u>" myth that all of North and East Africa were originally settled by "<u>Caucasians, Semites and Hamites</u>." Unfortunately, their African prodigies also engaged in the perpetuation of a <u>Caucasian image</u> for North Africa.

Anyone should readily see that Professor deGraft-Johnson had fallen for the "HAMITIC, SEMITIC, NEGRO"[22] mythology that has totally infected disciplinary scientific study and analysis in the various fields related to investigations into African history and prehistory. Not only did he use the racist coloquialisms that subvert basic scientific investigations common to his profession, he introduced his own stereotyped classifications of rank racism - the "<u>NEGROES OF THE NUBIAN RACE.</u>" This frequently happens to very well-meaning African scholars of any discipline who have to depend upon foreigners as the "AUTHORITIES" of African culture and history. One can only wonder if the "AUTHORITIES" he depended upon would have used him, or any other African, as a "AUTHORITY" of European history - even of tiny LITCHESTIEN'S history? There is only one major reason for this sabotage; the professor could not remove himself from the role of African student under the tutelege of his European teachers and colonial masters. This type of manipulation of the English language was designed to remove every trace of the so-called "Negroes" and "Bantus" from their heritage in all of North Africa, and make it Caucasian (European). It hurts much more so when one finds that Africans, many of them, still prattle the same racist and stereotyped history against their own people, not knowing just what they are saying or doing.

Professor J.C. de-Graft-Johnson's book, AFRICAN GLORY, never-the-less, except for his acceptance of such types of stereotype, is a very informative gathering of information for anyone who is not familiar with any North or West African history; especially in areas that involve the early North African Church, the Vandals in North Africa, some sketches of the Africans that became the first marytrs of Christendom, and the FATHERS OF THE CHURCH, along with many facts about the three of the most commonly known West African empires that existed in Africa before the arrival of the European-style Christian missionaries - Ghana, Melle and Songhai.* It is sorrowful that the professor was involved in this type of <u>follow the master</u> historical hypothesis. He should have known that before the 17th Century of the Christian Era (C.E.) the word "NEGRO" was not in use anywhere with respect to any of the peoples of the continent called "AFRICA." And, even with its universal acceptance among Europeans and European-Americans, he, as an African educator, should have refused to give it honor. It is only when Africans stand up against insults to their integrity and cultural heritage as men and women, will they eventually control their own destiny.

Certainly, there were no "NEGROES" in Dynastic Egypt. "NEGROES" were not manufactured by the Portuguese as yet since there were no Portuguese, or any other European and European-American nationals that exist today during the period when the Africans

---

*One needs to remember that the spelling of these empire names vary entensively. Those shown above are of African origin.

had their dynasties along the banks of the Nile Rivers, both BLUE and WHITE. "Negroes" are daily created for places where there were none by European-American historians and anthropologists;[23] just as "INDIANS" were created by the same "AUTHORITIES" for the Americas and Caribbean Islands. It is, therefore, quite difficult to distinguish who were the "NEGROES" in African history, to say the least, when in fact everyday some group of Africans is removed from "NEGRO" to "HAMITE" and from "HAMITE" to "CAUCASOID:" some even make it all the way to "CAUCASIAN" - which is the final step to PURITY, at least this is what is being implied everyday in the educational institutions of the United States of America. For an example: To say that the ELAMITES (originally Africans from East Africa) that settled in Persia (Iran) were "NEGROES" would be ridiculous. Yet they were of the same African people as the Africans one sees today all over the African continent (i.e. the earliest Egyptians and Ethiopians of yesteryears). What then is the difference, if there is any? The answer is that the ancient Africans, Asians, and the Europeans, did not suffer from ACUTE NEGROPHOBIA and indigestion from ENIGMA. The ancient Europeans did not know that they were "CAUCASIANS" - light-skinned or dark-skinned. These terms were designed in much later societies by very sick people who were in need of a sense of superiority over others. Their own feeling of their inferior position brought on this sense of feelings, and promulgated the genocide that was necessary to reach the position that made them feel that in reality they were, and are, SUPERIOR.

One must realize that none of the above stereotypes, nor nothing else resembling them, were in existence before "<u>Modern Man</u>" became a world-wide conqueror. This position was best stated in one of Egypt's most famous historical documents dealing with the question of the BLACKS ("Negroes, Bantus," etc.) in Egypt after that nation was already occupied and ruled by foreign invaders from Asia and of European-Asian mixture. Of course the period in which this historic reference is being made preceded the arrival of the present Arab invaders who arrived in Egypt during 640 C.E. (AH 18). Thus it is shown that Usertsen II^{24a} (fifth Pharoah of the Twenty-first Dynasty, conqueror of certain parts of Nubia - UPPER EGYPT) set up his stele at Samnah for the purpose of barring the Nubians* whom he had defeated in battle. The inscription also mentioned that he had driven the Nubians out of certain parts of Lower Egypt; and, that he was himself not indigenous of either Nubia or Egypt (Kimit). The following was translated into the English language from its original Hieroglyphs:

> I am the king; (my)** word is performed. My hand performs what my mind conceives... I attach my attacker.... The man who retreats is a vile coward;

---

*These Africans are called "NEGROES" by most "Western" educators. They occupied the land now called SUDAN. They have also ruled all of Egypt during several periods in ancient history.
**This word was inserted where one was omitted on the original.

> he who is defeated on his own land is no man. Thus
> is the <u>Nubians</u>.* He falls down at a word of command,
> when attacked he runs away, when pursued he shows
> his back in flight. The <u>Nubians</u> have no courage,
> they are weak and timid, their hearts are contempt-
> ible. I have seen them, I am not mistaken about
> them. <u>I seized their women</u>, I took their goods, I
> stopped-up their wells, I slew their bulls, I reaped
> their crops, I burnt their houses. I am speaking
> the truth.... My son who maintains this boundary is
> indeed my son; he who allows it to be thrust back is
> no son of mine, and I never begot him. I have set up
> a statue of myself here, not only for your benifit,
> but also that you should do battle for it.

Obviously Usertsen II must not have done his own homework on the fellow Africans he had just conquered, or he would have seen that the Egyptians also "<u>turned their backs</u>" to the Nubians in war. But, one must realize that these type of slurs were always commonly thrown by one conqueror or another against his conquered victims, even when the victims were the former conquerors. There are many fundamental points brought out in this inscription that bear directly upon the current color question about "NEGROES" and "AFRICANS SOUTH OF THE SAHARA" (Blacks) in Egypt, and when did they arrive there; also proof, on the positive side, that they were in Africa before the arrival of the "LIGHT-SKINNED CAUCASIANS" of Professor Jeffreys. A breakdown detail of Pharoah Usertsen II's proclamation follows:

   1. The word "NEGRO", nor anything resembling it was
      never mentioned; this of course does not stop many
      "<u>Western</u>" historians from inserting it in their
      own translation and racist interpretation. Some of
      them use the word "BLACK" instead, which is in this
      case no better than "NEGRO".

---
*The words underscored are for emphasis by the author.

2. The word "NUBIANS" has been used to designate the indigenous Africans of the area adjacent to the southern borders of ancient Egypt. This area is today called SUDAN by the Arab invaders. It must be noted that nowhere in the inscription is the word WHITE mentioned, and it should not be assumed. The peoples of the ancient world did not deal with each others in terms of colors as modern man in his racism; neither was CAUCASIANS mentioned.

3. NUBIA was a part of UPPER EGYPT during the periods of the Egyptians of LOWER EGYPT's rule over the Lowlands of the Nile River Valley. Equally, EGYPT became part of Nubia when it was ruled by the Nubians.

4. "I SEIZED THEIR WOMEN" was the direct statement of Usertsen II. Why did conquerors seize their victims' women? To rape them. When they were raped the offspring were treated as any of the victor's children. Certainly the Nubians did the same to the Egyptians when they were the victors.

5. The typical slurs thrown against the Nubian losers were the same thrown against many European nations by the Greeks and Romans. Even Adolph Hitler and his Nazis Germany employed this technique in the Second World War during the later 1940's C.E. When the Romans and Greeks belittled their much lighter-skinned Nordic enemies it did not make the blondes less European [25] than their swarthy southern European conquerors. Why would the conquest and slurs in the case of Egypt make the Nubians less African than the Egyptians?

6. The Nubians have been described as having produced a High-Culture (civilization) worthy of being ravaged by their Egyptian neighbors. Nothing in Egypt was beyond the development the Nubians had. When one looks at the map of the Nile Valley there is abundant proof that many of the remaining structures that were generally ascribed to Egypt were in fact Nubian. Note these sites on the map on pages ix; 682 and 684.

7. This historical data refutes the missionary stories about the "AFRICAN NEGROES NOT PRODUCING ANY CIVILIZATION IN AFRICA BEFORE THE EUROPEAN CHRISTIAN MISSIONARIES ARRIVED IN AFRICA", etc.[26]

The above comments by European and European-American-style Christian missionaries were, and still are, very easy to contradict, as Africans were also Popes of the Roman Catholic Church for centuries prior to the arrival of the first WHITE MAN in West Africa,[27] many of whom established dogmas which are still used by the world of Christendom.* (see, J.C. de-Graft-Johnson, AFRICAN GLORY; J.A. Rogers, WORLD'S GREAT MEN OF COLOR, Vol. I & II; HARMACKS, MISSION AND EXPANSION: Jane Soames, COAST OF THE BARBARY: Mrs. Steuart Erskine, THE VANISHED CITIES OF NORTH AFRICA; Augustine (St.) CONFESSIONS: ON CHRISTIAN DOCTRINES; and Tertullian's, DeANIMA).

Reflecting back into the past it is also revealed that Pepi I - also known as Merira (third Pharoah of the Sixth Dynasty) - cooperated with the Nubian Pharoahs (Kings). He joined one in a highly successful adventure in the capture of the Hebrews of Palestine. This was long before the Twelveth (12th) Dynasty, when there were serious conflicts between Nubia and her sister State, Kimit (Sais or Egypt); which eventually caused Pharoah Usertsen II to attack Nubia and finally capture her. This is added proof that the Nubians were prominent and honored people in Egyptian life, even up to the reign of Usertsen III.[28] Other documents show that Nubians were in Egypt as long as human beings occupied that land. The main differences between the Egyptians

---
*See Y. ben-Jochannan, AFRICAN ORIGINS OF MAJOR "WESTERN RELIGIONS."

and Nubians were political and cultural, nothing else. (see, Sir E. A. Wallis Budge, BOOK OF THE DEAD; Count C. F. Volney, RUINS OF EMPIRE; G.G.M. James, STOLEN LEGACY; J. A. Rogers, WORLD'S GREAT MEN OF COLOR, Vol. I; Herodotus, THE HISTORIES; Sir James Frazier, GOLDEN BOUGH; and Homer W. Smith, MAN AND HIS GODS).

It was Herodotus (the Greek citizen, who originally came from the Egyptian colony called Ionia in Asia Minor) in describing the largest statue of the world - the SPHINX OF GHIZEH - who wrote that it was:

...BUILT BY KHEOPS....

Why did Herodotus call <u>Khufu</u> by the name "KHEOPS" or "CHEOPS"? For the same reason that he and other Greeks called Pharaoh AHA (or NARNMER) by the Greek name - MENES. The following are only some of the basic reasons why Herodotus and many of the other Greeks and Romans of the ancient world referred to the ancient Africans of the Nile Valleys by names other than those the Africans gave themselves:

1. The Greeks of Herodotus' era could not pronounce certain Nile Valley language (Eyptian in particular) words.
2. Herodotus received his education from the indigenous Africans of Egypt (Kimit, Sais) while he was a student of the Mysteries in Egypt. There he was in the studies of every discipline, including "HISTORY," which most "Western" historians and other educators attributed to him as "FATHER." He had to translate his new knowledge to the understanding of his fellow Greek citizens* in terms

---
*Herodotus was not of Greek birth. He was an Ionian.

and sounds which they could comprehend. Also, there were no sufficient Greek characters in the Greek alphabet to produce certain indigenous African sounds in the Greek language word construction.

3. There are untold facts known to present day egyptologists about Egypt which the Egyptians of Herodotus' era kept secret from him and all of the other Greek and Ionian nationals before and after him. It must be understood that certain secrets of Egyptian society (religious, political, cultural, and otherwise) could not be revealed to Herodotus or any other foreigner. Like today in the United States of America, even friendly governments are not allowed to know everything the inner-circles of the government are doing or contemplating. The Egyptians and other Nile Valley African peoples were no different in this respect.

One should recall that Sir Ernest A. Wallis Budge wrote the following English comments about people like Herodotus:

"PEOPLE OF IGNOBLE BIRTH WHO CAME FROM EASTERN PARTS."

He was dealing with "PEOPLE" who were foreign to Egypt during the reign of Timaus' invasion of Egypt. Sir Ernest was quoting from the works of the Hebrew (Jewish) historian - Flavius Josephus (c 37 - 95 C.E.). He further stated that the invaders were:

"ARYANS"

who were also called "SHEPHERD KINGS" and "HYKSOS", not ARABS[29] as inferred by certain "Western" historians. (See, Sir Ernest A. Wallis Budge, EGYPT, p. 94). The so-called "ARYANS" were also from the same area that the Haribus came in about 1640 B.C.E. Yet they arrival was in 1675 B.C.E., which would caused grave doubt that the Hyksos and the Haribus had anything in common with respect to their arrival in Egypt.

The above revelation about the people from Asia that invaded Kimit (Sais, Egypt) around the year 1675 B.C.E., of course, refreshes one's memory of the major battle that was fought against these invaders by the African Prince, Seqenenra III.* It was a direct result of this battle that the prince lost his own life. The evidence of the most violent death he suffered is preserved with his mummy in the Cairo Museum, Egypt. The following details are indicative of said agony:

> His lower jawbone is broken, skull fractured, and brains protrude beyond the cranium case. His tongue is bitten through, and a dagger is thrusted above one of the eyes.

The death of this prince occurred during 1580 B.C.E. (XIIth Dynasty - 1580 - 1340 B.C.E.), This is the same year Pharoah Ahmes I - the son of Pharoah Seqenenra III - mounted the throne of Egypt after the death of his father. It was also Pharoah Ahmes I who finally drove the Hyksos invaders out of Kimit and pursued them all the way to Palestine, thereby placing the Hebrew City of SHARUKHANA under total seige. This is the same City mentioned in JOSHUA XIX, 6, of the Hebrew TORAH, as the <u>City of Sharuhen</u>. Note that this is to be found in the Christian OLD TESTAMENT, which is a version of the Torah. Add this to the fact that the Hebrew TORAH, Christian HOLY BIBLE, and Moslem (or

---

*This prince was one of the major personalities who Western historians assigned to the mythical "BLACK BELT" of Egypt.

Muslim) KORAN (or Quran), are sources of data about the indigenous Africans of the entire continent of Africa's (ALKEBU-LAN'S) history. These works are part and parcel of the materials that make up what is today being called "BLACK HISTORY" and/or "BLACK STUDIES", not "NEGRO HISTORY". But, in reality such studies should be a part of AFRICAN STUDIES DEPARTMENT everywhere, just as they are in other so-called "ETHNIC STUDIES DEPARTMENTS" or "SCHOOLS".

The pages of history reveal that the "light-skinned Caucasians" (Europeans and European-Americans) of Professor Jeffreys, and others like him, did not really established themselves in KIMIT (Sais or Egypt) until the entrance of Alexander "the great" (the son of Philip of Macedon), as conqueror, very late in the year 332 B.C.E. One has to remember, however, that the leader of the invasion, Alexander, depended to a major extent on the indigenous Africans of Egypt for their aid in driving out the then existing slavemasters of the Africans - the Persians. This was only possible because the Africans despised the Persians much more than they did the newcomers, who were in every sense of the word invaders and conquerors, also. It must be understood, at this point, that the usual references by certain "Western" educators as to the "racial" make up of the Persians (Brown) had nothing to do with the Africans preference for the Greeks (White). The Africans joined in the expulsion of the Persians because of the barbarity of Persian rule at that period in human history.

Yet, this period proved to be the beginning of the "LIGHT-SKINNED CAUCASIANS" rule over the Africans of Egypt (in UPPER and LOWER Egypt.) This was also the beginning of the end of the indigenous Africans' rule in Kimit (Sais or Egypt). It was to be the beginning of major Greek enlightenment into the AFRICAN MYSTERIES SYSTEM of the Nile River Valley High-Cultures, and the centre of major institutionalized learning for the Greek students who were imported for just such purpose by Aristotle. From this point onwards, up tò the present 20th Century C.E., the Africans of Northern Africa, most of whom are called "NEGROES, BANTUS, AFRICANS SOUTH OF THE SAHARAH, BLACK AFRICANS, NIGGERS, HOTTEN-TOTS, and a host of other such names of European and European-American labeling, had to endure every sort of dehumanizing confrontation with their Asian (Arab) and subsequent European conquerors. From this point onwards they were also forced to disperse all over the southern parts of what is today notoriously called - "AFRICA SOUTH OF THE SAHARA."

Alexander "<u>the great's</u>" death brought back to Kimit the same murderous rule that the equally ruthless Hyksos and Persian invaders had employed against the African people of the Nile before they were finally driven from North Africa. For example: From the lineage of the Ptolemies (descendants of General Soter, who declared himself "PHARAOH OF ALL EGYPT" at the death of Alexander "<u>the great</u>," and named himself "PTOLEMY I , came the dictators of Egypt. All of them were in direct revolution and rebellion against the government in Greece, since Ptolemy I had refused to rule Egypt in behalf of Alexander's brother - Prince ARRHIDAEUS - the second son of Philip of Macedonia, Alexander's father. This usurpation of the Greek's colonial entity, Egypt, by Greek and other mercenaries that formerly served under Alexander "the great," caused the beginning of the worse "BLOOD BATH" in Egypt's more than forty-thousand years of recorded and pre-recorded history. This was the Greek's major contribution to the Egyptian throne and history. The Ptolemies' ruthlessness also introduced the end to Dynastic and Pharonic Egypt. The following chronological high-lights are very few of the major incidents of the niggardly behaviour of the Ptolemies (mixed European-Africans - beginning with General Soter, Ptolemy I, and his African wife, up to and including Ptolemy XIV - Cesarion, Emperor Julius Caesar's son with Queen Cleopartra VIII - daughter of Ptolemy XIII).

A CHRONOLOGY OF THE GREEKS "BLOOD BATH" IN ANCIENT EGYPT

(a) 311 BCE Alexander II ("the great") died mysteriously.

(b) 306 BCE General Soter, formerly of Alexander's High Command, and Governor of Egypt for Alexander, proclaimed himself PHAROAH OF ALL EGYPT and took upon himself the title PTOLEMY I. It was this same Soter who, with Aristotle, sacked the libraries and lodges of the Mysteries System.*

(c) Ptolemy II (Philadelphus) son of Ptolemy I (General Soter and an African princess - Hadra-of Kimit (Egypt). He started the PHAROAH LIGHTHOUSE. This structure be-

---

*See CHAPTER IX - AFRICAN ORIGINS OF GREEK PHILOSOPHY - for details on how Aristotle and others raped Egypt.

came one of the "WONDERS OF THE WORLD." During the
same period the Hebrews and Greeks allegedly translated the Hebrew TORAH from Hebrew to Greek. The
TORAH is also known as the Christian "OLD TESTAMENT."
It was, also, during this period that the African-
European (of Greek and Egyptian parentage) - MANETHO -
published his historical chronology called DYNASTIES.
The overall work in which the chronology was published
is called "HISTORY OF EGYPT."[30] This was about the
only true creative period of the so-called "light-
skinned Caucasians" of Professor Jeffreys' colonial
rule in Kimit.

(d) The beginning of the disintegration of Greek rule in
Kimit. Also, the last days of the Ptolemies' untold
murders and palace intrigues with the royal family
turning against itself. This began with Ptolemy IX's
overthrow of his brother - Ptolemy VIII.

(e) Ptolemy X murdered his wife - Cleopatra Bernice.

(f) Ptolemy XII chased his sister - Cleopatra VIII - off
her throne. He saw to it that his guardian - Pompey -
got killed just a few days before the BATTLE OF
PHARSALIA.

(g) Julius Ceasar reinstated the dethroned Cleopatra VIII
on her throne in 47 BCE. This most infamous Pharoah
(Queen) was of European (Greek, White) and African
(Egyptian, Black) parentage. Her "Caucasian" lineage
was from General Soter (Pharoah Ptolemy I); her African
lineage was from Ptolemy's wife - Princess Hadra.
All of the Ptolemies were descended from this
beginning.

(h) Ptolemy XII was murdered. He was drowned at the
hands of his own sister - Cleopatra VIII.

(i) Ptolemy XIII was appointed Co-Regent with Cleopatra
VIII. She immediately thereafter planned and aided
in his execution.

(j) Julius Ceasar (Emperor of Rome and colonial ruler
over Egypt, etc.) appointed his son Ptolemy XIV,
(also the son of Cleopatra VIII), - named CESARION,
to rule jointly with his mother as Co-Regent.

(k) Cleopatra VIII committed suicide after being discovered in a plot with Marc Antonio (Mark Anthony)

to murder Julius Ceasar.

(1) Octavianus, later on called AGUSTUS CAESAR, defeated Marc Antonio in the BATTLE OF ACTIUM during the year 30 BCE. At this juncture the end to the African-European (Egyptian-Greek) Pharoahs (Kings and Queens) became reality. Kimit, which the ancients called "SAIS", and the Haribus (Hebrews) renamed "EGYPT," became a Roman PROVINCE under the direct rule of the Caesar in Rome. The glory which was once that of the Africans of the Nile Valleys and Great Lakes High-Culture in Kimit was gone forever. The indigenous Africans, called today all sorts of derogatory names such as - "NEGRO, BANTU, AFRICANS SOUTH OF THE SAHARA, BLACK AFRICANS, HOTTENTOTS, PYGMIES," etc., have never been able to recapture their homeland; the vast majority of them had been driven south into Nubia (Sudan), Kush (Ethiopia), Uganda, Kongo (Congo), and other parts south throughout Alkebu-lan. See page 313 for the actual chronology by dates for the successions of Ptolemy I to Ptolemy XV.

The preceding information contains sufficient pertinent background material to enter into current studies of the history of Mother Africa, ALKEBU-LAN. However, it is much more advantageous to look somewhat deeper into Africa's past, so that once and for all time the NEGROPHOBES and NEGROPHOBIA can be placed in their final resting place in history. Then, hopefully, African, African-American and African-Caribbean historians and other writers will write about their heritage in north and east Africa. Only at this time will the true history of their past be accurately and forcefully presented in its proper perspective.

H. G. Wells, in his book, A SHORT HISTORY OF THE WORLD, pp.49-50, was moved to write the following paragraph with respect to the racism that makes the Africans of Egypt "CAUCASIANS, SEMITES, HAMITES," and others; all of which allegedly had nothing to do with "AFRICANS SOUTH OF THE SAHARA."

> We have to remember that the human race can all interbreed freely and that they separate, mingle and reunite as clouds do. Human races do not branch out like trees with branches that never come together again. It is a thing we need to bear constantly in mind, this remingling of races at any opportunity. It will save us from many cruel delusions and prejudices if we do so. People will use such a word as race in the lowest manner, and base the most preposterous generalization upon it. They will speak of a "British" race or "European" race.[31] But nearly all the European nations are confused mixtures of brownish, dark-white and Mongolian elements.

H.G. Wells' remarks have clearly undermined the racist theory of the Jeffreys and Wiedners who advanced their "CAUCASIAN" north African myth under the protection of the word "HYPOTHESIS." He has shown that the Europeans, as all other peoples of the world, are a combination of mixtures of everyone in the world. And, that the common missuse of the word "RACE" is intentional; purposefully arranged and manipulated by those who are in the position to have others drugged by it. He did not forget the various invasions of Europe, and colonial periods, by the MONGOLS from far-off China and Mongolia. That most of the entire eastern half of the continent called "EUROPE" was Mongolized; just as the Europeans began their Europeanization of the Africans in 1830 C.E.

It was a very sad day indeed when the originators of the disgusting term - "RACE" - introduced it to mankind as a "SCIENTIFIC EXPLANATION" for the apparent physical difference which is only face value. This difference, which is also called "ETHNIC

GROUPING" as another attempt to circumvent the vicious terminology - "RACE", is only valuable to those who need the support of the crutch it brings them. Between the despicable terms, RACE and ETHNIC, with the term "RELIGION" added, mankind has created the abyss which will, one day, help to destroy all that he now calls "CIVIL LIVING."[32] This will certainly come to pass, should sanity continue to evade man, while racism and bigotry remain in control of the pathological historians and other educators who serve their fellowmen and gloat and languish in the cultural deprivation and physical torture of others who are now their conquered colonials or neo-colonials.

Africa, today, is still being systematically raped spiritually, materialistically, economically, politically and all other ways imaginable under the Sun; in part, due to the causes and effects resulting from "RACE" and "RELIGION". The earliest slave traders from Europe, and later on from the United States of America to Western, Eastern, Southern and Central Africa, and the so-called CHRISTIAN MISSIONARIES - most of whom knew little and cared less about Christianity as it went from North Africa to Europe (ROME) were the two evils. However, the destruction of the indigenous African religions caused bedlam to break loose in Africa,[33] the end result being the metaphysical disarrangement of the African's mind. Added to this dilemma was the African's forced conversion to European-styled Christianity and Asian Islam; beginning from the year 640 C.E. or 18AH with the Moslem invasion of North

Africa; followed by the French and other Europeans' invasion of North Africa in the year 1830 C.E., continuing to the present day, and one has what is more commonly referred to as the disenchanted, disorganized, denuded and dehumanized "...AFRICAN BODY WITH A EUROPEAN MENTALITY." Such a "BODY" is also otherwise called "NEGRO." Therefore, "WEST INDIAN NEGRO, AMERICAN NEGRO, AFRICAN NEGRO, OUR NEGRO", and a host of other "NEGROES" are made to suit each condition that would deny the same people of African origin and birth their North and East African heritage. One would better understand how low men have sunk in their attempt to belittle the people they have labeled "NEGROES." In this respect Dr. Lothrop S. Stoddard, one of the so-called "AUTHORITIES ON AFRICA," in his book, THE RISING TIDE OF COLOR, p. 90, wrote the following;

> From the first glance we see that, in the Negro, we are in the presence of a being differing profoundly not merely from the white man but also from those human types which we discovered in our surveys of the brown and yellow worlds. The black man is, indeed, sharply differentiated from the other branches of mankind.

Before continuing any further with his obvious state of Negrophobia, one needs to look at the fact that this man even created worlds of various colors; thus, the "...BROWN AND YELLOW WORLDS." He is already establishing that the "NEGRO" is not even human as the Brown or Yellow races, much less the "GREAT WHITE RACE" one has heard so much about in the pages of history written by his fellow "light-skinned Caucasians." All of this becomes obvious as the good doctor continued:

> His outstanding quality is uper-abundant animal vitality. In this he easily surpasses other races. To it he owes his intense emotionalism. To it, again, is due his extreme fecundity, the Negro being the quickest of the breeders. This abounding vitality shows in many other ways, such as the Negro's ability to survive harsh conditions of slavery under which other races have succumbed.

Again it has become necessary to interrupt the good doctor. This must be done in order to analyze the major thesis upon which European-America has based its major fears about the "...EXTREME FECUNDITY...,"etc., of the "Negro" male. The "...ABUNDANT VITALITY...," etc., which the "Negro" allegedly has, is supposed to make him like a lion or ape and not a human being, one will gather from this "authority" on "NEGROES" and NEGROPHOBIA. The fact that he felt so inferior, because of his own WHITENESS, should not have been blamed on the VITALITY of the Negroes or on the fact that they were able "...TO SURVIVE HARSH CONDITIONS OF SLAVERY UNDER WHICH OTHER RACES HAVE SUCCUMBED." With respect to the latter reference, and others, the good doctor continued on:

> Lastly, in the ethnic crossings, the Negro strikingly displays his prepotency, for black blood, once entering a human stock, seems never really bred out again.[34]

One really has to pity men such as Dr. Stoddard who, instead of showing that his "NEGRO" is inferior to his "WHITE MAN," is in fact really displaying the "NEGROES" superiority over the WHITES. It also causes one to wonder how can a man who holds

117

the highest degree an institution of higher learning (even in the "Western World") can bestow, and lavish such stereotyped cliches and downright racist ignorance in his public utterances, such as you have just witnessed in Dr. Stoddard's conclusion on his so-called "NEGRO". Due to such utterances, however, one can readily understand why there is so much fear among the European and European-American males of the African and African-American counterpart, as stated before. For it is declarations such as Dr. Stoddard's which Anglo-Saxon Judaeo-Christian Greek oriented European and European-American society is nourished upon today, and was so nourished on for over the last 400 years.35 This is especially true throughout the most formative years in the life of each and every White American youngster in his or her church, synagogue, mosque, temple, school, place of employment, institution of academic learning, and all other places of every-day living experiences, from their cradle on to their grave; mostly because of men such as the Stoddards who make them fear that someday this type of "NEGRO" specified in this racist dogma will take over the "<u>lily-white</u>" females of Europe and the Americas and make it so that the "GREAT WHITE RACE," will never be able to "...REALLY BREED OUT AGAIN..." such "...BLACK BLOOD." Of course "BLACK BLOOD" is something which Africans do not want either. Such a type of blood would be dangerous to anyone. "<u>Black blood</u>" must be full of all kinds of things which RED BLOOD does not have. Most Black people will settle for RED BLOOD or none at all, since they only know of this kind; and they are the ones who are supposed to have originated from beings less than human, according to the good doctor.

One must also understand that the Haribus (misnomered Jews)[36] claimed to have survived bondage in Kimit (Egypt),* equally the English under the Romans - including the period when the indigenous Africans, Septimus Severus and his son Caracalla, were emperors of Rome. Did they too survive the conquerors' wrath and enslavement because of the ability of EXTREME SEXUAL PROGENATION according to Dr. Stoddard's theory? If one is to conclude such is the case, then it is necessary to have some sort of scientific facts submitted to prove the outright unscientific conclusions on the so-called "NEGROES" of Dr. Stoddard and Professor Jeffreys.[36a] But, in these days of the superhuman-type "MODERN MAN," "LIGHT-SKINNED CAUCASIAN" and "HERRENVOLK" philosophy that "THE WHITE MAN MUST REIGN SUPREME," it is obviously apparent that the racist theories of men like Stoddard, Wiedner and Jeffreys shall continue to be the basis upon which Africa's sons and daughters shall continue to be prosecuted and persecuted.[37] Let one not forget that Aristotle once said:

"THAT WHICH IS NOT GREEK IS BARBARIAN...," etc.

Today Aristotle's racism is being echoed as:

---

*The Jews could not have been involved with an EXODUS from Egypt to a free land. Egypt controlled all land around her during that time.

> THAT WHICH IS NOT MODERN MAN OR LIGHT AND DARK-
> SKINNED CAUCASIAN* IS OVERSEXED, CANNIBALISTIC
> AND SUBHUMAN AND ONLY FIT TO SERVE AS A SLAVE, ETC.

In too many cases historians and other educators of Europe and European-America still do not give credit to peoples of African birth and/or origin of being human or even sub-human. This was best observed in the United States of America's Federal Constitution; a document that proclaimed for generations that it was born of...

> FREEDOM-LOVING PEOPLE IN A LAND OF THE FREE AND THE
> HOME OF THE BRAVE....

All of these words did not have any bearing on the Africans or African-Americans at the time when they were written, and very little comes to bear at this very instance in reality and practice, as it too did not consider the Africans, who were at the time chattel not human beings.[38] This was so true that the "Father of the United States of America," GEORGE WASHINGTON, sold some of his African slaves to other Europeans in Barbados, British West Indies (Caribbeans), for a few hogs-head of rum shortly after the Whites of the colonies had become free of the Whites from Britain. And it would seem that most European-Americans would prefer that those days were still here today since they are not willing to remove their mental state from the former official position on slavery of their government before the addition of the FOURTEENTH (14th) AMENDMENT to the United

---

*Europeans and European-Americans (Whites).

States of America's Federal Constitution. They still feel that the Africans and African-Americans are their "NEGROES" to hold, own, and keep forever.

The question of just who was, or is, an African; and what type of an African occupied what area of Africa, has bothered European and European-American advocates of CAUCASIANISM for many centuries of late. Even the honored historian and egyptologist, Sir Ernest A. Wallis Budge, in his work entitled EGYPT, on pages 21 and 22, was obliged to write the following:

> THE HISTORIC NATIVE OF EGYPT, BOTH IN THE OLD AND NEW STONE-AGES, WAS AFRICAN.[39]

Strange as it may seem, the same Sir Wallis Budge in many of his works indicated that the Egyptians were not NEGROES, even though they were Black, but may have had <u>Negroid strain</u>. Sir Wallis Budge continued:

> ...THERE ARE MANY THINGS IN THE MANNERS AND CUSTOMS AND RELIGIONS OF THE HISTORIC EGYPTIANS, THAT IS TO SAY, OF THE WORKERS ON THE LAND, THAT SUGGEST THAT THE ORIGINAL HOME OF THE PREHISTORIC ANCESTORS WAS A COUNTRY IN THE NEIGHBORHOOD OF UGANDA AND PUNT.[40]*

The citations just quoted from Sir Wallis Budge's EGYPT certainly nullify Professor Jeffreys' geographic line of demarcation with regard to his origin of the "LIGHT-SKINNED" and "DARK-SKINNED CAUCASIANS" (Modern Man, Europeans and European-Americans, White People) hypothesis, described in Dr. Donald L. Wiedner's

---

*Both of these countries are located around central-east Africa.

map which he entitled "ETHNOGRAPHY OF AFRICA Before 300 B.C.," shown on page   of this volume. For both of these men included the indigenous Africans which they call "AFRICANS SOUTH OF THE SAHARA, BANTUS, NEGROES," etc.; most of these Africans are indigenous to the soil of Kenya, Punt (the areas that present-day Somali Republic and the French Somaliland occupy) and Uganda. At the time when Egyptian history was the recorded events of solely indigenous Africans much of what is today called the Republic of Tanzania (Tanganyika) was only a part of Uganda. Why is this geographical delineation so important today? Because it is in this area that the oldest known fossil of an "ape-like man" or "man-like ape" by the name of ZINJANTHROPUS BOISIE[41] was unearthed by Drs. Mary and Louis S.B. Leakey. Why is this find of a fossil much more important than all the other fossils of this kind to be found in Africa, Asia, Australia or Europe? This one has, to date, proven to be the oldest known "LINK BETWEEN MAN AS WE KNOW HIM TODAY AND HIS MOST ANCIENT ANCESTORS FROM THE BEGINNING OF MAN'S EVOLUTION TO WHAT HE IS." If this is true, and that is what the facts have proven to be, then one can understand why there is so much rush to reclaim the "DARK CONTINENT" which Europeans and European-Americans for centuries had concluded was only occupied by SAVAGES, UNCIVILIZED PEOPLES, NATIVES, CANTIBALS, PRIMITIVES, and others who are not fit for civilization. These claims were only rescinded with respect to the "EUROPEANS," who many have camouflaged with the term "CAUCASIAN" in order to cop the culture and history of the Africans of this area of Africa; all in the process of also copping ZINJANTHROPUS BOISIE.

One can only wonder when the Nile Valleys (Blue and White, also the Atbara River) will be subjected to re-identification by those who are responsible for making CAUCASIANS out of AFRICANS. They will also change the Nile River from its northerly flow, and stop it from its source in Uganda and Ethiopia, both lands of indigenous Africans who are today called "NEGROES" and "BANTUS." But they will continue to let it pass through Sudan among the Nubians, because they were supposed to have been the "NEGROES" of the days of Dynastic and Predynastic Kimit (Egypt). In other words, there would, again, be another situation where the CAUCASIANS lived and originated in Kimit and Uganda, but in Sudan (Nubia or Meröwe) the "NEGROES" would once more live and originate there. Certainly this is confusing. It is more than confusing. But, it is the height of the racist hypotheses that is still being peddled by European and European-American educators and their African under studies with the pretext of academic discipline. It is a discipline which demands that all who challenge this type of racism must do so without exhibiting any emotional feelings in their work. This in itself is hypocritical and subjective, for no one can write on anything without exhibiting emotion. The mere fact that the writer thinks about writing in itself begins the emotional processes which are necessary to produce anything. Also, to say that a work is "An UNBIASED PRESENTATION" of anything is in itself BIASED. No one can be totally removed from the prejudices of the world in which he or she lives and write completely free of the effects of the strain the environment places upon him or her. It is for these same reasons that the contents in this volume bear the testimony of history as seen through the eyes of a person of African origin. This could not be done from the eyes of a person of European origin; as much as he or she would have wanted to be unbiased or without prejudice. So, then, just as the Nile Rivers flow north, so did the indigenous Africans of Africa travel north with the flow of the Nile waters until they arrived in what is today called EGYPT and built their High-Culture (civilization). All of this they did before the arrival of the first "CAUCASIAN" in Africa.

With respect to the Africans' identity, especially those of Eastern and Northern Africa, not a single attempt is being made to see to what extent they had Africanized ancient Europe; or, just why the southern Europeans, particularly the Greeks, Spaniards, Romans (Italians), Portuguese, Slavs, French, and those of the Islands of the Mediterranean, are so brown[42] and the other Europeans further north are so white and blonde. Furthermore; no questions are being asked about those Europeans of Sweden, Norway, Denmark, Germany, and Ireland, among all of the other national groupings of Europe, who show definite "NEGROID

PHYSICAL CHARACTERISTICS" of which Sir Harry H. Johnston and H.G. Wells refer to in their historic works. Yet, if an African has a pointed nose, thin lips, and light pigmentation all sorts of theories as to his or her being not of "NEGRO origin," but only showing a "NEGROID appearance," are brought forward. Why? What purposes can such information serve, other than to project the racist philosophies and needs of the conqueror against the helpless victims of conquest - the so-called "NEGROES?" Victims who have for a little more than four-hundred (400) years suffered every form of persecution and genocide from the ancestors of those who will now even deny them the one thing they still have left - THEIR HISTORY OF BEING THE FIRST TO DEVELOP WHAT IS TODAY CALLED EGYPTIAN CIVILIZATION. This being the culmination of the hundreds of High-Cultures the indigenous Africans, the so-called NEGROES, BANTUS, etc., created from the dawn of man's appearance on the Planet EARTH. The silent cessation by the Africans of their North and East African heritage should never have been expected to go on forever unchallenged. Because of this, one must examine the facts to find the answer as to the WHY asked in the above sentence. In so doing the following revelations become evident:

(a) Michaelangelo[43] painted the Europeans' version of their European-type Christian God - JESUS CHRIST - to appear in the image of any northern Italian one could have found during his lifetime. He and the Pope of the Roman Catholic Church in Rome created what is today among all of Christendom, except Ethiopia, the official picture of the blonde GOD-HEAD. His selection

was a very natural one, for he too was a part of the
image he projected as JESUS CHRIST and the DICIPLES
at the PASSOVER or LAST SUPPER.* He thereby, made
his GOD IN HIS OWN IMAGE, COLOR, and PHYSICAL APPEAR-
ANCE in conjunction with the biblical teachings
according to the Europeans. God, or Jesus Christ, has
since become a "WHITE MAN, CAUCASIAN," to every man,
woman and child of the "Western" Christian Religion;
even to the extent that BLACK Christians are afraid
to think of the possibility that Jesus Christ could
have been a BLACK MAN from a BLACK COUNTRY in Asia.

(b) The statue of ISIS and OSIRIS, depicting the indigenous African (BLACK) Goddess and God of Kimit
(Sais or Egypt), has been imitated and projected
as the "BLACK MADONNA AND CHILD."44 Yet, the child -
JESUS CHRIST - grows up to be a CAUCASIAN BLONDE
(European) with long curly BLONDE HAIR, BLUE EYES,
and KEEN FEATURES - called "CAUCASOID." His mother -
MARY - turns out to suit the image and color of her
European female worshippers, her Asian and African
origin through her Haribu (Hebrew or Jewish) background being completely ignored. Yet, the model,
ISIS and OSIRIS, still remains BLACK, the same as
the original MADONNA AND CHILD statues that were
originally imported into Europe during the earliest
days of Christendom when the Africans were the
religious leaders of the Christian world. One of
these statues still adorns the hall of St. Peter's
Church in Rome.

(c) There is a deliberate attempt to remove every trace
of BLACKNESS from the AFRICAN-MOORS also; thereby
making all of the BLACK PEOPLE who conquered and
colonized the Iberian Peninsula - SPAIN, PORTUGAL
and part of SOUTHERN FRANCE - appear to have been
ARABS, and it is conveniently forgotten or ignored
that there were two cultural groups of MOORS that
entered the Iberian Peninsula as conquerors during
the first half of the Eight (8th) Century C.E. or
First (1st) Century A.H.45 The first of the two
groups were the indigenous Africans, the so-called
"NEGROES, BANTUS, AFRICANS SOUTH OF THE SAHARA,"etc.,
under the command of a fellow African Moslem -
GENERAL TARIKH - for whom the ROCK OF GIBRALTAR is

---

*It is without doubt that Michaelangelo and the Pope were aware
of the fact that Israel was a hot country and the home of Blacks.

named, which derived from the words GIBRAL TARIKH or ROCK OF TARIKH.*[46] Why is there an attempt to remove the image of the African-Moors from this aspect of World History? Dr. Goebbels (Adolph Hitler's Nazi Propaganda Minister) provided the answer quite vividly in his attempt at "ARYANIZING" all of Europe; not CAUCASIANIZING it. Adolph Hitler himself echoed it much more succinctly in his book entitled - MEIN KAMPF; Professor M.D.W. Jeffreys answered it in his "NEGRO ENIGMA" as cited before in this volume; Dr. Donald L. Wiedner outlined it in his ETHNOGRAPHIC MAP OF AFRICA" with his CAUCASIAN ONLY North and East Africa; Dr. Heinrick Voerword of the Union of South Africa set it up in his concentration Camps called "NATIVE RESERVES"[47] in his program of "APARTHEID;" George L. Rockwell (the United States of America's late self-styled fuehrer) echoed it for all of the American Nazi-type and Facist Nationalists and other equally racist organizations that hide under the banner of SUPER-PATRIOTISM but maintain their "PURE WHITE CAUCASIANISM; just as King Leopold II of the Belgians and Henry Morton Stanley of "DARKEST AFRICA" noteriety planted it in genocide in the Congo along with the hundreds of so-called European and European-American "ENTREPRENUERS." It is, in all of its ugliness, called "WHITE SUPREMACY." It has proven to be the greatest murderer of the last four hundred (400) years. It is the beginning of an end. The "END" being the impending holocaust of the "Non-WHITE" peoples of Africa, Asia, Australia, South and North America, and the Caribbean (West Indies) Islands against the "WHITE" peoples of the UNITED STATES OF AMERICA and EUROPE; only because those who are in military and economic control of the world and its people have decided that some "GOD" or another COMMISSIONED THEM TO SAVE ALL OF MANKIND ON THIS PLANET - Earth.[48] In order to accomplish said goal (end) certain groups have been marked for eventual extermination - the AFRICANS (Blacks), the so-called "NEGROES, BANTUS," etc., being the selected VICTIMS, to be closely followed by all other non-WHITE peoples.

In order to better understand what has been said with respect to the identification and destruction of the Africans and their

---

*Note that this "ROCK" was originally called "MONS CALPE" by the original Iberian inhabitants the Africans conquered and ruled.

historical heritage, one needs to examine further the works of another of the European "AUTHORITIES" on the issue of the INTERMINGLING and AMALGAMATION of the ancient peoples of Africa, Asia, Europe and the islands connected thereto. It will be noticed, however, that much have been said by this individual before, never-the-less, because of his major projection in intellectual circles, it becomes necessary to quote from him once more. Thus, Sir Harry H. Johnston concluded in his book, A HISTORY OF CIVILISATION OF AFRICAN, page 48:

> ...These are the only recorded attempts of the Romans to reach the Sudan across the Sahara Desert;* but that intercourse had been going on for hundreds, if not thousands, of years between the Libyans and Hamites of Northern and North-Eastern Africa on the one hand, and the Negroids and Negroes of the Lake Chad** and Benue regions and of the whole Niger basin on the other. There can be little doubt, from a variety of evidence.^{49}

At what point in a racially-loaded statement of Negrophobia as this does one try to untangle the confusion which has been perpetrated on the reading public as academic scholarship? Is it at the point where the "LIBYANS, HAMITES, NEGROIDS, NEGROES," and other "RACES" come into play? Or, is it at the mere suggestion of the ridiculous usage of the term "RACE" itself, as displayed in Sir Harry's _racially_ imgregnated stereotyped presentation of what some may select to call _African History_? When did the

---
*Note that the term "SAHARA DESERT" is incorrectly used. The word "SAHARA" alone means "GREAT DESERT" in ancient Arabic, its source.
**The proper spelling of this word is "TCHAD".

LIBYANS became a distinctly different RACE from the other Africans of North Africa, or of Eastern Africa? And, to what RACE do the "NEGROIDS" belong? At what point did the LIBYANS stop being "HAMITES", the name they have been called by most "Western" educators for the past two centuries? Although these facts were projected in the sense of questions, they are meant to be citations of the depth to which European and European-American historians and others who are generally called "EDUCATORS" will go in order to disprove the presence of indigenous Africans, the so-called "NEGROES" and "BANTUS", etc., in Northern and Eastern Africa (Alkebu-lan) before the arrival of the Europeans and Asians of antiquity and ancient times. This is before the arrival of the HYKSOS or SHEPHERD KINGS in Kimit (Egypt or Sais) about 1675 B.C.E.*

Why have the ancient Libyans been removed from their established listing by other European writers? Even Professor Jeffreys conceded their indigenous African origin. Libya is in Africa; not only is this fact TRUTH, but Africa was once known as "LIBYA"** by the most ancient of the Caucasians (Europeans) - Romans and Greeks. Libya has always bordered on Kimit, and at one time in history she was sandwiched between Kimit and Numidia;

---

*See chronological listing of the arrival of the Hyksos and other peoples in Northern and Eastern Africa in this volume under the chapter heading - PREDYNASTIC AND DYNASTIC KIMIT, LIBYA, AND CUSH (Egypt, Libya, Ethiopia), pages 306 through 313.
**See MAP OF AFRICA, 1968 A.D., in this volume, located on page 700.

this being during the period in history when the Africans of Carthage were the masters of the Mediterranean Sea and all the nations bordering on it. Furthermore, there were no "HAMITES" before the <u>Haribus' myth</u> about "NOAH AND THE ARK DURING THE FLOOD" when the "WORLD WAS FLOODED BY GOD", according to the story. Or, is the good gentleman saying that the Haribu TORAH is lying when it states that:

> "...MOSES LED THE HEBREWS AND A MULTITUDE OF OTHER PEOPLES OUT OF EGYPT UNTO THE PROMISELAND...," etc.?

Sir Harry either got his theory mixed up with biblical mythology or the TORAH is certainly lying. One can easily prove this, as shown in the chronology of the different periods of the Egyptians' dynastic rule, because LIBYA was in existence before the birth of the first Haribu - ABRAHAM - a few generations before the year he arrived in Kimit (Egypt) - c1640 B.C.E., as mentioned in the FIRST BOOK OF MOSES - also called THE BOOK OF GENESIS.**

The conclusion reached by Sir Harry H. Johnston with respect to the Roman penetration into the SAHARA and SAVANNAHS of Central-West Africa to reach the NIGER BASIN with the Africans that guided them there in their return trips from North Africa and Europe, is phenomenal. However, such crossings had been made by General Septimus Flaccus in the year 50 B.C.E., and by the military explorer - Julius Maternus - who reached the Lake Tchad area and

---

*The Haribus that left Kimit with Moses had to end their EXODUS in Kimit territory, as Kimit ruled the entire area in 1232 BCE.
**Also see Christian HOLY BIBLE, or any "VERSION" of OLD TESTAMENT.

Bornu (Upper Nigeria) about 30 B.C.E. Both Flaccus and Maternus were Romans of European (White, Caucasian) origin.* Their success in crossing the Sahara depended totally upon the assistence they received from the Africans who traded by means of their caravans that transversed the GREAT DESERT, along very well established routes by said Africans[49a] whom "<u>Western</u>" historians and other "<u>educators</u>" continue to call "NEGROES" and "BANTUS", also "AFRICANS SOUTH OF THE SAHARA", in their obsession to CAUCAS-IANIZE North Africa.

The intercourse between the ancient indigenous Africans and the Romans (Whites, Blacks, Browns, Yellows) was so extensive that it was impossible to avoid free INTER-BREEDING (amalgamation) between the various African, Asian and European peoples, since color of one's skin was never a factor in those days; neither was the physical appearance of a man (asthetic - GOOD or BAD - looks). It was not because of any of these reasons that so many Africans became great and noted generals and other officeholders in the Roman Empire with a few even gaining the mantle of Emperor of Rome.[50]** However, those indigenous Africans were never recorded in the pages of history as being "NEGROES"*** or "BANTUS." Why? Because these terms were unknown to the ancients of Africa

---
*Like the Greeks, the Romans were not all indigenous to Europe. This word, "ROMAN", included many different peoples of Asia and Africa amongst the vast majority that were Europeans.
**Septimus Severus and his son - Caracalla.
***The Portuguese around the 17th or 18th Century C.E. introduced "NEGRO" and "NEGROLAND". The British introduced "BANTUS".

and Asia; even the Europeans did not know them, Europeans hundreds of years later were the ones to introduce them. The indigenous Africans were called, among many other names, "ETHIOPIANS, LIBYANS, CARTHAGINIANS, NUMIDIANS, NUBIANS, EGYPTIANS, BLACKS, AFRICANS, MOORS, PUNTS", etc., but never "NEGROES, BANTUS, HOTTENTOTS, BUSHMEN, FUZZY WUZZIES", nor any other such labels of inferior status. Even the indigenous Africans from as far south as the Niger basin were never called by names other than what they called themselves, which of course did not include any of the racist terms placed upon them by the Europeans and Asians (Arabs) of the colonial and slave-trading eras, with the Asians beginning in the early half of the 8th Century C.E. (18 A.H.), and the Europeans beginning about the 16th Century C.E. At least they could have called the Africans around the NIGER RIVER basin "NEGRO" from a semantical basis; but the fact is that it just did not happen that way. The word "NEGRO" in no way what-so-ever has the right of attachment to any segment of any of the indigenous peoples of the continent of Alkebu-lan, which the Greeks and Romans misnomered "AFRICA". It is a name that had its origin in the ENSLAVEMENT OF THE AFRICAN PEOPLES OF WEST AFRICA by the Europeans and Arabs along with its partner "NEGROLAND";* and as such was forced upon the peoples of said area by the slavemasters, and adopted by European-Americans later. It

---
*NEGROLAND appeared on many maps of the 17th through 18th Century C.E. See map on page 701 of this volume.

is a name which any self-respecting African or person of African origin cannot take pride in, and must reject and despise for the history of contempt it harbors against the well-being of the general African communities of the world.

One has to remember that Rome was not the cultural center of a particular homogeneous <u>ethnic</u> group of people. It was, in fact, the home of a number of so-called "RACES" or "ETHNIC" groupings, etc. For example: SAUL (Paul) was a Roman citizen; yet, he was a Haribu.* SENECA, the philosopher on politics, who was from Spain,** was a Spaniard and Roman citizen. SEPTIMUS SEVERUS, who became Emperor of Rome, was an indigenous African (Black man, "Bantu, Negro", etc.).[51] Emperor Septimus Severus' son, CARACALLA, was also Emperor of Rome - succeeding his father, was of African (Black) and Asian - Syrian (Brown) parentage.*** Of course these are only a very few of the noted Romans of history during the Christian Era. But, there were countless others through ordinary marriages and common-law relationships before, and after, the birth of the Christians' God - JESUS CHRIST. From these relationships came literally millions of offsprings; thus every MIXTURE and COMBINATIONS of African-Asian-European imaginable resulted in Rome, the same being true for ancient Greece, a condition which

---

  *This was the name the original people called "JEWS" were called by the ancients. Europeans changed the name to Jews, which represented only one of the Haribu tribes - "JUDAH".
 **Spain was originally part of the IBERIAN nation of people.
***The mother of Caracalla, the wife of Septimus Severus, was of Syrian birth and upbringing.

later on took place in all of North Africa, Egypt in particular. With regards to this historical fact an English "authority" on this area of history, Jane Soames, in her book - COAST OF THE BARBARY, pp. 30-31, was obliged to write the following:

> At the height of Roman power in North Africa the population of Italy was actually declining and there was never any vast number of Roman colonists in the racial sense of the word. The Romans knew nothing of those modern emotions which are to us so powerful and omnipresent that we can hardly imagine a civilsation from which they should be absent; She had neither color prejudice nor religious intolerance in the days of the Republic. The Christian martyrs of the early church suffered because they were felt to be a menace to the State, propagating doctrines subversive to good order and discipline: they were regarded as the Communists of their day. But highly cultivated Roman opinion considered all religions to be essentially the diverse manifestations of one great truth, and no conception of the white heat of missionizing zeal would put whole populations of unbelievers to the sword and send men to the scafold and the fire for the sake of a disputed theological definition.*

The remarks by Jane Soames should have been sufficient proof for anyone to submit in refuting the racist anti-African ("Negroes, Bantus", etc.) propaganda that is still so common among current history professors and other educators dealing with Africans, African-Americans and African-Caribbeans. She continued further in another paragraph:

> ...All that part of the make-up of men's minds (religious bigotry)** came later, as did the acute sense

---

*The words underscored are for emphasis on the points dealing with prejudice, religious bigotry, and racism with respect to the ancients of Rome, Roman North Africa, Europe and Asia.
**The words in brackets are by the author of this volume.

> of differentiation of race and consequent antagonism
> which may be summed up in the phrase '<u>colour bar</u>.'

Continuing on further on page 45 of her book, opening tremendous insight on the indigenous African ("Bantu, Negro", or whatever-else) who ruled Ireland, Scotland, Wales, England and all other lands of the Roman Empire during the years 193 - 211 C.E.:

> ...It is of peculiar interest to remember that this amazing career terminated in Great Britain. Faithful to his life-long preoccupation with military matters, Septimus Severus, spent the last three years of his reign in Britain reorganizing and strengthening the defenses of its northern frontier. He was accompanied by his son, Caracalla, who succeded him, and it is said that so long a sojourn in one of the most distant and <u>barbarous</u> of the provinces was in part due to an attempt to keep that son away from the deleterious and corrupting influence of the Court (in Rome).

It is rather amusing that the peoples of Great Britain were considered "BARBAROUS" during the reign of an indigenous African Roman Emperor, Septimus Severus, over them. Here one can see why the Europeans and European-Americans must continue their struggles to make all of North Africa "CAUCASIAN". For history revealed that too many Africans of the type presently called "AFRICANS SOUTH OF THE SAHARA" were the educators, conquerors and "CIVILIZERS" of too many Europeans - "CAUCASIANS" and "CAUCASOIDS".

It was the heavy task on Emperor Septimus Severus that finally caused him his life in England. He died in York in the year 211 C.E., during the month of February. Of course England's adverse climate also proved very much to the detriment of this African who was definitely more at home in the hot temperature of his native North Africa than in the cold and dreary British Isles.

R.G. Collingwood in his book, ROMAN BRITAIN, along with many other "<u>Western</u>" historians who were not ingrossed with racism, supported Jane Soames' conclusions. The facts of history, and the physical results which are still visible in the peoples of the Mediterranean borders of Europe, particularly in Italy, Sicily, Greece, Spain, and even Portugal on the Atlantic Sea, demonstrate the reality of her conclusions.[51a]

The entire world of Christendom owes its greatest successes to many indigenous Africans who would be today, were they alive in the United States of America and Europe, called "NEGROES, BANTUS", and other such names. In this regard, one must remember that the "FIRST MARTYRS OF CHRISTENDOM" were the indigenous Africans of North Africa; the very first being "NAMPHAMO".[52] Namphamo was a native of Numidia, an African nation that occupied an area between present day Libya and Algeria. The names, TERTULLIAN, ST. CYPRIAN, and ST. AUGUSTINE, are other great names in the heritage of the PATRONS and SAINTS of early Christendom.[53] All were indigenous Africans of the type anyone can observe in the Harlems of the United States of America today. Christians do give honor and lavish honor and praise to them in their churches, irrespective of denominations or sects. The greatness of the last three mentioned was so dynamic it forced the so-called "AUTHORITY" on Christian missionary, European-Style, in Africa - C.P. Groves, in his book, THE PLANTING OF CHRISTIANITY IN AFRICA*, to query:

WHO WERE THE THREE "...FATHERS OF CHRISTENDOM"?

Obviously they were indigenous Africans who are today called euphemistically "NEGROES" and other such names of slave-trading periods. Thus they are, according to Mrs. Steuart Erskine in her book, VANISHED CITIES OF NORTHERN AFRICA, page 80:

> The three great names that bring honour to the African Church are Tertullian, the first of the Church writers who made Latin the language of Christianity;[54] Cyprian, Bishop and martyr; and Augustine, one of the greatest of the most famous "Fathers of the Church".

The strength and depth of personality of one of these three greatest of the "FATHERS OF THE CHURCH" is felt in the following excerpt from his work. He wrote:

> Surely a glance at the wide world shows that it is daily being more cultivated and better peopled than before. All places are now accessible, well known, open to commerce. Delight farms have now blotted out every trace of the dreadful wastes; cultivated fields have overcome woods; flocks and herds have driven out wild beasts; sandy spots are sown; rocks are planted; bogs are drained. Large cities now occupy land hardly tenanted before by cottages. Islands are no longer dreaded; houses, people, civil rule, civilisation, are everywhere.

The above extract is taken from Tertullian's, DeANIMA, as translated from the original Latin text by Hanach in his MISSION AND EXPANSION, Vol. III, p. 275. It shows the depth of Tertullian's involvement with the economic life of the community in which he

---

*This is a 4 volume work on the co-colinization of the Africans by the military-religious compact in the partition of Africa.

lived and the manner in which he was able to interpret said life into religious significance so far as it concerned his Christianity. Also, it shows he was very keenly aware of the socio-political and religious implications involved with the total economy of various areas of Northern Africa during his lifetime. And, that he saw no separation between Church* and State,** thereby his religious interpretations above were economically moulded.

What revelations have come forward as a result of the information so far exposed to the average reading public which had been heretofore hidden?

(a) That it should be obvious, by now, that the Africans whom the Europeans would like to remove from the history of North and East Africa, were totally involved with the Europeans who were instrumental in making Europe what it is today;

(b) that they too helped to lay the foundation for Europeans to build upon, up to, and including, the present 20th Century C.E.;

(c) that the ancient indigenous Africans were responsible for much of the basic tenets of present day Christendom, just as they were in the past;

(d) that the Africans were not "CIVILIZED" in anyway by anyone other than themselves;

(e) that Christianity is nothing new to the indigenous Africans. They have worked with it from its creation, and along with the Romans and Greeks during later periods;

---

*The Church in question was that which was owned and controlled by the Africans of North Africa.
**The State was the Roman Empire with its power-base centered in Rome. This concept is still not workable (SEPARATION OF CHURCH AND STATE) anywhere including the United States of America.

- (f) that the indigenous Africans sired as many Europeans bearing the name "CAUCASIANS", as did the Europeans equally sire many Africans having been labeled "NEGROES".[55]

- (g) that racism is the disease of a sick and fearful "MODERN MAN";

- (h) that the BLACK MAN'S (the indigenous African and his descendants) history in Alkebu-lan (Africa) exists for as long as mankind itself exists; and,

- (i) that no amount of wishful hypotheses can change these facts, regardless of the so-called "AUTHORITIES" on "NEGRO HISTORY" and their proclamations and hypotheses to the contrary, or by the teachings in their "INSTITUTIONS OF HIGHER LEARNING" that remain in Europe and the Americas and decide what is established criteria for the African peoples and Africa.

What influences overshadowed the contributions of the early Africans to Christendom? What happened to remove the indigenous Africans from leadership in Christendom? Part of the answer is that there were many causes which changed the course of African leadership in the Christian Church of North Africa and Southern Europe, especially in Rome.[56] They go back very far indeed; even before the advent of the Christians' God-Head - JESUS CHRIST.[57] One cause was the indigenous Africans' ("CARTHAGINIANS") defeat of the Romans during the First (1st) and Second (2nd) PUNIC WARS,[58] which should have been settled by the Africans' defeat by the Romans in the Third (3rd) and final PUNIC WAR. Historians, and other "educators", such as Dr. Stoddard and Professor Jeffreys, who seemed to have suffered from acute "NEGROPHOBIA" in their works, also helped. For example: Dr. Lothrop Stoddard felt it necessary to write in his work, THE RISING TIDE OF COLOUR, page 68, added proof to support the Africans' fall amongst their European-Christian counterparts:

> Of course Christianity has made distinct progress in the <u>Dark Continent</u>. The natives of the South African Union are predominantly Christianized. In east-central Africa Christianity has also gained many converts, particularly in Uganda, while on the West African Guinea coast Christian missions have long been established and have generally succeeded in keeping Islam away from the Seaboard.

Before completing Dr. Stoddard's major premise, which shows that this type of "TRUE CHRISTIANITY" was very similar to that of Propaganda Minister Dr. Goebbels of Nazis Germany and Dr. Verwoerd's of the Union of South Africa,* one must recall that the history of the Christian Church, from its infancy, shows that Christianity was in North, East, and West Africa before the birth of the first Western European Christian, much less Dr. Stoddard.[59] And, that, what he and his fellow Europeans and European-Americans brought to the Africans of West Africa was "WHITE SUPREMACY" and "CAPITALISM" under the disguise of a Europeanized version of the Christianity the colonist missionaries adopted. Dr. Stoddard continued on pages 96 and 97 of his book:

> ...Certainly, <u>all white men</u>, whether professed Christians or not, should welcome the success of missionary efforts in Africa. The degrading <u>fetishism</u> and <u>demonology</u> which sum up the native pagan cults cannot stand, and all Negroes will be someday either Christian or Moslem. In so far as he is Christianized, <u>the Negro's savage instincts</u> will be restrained and he will be dis-

---

*The Union of South Africa was originally called "MONOMOTAPA" by the Africans that settled there thousands of years before the arrival of the first Europeans in 1488 C.E.

posed to acquiesce in white tutelege. In so far as he
is Islamized, <u>the Negro warlike propensities</u> will be
inflamed, and we will be used as the tool of Arab
Pan-Islamism seeking to drive the white man from
Africa and make the continent his very own.

The words underscored were so done in order to emphasize the racist colonial attitude that was prevalent, and still is, among the general so-called CHRISTIAN MISSIONARIES who came from Europe and European-America to Africa to:

"CHRISTIANIZE AND CIVILIZE THE HEATHEN NATIVES."
This Europeanized Christian zeal of the colonist missionaries was also transferred to Africans and other peoples of African origin who joined in with the colonial administrators over the Africans in Africa. And, most certainly, the declarations by Dr. Stoddard and others like him set the stage and established the criteria used against the indigenous African religions the Europeans met when they arrived in Africa as colonists. This was the basis upon which they also operated in Ethiopia, East Africa, even though the Africans of Ethiopia had a Christian religion and an official CHRISTIAN NATION before Rome became Christian under Emperor Constantine in the Third (3rd) Century C.E. These same sentiments and declarations are motivating factors that still drive the majority of the so-called "JUDAEO-CHRISTIAN MISSIONARIES" who arrive in Africa under the subterfuge of BROTHERLY LOVE AND HUMAN FELLOWSHIP.

It is very necessary to analyze certain other aspects of the good doctor's obvious ENIGMATIC NEGROPHOBIA which Professor

Jeffreys also demonstrated, all of which contained the same type of racist cancer only to be found in a mind that is obsessed with self-pity and an apparent inner inferiority which one may feel with regards to <u>the inherent power and strength</u> ascribed to the "NEGROES" and others of indigenous Africa. However, Dr. Stoddard's arrogance, in his own Negrophobia, was very typical of the Christian missionaries of his days; and as stated before, including those of the 20th Century C.E. which is totally institutionalized and taught in the various RELIGIOUS SEMINARIES where Africans and peoples of African origin receive their training to go out and teach the same <u>racist theology</u> and religion.

The following points were the most bigoted of the intemperately crude remarks and racist sentiments projected in the extract from the writings of Dr. Stoddard's book, THE RISING TIDE OF COLOUR:

(1) He began with the usual racist premise most White bigots hold about Africa and things African - that Africa is some sort of Henry Morton Stanley's fantastic...DARKEST AFRICA...where the <u>White</u> Man had to come to save the NATIVES from eating themselves. This, of course, was to make his White audiences imagine that they could even see NATIVE AFRICAN CANNIBALS creeping all over Africa until the "GREAT WHITE FATHERS AND MOTHERS" arrived with the magical book, THE HOLY BIBLE, to stop it all. The European Christian missionaries he presented appeared as the COMMUNIST BOGEY MAN of the COMMUNIST CONSPIRACY everyone seemed to be afraid of in the United States of America for the past few generations. The only difference was their alleged "CALLING".

(2) His assumption that "ISLAM" and its teachings would only bring forward the "...SAVAGE INSTINCTS" in the "NEGROES". This theory was designed to prove that

the Africans did not have the ability of even using
their brain; for they, according to the good doctor's
findings, could only depend upon their "INSTINCT".
Thus, it would seem that savagery refers only to all
non-Whites, especially the doctor's "NEGROES"; the
good doctor forgetting that the Romans also said that
"...THE ANGLO-SAXONS WERE TOO STUPID EVEN TO MAKE
SLAVES OF THEM...," etc. This would also mean that the
imfamous slave trade, which was supported by all of
European and European-American Christendom, including
the HOLY SEE in Rome through its bishops-starting with
Pope Martin V[60] and Bishop Bartolome de Las Casas, and
the citadels of Protestantism - particularly Great
Britain, were not "SAVAGES". Nor were "THE FOUNDING
FATHERS" of the United States of America who sold
Africans as they sold molasses, and exterminated the
indigenous peoples of America whom they labeled "INDIANS"
and "SAVAGES" after murdering them and taking all of
their earthly possessions in the name of "CHRISTIANITY"
and "CIVILIZATION". That, even the "butcher" King
Leopold II of Belgian[61] and Adolph Hitler - Dictator
of Nazi Germany, accordingly, were not "SAVAGES", on
the sole basis that they were "...ALL WHITE MEN, WHETHER
PROFESSED CHRISTIANS OR NOT." They were the type Stoddard
appealed to. One is expected, according to the position
taken by Stoddard, to accept that the Europeans mentioned, and the European-Americans that were involved
with them, could not possibly be "SAVAGES" solely on
the basis that they were the same type of "LIGHT-
SKINNED CAUCASIANS" spoken of by Professor Jeffreys and
called "WHITE MEN" by Dr. Stoddard.

(3) "...THE DEGRADING FETISHISM AND DEMONOLOGY...,"etc.,
which the **good** doctor seemed to have abhored within
the Africans is still being practised by Europeans
today in European-style Christianity, just as they were
in those days; and the Africans also continue practicing
theirs, the only difference of note is that the Africans
maintain the right to have their own home-grown versions
of "DEMONOLOGY". But, those **who stop their own** to
question what RIGHTS the Africans have in practicing
their type of religiosity should have first questioned
what RIGHT the good doctor had in leaving his own homeland in Europe to challenge the Africans in their own
homeland; the Africans having every right to practice
any form or religion they deemed appropriate for their
own need.

(4) He appealed to the lowest element of <u>White racism</u> when he wrote the following: "...CERTAINLY ALL WHITE MEN, WHETHER PROFESSING CHRISTIANS OR NOT, SHOULD WELCOME THE SUCCESS OF THE MISSIONARY EFFORT IN AFRICA." Here again the good doctor really displayed the height of the purpose which European and European-American-style Christian missionaries reached in trying to "CHRISTIANIZE AND CIVILIZE" the so-called "DARK CONTINENT". One sees, or should be able to see, that the basic aim of the Christians then, as it is now, is to use JESUS CHRIST and CHRISTIANITY as the tools and weapons which are necessary in the continued <u>colonization and neo-colonization</u> of the peoples of the world, the Africans in particular, since Africa represents the RICHEST PIECE OF REAL ESTATE ON THE PLANET EARTH.

With the above historical background, and all of the racism and bigotry it conveys, is it at all suprising that all over the world European and European-American-style CHRISTIAN MISSIONARIES and their colonial proteges are being slaughtered daily?[62] For, after all, Dr. Lothrop Stoddard was only expressing the prevailing sentiments held by most Europeans and European-Americans of every religious and secular persuasian about all non-White peoples the world over. In this specific case it is the Africans. To support this position another European (CAUCASIAN, WHITE) named Henri Junod, in his book entitled, BA RANGA, page 482 (as quoted by Raymond Michelet) wrote similarly:

> I speak of resignation. It is necessary to the Blacks, for despite all that has been written on the fundamental axiom of the absolute equality of mankind, they are an inferior race, a race made to serve.

Is it not strange that Junod is still rated within intellectual circles, "AN OBJECTIVE PROTESTANT ETHNOGRAPHER"? What kind of OBJECTIVITY does he reveal in the following statement?

"...THEY ARE AN INFERIOR RACE, A RACE MADE TO SERVE."
Even if one is to assume that the entire concept and theory of
this racist mythology is correct, what criteria has been established that will make one RACE INFERIOR and another RACE SUPERIOR.
Maybe JESUS CHRIST, or one of his PROPHETS, came to the Junods of
the Christian missionaries in a midnight's dream and revealed
<u>heaven's master plan</u> for all races, since this is the way (by
(MASTERFUL DREAMS) most of religion's racist edicts came down
from heaven. The angel-in-charge of dreams must have told Junod
that Africans, which he too prefers to call "NEGROES", were
designed, not created, by his Caucasianized White God - JESUS
CHRIST - "TO SERVE" all White people. But, these type of racist
expressions by the Junods, Jeffreys, and others like them, have
been the basis upon which so-called "NEGRO HISTORY" was written
in the past. It was, and still is, taught in the same manner in
the educational institutions throughout the United States of
America and Europe. This is the major reason why AFRICAN STUDIES,
misnomered "BLACK STUDIES", is today the challenge to most European-American <u>educators</u> of every religious persuasion. For
most of what they have been teaching as "TRUTHS" with regards to
the history and peoples of the world who are non-White, particularly people of African birth and/or origin, must now be discarded.

Once again it becomes necessary to reflect a bit, and of

course return to the origin of Christianity to see upon what basis the early White (European, Caucasian) Christian missionaries of Europe got the idea that a God named "JESUS CHRIST", or JEHOVAH, ordained them to convert African people. In so doing it is also necessary to read a quotation from a Roman Catholic Monk by the name of Salvianus (also Salvian), who was a noted Christian writer of Europe. At the time of his writings he too was living off the spoils of the African peoples and continent, just as most of his leaders were doing then, and as others are still doing now. This man who has been quoted as much as most of the so-called "AUTHORITIES" on this subject, wrote the following:

> Where are there more abundant treasures than with the Africans? Where can we (European Christian missionaries) find more prosperous commerce - shops better stocked? The Prophet Ezekiel said of Tyre "Thou has filled thy treasury with gold and silver by the extent of thy commerce," but I say of Africa that her commerce enrich her so much that not only were her treasuries filled, but she seemed able to fill those of the whole universe... Carthage, formerly the rival of Rome as regards power and warlike quality, was she not afterward her rival in splendor? And in imposing majesty? Carthage, the Rome of Africa, held in her bosom all the treasuries of the State; here was the seat of government and all the instituters of the State; here were the schools for the liberal arts, audiences for philosophers, chairs for professors of all languages and for every branch of law.

After reading the above account of the Africans and their State, Carthage, is there any reason why one cannot understand the European and European-American educators' refusal to accept that North African High-Cultures were developed by the same type of Africans that were placed in chains by the colonizers and slave owners, most of whom were ministers and other high dignataries in the European and European-American versions of Christianity? This is as great a summary of the achievements of a people who are only fit "...TO SERVE..." that mankind have ever seen. One has to wonder if Henri Junod ever read this account by his fellow European (White) Christian missionary writer? If he did, and one must assume that this is true, being that he was supposed to be the type of scholar he was rated to be; then, the mystery surely sharpens as to why this man could have written what he did about the people who once taught all of ancient Europe what they knew about the God they now feel is their exclusive property.

Of course, anyone familiar with the history of the RAPE OF AFRICA AND HER PEOPLES knows that European colonialists (many of whom were called "CHRISTIAN MISSIONARIES) involved in the partition of Africa from 1830 to the present 1970's C.E. dared to suggest that the HOLY OF THE HOLIES of the ancient Monomotapa Empire's seat of government, ZIMBABWE,* must have been built by Greeks, Romans or shipwrecked European mariners. But none of the "AUTHORITIES" who brought forth this nonsensical hypothesis suggested, or in any way pointed to, one bit of evidence to sub-

---

*The area of Africa that was originally called "ZIMBABWE" by the indigenous Africans was renamed "RHODESIA" by British colonialists and slave traders in honor of the murderer Cecil Rhodes.

stantiate any of the declarations. This type of statement, never the less, reeks with the same type of baseless conclusions that is apparent in all of the other statements made by the so-called "HISTORIANS" and other "EDUCATORS" on Africa and African peoples so far examined in this volume and chapter. All that the Europeans and European-Americans could vision was that...

IT COULD NOT BE THE WORK OF THE HEATHEN NATIVES.
Of course the "NATIVES" is just another name for the so-called "BANTUS" and/or "NEGROES", "AFRICANS SOUTH OF THE SAHARA", and a host of other such Africans that were manufactured by the colonialists, slaveholders, sellers and buyers of the African peoples, including their economic exploiter who hid behind the title of CHRISTIAN CLERGY, HEBREW CLERGY, MOSLEM CLERGY, ENTREPRENUERS, etc. But truth was yet to be served, as Dr. Gertrude Caton-Thompson (an accomplished English cultural anthropologist) subsequently laid the ridiculous disclaimer to rest in her timely book, THE ZIMBABWE CULTURE.[63] Dr. Caton-Thompson was very shortly after followed by numerous other anthropologists, historians and educators of varied disciplines, all of whom went to the area of the HOLY OF HOLIES of the Zimbwe and Rozwis people who are the descendants of those who originally created and developed the High-Culture (civilization) that produced it. This was after the majority of them had renamed Zimbabwe's Holy of Holies the "AFRICAN METROPOLIS". It is obvious that the African name was not good enough for the

CIVILIZED WHITES, most of whom are bent on the position that everything must have a Greek-centered Anglo-Saxon Judaeo-Christian origin or it is of no major value in human existence. Of course THE ONLY TRULY CIVILIZED PEOPLE IN THE WORLD ARE EUROPEANS AND EUROPEAN-AMERICANS; at least this is the impression one can see in all of these allegedly "AUTHORITATIVE" works being examined with regard to the African's identity. This being the prevailing thought of White America and Europe, the institutions of learning had to be geared to keep up this myth. The churches, synagogues, temples, mosques and every other means of cultural development of European-America had African-Americans being no less subjected to the same brain-washing process in the same institutions or in others et up for them by the same people who own and control the White ones.

One can easily see the same parallel in the following extract from Stanley Lane-Poole's book, THE MOORS IN SPAIN, as he wrote:

> The misguided Spaniards knew not what they were doing... The 'infidels'[64] were ordered to abandon their native and picturesque costumes, to assume the hats and breeches of the Christians, to give up bathing and adopt the dirt of the conquerors, to renounce their language, their customs and ceremonies, even their names.

Again one must wonder how could the Africans be considered "UNCIVILIZED" even today in the 20th Century, C.E., when it is known by each and every historian from the MIDDLE-AGES (and also from ancient times) that they even introduced the "COMMON BATH" to the Europeans of the Iberian Peninsula - Spain, Southern France and Portugal.[65] Stanley Lane-Poole's explanation of how these Europeans also demanded that the Africans (Moors) "...GIVE UP BATHING..." was of major significance to those who have always considered the africans "LESS CIVILIZED" than they are. He continued:

> It is stated that no less than three million of Moors* were banished between the fall of Granada and the first decade of the seventeenth century... But the Spaniards did not understand that they had killed their golden geese. For centuries Spain had been the centre of civilisation, the seat of arts and sciences, of learning and every form of refined enlightenment. No country in Europe had so far approached the cultivated dominion of the Moors.

It is very necessary to break into the declarations of this writer in order to maintain a very important trend of thought at this juncture. For here it is the Africans again who are the "CIVILIZATION BEARERS" of Europe, in this case among the Iberian peoples who carried it into the outer reaches of Northern and Eastern Europe; while in more ancient times it was the Ethiopians and Egyptians, including the Nubians and other peoples of the Nile Valleys and Great Lakes, who carried it into Southern Europe until it spread into what was later called "GREEK PHILOSOPHY". It was not only Spain that "KILLED THEIR GOLDEN GEESE", the entire peoples that took part in the de-africanization of the African HIGH-CULTURE introduced to Europe from the 8th Century when the Africans under the leadership of General Tarikh invaded and

---
*The MOORS were Africans who originally came from the area now called MAURITANIA, the colonialists also called it "MAURITUS".

conquered Iberia in 711 C.E., "KILLED THEIR GOLDEN GEESE".

Stanley Lane-Poole's historical revelations continued:

> The Moors were banished, and for a while Christian Spain shone like the moon, with a borrowed light; when came the eclipse, and in the darkness Spain has grovelled ever since. The true memorial of the Moors is seen in the desolate tracts of utter barrenness, where once the Moslem* grew luxuriant vines, olives and yellow ears of corn; in a stupid ignorant population where once art and learning flourished, in the general stagnation and degradation of a people which has hopelessly fallen in the scale of nations and has deserved its humiliation.

The amazing phoenomena about the African-Moors in Spain is, that, they extended their rule for two-hundred (200) years - from 1285 to 1485 C.E. - in Granada; when in all other parts of Spain the Arab-Moors had already been driven out by the Christian Spaniards in 1285 C.E. The African-Moors, the first to enter Spain - in 711 C.E. - were in fact the last to leave, in 1485 C.E., which was only seven (7) short years before an African-Moor named PIETRO OLONZO NINO became Captain of the Flagship SANTA MARIA, which was the lead ship of the expedition that Cristobal Colon** commanded as admirante (admiral).

There are certain basic facts which one must remember about this period of history when the Africans ruled the Iberian Peninsula. Spain was captured by the African, General Tarikh,

---

*The only thing Arabic about the Moors was that they too were Moslems, having adopted the faith of Islam after the Arab invasion of North Africa in the year 640 C.E. or 18 A.H.
**This was the original name of the man called "CHRISTOPHER COLOMBUS" in the history books of the United States of America. The African who sailed the ship on which Colon served as "ADMIRAL" and "EXPLORER" was born in what is today called "MOROCCO".

quite a few years before the arrival of the Arab-Moors in Spain.[66] And history is quite definite in its description that Tarikh was a "BLACK MAN" just as any other Black Man one is subject to see on the streets of the United States of America who is being called "NEGRO" and other such names not of his making or selection.[67] General Tarikh was the first of the Moors to capture the very first part of the Iberian Peninsula. He accomplished this feat in the year 711 C.E.[68] He had also fought against the Arab-Moslems from Arabia in c680 C.E., this before his own capture by them and his subsequent conversion to Islam to save his own life and to maintain his status as a general.

With the African-Moors and Arab-Moors in Spain the inter-Christian-Moslem marriages and conversions of Christians to the Moslem faith (Islam) became widespread, just as it was to be expected when any conqueror enters any conquered people's homeland. In simple words, the Africans and Asians INTER-BRED and AMALGAMATED with the European population they met on the Iberian Peninsula, just as former indigenous Africans had done with the Romans during the First (1st) and Second (2nd) PUNIC WARS, or with the Anglo-Saxons (particularly the English, Irish, Scots, Welch, and Gauls) during the reign of the African Emperor of the Roman Empire - Septimus Severus;[69] equally as the Europeans did with enslaved Africans and the so-called "AMERICAN" and "WEST INDIAN

NEGROES".*

There has been a jump of almost 700 to 1000 years ahead of the basic point of this Chapter, due, only to the necessity of the pertinent references which were cardinal to this area of the African's identification in world history, in particular, their involvement with the early southern peoples of the European side of the Mediterranean Sea. If these conclusions, which one has been able to observe, had been challenged by Africans and African descendants throughout the world, most of the ill-conceived racist NEGROPHOBIA which men of letters and high rating within the present structure of academia have perpetuated through the cover of academic pronouncements could have been stopped, or at least deterred. And, the peoples of the entire world would have been that less confused as to the heritage and history of the glorious peoples of Africa, which would have certainly removed the possibility of said peoples having to be judged SOLELY UPON THE BASIS OF THEIR BLACK COLOR, "RACE", RELIGION AND/OR GEOGRAPHIC LOCATION OF BIRTH, and for whatever other reasons man and woman superficially discriminate against his or her brother and sister human beings.

Professor James H. Breasted in his book, ANCIENT RECORDS OF

---

*It should be noted that the Africans brought to the Caribbeans (from 1503) and the Americas (1619 or 1620 in the case of the United States of America) - while still a British colony - did not change to "NEGROES" because historians and other European and European-American educators warranted it to be so.

EGYPT, Volume I, page 358, wrote the following:

> This nobleman of Aswan in the Middle Nile was sent by Pepi II - late third millenium B.C. - on two imperial expeditions southward into Nubian lands of Wawat and Irthet, thus preparing the way for later conquests. His inscriptions survive.

Professor Breasted was dealing with the building of the early Egyptian Empire, indicating that the contact that existed between the indigenous Egyptians and Nubians, both of them of what is today called "NEGROID STOCK". They were not "NEGROES" or "NEGROID" peoples.[70] Such names, which the European and European-American writers and historians continue to call indigenous African peoples, were never used in ancient times, the ancient being ignorant of these terms and the emotions that engendered them. Yet, they to continue using such names as the least resistance to criticism from those in power that control the economic livelihood of Black peoples with the white academic community not excluded.

In Volume II, on pages 486 and 487, of the above work, Professor Breasted also noted:

> From very early times the Egyptians also traded with Punt, which may be placed at the southern extremity of the Red Sea and at the north coast of Modern Somalia. One great expedition ordered by Queen Hatshepsut (1490-1468 B.C., by Gardiner's conjectural dating) is marvelously recorded in the queen's temple at Deir-el-Bahri.[71] Here, together with many inscriptions, are depicted scenes of Punt, a "potrait" of the chief Punt and another of his wife, who resides upon a donkey: the earliest pictorial records of Africa "South of the Sahara", together with an explicit list of "the loading of the ships very heavily

with marvels of the country of Punt."⁷²* Hatshepsut's coeval, Authmosis III (1490-1436 by conjectural dating), continued the trade.

The errors, or willful distortions, of Africa's history were not only written by European and European-American historians and other educators of various disciplines during, but since, the African slave trade. Herodotus, the first of the European historians,** also engaged in injecting his own European values into African history while describing what he believed to be "ETHIOPIAN (Kushite) CUSTOMS OF WORSHIP". Thus he wrote, according to the English translation by Aubrey deSelincourt's, HERODOTUS: THE HISTORIES:

> After crossing the lake one comes again to the stream of the Nile, which flows into it.*** At this point one must land and travel along the bank of the river for forty days, because sharp rocks, some showing above the water and many just avast, make the river impracticable for boats. After the forty day journey on land one takes another boat and in twelve days reaches a big city named Meroe, said to be the capital of the Ethiopians. The inhabitants worship Zeus and Dionysus alone of the Gods, holding them in great honor. There is an Oracle of Zeus there, and they make war according to its pronouncements, taking from it both the occasion and the object of their various expeditions.

First, it must be noted that Herodotus touched on one of the

---
*See page 160 of Chapter, "A PICTORIAL REVIEW OF ANCIENT EGYPT." "IN BLACK MAN OF THE NILE", by Yosef ben-Jochannan, 1970.
**Most European and European-American educators give the impression that "HERODOTUS WAS THE FATHER OF HISTORY". This would be correct if they were only referring to European history. He went to Africa to learn the fundamentals of history, as will be seen in Chapter IX, AFRICAN ORIGINS OF "GREEK PHILOSOPHY".
***Herodotus knew very little about the Nile. See his map on page of this volume, which he drew in the year 450 B.C.E.

major reasons why Alexander II ("<u>the great</u>") invaded Kimit in the year 332 B.C.E. to speak and consult with the famous Oracle that was living in Amon. Second, the argument about the ancient nation of Kush (Cush) not being within the limits of modern Ethiopia was proven to be incorrect according to his findings, in which he noted that:

> "...A BIG CITY NAMED MEROE, SAID TO BE THE CAPITAL CITY OF THE ETHIOPIANS..."

It should be remembered that Herodotus spent enough time travelling along the Nile Valleys to know the people with whom he lived that he could have described them with pin-pointed accuracy, which he did in the following manner:

> "THE COLCHIANS, EGYPTIANS AND ETHIOPIANS HAVE THICK LIPS, BROAD NOSE, WOLLEY HAIR, AND THEY ARE BURNT OF SKIN."

Referring back to the description of Herodotus' journey along the Nile, it is very much apparent that he attempted to speak as an "AUTHORITY", as do so many modern educators, on the religion of Ethiopia, even though he admitted that he had not seen the inside of an Ethiopian temple or studied their religion. He made the same error as Professor Jeffreys' "MODERN MAN" with respect to Africa and Africans. But, Herodotus went on further to suggest that:

> "...the Ethiopians worship the Gods of the Greeks, Zeus and Dionysus."

In another sentence the following is written:

> "...could not enter Ethiopie, the Nile was not

navigable."

Who "could not enter Ethiopie" (Ethiopia, Kush or Cush)? Herodotus. Why? Because of the natural barriers formed by the various Cataracts he had encountered. Obviously, he had reached the First (1st) Cataract, which would have placed him within the boundary of UPPER EGYPT or modern Sudan before the Berlin Conference of 1884-1885 C.E. removed the boundary back in a southward position.

When Herodotus referred to:

"...THE STREAMS OF THE NILE, WHICH FLOWS INTO IT," he was obviously directing one's attention to the ATBARA RIVER with its beginning in the Highlands of Ethiopia and connects with the Blue and White Nile at ATBARA in the Sudan, just a little south of the First (1st) Cataract.

In other words, it could be safely said that Herodotus made his conclusion on the Ethiopians worship solely on hearsay evidence. Yet, thousands of European and European-American ("Western") historians and other writers wrote millions of volumes echoing Herodotus' description of the Ethiopians' religion as "TRUTH", ignoring Ethiopia's historians that protested the inaccuracies of such reporting. This continued until the late twentieth century C.E. before the "Westerners" finally accepted the fact that Ethiopians did not in fact worshiped ZEUS or DIONYSUS in Ethiopia (Kush or Cush).

There is another major aspect to the NEGROPHOBIA among present

day historians who project WHITE SUPREMACY as history; many of
whom will, and have, destroyed the image of any African (Black
Man) whenever they have failed to established in other's mind
the African's non-existence in ancient north and south Africa.
Their theory is:

> IF YOU CANNOT CONVINCE PEOPLE THAT THE AFRICANS DID
> NOT EXIST AT ALL IN A PARTICULAR SOCIETY IN AFRICA,
> THEN SAY THAT HE HAD A WHITE MOTHER OR FATHER, etc.

And if this still does not do the required trick and accomplish
the desired goal, they always have the countermeasure that the
African:

> RULED AS A DESPOT; HE MURDERED UNSCRUPULOUSLY;
> HE DID NOT TREAT HIS OWN PEOPLE AS HE SHOULD.

This type of behaviour presented itself as far back as the
charges made against the African Emperor of Rome, Septimus
Severus, who allegedly:

> STARTED THE PERSECUTION OF THE CHRISTIANS AND
> THEIR INSTITUTIONS DURING THE YEAR 193 A.D.[73]

The same CHURCH and INSTITUTIONS which Septimus Severus is charged with persecuting were also charged to his son who succeeded him at his death.[74] For it was Caracalla who was actually Emperor of the Roman Empire at the beginning of the prosecutions of those who were disrupting Roman "LAW AND ORDER", which included Hebrews (today called "Jews") and other Roman citizens of a multitude of other religious beliefs, but of which the orthodox Christians were the greatest in numbers.

   The above type of propaganda against the greatest of the

African Emperors of the Roman Empire is a feeble attempt by Christendom's self-appointed protectors of the world for JESUS CHRIST to bismirch his character. This, however, is if one can assume that the conduct of Emperor Caracalla was wrong in persecuting the Christians and others who were disrupting LAW AND ORDER and PEACE AND TRANQUILITY in the Roman Empire. If this is the position to be taken, then one must also note that the same type of pressures placed upon those who disrupt LAW AND ORDER and PEACE AND TRANQUILITY in the 1970's all over the United States of America must be rated in the same manner as the persecuted Christians of the days of the Emperor Caracalla in Rome - that is providing the standards of JESUS CHRIST and JEHOVAH do not change from country to country, or from race to race. But, it is also obvious that Emperor Septimus Severus has been tried in the White history books of most "Western" writers other than for his actions as the Emperor of the Roman Empire or State. He is still being tried because of his Africaness - BLACKNESS.[75] Of course this rationale does not hold true for Christian historians who were his contemporaries. For it is only for the last two centuries that the protaganists of the CAUCASIAN NORTH AFRICA AT ALL COSTS started to imply, and did state, that Emperor Septimus Severus was...

"A DESPOTIC EMPEROR ...," "etc.,

by virtue of the fact that he was an African - a BLACK MAN; or as many would prefer to state it: A MEMBER OF THE NEGRO RACE.

However, if the first part of the BIG LIE technique is deflated, and this have been proven a fact, the other parts remain discredited also, and further comments need not be made in the emperor's behalf. It must be also remembered that the Church of Rome, in its own historical pronouncements and writings, stated that:

> "ON JULY 19, A.D. 180, FELICITAS AND PERPETUA WERE MARTYRED BY THE SOLDIERS OF EMPEROR SEPTIMUS SEVERUS."[76]

Of course it is assumed by many "<u>Western</u>" historians who project their NEGROPHOBIA constantly, that their readers will never remember the date when the African Emperor of the Roman Empire, Septimus Severus,[77] mounted the throne in Rome; which did not occur until thirteen (13) long years after the alleged martyrdom of NAMPHAMO, FELICITAS, and PERPETUA, all three of whom were allegedly:

> "THE FIRST CHRISTIAN MARTYRS."

Stranger yet, they were all indigenous Africans as the Emperor himself; all four being of Carthaginian birth. All of them would have had to register in the 1970's <u>Federal Census</u> of the United States of America as "NEGROES", or at least AFRICAN-AMERICANS. Even the term "Mulatto" would not have fitted them.

One will inquire why so much time is being spent on the role of the CHURCH OF ROME with respect to the history of the African (Black Man)? The answer is strictly fundamental. Thus: The ROMAN CATHOLIC CHURCH, with its seat of government in Rome, Italy, through its "CHRISTIAN MISSIONARIES" (European-style), along with the colonialist governments of Spain and Portugal and others throughout Europe, were equal partners, and equally shared in the destruction of many of the African High-Cultures (civilizations) and the distortion of their history. This was not only true of North Africa, but of West and Central Africa. Protestantism is not exempted; the only difference being that the PROTESTANTS entered the prosecution and persecution of the African peoples and their institutions after the ROMAN CATHOLICS and ARAB MOSLEMS had already begun.[78] And of course in this role all of them equally assumed and reaped enormous economic benifits during the earlier periods in North Africa (as detailed by Sylvianus the Munk) and up to the present day throughout most of Africa, particularly where Spain, France, Portugal, Belgium and Italy dominate or their insphere of influence still control.[78a]

Completing the rationale on the greatest African Emperor of the entire Roman Empire, including England (Angloland) and all of the Islands associated thereto, once again it is necessary to quote from another author and "authority" on this phase of African history and identity of the African peoples, Jane Soames, from her book, THE COAST OF THE BARBARY, page 47:

> Just as Gibbon started from the presumption which was in reality a prejudice and based all his work upon it, so today we will tend to emphasize those elements contributing to the death of Rome which march with our own preoccupations and appear to bear out the contemporary economic, social, religious, and <u>racial theories which happen to appeal to us</u>. There is,

> however, general agreement upon the fact that Rome
> was not murdered, but died of a mortal disease the
> symptoms of which were apparent long before the
> final crisis set in, and the African Emperor
> Septimus Severus was probably not far wrong in the
> palliative he adopted to stave off the evil day.
> His preoccupation with efficiency of the army,
> quite apart from personal considerations, arose
> from instinctive knowledge that without it all
> was lost.

Current WHITE SUPREMISIST, many of whom call themselves "CHRISTIAN THEOLOGIANS", do not sum-up the beginning of the fall of the Roman Empire under this African Emperor of Rome with the same type of rationale employed in the above extract by Jane Soames. They insist that it was some sort of:

> "...MYSTERIOUS FORCE FROM JESUS CHRIST THAT CRUSHED
> THE ROMAN EMPIRE AND ITS DEVILISH AFRICAN EMPEROR."[79]

How many times has this last citation of religious jargon been preached in the pulpits of so many "CHRISTIAN CHURCHES"? How many times were people of African origin not the main audience listening and digesting this racist line of character assassination of one of their fellow Africans, all in the name of their being in the service of the LORD JESUS CHRIST, which blinded them to the point where anyone can say and do anything against one of them without any response against the perpetrator? Yet, it goes on and on as:

> "...THE WORDS OF THE LORD GOD - JESUS CHRIST - AND
> HIS MINISTRY," etc., etc., etc., Amen.

Of course, since God, himself, is supposed to have...

PLACED IT INTO THE MINDS OF HIS EARTHLY REPRESENTA-

TIVES* THROUGH INSPIRATIONS AND DREAMS..., the representatives remain infallable, and their pronouncements unquestionable. They have been placed above and beyond the limits of interrogation by the mere evidence of their profession, which they prefer to label their "CALLING". But to the inquiring mind this type of malicious characterization of any African or group of Africans cannot be allowed to stand unchallenged in this - the latter half of the twentieth century C.E. For no longer can the TRUE HISTORY OF AFRICA AND THE AFRICAN PEOPLES remain distorted just to save the sanctity of certain past,and present, "CHURCH FATHERS" and their underlings from exposure which has been necessary for too long.

The traditional misinformation in the Christian Church History, Roman Catholic and Protestant alike, espouses all sorts of propaganda - of which too many so-called "NEGROES" - repeat like parrots without question. These "NEGROES" pay millions of dollars daily and many more millions on Sundays to hear certain members of the clergy, also known as "MEN OF THE CLOTH", tell them how much less than human the Africans and the Africans' descendants (themselves) are, but the greatness of the Europeans and their descendants (Whites) of the United States of America and Europe who journey to Africa is extolled under the label of "CHRISTIAN MISSIONARIES".[80] But, the real irony of this tragedy

---

*Priests, rabbis, ministers, imans, and others entitle "MEMBERS OF THE CLERGY."

comes when a "NEGRO MINISTER" stands before an all-"NEGRO" congregation and tells them:

> "YOUR HEARTS HAVE GOT TO BE WHITE AS SNOW BEFORE
> YOU CAN ENTER THE GATES OF THE KINGDOM OF HEAVEN."

One's imagination must stretch very far indeed to see such a fete;

A BLACK MAN WITH A WHITE HEART.

Maybe this too is possible under current CHRISTIAN MISSIONARY teachings; since one is to understand that such teachers received those words:

"DIRECTLY FROM HOLY MEN INSPIRED BY JESUS CHRIST,"

some words were received by the entrance of:

ANGELS SENT DOWN FROM HEAVEN WITH MASTERFUL DREAMS,

which are in turn passed on to the congregations who are not so endowed with the power of receiving DREAMS. At least, this is the impression given by these men who enter into areas of which they know very little or absolutely nothing about, but of which they pretend and act as authority; this they have been guilty of by spreading false rumors about Africa and her sons and daughters. Most of them are aware of the various VERSIONS of every BIBLE, but know practically nothing about the development of the history and culture of the people to whom that book alludes; nor are they aware of the history of the institutions that manufacture said book and other works that stem from it;[81] all of which is designed to maintain the image of WHITE SUPREMACY and a CAUCASIAN NORTH AND EAST AFRICA, since most of the biblical characters in the foundation of JUDAEO-CHRISTIANITY were for the most part NATIVES (indigenous Africans), otherwise today called NEGROES, etc., OF NORTH AND EAST AFRICA.

One is to expect that these revelations will cause certain violent reactions by many who may assume that their religion is being attacked, because their church leaders have kept them in ignorance of church history, bearing in mind that not too often the ministers themselves are not aware of the works holding such information. For very good reasons this is so arranged by those whose livelihood depends upon an ignorant clergy and an equally ignorant congregation. Why is this TRUTH so basic? Because most "MEMBERS OF THE CLERGY" - Christian, Hebrew (otherwise called "Judaism"), Moslem - have been involved in the colonization of the African peoples and/or have inherited the proceeds of such through the role their respective religion played in the slave trade from Africa to the Caribbean Islands, to the Americas, and to Europe. Neither can they explain why there are no pictures of...

> BLACK, BROWN, YELLOW, or RED ANGELS FLYING AROUND HEAVEN WITH JESUS...

as the WHITE BLONDS one sees every day; the same for the...

> DISCIPLES SITTING AT THE TABLE WITH JESUS DURING THE PASSOVER FEAST...

which the Christians called "THE LAST SUPPER". This too applies equally to the BLONDE JESUS CHRIST at the table with his BLONDE DISCIPLES with nothing but BLONDE ANGELS flying around them in a

BLACK or BROWN Palestine (also called Israel in error); when in fact anyone familiar with world history must know that the area in which all of this supposedly took place is the land of people who were in no respect akin to that which is today called "CAUCASIANS", LIGHT-SKINNED or DARK-SKINNED. It is for this very reason that Herodotus' description of the peoples of this general area must be hidden or otherwise distorted. He wrote:

> THE COLCHIANS, EGYPTIANS AND ETHIOPIANS HAVE THICK LIPS, BROAD NOSES, WOOLY HAIR, AND THEY ARE BURNT OF SKIN.

The above description was typical of the people who once occupied the area in which the "LAST SUPPER" was supposed to have taken place, regardless of what Michaelangelo was commissioned to paint for the HOLY SEE of ROME. At least if the picture was showing the people involved as being somewhat TAN from the hot scorching Palestinian SUN and DESERT there could have been some ground for its acceptance with a little stretch of the imagination. But today, as late as the latter half of the twentieth century of the so-called "CHRISTIAN ERA", AFRICANS (Blacks) and other peoples who are not labeled "CAUCASIANS", and whose heritage and homeland are as much more in Palestine (or Israel) than European Caucasians (Whites) are questioning:

> WHY HAVE WE BEEN BOTH PHYSICALLY AND MENTALLY EXCLUDED FROM THIS, OUR HERITAGE, BY YOU* FOR

---

*YOU, in this case, refers to all of the so-called "AUTHORITIES" who have for whatever reason distorted the pages of WORLD HISTORY in order to perpetuate the BIG LIE and MYTH of a world that centers around a PURE and GREAT WHITE RACE that is otherwise called "CAUCASIAN"; with all of man's knowledge going back only to the GREEKS whose history dates only to 3000 B.C.E.

SO MANY HUNDREDS OF YEARS OF OUR ENSLAVEMENT?

What will the answer be? Who will give the TRUE answer? Who is ready to revise the textbooks on WORLD HISTORY as taught in the United States of America and Europe...

TO TELL THE TRUTH AND NOTHING BUT THE TRUTH?[82]

CHAPTER III

HISTORIC QUOTATIONS AND COMMENTS ABOUT AND OF THE AFRICANS

This topic is of major importance in the sense that one can observe that in ancient times and the not too distant past the peoples of the entire world revered the indigenous Africans who are despised by the children of those who once worshipped them. These quotations are from LIGHT-SKINNED CAUCASIANS as well as the DARK-SKINNED ones; and of course from BLACK-SKINNED AFRICANS and others who are of African origin - people who are now called "NEGROES, BANTUS", and other such names of inferiority which the colonialist Europeans and European-Americans placed upon the African peoples during their enslavement.

The first quotation comes from the distinguished French "authority", a Black man named Felix DuBois. He wrote:

> This accomplishment brings the greatest honor to the black race and merits, from this view point, all our attention. In the 16th Century, the Songhay land awoke. A marvelous growth of civilisation mounted there in the heart of the Black continent... And this civilisation was not imposed by circumstances, nor by an invader, as is often the case even in our own day. It was desired, called forth, introduced and perpetuated by a man of the Black race.

The above is taken from Felix DuBois' work in which he described West African societies and cultures, TIMBUCTOO THE MYSTERIOUS.[1]

> When Arab merchants came to the Sudan, about 1000 A.D., they already found a well-arranged system of commerce. When the Arabs first visited <u>Negroland</u> by the Western route in the 8th and 9th centuries of our era, they found the black kings of Ghana in the height of their prosperity.

The above comment was written by the wife (Lady Flora Shaw Lugard) of the British colonialist and master of genocide in Africa - Captain (Lord) Lugard. It is noted that the good Lady used the term "NEGROLAND",[2] which has been underscored by the author of this volume for comment. Why? Because "NEGROLAND" was the continuation of the insult to the peoples of West Africa spoken of so proudly by Felix DuBois in the previous extract from his book of world renown. NEGROLAND was a creation of the imaginative and mythological fiction of the colonialist European's mind of Lady Lugard's era. It was incorporated on the maps made by Europeans, such as her husband. (It started with the Portugese.) Lugard, as Cecil Rhodes and King Leopold II of Belgian,* was responsible for the brutal murder of millions upon millions of Africans in South and West Africa. These men, and others like them, committed a type of genocide in Africa that was not equalled even by Adolph Hitler and his Nazis at the height of the massacre of the Jews of Europe or Benito Mussolini's rape and murder of Ethiopia and the Ethiopians of East Africa. It is conservatively estimated that between them they killed more than 100 million indigenous Africans in their quest for the natural resources and free labor of Africa and the African people. (See map on page 701 at the rear of this volume for the area of West African demarcated "NEGROLAND" by the Portugese and all of the other European

---
*Note that scores of European-American colonialists under the name of "ENTREPRENEURS" joined Leopold in what they choose to call "THE CONGO FREE STATE".

imperialists and colonialists who also joined-in with the PARTITION OF AFRICA at the Berlin and Brussels conferences of 1884 to 1896 C.E.)

> The virile peoples of the Western Sudan have always been distinguished for commercial enterprise, masterful ardour, and aptitude for the art of government. From the happy combination of these qualities there sprang a number of political States to which the <u>grandoise style of empire is often loosely assigned</u>. None, however, can challenge the fairness of its application to the great Mandingo Kingdom which is known as the empire of Mali or Mande, and is sometimes called the Mellestine.

The above extract came from E.W. Bovill, CARAVANS OF OLD SAHARA, page 67. It is to be noted that "MALI" or "MANDE" was not the correct name of this empire, it was MELLE, and the Africans who built it were of the MENDE people and culture. "MANDINGO" is of strictly European colonial origin. The words underscored by the author of this volume are for the purpose of pointing out that even when Europeans and European-Americans, on the whole, try to speak in praises of the African peoples, certain disparaging remarks generally have to be thrown in for good measure. Is Bovill insinuating that all of the nations of Europe which were also called "EMPIRES" were in fact that? Or that tiny little tribal units such as Latvia, Estonia, Lithuania and other such political entities of Europe were in fact not TRIBAL STATES such as those in Africa today?

> For mine owne part, when I heare the Africans evil spoken of, I will affune myselfe to be one of Granada: and when I perceive the nation of Granada to be discommended, then I professe myselfe, to be

170

an African.³*

The above extract is taken from one of the many great works by the noted African historian and traveller Leo Africanus (Leo the African) entitled, THE HISTORY AND DISCRIPTION OF AFRICA, as translated by John Pory and edited by Dr. R. Brown, Hakluyt Society, London, England.³ᵃ One notices that this African spoke of his culture without excuse for same. Also of the fact that he was proud to be an African, and wanted no man to speak of "...THE AFRICANS EVIL..." This he felt, even though at the time of his writing the Africans called MOORS were still the center of the culture and figures of greatness in the Iberian Peninsula.

> Forced to defend themselves against slaving raids and eager to break the coastal monopoly on the import of European goods, notably firearms, <u>the Fons of Dahomey broke through in the sea in 1724</u>. They became a power with whom the Europeans had to reckon and so soon learned to respect.

The short excerpt shown above was written by Archibald Dazell in his book, HISTORY OF DAHOMEY, London, 1793, and appears on page 60. What Dazell failed, in his work, to point out was that the Fons break-through to the West Coast of Africa was at the same period when the entire West African sea coast was dominated by European <u>slavers</u> and <u>colonialists</u>. The Fons were forced into the slave trading enterprise like all of the other Africans after them. This was the first time in the history of slavery that the

---

*The Old English is not in fact the manner in which Africans spoke, but in fact the manner in which the English could convey the African's message to their own people of England.

Africans actually became involved in selling each other to the Europeans and European-Americans; they had to succumb to the superiority of gunpowder over spears, bows, and arrows. This major episode in the entire sordid history of the enslavement of the African people is always corrupted to remove the Arab and European slave traders' guilt for the demography and rape of Africa and her sons and daughters. It is important that each reader spend some time on this period and people of West Africa; these being the ones responsible for the women army of AMAZONS - the Fons of DAN and HOMY,* which the French corrupted into "DAHOMEY". Recommended for easy reading in this area are the works of B. Davidson, specifically his THE AFRICAN PAST, pages 233 and 234, New York, 1964. This is not an endorsement of Davidson's work, it is a recommendation because in the general assemblage of works by Europeans and European-Americans on this area his is the least offensive to the Africans. It must be noted that Dazell was also governor of the English trading station and castle at Cape Coast. He also spent four (4) years at Quidah, where he became personally involved with the then rising nation of Dan and Homy - Danhomey or Dahomey (Home or Land of the Fons).

> In Kilwa there are many strong houses several
> stories high. They are built of stone and mortar
> and plastered with various designs. As soon as

---

*Dan and Homy were African kings who fought over the land Dan won at the death of Homy who he had killed. This was the typical manner in which European monarchs also settled disputes.

> the town had been taken without opposition, the
> Vicar-General and some of the Franciscan fathers
> came ashore carrying two crosses in procession
> and singing the TE DEUM. They went to the palace,
> and there the cross was put down and the Grand-
> Captain prayed. Then everyone started to plunder
> the town of all its merchandise and provisions.
> Two days later d'Almeida fired the town, destroy-
> ing, as the account in deBarros explains, "the
> greater part of this city abomination."

The above extract taken from Basil Davidson's work, THE AFRICAN PAST, p. 136, which is the best English translation available to date. It also highlights the reason why so much attention was given to the role of the European Christian missionaries who were fellow colonialists and imperialist adventurers in the exploitation of the Africans and their continent. Here one clearly sees the role of the clergy as they became involved with the destruction of another peaceful non-violent community of Africans who made no defense as their "...TOWN HAD BEEN TAKEN WITHOUT OPPOSITION". Their (the Africans) palace was looted as the Franciscan fathers planted their crosses. All of this having taken place at Kilwa, East Africa, by "CIVILIZED EUROPEANS" against "UNCIVILIZED AFRICANS" in their own homeland, and for their own good. In turn they were given European-style Christian bibles and a chance to be slaves.

> There is another habitation of Moores two
> Caliver shots from the Castle, poore and misserable,
> which live by serving the Portugals. The women
> performe there the offices of Tillage and Husbandry;
> as also doe the Moores. They pay tithes to the
> Dominicans Church. The fortress was built in 1505
> by Pero da Nhaya, with consent of the Moorish King
> Zufe, a man blinde of both his eyes (in both senses,

> external, religious and politike) who too late
> repenting, thought to supplant it with trecherie,
> which they returned upon himselfe and slew him.
> In old times they had petty Moorish* Kings on
> the coast, few of which remaine by reason of the
> portugall Captynes succeeding in their places,
> and in their amitie and commerce with the Quitene
> King of these countries.

The remarks above are from a Dominican Priest's, Joa dos Santos, book entitled ETHIOPIA ORIENTAL (as translated into English in Purchas, HIS PILGRIMS, reprinted in Glassgow, Scotland, 1905. See also, J. Pinkerton, A GENERAL COLLECTION OF THE BEST AND MOST INTERESTING VOYAGES AND TRAVELS, Vol. 16, London, 1814.) One must wonder if this priest believed that there would ever come a day when this type of barbarous behaviour on the pretext of carrying "CIVILIZATION" and "CHRISTIANITY" to the "NATIVES" would be brought to the bar of justice on earth before Jesus Christ? What about these missionaries deportment, were they CHRISTIAN-LIKE, also? It is also strange that this report is dealing with the period of 1586 C.E., during the same period when the Boers (Dutch) were just arriving in Monomotapa, yet they have contended that when they "arrived at South Africa there were no BANTUS and NEGROES living NEAR" OR/AT "THE CAPE." Certainly they did not meet any "NEGROES" AND "BANTUS" there.

---

*The word MOORES is herein used to represent all the Africans of the Moslem (Muslim) religion - also called Islam. All of the Moslem inhabitants of Africa were called by this name during this period in African history and before the arrival of dos Santos. Yet, the majority of them were later recorded as "SWAHILIS" by European colonialists, missionary historians, and others.

This type of Africans was not yet invented for Africa by the Portugese and the British imperialist historians and colonial charters and map makers.

Joa dos Santos, who wrote the earliest known European reports on Central East Africa was himself a Dominican Priest of the Roman Catholic Church. He first visited Africa's East Coast in 1586 C.E. He served in Sofala until 1590, and he also travelled to Zambezi, Tete, and Monomotapa (at the seat of the kingdom called ZIMBABWE, which the Portuguese called "ZIMBOAE"). Upon his return to Portugal, he remained for approximately ten years (some European writers say eleven years) before he begged to return, and did return, to Africa, where he then wrote his ETHIOPIA ORIENTAL in 1609 C.E. and published it at Evora. It was later translated from the original Portugese into English by many scholars.

> I, the Emperor of Monomotapa, think fit and pleased to give to his majesty <u>all the mines of gold, copper, iron, lead and pewter</u> which may be in my empire, so long as the King of Portugal, to whom I give the said mines, shall maintain me in my position.

The above extract is taken from Diogo Simoes report to the King of Portugal in a letter allegedly written by the Monomotapa (Emperor) in the year 1607 on August 1. Simoes was at the time KEEPER OF THE ARCHIVES AND CHRONICLEER OF INDIA. Parts of India were under Portuguese colonial rule. One sees in this drama a little of the political manuevering that caused the Africans to lose all of their countries to the European colonialist. For exchange of the European's cannons and gun powder they surrendered much of their natural resources. This is not to say that the African continent was taken in this manner only; it never the less points to the fact that one group of Africans allowed the Europeans to help them fight another with the Europeans becoming the victor over both at the end of the conflict. Not only is this obvious, but another factor is that the Europeans are seen in light of the major reason for their coming to Africa and Asia during the early part of the 15th century C.E., it was for the natural resources they could get to feed a hungry Europe, particularly Portugal.

On the following page is a picture of the magnificent figure called LE GRAND ROY MONOMOTAPA - <u>The Great King Monomotapa</u>. One must note that the word MONOMOTAPA meant <u>King</u> or <u>Emperor</u>. The early Europeans who came to the empire (all of the southern end of South Africa, including the Cape) did not understand that the name of the empire was also the first part of the Emperor's title. The same custom was apparent in other parts of the entire African continent. For example: Ghana was named for King Ghana, Melle for King Melle. This was not always true for every nation in Africa. See page 177 and read the English translation or the French original about Le Grand Roy Monomotapa. Note the wealth of his garment and the crown on his head. All of which is supposedly the manner in which an "UNCIVILIZED HEATHEN NATIVE"

(Partial English Translation): "The Great King, Monomotapa. Very rich in gold. Several kings are tributary to him. His territory comprises lower Ethiopia.... His empire is very large and has a circuit of 2400 miles. His court is at Zimboae. There are women in his guard....He has a great number of elephants. His subjects are black, brave and swift runners, and he has very fast horses. Idolaters, sorcerers, and thieves are severely punished." Note that Zimboae is the Portuguese for ZIMBABWE.

177

lives.

Antonio Boccarro, whose work was translated into English by Theal in his own book, RECORDS OF SOUTH EASTERN AFRICA, Vol. 3, 1900, followed dos Santos and Simone. He too dealt with the manner by which the Portugese exploiters, nefariously called "DISCOVERERS and EXPLORERS", got fabulously wealthy by way of gunpowder and the misuse of the European-style Christian religion - by priest and layman alike - all with the approval of Rome. The later arrival of the Protestants made no difference in terms of betterment for the Africans. To the contrary. Nor did it remove the control of Arab slavery which had been running rampant for more than 100 years before the arrival of the Portugese to East Africa in 1496 with Vasco daGama.

Speaking about archives, the following data from the British Museum Archives should prove quite an interesting point on which to examine certain "TRUTHS" - as stated in the Hebrew TORAH and Christian HOLY BIBLE. It is a document surrendered to the Museum by the world's once famous egyptologist, Sir Ernest A. Wallis Budge, who became the work's first editor. Note the striking similarity that exists between the papyrus entitled "THE TEACHINGS OF AMEN-EN-EOPE"[4] and that of the alleged Hebrew "PROVERBS OF SOLOMON" - the so-called "CANONICAL BOOK" on page 179.

Before examination of these two works the reader must remember that King Solomon was not known to have written any book before

THE COMPARATIVE WORKS

ISRAEL (Asia-Minor)	EGYPT (North-Africa)
PROVERBS XXII. 17-XXIII. 14;	THE TEACHINGS OF AMEN-EM-OPE
The "teachings of King Solomon" (c970 BCE) of Israel	(c1300 BCE) Pharoah of Egypt

1. Incline thine ear, and hear my words,
   And apply thine heart to apprehend;
   For it is pleasant if thou keep them in thy belly,
   That they may be fixed like a peg upon thy lips.

1a. Give thine ear, and hear what I say,
   And apply thine heart to apprehend;
   It is good for thee to place them in thine heart,
   Let them rest in the casket of thy belly.
   That they may act as a peg upon thy tongue.

2. Have I not written for thee thirty sayings
   Of counsels and knowledge!
   That thou mayest make known truth to him that speaketh.

2a. Consider these thirty chapters;
   They delight, they instruct.
   Knowledge how to answer him that speaketh,
   And how to carry back a report to one that sent him.

3. Rob not the poor for he is poor,
   Neither oppress the lowly in the gate.

3a. Beware of robbing the poor,
   And of oppressing the afflicted.

4. Associate not with a passionate man,
   Nor go with a wrathful man,
   Lest thou learn his ways
   And get a snare to thy soul.

4a. Associate not with a passionate man,
   Nor approach him for conversations;
   Leap not to cleave to such a one,
   That the terror carry thee not away.

5. A man who is skilful in his business
   Shall stand before Kings.

5a. A scribe who is skilful in his business
   Findeth himself worthy to be a courtier.

he mounted the Hebrew throne about 970 B.C.E., which was during the rule of the Twenty-first Dynasty of Kimit (Egypt), at which time the pharoahs were Tanites of the Late Kingdom Period. On the other hand the Pharoah, Amen-em-eope, had written many of the major works dealing with this type of approach to the God of Kimit. This specific papyrus was written during the year 1000 B.C.E., at least thirty-one (31) years before Solomon mounted the Hebrew throne and was credited with writing what is called the "PROVERBS".

The revelations on page 179 should be of no surprise to anyone familiar with the origin of the so-called "WESTERN RELIGIONS" with respect to Africa and their African creators, especially in the case of Judaism which had its real birth in Africa - Kimit. Those who have done research in this area are fully aware that the basic "MOSAIC LAWS" (Commandments and Diety concepts) came from training that Moses received in the LAWS of the MYSTERIES OF EGYPT while a boy,[4a] and later as a grown man. This is according to the oldest document on Moses - THE BOOK OF EXODUS, as GENESIS was before his birth and ended with Joseph's death. EXODUS also dealt with Moses as an African of the type Herodotus described in his HISTORIES, which has been quoted earlier in the pages of this volume. The TORAH or Christian HOLY BIBLE's (any version) OLD TESTAMENT should be read in conjunction with this revelation and the following works listed in the special bibliography.

SUGGESTED BIBLIOGRAPHY ON THE COMPARATIVE WORKS

Griffith, Ranke (In: Gressman), Sange, DAR WEISBEITSBUCH DES AMENEN EOPE, 1925 (English translation: Amen-em-eope Teachings).
Blackman's essay in "THE PSALMISTS", (ed. by D.C. Simpson), 1926.
Osterly and Robinson A HISTORY OF ISRAEL, (1934).
Hooke, S.H. (Ed.) MYTH AND RITUAL (1933).
Jack, J.W. THE DATE OF THE EXODUS, (1925).
Blackman's English translation of, DIE LITERATUR DER AGYPTER (1933).
Breasted, J.H. ANCIENT RECORDS OF EGYPT: THE HISTORICA DOCUMENTS.
Cook, S.A. THE RELIGION OF ANCIENT PALESTINE IN THE LIGHT OF ARCHAEOLOGY (1930).
Smith, Homer W. MAN AND HIS GODS, (1953).
Buchler DIE TOBIADEN UND DIE ONIADEN, (1899).
Frazier, J. THE GOLDEN BOUGH, (1922).
Cowley JEWISH DOCUMENTS OF THE TIME OF EZRA, (1919).
Wallis Budge Sir. E.A. BOOK OF THE DEAD, (1959).
ARAMAIC PAPYRI OF THE FIFTH CENTURY B.C., (1923).
Higgins, Sir G. ANACALYPSIS, (1840).
Peet's EGYPT AND THE OLD TESTAMENT (1922).

Sir John Harris explaining the economic motives of one of Africa's most despotic colonialists and imperialists of the Victorian Era who come from England; wrote:

> It was the scintillating gleam of gold in the rock-strewn ground of Matableland that forced Sir Starr Jameson's hand and compelled him to invade Matable from Fort Victoria, and adds, the effect of this impact upon <u>the backward peoples</u> has always been acutely violent; coupled with bloodshed and cruelty upon an atrocious scale.

The above extract was taken from Sir John Harris, SLAVERY OR SACRED TRUST?, p. 68.[5] Here again one can see the same old so-called "<u>liberalism</u>" that the GREAT WHITE FATHERS have displayed in behalf of the Africans, and allegedly against their fellow Europeans and European-Americans engaged in the rape of the African peoples and their homeland. Thus one sees Sir Harris apparently challenging the genocide imposed upon the Africans of Monomotapa by Cecil Rhodes' hangman - Sir Star Jameson. But what made Sir Harris expound the theory that the Africans within their own homeland and in their own culture were any more "...BACKWARD..." than the peoples he left in Britain and other parts of Europe during the same period? This type of racist attitude is the common pattern of behaviour up to the present time with regards to Africa, her sons and daughters and their offsprings everywhere.

There is, in fact, the opposite feeling expressed by Sir Harris and others who feel that their "<u>liberalism</u>" must make them speak out against the genocide the Africans suffered at the hands of the European and European-American colonialists and imperialists. Never the less they are in the very minute part of their nation's general scheme of things relating to the international exploitation of the African peoples and their natural resources, from which the so-called "liberals" also reap untold benefits.

Strange as it may seem, the racist colonialists and other imperialists who took turns exterminating the Africans by means of genocide also took pride in debasing each other over their stolen lands and captured slaves - the indigenous African peoples. Thus one sees William Polmer in his book entitled, CECIL RHODES, page 73, saying the following with respect to Boer President Kruger's appraisal of his most hated rival - Cecil Rhodes; yet both Kruger and Rhodes' anxiety about each other resulted from their struggles over who was to be the one in control of the extermination and enslavement of the African peoples of the "Great" Monomotapa (South Africa). They fought for the confiscation of their personal belongings, which also included their herds of cattle, and natural resources, and of course all of the diamond and gold mines presently being exploited by Europeans and European-Americans, and enjoyed by European-Americans of every economic level in the United States of America as it is in Europe, the British Isles included. Kruger allegedly stated:

> Rhodes* was one of the mos unscrupulous characters that ever lived;...No matter how debase, no matter how contemptible; be it lying, bribery or treachery, all and every means were welcomed subjects.

What kind of a man could Rhodes have been? This question must certainly make people of African origin wonder why this type of "UNSCRUPULOUS CHARACTER" is not mentioned as such in the history books of the United States of America's schools, especially those written by "liberals" and "Christian missionaries" who are so much in love with justice and pursue the democratic rights of all free people the world over. If Kruger and the Boers (Dutch ancestors of the present White supremists who rule South Africa under a system that surpassed anything introduced by

---

*The same Cecil Rhodes is the man for whom the "RHODES SCHOLARSHIP" is named. This type of infamy is equivalent to naming a scholarship THE ADOLPH EICHMANN SCHOLARSHIP and offering it to Jewish students. Shamefully enough Africans and other Black students over the world are the recipients of many of these "Rhodes Scholarships'.

Adolph Hitler and his Nazis Germany, named "APARTHEID") were the type of murderers history has shown them to be; one can only wonder what depth did Rhodes sunk to in order to out-fox Kruger, and what must have been the fate the African peoples of Monomotapa suffered at the hands of both men. Maybe someday in future history, someone of the "<u>liberal</u>" and/or "<u>Christian missionaries</u>" camps will release the withheld information that will really reveal the depths of the quagmire to which they had sunk in the genocide of millions upon millions of Africans they destroyed, maimed, tortured, enslaved. Their descendants do the same today in the latter half of the 20th century.

The following remarks by Sir Godfrey Higgins, once Premier and Minister of Native Affairs of Rhodesia, addressing the Colonial Overseas League in London, England, on July 12, 1934, stated the general position of the European and European-American peoples, which includes the so-called "WORKING CLASS". Thus Sir Higgins said:

> It is time for the people in England to realize that <u>the white man in Africa is not prepared and never will be prepared to accept the African as an equal, socially or politically.</u>

The above statement should not shock anyone in the United States of America, as what Sir Higgins stated is the general feelings of European-Americans with regards to the African-Americans within continental North America and the United States of America's colonies - otherwise called "POSSESSIONS" and

"COMMONWEALTHS" in the Caribbeans and the Pacific.

Sir Godfrey Higgins continued further with his expressed racism during a speech on March 30, 1938 to his fellow White colonialist settlers at Bulawayo, Zimbabwe (colonial Rhodesia).[6] He labeled the White settlers' community:

> ...an island of white in a sea of black, with the white artisans and tradesmen forming the shores and the white professional classes the highlands. Was the native to be allowed to erode the shore and gradually attack the highlands? To permit this would mean that the leaven of civilization would be removed and that the blacks would inevitably revert to barbarism, because the ancient control, such as tribal authority, had gone, never to return, leaving only the white man's law, religion and example. While there was yet time and space, the country must be divided into seperate white and black areas.

One will notice that what Sir Higgins had established in the Africans' homeland, his fellow colonialists had established all over the Planet Earth wherever they were in control, including the United States of America in the case of the indigenous peoples the Europeans labeled, "INDIANS". The good Premier continued with his rank racism, forgetting that the people of whom he was speaking are in fact the rightful owners of the land which he (and others like him) were usurping; and that one day he and others must pay the price of their action. He said:

> In the white areas the natives would be welcomed, but on the understanding that he merely assist and not compete with the white man. Native education should be by missions and not by the State till natives had a background in Christianity.

There are many areas in the above statement that have direct bearing on the present situation in Zimbabwe between the White racists that now rule the country under Ian Smith and those he forced to his will under the rule of the present Queen of Britain, Elizabeth II. First; what this man was saying was implemented by the British government under the direction of Elizabeth's father, George VI. Second; all of the members of the United Nations Organization are aware of the history of the British colonialist <u>entrepreneurs</u> and <u>missionaries</u> to whom the good man alluded when he said they should control "<u>native education</u>". Third; the separation of the races is common in every country under the control of Europeans or European-Americans; even in many countries that are <u>supposedly independent</u> from their former colonialist administrators such as the Philipines, Kenya, Ghana, Malawi and many others too numerous to mention here.

Sir Godfrey Higgins' position still expresses the feeling common among all of the Whites in Africa to date, and of course, among the missionaries who also hope that they can continue selling their European version of economic, religious, and racist philosophy under the pretext of "BRINGING CHRISTIANITY TO THE NATIVES". "<u>Christian ideals</u>", the outward expression of contempt for the African peoples by those who claimed then, and do now, became so intense that even certain White Hebrew (misnomered "<u>Jewish</u>") writers (themselves not too long removed from servitude for their fellow Europeans the Christians and some Moslems) such as C.G. Seligman, in his book, RACES OF AFRICA, page 96,

New York, 1924 (reprinted in 1930 and 1968)[7] wrote:

> Apart from relatively late Semitic influence...the civilizations of Africa are the civilizations of the Hamites, its history the record of these peoples and their interaction with the two other African stocks, the Negro and the Bushman, whether this influence was exerted by highly civilized Egyptians or by such wider pastoralists as are represented at the present day by the Beja and Somali...The incoming Hamites were pastoral 'Europeans' - arriving wave after wave - better armed as well as quicker witted than the dark agricultural Negroes.

The Semitic racism displayed by Seligman was in no sense original by Jews with regards to their African brothers; it followed much worse pronouncements by such as <u>Benjamin of Tudela</u> who wrote the following:

> ...There is a people...who, like animals, eat of the herbs that grow on the banks of the Nile and in their fields. They go about naked and have not the intelligence of ordinary men. They cohabit with their sisters and anyone they can find...they are taken slaves and sold in Egypt and neighboring countries. These sons of Ham are black slaves.

The above extract was taken from the English translation in R. Hess, TRAVELS OF BENJAMIN OF TUDELA. Although there are ample reasons to further examine the racist and bigoted remarks of this man who himself was suffering from all sorts of religious and racial persecutions, there is one point in his presentation which should be specially observed. He spoke of the Africans as:

"...THESE SONS OF HAM ARE BLACK SLAVES."

Here the usage of the word HAM and HAMITE are used with relationship to the identity of those who are now called "NEGROES, BANTUS, AFRICANS SOUTH OF THE SAHARA", etc. But the Semitic procrastinators did not begin with Benjamin of Tudela; as early as the Sixth (6th) century C.E. (A.D.) <u>Rabbinical Scholars</u> of the Babylonian Talmud produced the following:

> 'Now I cannot beget the fourth son whose children I would have ordered to serve you and your brothers! Therefore it must be Canaan, your firstborn, whom they enslave. And since you have disabled me... doing ugly things in the blackness of night, Canaan's children shall be borne ugly and black! Moreover, <u>because you twisted your head around to see my nakedness,</u> your grandchildren's hair shall be twisted into kinks, and their eyes red; again because your lips jested at my misfortune, theirs shall swell; and because you neglected my nakedness, they shall go naked, and their male members shall be shamefully elongated! Men of this race are called Negroes, their forefather Canaan them to love theft and fornication, to be banded together in hatred of their masters and never to tell the truth.'

The above extract is taken from R. Graves and R. Patai, HEBREW MYTHS, page 121, New York, 1964. Of course this was only a Jewish attempt at correcting their fellow Europeans' myth that centered around the Calvinist Christian teachings that the incident took place with HAM instead of CANAAN. The fact is that the TORAH has the myth in the following manner:

> Curse be Canaan;
> A servant of servants shall he be
> unto his brethern.
> And he said,
> Blessed be Jehovah, the God of Shem;
> And let Canaan be his servant.
> God enlarge Japhet,
> And let him dwell in the tent of Shem;
> And let Canaan be his servent.

Obviously there must have been some mistake made by the truly original writers of the Torah or those who later on wrote the above in the Sixth century C.E. Babylonian Talmud. One must wonder what would make people who annually <u>note their own historical bondage to others</u> speak of people who are alledgedly made by some God or another to be their "SERVANTS"; in reality their SLAVES.

Seligman wrote in the same work:

> ...It would be very wide of the mark to say that the history of Africa South of the Sahara is no more than the story of the permeation through the ages, in different degrees and at various times, of the Negro and Bushman aboriginals by <u>Hamitic blood</u>* and culture.

Such recklessly loose remarks were, and still are, the order of the day, as they linger on in the works of Professor Jeffreys to the present (the latter part of the 20th century C.E.). What does Seligman mean by "HAMITIC BLOOD"? Is it possible that the Black peoples of Alkebu-lan, North and East, sprung from a mythical Jew (Hebrew) by the name of "HAM"? Is it not a proven fact that Africans all over Alkebu-lan (Africa) existed for centuries before the first Haribu (Hebrew or Jew) - ABRAHAM (Avram) - was ever heard of in world history? The Haribus (Jews) had no beginning before the year c1675 B.C.E. There are abundant documents that recite the glorious history of indigenous African societies even before the Haribus created their "ADAM AND EVE" for their "GARDEN OF EDEN" hundreds of years after an African

---

*This indicates how low certain "authorities on Africa" stoop to prove their racist theories. What is "HAMITIC BLOOD"?

named "MOSES" gave them a way of life, now called "JUDAISM". These facts hould be looked at in what is today called the "FIVE BOOKS OF MOSES" or HOLY TORAH. Because of the almost limitless proponderance of works on this area of African history no student of history should be ignorant of the facts mentioned herein. At least no professor of history or cultural anthropology should be without knowledge of these background facts and myths of and about the Africans who are presently called all sorts of disparaging names shown in this text and others with which most "<u>Western educators</u>" are very familiar. The TRUTH about the Africans must be brought forward, especially that which presented the greatness of the Africans in their role as economists, sociologists and political scientists; and, the BIG LIE about them must be deflated.

In all of the vileness perpetuated against <u>Mother-Africa</u> (Alkebu-lan) and her indigenous peoples, a few voices in White Europe and the United States of America still managed to speak in praise of Africa's former GLORY: Note James Montgomery's poems in 1841 C.E. In one of them he wrote:

>   Utterable mysteries of fate
>   Involve, O Africa! , thy future state
>   Dim through the night of these tempestuous years
>   A Sabbath dawn o'er Africa appears:
>   Then shall her neck from Europe's yoke be freed,
>   And healing arts to be hideous arms succeed;
>   at home fraternal bonds her tribes shall bind,
>   Commerce abroad espouse them with mankind...

Ancient and modern European and Asian greats who worshipped

and praised Africa and the Africans did so orally, as well as in their most precious writings. Some samples of these follow :

Pliny quoted an ancient Greek saying in his work entitled, ROMAN HISTORY, written sometime between c23 and c79 C.E. (A.D.). He wrote:

> EX AFRICA SEMPER ALIQUID NOVI. (English translation: "<u>Out of Africa comes something always new.</u>")

The following is from an ancient Arabian saying that predates the conquest of the Congo by Arab slavers:

> He who has drunk from the waters of Africa will drink again.

The English playwright and dramatist of world renown Sir William Shakespeare in his work, HENRY IV, v. III, wrote:

> I SPEAK OF AFRICA AND GOLDEN JOYS.

The honoured English historian, author and physician, Sir Thomas Browne, 1605-1682 C.E.; wrote:

> THERE IS AFRICA AND ALL HER PRODIGIES IN US.

Dr. Victor Robinson, one of the world's most noted authors in his book, CIBA SYMPOSIA, 1940; wrote:

> It is one of the paradoxes of history that Africa, the Mother of Civilisation, remained for over two thousand years the DARK CONTINENT.[8] To the moderns Africa was the region where ivory was sought for Europe, and slaves for America. In the time of Jonathan Swift (1667-1745), as the satirist informs us, geographers in drawing maps fill in gaps with savage pictures. Where towns should have been they placed elephants.

Even in praising Africa and the Africans the "DARK CONTINENT" mythology established by Henry Morton Stanley must always come forth. Stanley's image is highlighted in the words below.

"WHERE TOWNS SHOULD HAVE BEEN THEY PLACED ELEPHANTS." What an indictment against those whose history reverts to Europe and the Europeans with respect to their "SUPERIORITY OVER THE AFRICANS". This, however, was no different than the fact that in West Africa: WHERE THERE WAS ANCIENT SONGHAI THEY PLACED NEGROLAND AND NEGROES from the 17th century C.E.

In the book entitled HISTORY OF NATIONS, vol. 18, p. 1, New York, 1906, it is written:

>The African continent is no recent discovery; it is not a new world like America or Australia... <u>While yet Europe was the home of the wandering barbarians one of the most wonderful civilization on record had begun to work its destiny on the Nile</u>...

The underlined words point out quite vividly why the African nations of the ancient Nile Valleys High-Cultures had to be re-recorded and history altered to make them appear as "CAUCASIANS, SEMITES, HAMITES", and all other forms of mankind except those who are now designated "NEGROES, BANTUS," etc., by the descendants of the "WANDERING BARBARIANS" of their home in Europe. The more one reads the earlier works, the more the beauty and glory that was Africa and her sons and daughters unfold in splendor.

Count C.F. Volney saw the ruins of the Colossal Black Monuments there in Upper Egypt (Nubia, Sudan, Ethiopia), He wrote:

>There a people now forgotten discovered while others were yet barbarians, the elements of the

> arts and sciences. <u>A race of men now rejected from society for the sable skin and wooley hair,</u> founded on the study of the laws of nature those civil and religious systems which still govern the Universe.

There could be no doubt that the same type of Africans described by Herodotus in his HISTORIES are the same people thousands of years later Count Volney described; people who fit into the same description called "NEGROES", sometimes even "NIGGERS", in the United States of America today. Certainly it was also Count C.F. Volney who visited Egypt in 1787 C.E. and stated that Herodotus had solved for himself the problem of why the people of Egypt (Kimit or Sais) were so:

"BLACK AND WOOLY-HAIRED;"

and we learn of the:

GREAT SPHINX OF GHIZEH -

the <u>Supreme Symbol of worship and power</u>. Reflecting on how he met the State of Egypt in its reduced image of grandeur the Count also wrote:

> To think that a race of Black men who are today our slaves and the object of our contempt are the same ones to whom we owe our arts, sciences and even the very use of speech.[9]

One should readily understand why books such as those written by men of the calibre of the Volneys are kept away from the general student population of the major institutions of higher learning and the general public at large. For if this type of information was available to students in secondary schools it would have been impossible to have the type of <u>object racism</u> and <u>bigotry</u> of the most vicious character displayed against the sons and daughters of the conveyors of man's first peep into the universe of knowledge. (See Count C.F. Volney, RUINS OF EMPIRES, pp. 16-17, (1890); also, Volney, OEUVRES, vol. 2, pp. 65-68, (1825).

Two other most respected European scholars of Volney's era who saw the SPHINX OF GHIZEH in its greatest splendor before "Napoleon de Bonnepart's soldiers blew its face asunder" were Baron Denon and Gustav Flaubert, both of whom expressed similar opinions. Baron Denon, in particular, made a first hand sketch of the great statue in 1798 C.E. He said of it:

> The character is African... the lips are thick... Art must have been at a high pitch when this monument was executed.

See Baron Denon, TRAVELS IN UPPER AND LOWER EGYPT, vol. I, p. 115, (1910). Flaubert identified its African group in 1849 C.E. in the following manner:

IT IS CERTAINLY ETHIOPIAN. THE LIPS ARE THICK.[10]

(See Gustave Flaubert, NOTES de VOYAGE, p. 115; picture and sketch of the Sphinx of Ghizeh by Baron Denon showing its "<u>thick</u>" African "<u>lips</u>" before they were blown asunder, on page 195.)

Here there is insight into one of the names by which the ancient Africans were called. The ancients also called the entire continent "ETHIOPIA". (see map on page 679)

In 1910 C.E. the German explorer, scholar, and historian,

The <u>Sphinx of Gizeh</u> as it appeared to Baron Denon in 1798 C.E., from one of his own drawings he made first hand. Note the relative indigenous African characteristics - nose, lips, etc. This was the way it appeared before Napoleon's soldiers blew its face assunder in distaste of its "NEGROID FEATURES". This took place during France's invasion of Egypt. Why was this picture withheld from students and the general public?

AKHET KHUFU
(Horizon of Khufu)

The <u>Sphinx</u> as it appears in 1970; showing the temple and dream-stele.

Leo Frobenius, furthered Count C.F. Volney's work as he influenced the recording of African history by subsequent European scholars (also a few European-Americans later on) by taking a completely new posture because of his own in-depth researches and writings on, and about, the African people and the great cultures they had produced before, and during, his lifetime. In his most basic work on Africa, UND AFRIKA SPRACH (English translation: <u>The Voice of Africa</u>; or <u>Africa Speaks</u>), Frobenius urged his colleagues:

> Let there be
> Light in Africa. In that portion of the globe to which the stalwart Anglo-Saxon Stanley gave the name "dark" and "darkest". Light upon the people of that continent whose children we are accustomed to regard as types of natural servility with no recorded history. (But) The spell has been broken. The buried treasures of antiquity again revisit the sun.

With the above extract from Frobenius' work this chapter could be brought to close without further comment; however, one of the main highlights in it must be magnified somewhat. Frobenius touched on the main issue of modern times that has caused the Africans the untold miseries they have suffered, and are still suffering at the hands of the European and European-American slavers, colonialists, Christian missionaries, and so-called "entrepreneurs." <u>It is the mark of "inferiority" Henry Morton Stanley placed upon them during the latter part of the 19th century C.E.</u> Frobenius cited the Stanley myth in the following manner:

IN THAT PORTION OF THE GLOBE TO WHICH THE STALWART ANGLO-SAXON STANLEY GAVE THE NAME "dark" and "darkest."

Herein lies the major problem which "Western educators" have never been able to overcome, the sense of arrogant "superiority" over the African epople which they have adopted from the racist words of Henry Morton Stanley. Never-the-less this chapter closes, although the surface of the overwhelming amount of evidence and testimony to the greatness of the Africans and their continent - Mother Africa - was slightly scratched by the preponderance of documented data submitted in this chapter, the preceding chapters, and the following chapters. That which follows, however, will more than explain many of the laudatory comments already made, and about to be made. It will also introduce others, but of course all cannot be dealt with because of the limited space in a volume such as this. The following adverse comments, equally stated to provide the necessary academic investigation for the service of TRUTH, are to be give full attention too with respect to the sons and daughters' of Mother-Africa's TRUE history (before hidden) all through the existence of MANKIND, even before the appearance of ZINJANTHROPUS BOISIE more than 1,750,000 years ago. However, one must hope that the general student body, as well as the reading public, have learned some new aspects about Africa and the African peoples other than the adverse racist and religiously bigoted information that has generally been forced upon them by most so-called "WESTERN

EDUCATORS" in the past. Much of this information continues in the present; all of which give every indication that it will continue in the future if other works such as this are not placed before the students of the institutions of higher learning in the United States of America and elsewhere throughout what is still being called "THE WESTERN WORLD". At least through works such as this one can see another aspect of the TRUTH.

BIBLIOGRAPHY FOR CHAPTER III

Dazells, Archibald	HISTORY OF DAHOMEY, London, 1793.
dos Santos, Joa	ETHIOPIA ORIENTAL (In: Purchas, HIS PILGRIMS, Vol. 9, Glasgow, 1905).
Pinkerton, J.A.	A GENERAL COLLECTION OF THE BEST AND MOST INTERESTING VOYAGES AND TRAVELS, vol. 16, London, 1814.
Theal, G.M.	RECORDS OF SOUTH EASTERN AFRICA, Vol. III, 1900.
Pliny	ROMAN HISTORY
Flaubert, Gustav	NOTES de VOYAGE, 1910.
DuBois, Felix	TIMBUCTOO THE MYSTERIOUS, 1924.
Bovills, E.W.	CARAVANS OF OLD SAHARA
Lugard, Lady F.S.	A TROPICAL DEPENDENCY, London, 1880.
Africanus, Leo	A HISTORY AND DESCRIPTION OF AFRICA (trans. by John Pory to English; edited by Dr. R. Brown, Hakluyt Society, London).
Davidson, Basil	THE AFRICAN PAST, New York, 1964.
Wallis-Budge, Sir. E.	BOOK OF THE DEAD, New York, 1959.
- - - - -	THE TEACHINGS OF AMEN-EM-EOPE, (Papyrus collections. Written about 1001 B.C.E. or earlier, London Museum of Natural History).
Harris, Sir John	SLAVERY OR SACRED TRUST?, London
Polmer, William	CECIL RHODES, London
Shakespeare, Sir W.	HENRY IV, London
Robinson, Dr. Victor	CIBA SYMPOSIUM
Volney, Count C.F.	RUINS OF EMPIRES, Paris 1789 (latest New York edition 1950).
Denon, Baron Viviant	TRAVELS IN LOWER AND UPPER EGYPT, vol. I, Paris, 1803.
Frobenius, Leo	UND AFRICA SPRACH (English translation: <u>Voice of Africa</u>; or <u>Africa Speaks</u>), Berlin.

PEOPLE WHO MADE NILE VALLEY HISTORY YESTERDAY AND TODAY

THE DAWN OF NILE EXPLORATION

THE first men who entered Egypt and travelled up the valley of the Nile came, almost unquestionably, from the east, and were part of those radiations from the central focus of humanity, India. It is possible that the first men who entered the valley of the Nile from this direction may have been of so primitive, simian, and undetermined a type — so "Neanderthaloid" — as not to belong definitely to any one of the three main species of humanity. At that distant time, however (let us say at the end of the Pleistocene period or beginning of the Quaternary Epoch), there was undoubtedly a land connection over the south as well as over the north end of the Red Sea, joining Arabia to Ethiopia as well as to Egypt; and across this bridge came many types of Asiatic mammals, also man, — possibly in the form of a low Negroid, a type represented to-day (much changed and modified, of course) by the Congo Pygmies and South African Bushmen. As regards the history of humanity, however, the valley of the Nile has been divided into two very distinct parts. The southern half of its basin — in common with all Africa south of the Sahara and the fifteenth degree of north latitude — was peopled from the east, through southern Arabia, and by the Negro species in the main. Egypt proper and the adjoining regions of Arabia once lay within the domain of the Negroid Pygmies, but these indigenes were overwhelmed at a relatively early period by more or less "negrified" branches of the Caucasian stock coming from the direction of Syria or from Libya. Before the dawn of the historical epoch — say nine thousand years ago — an element in the population of Lower Egypt certainly showed Bushmen affinities. These steatopygous Bushmen were perhaps Proto-negroes, who may have branched off from the Nigritic stock when first that species reached the Mediterranean regions. This Bushman element in Egypt was for some time distinct, prior to the historical period, as the characteristic type of the servile class. Following on these dwarfish people came races bearing some slight resemblance to the Dravidians of India.

I could find no more appropriate manner in which to commence

199

this lecture than the above comments and citations extracted from Sir Harry H. Johnston, THE NILE CONQUEST, Federick A. Stokes Company, New York, 1903, pp 1 - 2. The same man who wrote the above also made the following remarks on page 30 of the same book under the subtitle in Chapter III,"ABYSSINIANS AND JEWS," with respect to the "...KINGS OF THE ETHIOPIAN RACE..." (Gala dashed with Arab and Jew)...,etc. He wrote:

> The history of Abyssinia - if it is to be written with regard to truth - is still obscure. This country of lofty mountains and temperate climate is bordered on the east by the land of Afar,[1] an inhospitable desert inhabited by <u>fierce Hamites</u>* (Danakil)."

On page 31 he continued:

> Originally <u>no doubt Abyssinia was peopled by the same dwarf Bushman race as that which formed the lowest stratum</u> of all the African populations. Then a portion of the country came into the possession of the <u>big black Negroes</u>[x] who still inhabit its western flanks. These again are superceded and partially absorbed by the <u>superior race of Hamites</u>,[+] the ancestors of the Gala, Somali, and ancient Egyptian. This <u>Hamite race of Caucasian stock with some Negroid intermixture</u> forms the basis of the Abyssinian population of the present day.

When one considers that it is people like Sir Harry H. Johnston that the "Western World's" educators termed "AUTHORITY ON AFRICA;" it is a wonder that many more people are not still clamoring for the return of AFRICAN CHATLE SLAVERY. Just who, or what, gave this man the right to refer to anyone as "...THAT WHICH FORMED THE LOWEST STRATUM...," etc. Stranger yet, Sir Harry H. Johnston is still considered by most "modern" historian of Europe and European-America as an "AUTHORITY ON THE AFRICAN PEOPLES."

---
1. Modern Afars; the name the French colonialists reinstituted for their east African colonies is still to the Africans living there the French colony of Somaliland until they are gone. Words in parentheses by the lecturer for clarity only.

The "...FIERCE HAMITES...", Johnston speaks about, obviously, were suposedly much more CIVILIZED than the "...BIG BLACK NEGROES...."+ But these "...FIERCE HAMITES..."* were also descendants "...OF CAUCASIAN STOCK..., WITH SOME NEGROID INTERMIXTURE...." Certainly we are to conclude that their African FIERCENESS was inherited from their "...BIG BLACK NEGRO..."ancestors. Yet these "...BIG BLACK NEGROES..." were not racially moderated by "...THE SUPERIOR RACE OF HAMITES..." Sir Harry H. Johnston, and others like him, invented for Ethiopia and areas of Africa not covered in his racist comments. They are descendants of the fossils his "CAUCASIAN STOCK" is presently digging up and claiming in east-central Africa today.

This man, Johnston, formulated much of what is being taught throughout western Europe, the British Isle, the Americas, with regards to African peoples everywhere in all levels of institutionalized education. As you must have noticed already, the HAMETIC-SEMITIC syndrome was prevalent very far back into the 18th and 19th century C.E. among European and European-American historians.[1] They ignored the fact that the entire north and east-African landmass, which they considered totally inhabitted by "NATIVES OF CAUCASIAN, HAMITIC, NEGROID" and "PYGMY ADMIXTURE" was in fact, and still is, the same area the oldest known fossil-men are still being unearthed – the true GARDEN OF EDEN. The racist historians during this period were very few of European (White)-Jewish origin, thus the "SEMITIC" aspect of the racial and ethnic syndrome was very much underplayed. This aspect of European and European-American racism and religious bigotry subsided, only be-

---
1. H.R. Rappaport, AFRICAN RACES AND THE SEMITE, 1798; also M.A. du Audrey, PEOPLES OF AFRICA, EGYPT AND ETHIOPIA, Paris, 1749.

cause Jewish historians (at the same period) were themselves, in Europe and the United States of America, underdogs like the African people so many of their descendants have joined in with their fellow White Christians of Europe and European-America in degrading of late.[1] This does not negate the role of the Sixth (6th) century C.E. Babylonian Talmudist scholars, God's "CHOOSEN SCRIBES and "INSPIRED PROPHETS" of European Jewish ghettos, who wrote the following about the "NEGROES" with respect to their being the "...DESCENDANTS OF CANAAN..." and "...HAM...."

> 'God's curse upon Canaan! May his brothers make him a slave of slaves! But blessed be the God of Shem, whom Canaan shall serve. May He also enlarge Japheth, to dwell in the tents of Shem; and Canaan shall serve them both.'

> 'Now I cannot beget the fourth son whose children I would have ordered to serve you and your brothers! Therefore it must be Canaan, your first-born, whom they enslave. And since you have disabled me from doing ugly things in the blackness of night, Canaan's children shall be born ugly and black! Moreover, because you twisted your head around to see my nakedness, your grandchildren's hair shall be twisted into kinks, and their eyes red; again, because your lips jested at my misfortune, theirs shall swell; and because you neglected my nakedness, they shall go naked, and their male members shall be shamefully elongated.' Men of this race are called Negroes; their forefather Canaan commanded them to love theft and fornication, to be banded together in hatred of their masters and never to tell the truth.[5]

5. B. Sanhedrin 72a-b, 108b; B. Pesahim 113b; Tanhuma Buber Gen. 49-50; Tanhuma Noah 13, 15; Gen. Rab. 341.

Here, too, we see that the European and European-American (White) Jews, who have been continually claiming that "...JEWS AND NEGROES ARE TREATED UNFAIRLY..." and are "...EQUALLY MINORITIES IN THE UNITED STATES OF AMERICA...", never-the-less failed to decry the part earlier European Jews played in creating the myth that their fellow Europeans used in morally justifying the

---

1. All sort of anti-Semitic charges may arise from this historical citation; never-the-less the proof is voluminous. See Seligman, RACES OF AFRICA, New York, 1930; also R. Graves and R. Patai, HEBREW MYTHS, New York, 1967.

"NEGROES" enslavement. Of course this fact will be labled "anti-SEMITISM." But, a BLACK HEBREW cannot be "anti-SEMITIC"; maybe anti-EUROPEAN-AMERICAN TALMUDIC JUDAISM would be much more appropriate, if such was the case. Why would it be ANTI anything when one points out and submit documentary evidence? Is it not "anti-AFRICANISM" or "anti-BLACKISM," and even "anti-NEGROISM," is being pointed out here? Your instructor is doing neither. To me there is no difference between the rabbis of the 6th century C.E. and Sir Harry H. Johnston who wrote in the manner shown. The same holds true for modern scholars like Dr. Donald Weidner who wrote in his book, A SHORT HISTORY OF AFRICA SOUTH OF THE SAHARA..., p.12., the following comments about Africa and her indigenous sons and daughters:

Caucasian types also began to appear in western Kenya. They are known variously as Capsian people, early Cushites or early Hamites, but there is no agreement whether this was an evolution from Bushman ancestry or another independent development. These people, it is believed, migrated northeastward into Arabia and western Asia as well as northwestward into Egypt and North Africa. Recent scholars (notably Joseph H. Greenberg)³ have suggested that the term Cushite be applied to this parent Caucasian race, and that their basic language be called Afroasiatic (formerly Hamitic). Bushman would then be the name of another race, whose speech is called Khoisan. Nothing definite is known about original Pygmy language, since his race adopted completely the languages of its later conquerors.

The origin of the Negroes has been the greatest enigma. A variation within the Cushites, or a combination of Cushites with either Bushmen or Pygmies, has been considered. Older theories, involving Negroes in India or Indonesia who mysteriously migrated but left no evidence on their way, are now discredited.

Dating of these prehistoric developments is necessarily approximate and relative, pending further research, but it appears that: (1) Cushites, Bushmen and Pygmies were quite distinct before 10,000 B.C., (2) Cushites who were developing Caucasian characteristics penetrated Egypt about 5,000 B.C., but (3) Negroes cannot be distinguished before about 6,000 B.C. (some suggest even as late as 4,000 B.C.). When they did appear, they were in the Sahara, well above the rain forest but not touching

³ Joseph H. Greenberg, *Studies in African Linguistic Classification*, New Haven, 1955, pp. 54-55. The older summary by C. G. Seligman, *Races of Africa*, New York, 1930, is outdated.

See BLACK MAN OF THE NILE, page 10, for racist map by Weidner in which he assumed to have the knowledge of just what RACE the people of north and east Africa were thousands of years before the Christian era. It should not supprise you to note that this "AUTHORITY ON AFRICA" found no place in either east or north

Africa where his "AFRICANS SOUTH OF THE SAHARA" existed before 6000 BCE. Of course his "CAUCASIANS" and "SEMITES" were all over north and east Africa from the time of the first man; they obviously changed place with the Tigris and Euphrates for the Nile River Valley and the African Great Lakes region.

Should the BLACK man in the "Western World" (the so-called "Americas"), professors or not, continue in silence while other so-called "ETHNIC GROUPS" spew the same ancient racist and riligious MYTHS about African peoples without the least sign of righteous indignation on his part? No one in his or her right mind should expect this; the BLACK MAN, not the "Negro," will not allow these MYTHS and their propagandists any further comfort.

In ancient times, even as late as the African-European amalgamated Ptolomies - I to XV (c327-47 BCE), the Europeans did not speak of the indigenous Africans in the manner I have described. The most offensive reference to the Ethiopians in ancient times came from Herodotus around the years c457-450 BCE, when he stated that:

> "...THERE WAS IN ETHIOPIA, A CIVILIZED CITY AT THE THE NILE'S BEND AT MEROE BEYOND WHICH NOTHING IS KNOWN...," etc., etc., etc.

Aristotle, the so-called "<u>philosopher</u>," who stole an entire library of the Africans of Kimit's (Egypt's) works and placed his name as author on many of them, around 300 BCE, stated that:

> "...TO THE SOUTHEAST (of Ethiopia)[1] THERE WAS A PYGMY RACE OF ETHIOPIANS WHO OFTEN FOUGHT WITH THE OVERSIZED CRANES" (ostriches).[1]

On the otherhand Eratosthenes[2] (the mixed African-European geog-

---
1. Words in parentheses by your lecturer for clarity only.
2. The son of European and African parents; born in north Africa.

rapher of Cyrene or Cyrenica, North Africa - where he was born in c276 BCE; later on a librarian in the Alexandrian Library of Alexandria, Egypt'; the first to write a history of the Nubian beyond the Second (2nd Cataract) spoke not of any of the Africans in terms used by Sir Harry H. Johnston or anyother of the so-called "modern" historians. For example: We find Sir Harry H. Johnston saying on page 2 of the same book mentioned above:

> EGYPT PROPER AND THE ADJOINING REGIONS OF ARABIA ONCE LAY WITHIN THE DOMAIN OF THE NEGROID PYGMIES, BUT THESE INDIGENOUS WERE OVERWHELMED AT A RELATIVELY EARLY PERIOD BY MORE OR LESS "negrified" BRANCH OF THE CAUCASIAN STOCK COMING FROM THE DIRECTION OF SYRIA OR FROM LIBYA.

The ignorance and racism exhibited by Sir Harry H. Johnston was much more confusing and assinine than is normal among most writers of his ilk. How did the so-called "NEGROES" get to become a "NEGRIFIED BRANCH OF THE CAUCASIAN STOCK...," etc.? Obviously the ancient "CAUCASIANS" must not have thought of themselves as a "...SUPERIOR RACE..." like their descendants do today. Or, it must have been that they had become, at this most earliest period in man's prehistory, the "NEGRITIC PEOPLE'S" slaves. The sad condition of Sir Harry's mind was further reflected in the following statement he made on page 2 before the latter remarks:

> The southern half of its (the Nile)[1] basin - in common with all Africa south of the Sahara and the fifteenth degree of north latitude - was peopled from the east, through southern Arabia, and by the Negro species in the main. Egypt proper....

Sir Harry really surpassed Herodotus' description of the Egyptians and Ethiopians when he wrote, on page 3:

> In these countries (Galaland, Somaliland, or Abys-

---

1. Words in parenthesis by the lecturer for clarity only.

> sinia where he said the ancient Egyptians originated),[1] or originally perhaps in southern Arabia, there was formed a handsome race mainly of Caucasian stock, but which had mingled somewhat with the proto-negroes and Dravidians in Arabia and in northeast Africa, and so had acquired darker skins, and hair with more or less tendency to curl.

The clincher to Sir Harry's racist confusion came when he noted:

> Their (Gala, Somali, Danakil, Ethiopians)[1] degenerate descendants continue to exist with but little altered type in the Danakil, Somali and Gala of the present day, but in the northern half of the Nile Valley they became in time the main stock of the Ethiopian population.

Quoting Sir Harry H. Johnston further at this junction in my lecture would only add much more of the racist type of logic that preceded Adolph Hitler and his Nazis bible - MEIN KAMPF. It does not mean that this so-called "authority" on Africa and African peoples will be forgotten. It does mean, however, that for the time being, in this lecture at least, others of his ilk shall be cited equally.

In the book, ART OF EGYPT, published by Charles Scribner's Sons, New York, 1892, on page V of the PREFACE, professor Gaston Maspero wrote:

> Primitive Art in Egypt before Menes (Aha or Narmer)[1] - Thinite Art and its Remains: Architecture, Fortresses, Places, Temples, Tombs - In it we may trace the Principles and Forms which, developing in the course of centuries, gave to Egyptian Art its characteristic aspect - Memphite Art was developed by contact with it.

Professor Maspero went on to show a multiplicity of paintings and sculptured statues with all forms of varied featural characteristics which are very seldom exhibited to the general public, all of them with their nose intact; most of the photographs of

---

1. Words in parentheses by your lecturer for clarity only.

them by Dr. E. Brugsch, and held in the Museum of Cairo, Egypt (North Africa). But where are they today? Why are they missing from our institutions of higher-learning?

William Palmer in his own religiously oriented works, EGYPTIAN CHRONICLES (Longman, Green, Longman, and Roberts, London, 1861, Vol's. I & II), relied very heavily on the works of the African High Priest - Manetho, Eusebius, and Syncellus. He also quoted from Josephus' works frequently; and placed very high confidence in the "Hieratic writings of the Africans" spoken of by the Greek chronicler - Diogenes Laertius. He pointed out that the "origin of all writings in the world" began first along the beginning of the Nile River below 15° (degree) north latitude, the same area Sir Harry H. Johnston felt was inhabited by "BIG BLACK NEGROES" whom he considered to be "BRUTISH." In showing the origin of the Narative in EXODUS (Second Book Of Moses of the Hebrew or Jewish Holy Torah, Christian Old Testament), Palmer wrote in Volume I, page xix of the "INTRODUCTION:"

> A still earlier King, Thotmes III (the fourth or fifth of Dyn. XVIII, according as his elder sister and her consort Thotmes II, are reckoned or omitted), is set by the monuments in a light in the highest degree remarkable. It is from his death that the narrative of the Exodus in the Scriptures commence: he was himself the chief oppressor of the Hebrews: and it is in a tomb of his reign that the Hebrews with their semi-Nubian taskmasters are still to be seen painted in the act of making bricks for the temple of Ammon.

Palmer did not qualify what he meant by a "semi-Nubian." That is equivalent to a 'semi-Negro,' since the Nubians have been designated "TRUE NEGROES" by most of the European and European-American educators - Jewish scholars included. Is Palmer indicating that the Jews, the so-called "Semites", were forced to associate with the "<u>Negroes</u>" - the"<u>anti-Nubians</u>"- and not mix with their fellow "<u>Semites</u>" - the <u>Egyptians</u>? The kings preceding, and immediately following Thotmes, were,by most of the European and European-American educators I **have** so far quoted, "<u>negrified Hamites</u>" or "<u>negrified Caucasians</u>." On page 57 of the same book Palmer wrote the following:

> Ham, perhaps, the ancestor of the Egyptians and Phoenicians, being the father of such as live in villages and towns, and Magus, who may stand for Shem the father of the Magi, being the father of such as keep flocks.

Palmer certainly knocked down two of the most favorite myths of modern educators in the field of history. The first: The "Phoenicians" as the children of "Ham;" thus they too were "CURSED" like the "NEGROES." Second: Shem, from whence the so-called "SEMITES" originated, also came from the same "CURSED" source; and of course the "Egyptians;" the latter of "CAUCASIAN STOCK" according to "modern" historians and other educators.

How is it that"modern" (or "Western") man of the late part of the 20th century C.E. could still give credence to the type of religous bigotry and racial hatred we find among so many of the 18th and 19th century C.E. Egyptologists, historians and religious theologians dealing with African history - or the racism they so designated by that name? We can see how such arrogance began and developed in the case of Burton and Speke, both Englishmen, with reference to their alleged "<u>discovery of the source of the Nile River</u>" on "<u>August 3, 1858 A.D.</u>" This he accomplished while the indigenous Africans of the Bonyoro Kingdom, modern Uganda and Buganda, watched him DISCOVERING it. This account is also mentioned in Sir Harry H. Johnston's book, THE NILE QUEST, Page 120. Sir

Harry wrote:

> Speke gathered together a caravan, and on the 30th of July ,1858, he saw the Mwanza creek,[1] one of the southernmost gulfs of the Victoria Nyanza.[2] The extremity of this he (Speke) named "Jordans Mullah."[3]

However, on page 121 Sir Harry H. Johnston continued his own description of Speke's "...DISCOVERY OF THE NILE'S SOURCE" in the following remarks:

> Speke inquired from the natives[4] the name of this fresh water sea, and they replied "NYANZA," which in varying forms such as Nyanja, Nyasa, Kianja, Luanza (according to prefix), is a widespread Bantu root for a large extent of water, - a river or a lake. To this Speke added the name Victoria (the despotic and murderous Queen of England he was serving at the time during her direction of British colonial expansion and partition in Africa)[5] after the Queen of England.

Just imagine naming the largest lake in Africa after a woman who was responsible for the murder of more Africans than Adolph Hitler killed Jews in his maniacal drive throughout Europe. Victoria was one of the original masters of genocide of the Christian Era.

The main points of the quotation from Speke, and the previous comments by Sir Harry H. Johnston, only indicate the extent to which the so-called "EXPLORERS" of the 19th century C.E. from Europe and Great Britain (England, Scotland, Ireland, Wales), and to some extent the United States of America, not only failed

---

1. "MWANZA" is the name of the largest lake in Africa. Here the Nile begins. "NYANZA" is the word for Lake in Kenda-based languages - such as KiSWAHILI.
2. "VICTORIA" is the name Speke used to substitute the Africans' "MWANZA" in his notorious contempt for the Africans.
3. This name Speke made up from a combination of two (2) words: "JORDAN" named after his home in Somersetshire, England; and "NULLAH" - a corruption of an East-Indian word for creek," ǎlla.
4. Did these African peoples have names? Who are "THE NATIVES"?
5. Words in parentheses by the lecturer for the sake of clarity.

to give recognition to the people and cultures they met in Alkebu-lan (Africa), but; how they also took upon themselves the "authority" of renaming people and things in total disregard and contempt of their African hosts - the indigenous people. In the first place "MWANZA" was, and still is, not the name of a "creek." It is still the name of the "LAKE" Speke selected to add the name of one of the most vile personality in world history - Queen Victoria of England. To the Africans this insult is similar to Adolph Eichman entering Israel and renaming the Negev in honor of Adolph Hitler of Nazis Germany - his Furher. For, to the African people who had the unfortunate fate of dealing with Victoria and her ilk, through her so-called "explorers" and "entreprenuers" (storm troopers) such as Speke and Burton, Rhodes[1] and Lugard, Stanley (also of America - the U.S.A.), and a host of other despots like herself that raped Africa and her people, even before the birth of Adolph Hitler and Adolph Eichman, she was worse than any CURSE mentioned in the Hebrew, Christian and Islamic Holy Scriptures; and more bestial than any despot that ever lived before and after her. Academic "scholarship" requires that my comments with respect to Victoria be much more subdued. Why should any writer of African origin so act in cases such as this; in view of the BLACK EXPERIENCE she caused, along with others of her ilk, to be ranked with genocide, racism, and religious bigotry against African peoples up to the present day? These comments are in answer to atrocities committed by many of those whom you may have considered major contributors to "Western civilization" or "the American way of life;" either term which in itself cannot be correctly separated from the definite carry-over from the dommi-

---

1. The man for whom the "RHODES SCHOLARSHIP" is named. 19th century master of genocide against the Africans of South and South-east Africa.

nant influence Africa and Asia played in them; and the reverberation they in turn have to the present time in the so-called "BLACK-WHITE CONFRONTATION in the United States of America.

John Hanning Speke - a native of Britain, born on May 27, 1827, at Orleigh Court, Bedford, North Devon,- was himself a result of name changing, his ancestors having changed their family (or Sir) name from its original Norman - "L'Espec"- during the 13th century C.E. One could sympathize with Speke; since the original name stands for "PORCUPINE" or "SPIKE NAIL," both being of one of the original names for Norman slaves; and both having appeared on his family's CREST. His father, William Speke, made his living and fortune off two (2) churches of the Christian religion (Anglican Church, an English sect of the Christian religion) which he, like most of the other "members of the cloth " during said period, and to a large degree today, operated for his own personal benifit and extensive fortune through its profits. Speke was an officer in the Indian army Britain established for the control and enslavement of the so-called "SUB-CONTINENT OF ASIA" - India - and its peoples. It was, however, the "SOMALI EXPEDITION" in which the British military forces slaughtered the African population to seize their homeland and natural resources that Speke joined (Sir) Richard Burton as his surveyor, upon orders issued by Colonel Sir James Outram - who over-ruled Speke's commander at Bombay, India (an opponent of the "EXPEDITION" that was launched in 1857 C.E.).

The "EXPEDITION TO THE HEAD WATERS OF THE Nile" also included many other crack sharpshooters of the British militia, even Captain James Augustus Grant - who served with Speke and

Burton in the British attempts at genocide against the Indian people in their efforts to subdue them in order to steal their natural resources, which they finally accomplished until their expulsion by Mohandas Karanchand Ghandi and his followers.

Since this lecture is not geared to the life and times of Speke or Burton, I must return to the main point; but, I must first cite that Burton and Speke fell out over their African enterprise; Speke having gotten the robbery bug before Burton did and left him for their own native homeland - England - in 1859 C.E. where he immediately, upon landing, proclaimed that he alone had "...DISCOVERED THE SOURCE OF THE NILE RIVER...," etc. Speke's lies eventually caught-up with him upon the subsequent arrival of Burton in England; and the presentation of substantial proof and documents by Burton indicating that he was in fact the FIRST EUROPEAN (Englishman, and that is all he was) to see the "...SOURCE OF THE NILE..." (the White Nile) in central Africa. He was not its "...DISCOVER...;" a claim he made. Why not? Because there were millions upon millions of indigenous Africans - the so-called "Negroes, Bantus, Africans South of the Sahara," etc., who lived and visited along the entire Nile River and its source - MWANZA NYANZA - before any European, including the Greeks of Herodotus' era (c457 BCE) who wanted to find out the same information. Speke and Burton (as well as hundreds more from Europe and European-America) sought.

In 1860 C.E. the ROYAL GEOGRAPHICAL SOCIETY of Great Britain did award Burton its Gold Medal for his "...DISCOVERY..." and withdrew its recognition of Speke. It was neccessary to cite the background of these two major characters in order that you can clearly visualize the type of Europeans and European-Americans that came to Africa (Alkebu-lan) with the title of "ADVENTURER, EXPLORER, CHRISTIAN MISSIONARY," etc., etc., etc.; almost endlessly the titles were, and still are to the present day.

"THE NILE QUEST" did not bring to the areas of central Africa Speke and Burton alone. There were countless others, as I have indicated before, many of whom became such failure in their military adventures that their own European, British, or European-American history failed to mention their existence as subjects or citizens, muchless "EXPLORERS." Of those who did not make history for themselves like Burton and Speke, the most outstanding were: Samuel White Baker of London, England - son of the owner of a most extensive slave plantation on the Island of Jamaica, British West Indies, and Mauritus in the Indian Ocean (an island laying off the coast of today's Malagasy Republic, formerly called Madagascar by the French colonialist that invaded and conquered it); the French Jesuit priest - Father Brèvedent - early as 1699 C.E.; the Pope's own personal missionary representative, a Maronite priest, Father Gabriel, whom the Pope dispatched from his Cairo, Egypt, base to find one Father Poncet - who had succeded Father Brèvedent upon his death in Ethiopia (called "Abyssinia" at the time); Joseph le Roux - the Count of Deseval, a former nobleman in the Danish Navy (of French birth) in 1739 C.E. left out from Cairo, Egypt, and reached as far as Nubia (modern Sudan). The <u>Portuguese</u> (at the time called "Portugals") sent more Roman Catholic priests, such as the Jesuits - Alvarez, Lobo, and Paez. These Portugals received their information from data collected by the German philologist - Ludolf, who relied heavily on information received from

Ethiopian ambassadors and travelers in Italy. In 1772 C.E. a Frenchman named D'Anville published a fantastic story and map purported to be the geographical area at the "NILE'S HEADWATERS;" at the time the Blue Nile in Ethiopia, which begins at Lake Tana in the Ethiopian highlands, was considered the only source of the main Nile River that flows into the Kimit Sea (today's Mediterranean Sea). The map and/or graph published by D'Anville he did compose in his own studio from bits of information he gathered while speaking to German, Portuguese and Dutch travelers who had visited Ethiopia and Nubia for the purpose of their own "NILE QUEST." Jean Baptiste Bourguignon d'Anville, born at Paris, France, in 1697 C.E., had stirred-up enough fantacy among his fellow Europeans over the "Nile's Headwaters" to cause sufficient panic that they revived the age-old "KING SOLOMON'S MINE" myth in the same area of the "HEADWATERS." Some even claimed that at the "Headwaters" was the "...ORIGINAL PLACE OF THE TRUE BIRTH OF JESUS CHRIST OF NAZZARETH...." Others claimed that "...IT WAS IN ABYSSINIA...." (modern Ethiopia).

The following is a facimile of the map by D'Anville. It is displayed for your examination, because it was not disputed until after Burton actually became the first European (a Britisher) to see the "true Headwaters of the Nile River" at Mwanza Nyanza. In order to make a comparison between Burton's finding and D'Anville's hipocracy, I have also included Burton's map of December 1864 C.E., erroneous as that too is.

There were literally hundreds of other maps filed all over Europe, England and the United States of America that prentended to be "...A TRUE MAP OF THE SOURCE OF THE NILE RIVER," etc. The

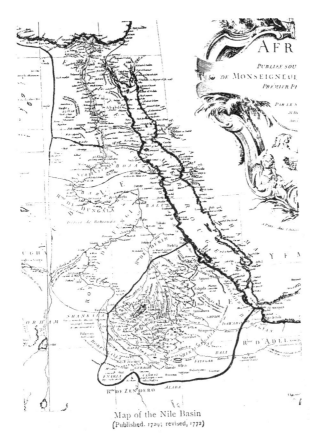

Map of the Nile Basin
(Published. 1729; revised, 1772)

Map by D'Anville in 1772 C.E.

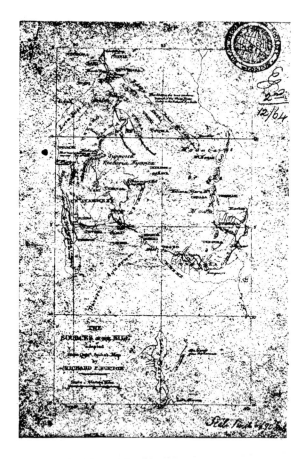

MAP by Burton in 1864 C.E.

first European map of the Nile dates back to Herodotus; but it was the Ptolemies who most educators generally look to for the earliest map of the area. The following map is one of them, a version dated back to 930 C.E., which is still in the possession of the Mount Athos Monastery.

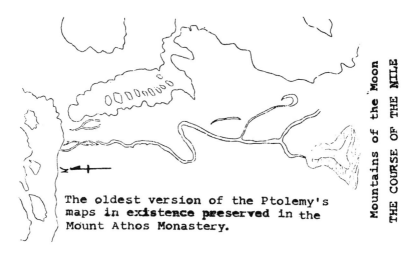

The oldest version of the Ptolemy's maps in existence preserved in the Mount Athos Monastery.

MAP of Ptolomey 930 C.E.

Continuing the list of "DISCOVERERS" of the Nile's source; we find that one Samuel Baker, whom I have described partially before, according to his biographer - Douglas Murray, was a <u>soldier of fortune</u> at the end of the Crimean War. He became the "...<u>general-manager of the British-built and operated railroad</u> ..." that operated between the Danube and the Black Sea, where he met and married a Hungarian woman named Florence Ninian von Sass (later on Lady Baker). In 1861 C.E. both Baker and his wife arrived at Cairo, Egypt, for his fling at the <u>Nile's source</u>. He then challenged the Atbara River, rather than attempt the southern route beyond Gondokoro Thus, he became one of the first European to see the last tributary of the main Nile before it enters Kimit (Egypt) from Nubia (Sudan). He turned back before he could reach Khartoun, which he called "KHARTUM." Baker and his wife started out to find Speke's source in March 1863 C.E., and wound up at what he selected to call "ALBERT NYANZA" (or "Lake Albert") in honor of his king- Albert of England, thereby refusing to recognize the correct name the Africans of the region named their lake thousands of years before there was an England in world history; they named it - "LUTA NZIGE."

Is it not very peculiar to you that no one named any of the so-called "DISCOVERIES" after one of the thousands of African names in the area; or even allow at least one of the places with the name they found? It should not be. Why? Because the history of these alleged "EXPLORATIONS" and "EXPLORERS" were written in a manner to make the <u>colonialist exploiters</u> (both male and female, most of whom were misfits in Europe, Great Britain and the United States of America) appear to be heroes and heroines. The indigenous Africans, whom the so-called "EXPLORERS" preferred to call "<u>Hamites, Nilotics, Negroes, Arabized Negroes</u>," etc., for the most part, looked like the pictures following (from Baker's

A Man of Unyoro

A Swahili Arab Trader

and Speke's portfollios. Of course you are, by now, confused as to just who or what was, and is, an "ARAB, SWAHILI" or "NEGRO" - according to the professors you have had in "African Studies" and/or "Black Studies" courses. It is true that these men, under any circumstance whatsoever, could not reach one (1) solitary mile beyond the Mediterranean Sea were it not for the hundreds of indigenous Africans whom they preferred to call by their sir name - "NATIVES")who commandered them to "...THE SOURCE OF THE WHITE" or "BLUE NILE" and "ATBARA RIVER;" yet, not one of these Africans do we here in the United States of America's system of higher education know by any of their African names. Why? Because of racist arrogance on the part of the so-called educational system established by those who think and act in the same manner as the so-called "EXPLORERS" and "AFRICAN HISTORIANS" who write biographies and other adventure stories related to Africa and African peoples. This is the same reason why we can still display pictures of "SCOUTS, PORTERS, GUIDES, CONFIDANTS," etc., but no 'co-EXPLORERS' or 'co-DISCOVERERS' of indigenous African origin in their own continent's history written in our textbooks. Not even 'ENTERPRETERS' are connected to the name "NATIVE" or "THE NATIVES" given the Africans by their slavemasters. In the same vein reports, now labeled "HISTORY," of alleged "EXPLORERS" are, and were, written, and will continue to be written by such European and European-American-types, until Africans and their fellow African peoples in the so-called "Western World" begin to set their own AUTHORITY over NORTH, NORTHEAST and EAST African history and heritage as they are now beginning to do with respect to all of West and West-Central Africa. Because of this reason

I do not hold European and European-American (White) writers of current vintage culpable; for no man should be expected to write objectively of another man (in equal honor) unless they are both from mutual beginning or origin. The slavemaster equally cannot be expected to write about the slave as he writes of himself. For the same reason no one can teach Africa's history as well as an African historian of nationalist orientation can. I know these two sentences will bring down the cries of the "LIBERALS" and other "DO-GOODERS;" but, I rely solely upon the evidence (called "FACTS"), and look about and around you for my conclusion. Check the holdings in your college's library, and all the other libraries of the other major institutions of higher learning, religious and secular, also your book stores, and see if you do not reach the same conclusion I have reached.

You may not have connected my reason for being emotionally bitter about the insult to the African people by the changes of their names and their personal properties or lands and other things by European and European-American "EXPLORERS, ENTREPRENUERS, CHRISTIAN MISSIONARIES" and others, including 'BIG BAD GAME HUNTERS on Safaris. If you have not, consider the problems their caused the Africans, even locally in their school rooms under European and European-American so-called "MISSIONARIES", most of whom were totally qualified solely for the role as MIS-EDUCATORS; all of whom had no use for anything BLACK in color other than to allegedly "...CARRY THE WORDS OF JESUS CHRIST TO THE HEATHEN NATIVES." Of course it is Michaelangelo's conception of a northern blonde Italian God, JESUS CHRIST, from a black or brown Palestine or Israel is the God in question presented to the

"...HEATHEN NATIVES...."

The NILE QUEST became so impulsive that the United States of America also joined the mad rush to the Nile's headwaters. The entries from the "New World" were two: - C. Chaille-Long and Dr. Donald-Smith. The latter traversed an area of Africa in 1900 C.E. bounded on the north by Lake Asua (renamed "RUDOLF" by the British colonialists) and to the southern limits by the rivers Tu, Kos and Oguelokur. The Kos River flows in a northerly direction like the White Nile, and to its north is the Mountain of the Nile and its branch water - the Giraffe River.

On pages 319-321 of Sir Harry H. Johnston's THE NILE QUEST the following partial list of Europeans and European-Americans, including Britons, who tried to chart the course of the Nile River and its tributaries up until the early part of the 20th century C.E. is given. This list only includes those who made attempts at establishing geographic maps and charts in which they plotted land and water routes for future colonialist exploitation and the PARTITION of the African continent. Included are 3 European-Americans, 34 Britishers (21 English, 2 Irish, 8 Scots and 3 Welch), 10 Germans, 13 Frenchmen, 4 Italians, 3 Portuguese, 2 Dutchmen, 2 Belgians, 2 Swiss, 3 Austrian-Hungarians, and 1 Turk; all of whom were <u>misfits</u> in their own homeland but found recognition and glory in the missery they caused the indigenous Africans.(U.S.A. citizens and Britishers, pp 221-222; others p 227)

NAME	NATIONALITY	NAME	NATIONALITY
C. Chaillé-Long	United States.	M. S. Wellby	British (English)
Mason (Bey)	United States.	H. H. Austin	" "
Donaldson Smith	United States.	R. G. T. Bright	" "
Malcolm Peake	British (Scottish)	C. W. Hobley	" "
Weld Blundell	" (English)	Ewart Gregan	" "
Benjamin Whitehouse	" "	J. E. S. Moore	" "
G. W. Gwynn	" (Welsh)	Malcolm Fergusson	" (Scottish)

221

NAME	NATIONALITY	NAME	NATIONALITY
Richard Pococke	British (English)	William Browne	" (English)
James Bruce	" (Scottish)	Joseph Thomson	British (Scottish)
Charles George Gordon	British (English)	Frederick Dealtry Lugard	" (English)
Henry Moreton Stanley	British (Welsh)	Seymour Vandeleur	" (Irish)
Mansfield Parkyns	British (English)	G. F. Scott-Elliot	" (Scottish)
Charles T. Beke	" "	H. H. Wilson	British (English)
C. T. Wilson	British (English)	E. A. Stanton	British (English)
R. W. Felkin	" (Scottish)	William Garstin	British (Irish)
C. M. Watson	British (English)	John Hanning Speke	British (English)
John Petherick	British (Welsh)	James Augustus Grant	" (Scottish)
James R. Lennox Macdonald	British (Scottish)	Samuel White Baker	" (English)
		Charles Delmé Radcliffe	" (English)

It was, however, not until 1901 C.E. that Major C. Delmé Radcliffe, another British military catagrapher , made the first truly comprehensive map of the Nile River - from Luta Nzige (Lake Albert) to Godokoro, showing the true affluents of Lake Asuas (Lake Rudolf), other minor streans related thereto, and the highlands of the Acholi and Nadi region, along with the stretch of land Gondokoro and Luta Nzige.

But, what impelling magic caused these 19th and 20th century military pirates to search for the headwaters of the Nile River? It was Sir Edwin Arnold, another of the almost endless British colonialists, who first demanded that Britain's influence be not only diplomatic between the so-called Cape of Good Hope (the tip of the Monomotapa Empire - South Africa) to Cairo (the tip of Kimit or Sais; today's Egypt or United Arab Republic - U.A.R.) but, also, in land area. This imperialist declaration was made as early as 1876 C.E., and adopted by the man from whom Adolph Hitler of Nazis Germany must have copied a few tricks in his pattern of genocide in Europe against the defenseless Jews - one Cecil Rhodes in 1892 C.E. Rhodes' hangmen, Ewart Grogan and Major C. Sharpe, attempted to carryout this task when they established their route from the Cape but were only able to reach no further than Lake Gallop (the British colonialists renamed it Lake Albert-Edward). The same course established by these three colonialist pirates was later followed by two more colonialist British military geographers - Major A. St. Hill Gibbons in 1900, Lionel Decle in 1901, and sometime between 1898-1902 Colonel E. A. Stanton - who surveyed a path along the Bahr-al-Ghazal and the low-lands of the Mountain of the Nile - follwed suit.

What has been unfolded before you, my students and auditors of this course, is THE NILE QUEST from the time of the Roman Emperor Nero's two (2) centurions attempt to reach beyond the Second Cataract in Nubia around the year 66 C.E. to Speke and Burton's partial success in the "modern" or "Christian Era;" and the earlier attempts by Herodotus in 457 B.C.E. and others after until Nero; all of whom tried to scale the Nile Valley high-lands of central-north and central-east Africa in search of the BLUE and WHITE NILE sources, also the ATBARA RIVER.

What other significant factor we must take very serious note of in these militarist "EXPLORATIONS" of the Nile River and its affluents and tributaries? The answer to this question was given by Sir Harry H. Johnston on page 276 of the same work we are presently surveying. Under the heading - "THE EASTERN BASIN OF THE NILE," Chapter XXVI, he wrote the following:

> Bruce had broken the spell which rested on this strange country (Ethiopia, which Johnston called Abyssinia)[1], so facinating to Europeans, because while being alsolutely "Africa" it was ruled, and for the most part inhabited, by more or less <u>Caucasian races</u>,[2] its rulers having a <u>Semitic history</u> which attached them to the fountains of civilizations.

---
1. Words in parentheses by your professor for clarity only.
2. Words underscored for special emphasis in further explanation and analysis.

It is needless for me to belabor the words and phrases underscored in the above statement. Never-the-less, in closing this lecture-essay, I would like that you remember that Sir Harry H. Johnston, like all of the others who claimed "CAUCASIAN" or "SEMITIC" origin for north and east Africa, has not, to this very day in history, submitted one iota of evidence to substantiate his racist and bigoted theories or claims. What is a "CAUCASIAN"? What is "SEMITE"? Who decides just who fall into these catagories? How many known as "CAUCASIANS" and "SEMITES" today who cannot pass this test are there? How many "NEGROES" or "NIGGERS" were, and still are, most honoured members of the "CAUCASIAN" and "SEMITIC RACE" within your own group? These are but a very few of the questions you are confronted with, and you must answer sooner or later. The most challenging of them is:

> WHO CAN TRACE THEIR ANCESTRY BEYOND A BLACK
> HERITAGE AFTER THE CARTHAGINIANS, ETHIOPIANS,
> MOORS, EGYPTIANS, NUBIANS AND OTHER AFRICANS
> ENTERED EUROPE AS CONQUERORS?

And, who will dare challenge their African (Ethiopian or Black) ancestry after....

> MOSES AND ALL OF THE HEBREWS FROM c1630 B.C.E.
> OR EARLIER TO c1298-1232 B.C.E. WERE BORN IN
> SLAVERY TO "BIG BLACK AFRICAN NEGROES" IN
> KIMIT (Egypt); MOSES' WIFE (the daughter of
> the High-Priest of Kush, Ethiopia or Abyssi-
> nia) BEING HERSELF A "NEGRO".

Less we forget; the "SEMITES" came to Kimit and other lands of the Nile Valley and the African Great Lakes to receive their

FIRST GLANCE into CIVILIZATION; not the Africans entered Asia or Europe for said experience. What is being noted here with respect to the "SEMITES" equally applies to the so-called "LIGHT" and "DARK-SKINNED CAUCASIANS."

A BRIEF SUGGESTED BIBLIOGRAPHY FOR THIS LECTURE

Sir E. H. Bunbury, HISTORY OF ANCIENT GEOGRAPHY, London, 1879.
T. Desborough Cooley, PTOLEMY AND THE NILE, London, 1854.
W.M. Flinders Petrie, HISTORY OF EGYPT, London, 1902 (4 vols.).
Sir E. A. Wallis Budge, HISTORY OF EGYPT, London, 1902 (13 vols).
Dr. J. Scott Keltie, PARTITION OF AFRICA, London, 1895 (2nd Ed.).
Bartolomeo Tellez, A VOYAGE TO ABYSSINIA, London, 1735.
C.S. Sonnini de Manoncourt, TRAVELS IN UPPER AND LOWER EGYPT (transl. by H. Hunter into English), London, 1799.
Count. C.F. Volney, RUINS OF EMPIRE, Paris, 1830.
William G. Browne, TRAVELS IN AFRICA, EGYPT, AND SYRIA, London, 1860.
A. Linant de Bellefonds, JOURNAL OF NAVIGATION ON THE BAHR-EL-ABIAD OR THE WHITE NILE, 1828 (African Associates), London.
John Louis Buckhardt, TRAVELS IN NUBIA, London, 1819.
John Petherick, EGYPT, THE SUDAN, AND CENTRAL AFRICA, London, 1861.
Mansfield Parkyns, LIFE IN ABYSSINIA, London, 1867.
Sir Samuel Baker, M.A., THE ALBERT NYANZA, London, 1866.
Dr. J.L. Krapf, TRAVELS, RESEARCHES, AND MISSIONARY LABOURS, 1860.
Captain J.H. Speke, WHAT LED TO THE DISCOVERY OF THE NILE SOURCES, London, 1864.
R.F. Burton, THE LAKE REGIONS OF CENTRAL AFRICA, 1860.
J.H. Speke, JOURNAL OF THE DISCOVERY OF THE SOURCE OF THE NILE, 1864.
H.M. Stanley, THROUGH THE DARK CONTINENT, 1877 (2 vols.).
Sir E.A. Arnold, Colonel J.A. Grant, et al., REMARKS ON A PROPOSED LINE OF TELEGRAPH OVERLAND FROM EGYPT TO THE CAPE OF GOOD HOPE, London, 1876.
Colonel C. Chaille-Long, CENTRAL AFRICA: NAKED TRUTHS OF NAKED PEOPLE, London, 1876.
Dr. Wilhelm Junker, TRAVELS IN AFRICA DURING THE YEARS 1875-78; 1879-1883; 1882-1886; 1890, 1891, 1892.
H.M. Stanley, IN DARKEST AFRICA, 1890 (2 vols.).
E. Grogan and A. Sharp, THE CAPE TO CAIRO, 1900.
J.E. Moore, THE MOUNTAINS OF THE MOON, 1902.
Captain M.S. Wellby, KING MENELIK'S DOMINIONS AND THE COUNTRY BETWEEN LAKE GALLOP (Rudolf) AND THE NILE, London, 1900 (Geographical Journal for September).
Dr. Robert Brown, THE STORY AFRICA (4 vols.), 1893-1895.
Colonel Stanton's articles), THE JOURNAL OF THE AFRICAN SOCIETY, London, 1955 (4 vols.).

All of the works mentioned I have personally examined or read in their entirety; the vast majority of which you have had the opportunity of being exposed to. Except for Count C.F. Volney's RUINS OF EMPIRE, and Professor C.P. Groves' THE PLANTING OF CHRISTIANITY IN AFRICA, they were all used by sir Harry H. Johnston in the preparation of his work, THE NILE QUEST. You may still use my personal library for all of the works written by Sir Harry H. Johnston, Speke , Burton, and a host of the other so-called "EXPLORERS" and "CHRISTIAN MISSIONARIES" who came to Africa under the pretext of "DISCOVERERS". The <u>Arthur Olonzo Schumburg Collection</u> of the Cuntee Cullen Public Library of the City of New York, Harlem, New York City, is another major source which you can use in the preparation of your own essay on this topic. The Central Library of the City of New York at 42nd Street is another source to be peruse in this regards. Suggested private collections of works on this area and others related to the entire course outline are the following: <u>Professor John Henrike</u> Clarke's Collection; Richard B. Moore's Collection; Clarence <u>Holt's Holte's Collection; Professor Sieffert's Collection</u>. The last three collections are all located in the Harlem area also. Of all the <u>Collections</u> the Schumberg is the most complete and extensive. Neither of them are you permitted to borrow any of the works; most of which are out of print at the present time.

 For extra information towards accomplishing the best essay you can prepare the following works should be added to your already extensive list: Sir Edward Hertslett, THE MAP OF AFRICA BY TREATY, London, 1898 (3 vols.); Parker T. Moon, IMPERIALISM AND WORLD POLITICS, New York, 1930; and George Padmore, AFRICA: BRITAIN'S THIRD EMPIRE, New York, 1946.

  The NILE QUEST is just another story of how the Africans

were used and misused by pirates and other thieves under the disguise of "ENTREPRENUERS, EXPLORERS, CHRISTIAN MISSIONARIES, WHITE, SETTLERS, BIG GAME HUNTERS, FRIENDS," etc., etc., etc., almost without end. Yet, it was these same characters who were the ones taht turned out to be the <u>enslavers</u> of the African peoples and the <u>rapers</u> of their land - Alkebu-lan, "MOTHER AFRICA."

(list from p.p. 221-222 cont'd)

NAME	NATIONALITY	NAME	NATIONALITY
Johann Ludwig Burckhardt	Swiss.	A. H. Dyé	French.
Frederic Cailliaud	French.	J. B. Marchand	"
Adolphe Linant de Bellefonds	Belgian.	Franz Stuhlmann	German.
Prokesch von Osten	German.	Oscar Baumann	"
Eduard Rüppell	German.	Vittorio Bottego	Italian.
Selim Bimbashi	Turk.	Romolo Gessi	Italian
Thibaut	French.	Lionel Décle	French.
D'Arnaud	"	WILHELM JUNKER	Russo-German.
FERDINAND WERNE	German.	Edouard Linant de Bellefonds	Belgian.
Brun-Rollet	French.	Oscar Neumann	German.
Ignatz Knoblecher	Austrian.	Alfred Peney	French.
ANTOINE THOMSON D'ABBADIE	French-Irish.	Lejean	"
Arnaud d'Abbadie	" "	Werner Munzinger	Swiss.
Johann Maria Schuver	Dutch.	Theodor von Heuglin	German
Ernest Marno	Austrian.	Alexandrine Tinne	Dutch.
EMIN (EDUARD SCHNITZER)	German (Silesia).	De Malzac	French.
Florence Baker	Hungarian.	De Bonchamps	French.
Giovanni Miani	Italian (Venetian)	Francisco Alvarez	Portuguese.
GEORG SCHWEINFURTH	Russo-German.	Pedro Paez	"
Piaggia	Italian.	JERONIMO LOBO	"

Submitted: November 1970 for students perusal, analytical analysis, and citicism. A paper of at least 2,500 words (properly documented) is expected.

RACISM, HISTORIANS, AND ETHIOPIA

A Lecture-Essay

by

Yosef ben - Jochannan
Adj. Assoc. Prof. Pace College, N.Y.C.

If I was asked;which nation in Africa "Western" historians and other "educators" exert most of their racist interpretations on its history and people? I would be compelled to say it is no other than Ethiopia, East Africa. Even the so-called "LIBERAL WRITER" on Africa and things African, Basil Davidson, found it necessary to exert his own subtle type of White racism when the question; who were the Ethiopians? arose. Thus, on page 46 of his book, THE AFRICAN PAST: CHRONICLES FROM ANTIQUITY TO MODERN TIMES, Little, Brown and Company (Boston, Toronto), 1964, we find Davidson saying:

> On circumcision, for example, "as between the Egyptians and the Ethiopians [that is, the Kushites], I should not like to say which learned from the other . . ." As to the skin color of the Egyptians, he recalls the story of a dove connected with the Egyptian oracle at Dodona. This bird was said to have been black. Why black? "As to the bird being black," says Herodotus, "they merely signify by this that the woman was an Egyptian." Explaining why the Colchians "are of Egyptian descent," he suggests that they may have descended from Egyptian soldiers who had served under Sesostris, a Pharaoh whose armies had invaded the Near East. But "my own idea on the subject was based first on the fact that they [the Colchians] have black skins and woolly hair (not that that amounts to much, as other nations have the same), and secondly, and more especially, on the fact that the Colchians, the Egyptians, and the Ethiopians [the Kushites] are the only races which from ancient times have practiced circumcision." "Black" notwithstanding, it will be rash to build any "racial" conclusions from this much-commented passage: what interested Herodotus was not the "racial" origins of people but their habits and relationships.

Why was it necessary for Davidson to vere completely from the context of his subject to interject that "...WHAT INTERESTED

HERODOTUS WAS NOT THE RACIAL ORIGINS OF THE PEOPLE"(Colchians, Ethiopians, Egyptians) "BUT THEIR HABITS AND RELATIONSHIP...." Herodotus did pay very special and articulate attention and deepest interest to the racial origins of the Colchians, Ethiopians and Egyptians all over his most noted work, THE HISTORIES; and he most definitely referred to their color, texture of hair, facial characteristics, and "<u>burnt skin</u>." I believe Davidson gave the answer to his own racism on page 7 under the sub-title, "<u>The Stages of the Past</u>." He wrote:

> Most historical writing has reflected man's disunity. In spite of the liberal example of Herodotus, whose sympathies and interests far outleaped the borders of the Greek world, historians have generally written (and no doubt it could not be otherwise) from a firmly and even narrowly national standpoint. The good ones made the best of this limitation; the bad ones, becoming xenophobic, made the worst of it: with few exceptions none achieved or desired to achieve, or even thought they could achieve if they had wished, what is now called a world view. This is why great segments of historical experience have often become lost or undervalued.

Why was it necessary for Davidson, like most of the other European and European-American self-proclaimed "AUTHORITIES" on Africa and the Africans, to deny Herodotus' RACIAL interest in the indigenous Africans of the Nile Valley and other parts of North and East Africa? To support the <u>long-standing racist myth</u> of a "SEMITIC" and "CAUCASIAN" north and east Africa that was free of the so-called "TRUE NEGROES, BANTUS, AFRICANS SOUTH OF THE SAHARA," etc. Said "FREE" area also included "NUBIA" and the "NUBIANS" - who, although located between the Kushites (Ethiopians) and Romiti (Egyptians), are said to have been "TRUE NEGROES;" but not their neighbours - Romiti and Kushites - to their north and east. If Herodotus' conclusion on this very point is to go unchallenged, it mean that almost everything created and developed in Kimit, Kush and Colchis up until c1675 B.C.E. were done by people whose descendants are today called "NEGROES, NIGGERS," and "INFERIORS," etc. among other degrading names. For it was not until c1675 B.C.E. that the first non-indigenous African peoples entered ALKEBU-LAN (Africa by the Greeks and Romans). These foreigners came from around the Oxus River valley region of what was once called ASIA-MINOR, later on EUR-ASIA, today's MIDDLE-EAST. Up until this period there is no record available to show that the first "CAUCASIANS, SEMITES", or "HAMITES" were even in existence in the Caucaus Mountains where they were supposed to have originated. Certainly Basil Davidson is aware of these facts. If he is not, one must assume that he is not much of a reliable source on which to depend for information relating to "THE AFRICAN PAST," which, incidentally, is the title of his book in question. If Davidson's book was unique in its <u>racist interpretation</u> of basic African heritage and High-culture, I would have been disturbed; but, it is quite normal for Europeans and European-Americans (Caucasians, Semites, Indo-European-Aryans - Judaeo-Christians included) to write everyone's history from a <u>racist reference</u> of their own history, traditions, religion and culture, relating everything from the Greeks; and all that falls short of their own origin must be treated as "PRIMITIVE PAGAN INFERIORITY," etc.; they, knowing too well that it is all based upon a NEGROPHOBIC SYNDROME. Being aware of all of this, I must state that this continues because of the callousness of African-American and African (Black or Ethiopian) historians and other educators inside and outside of so-called "BLACK STUDIES" courses departments throughout intitutions of higher-learning. Why? Because it is they who sit idly by and allow everyone to write contemptuously about Black People - the so-called "NEGROES". The same people who would cry <u>bloody murder</u> should the Africans or African-Americans even suggest they intended to write as AUTHORITIES on CAUCASIAN, SEMITIC or INDO-EUROPEAN-ARYAN history and culture (civilization). In this regards one must remember how Basil Davidson, C. G. Selligman, Professor M.D.W. Jeffreys, Dr. Donald Weidner, and others of their ilk, would respond if an African or African-American historian dared suggest that 'THE JEWS ARE NOT A RACE;' or that one could be a "NEGRO" and still qualify as a "SEMITE;" both of which are TRUE; never-the-less they are not commonly taught as such by any of the men named, nor most of their contemporaries.

How was it possible for the Cushites (Ethiopians or Blacks) directly to the south of the Nubians (Sudanese) - the so-called "TRUE NEGROES", and the Romiti (Egyptians, also called Ethiopians by the ancient Greeks and Romans) directly to the Nubians' north, not to have been one common "RACE" of people after living together for thousands upon thousands of years; each having ruled over the others politically and militarily at various intervals throughout antiquity; even as late as the dynastic periods.

Ethiopia is especially important in the sense of its religious significance, if nothing else, to the Haribus (Hebrews or "Jews") of today; particularly for those presently living in its north-western regions of Gondar Province - the BETA ISRAEL, otherwise called "FALASA" or "FALASHA", correctly "CHILDREN OF THE HOUSE OF ISRAEL" or "HOUSE OF ISRAEL." For it is with the

Ethiopian Hebrews ("Jews" as a misnomer) that the so-called "TABLET OF MOSES" was intrusted after the founding of the SALOMONIC DYNASTY by Ethiopia's first Emperor - Melenik I, the "SON OF KING SOLOMON OF ISRAEL AND QUEEN MAKEDA" (Queen of Sheba) " OF AXUM" (the ancient capital of Etiopia) - according to the ETHIOPIAN CHRONICLES or KEBRA NEGAST (Chronicles of the Kings). For added data on the meeting and mating of this great African Queen, once "the greatest beauty of all women," who boasted:

"I AM BLACK AND COMELY"

to King Solomon, contact the Hebrew HOLY TORAH (Christian OLD TESTAMENT), Book Of Kings I : X, before it was changed to read:

"I AM BLACK, BUT COMELY",

by racist and bigoted so-called "theologians" and other self-proclaimed "INSPIRED " revisionists of Europe and the United States of America, Great Britain included. I KINGS X, states:

> "...When the Queen of Sheba[1] heard of the fame of King Solomon concerning the name of the Lord (the Jews' God - Ywh or Jehovah)[2], she came to prove him with hard questions. And she came to Jerusalem with a very great caravan, with camels that bare spices, very much gold, and precious stones.... And King Solomon gave unto the Queen of Sheba all that she desired, whatever she asked for, beside that which Solomon gave her of his royal bounty. She then returned to her own land."

Besides these things, according to ancient Hebrew writings by the Ethiopian Falasha "HOLY SCRIBES", Queen (or Empress) Makeda also returned to Ethiopia, or Axum, "...PREGNANT FOR KING SOLOMON OF ISRAEL;" said pregnancy resulting in her one and only child, Emperor Menelik I, for whom she abdicated her throne; he, thereby,

---

1. This is another of the many names by which MAKEDA was called by the ancients of her time. Sheba was a colony of Ethiopia.
2. Words in parentheses by your lecturer for clarity only.

establishing Ethiopia as "...A HEBREW NATION...," etc. The entire details of this historic account could be seen in the KEBRA NEGAST or GLORY OF KINGS. The present vintage follows the revised version that dates back to approximately c125 C.E., when Ethiopia had already become a <u>Coptic</u> (or Koptic) <u>nation</u>. It is to be noted that the KEBRA NEGAST refers to Emperor Menelik I as "EBNA-HAKIN." Another work in which details relating to this aspect of Ethiopian history is called the "SERATA-MANGEST" or ORDER OF THE REALM. It is the book from which the history of Ethiopia was read during the CORONATION CEREMONIES of a new Emperor or Empress. This custom has continued unabated since the founding of the first capital city - AXUM or AKHSUM (also Aksum); presently it is performed infront of the Cathedral of St. Mary of Zion.

Queen AZEB - the correct Ethiopian name for the Queen of Sheba - was also "QUEEN OF THE SOUTH," which included Puanit and lands extending all the way into India in southern Asia. Fantastic accounts of her beauty that spread all over the known world of her era did not surpass her skill and cunning as a ruler and conqueror; all being no reason why she declared, according to the Hebrew "SACRED SCRIPTURES".

"I AM BLACK AND BEAUTIFUL YE DAUGHTERS OF ISRAEL."
Is it not shameful that so-called "modern theologians" and "historians" have the world's most beautiful woman of her day saying to the King of Israel, Solomon, her equal in rank:

"I AM BLACK, BUT COMELY".

Does it make sense that this woman, wealthier than Solomon by degrees beyond imagination, head of an empire more than five (5) times the size of Solomon's Israel, wise as Solomon, rated the

"MOST BEAUTIFUL ON EARTH," would have felt remorseful over the COLOR OF HER SKIN; particularly when the "WORLD'S MOST POWERFUL MAN and RULER," also "WISE MAN," had fallen for "BLACK BEAUTY" - (actually lossed his mind over BLACK IS BEAUTIFUL)? Can one imagine the FIRST LADY of the United States of America, regardless of how UGLY she was, telling the King of any European country or President of an African nation;

'I AM WHITE, BUT COMELY?'

Not at all; never by any stretch of ones wildest dream. This type of figment of the imagination of the <u>racist</u> who wrote the "BUT" into the drama would have been abnormal in antiquity; and it becomes more and more obnoxious as time continues to see such <u>racism</u> in a so-called "HOLY BOOK "(Torah or Old Testament or else).

Ethiopian history before Emperor Menelik I is pretty-much integrated with that of Nubia, Puanit and Kimit (Sudan, Somalia and Egypt); and of course of all other nations of Alkebu-lan's (Africa's) antiquity. But, following Menelik I came emperors or Kings that bismirched its great history. However the emperor directly following Menelik I, Gedur of the City of Nouh - whose stele was recently unearthed along with a monument of himself - was very much like Menelik I and his mother Empress Azeb (Makeda or Queen of Sheba). They are other monuments and artifacts unearthed that testify to this aspect of Ethiopia's ancient history, many already cited in the BOOK OF AKSUM, including references to the birthplace of Ebna-Hakim (Menelik I) at a site very near the present city of MASSAWA. Further southeast of Hauzien is DONGOLLO, an enormous site of many ruins that testify to this part of Ethiopia's glorious history and ancient culture; this area presently called "DEBRA-MAKEDA" in honour of the world's once "MOST BEAUTIFUL WOMAN." Unearthed also, and re-established recently, are the old capitals - ATSABA and AZABAR, each having distinguishingly different difine structures which were identified as SEPULCHERS that preceded Emperor Menelik I, Emperor Kaleb, and Emperor Gabra-Maskal, as well as some built by each of them. The volume of work on Cushitic antifacts made for the cathedral of the HOLY CITY OF AKHSUM , already mentioned above, contains a two-page preamble detailing the antiquities of the entire area. One such account refer to the tomb (equivalent of the Egyptian pyramid) of ITYOPIS (Ethiopia) - the son of Kush and grandson of Shem. According to the Hebrews the story has been reversed; Kush is shown as one of the sons of Noah - a brother of Ham and Shem. A recapitulation of his biblical story according to THE BOOK OF AKHSUM, written by "GOD INSPIRED HOLY MEN," reads:

> The genealogy of the fathers of this temple is: Kush, the son of Shem, begot Ityopis (Ethiopia), father of Akh-sumawi, whose descendants founded the Holy City, Akhsum, each sector having been named for each of his offspring.

The above story, obviously, makes the JET BALCK Itiopis (a word from which the Greeks' "Ethiopæa" is fashioned) people of northeastern Alkebu-lan (the Greeks and Romans' "Africa") <u>Shemites</u> - the direct brothers and sisters of European and European-American ("Caucasian" and/or "White") <u>Jews</u> or <u>Semites</u>. Thus one can readily see that the term "anti-SEMITISM" as presently used in the United States of America is a misnomer, being that it is applied to designate a "RACE" of people; primarily the European and European-American (White or Caucasian) "JEWISH RACE," of

---

1. Name of a mythical character; supposedly the man who "SAVED THE WORLD FROM THE FLOOD" Jehovah imposed on the ancient world.
2. Two of the sons of "NOAH" of the Hebrew HOLY TORAH.

which there is actually no such thing or person in reality. The
most incredulous usage of this misnomer is as follows:

"HE (or she) HAS A SEMITIC NOSE."

In the first instance; the term "SEMITE" or "SEMITIC" refers to
a LANGUAGE or LANGUAGE-GROUP. The Nubians, Ethiopians, Colchians,
Puanits and Egyptians, also other indigenous peoples along the
banks of the White and Blue Niles, and along the banks of the
central African Great Lakes all of whom Herodotus - the "FATHER
OF EUROPEAN HISTORY" - described as having:

"...THICK LIPS, BROAD NOSE, WOOLY HAIR, AND
THE ARE BURNT OF SKIN" (Black), etc.,

spoke one kind or another of a language which "Western" historians
and other "educators" of varied disciplines also call "SEMITIC
LANGUAGES." This, then, is one of the basic reasons why the expressed BIGOTRY and RACISM relative to Ethiopia's history of the
ancient past and present persist by said "modern" men of Europe
and European-America Great Britain included. Ethiopia's history (the history and cultural heritage of its people, who from
time to time have been designated "NEGROES" and "HAMITES"), in
fact, proved to be the predecessor of the name-givers. For historically Ethiopia's existence predated that of Egypt by thousands of years. The Romiti themselves testified to this in their
own works giving praises to the Gods of Ethiopia and Puanit, also
to the Gods of other African nations further south. It was, in
fact, the ancient Ethiopian trade along the Green Sea (today's
Red Sea) which the ancient Egyptians (Romiti) used to reach Puanit (Punt, today's Somalia) to secure most of the nedded supply
to build their pyramids, develop their scientific programs, em-
balm their deads, worship their Gods including the PRIESTS they

imported to teach at the Lodges of the MYSTERIES SYSTEM with its mother Lodge at LUXOR from Puanit and Ethiopia..."THE LAND WHERE THE GODS LOVE TO BE..." according to the Egyptians' own BOOK OF THE DEAD and the PAPYRUS OF ANI.

The Egyptians spoke very highly of their Ethiopian teachers and those of Puanit from whom they learnt their religion. They called the land of Puanit: "GOD'S LAND." Ethiopia, they said is the: "LAND WHERE THE GODS LOVE TO DWELL."

Herodotus, using Egyptian sources, tells of Pharaoh Sesostris being hnonoured with a stele erected by the Ethiopians at the city of DEIRE; a story that was confirmed by the African geographer from Cyrene (today's Cyrenica of north Africa) - Eratosthenes. Pharoah Pepi II, around the year c2401 B.C.E., made a very long pilgrimage to Ethiopia and Puanit, being followed by one of the Romiti's most famous queen, Hatshep-sut, around c1521-1483 B.C.E. But the ETHIOPIAN CHRONICLES placed much more importance on the Eleventh (11th) Dynasty voyages, most of which took place under the direction of Pharaoh Mentuhotep IV around c2015-2005 B.C.E. He had imported into Kimit from Ethiopia "...HUNDREDS OF TONS OF RARE PRODUCE...." Reports of Queen (Pharoah) Hatshepsut's most famous voyage to Puanit can be seen in an inscription on the walls of her temple at Deir-el-Bahir, Egypt, which reads:

> No one yet knew the way to God's Land; no one trod the Myrrh-terraces, which the people knew not, but it was heard of from mouth to mouth by hearsay of the ancestors....

The above quotation is taken from Conti-Rossini's STORIA d'ETIOPIA; a translation of the Hieroglphic inscription which is also seen on page 160 of BLACK MAN OF THE NILE. The queen answered her own riddle when she stated:

"...but I have led them on water and on land, to explore the waters of inacessible chanels, and I have reached the Myrrh-terraces."

The "...INACESSIBLE CHANNELS..." had to be Ethiopia, for Puanit sets out at the Cape of Puanit where the Green Sea (today's Red Sea) and the Eastern Ocean (today's Indian Ocean) converge with each other. The voyages and expeditions by this queen followed the advise from the extensive knowledge of Pharoah Thutmose III which he gained from other great Ethiopians he met from such cities as Hamasu, Tekaru, and Outoulit, all of them located in Ethiopia, as witnessed in the inscriptions on the walls of his pyramid. Pharoah Harenheb - c1340-1320 B.C.E., also, wrote extensively about the "KINGS" and other "DIGNITARIES" he "RECEIVED FROM ETHIOPIA AND PUANIT...," etc.; all of whom "BROUGHT" him "GREAT TRIBUTES OF GOLD, AROMATIC GUM, OSTRICH PLUMES...," etc. Pharoah Seti I - c 1318-1298 B.C.E., his son Pharoah Rameses II - c1298-1232 B.C.E. (who chased Moses and the Haribu Africans out of northwestern Kimit), and his other descendants - Pharoahs Rameses III -c1198-1168 B.C.E,, and IV, made further references to the great importance of "THE LAND OF THE GODS" and "THE LAND WHERE THE GODS LOVE TO BE" in inscriptions on the walls of their temple, also.

Ethiopia and Egypt (Itiopis and Kimit), at various times in their history, along with Nubia and Puanit, became one common country under one common ruler or pharoah. The first time was during the period when the Africans were moving northerly in the direction from their original home - the GREAT LAKES area of central Alkebu-lan (Africa) and the head-waters of the White Nile at MWANZA NYANZA (the colonialists renamed this "Lake Victoria").

The second period was during the era when the Ethiopians descended the plains of their highlands, along the Blue Nile and the Atbara rivers, and moved northerly towards the DELTA (Lower Egypt) at the Kimit Sea (today's Mediterranean Sea). These facts were recorded thousands of years prior to the existence of the Ionian historian, Herodotus,[1] whom the Greeks adopted as one of their own citizens, and recorded his treatise about the lands of Ethiopia, Nubia, Punt (Puanit) etc. These records, and millions more not mentioned herein, even predated the so-called "TWENTY-FIFTH (25th) or "KUSHITE" (Ethiopian) DYNASTY FROM THE SOUTH" in which many Ethiopian pharoahs, the most noted of them being Piankhi, ruled Kimit - from c751 to 656 B.C.E.[2] Others most frequently mentioned by "Western" historians are Shabaka[3] (Sabacom) - c716-710 B.C.E. and Taharqa -c690-664 B.C.E.; all of whom also ruled Nubia and Merowe at the same period; Merowe being at that time the center of Ethiopian rule after the Ethiopians were finally defeated by their African brothers of Kimit. But European and European-American writers and educators who have set up themselves as "AUTHORIES" on Africa and African peoples purposefully underplay the role of the Ethiopians in the creation of the HIGH-CULTURE (civilization) that reached its ZENITH in Kimit thousands of years before the arrival of the first foreigners - the HYKSOS in c1675 B.C.E. from Asia and the Greeks (the first Europeans) in approximately 600 B.C.E.; all of which occured before the Europeans became rulers in Kimit through the conquest of said Alkebu-lan nation by Alexander II ("the great") in c332 B.C.E.

---

1. Ionia was a colony of the Africans of Egypt during the time of Herodotus' birth. He received all of his education from African Priests in his native Ionia and in Kimit as an adult.
2. These dates vary slightly, depending upon which historian one reads at a given time; also the historian's interest.
3. Not to be confused with SHABATAKA.

Although the Ethiopians rule of dynastic Egypt started with Pharoah Kashta -c751 and ended with Pharoah Tanutemun c653 B.C.E. there were many other pharoahs of Kimit who were born in Ethiopia and of Ethiopian parentage in Kimit and Nubia, but they did not rule due to any invasion and occupation of Kimit as did those between 751-653 B.C.E. They were politically Egyptians by nationality; the same as Herodotus and others who were given the name Greek "PHILOSOPHERS" became "GREEK CITIZENS" politically and not by birth in Greece, even when this European nation was known by the name "PYRRHUS." There was King Arwe, also called "ORI" by "Western" scholars, who gave Koptic (or Coptic) Christian-Ethiopian literature its demonic, angelic, moral, and mythological characteristics from the BOOK OF THE DEAD; thus, the "...LEGEND OF THE KING-SERPENT ARWE" found in the teachings of Ethiopian ORAL traditional history, especially around the area of Tigre and its surroundings; yet, it originated in the HOLY CITY OF AKHSUM at the highlands of Ethiopia. Even the modern indigenous scholars of Ethiopia continue the teachings of their ancestors traditional history with respect to "...THE DRAGON, ARWE, THAT DWELLS IN THE PLAIN OF HASEBO...." This story led to the most famous "SAINT (King or Emperor) GEORGE AND THE DRAGON" myth of the early part of the Christian Era (C.E.); a fairy tale that that was adopted lock-stock-and-barrel by European Christians from their Ethiopian forerunners.

The INTRA and INTER-RELATION influence on Egyptian culture by the Ethiopians, noted above, contributed to Bruce and other early "Western" European colonialists errors in associating all of Ethiopia's monuments to "EGYPTIAN OBELISKS" and "PYRAMIDS" they saw in Akhsum and other parts of Ethiopia. Of course there was a possibility that "EGYPTIAN INFLUENCE" permeated Ethiopian culture when the Egyptians became the rulers of the world of antiquity; just as it was the opposite way, as all of the Nile Valleys and Great Lakes High-Cultures (civilizations) drew upon each other for resources in every phase of life's existence and culture.

When Homer wrote his ILIAD he, too, found it necessary to have the Greek God - ZEUS - pay a visit to Ethiopia "...TO JOIN THE VIRTUOUS ETHIOPIANS..." at the feast of the Gods. Diodorus surpassed Homer in his praises for these African people, to the extent of saying that:

> "...from the Ethiopians the Egyptians derived
> their worship of the king, their conservation
> of their royal sepulchre, their acheivements
> in sculpture, and also their language and
> script."

It was about the same Africans that Aeschyylus (another of the most noted Greeks of ancient times) wrote the following:

> "...There, are sacred waters of the Erythraen
> Sea break a bright red strand, and at no great
> distance from the Ocean lies a copper-tinted
> lake - the lake that is the jewel of Ethiopia,
> where the all-prevading Sun returns again and
> to plunge his immortal from, and finds a solace
> for his weary round in gentle ripples that are
> but a warm caress...."

The above quotation is taken from Aeschylus, FRAGMENT 67.

Pursuing Ethiopia's antiquity further, prior to the entrance of the Greek conquerors of Egypt with Alexander II - "the great", and subsequently under the rule of the Greek-Egyptian (European-African) mixed Ptolemies, beginning with the Greek general, Soter (a Macedonian) - who renamed himself "PTOLEMY I" and claimed to be the "RULER OF ALL EGYPT," and his Egyptian wife, a period beginning in c332 B.C.E. and the ending with the conquest of Egypt by the Romans in c47 B.C.E , probably, would not add to the changing of anyone of the so-called "EGYPTOLOGISTS" confusion with respect to Ethiopia's influence on their prize SACRED COW - Egypt. Never-the-less I do hope that you, my students, shall open the flood-gate to further information on Ethiopia's history, and let the <u>waters of</u> (said) <u>knowledge</u> inundate the closed mind of the uninformed, as the flood-waters from the Ethiopian highlands along the trails of the Blue Nile and Atbara River inundate the lowlands of Nubia (Sudan) and Kimit (Egypt). This I bid of you, even though the few converts which I have to add in this lecture are only supportive of the preceding ones. Yet, it is of grave importance that you never fail to asses the Africans and their history, particularly that of north and east Africa (Alkebu-lan) as the history of the indigenous African peoples; and the term "AFRICAN PEOPLES" should only apply to "AFRICANS" with respect to differences in culture and nationality, not "RACIAL"- as commonly used by so many European and European-American racists whose only purpose is to maintain their own SUPERIORITY image over the rest of the entire world. You are further charged with the responsibility of not accusing all Europeans or European-Americans with the act of distorting the history of Africa and the African peoples; remembering that the very few who failed to do likewise are never-the-less worthy of your praise. At the same instance, it is equally important that you leave no stones unturned in your pursuit of correcting the untold myths about the "NEGROES, BANTUS, AND AFRICANS SOUTH OF THE SAHARA" not being involved with "...THE ORIGIN AND DEVELOPMENT OF THE CIVILIZATION

OF EGYPT AND ETHIOPIA...," which is the current propaganda being taught in most of the United States of America's educational system, both private and public parochial included.

A. Pinkoff and E. Drioton, in their most distinguished work, THE BOOK OF THE DAY AND THE NIGHT, Le Caire, 1942, page 89, plate I, wrote:

> "...Their dwelling place is the Land of Punt.[1] They live in the country of the Ape-like[2] Ones, close to the land of the Outnet and the Eastern Sea.[3]

The ancient Egyptians referred to this region of the "APE-LIKE GODS" as the original home of man - "PARADISE." The reverse face of a coin used throughout Ethiopia during the period the Egyptians spoke of Ethiopians as "APE-LIKE GODS " shows a typical Ethiopian of the type described by Herodotus in his HISTORIES,

---

1. In this specific case the "Land Of Punt" was identified as the geographic area of Ethiopia, according to the Egyptians themselves.
2. Note that the "Ape-like Ones" were in fact Gods and not Apes.
3. The Indian Ocean was known by this during antiquity.

Book II, quoted before in this and many other lectures.

So far, practically everything I have said is exclusive of Ethiopia's role as the land from whence much that is called "Christianity" today originated. On the otherhand, one cannot speak of Ethiopia and Ethiopians without refering to this basic part of their history and heritage (significantly included.) In this regards it is most important that I quote, somewhat, from THE JOURNAL OF THE ASSOCIATION OF SOCIAL SCIENCE TEACHERS, December 1963. In that issue, under an article entitled - "ALLEGED ETHIOPIAN ORIGINS OF CHRISTIANITY," by John F. Hatchett of Bennett College (paraphrasing and quoting from Sir Ernest A. Wallis Budge, A HISTORY OF ETHIOPIA, p. 129;* and David Talbot, CONTEMPORARY ETHIOPIA, pp. 26-29;* also, Ernest W. Luther, ETHIOPIA TODAY, 9; cf. p. 29 ⁺), he wrote:

> The indigenous people of Abyssinia have been since time immemorial Negroid.* The country was invaded around 500 B.C. by Arabs who racially are not Caucasians but a mixed type of Caucasoid and Negroid strain.+

Although Hatchett wanted to prove the "indigenous" character of the Africans of Ethiopia, whom he called "Abyssinians "(a word that is the equivalent to Ethiopians as "Nigger" is to Africans or African-Americans); and to show that the word "CAUCASIAN" is equally nefarious in kind, semantically. He, never-the-less, erred very seriously when he selected to adopt the usage of the word "NEGROID" with respect to any group of African peoples. This word, from Porutuguese imperial "NEGROLAND" origin was started and perpetuated during the Africans' castration by Western Europeans during chattel slavery to the Americas and the Caribbean islands; and it cannot be tolerated by African peoples in any of its forms;

and must be challenged even when the intent is to be complementary. In dealing with the alleged invasions by the Arabs, Hatchett stated:

> "Of the many (Arab)[1] tribes occupying Ethiopia, the Habashat has given the country the name Habesh by which it is still known to the Arabic speaking world and from whence is derived the European name of the country, Abyssinia." Another, the Ag-azi has given its name to the classical language of the country, Ge'ez, in which all its ancient literature is written and which is still the liturgical language of its church.

The above extract is heavily weighted with quotations and references from the work of A.H.M. Jones and Elizabeth Monroe, A HISTORY OF ETHIOPIA, p.7. Appearently Hatchett failed to show the resemblance, if any, between the Ethiopian language called "GE'EZ" (Ghez) and anyone of the "ARABIC" languages he claimed it was adopted from. He, as so many other writers on Ethiopia, has failed to really delve seriously into Ethiopia's history of antiquity; thus he too ignored the fact that AGU, Ethiopia's most ancient language, is in truth the origin of all of Ethiopia's following languages - including its present "NATIONAL LANGUAGE," Amheric. Nowhere in the article has Hatchett shown that any, or all, foreign language was resisted, and rejected, by the indigenous people in order to protect their overall High-Culture (civilization) from foreign corruption. It is also very obvious that hardly any personal investigation in the direction of Ethiopia's traditional culture was done by Hatchett himself; also, that he did not approach local documentary sources, except for a mostly modern work by David Talbot (formerly the editor and publisher of Ethiopia's most noted daily newspaper and author) , CONTEMPORARY

---
1. Words in parentheses by the lecturer for clarity only.

ETHIOPIA, already cited.

It must be understood, very carefully so, that for the most part I endorse Hatchett's work. However, what I do object to, is the inaccuracies relating to the usage of common terminologies of a racist nature, which he adopted from the same people his article criticizes. For Hatchett touched on many issues, defending each admirably; issues which many so-called BLACK STUDIES PROFESSORS avoid for less meaningful rhetoric of the so-called "REVOLUTIONARY DIALECTIC MATERIALISM," whatever this is. Quoting Sir Ernest A. Wallis Budge's, ETHIOPIA TODAY, page ix, Hatchett wrote:

> According to E.A. Budge, the only trustworthy historical insrciptions dealing with Abyssinia which have come down to us are those which were written in Greek during the reign of Ptolemy III, Ptolemy IV and Zoscales, and the great trilingual inscription in Greek, Sabaean, and Ethiopic which discovered by the German-Aksum Expedition.

The reason for Sir E. A. Wallis Budge's apprehension, with regards to Ethiopia's history and language, was his own failure to give the necessary respect to the indigenous Ethiopian scholars and priests who wrote in scripts which are still being called "MEROTIC WRITINGS;" this Budge would have realized had he treated the Africans of Ethiopia's languages he saw with the same respect he gave to the ancient writings of the Greeks he found in Egypt. It must be remembered that,although Sir E. A. Wallis Budge was one of the greatest of the "EGYPTOLOGISTS" from Europe - Great Britain in this case, he never-the-less suffered from the same ACCUTE NEGROPHOBIA as most of his fellow Europeans and European-Americans of the 19th through 20th century C.E. with respect to any and all things African which show the Africans as the originators of anything Caucasians cherish. Yet, Budge was forced to concede certain basic facts about Ethiopian history from indigenous African historians; of course only that which he considered "TRUSTWORTHY" from a European point of reference, being that he assumed the stature of GRAND CENSOR; thus setting-up himself as the "AUTHORITY" on what is TRUE or FALSE in African history, particularly that of the Nile River Valley; a position which Africans cannot, and will not, tolerate for one solitary split second. In this regards Hatchett also wrote:

> He (Sir E.A. Wallis Budge)[1] goes on to say that ultimately we are driven to construct a history of Ethiopia or Abyssinia from the Royal Chronicles and chronological works which have been compiled at various times by native authors.

What other sources did Budge expected to quote other than "...NATIVE AUTHORS..."? And; who are the "WE" and "US" that "WERE DRIVEN TO CONSTRUCT A HISTORY OF ETHIOPIA"? No African ever drove Budge or anyother European or European-American to write of their history. The reason the "WE" and "US"..."WERE DRIVEN TO CONSTRUCT A HISTORY" of any part of the continent of Alkebu-lan (Africa) was adequately described in the answer by Dr. William Edward Burkhardt DuBois', THE WORLD AND AFRICA, pages 85 and 86, as quoted by Hatchett:

> "What are the peoples who from vague prehistory emerged as the Africans of today? The answer has been bedeviled by the assumption that there was in Africa a 'true' Negro and that his pure aboriginal race was mixed with a mythical Hametic race which came appearently from neither Europe, Asia, nor Africa, but constituted itself as a 'white element' in Negro Africa...."

The above statement by Dr. DuBois is the crux of the entire

Words in parentheses by the lecturer for clarity only.

RACIST ATTITUDE of the type that permeates the thinking process of most of the so-called "SCHOLARS" and "AUTHORITIES" of Europe (including the British Isle), also European-America, who make their livelihood writing about Africa and her indigenous sons and daughters' heritage and history from antiquity to the present. However, Dr. DuBois needed to include in his remarks that there is no difference in the case of the equally "SEMITIC RACE" myth which is being imposed today by those who consider themselves both of a "Caucasian" as well as a "Semitic" RACE. It is certain members of this so-called "SEMITIC RACE" who now take it upon themselves to interpret the cultural, historical, and social heritage of the Africans and African-descended peoples of the United States of America; thereby establishing themselves, along with their fellow European and European-American (White people all) of the Christian faith, as the "AUTHORITIES" on all things BLACK. On the otherhand, people so designated are extremely jealous and zealous about what others not bearing such racial designation write about them; and when such is the case it is not to infrequent that the outcry of "anti-SEMITISM" rings out in the air. Using "SEMITE" to designate a "RACE" rather than a LANGUAGE, is no better than using the word "NEGRO" or "NIGGER" to designate the African race. What is a RACE anyhow?

    The introduction and the constant alluding to some sort of a "SABEAN" and "ARAB" predominant influence in Ethiopia, according to "Western" historians and other educators and their "Negro-American" proteges that act as their parrots with respect to Ethiopia, is no different to the racist depiction of West Africa being "UNCIVILIZED BEFORE THE ARRIVAL OF THE WHITE MAN" from

Western Europe, England, and the United States of America with his Judaeo-Christianity and imperialism. This common racist propaganda dates back to Henry Morton Stanley's DARKEST AFRICA, which became the MEIN KAMPF of most of today's "AUTHRORITIES ON AFRICA" and things "AFRICAN."

I must close this lecture-essay on certain biblical citations dealing with the same Ethiopia of the continent of ALKEBU-LAN, the "...LAND WHERE THE GODS LOVE TO BE..." according to the Egyptians' BOOK OF THE DEAD of at least 4000 B.C.E.[1] It is, therefore, befitting that I quote all of the biblically historical data in PART III of Hatchett's article, ALLEGED ETHIOPIAN ORIGINS OF CHRISTIANITY.

Why is the story of the Ethiopian eunuch and his Queen Candace so pertinent to our thesis that Christianity had its origin in Ethiopia in the first century A.D.?

Supreme importance has been attached to the story of the Ethiopian eunuch, because this episode is one of the tiny, but historically plausible, strands of knowledge upon which our central thesis rests. We are able to verify the date for the *Acts of the Apostles*, written by Luke. It is ca 75 A.D.[26] Luke knew Philip and even if he were employing the story to prove a point, i.e., the spreading of the faith to the Gentiles (those outside the Jewish faith), how account for the specific reference to a specific Queen, obviously known to either Philip or Luke. It seems to the author that this is a "historical" passage rather than an allegory. And the conversion of the eunuch which took place before the writing of *Acts*, and the subsequent events which took place after the conversion, squarely place the origin of Christianity in Ethiopia in the first century A.D., long before the coming of Frumentius.

Another extremely early and valuable source of information which sheds some light on our central thesis is to be found in Eusebius' *Ecclesiastical History*. Eusebius was an articulate and accurate chronicler of the faith. "Part of his great claim to distinction is that when writing philosophy he never neglects history, or philosophy when writing history."[27] Eusebius accepts the account of the Ethiopian eunuch in the *Acts of the Apostles* and makes this rather pointed assessment of it.

While the saving preaching was daily progressing and growing, some providence brought from the land of the Ethiopians an officer of the queen of that land, for the nation, following ancestral customs, is still ruled by a woman. Tradition says that he, who was the first of the Gentiles to receive from Philip by revelation the mysteries of the divine word, and was the first-fruits of the faithful throughout the world, was also the first to return to his native land and preach the Gospel of the knowledge of the God of the Universe and the sojourn of our Savior which gives life to men, so that by him was actually fulfilled the prophecy which says, "Ethiopia shall stretch out her hand to God."[28]

This passage also indicates that Eusebius was quite familiar with at least some of the Old Testament references to Ethiopia.

On these two early sources and the background material i n t r o d u c e d throughout it can be contended that Christianity had its beginning in Ethiopia in the first century A.D.

[27] Eusebius, **The Ecclesiastical History**. English translation by Kirsopp Lake, p. XV.
[28] Ibid., pp. 109-111.

---

1. B.C.E. (B.C.) = Before the Christian Era. C.E. (A.D.) The Christian Era. These designations have been used in order to show respect to those who do not accept that there was in fact a God who came to earth named "JESUS CHRIST."

To keep in mind the basis of this lecture-essay the following is taken from page 153 of Jean Doressee's, ANCIENT CITIES AND TEMPLES: ETHIOPIA, Frederick Ungar Publishing Co., New York, 1959 (as translated from the French to English by Ela Coult):

> Westward (of Ethiopia)[1] lay the Sudan and Nubia, the lands of the Nile, once Christian and now under Islam; through these territories lay the route to Egypt. To the south-east stretched the pagan realms of Black Africa.

The picture below is alleged to be that of the likeness of the present Emperor of Ethiopia, Haile Selassie I, otherwise called the "CONQUERING LION OF JUDAEH," etc. One can see what has been done to the feature of the African people to make them appear "non-NEGROID, CAUCASIAN, HAMITIC, SEMITIC," etc. for centuries of European and European-American RACISM and RELIGIOUS BIGOTRY. This is assuming that to be a so-called "TRUE NEGRO" one has to have "THICK LIPS, BROAD NOSE, WOOLY HAIR" and VERY BLACK SKIN. This is the MYTH used by so-called "CAUCASIANS, SEMITES," and others to co-opt the indigenous Africans of North and East Alkebu-lan's (Africa's) history and heritage. This is a living example of the plagerism that took place with the pictures and statues of African peoples of north and east Africa.

---

1. Words in parentheses by the lecturer for clarity only.

This lecture-essay, one minutely infinitisimal aspect of Alkebu-lan's contributions to WORLD HIGH-CULTURE (civilization), should, at least, prove the extent to which professors in BLACK STUDIES courses must go in order to counteract the RACIST theories about indigenous African peoples being of "...DIFFERENT RACES..." which have been manufactured for them by Europeans and European-Americans who call themselves "ANTHROPOLOGISTS, PALAEONTOLOGISTS, EGYPTOLOGISTS," and a host of other names which tend to indicate "AUTHORITY." It shows that major works such as C. G. Seligman, RACES OF AFRICA, New York, 1969 (first published in 1930), only adds to prove that difference in physical characteristics between Europeans do not qualify them as seperate RACES - according to European and European-American "AUTHORITIES" on Kosher RACES; whereas, any slight physical difference or variance between any two (2) Africans make them qualify as members of two (2) seperate RACES by the same "AUTHORITIES" standard. Thus, an EGYPTIAN and a SOUTH AFRICAN are two (2) Africans of two (2) seperate RACES; whereas a GREEK and a SWEDE are both of the same "CAUCASIAN RACE." In order to satisfy this RACIST idiocincracy the subjects and disciplines of "PALAEONTOLOGY" and "PHYSICAL ANTHROPOLOGY" were created by the "AUTHORITIES". These two areas of of "HIGHER-EDUCATION" have been carefully guarded by the alleged "AUTHORITIES;" only the most obedient adherents being able to acheive membership and the GOOD SEAL OF APPROVAL - the Ph.D. Degree in either one. Yet, both disciplines have proven no better than their founders or perpetrators; they fall short of scientific reality; though they, recently, pretend to be scientific and responsive to more meaningful application with regards to the bigoted term "RACE." Most of the closed-circuit membership organizations within these two (2) disciplines have dropped "RACE" for another equally ridiculous term - "ETHNIC;" which in fact is used in the very same manner as the term it was supposed to replace. But the day will still come, this being not to far off in the distant future, when the people of Alkebu-lan will again have the previlege of reaping the benifits of their biblical teachings that say:

> "AND ETHIOPIA SHALL STRETCH FORTH HER HANDS UNTO GOD AND SHE SHALL BE SAVED."

But the children of Ethiopia, her sons and daughters, will not await a MIRACULOUS turn of history to be "SAVED." She, and her sons and daughters are also aware of another of her teachings:

> "GOD HELP THOSE WHO HELP THEMSELVES."

THE RETURN OF KIMIT, ZIMBABWE, AND NUBIA TO THE CONTINENT OF ALKEBU-LAN

Northeast Africa - KIMIT- The Light of Antiquity: Before the Foreigners Came as Rulers.

The most common beginning of Egyptian history, written by "Western" historians or Egyptologists, is that:

> 'A few thousands years ago, about 6000 B.C., Semitic and Hametic peoples from Asia invaded the Nile Valley and began Nile Valley civilization...,' etc., etc., etc.

The fact of the matter is, they have failed, miserably so, to produce one iota of evidence to justify this claim. On the other-hand, they have shown consistent collusion with respect to presenting only those papyri that tend to indicate "SEMITIC, HAMITIC" and/or "CAUCASIAN" features; whatever these terms mean. Of course POINTED NOSE and THIN LIPS are always two of the basic requirements one would need to qualify for any of the three terms mentioned - "<u>Semitic, Hamitic, Caucasian</u>." This is irrespective of the fact that millions of Africans all over the continent fit this description, yet they are called "NEGROES," etc.

It is rather very significant that some European and European-American egyptologists and historians do indicate that.."THEY WERE SOME NEGROES IN EGYPT FROM ANTIQUITY." But, even these must always quickly add:

"THEY SERVED IN THE ARMY; or, THEY WERE SLAVES."

There is no need to give any bibliography on the above quotation, as practically any book on Egyptian antiquity by said "scholars" will so recite. Thus; this work is intended to show that Kimit , which shall be called EGYPT - [the name given this nation of Alkebu-lan (the Greeks and Romans AFRICA) by the ancient Haribus (Hebrews or "Jews") and Greeks] , for the convenience of the student and general reader, was , in fact, originally settled and developed by the Romiti (the original name for the people called EGYPTIANS , whose descendants are today called "NEGROES" and other such degrading terms by "Westerners" and fellow Africans who know no better.) For, it was not until approximately c1675 B.C.E. (Before the Christian Era, or B.C.) that Asians, called "HYKSOS", invaded the land of Egypt and became the first non-African peoples to rule over any piece of African land. References to this area of information, and all to follow in this lecture-essay, historically that is, it will be noted, are taken from original sources; thus, I refrain from the otherwise speculatively wild and outrageous hypothetical conclusions by most of my European-American colleagues of the title - "HISTORIAN."

Let us begin with the main cause for the plagerization of the indigenous Africans of Egypt's history and cultural experience. We find that it all began on 19 May 1798 C.E.; when a French fleet commanded by General Napoleon Bonaparte sailed into the EGYPTIAN DELTA from Toulon, France, with the intent of establishing a military base of operation for the purpose of dislodging Great Britain as the power in India; thus, causing same to fall into the hands of the French imperialists. Napoleon's abortive adventure ended in total catostrophic dilemma, the result of his own political problems at home in France, forcing him to withdraw hurriedly back to France the following year - 1801 C.E. One would, most definitely, begin to figure that the French should have been out of the picture of the affairs of the Africans of Egypt at this point, and would not have been the first plagerizers of their history, religion, culture, etc.; but this would be very far from correct. It was just the reverse.

The entrance of French military might with Napoleon Bonaparte in Egypt permitted Europeans by the dozens, for the first time in history, to go beyond the limits of the Nile River Valley anyother European did prior to that period. In so doing, they were able to unlock much of the information that was hidden in secret from the indigenous African inheritors for the next few hundred years to follow; said SECRET being entombed in the languages of the African High-Cultures of the greater Nile Valley and the Great Lakes regions; and particularly one - HIEROGLYPHIC. Of course there were many other scripts left by the ancient Africans of Egypt (Romiti), everyone of them much more ancient than the beginning of the first European nation - PYRRHUS or GREECE c3000 B.C.E.; the vast majority of them having been created and developed by the Nile Valley people Herodotus (the Ionian native turned Greek citizen) described as having:

"...THICH LIPS, BROAD NOSE, WOOLLY HAIR, AND THEIR ARE BURNT OF SKIN."[1]

The penetration of the French also permitted them to come in contact with the ruins of temples and other Shrines of the period when their builders - the Africans indigenous to Egyptian antiquity - had already reached their zenith, which was hundreds of years before the birth of the first so-called "SEMITE" or "HAMITE"; the

---

1. See HERODOTUS HISTORIES, Book II (as transl. by A. Selincourt). Note that the "thick lips, broad nose,"..is edited-out in Selincourt's late work; but not in Wilson Armisted, A TRIBUTE FOR THE NEGRO, London, 1848, p. 122, etc.

latter two terms being of modern usage for the compliment of the word RACE, but originally used as language-group designations. Many of these monuments, or ruins, were sacked and their contents stolen by the French; among them being thousands of folios and other basic volumes that were laid to rest with their owners of origin - the PHAROAHS of thousands of years before the grave-snatching Frenchmen. But the overwhelming amount of the French loot, stolen from the temple-ruins and other structures of Egypt's antiquity, were re-confiscated by the British commander of operations, General Menou, when he defeated Napoleon and forced the French military forces to surrender at Alexandria. The bulk of this stolen treasure them became the illegal property of the British Museum under the name - "EGYPTIAN ANTIQUITIES."

Although the British had stolen from the French that which had been originally confiscated from the indigenous Africans, they also had no way of knowing the secrets locked into the inscriptions of the papyri and other written treasures in their possession - the KEY. The answer (KEY) remained in that which was to be called, later on, "THE ROSETTA STONE." A piece of a stone slab with many distinctly different scripts, all of which were written in languages unfamiliar to both the French and British at first examination. It was not until Jean François Champollion, a Frenchman, in September 1882 C.E. - (approximately eighty- 30) years after the ROSETTA STONE was stolen from its African owners) - was able to decipher two of its scripts: the GREEK and the HIEROGLYPS; thus announcing that he had accomplished his goal (in French):..."Je tiens l'affaire!"

On 28 September (the same year), a very few days after noting that the Greek words matched the same pattern of consistency as the Hieroglyphs, Champollion exposed his findings to his French coleagues, and later on to the rest of the European and European-American (White) world. Of course the people from whom the ROSETTA STONE was confiscated, the indigenous Africans and their descendants, not one of them, were not invited to the presentation of the "UNLOCKING" of the ancient knowledge of <u>their ancestors' writings</u>; KNOWLEDGE which was last familiar to them up until the arrival of the Muslim Arabs from the Arabian Peninsula with their JIHADS (Holy Wars) during the seventh (7th) century C.E. (640 CE or 18 AH), most of which had already been stolen by the Greeks with Alexander II ("the great") - including Aristotle and General Soter (who later renamed himself "Ptolemy I, Pharoah of All Egypt and Nubia ").

The ROSETTA STONE'S inscriptions, which Champollion deciphered, dealt with a decree honoring Pharoah (King) Ptolemy V -also known as EPIPHANES (c205-180 B.C.E.). The text is written in many languages besides Greek and Hieroglyphics; the former Champollion noticed was written in an older form of Greek script than that which was in general use at the time of its tranlastion . The style was dated to have been written around 196 B.C.E. by the Priests of one of the subordinate LODGE of the MYSTERIES SYSTEM at Memphis -the capital city of Kimit (Egypt) at that time. A sample of the ROSETTA STONE, as it appears in the British Museum, London England, today, (see BLACK MAN OF THE NILE, P. 2).

The inscription cited the pharoah, Ptolemy V, for his generosity shown to the people; also, the praises they bestowed upon him for said deed. In order to make these facts known to all who resided within the geo-political boundary of the state of Egypt, it was ordered, according to the inscription on the ROSETTA STONE, that said doings be engraved on a tablet of stone...

"BEARING THE SACRED WRITINGS,[1] IN THE NATIVE SCRIPT, AND IN GREEK LETTERS."

One must realize that by the time the ROSETTA STONE had been written the Greeks were already in total control of the ballance of their <u>stolen booty</u>, which they seized following their conquest of Kimit in 332 B.C.E. under the leadership of Alexander II ("the great"). Their rule in Kimit (or Egypt), and their bastardization of Egyptian culture (the end of which came at the hands of Aristotle and Ptolemy I - General Soter), caused the language of the indigenous African peoples of Egypt (Romiti or Egyptians) - Hieroglyphs - to become a "...DEAD LANGUAGE...." This was done after the Greeks had already forced the African High-Priest, Manetho, in approximately 300 B.C.E., to write down the chronological order of each and every pharoah's reign over Egypt from the beginning of the first one, AHA , whom the Greeks later on called "MENES." Manetho compiled and divided said chronological and historical data into "THIRTY (30) DYNASTIES " or "ROYAL HOUSES." The dates and other data relating to the dynastic chronology appears on pages 509 through 514 of your textbook - BLACK MAN OF THE NILE. This dating process by Manetho was to , later on, present those who followed him (as Egyptologists) with the "KEY" to the calculation of the time in which each pharoah reigned over Egypt before the "...BIRTH OF JESUS CHRIST OF NAZZARETH." It was

---

1. Ptolemy V to XV were all descendants -paternally- from General Soter of Macedonia, one of Alexander's greatest generals - who declared himself "Pharoah" at Alexander's death. His mother was an indigenous African ("Negro"); Cleopatra I - XII being of the same family; the VIIIth was Julius Ceasar's lover.

proclaimed by Asians and Africans who later called themselves "CHRISTIANS," all of whom at that time were for the most part of the HEBREW RELIGION - worshipers of the God, JEHOVAH.

We have trespassed this far into Egyptian antiquity without once identifying Egypt's land geographically and politically - at the period in question. The Egypt (Kimit or Sais originally), and her Egyptian African peoples - who originally called themselves "ROMITU"(singular) or "ROMITI" (plural), which is being refered to here, began at an emaginary line somewhere below the Second (2nd) Cataract and crossed easterly and westerly to the borders with the <u>Green Sea</u> (currently the RED SEA); thence - crossing the <u>Lebu</u> (the Greeks and Romans' "Libya") <u>Desert</u> - part of today's Sahara Desert. To the north was the SEA OF KIMIT - today's <u>Mediterranean Sea</u>. The people were of different physical chracteristics than the present Egyptian population, for the most part; the vast majority as described by the ancient Ionian of Greek fame - HERODOTUS, who stated in his HISTORIES, <u>Book II</u> (already mentioned; and as translated by Wilson Armisted in his book, A TRIBUTE FOR THE NEGRO, p. 122); they are...

>"...WOOLLY-HAIRED BLACKS, WITH PROJECTING LIPS...," etc.

There are many other translations of this description by Herodotus, each differing to some degree or another, all agreeing to the "...<u>woolly hair</u>" and "<u>black</u>" color of the indigenous Africans of Egypt - the <u>Romiti</u>. The late work by Frank W. Snowden, <u>BLACKS OF ANTIQUITY: Greco-Roman Experience</u>, (Harvard University Press), 1970, should add further to one's acceptance of the description by the "FATHER OF"(European)"HISTORY" - Herodotus.

Herodotus' statement, written sometime between 457-450 BCE

(at least one-hundred and eighteen - 118 - years prior to the conquest of the Africans of Egypt by the Greeks, and one-thousand two-hundred and eighteen - 1218 - years after the first foreigners occupied Egypt), still stands as one of the most directly descriptive physical identification of the indigenous Africans of Egypt known to date, all of which have been further documented by other ancients of Europe and Asia who were not disturbed by it. In this former period, as mentioned before, there were no "SEMITES" and "HAMITES" known anywhere on the planet Earth, not even a <u>Hebrew people</u> or <u>nation</u>. This was around c1675 B.C.E.; just about the time when <u>the first of the Haribu</u> (misnomered "Jews") <u>people</u> were spiritually born - a man named AVRAM (Abram or Abraham) - in the nation of Chaldea, at the City of UR. At the period before the entrance of the foreign invaders - the HYKSOS, from Asia, who came from around the bend of the Axus River, there were already Asians who had visited Egypt from as far east as Persia and India. But before them there were common traders and visitors, official and non-official, between the royalty of Ethiopia (Cush or Kush), Somalia (Punt or Puanit) and Meröe (Mërow or Merö), according to recorded history of all three nations mentioned.

The death of Jean Francois Champollion in 1832 C.E. left much of the task of further deciphering the <u>Egyptian Hieroglyphic texts</u> (stolen out of Egypt by Frenchmen and Britons alike) to a few men who were able to take up the mantle, being that he had already completed an extensive Egyptian language (Hieroglyphic) dictionary and gramatical structure. Said works were to be later on followed by the so-called "...<u>earliest of the 19th century Egyptologists</u>..." like Gaston Maspero, I. Loti, Sir Ernest A. Wallis Budge, James H.

Breasted, and others (all of whom are to be mentioned individually for specific contributions, or were already so detailed). It must be noted, however, that before Champollion's work was completed and announced to the European and European-American public one Thomas Young , an English physicist, had independently deciphered Pharoah Ptolomey's name and many other of the words in the inscription on the "ROSETTA STONE; but he failed to make his findings public before Champollion's.

The fact that Kush, Puanit, Nubia and other African High-Cultures (civilizations) along the southern end of the Nile River valleys existed before indigenous Africans travelled from them to establish and developed what was to be known as KIMIT later SAIS (today's EGYPT as renamed by the Haribus in their mythology about"<u>Noah and the flood</u> "), suggests further proof of the type of people the ancient east and northeast-Africans were before their description by Herodotus, and subsequently before their conquest by the Europeans (Greeks and Romans) - AN ADMIXTURE OF PEOPLE WITH FACIAL CHARACTERISTICS TODAY CALLED "NEGRO" or "NEGROID." This revelation pictures a composite example of the similarity between the Africans of both Kimit and Puanit (Egypt and Punt - Somaliland). Here we see, below, a picture of the QUEEN OF PUNT and member of her royal guests from Kimit who came to pay her special homage. It will be noted that the people of Puanit also wore the same type of long-tailed wigs as the Romiti of Egypt in high office. The following picture of the queen and guests are taken from page 103 of the book, WHEN EGYPT RULED THE EAST. This picture can be also seen in the Cairo Museum, Cairo, Egypt, under the caption-" THE QUEEN OF PUNT." Note that the ancient people of Puanit were shown of the same color and general physical characteristics as their northerly neighbours of Kimit, Nubia, Kush and Meröwe; this does not exclude those of Numidia, Lebus (libya), Khart Haddas (Carthage), etc.

The Queen of Punt (Cairo Museum)

Besides the common characteristics of the Nile Valley African peoples in the above picture; it will be noted that they also used similiar types of transportation which "Western" writers have given the impression were only used by the Egyptians. Also, that there was nothing "SEMITIC" or "HAMITIC" about these Africans than their fellow Africans of anyother section of Alkebu-lan (Africa according to the Greeks and Romans). Certainly none of them could be called "CAUCASIAN," neither "LIGHT-SKINNED" or "DARK-SKINNED" - according to Dr. M.D.W. Jeffreys and others who expound their racist theories (otherwise called "HYPOTHESES") about "...Caucasian" and "Semitic North Africa" that minus their "Negroes" and

"Negroids." The following picture, also taken from the same source as the above, entitled "NUBIAN ROYALTY PAYING VISIT TO EGYPT AND PHARAOH TUTANKHAMUN, shows the reverse scene; in this case it is the Africans of Puanit paying homage to their Romitu hosts (Egyptian hosts).

NUBIANS BRINGING TRIBUTE TO TUTANKHAMUN
(THEBES, TOMB OF HUY)

(The above is from the Tomb of Pharaoh Huy)

Predynastic Egyptian history, according to High-Priest Manetho (c300-210 B.C.E.), ended just before the beginning of the OLD KINGDOM (3rd to 4th dynasty - c3200-2258 B.C.E.), which was following the reign of the first pharoah (king) - AHA (the Greeks called him "MENES") or NARMER to Pharoah PEPI II. This was the period when the Romiti had to import most of what they needed for their own subsistence through foreign trade at points further south in Alkebu-lan (such as Nubia, Merowe, Kush, Puanit, Bonyoro); the latter countries also trading with other African nations further south and southwest such as Monomotapa's capital -ZIMBABWE.

It is from these southern countries the Romiti got their lions, elephants, ostrichs, sweet incense, myrrhs, fine woods and ivory, etc., none of which was native to the Kimit Desert (Egyptian Desert, today's SAHARA - according to the Arab invaders that entered Egypt in 640 C.E. or A,D., also 18 A.H.) or the fertile banks of the northern end of the Nile River which empty's into the Kimit Sea (today's Medeterranean Sea). There were no highlands for the ostrichs, and no praries for the lions and elephants in Kimit; neither were these animals or birds native to the desert-lands of the Middle East. Some "Western" historians and Egyptologists disagree with the High-Priest Manetho and designated the OLD KINGDOM dynastic period as being from the IInd to VIth dynasty (c2680-1258 B.C.E.) - from Pharoah KHASEKHEMUWY to Pharoah PEPI II. They excluded AHA (Narmer, sometimes also called "ABA"), indicating, also, that he was "...the last of the Archaic Period Kings." Regardless of how High-Priest Manetho or any of the "Western" Egyptologists chronologically listed the dynasties, it is the period from the SEBELIANS - I, II and III (25,000-6000 BCE) - the SILT TERRACES builders, to the Pharoahs of the beginning of the Second Dynastic Intermediate Period - VIII-XVII Dynasty (c1676 BCE), that I am most interested in at this juncture of our excursion into the African-American past - THE BLACK EXPERIENCE-in north and northeast Alkebu-lan (Africa, Ethiopia, Libya, Ortegya, etc. See page 266 of BLACK MAN OF THE NILE for series of names of AFRICA before it was so named by the Greeks and Romans . It is also during this same period, approximately 23,324 years before the first foreigners arrived in Kimit (Egypt), North Alkebu-lan (Africa), that the Romiti (Egyptians) commenced the final stage of the zenith of their High-Culture; and at that last date (c1676 or 1675 BCE) came to their end as a result of an invasion by,.:"illiterate Asians who knew not what they were destroying"..(according to A.D. Thomas, NEGRO NORTH AFRICA, London, 1804); these "ILLITERATES" bearing the name HYKSOS or SHEPHERD KINGS OF BEDUINA.

Since we are not to hear about the mythical theory of "NOAH AND THE GREAT FLOOD", when the Haribu (Hebrew, later "Jewish") peoples' world "CAME TO AN END" in their HOLY TORAH (the Christian OLD TESTAMENT) during this period; it is also obvious that there were no "Noah's sons" also. If NOAH and his SONS did not exist, therefore no SHEM and HAM. If no SHEM and HAM, equally there could be no SHEMITIC or SEMITIC and HAMITIC languages or peoples one hears so much about lately. But, we are to base all of mankind's history on this bit of Hebrew (Jewish) mythology, even though other people's history have no such characters or myth; at least this is what is being taught to each and every American citizen in these United States of America, irrespective of race, creed or color and sex, or national origin (this being one of the only area in which there is equality in the so-called "AMERICAN DREAM" or the "WHITE EXPERIENCE.")

The cut-off date we are interested in, on the otherhand, is c1675 BCE, more than five-hundred and eighty-three (583) years after the last of the MAJOR PYRAMID BUILDERS - Pharaohs DJOSER, KHUFU, KHAFRA and MENKAURE (3,100 or 2258 to 1675 BCE) had already built their pyramids (tombs or houses of the Nether World - Amenta) and died; thus, not a single "SEMITE", at least not of HEBREW or JUDAEO-CHRISTIAN origin, being involved in said building or "SLAVING", on either of them. This means that the "Christian OLF TESTAMENT" or the Hebrew HOLY TORAH's SECOND BOOK OF MOSES (also known as the <u>Book of Exodus</u>) story about the Haribus (Hebrews or "Jews") slaving for at least four-hundred (400) years on the building of the pyramids in Egypt does not apply to this area or these pyramids in Egyptian history. This aspect of history even covers the period before the Hebrews' God - JEHOVAH or ADONI allegedly "...GAVE THE TEN COMMANDMENTS TO MOSES ON MOUNT SINAI;" as this African - Moses - was not yet born in Africa - Kimit or Egypt. It is, also, before there was an "ADAM AND EVE IN THE GARDEN OF EDEN"(spoken of in the FIRST BOOK OF MOSES, the <u>Book of Genesis</u>, which also came from JEHOVAH through the African of Kimit, Moses, teachings about his Mount Sinai's adventure with the same **SUPREME BEING**., These biblical stories, mythological or not, had to be clarified before further historical investigation and presentation could be made with respect to the true history of the African peoples of Kimit and others along the Nile Valley and Great Lakes. Since there was no Greek nation or people in existence during this period; thus, no CAUCASIAN as yet from the Caucas Mountains of Asia or Eur-Asia in Kimit to CAUCASIZE the indigenous Africans'("Negroes" etc.) history or High-Culture at this juncture. Repugnant as these racially-inpregnated anthropological terms are in this lecture-essay, especially as they are used at this point, they are never-the-less what I must use in order to point out effectively that <u>Egyptian antiquity was in fact an indigenous "AFRICAN-AMERICAN" experience that began with their ancient African ancestors who created, developed and reached their zenith in north and east Africa</u>; and that <u>they were no different to the people presently being called "NEGROES, BANTUS, NIGGERS,"</u>

etc. by so-called "AUTHORITIES ON AFRICA" and "NEGRO HISTORY."

The PALEOLITHIC PERIODS indigenous Africans of Kimit were once equated to the so-called "HAMITIC TRIBES OF ARABIA." These "HAMITES" (a term once applied to people who are now called "Africans south of the Sahara, Negroes," etc., all, names denoting the inferiority of the Africans to Europeans and European-Americans - Whites or Caucasians) were once considered to be the indigenous people of Puanit, Kush and Kimit; that was, of course, before the so-called "ROSETTA STONE" and other works from Kimit (Egypt) became of supreme importance to the origin of "Western" man - "DARK-SKINNED" and "LIGHT-SKINNED CAUCASIANS;" <u>works which were stolen out of Africa and still held illegally</u> in so-called PRIVATE and PUBLIC COLLECTIONS throughout European-America and Europe (including the British Isle - Ireland, Scotland, Wales and England).

In all of Egypt's history, prior to the conquest of its Delta region by the Hyksos invaders from Asia, it was the people at the southern borders which the Egyptians, themselves, worshiped. For example: It was in Puanit that they said "...THE GODS WERE CREATED;" but, it was in Kush they believed that "...THE GODS LOVED TO BE." Furthermore, it was in Nubia they believed "...THE HEADWATERS OF THE GOD - HAPI" (the Nile River) "WAS BORN" (began); they, not knowing that it really began at Mwanza Nyanza (called "Lake Victoria" by the British colonialists) in central Africa (Uganda) and Lake Tana at the Ethiopian highlands - equally the Atbara River.

Along the Nile River Valley of Egypt there were, in fact, two seperate kingdoms collquially called "UPPER EGYPT" and "LOWER

EGYPT. The UPPER area, once also a part of Nubia, was symbolized by its capital city established at OMBOS; whereas, it was at BEHDET for the northern capital. In the south, where both kingdoms originally started, the standard or colour was symbolized by the WHITE CROWN worn by its pharoahs; in the north it was a RED CROWN. The southern standard emblem was further marked by the national plant, the LILLY or LOTUS; in the north it was the PAPYRUS plant from whence the world's first paper was manufactured. All of these signs and symbols are traceable through one of the most ancient documents produced by the Egyptians (including the PAPYRUS OF ANI and the BOOK OF THE DEAD), as well as other totems and monuments further south in Ethiopia and Puanit. Dr. Albert Churchward's, SIGNS AND SYMBOLS OF PRIMORDIAL MAN, and, ORIGINS AND EVOLUTION OF RELIGION, show that these signs, and mostly all others used by other High-Cultures along the 4,100 miles Nile Valley, were first used by the TWA (so-called "Pygmies" by the colonialists from Europe and America) people of central Africa before they reached Puanit, Ethiopia, Nubia, and then Egypt and other parts of northern Africa before crossing into Asia-Minor and Europe - Greece. On the other hand, Sir Geoffrey Higgins was of the opinion that they all "STARTED IN INDIA," as shown in his books, ANACALYPSIS, Vols. I & II, London, 1834.

The change of the two Egyptian kingdoms, UPPER and LOWER, came when the northern (UPPER) captured the southern (LOWER) and forced the southerners into a united Egyptian Kingdom (one pharaoh). The two capitals were abondoned (politically) as capitals; and the city of ON[1] - The City of the Sun, HELIOPOLIS according to the Greeks, a city bordering near modern Cairo, became both the

---

1. Mentioned in the Hebrew HOLY TORAH, Christian OLD TESTAMENT.

religious and political capital of the union of UPPER and LOWER Egypt. This state of affair was only temporary, however; as the records show (no date given) that the southerners soon after revolted against their northern brothers and won their seperation once more. BUTO, also known as DEP and PEE, or the "DOUBLE METROPOLIS," was the capital of the northerners; the southerners having selected a site near ELKHAB, a city also divided and rul - ed by two pharaohs as the north, called NEKHEB and NEKHEM. In the ensuing wars that followed the southerners returned the loss to the northerners and reunited the country under southerners who were primarily from Nubia, Puanit and Ethiopia. From this point onwards one is to note the beginnings of what was later to become the "DYNASTIES" that the High Priest Manetho mentioned, all thirty (30) of them, from the Pharaoh AHA to conquest of Kimit by Alexander II ("the great") in 332 BCE. And it was Pharoah AHA who was the last of the indigenous Africans of Kimit to unite both UPPER and LOWER halves to commence the DYNASTIC PERIODS.

The PreDYNASTIC kings, or pharaohs, were equally great. There are many monuments of their creative genius left for us to attest to their greatness. NEKHEM, "The Scorpion," was one of the greatest of those pharoahs. He was a southerner from Hierakonpolis, the city where the oldest written language in existence - HIEROGLYPHICS - was created; and from whence he waged his most successful wars against the northerners. Some "Western" historians are of the opinion that he even "...penetrated all the way north to TURA," which was north of the city of MEMPHIS; others, yet, claimed that it was all the way "...into the Delta..." region on the Kimit Sea (Mediterranean Sea).

Pharaoh AHA, who is most noted in Egyptian history as "NARMER" (a name given him by the ancient Greeks), recorded his envolvement in the re-unification of UPPER and LOWER Egypt on a palette shown held in his hands. This historical recording took place at least two-thousand five-hundred and twenty-three (2523) years before the birth of the so-called "FATHER OF HISTORY"- Herodotus of the Greeks. Whereas, some "Western" historians also declared that the religious recordings of the Egyptians with relationship to their secular activities and those of their Gods could not be called "HISTORY" in the same sense as Herodotus' account of Egyptian life. Yet, the account of Egyptian history by Pharoah AHA was in every detail complete of the argument and analytical questions and answers found in Herodotus' work, HISTORIES, covering the period of AHA's reign. It "<u>fall into the area of poetry</u>" others continue saying; thus, they failed to note that poetic language and dialouge were methods used by the ancient Africans all over Alkebu-lan (Africa) in every aspect of their recordings of their living experiences and that of their religious outlook; they, not distinguishing any difference between the spiritual and the secular. Modern-day Africans to a great degree have continued this custom. The Africans' form of history preceded Herodotus; as such, they had no reason to change their style to please their student - HERODOTUS.

Except for the great achievements AHA made in his war efforts; and inspite of the fact of the "<u>great general</u>" and "<u>king</u>" he was, the First Dynasty did not really begin the major building period of the temple and pyramid structures that impress all of mankind to this very day; none of his works in this direction displayed the great genius of the Africans in their structures they built for the worship of their Gods. But, it was still this pharaoh of the First Dynasty that led the unity which was to set the pace to produce the following peaceful mode that created the architectural and engineering genius of the Third Dynasty. The first pharoah of the Third Dynasty, DJOSER (the Greeks called him ZOZER), was the first of the major pyramid builders. He was joined by a southerner named IMHOTEP - architect, physician, prime minister, poet, historian, fablist, etc., etc.,the one who designed and built the "first STEP PYRAMID," at Sakhara (the Greeks called this place "Saqqara").[1] Imhotep and Djoser introduced the GREAT PYRAMID AGE that lasted until c2565, ending with the death of Pharaoh KHAFRA; all of this having begun and ended more than 890 years before the first foreingers into Alkebu-lan arrived there from Asia - people called "HYKSOS".[2]

THE FIRST non-AFRICAN INVADERS IN KIMIT (Egypt):

Josephus, the Hebrew (Jewish) historian that wrote much of the earliest information of the Christian religion and its God - Jesus Christ of Nazzareth; and who also salvaged much of the historical information we know about the ancient Africans of Egypt and their country - as written by the High-Priest Manetho, was also duplicated by others. He exhibited the same type of respect for Manetho's work, THE HISTORY OF EGYPT, as did Eusebius, Leo Africanus (Leo the African) and others; and described the

---

1. He was a "great physician" and called the "God of Medicine" more than 1300 years before the birth of Europe's first physician -HIPPOCRATES.

2. These people is said to have originated around the OXUS RIVER bed of Asia; and, that, they crossed into Alkebu-lan through the Sinai Peninsula. See BLACK MAN OF THE NILE.

foreigners - HYKSOS - that invaded Egypt in the following manner:

> "...a blast of Rē (God)[1] smote us unexpectedly from the regions to the East (Sinai Peninsula), <u>invaders of an obscure race</u>[2] marched with vengance on our land (Kimit, Sais or Egypt). By sheer manpower they quickly seized our land without hardly a blow; having overpowered the Lords of our land, they hurriedly set fire to our cities ruthlessly, they razed to the earth our temples of the Gods, and abused our people with a cruel brutality....And finally, they appointed one of their own numbers, one called Salitis, as Pharoah (King).

Josephus' recapitulation of Manetho's[3] documentation of the Africans ("Negroes, Bantus, Niggers," etc.) of Egypt's history, with respect to their invasion and capture by foreigners who were the first to enter Alkebu-lan from any other continent, in this case ASIA. The quotation made it quite clear that the invaders were not the same as the indigenous Africans they met in Kimit (Egypt). He quoted Manetho as saying that the invaders were "... AN OBSCURE RACE...," etc. This very fact that the Egyptians (correctly "ROMITI") made it their business to record the physical difference between themselves and the invaders (their enslavers) is added proof, unchallengably so, that they wanted their descendants (African-Americans included) to remember that a people who were not Africans, as their ancestors, had "INVADED" and "ABUSED" them. Therefore, the Hyksos- whom "modern" historians called "SEMITES"- were the so-called "WHITE HOPE" that failed to materialize under strict historical scrutiny; they proved to be no link in the so-called "CAUCASIAN" or "SEMITIC NORTH AFRICA" myth

---

1. Words in parentheses by your professor for clarity only.
2. Words shown underscored is for special emphasis, and related to comments to follow in citing specific details which they have in the following work.
3. African High-Priest under the reign of the Greeks who invaded Egypt with Alexander II and Aristotle, also Ptolemy I (Soter).

so prevalent among European-American historians and Egyptologists of the 19th and 20th century.

Since the Hyksos (pronounced HICK - SUS) have been declared to be the "...FIRST OF THE SEMITIC RACES THAT OCCUPIED EGYPT...," etc. according to most "Western" educators, and they did not enter Kimit before 1675 BCE, it is clearly obvious that the "SEMITES" could not have built-up the High-Culture of Kimit or anyother of the African nations along the Nile Valleys, Great Lakes region, or other parts of north and northeast Africa before the so-called "NEGROES" or "BANTUS" did.

Most "Western" educators have recently made it their common practice to disclaim the accuracy of Manetho's characterization of the HYKSOS, even though he saw the remnants of them in his native Kimit. The disclaimer, however, is no different than their contempt for their own "FATHER OF HISTORY", Herodotus, description (already given in other lectures) of the indigenous people of Egypt that would have appeared to resemble any African-American one would see on the streets of the Harlems of the United States of America today; and we must rember that both Manetho and Herodotus were living in Kimit hundreds of years before the birth of the Christians' Jesus Christ, and thousands of years before the so-called "modern historians" and "Egyptologists." These facts are further demonstrated in Herodotus' THE HISTORIES; as well as Manetho's THE HISTORY OF EGYPT; both books you have been exposed to in many class sessions in this course. It is, therefore, unnecessary to provide any further bibliographical references to cover this point. If such is not the case, I say to you who need further details in this matter, take up anyone of the works dealing with this period of African history in our college's library, or that of anyother "INSITUTION OF HIGHER LEARNING" throughout the United States of America and its colonies (including those called "Commonwealth," such as Puerto Rico), and practically all of them will verify my contention.

But, you must also note that it was not until 525 BCE that another "OBSCURE RACE" of people entered Kimit, North Africa, as conquerors - PERSIANS; this having takem place 1055 years following the expulsion of the HYKSOS (Shepherd Kings or Keeper of Shepherds)-1580,[1] according to the High-Priest, Manetho, of Kimit. These people were (at the time of their invasion of Kimit in č1675 BCE) already former captives of an Egyptian army that extended itself to the banks of the Indus River - today's GANGES RIVER (named in honour of the African general of the army of Kush -Ethiopia- that invaded and captured much of India). Although some of the same educators have claimed, without the least bit of documentary evidence to substantiate their hypotheses, fantastic developments by the Hyksos during their "BRUTAL" reign in Kimit over the Romiti (Egyptians), they are unable to cite one aspect of change the Hyksos made to the African's religion, burial rites, method of construction of their temples and other buildings, agriculture, medical science, astronomy, mathematics, phi-

---

1. This depiction by Manetho also caused "modern" educators on Egyptian history to create many versions and interpretations of history in order to make the Hyksos appear to be of the same "SEMITIC RACE" as the indigenous Africans they met in Kimit (Egypt). George Steindorff and Keith C. Seele in their book, WHEN EGYPT RULED THE EAST. The Univ. of Chicago Press, Chicago & London), 1942, p. 24, even suggested that the word HYKSOS, originally called "HEKU SHOSWET", was later pronounced "HYKU SHOSE,"and means "RULERS OF FOREIGN LANDS." The conflict between "modern" educators on this point still retain its most racist characteristics never-the-less.

losophy, or anyother desciplines in which the indigenous people of Kimit were engaged in. Why is this practice still active among so-called "modern" educators on the history of the peoples of north Africa? Because the HYKSOS were their only hope to connect "DARK-SKINNED" or "LIGHT-SKINNED CAUCASIANS" and "SEMITES" to NORTH AFRICA'S High-Culture of antiquity. But the HYKSOS were not known at any period in history, prior to the invasion of Kimit, to have built one building of stone any where, or to have developed any system of High-Culture (civilization) of the type they met in Egypt, not even remotely similar to the least of that which they met on the borders of the Sinai Peninsula that were colonies of Kimit at that period in history. Thus,"<u>the fortifications at Tell el-Yahudiah and Heliopolis</u>," attributed to the "<u>HYKSOS inginuity</u>" by "modern" educators were, in fact, African; such construction also showing no marked change in the characteristics of other construction built before the arrival of these foreigners. Of course, I am not ignoring the fact that there were great builders of equally magnificent structures in other African nations during said period — such as Nubia, Kush, Zimbabwe, Dhlo Dhlo; also in Asia-Minor - today's Middle East, all of which had no connection with the invading Hyksos that arrived in the Egyptian Delta in c1675 BCE. What I am saying, however, is that <u>the Africans of Kimit (Egypt) structural engineering cannot, with any degree of documentary proof whatsoever, be correctly attributed to the Hyksos or anyother so-called "SEMITIC RACE" that did not already come in contact with Africans of Kimit, Nubia, Puanit, and other Nile Valleys and Great Lakes High-Cultures before they were built</u>.

Since I have already introduced two new names of indigenous African High-Cultures in my reference, at this juncture, the following chapter will give some brief details on ZIMBABWE, DHLO-DHLO, and some of the other related areas and nations of central and southern Alkebu-lan (Africa) of antiquity; all of them almost unheard of by the average African, much less European and/or European-American and African-American. I will not include Kush (Cush or Ethiopia), Nubia (Sudan), Puanit (Punt or Somaliland - parts of Kenya and Ethiopia), all three of which, by now, you are, or should be, quite familiar historically and socio-politically.

Returning to the African-Egyptian High-Culture (civilization) of antiquity, which European-American Egyptologists, even such noted ones as Gaston Maspero, E. Loti, Sir E.A.Wallis Budge, and hundreds more before the United States of America's professor James Henry Breasted and other late-commers to the field tried to "CAUCASIANIZE" or "SEMITICIZE," and even "HAMETICIZE," North Africa - Egypt in particular, we find Hetcaeus of Miletus (? - c510 BCE) who wrote a HISTORY OF EGYPT (before Herodotus of Halicarmassus c484-430 BCE) relative to the African-Egyptian's "...LIFE IN THE DELTA..." and the "...PROBLEMS OF THE NILE FLOOD, FORMATION OF THE DELTA...", and "...FAUNA OF THE NATION." Hectcaeus called his work,"A SURVEY OF THE EARTH." Of course the "EARTH," at that period in antiquity, only included the extent of the Indus River (Ganges River) at the East, southern China at the furthest point northeast, crossing Asia diagonally east by west above the FERTILE CRESCENT at the Black Sea, and then into Europe at Pyrrhs (Greece) to the eastern side of the Itali-

an Peninsula, and back across the Egyptian side of the Kimit Sea
(Mediterranean Sea) into Alkebu-lan (Africa). This latter point
I have raised, only to show that Herodotus was not the "...FIRST
HISTORIAN...," European or otherwise, as claimed by so many so-
called "modern historians" and others of related desciplines. But,
Herodotus, in the SECOND BOOK of his work, which he called "<u>EU-
TERPE"-After the Muse</u>, deals primarily with the people of Egypt
(already described in details earlier in this series of lecture-
essays) conflicts with foreigners of Africa and those from Asia;
the wonders of the country - which included its educational system of science, astronomy, philosophy, astrology, agriculture,
religion, mathematics, engineering, law, architecture, etc. These
observations he excelled in - due to his ability for narratives,
and as such he was able to compile some of the most valuable
historical data on his expidition up the Nile River Valley to
the First Cataract about c457 or 450 BCE. Like Herodotus, however, Hecataeus also wrote of the "...BLACKNESS..." of the indigenous Egyptian people. Most historians of European and European-American origin, on the other hand, dared to suggest that
the word "BLACKNESS," only in this case, had nothing to do with
the indigenous Africans of Egypt's "...COLOR OF SKIN;" but, instead said writers were referring to a "...CONDITION OF CULTURE"
or some other sophisticatedly contrived hypothesis of a semantical nature common among so-called "modern educators" today. Yet,
Herodotus included in his work a list of the indigenous African
PHAROAHS, from Psametichus I (c664-610 BCE) up to those of the
date of his writing (c457 or 450 BCE). This man, of whom Cicero
gave the title - "FATHER OF HISTORY," was the first to translate

the Africans of Kimit's language, **OF HISTORY** into the language of the indigenous Europeans of Greece - GREEK- for the pleasure of his fellow Greek citizens information; even though he was not a Greek by birth, but an Ionian of Egyptian training. It was his translation, in terms which the Greeks could understand and digest, which made Cicero proclaimed that "HERODOTUS' WORK..." was "...DIFFERENT TO THE POETIC WORKS OF THE EGYPTIANS...," etc. He also stated that "...HERODOTUS WAS THE FIRST HISTORIAN...." This conclusion on the part of Cicero about the history of Kimit, as written by African historians that predated Herodotus, has been the basis upon which so-called "modern historians" also hold that "HERODOTUS WAS THE FATHER OF HISTORY", and "THE FIRST HISTORIAN." This is similar as saying that the Hebrew HOLY TORAH (Christian OLD TESTAMENT) is not the history, as well as religious mythology, of the Haribus (Hebrew or Jewish peoples). Yet, it is Herodotus' BOOK TWO (II) which most of the same so-called "modern historians" and "Egyptologists" rejected for its references to the "...<u>COLCHIANS, CUSHITES AND EGYPTIANS" color of skin, size of lips, texture of hair and other aspects of a physical nature usually ascribed to the so-called "NEGROES" or "NEGROIDS</u>," calling it "<u>FICTICIOUS</u>" - among other names much more derogatory than this one. Herodotus not only found these things to be true, he also corroborated similar findings by Hecataeus of Miletus; and he too was corraborated in the writings of Diodorus Siculus of Greece's work, GENERAL HISTORY, Book I. Yet, Diodorus came to Kimit (Egypt) about 391 years (c590 BCE) after Herodotus had already written his HISTORIES- c457-450 BCE . It was Diodorus who gave Pharoah AHA the name - "MENAS," which has been further corrupted into the modern-day "MENES. It was he who also stated that AHA was "...THE FIRST OF THE EGYPTIAN KINGS;" but failed to name any of the others who were just as prominent in Egyptian history, except for an occasional mention in his footnotes throughout his work.

There is no doubt that both of the aforementioned foreign writers, Herodotus and Diodorus, as well as Hecataeus, made certain errors with regards to much that they learnt through hearsay evidence. Some of their errors also had to do with what they actually saw. Because much of what they saw they could only interpret in terms of their own experiences in Greece and Ionia; settings which had indigenous African origin, but of local rearrangement. Never-the-less, <u>it was impossible for them to make errors about the color of the people they met and live with, including the people's physical characteristics they described in such details</u>. It must be remembered that they lived with the **Africans**, and studied under their priests ; this they did in Nubia and Merowe, as well as Kimit; and these priests came from as far off as MONOMOTAPA - the southernmost end of the continent of ALKEBU-LAN (Africa) - presently called "THE REPUBLIC OF SOUTH AFRICA (a racist government that excludes the children of the indigenous peoples who once comprised the population of KIMIT, KUSH, NUBIA, MEROWE, etc. - High-Cultures, civilizations , that reached their zenith all along the Great Lakes regions and the head-waters of the more than 4,100 miles long Nile River).

ZIMBABWE, DHLO-DHLO, etc.: THE KIMITS OF
SOUTHERN ALKEBU-LAN - <u>Monomotapa Empire</u>

To say that Africans "<u>South of the Sahara</u>", the so-called "BANTUS, NEGROES, PYGMIES, HOTTENTOTS, BUSHMEN," etc. (all of these names of inferiority placed upon indigenous African peoples in their own homeland by 19th and 20th century conquerors and slavers from imperial Europe, European-America and Great Britain - including Scotland, Ireland, Wales and England) built and developed High-Cultures equivalent to that of Kimit, would be equally as ridiculous to "Westerners" as saying that the Africans of Kimit, before the invasion of that nation by the Hyksos, were like their physical description given by Herodotus and others like himself. Never-the-less <u>Zimbabwe, Dhlo-Dhlo, Bulawayo, Chiwona, Hubvumi, Mshosho</u>, and other southern and central African High-Cultures of antiquity, equalled the Africans of Kimit's zenith in many aspects, surpassed them in many others, and were behind in quite a few.

When the first of the Europeans (Portuguese mariners) arrived at CABO de TORMENTOS ("Cape of Storms") in 1486 C.E. with captain Bartolome Dias, and his men forced to seek refuge among the Africans of the Empire of Monomotapa, there were no theories existing about "AFRICANS SOUTH OF THE SAHARA, SEMITIC AFRICA, CAUCASIAN AFRICA;" not even "NEGROID AFRICA." Before other Europeans turned the "CAPE OF GOOD HOPE" and reached ZIMBABWE (the seat of government of the Monomotapa Empire) in 1496 C.E. with captain Vasco da Gama, they met indigenous Africans in their boats, and on land, all along the coast of the Empire; all of whom appraised the European (Portuguese) foreigners of their great TEMPLE OF THE GODS.[1] The TEMPLE OF THE GODS is a series of major stone mason-

---

1. See the following works: Y. ben-Jochannan, BLACK MAN OF THE Nile; Basil Davidson, THE AFRICAN PAST; LOST CITIES OF AFRICA; G. Padmore, AFRICA: BRITAIN'S THIRD EMPIRE; J.C.deGraft-Johnson, AFRICAN GLORY; J.A. Rogers, WORLD'S GREAT MEN OF COLOR (2 v.); J. Jackson, AN INTRODUCTION TO AFRICAN HISTORY; L. Labourete, AFRICA BEFORE THE WHITE MAN; L. Froebenius, AFRIKA SPRACK; etc.

ry structures that were later on to be wrongfully renamed by European and European-American colonialist adventurers that invaded the area for the purpose of enslaving the indigenous African peoples and confiscating their "GOLD-LADEN ELIPTICAL BUILDINGS AND ACROPOLIS." Here, at these sites, the indigenous Africans had untilized the natural formation of bed rock for the foundation of their multi-story structured TEMPLES OF THE GODS they built for prayers to their Gods and other functions. On the otherhand, their fellow indigenous Africans of North Africa, Kimit in particular, had to work through sandy top soil to delve deep into the inner-earth (ground) to find a sub-strata equal to the weight of the super-structure of their TEMPLES to their GODS. These two major factors affected seriously the basic differences why the African structures of the north took on opposite characteristics in design to those of the south. These factors also affected greatly the type of cultures which were to develop in each area. The basic fauna and other natural geographical considerations, especially the northern GREAT DESERT (the Arabs' "SAHARA"), as against the southern FERTILE HIGHLANDS, in each respective area, north and south, made further differences in cultural considerations necessary. In the central and southern High-Cultures (civilizations) there were an abundance of food, animals, birds, materials for construction, skins and other materials for clothing, and mountains in which "...THE GODS DWELL" -the same as the "GODS" that their Egyptian, Ethiopian, Nubian and Puanit fellow indigenous Africans of the north and northeast adopted from the TWA Africans of central Africa - whom European colonialists and slavers renamed "PYGMIES."

As to which European or European-American between the 19th and 20th century C.E. was the first to visit any of the ruins there is quite a lot of confusion. However, it is R.N. Hall, D. Randall MacIver and Gertrude Caton-Thompson (Ph.D.) who most Europeans and European-Americans quote as "AUTHORITIES" on this aspect of the indigenous Africans' EXPERIENCE. These are Europe's and the United States of America's cultural, anthropological, archaelogical, and historical makers of the history and heritage that have been so far pedled as "AUTHORITATIVE SOURCES" and "AUTHORITIES." I shall not hesitate to use all three sources whereever and whenever necessary; nor would I fail to introduce others of the same chracterization. However, I also reserve the right, as an African son whose heritage it is the so-called "AUTHORITIES" wrote about, to point out their errors, racist conclusions, and willful distortions constantly being manufactured about these societies - High-Cultures, just as I have done with respect to those of north and northeast Africa. This position I have taken, irrespective of any stance to the opposite taken by the COUNCIL OF BRITISH ASSOCIATION, the ZOOLOGICAL SOCIETY OF SOUTH AFRICA, the RHODESIAN SOCIETY OF ANTIQUITIES, or any other European-based organization that assumed the "AUTHORITY" of speaking for the Africans and their descendants inside and outside of my "MOTHERLAND" - Alkebu-lan (Africa). The 1st two "AUTHORITIES" which I wish to cite with regards to their inadequacies in this area are the BRITISH MUSEUM HANDBOOK to the Ethnological Collections and the ENCYCLOPEDIA BRITANICA. Thus, one finds in the latter's 11th Edition the following description of ZIMBABWE:

>   Zimbabwe was the distributing centre for the gold traffic carried on in the Middle Ages be-

> tween the Monomotapa and the Mohammedans (Arabs)[1]
> of the coast.... It may therefore be dated to a
> period not earlier than the 14th or 15th century
> A.D. and attributed to the same Bantu people, re-
> mains of whose stone-fenced kraals are found be-
> tween the Limpopo and the Zambesi (rivers).

On the otherhand the former states on page 216 of its 1925 Edition, the following:

> The origin of these ruins has been the sud-
> ject of much controversy;[2] but from archaeolog-
> ical evidence it appears that the most import-
> ant of these structures cannot referred to a
> period prior to the fourteenth century, and no
> remains have been found which connect them with
> any race but that of the negro.[3]

Which one of you would have figured, or accepted on my say so before this date, that even these two sources of European and European-American "AUTHORITY ON AFRICA" are purposefully racist and erroneous   But, why the "...it may therefore be dated to a period not earlier than the 14th century A.D." etc.[1] when, in fact, they do not know the truth of what they speak?

R.N. Hall (one of the first of the "Western" writers on Zimbabwe - The Maund Ruins) characterized them according to "LOWER, MIDDLE" and "UPPER VALLEY RUINS" in his book, GREAT ZIMBABWE, Methuen, 1905. On page 364 he wrote the following:

> The Upper Grouping includes the No. 1 Ruins;
> Ridge Ruins; Mauch Ruins; and East Ruins. The
> names commemorate the earliest explorers of
> Zimbabwe, beginning with Adam Renders, who 'dis-
> covered' it in 1869, and Karl Mauch, who, three
> years later, gave to the world fuller details
> concerning it.

---

1. Words in brackets by the lecturer for clarity only.
2. Words underscored for special emphasis in the following remarks relating to same.
3. Note that the word "negro" was not even capitalized. The "negro" was, and still is, a "thing" or "property" in the eyes of the Europeans and European-Americans.

I have underscored two sets of words above. The first deals with the alleged "DISCOVERY OF ZIMBABWE" by a European who was told about its existence like thousands more before him from 1496 C.E. The second deals with the '<u>world</u>' which these men wrote for; a '<u>world</u>' that excluded even the descendants of those indigenous Africans who engineered and built Zimbabwe; Africans who were at the time of the alleged gift "<u>to the world</u>" slaves of Mauch's fellow European and European-American imperialist and colonialist settlers in southern Africa, as well as other areas of the continent. As to <u>discovering it</u>; that is equivalent to saying that I can '<u>discover twenty dollars on your living room table which you placed there before I even knew where you lived</u>'; a <u>discovery</u> that is equal to that Cristobal Colon and other Spaniards and Portuguese, the so-called "explorers," to Asia, Africa, and the Americas - including the Caribbean Islands <u>where the indigenous peoples were unaware they were being discovered</u>.

Attempts at dating this "metropolis," Zimbabwe, brought on all sort of declarations; from, "...<u>it was built by shipwrecked Greeks</u>...," to; "...<u>it was built by Chinese merchants</u>...," etc. The latest placed its building "...<u>by Arab merchants from Arabia in the 10th century A.D.</u>...,"etc. The exception to these stories before Dr. Gertrude Caton-Thompson's historic cultural-anthropological work was always known by Africans indigenous to the area of which these "<u>ruins</u>" stand. The history of the structures, before they were "<u>ruins</u>," having passed down from generation to generation orally, just as the history of the ancient Hebrews before Moses (and after) to the rabbis of the Great Synagouge, the ancient Greeks up to and after Herodotus, and all other ancient peoples of antiquity. MacIver (the Scot..) was certain that...

> "Not a single inscription has ever been found in the country."

The "country," today, is called "RHODESIA" (formerly Southern Rhodesia); but, before the arrival of the European imperialist slavers the indigenous Africans had already named their country "ZIMBABWE." MacIver also claimed that:

> Seven sites have been investigated, and from not one of them has any object been obtained by myself or by others before me which can be shown to be more ancient than fourteenth or fifteenth century A.D.

In both of the above quotations MacIver, like those he termed "...others before me...," etc., and those after him until Dr. Gertrude Caton-Thompson in 1928 C.E., failed to take note of the signs and symbols (African writings never-the-less) on the interior and exterior walls of the "RUINS." He too failed to accept that written communication does not necessarily have to follow that which Europeans and European-Americans consider to be "WRITING" or "SCRIPT." It is because of the same reason that the totems of the indigenous Americans (the so-called "Indians") history, 'written history' that is, has evaded the Europeans and European-Americans to this very date - 1971 C.E. - some 479 years after the first of them entered their "NEW WORLD", which they also called "AMERICA" and "WESTERN HEMISPHERE."

Hall, as MacIver, on page 306 of his book, GREAT ZIMBABWE, states that:

> "...three large black beads with white lines, possibly identical with a similar bead found by Bent[1]

---

1. Theodore Bent, THE RUINED CITES OF MASHONALAND, Longmans, London, 1893; also, THE RUINS OF MASHONALAND and EXPLORATIONS in the COUNTRY, Geographical Journal, May 1892.

...to which he ascribes a very great age...;"etc. Hall was later on to place the entire "METROPOLIS OF ZIMBABWE" to an origin "...<u>not earlier than the fourteenth century A.D.</u>;" a position which has been totally descredited by his fellow Europeans and European-Americans, including Dr. Caton-Thompson. The current disrespect for the Africans is typical of Hall and others who renamed the "RUINS" (each site) in honour of their fellow European, a so-called EXPLORER, even though they were very well aware of the names the indigenous Africans gave to their own homeland and sites; this type of contempteous behaviour being equal to the renaming of certain indigenous African peoples-"NEGROES" (with a common or capital letter), "PYGMIES," etc.; the names "SEMITIC" and "HAMITIC," as "CAUCASIAN," being no better when refering to the indigenous African peoples. One must realize that it was not to very long ago the type of '<u>therefore it is this, thus, and so</u>' history of West Africa was written by European and European-American so-called "AUTHORITIES ON AFRICA," all of which have not stopped in any way up to this present lecture; and none of which there is any indication of change in the very near future, as long as "BLACK STUDIES" and "AFRICAN STUDIES" departments and/or courses in European-American institutions of higher learning continue to be controlled by people other than those whose history is being written and taught - African peoples.

A goodly number of the European and European-American authors who wrote about the Monomotapa Empire (which they have broken down into subject-nations of same: such as Mashonaland, Zululand, Barotseland, Swaziland, Bechuanaland, Zimbabwe, etc. in their so-called "authoritative works") are listed in the following bibliographic compilation: - Thomas Baines, GOLD REGIONS OF SOUTH-EASTERN AFRICA, 1877; Harry Balfour, FLINT ENGRAVED POTTERY FROM THE RUINS AT KHAMI AND DHLO-DHLO (in: Rhodesia Man), Feb. 1906; S.S. Dorman, RHODESIAN RUINS AND NATIVE TRADITION (in: South African Journal of Science), June 1916; H.B. Douslin, RECENT EXPLORATIONS AT ZIMBABWE (in: Proc. Rh. Sc. Ass., Vol. XX), 1921-22; H.W. Garbutt and J.P. Johnson, HUT AT KHAMI RUINS (Rhodesia Man, 56), 1912; R.H. Hall, PREHISTORIC RHODESIA, 1905; R.H. Hall, HUMAN REMAINS IN RHODESIAN RUINS (in: Geographical Journal), Nov. 1909; D. Randall MacIver, MEDIAVAL RHODESIA, 1906; D.R. MacIver, THE RHODESIAN RUINS:THEIR PROBABLE ORIGIN AND SIGNIFICANCE (in: Geographical Journal), April 1906; Karl Maunch, REISEN IM INNEREN von SUD-AFRIKA, 1865-72; H.B. Maufe, THE EARLY INHABITANTS OF RHODESIA, 1924; etc. All of these works I have placed before you at various times for your independent examination and research beyond this lecture series. I expect that you will pursue them in the most exhaustive manner possible, and that your thesis shall reflect support, opposition, and difference if you may, to them and my lecture as you deem appropriate; that is providing you support all of your contentions by evidence on all sides of the picture; and when you are presenting your own hypothesis, that you state so very clearly and succinctly.

You will note that the CONE TOWER TEMPLE, called the "ZIMBABWE HOLY OF HOLIES" by European and European-American writers, was constructed in a manner whereby the sun's rays always beamed upon its ALTER OF SACRIFICE. And, that this structure was also built on an orientation that would use the sun's rays falling on the CONE TOWER as a SUN DIAL. This structure, of which only the <u>ruins</u> remain, was said to be the "...RUINS OF THE PRIESTESS OF THE MONDORO CULT", also "...THE BURIAL PLACES OF CHIEFS." Here again, as in all High-Cultures of which European and European-American educators believe were not responsible for their own education and "civilization" ("Western Judaeo-Christian Greek" orientation), we can see "Western educators" designating the indigenous religions as "CULTS," and the heads of state as "CHIEFS." It is obvious that a metropolis of the magnitude of DHLO-DHLO and ZIMBABWE, much less the Monomotapa Empire, had to have had a head of state way above the esteem of the rank of "CHIEF." In the very same light, the religions of Kimit, Kush, Puanit, Nubia, Merowe and other African nations of the north and northeast are still called "CULTS;" whereas, those of ancient Rome, Greece, Israel, Persia and other parts of the <u>Middle East</u> and Europe are-called "INDO-EUROPEAN ARYAN ORIGIN RELIGIONS." Likewise, the religion of Zimbabwe (the worship of the same Sun GOD - RĀ or RĒ), as those of ancient Kush, Nubia, Carthage, Kimit, etc. (all of them foundation nations upon which Judaeo-Christianity and Islam must also rest) is also termed "IDOLATROUS"or "PAGANISTIC;" not Judaism, Christianity and Islam - the latter three being outgrowths of those so deemed "CULTS." As such, we find Charles Bullock in his work, THE MASHONA, Juta, 1928, saying the following on page 38:

> "...the minature <u>huts</u>[1] (stone houses)[2] built at a place of sacrifice to the tribal spirit. I hazard (without native confirmation)"Lo! A great house."

Even <u>stone houses</u>, called DZIMBA DZA MAHWE (house of stone), by

---

1. Word underscored by the lecturer for emphasis and comments.
2. Words in parentheses by the lecturer for clarity.

the indigenous Africans of this region are referred to as "HUTS" by these foreigners who always declare that they only write (academically) "...true and impartial history." Yet any hovel in Europe produced by ancient Europeans does not gain the name "HUT" by the same writers. Semantically they are called all sorts of sophisticated anthropological and archaeological names that place them respectfully within a "non-primitive" stature. There is no doubt that these "STONE HOUSES" or "HOUSES OF STONE" - DZIMBA DZA MAHWE - are similar, and for the same purpose as "ANTI-TEMPLES" were to "TEMPLES" in Kimit. This method of construction was typical in Kush, Puanit, Nubia, Merowe, Kimit and among many other places in Alkebu-lan, including the West-African Empires. Thus, we find them as far back into antiquity as the MASTABAS built attached, or appart, of the main pyramids of Kimit as early as 6000 to 4000 BCE. Just emagine "HUTS" built with "GRANITE CEMENT FLOORS" and "CRUSHED FRAGMENTS OF DECOMPOSED GRANITE MIXED WITH LARGE PROPORTION OF LIME," as described by R.N. Hall in his book, GREAT ZIMBABWE, page 187; or the "SUPERIOR MATERIAL" (to Hall's description)[1] employed by the Africans at DHLO-DHLO..."IN PLACE OF CLAY THEY HAVE USED A HARD CEMENT (made apparently with powdered granite) SIMILAR TO THAT WHICH WE SHALL FIND AT NANA-TALI, KHAMI AND ZIMBABWE...," as stated by D. Randall MacIver in his book, MEDIAEVAL RHODESIA, Macmillan, New York, 1906. Dr. Gertrude Caton-Thompson in her work, THE ZIMBABWE CULTURE, The Clarendon Press, Oxford, England, 1931, on page 12, under the sub-title "Zimbabwe: The Maund Ruins," with respect to the more than 500 RUINS that comprise the "GREAT ZIMBABWE METROPOLIS," wrote:

> As one gazes over wide stretches (from an airplane which she was riding)[1] of the country from

---

1. Words in parenthesis by your lecturer for clarity only.

> the Summit of the Acropolis Hill, raised some 350 ft. above the surrounding land, or better still as one circles far above it in an aeroplane, the full excellence of the position is borne home. Truly the founders (indigenous Africans called "Negroes")[1] of Zimbabwe balanced the merits of two worlds, <u>and, being undecided</u>, chose both.

It was impossible for an area covered with 500 or more stone structures, <u>ruins</u>, of the type we are considering not to have been as developed in every manner in a High-Culture similar to that of **Kimit**, Colchis, Kush, Nubia, Sumner, Babylon and other nations of antiquity, including Greece later on - the baby of all so far mentioned. The comment by J. Willoughby in his book, FURTHER EXCAVATIONS AT ZIMBABWE (George Philip, 1893), page 27, testify to the magnitude of the construction undertaken by the Africans of Zimbabwe and the other sites directly surrounding. He wrote:

> The absence of any quarry from which the stone was obtained is not to be wondered at, for everywhere in the neighborhood, and particularly in the valley to the eastwards, huge slabs or scales of granite, varying in thickness from one to twelve inches, are lying about ready to hand.

Willoughby's comment is most significant, being that there were others who could not understand why there were entire sections of the "RUINS" missing from the sites and no trace of the stones being present. But, it is only obvious that the <u>stones</u> were removed before the "Westerners" arrived there to write about the area (after their forerunners had all but exterminated the entire population of indigenous Africans to whom the RUINS belonged). The same type of situation occured when the indigenous people moved

---
1. **Words in parentheses** by the lecturer for clarity only.
2. **Words underscored** by the lecturer for specific emphasis and for future citations.

their operations for the mummification of bodies to a hiding place in recent years. With regards to the Europeans concern over the removal of the <u>stones</u> from the "ruins" M.C. Burkitt in his book, SOUTH AFRICA'S PAST IN STONE AND PAINT (Cambridge University Press, 1928), on page 161, noted:

> It is significant that just around Zimbabwe most of the natural scalings seem to have disappeared, doubtless having been removed for the construction of the building.

The above comment was answered by Willoughby's statement above, and by other writers that subsequently followed him.

The Africans of Zimbabwe developed their "STONE STRUCTURES" to the point of consideration for EXPANSION JOINTS between the new and old, high and low, structures. To accomplish this fete way back in antiquity they had to introduce the principle of "STRAIGHT-LINE JOINTS" before "modern" man. J.F. Schefield's, ZIMBABWE: A Critical Examination Of The Building Methods Employed, (South African Journal of Science, Dec. 1926), page 974, states:

> The practice of making straight joints whenever they had to connect new work to old seems to have been the invariable custom of the old builders. It is a simple way of getting over the very real difficulty of bonding into dry rubble work.

You can examine the various documents and excavation stratification data in all of these works I have submitted before you for further verification of the magnitude of the engineering and architectural skills that were necessary to produce this monsterous "METROPOLIS." In many of their own particularity the Zimbabwe and Dhlo-Dhlo structures were much more critical to calculate than their apparent equal in engineering among the RUINS of Kush, Nubia, Carthage, Lebus, Kimit and other areas of north and east Africa (Alkebu-lan).

NUBIA - MOTHER OF KIMIT - GATEWAY TO THE NORTH

Other than COLOR OF SKIN and FACIAL CHARACTERISTICS what make "Western" historians and anthropologists hold that the Nubians were "NEGROES"? Some say it was "PHYSICAL CHARACTERISTICS." But, Herodotus and other ancient European historians who lived among all of the Nile Valley indigenous Africans below the First (1st.) Cataract disagree with the "Westerners" in both cases. The ancients also referred to both, Egyptians and Nubians, as "ETHIOPIANS."[1] Yet, if there is a country and people in history that should receive the MOST MALIGNED award it is Nubia and the Nubians - the so-called "NEGORES." Why? Egypt and Nubia, as Merowe, and sometimes Kush, shared identical writing, culture, Gods, agriculture, science, medicine; and at varied times they also shared common HEAD-OF-STATE called "PHAROAH" (King). Pharoah Piankhi, the best known of the pharoahs that ruled both nations jointly, is shown on the STELAE OF PIANKHI, MERI-AMEN, with the same type of facial characteristics as any other Egyptian pharoah on record except the foreigners from Asia and Europe who came as conquerors with the Persians, Assyrians, Greeks, Romans, and the first of them all - the Hyksos in c1675 BCE. The following picture taken from Sir E.A. Wallis Budge's, BOOKS ON EGYPT AND CHALDEA: EGYPTIAN LITERATURE (Vol. II, Anals of Nubian Kings...,etc.), London, 1912, page li, supports my contention.

The similarity of Hieroglyphics in Egypt and Nubia can be best observed in the inscription on the STELE OF MATISEN, showing a queen of Napata's "DEDICATION" and "ENDOWMENT." The following

---

1. See Frank M. Snowden, BLACKS OF ANTIQUITY : The Greco-Roman Experience, Harvard University Press, Cambridge, Mass., 1970.

picture of said inscription is taken from page xcviii of the works of Sir Ernest A. Wallis Budge already mentioned.

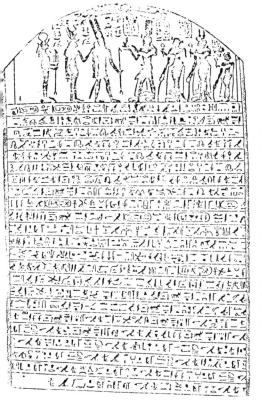

THE STELE OF QUEEN MĀTISEN, OR MĀTISENEN.
DEDICATION OF AN ENDOWMENT BY A QUEEN OF NAPATA.

THE text of this interesting document is cut in hieroglyphics upon a granite stele, which was set up in the temple of Åmen-Rā at Gebel Barkal, in the third year of the reign of Áspelta, to commemorate an endowment made by his queen Mātisen. When and by whom it was found is not known, but it is tolerably certain that it formed one of the group which stood close to the great Stele of Piānkhi. It was acquired by Linant Bey, and then it passed into the possession of Prince Napoleon, and subsequently into the hands of E. de Rougé, after whose death it was given to the Louvre by Monsieur J. de Rougé. It now stands in Salle Henri IV. The text was first published and translated by Pierret in 1873,[1] and an English translation by the same Egyptologist appeared in 1876.[2] The text was republished with a German translation by Dr. Schäfer in 1895,[3] and a facsimile of the text, made from a tracing, was given with a summary of its contents by myself in 1907.[4]

[1] *Études Égyptologiques*, tom. i., p. 96 ff., pl. 2. Paris, 1873.
[2] *Records of the Past*, Old Series, vol. iv., p. 89 f.
[3] *Äg. Zeit.*, 1895, p. 101 ff.; see also *Urkunden*, iii., 101 ff.
[4] *Egyptian Sûdân*, vol. ii., p. 66.

This granite <u>stele</u> deals with a historic detailing of the "ENDOWMENT OF QUEEN MATISEN during the third year of the reign of Pharoah Aspelta. The <u>stele</u> was set up in the <u>Temple of Amen-Rā</u> at Gebel Barkal. It was one of the many stelae stolen from Kimit[1] and Nubia by Prince Napoleon Boneparte and his subordinates dur-

---

1. Napata was at one time the capital city of Kimit when the Nubians and Kushites ruled all three countries jointly.

ing the French invasion of Kimit (Egypt). An English translation of the entire text of the <u>stele's</u> inscription appears in Sir E.A. Wallis Budge's EGYPTIAN SUDAN, Vol. ii, p. 66; the original work was written by Pierret in his book, ETUDES EGYPTOLOGIQUES, tom. i., p. 96ff, and shown on plate 2, Paris, 1873, which he later on translated into English.

Another of the major Nubian <u>stelae</u> is of a "DECREE OF EX-COMMUNICATION" (date unknown) by Pharoah Aspelta. It was made out of a slab of at least 4 feet 4 inches high, by 2 feet 3 inches wide. This <u>stele</u> was also found along with the STELE OF PIANKHI at Bebel Barkal. It is presently housed in the Egyptian Museum, Cairo, Egypt. It **must** be noted, however, that professor Gaston Maspero also mentioned this <u>stele</u> in his work, GUIDE (1910 Edition), p. 215.

In all of the inscriptions dealing with "LIFE" we see the Nubians using the same symbol - ANKH ☥ ; this symbol having been used from periods long before the existence of either Kimit or Nubia. It was first introduced to the world by the TWA people of the Great Lakes region of central Africa, the so-called "PYGMIES." We can substantiate this fact best by referring to Dr. Albert C. Churchward's works, SIGNS AND SYMBOLS OF PRIMORDIAL MAN, London, 1920; also, THE ORIGIN AND EVOLUTION OF RELIGION, London, 1925; both books, I have submitted to you on previous meetings of this class.

Following, we find a drawing by one Hoskins in Sir Ernest A. Wallis Budge's, BOOKS ON EGYPT AND CHALDEA, Vol. II, p. lxxvi, plate II, entitled -"<u>Ruins of the Temple of Tirhâkâh at Gebel Barkal</u>."

"RUINS" OF GEBEL BARKA

The "Ruins" of Gebel Barka is located about ten (10) miles from the Fourth (4th) Cataract in Nubia (modern Sudan). The main subject of the "SEVEN STELE" most often quoted (which originally was located in a group within the temple) was in regards to the conquest of Kimit by Prince (general also) Piankhi in c721 BCE; and the invasion of Kimit by Tamut-Amen between c663-661 BCE; also the "DECREE OF ASPELTA AGAINST TRAITORS;" lastly, the "DEDICATION" and "ENDOWMENT OF QUEEN NATISEN TO AMEN-RA" - which has been detailed before. The queen's role occurred during the 7th century before the Christian era (BCE). There are also references to the defeat of the Persian pharoah of Kimit, Cambysess, by Nastasen; also of his military exploits in eastern Nubia about c520 BCE.

We must remember that the period in which the indigenous **Ithiops** controlled Kimit covered the years c750 to c500 BCE approximately, a total of at least 250 years. And, we must also remember that the city of Napata was in fact the capital of three

Nile Valley nations - Kush, Nubia and Kimit.[1] Thus, it should not supprise anyone to know that many of the pharoahs believed to have been Romiti (Egyptians) were in fact Nubian by birth - "Negroes" or "Negroids" according to the "Westerners." These pharoahs were primarily involved with the joint Kimit-Nubia common development from the reign of Pharoah Seneferu of the IVth Dynasty to the reign of Pharoah Piankhi. It should also be remembered that Pharoah Seneferu led the Romiti in the scourge of Nubia, and was himself driven out of Nubia after he had "...RAVAGED THE WOMEN OF HIS NEIGHBORS (Nubians)[2] AT THE SOUTH...," etc.

The confusion which exists between Western historians and Egyptologists over the original Nubians and Romiti's (Egyptians) physical characteristics, as described by Herodotus and others of antiquity, is further strained by those who mistakenly forget that present-day Arabs (Asians from the Arabian Peninsula - mostly of the Muslim faith) are not descendants of the original indigenous Africans of Kimit, Nubia, Merowe or Kush. In Nubia most of the indigenous African descendants of the ancient occupants of all four (4) Nile Valley nations mentioned have been forced to the southern-most limits of the country by the descendants of the Arab conquerors who arrived there about c640 C.E. or 18 A.H. In the case of the indigenous Africans of Kimit, the very few that remained, or survived, after the Arab Muslims' "JIHADS" (Holy Wars) that began way back in c640 C.E., have had to take second-class citizenship status or leave for points further south in Uganda or Kush (Ethiopia). The Arab and African-Arab rulers of

---

1. The correct indigenous African name of Napata is NAPT. "Western" historians and Egyptologists gave it the former derivation without the approval of the African people of Nubia.
2. Words in parentheses by the lecturer for clarity only.

the 18th and 19th century, such as Juda Pasha and Sa'id Pasha, were equally responsible for the looting of the Africans of Egypt and Nubia artifacts we now see in many public and private "COLLECTIONS" in Europe, Britain and the United States of America; and of course, the so-called "CLEOPATRA'S NEEDLE" in Central Park, New York City. This charge is supported by the case of an Arab officer in the service of Sa'id Pasha in 1862 C.E. who tried to sell the PIANKHI STELE. Yet, Sa'id Pasha who founded the Bulak Museum of Egyptian Antiquities, also, personally, sold many of Kimit's and Nubia's artifacts to the British and French imperialists and colonialists (most of them called themselves "ENTERPRENUERS," and their government).

Speaking of Pharoah Piankhi's STELE. It measured 5 feet 11 inches high, 4 feet 7½ inches wide and 1 foot 5 inches thick, according to figures of its cast in the British Museum's SOUTHERN EGYPTIAN GALLERY. The inscriptions on it are written in Hieroglyphics on all of its four (4) faces (front, back, and two sides). It was cut from a massive slab of grey granite, and weighs approximately 2¼ tons (4,250 lbs.). There are many English translations of this stele's texts. In 1869 C.E. Lauth published his German translation of it under the title - " Sitzungsberichte der Kon Bay Akad," pp. 13-49 (Philos. - Philol. Classe). In the year 1873 C.E. Canon F.C. Cook translated Lauth's German work under the title - "The Inscription of Pianchi," Meramon, London, 1873, 8vo. Cook's work was also published under the title of the 1873 C.E. issue of Records of the Past, O.S., ii, p. 79. An English version of Dr. Burgsch's German works was written and published under the title- "Egypt Under the Pharoahs,"vol. ii. A United States of

America's version followed much later in professor James Henry Breasted's <u>Ancient Records of Egypt</u>, vol. IV. Of the many versions, most deal with the TEXTS from the standpoint of its similarity to certain Egyptian Stelae. Most of the translators were to busy trying to find distinctly different characteristics between their so-called "NEGROES OF NUBIA" and "SEMITES OF EGYPT" and failed to do justice to the historical similarities existing between all of the stelae. It is because of this reason why so many of them are hoping that the "DEMOTIC" and "MEROTIC" scripts written by the indigenous Africans of Nubia, Kush, Merowe and Kimit would never be decoded. For, in them, they see the unravelling of much of their erroneous and racist hypotheses they have passed down to generations after generations with regards to the Nubians being of a "...DIFFERENT RACE TO THE EGYPTIANS AND ETHIOPIANS;" of course never "...DIFFERENT..." to the Europeans and/or European-Americans who write such religiously bigoted and racist materials.

Is it very strange (at least it should not be to the students in my class) that the pictures shown in this <u>lecture-essay</u> and the bibliographical materials submitted for your examination were always available to so-called "EDUCATORS" who constantly crave their ignorance of same in order to continue teaching whatever they desire, while suppressing the TRUTH about the Africans of the Nile Valleys and the Great Lakes region with respect to their commonality. Such "EDUCATORS," never-the-less, continue telling their students that "...THE NEGROES OF NUBIA LEFT NO RECORDS OF THEIR CIVLIZATION...," etc.,etc., etc., almost endlessly. Nothing could be further from the TRUTH. Not a single word of the documentary data in this lecture was ever kept in secret by the Nubians or

Egyptians. Practically each and every historian or Egyptologist should have known of these works existence. If they do not, then they have been thoroughly mis-educated by others who crave the same type of ignorance as they do.

Nubia- like Zimbabwe, Dhlo-Dhlo, and other ancient nations of African antiquity - including Egypt, Ethiopia and Puanit, was the creation and development of African peoples who were almost genius to the last man; this being typical of the Nile Valley peoples - from Uganda (the former Bonyoro Kingdom) to the Mediterranean Sea (formerly the Kimit Sea , a distance of a little more than 4,100 miles) at that period in history; a period when there were no "SEMITES, CAUCASOIDS, HAMITES " and other ITES and SOIDS mentioned in world history; not even a Greece or a Europe. Even the so-called "SLAVES" during this period were recognized as HUMAN BEINGS; and they too contributed freely to the grandeur of their society or High-Culture (civilization) - Nubia, Kush, Merowe, Kimit, and others along the Nile Valleys and Great Lakes region.

THE CONCLUSION OF THIS LECTURE-ESSAY

This lecture, the last in the series on this topic for the semester, should have made you (the student) aware of the fact that there is a preponderance of historical evidence showing the Nubians, Ethiopians, Puanits, Lebus (Libyans),[1] Zimbabians, and other Africans along the Nile Valleys[2] and African Great Lakes. It should have made you realize that there are thousands of volumes on the history of each of these African nations which have been

---
1. Lebu is the original name the Africans called the land the Romans and Greeks renamed "LIBYA."
2. BLUE and WHITE; the ATBARA RIVER from Ethiopia included.

purposefully kept from students of history (all colors) for the past two (2) centuries or more. Unfortunately most of said volumes are alien to most of our "modern" professors of history and anthropology, including those bearing the title "AUTHORITY OF AFRICA;" this in no way exclude most called "BLACK STUDIES PROFESSORS." Thus, you are aware of the problems all of us face; that is, people who profess to speak "<u>authoritatively</u>" on Africa, and things African, without any knowledge of them except for certain aspects of the infamous SLAVE TRADE which was started by the Rt. Rev. Bishop Bartolome de LasCasas and His Holiness Pope Martin Vth of the Roman Catholic Church around the year 1503 or 1506 C.E. - CHATTLE SLAVERY, that is.

We can truly say that the surface of the INTER and/or INTRA relationships between the African High-Cultures from the tip of southern Africa - MONOMOTAPA (presently misnomered "<u>The Republic of South Africa</u>" by inheritors of its European colonizers and slavers) all the way through a northerly path along the African Great Lakes region of central Alkebu-lan, thence along the White Nile River Valley at Nubia (misnamed "Sudan" by Arab Muslim invaders and slavers), and further northerly until the White and Blue Nile rivers jointly meet in a tangent with the Atbara River flowing down from the highlands of Ethiopia (the name given Kush by the ancient Greeks); all of these bodies of water forming the most noted section of the NILE RIVER, the tail-end of this historic waterway, as it leaves Nubia and enters Kimit (the original name of Egypt , the latter being a misnomer by the ancient Haribus in the Noah myth) at the south and enters the Kimit Sea (today's Mediterranean Sea) at the northernmost limits of the so-called "EGYPTIAN" or "NILE DELTA."[1]

Certainly it is incumbent upon all of you to delve very much deeper into the annals of the history of these new countries I have introduced. This, in no way whatso-ever, does not mean that you can cease your research into the history of Egypt, for this African land's history has not yet been exhausted, as we are really just on the treshold of its <u>mysteries</u>. In fact, we are only on the surface of the history of every continent of the planet <u>Earth</u>. We have never studied any other TRUE history; and the calously infinitisimal attempt we have made to give the impression that such we have done **had been** based upon the imperialist colonial involvement between the European and European-American experience in the <u>Middle</u> and <u>Far East</u>. All of these military expeditions, traditionally called "EXPLORATIONS," began with the 15th century C.E. decision of the Roman Pope to divide the planet Earth:- the "<u>eastern half</u>" to Portugal, and the "<u>western half</u>" to Spain.

Before you today is a new history; a new cultural anthropology; a new world; all of which maybe a first time knowledge. Yet, although it is the last in a series, it is just the beginning of an area that require thousands of volumes to bring forward its hidden world to the general public; not **only** the so-called "ACADEMICIANS" who will continue treating them as if they did not exist, but **those who use** them in terms which only their own professional colleagues could understand.

With all of these facts fresh in your mind, I beg of those

---

1. The Greeks called this watery land of Egypt the "DELTA" because the shape of its contours appeared to them to be similar to the shape of their letter of said name in their alphabet.

who plan to make history a professional career and love of work to remember that the history of nowhere is complete; and that of all continents other than Europe is particularly non-existent if we are to use the library holdings in our "INSTITUTIONS OF HIGHER LEARNING" in the United States of America. You are responsible to change the manner in which history is presently being taught. You must teach history without the racist orientation it now has. You must be able to see others GOD with respect, and how their history is woven into their mythology as you see your own in what is popularly called "<u>Judaeo-Christian Theology</u>." You are charged with changing this world you rightly, and justly, stated has been corrupted by elders such as myself; but, you are also responsible for the label your descendants will give you when you have remolded OUR world. I should hope that the end result of your project will be a subject or study called, and is truely, WORLD HISTORY. And, that, at least one of every nation's historians will be represented on that body which will produce the materials to be taught in said studies, which must be also complimentary to all; just as it will be equally critical; and allow the masses of mankind to make their own decision as to RIGHT, WRONG, or INDIFFERENCE on the subject of WORLD HISTORY.

  This <u>lecture-essay</u>, as so many others I have submitted to you, must end with the following charge. The indigenous Africans along the Nile River Valleys High-Cultures wrote on the walls of their temples thousands of years before the theory of ADAM AND EVE was created; equally the same amount of time before it was copied by so-called "INSPIRED HOLY WRITERS OF THE HEBREW HOLY TORAH" and "CHRISTIAN HOLY BIBLE, these historic words which you must pass on to your students of history - WORLD HISTORY:

"MAN, KNOW YOURSELF, AND YOU SHALL BE FREE."

> Submitted for students critical analysis, comments, and other use: Yosef ben-Jochannan, Adj. Assoc. Prof. of History, Pace College (Westchester and New York campus), February 1970. **(edited and revised for publication).**

CHAPTER IV

PREDYNASTIC and DYNASTIC KIMIT, NUBIA, KUSH, and LEBU
(Sais or Egypt, Merowe, Cush or Ethiopia, Libya)

An Introduction:

The following chronological listings of <u>Predynastic</u>, <u>Dynastic</u>, and <u>Post-dynastic</u> Nile Valley monarchs (pharoahs, kings, queens, etc.) are presented to show the continuity of the ancient history of the High-Cultures ("civilizations").[1] These cultures that had their earliest beginnings around the African Great Lakes - <u>Mwanza Nyanza</u>, <u>Tanganyika Nyanza</u>, and <u>Malawi Nyanza</u>. The listing of the various 20th century references make it possible for cross-cultural relationship from the past to the present. However, the basic contents of this chapter specifically relate to periods before the Christian Era (B.C.E.) and just beyond the dawn of the Christian Era (C.E.).**

There are many dates which cannot be verified by currently available data. In such cases the date is prefixed with the symbols <u>"?"</u> or <u>"c"</u>. In some places the date is completely omitted. In other listings the dates are from B.C.E. to C.E.; in others it is just the opposite. <u>Care</u> must be taken in using this method of comparative studies in African geo-politics and histography. Such listings are not coincidental, they are intentional. This

---

*The word "NYANZA" is a Kenda-based word, also KiSwahili, for the English word "LAKE" or "LARGE BODY OF WATER". The use of the word "VICTORIA" as a name of Africa's largest lake is insulting to people of African origin; its name is MWANZA NYANZA.
**BCE = BC = Before the Christian Era. CE = AD = During the Christian Era. This context is observed in this volume.

method has been undertaken to prevent monotonous reading of the chronology, along with the necessity to place special emphasis on certain periods.

The comments, with respect to the High Priest Manetho of Kimit (Egypt or Sais) during the beginning of Greek rule, are prefixed by dates and periods in order that a picto-graphical image of the history being presented could be had by the student and other readers. Manetho was the original chronographer who set Egyptian history into "DYNASTIC, PRE-DYNASTIC, and POST-DYNASTIC PERIODS". All others dealing with this methodology of Egyptian history and High-Culture have copied and modified his.

The high point in this method of presenting history is to show the INTERPLAY and/or INTERCHANGE between the ancient Africans, Asians, and Europeans of antiquity in preference to giving any distorted picture of them being of seperate historical background on the mere premesis of PIGMENT OF SKIN or PHYSICAL CHARACTERIS-TICS as is the case in most history books written by people calling themselves "AUTHORITIES ON AFRICAN HISTORY". It also provides much of the needed periodic data for the background of the historical facts already revealed in the following chapters.[2]

CHRONOLOGY

CLASSIFICATION & DATES OF
EGYPTIAN HISTORY
B.C.E.

On the introduction of the solar calendar of/by the Egyptians....

                c. 4,500-4,441 B.C.E.

Prehistoric Epoch...	Palaeolithic [old stone] Period.... Neolithic [new stone] Period....... Tasian Period...................... Badarian Period.................... Predynastic Period.................	(Before) 3200 - BCE
Old Kingdom	Archaic Period: 1st and IInd Dynasties........3200 to 2780 - Pyramid Age: IIIrd to VIth Dynasties.......2780 to 2270 - VIIth to Xth Dynasties........2270 to 2100 -	
Middle Kingdom......	XIth to XIVth Dynasties.........2100 to 1675 -	
Hyksos Period..........	XVth and XVIth Dynasties........1675 to 1600 — XVIIth Dynasty..................1600 to 1555 -	
New Kingdom.........	Theban Period: XVIIIth to XXth Dynasties.....1555 to 1090 - Tanite and Bubastite Period: XXIst to XXIIIrd Dynasties....1090 to 718 - BCE	

B.C.E. = B.C. = BEFORE THE CHRISTIAN ERA

CHRONOLOGY

CLASSIFICATION & DATES OF

EGYPTIAN HISTORY
(con'td.)
BCE

Ethiopian and Saite Period:

    XXIVth to XXVIth Dynasties....718 to 529 - B.C.E.

Late Epoch.......... Old Persian, Mendesian Period.............616 -

    (Persian Invasion, under Chosroes II)

    XXVIIth to XXXIst Dynasties....525 to 332 -

    Ptolemaic Period................. 332 to 30 B.C.E.
Greco-Roman Epoch...
    Roman Colonial Period.... .... 30 B.C.E.-324 C.E.

Byzantine and Coptic Epoch........................... 324 to 640 C.E.

Arab Conquest (Period).............................. 640 to 1805 -

Ottoman Turks (Mohammed Ali, Khedivate)...............1805 to 1882 -

French Invasion Period.. ....1798 to 1801 -
                   * 1876 to 1872

British Conquest (Period)...........................**1882 to 1952 -

Arab-African Resumption of Control..................1952 to 1958 -

Egypt became United Arab Republic....................1958 to present

Syria was the ... second half of the two nations that comprised ....

The United Arab Republic. Syria withdrew unilaterally in 1961)³

---

* In order to gain control of the Suez Canal Zone France permitted, and encouraged the corrupt Khedive Ismail to borrow more money than he could repay. France then took over the canal that was started by Ismail. (G. Douin, "Historie du Rigne du Khedive Ismail", Cairo, 1937).
** Britain invaded Egypt on August 16, 1882. The invasion was commanded by Sir (General) Ganet Wolsely, who had been deployed to Cyprus and Malta by the British Government of July 20, 1882, in anticipation of the invasion. [Spencer Childers, "The Life...of Hugh C.E. Childers", 1901, II; R. Robinson and J. Gallagher with A. Denny, "Africa and the Victorians-the Climax of Imperialism", N.Y., Doubleday & Co., 1968. J.L. Garvin, "The Life of Joseph Chamberlain", 1932, I; J. Chamberlain, "A Political Memoir", 1880-1882, ed by C.D. Howard, 1953. H.L. Hoskins, "British Routes to India", 1928; C.W. Hallberg, "The Suez Canal: Its History and Diplomatic Importance", New York, 1931.

CHRONOLOGY

PRE-DYNASTIC PERIOD
EGYPTIAN EARLY STONE AGE CULTURES

Date B.C.E.	Classification	Ruler
8000-6000		Sebelian III
12,000-8000		Sebelian II
25,000- ?	Upper Palaeolithic Period	Sebelian I (Builder of the Silt Terraces)
100,000- ?	Middle Palaeolithic Period [(Handaxes-Levalloisian flakes 10 ft. Nile Terrace)]	
250,000- ?	Lower Palaeolithic Period [Handaxes-100 ft. Nile Terraces & 50 ft.]	

(? = Date not definite)

DYNASTIC PERIOD
or
HISTORIC EGYPTIAN and SUDANESE CULTURES

LOWER EGYPT (North) Date B.C.E.	PERIOD	UPPER EGYPT (South)
3000	Narmer* 1st Dynasty	1st Dynasty
3400-3200	Late Pre-Dynastic (or Gerzean period)	Late Pre-Dynastic (or Gerzean period)
3500-3400	Middle Pre-Dynastic (or Gerzean period)	Middle Pre-Dynastic (or Gerzean period)
3600	Early Pre-Dynastic	Early Pre-Dynastic (Amratian)-Shaheinab
3800	Fayum B	Badarian Culture-Khartoum
4000	Helwan (El Omari) Merimdeh	Tasian Culture
4400	Fayum A	

*Also AHA; and MENES according to the Greeks. There is some doubt as to whether he was the first pharoah of the First Dynasty.

CHRONOLOGY

EGYPTIAN CHIEF KINGS OF THE PRE-MIDDLE KINGDOM PERIOD

DATE B.C.E.	DESCRIPTION	KING
3200 - 2680	Archaic Period (Ist, IInd, & IIIrd Dynasties)	
3200 - 2980	Ist Dynasty	Narmer (Menes) Aha*

KINGS WHO BUILT THE GREAT PYRAMIDS
and
THE "DWARF" SIZE KINGS

DATE B.C.E.	DESCRIPTION	KING
2980 - 2780	IInd Dynasty	Khasekhemuwy
2780 - 2680	IIIrd Dynasty	[Zozer]**
2680 - 2258	OLd Kingdom (IInd & IVth Dynasties)	Snefru
		Khufu [Cheops]
		Khafra [Chephren]
		Menku-ra-re [Mycerinus]
2565 - 2420	Vth Dynasty	Unas
2420 - 2258	VIth Dynasty	Pepi I
		Mernera
		Pepi II
2258 - 2052	VIIth - Xth Dynasties (Beginning of the intermediate Period)	

*Names in brackets are given to the African pharoahs by the Greeks. The Greeks were unable to pronounce most of the African names.

CHRONOLOGY

MIDDLE KINGDOM CHEIF MONARCHS
(XIth and XIIth Dynasties)

[(2258-2052 B.C.E.) First Dynastic Intermediate Period-VIIth-Xth
Dynasties]

XIth DYNASTY		XII DYNASTY	
(2150-2000 B.C.E.)		(2000-1785 B.C.E.)	
Date B.C.E.	Monarch	Date B.C.E.	Monarch
2150 - 2090	Intef II	2000 - 1979	Amrnrhet I
2090 - 2085	Intef III	1979 - 1936	Senwosret I
2085 - 2065	Mentuhotep I	1936 - 1904	Amenehet II
2065 - 2060	Mentuhotep II	1906 - 1888	Senwosret II
2060 - 2015	Mentuhotep III	1887 - 1850	Senwosret III
2015 - 2005	Mentuhotep IV	1850 - 1800	Amenehet III
2005 - 2000	Mentuhotep V	1800 - 1792	Amenehet IV

[(1785-1580 B.C.E.) Second Dynastic Intermediate Period-VIII-XVII
Dynasties]

Date B.C.E.	Monarch	Date B.C.E.	Monarch
(beginning)		(ending)	
? 1676 - 1675	Hyksos * [mixed European-Asian entrance c1640. Allegedly the period Abraham and his family entered Sais (Egypt)]. **	1580	King Kamose, et al

[? Date subject to further verification].

---

*Saltis was the first of the Hyksos Monarchs to rule over LOWER EGYPT. He led the first invasion of the first foreigners on African soil — in Kimit (Egypt).
**See Yosef ben-Jochannan, AFRICAN ORIGIN OF THE MAJOR "WESTERN RELIGIONS," New York, 1970.

CHRONOLOGY

NEW KINGDOM CHEIF MONARCHS

(XVIIIth, XIXth and XXth Dynasties)

XVIIIth DYNASTY
(1580-1340 B.C.E.)

Date B.C.E.	Monarch
1580 - 1558	Ahmose I
1557 - 1530	Amenhotep I
1530 - 1515 ?	Thutmose I
? 1515 - 1505	Thutmose II
? 1515 - 1484	Hatshepsut

XVIIIth DYNASTY
(1580-1340 B.C.E.)

Date B.C.E.	Monarch
1504 - 1450	Thutmose III
1450 - 1415	Amenhotep II
? 1415 - 1405	Thutmose IV
1405 - 1370	Amenhotep III
1370 - 1352	Amenhotep IV (Akhenaton)
?* - 1349	Tutankhamun

XIXth DYNASTY
(? 1340-1200 B.C.E.)

Date B.C.E.	Monarch
? 1340 - 1320	Haremheb
1320 - 1318	Ramses I**
1318 - 1298	Seti I
1298 - 1232	Ramses II

XXth DYNASTY
(1200-1085 B.C.E.)

Date B.C.E.	Monarch
1232 - 1224	Merneptah
1200 - 1198	Setinekht
1198 - 1168	Ramses III (the commoner)
1168 - 1085	Rameside Kings

Note: Rameses II was the Pharoah of Kimit who was alledged to have driven his fellow Egyptian - Moses - out of Sucoth into Sinai. If this was true Moses did not cross the Red Sea by traveling south "INTO THE LAND FULL WITH MILK AND HONEY" according to the Hebrew TORAH - Bible or Christian OLD TESTAMENT.

[? Date subject to further verification or is unknown. No proof available].

*Some historians have given the date 1352 for this pharoah's birth; others claimed it is the date he mounted the throne for the very short time he ruled.
**The name of this man is spelled numerous ways.

CHRONOLOGY

LATE KINGDOM CHEIF MONARCHS

*1085-950 B.C.E. (TANITE) XXIst Dynasty

(LIBYAN DYNASTY: PRIEST-KINGS OF THEBES)

*(950 - 750 B.C.E.)

Date B.C.E.	Monarch	Date B.C.E.	Monarch
*950 - 925	Sheshonq I [Shashanq]	870 - 847	Osorkon II **
925 - 893	Osorkon I	847 - 823	Takelot II
893 - 870	Takelet I	823 - 772	Sheshonq II

817 - 715 B.C.E. XXIIIrd Dynasty

730 - 715 B.C.E. XXIVth Dynasty

Date B.C.E.	Monarch
730 - 720	Tetneket

(KUSHITE) XXVth Dynasty

(751-656 B.C.E.)

Date B.C.E.	Monarch	Date B.C.E.	Monarch
760 - 751	Kashta	701 - 690	Shabataka
751 - 716	Piankhy (Pianki)	690 - 664	Taharqa
716 - 701	Shabaka	664 - 653	Tanutemun

MEMPHITES SURRENDER TO THE ASSYRIANS

(Esarhaddon of Assyria-Conqueror)

671 B.C.E.

THEBIANS (Thebites) SURRENDER TO THE ASSYRIANS

(Ashurbanipal of Assyria-Conqueror)

663 B.C.E.

---

*This is the period King Solomon of Israel was born (976-936 B.C.E.), reigned, and died. Note that the PROVERBS -"The Teachings of Amen-em-eope" - were already written.

**He was also called USERTSEN II.

CHRONOLOGY

LATE KINGDOM CHIEF MONARCHS
(continued)

(SAITE PERIOD) XXVIth DYNASTY

(663 - 525 B.C.E.)

Date B.C.E.	Monarch	Date B.C.E.	Monarch
663 - 609	Psammetiches I (Psemthek I)	588 - 568	Apries
609 - 594	Necho (Neku)	568 - 525	Amasis
594 - 588	Psammetichos II		

(PERSIAN PERIOD) XXVII 525 - 404 B.C.E.
                  XXVIII 404 - 398 B.C.E.
                    XXIX 394 - 378 B.C.E.

Sebenytic Period
XXX DYNASTY

(378 - 341 B.C.E.)

Date B.C.E.	Monarch	Date B.C.E.	Monarch
378 - 360	Nectanebos I*	360 - 341	Nectanebos II

(PERSIAN PERIOD) XXXI 341 - 332 B.C.E.
(Alexander "the great" captured Egypt in 332 BCE)
(GREEK OR PTOLEMAIC PERIOD) XXXIInd DYNASTY

(320 - 30 B.C.E.)

Date B.C.E.	Monarch	Date B.C.E.	Monarch
332 - 323	Alexander ("The Great")	285 - 47 ?	Ptolemy [II-XIII]
323 - 283	Ptolemy I (Soter I)	? 47-30	Cleopatra VIII **

[? Exact date in dispute by many historians.]

THE POST DYNASTIES

ROMAN PERIOD 47 B.C.E.(± 1 BCE - 1 CE) 324 CE
COPTIC CHRISTIAN RULE (324 C.E. - 640 C.E.)
[African-European Theocratic Rule]

---

*Also written NECTANEBUS.
**Reinstated by Julius Caesar on the throne in 47 B.C.E. She was one of the Ptolemies. During this period JESUS CHRIST was allegedly born of Hebrew parents - Joseph and Mary.

THE EGYPTIAN DYNASTIES AND COMMENTS
by the High-Priest Manetho
(all dates B. C. E.)

3200-2780 **Ist and IInd DYNASTIES** (Thinite Dynasties):

The dynasties are called **Thinite** because the pharaohs (kings) of these two dynasties were buried at Abydos near **Thinis**. Their residences were at Nachen.

The Ist and IInd Dynasties were famous for astrological dating for their remarkable development of the fine arts, and for the use of precious jewels and various metals which were unknown to most of the world cultures at this period. A Ist Dynasty pharoah was tempted to regulate and divert the flow of the waters of the Nile River around the City of Fayum and its outreaches.* This attempt to change the course of the Nile waters for agricultural purposes was the obsession of most of Kimit's ancient monarchs, as well as its recently deceased resident, Gamal Abdul Nasser.

2780-2270 **IIIrd to IVth DYNASTIES** (Memphite Period):

Sometime within this period the royal residence was moved to Memphis. It was also within this same period that the ARCHITECTURAL LOVER, Pharaoh Djoser (the Greeks called him Zozer), had the first STEP PYRAMID at Sakhara designed and built by his most

---

*The headwaters of the Nile River have been diverted for the purpose of extending the Aswan Dam of Lower Egypt. This caused the removal of countless statues of the ancient past to higher ground and to museums under a project undertaken by the government of Egypt and member nations of the United Nations Organization in the latter part of the 1960's C. E.

famous architect-Imhotep, whom the Greeks called "AESCULAPIUS".*
Imhotep, before his death, was diefied and worshipped as the "GOD
OF MEDICINE". His knowledge of the medical arts was vastly superior
to any other physician's of his days; this being true even to the
Greek physician of recorded history, - APOLLO. He lived and died at
least 1,500 years before the European's "FATHER OF MEDICINE" -
Hippocrates of Greece - was born. The proof of this is best seen
in the OATH which 20th century physicians must take in respect to
this <u>African God</u> which the European's FATHER OF MEDICINE also
worshipped (page 316). It also proved that the Step Pyramid of
Sakhara was not one of the pyramids which the Haribus (Hebrews or
"Jews") claimed to have slaved on,** this having been built between 2780 and 2680 B.C.E.; for the first of the Haribus - ABRAHAM
(Avram) and his small family*** did not arrive in Kimit (Egypt)
until c1640 B.C.E. at the earliest. A picture of this African
and the Step Pyramid of Sakhara he designed and built appear on
page 317.

Note that it was 700 years later (200 C.E.) than the so-called
OATH OF HIPPOCRATES that the Roman anatomist of great renown,
Galen, also admitted his debt of gratitude to the Africans of

---

*Aesulapius (the African - Imhotep) was the name Hippocrates of Cos (Greece) called His God of Medicine - (Imhotep) - in the year 500 B.C.E. as shown in the so-called HIPPOCRATIC OATH.
**See the SECOND BOOK OF MOSES, also called EXODUS for the Haribu's story on how they allegedly toiled in the building of the pyramid for the pharoah. Of course they did not identify the pharoah in question, which had to be Rameses II on the throne.
***See the FIRST BOOK OF MOSES, also called GENESIS.

The Oath

I SWEAR by Apollo the physician, and Æsculapius, and Health, and All-heal, and all the gods and goddesses, that, according to my ability and judgment, I will keep this Oath and this stipulation—to reckon him who taught me this Art equally dear to me as my parents, to share my substance with him, and relieve his necessities if required; to look upon his offspring in the same footing as my own brothers, and to teach them this art, if they shall wish to learn it, without fee or stipulation; and that by precept, lecture, and every other mode of instruction, I will impart a knowledge of the Art to my own sons, and those of my teachers, and to disciples bound by a stipulation and oath according to the law of medicine, but to none others. I will follow that system of regimen which, according to my ability and judgment, I consider for the benefit of my patients, and abstain from whatever is deleterious and mischievous. I will give no deadly medicine to any one if asked, nor suggest any such counsel; and in like manner I will not give to a woman a pessary to produce abortion. With purity and with holiness I will pass my life and practice my Art. I will not cut persons laboring under the stone, but will leave this to be done by men who are practitioners of this work. Into whatever houses I enter, I will go into them for the benefit of the sick, and will abstain from every voluntary act of mischief and corruption; and, further from the seduction of females or males, of freemen and slaves. Whatever, in connection with my professional practice or not, in connection with it, I see or hear, in the life of men, which ought not to be spoken of abroad, I will not divulge, as reckoning that all such should be kept secret. While I continue to keep this Oath unviolated, may it be granted to me to enjoy life and the practice of the art, respected by all men, in all times! But should I trespass and violate this Oath, may the reverse be my lot!

---

* Aesculapius is the name the ancient Greeks gave to their AFRICAN GOD - Imhotep. This African, during his prominence as a philosopher, poet, architect, builder, physician, etc., predated the birth of the first European physician - Hippocrates - by more than two-thousand (2000) years - c2780-2680 B.C.E. See page 317 for picture of the "GOD OF MEDICINE" - Imhotep.

Imhotep: Builder, Architect, Prime Minister, Poet, Physician, Philosopher, and "GOD OF MEDICINE" of the Greeks; an indigenous African of Kimit (III Dynasty). See OATH to him on page 316.

PLAN of Step Pyramid of Sakharah designed by Architect Imhotep about c2780-2680 B.C.E. during the reign of Pharoah Djozer, whom the Greeks named "ZOZER." This was the first building of its kind. Note pylons for other major structures in foreground of pyramid.

the Nile Valleys, and to the Egyptians in particular, for all the knowledge in medicine which the Europeans knew.

The Vth DYNASTY was marked by the predominance of the religion of the God RA (the Sun God). Beginning from this period to the solitary reign of Pharoah Mankhurere of the IVth Dynasty the pharoahs named themselves "SONS OF RA". They also built their pyramid-temples at Abusir, near Sakhara; the most peculiar temple was NE-USER-RA. It was the first temple known to have used red granite with lotiform capitals, which in no way resembled the pillars of other temples.

During this reign the planning and erection of a very noted tomb by one of Kimit's most famous architects, TI,* was built at Sakhara. The completion of a TREATISE ON PHILOSOPHICAL MAXIMS by Path-hotep, and the building of the PYRAMID OF UNAS at Sakhara** — containing the first of the world's famous PYRAMID TEXTS,*** were further accomplishments. This was one of Kimit's most creative periods in fine arts, architecture, philosophy, and the physical and social sciences. It also marked one of the highest periods in the history of mankind because cultural greatness was the major objective of organized society, not the
___
*Second only to IMHOTEP in reputation as an architect; the latter had no equal even up to the present 20th century.
**The original spelling of this word is "SAKKARAH".
***A composition of prayers adorn the walls of one of his pyramids. These texts formed much of the data that appear in works such as BOOK OF THE DEAD"; OSIRIS; AFRICAN ORIGINS OF THE MAJOR "WESTERN RELIGIONS"; STOLEN LEGACY, and a host of other major works dealing with the development of "Western Civilization" by Africans in Africa.

accumulation of material wealth.

2270 - 2100   THE VIIth to Xth DYNASTIES...started with varied political disorders which were largely due to the incoming Asian peoples called "Hyksos" during the reign of Pharoah Pepi II. It was the beginning of Kimit's (Egypt's) functionaries of the courts abandonment of the royal residence to establish themselves in southern (Upper) Kimit as minor feudal Lords, from whence they moved up to become petty kings of very minor importance. But they were all assembled around one court, which was more powerful than the court in Memphis. Its residence was at Ahnasia-el-Medina, which the Greeks called "Herakleopolis". This court very soon became the rival of its counter-part in Memphis, and it challenged the Memphites' control of the area where they had taken over.

2100 to 1675   THE Xth to XIVth DYNASTIES (Middle Kingdom):... The beginning of the Middle Kingdom was marred by a series of royal family wars between the minor kings and lords of Ahnasia-el-Medina and those of Hermonthis (the present Arab population call this area ARMANT). It was the Dynasty of the Mentu-hoteps, however, that became authoritatively powerful, along with the supremacy of Thebes. From this point on the reunification of Kimit came under the sceptre of a unique and most mighty monarch, the glorious Amen-em-hat I. He immediately established the worship of the God AMEN* as the official religion of the people of

---

* This God is still honored in all Hebrew (Jewish), Christian and Muslim (Moslem) prayers ending with the word "AMEN". It is a farce to change the original meaning of the word to "SO BE IT".

Kimit. To this very day, however, the God AMEN is being worshipped by all whose religion is based upon the African religious philosophy developed by Amen-em-hat I. Thus one notes that at the end of every prayer the Haribus (Hebrews or Jews) and the Christians end with "praise to the God AMEN" (Ra). It is also noted that the Jews changed the meaning of the word AMEN to "SO BE IT." Of course the Christians, who were originally Jews, followed their ancestors with the same interpretation of the Greek and Anglo-Saxon version to the end of prayers. The same Amen-em-hat I was unable to subdue the nobles by force of arms, because they had grown too strong in the areas where they were allowed to reign as lords and minor kings. However, he did win a few of them over to his side through peaceful means by promising them power and glory over the others when he capture them. The others whom he did not eventually capture, never-the-less, remained constantly fearful of him.

Amen-em-hat I erected many temples in the main Delta* region as well as in Memphis, in the Fayum, and in Nubia (Upper Kimit - also Upper Egypt or Upper Sais). He also established his residence at Itet-taui (presently called Lisht). In order to secure his power Itet-taui was fortified to the point that it was declared an "impregnable city". This belief did much to save it from enemy attack. The very mention of its name brought awe to

---

* This area of Kimit (North Africa) was given the name "DELTA" because the Greeks said the formation of the land appeard to have the shape of the Greek letter bearing said name.

his followers and utter fear to the minds of his enemies.

The reign of Amen-em-hat III completed the line of the "GRAND PHAROAHS" (Grand Kings) of the XIIth Dynasty. His successors, members of the Sebek-hoteps family, were preceded by Amen-em-hat IV, and by one of the few women pharoahs (Queens) that actually ruled Kimit - Pharoah Skemiophris. Everyone of them failed to maintain the high standard of strength established by the illustrious Pharoah Amen-em-hat I. The lack of governmental skills and military power caused his successors to fall into the Hyksos' hands as colonials. The Hyksos were a group of people who were in fact only nomads from the Asian desert. These Asian people became the first of the non-indigenous African - Black, "Negroes, Africans South of the Sahara, Bantus", etc. - people to invade and capture Kimit; this being possible because they were able to know that the Africans had deployed their forces at that time across the Arabian Peninsula and were weak at home. All of this took place as a direct result of the fact that the Africans of Kimit had allowed too many of the Hyksos to enter their country a few years before, thus allowing a sort of Fifth Column to develop. As a direct result of this fact they were able to seize the country from within and without in 1675 B.C.E. Until this period the power over the entire continent of Alkebu-lan was the exclusive domain of the people who are now called "NEGROES" and other such degrading names that had their origin in the dastardly slave trading era. They first entered Kimit in the so-called

DELTA REGION. Their power stretched from the same "Delta Region" up to a good distance below the First Cataract, which placed them solely in control of what was then called "LOWER KIMIT," or as the area is presently called — "LOWER EGYPT". The Hyksos were originally Asian people who inhabited the regions around and about the Oxus River Valley, but who were eventually amalgamated to a very small extent by a few Europeans who staggered into the area which was one time called "ASIA MINOR". Some "Modern historians", many of whom are called "authorities on African history", implied that they were "SEMITIC PEOPLES"; of course others bearing the same title claimed that they were "DARK-SKINNED HAMITES FROM EUROPE". The latter type of declaration was very obvious in Seligman's works mentioned before in this chapter and others; certainly Jeffreys and Wiedner are masters of this hypothesis, and they have for years gone on with this piece of racist history without challenge by any African or African-American historian, most of whom seek out these same people for endorsement and also recognition as historians of their own ancestoral history. This is not to imply that other peoples did not come into Kimit from Asia and Europe before 1675 B.C.E. to live, learn, and work. Other indigenous Africans came from other parts of the continent as the Africans of Kimit went to their countries. But, it was, in fact, the first time in the history of Alkebu-lan (Africa)*

---

* It is of major importance to remember that "AFRICA" is the name given the continent of ALKEBU-LAN by the ancient Greeks and Romans, just as Egypt was the name given KIMIT by the Haribus.

that non-indigenous Africans were able to sieze control of any of the African thrones.

1676 - 1580   THE XVth and XVIthe DYNASTIES (Hyksos Period):

Somewhere between c1676 and c1675 B.C.E. is when "Western historians" say "...A RAMPAGING AND FANATICAL NOMADIC PEOPLE OF EUROPEAN AND ASIAN ORIGIN INVADED EGYPT AROUND THE DELTA." What they have failed to mention is that very few of them were in fact of European origin - they were mostly Asians; also, the people whose land they had invaded were the so-called "NEGROES" and "BANTUS" one hears so much about of late.

The invaders, the Hyksos, were led by clan-heads called "CHIEFS OF BEDIUNA" (Shepherd Kings). Their invasion was partly due to the effects of the mass movement of Europeans fleeing other Europeans easterly towards the direction of Assyria (Syria) and Babylonia (Babylon). It must be remembered that the Colchians also inhabited the region from whence the Hyksos came; and they were also said to have:

> "...THICK LIPS, BROAD NOSES, WOOLY HAIR, AND BEEN BURNT OF SKIN...," etc.,

according to the first of the European historians - Herodotus, about 450 B.C.E. (See Herodotus, HISTORIES, Book II). Thus the Hyksos were in fact primarily Asians who were amalgamated to a very slight extent with Europeans and Africans, both of whom are today called such names as "CAUCASIANS"and "NEGROES", among others. The Europeans were also nomadic tribesmen, equally as illiterate to the culture of Kimit as their fellow nomads from Assyria - around the Oxus River beds.

In a very short space of time the Hyksos had become extremely powerful. They were in control of most of the regions of northern, eastern, and western LOWER EGYPT (the Delta Region). They also settled in parts of the Middle Egyptian interior - just below the First Cataract, and ruled supreme over said area, which they occupied in great numbers. But the Hyksos also destroyed vast amounts of the temples, very important monuments and other structures they found in Kimit (Egypt). Following this they then set forth and forced their African captives into virtual slavery. They also established their own capital city at Avaris - in the Delta Region near the Kimit Sea (Egyptian Sea, presently the Mediterranean Sea). They, never-the-less, had destroyed practically everything they touched in Kimit. Why? Simply because they did not understand the indigenous African society and High-Culture ("civilization") they had invaded and taken over. This meant that they had to be constantly watchful, and they did not relate sufficiently to assimilate with or contribute to the High-Culture of the vanquished indigenous African victims.

1600 - 1555   <u>THE XVIIth DYNASTY</u>: This period marked the indigenous Africans' of Kimit struggle against the Hyksos. It was the beginning of their fight for independence from enslavement by a foreign people. Three Theban kings - SEQENEN-RA I, II, and III - directed the drive against the Hyksos for independence.

Pharaoh Sequenen-ra III was killed in one of the liberation battles with his weapons still clutched in his hands. The last of his three sons, AMHOSE I, in the year 1580 B.C.E., succeeded in driving the Hyksos out of Kimit, and followed them in hot pursuit to the city of Sharuhen in southern Palestine. * Amhose I (also called Ahmose I) had revenged his father's death. The defeat of the Hyksos by Ahmose I and the Africans of Kimit (Blacks) saw the Asians (Browns) depart from the Africa in haste with their European allies (Whites) and some of their African underlings (Blacks). This historical event is carefully recorded in the famous EL-KAB INSCRIPTION.

1555 - 1090   THE XVIIIth to XXth DYNASTIES (New Kingdom or Theban Period): Neb-pehti-ra Ashmes (Amasis) founded the mighty XVIIIth Dynasty that ruled Kimit for more than two-hundred (200) years. He occupied himself with the expansion of the Hyksos during the end of their final expulsion from his country, but he failed to watch the Nubians - the so-called "Negroes" - with whom his nation was at virtual warfare. These Nubians, fellow Africans of what was at various times called UPPER KIMIT (Upper Egypt), had taken advantage of Kimit's fight with the Hyksos; and as a direct result, the Nubians were able to conquer all of Kimit (Lower Egypt) from the Second Cataract north to the Mediterranean Sea. Ashmes ruled Kimit for a total of twenty-two

---

*Part of this area is occupied by the modern state established by European Jews under the name of "ISRAEL".

(22) long years until his death. He was buried in the Theban region.* His mummy is still in its preserved state in the Egyptian Museum of Cairo, Cairo, Egypt (presently called THE UNITED ARAB REPUBLIC, U.A.R.). Ashmes was followed on the throne of Kimit by his son - Amen-hotep I.

Amen-hotep III was the last of the honored pharoahs of the XVIIIth Dynasty. One of his greatest accomplishments was the conquest of neighboring Nubia. During his reign the world's most famous and often quoted "CORRESPONDENCE OF TELL EL-'AMARNA" was written in Babylonian cuneiform letters and script. This "Correspondence" dealt with certain royal marriages that were arranged between the African princes and princesses of Kimit (Egypt)-presently called "Negroes", and those of Asian Babylonia - generally referred to as "Semites" or "Brown". The proposed marriages were intended to cement diplomatically the political relationship and geographic dominance by Kimit over the countries surrounding Babylon and Kimit; and also guaranteed Babylon's independence from external invasion. They were, also, to be marriages of political expedience and convenience on the part of the Africans of Kimit. Of course they also offered the militarily weak Babylon some semblance of defensive protection from war and invasion by enemies of herself and Kimit. It was during this

---

*The present rulers of Egypt, Arabized-Africans, Arabs and a few remaining Africans who have no power in the existing government, renamed the area "DIRA ABU-N-NAGA".

dynasty that the contraceptive plan for <u>Fertility Control,</u> shown on page 159 of **BLACK MAN OF THE NILE** was developed; it was probably developed in an earlier period.

1580 - 1340   <u>THE XVIIIth DYNASTY</u> cannot be properly treated without mention of Pharaoh Tut-ankh-amen. Yet, he was not a direct successor to the throne of Kimit. He got there through one of Akhnaten's (Amen-hotep IV) seven daughters, the eldest, who he married.   It must have been a marriage when he was extremely young, as he died when he was only in his teens. He reigned only eight or seven very short years (1357-1349 B.C.E.). Smenkka-ra, a very much unknown prince, had remained hardly any time on the throne after inheriting it before Tut-ankh-Amen's (<u>The Living Image Of Aten</u>, or <u>Beautiful Is The Life Of Aten</u>) marriage to Akhnaten (<u>The God Aten Is Content</u>, or <u>Amen-hotep IV</u>) - his father-in-law's daughter. Even his name was given to him by Akhnaten, who made of Tut-ankh-amen (or Tut-ankh-aten*) a royal figure in order to protect the honor of his daughter.

According to a stele discovered at Karmak, Tut-ankh-aten** converted the Thebans to the worship of the ancient God of Kimit - AMEN - upon his return to Thebes from Lower Kimit's Delta re-

---

*He was also called "TUT" by many Western writers because of the length of his name. It is, however, incorrect.
**It is possible that he did not change anything for he was only 19 years of age when he died. His Grand Vizier (Prime Minister) made most of his decisions. He only served as pharaoh (king) from c1352-1349 B.C.E. The only justification for all the fuss being made over this pharaoh by certain "western historians" is the fact that his tomb's jewels were discovered intact.

gion. This was the beginning of the spread of the worship of the God AMEN throughout Kimit and all of the colonies under its control during this period.

1340 - 1200   **THE XIXth DYNASTY** began with Her-m-heb (Herun-n-heb). He was a general of the army and Regent during the reign of Pharaoh Tut-ankh-aten, whom he succeeded on the throne. After him came a very old man to sit on the throne of Kimit, Rameses. He was in no way related to the royal family of Her-m-heb or any other pharaoh before him. But for some unexplained reason and circumstance he was able to assume control of the entire Empire of Kimit (Egyptian Empire), proclaim himself Pharoah Rameses I in the year 1340 B.C.E., and he ruled until 1320 B.C.E. He was subsequently forced to step down and give way to his only son - Seti I - during the year 1318 B.C.E., due to his old age.
Seti I, also known as Sethos I, ruled until 1298 B.C.E. He was the pharoah of Kimit that conquered Palestine and had thousands of Africans (who are today called "NEGROES") ravage the country. This is one of the reasons why so many Jewish historians find it necessary to make certain that the impression of a "SEMITIC EGYPT" is maintained in the mind of the public at large. Yet, they cannot justify how North and East Africa became SEMITIC before there was a SHEM, in order to have the SHEMITIC MYTHOLOGY. It is also the major reason why the Ethiopian Haribus, otherwise known as "FALASHAS, BLACK JEWS, AFRICAN JEWS," and "BETA ISRAEL" - which they prefer to be called, are constantly shown by the same

"SEMETIC" sources as having originated through the biblical story of King Solomon of Israel and Makeda of Axum (Queen of Sheba)-Kush (Ethiopia), thereby, completely ignoring the fact that their origin dates back at least before Moses of the EXODUS marriage to the daughter of the High Priest of Kush; a "NEGRESS" - as African-American women were once called in the United States of America. (See SECOND BOOK OF MOSES, also known as EXODUS, in the Hebrew TORAH). It is to be noted that it was from this relationship with the Queen of Ethiopia (Africa) and the King of Israel (Asia), that Ethiopia got its first Hebrew ("Jewish") emperor - MENELIK I, "son of King Solomon and Makeda" - Queen of Ethiopia. It is because of this historical background any and all emperors of Ethiopia must take on the title of "LION OF JUDAH", etc., among many others, at his coronation.

Seti I was a very industrious pharoah. He restored many of the temples of the God AMEN, most of which were destroyed at a later period by Akhnaten (Akhenaten, Amen-hotep IV) Pharoah Tut-ankh-amen's father-in-law, the first of the entire world's "TRINITARIANS", and the "PRINCE OF PEACE" who preceded JESUS CHRIST by thousands of years. Seti I reigned for more than twenty (20) years (1318-1298 B.C.E.) before he died of natural causes. He was followed on the throne by his illustrious son - RAMESES II who ruled from 1298 to 1232 B.C.E., during which period the Haribus (misnomered "Jews") were allegedly driven from Kimit (Egypt) in what is commonly called the "EXODUS" in the Hebrew

TORAH. See BLACK MAN OF THE NILE for likeness of Rameses II. Note similarities between him and other Africans along the Nile Valley and other parts of Africa as shown on the other pages in Chapter VI, A PICTORIAL REVIEW OF THE ANCIENT NILE VALLEYS' HIGH-CULTURES.

Upon the death of Rameses II MENEPHTAH, his thirteenth son, mounted the throne. Menephtah immediately waged many successful wars against the African nation of Libya and the Asian nation of Palestine. He left an account of these wars on the famous "ISRAEL STELAE", where the name of "ISRAEL" is mentioned for the first time by the ancient historians of Kimit and others along the Nile Valleys and North Africa. Even the "PASSOVER" or "EXODUS" drama is not mentioned in any of Kimit's glorious history by any African historian (scribe)* who existed during the reign of Rameses II, under whose rule this major event in Africa's history was supposed to have taken place. Even Menephtah did not reveal anything about an EXODUS taking place in Kimit during his father or grandfather's reign as publicized by the Hebrews in their

---

*Note that it was contrary to common practice of the Nile Valleys' High-Culture not to have recorded as significant a historic event. For if Moses, a fellow Egyptian like Rameses II, was not being pursued for the crime of <u>murder</u> they would not have been any cause for a PASSOVER. This was more than forty years before the alleged EXODUS took place. It is stranger than fiction that Moses was supposed to have received the TEN COMMANDMENTS, of which one was: "THOU SHALT NOT KILL"..Never-the-less before he arrived at Mount Sinai, he is seen running from someone else who God also gave the "LAWS" before him. Why? Moses had committed <u>murder</u> by killing Rameses' (II)soldier. There was no Exodus because the Haribus were slaving on any of the major pyramids. All of them were already built hundreds of years before the first Haribu - ABRAHAM was born in the city of Ur, Chaldea.

mythological pronouncements in what is today called "THE SECOND BOOK OF MOSES" or "EXODUS". This was supposed to have taken place when the Haribus "BROKE THEIR BOND OF SLAVERY UNDER THE YOKE OF THEIR"(Africans, "Negroes, Bantus, Africans South of the Sahara," etc.) "EGYPTIAN SLAVEMASTERS". But <u>there was nothing to show that the Haribus could be physically distinguished from their other African brothers and sisters of those days</u>; their only differences were in respect to the worship of the God RA and/or AMEN as against the God JEHOVAH or YVAH; the God YVAM being a God brought into North Africa by the small group of shepherds arriving with Abraham during the year c1640 B.C.E., which had to be during the rule of the foreigners from the Asian desert who originally came from the banks of the Oxus River Valley - called <u>Hyksos</u>. However, the most recent excavations in the area of Kimit (Egypt or Sais), where this monumental historical feat allegedly took place, have not proven that such an event ever happened by any of the methods stated in the <u>Torah</u>, <u>Holy Bible</u>, or <u>Koran</u>, during any period in the history of the Africans of Kimit, including this - the XVIIIth Dynasty. In fact did it ever take place? For only in the XVIIIth Dynasty's inscriptions is there any mention what-so-ever of any historical events which may or may not have some sort of similarity to the Haribus' story about their EXODUS and PASSOVER. Moreover, the inscriptions deal with the Haribus being expelled, not voluntarily leaving on their own initiative as stated in the Torah - THE SECOND BOOK OF MOSES.

It would not have been possible for a band of unarmed slaves and the "MULTITUDES" who accompanied them - according to the story in the Torah. Also, it would have been impossible for the Haribus to have escaped the Pharoah's soldiers, for Pharoah Rameses II inherited the entire Empire of Kimit (Egyptian Empire), which included the land on both sides of the RED SEA, from his father. Mount Sinai was also a part of the colonial and imperial expansion that was Kimit during that period in world history. Never-the-less, the myth continues.

1200 - 1085   <u>THE XXth DYNASTY</u>: Rameses III, the son of a commoner named Set-nekht, mounted the throne of Kimit. He too commanded the indigenous African troops of Kimit in many successful battles against the Libyans and Aegeans (Europeans of Pyrrhus - ancient Greece). He then invaded Assyria and Palestine, carrying thousands of so-called "<u>Negroes</u>" into these areas after reducing them to vassal kingdoms under the control of his African governors, all of whom were typical of what is today called "BANTUS" by most so-called "AUTHORITIES ON AFRICAN HISTORY". *

The reigns of the so-called "RAMISIDE KINGS" followed Pharaoh Rameses III (1198-1168 B.C.E.). But very little is known to date about them. Their successions were ended very quickly; this being the major reason why so little has been recorded in their behalf, or by them. For example: Between the death of Rameses III

---

*See papyrus found by Harris, and subsequently misnamed "THE HARRIS PAPYRUS" instead of its proper and correct African name, for an account of these events in "BLACK HISTORY".

and Rameses IX there was an elapsed time of only twenty-one (21) years. This period also marked one of the worse periods in physical, spiritual and cultural decline in the history of Kimit and her African people. Looting was widespread, as many of the royal tombs (pyramids) and their mastabas (anti-tombs containing minor and major officials of the Pharoah) were violated. This dynasty came to its end under the corrupt landlords who violated every office during their control of Kimit. They brought to the empire the beginning seeds of the empire's eventual downfall to other groups of conquering aliens who followed.

1085 - 718 THE XXIst to XXIIIrd DYNASTIES (Tanite and Bubasite Period): Smedes and his son, Psusennes I, the XXIst Dynasty at Tanis. The Libyan Chief, Shashanq (Shishak of the Hebrew Torah) - who married a royal princess, became the first pharaoh of the Baubasite Dynasty (the XXIInd). Shashanq's reign came shortly after the death of King Solomon of Palestine (c976-936 B.C.E.). At this period in history the rivalry between Solomon's successor, Rhehoboan in Southern Palestine and the usurper Jeroboan in Northern Palestine, encouraged Shasanq to intervene in order to assert his control over Palestine. This revelation indicates very vividly why every attempt by "Western" (European - Hebrew, Christian, Moslem, all labeled "Caucasians") historians and other propagandists calling themselves "authority on African history" must be made to present ancient indigenous Africans as anything else other than "NEGROES, BANTUS, BLACK AFRICANS, BUSH-

MEN", etc. For it should be quite obvious that they had amalgamated with everyone along the Mediterranean Sea. This includes those whom they conquered, enslaved, and educated ("<u>civilized</u>".) Shashanq responded by taking Jerusalem in 930 B.C.E. He brought back to Africa (Kimit) many treasures from his campaign, among which were many artifacts from the "<u>Temple of Solomon</u>". Shashanq died about five (5) years after his conquest of the Hebrews, and was succeeded by his son - Osorkon I - in 925 B.C.E. and he ruled until 893 B.C.E. Osorkon I did not accomplish very much on the throne except to capture Kimit's neighbor Nubia and reduce it to a vassal state of serfs and other types of slavery* for other Africans of Lower Kimit along the Delta regions below the First Cataract. He also invaded and conquered much further into Palestine than his father before him had done.

After the reign of Osorkon II, Theban Priest-Kings began to dispute the title of the throne of Kimit (Sais or Egypt) along with their fellow Libyan usurpers. This period was quite obscure in parts of its history - according to all of the available data on this era; most of these missing links are still buried in the sands of time.

Another pharoah by the name of Piankhi - a Kushite (Cushite or

---

*Most "Western" educators state that the Nubians, who they prefer to call "Negroes", were not "Dark-skinned Caucasians" or "Semites" as the "Egyptians". Yet, they have failed to show in their works how it was possible for Kimit (Egypt) and Kush (Ethiopia) to remain on both sides of Nubia and maintain contact with each other without intercourse on all levels with the Nubians.

Ethiopian), succeeded in unifying the people of Kimit's power once more under indigenous Africans (so-called "NEGROES, BANTUS", etc.) control. A most important stelae, which is still in the Museum in Cairo, Egypt (presently United Arab Republic, U.A.R.), has recorded information of great importance of Piankhi's fete. During this period Assyrian invaders, after conquering most of Palestine, arrived at the borders of Kimit and demanded its surrender, to which the indigenous Africans refused, and followed their refusal with an attack on the alien forces.

718 - 525   THE XXIVth to XXVIth DYNASTIES (Saite and Ethiopian Periods): During the XXIVth Dynasty foreigners, mostly from the ports of Hellades, Greece (Europe) flourished throughout Kimit's Nile River Delta. These Europeans ("Caucasians") selected the City of Sais* to be their base of operation from whence to usurp the Africans' power and control of the Delta region; it later became their capital city. They also established their own separate commerce with other Mediterranean-European countries that by this period were also flourishing after having been developed through the influences the Africans had forced upon them. Most of their officials and heads of government had been taught in Kimit and other nations of Northern Africa by others who studied among the Africans in Northern Africa, or in colonies

---

*This name, SAIS, was originally a city in Kimit. It was also a name which Kimit was also called before the Haribus (Hebrews) renamed it "EGYPT" in their tale about Noah and his genealogy in the FLOOD drama spoken of in the First Book of Moses - Genesis. KIMIT is the earliest name which Egypt was called by Africans.

under the control of African colonialists and imperialists of the period. But the foreign usurpers in the Delta region, mostly Greeks, attempted to establish their own independent kingdom within the Kingdom of Kimit; these being headed by people who declared themselves "PHAROAHS". The first to call himself "Pharoah" was "TEF-NEKHT", one of the so-called "SAITE KINGS", the other being "BOCCHRIS". In reading the history of ancient Nile Valley High-Cultures ("civilizations") it is soon observed that these names were of foreign origin, none having followed the African names that preceded them. However, before they could become entrenched in the Delta region another Ethiopian Pharoah, SHABAKA (also known as Sabacon), invaded Kimit's Delta region along with his establishment of Ethiopian control all over LOWER KIMIT (Lower Egypt). This invasion and conquest established the XXVth Dynasty. Shababka's military Chief of Staff, his nephew, was later defeated by the Assyrians under Sennacherib. Taherq (the "TIRAHAKAH" of the Haribu Torah, the grandson of Pharoah Piankhi) followed Pharoah Shabaka, and also became Pharoah of UPPER and LOWER Kimit (Egypt). He established his official residence at the City of Tanis in Lower Kimit. This city was selected in order to be in a militarily favorable position to face the invading Assyrians on Kimit's eastern border. This was necessary because of the increasing strength of the Assyrian troops in Palestine and their constant deploying of troops from Palestine to the Kimit border. But Esarhaddon, the son of

Sennacherib, succeeded in penetrating the border defenses of Kimit and continued his conquest deep into the old city of Herakleopolis before he was temporarily halted by the Africans. He had captured the Princess of Kimit, and he exacted tributes from her for his native Assyria (the original name of Syria).

The Assyrian armies were finally expelled from Kimit during the reign of Ashurbanipal, the last of the Assyrian Pharoahs, by the African general of Kimit, Taherq, who later became Pharoah of All Kimit (Upper and Lower). But, two years later, Ashurbanipal, with the help of a Phoenician fleet, once again conquered Lower Kimit and secured his troops at the Walls of Thebes.

663 - 525   THE XXVIth DYNASTY (Saite Period): This period was started by Psemthek I. He established his royal residence at Sais, the capital city of the Delta region, and reorganized the army of Kimit with Carian, Ionian, and Syrian mercenaries as chief-generals and confidants. Africans of indigenous origin (the so-called "NEGROES, BANTUS", etc.) were generally excluded from top commands. Mentu-m-hat was placed as governor of the highly mobilized fortresses on the eastern frontiers of Thebes. He was later succeeded by Pharoah Necho (Neku or Necku), who is mentioned in Hebrew (Jewish) history as "the Egyptian general of the Battle of Carchemish", where he was defeated by Nebuchardrezzar. It was after this defeat that Nebuchardrezzar destroyed the Temple of Jerusalem.

525 - 332   THE XXVIIth to XXXIst DYNASTIES (Old Persian and

Mendesian Period): This was the era in which Cambyses, who had become Pharoah of Kimit, began the reconstruction of the temples and other structures of Kimit which his fellow alien predecessors had destroyed in their attempt at keeping the Africans in virtual and perpetual serfdom. He immediately dropped all foreign pretenses and pretexts. He reinstituted all forms of the traditional protocols and attributes of former indigenous African Pharoahs that preceded him. He then renamed himself:

SON OF THE GOD RA,

just as were all of the ancient African Pharoahs of Kimit and other Nile Valleys High-Cultures ("civilizations"). However, Cambyses conducted many unsuccessful military campaigns against the Africans beyond Nubia in the nation of Kush (Cush, Ethiopia, also at one time part of the far-off Upper Kimit) and the Kingdom near the Oasis of Siga in the Libyan Desert. He had depended upon other African peoples of the kingdom to the far-off Northwest, Khart Haddas; for use of their first fleet against other nations, but they refused to fight against their fellow Africans for the benefit of the foreigners - the Persians. Angered by the refusal of the Africans of Khart Haddas, Cambyses set forth destroying all that he had restored and others who were not destroyed by foreign invaders before the entrance of the Persians, even to the point of destroying the Gods of Khart Haddan influences. He

---

*This means "NEW TOWN" in English. It is also called "CARTHAGE". KHART HADDAS is the original name the Africans named that area that is today called "TUNISIA".

destroyed their statues, demolished their temples, and actually killed one of the "SACRED APIS BULLS". This last act infuriated his African captives to the point that civil war was about to ensue, giving rise to Cambyses' recall to Persia in the year 521 B.C.E., and his replacement with Darius I, the son of Hystaspes - the Emperor of Persia. Darius was then made, or proclaimed, PHAROAH OF ALL EGYPT by his father, but in fact did not control most of UPPER EGYPT which was in rebellion when Cambyses was withdrawn.

404 - 394   THE XXVIIIth DYNASTY was founded by Amyrtaeos of Kimit (Sais, Egypt), its only Pharoah. Nothing of major significance in the history of the nation happened during this period. It was also during this era, however, that the indigenous Africans ushered in their withdrawal from the northern reaches of the Nile Delta up to the further highlands in Upper Egypt in order to protect themselves against further foreign intrigues which they realized they could no longer withstand without the aid of other African nations along the more than 4,100 miles long Nile Valleys (from the Mediterranean Sea all the way to the largest of the Great Lakes - Mwanza Nyanza, which the British colonialists re-named "Lake Victoria".) Most of them first settled in Nubia (today's Sudan), others went as far south as Central Africa around the basin and crater that forms the "Great Depression" from West-Central to East-Central Alkebu-lan (Africa). It should be clearly stated that this march led the indigenous Africans in a south-

westerly direction as it did southeasterly. And this march carried many of them all the way down to the southern tip of what was later called "MONOMOTAPA", today renamed by colonialists and imperialist slavers as the "REPUBLIC OF SOUTH AFRICA". Presently such Africans' descendants comprise many of who are today being called "AFRICANS SOUTH OF THE SAHARA".* It was also during this era that the TUTSI (called "<u>Watusi</u>") and the TWA (called "Pygmy") fled Kimit and Nubia (UPPER and LOWER Kimit) in mass migrations - according to their own traditional history which they do not hesitate in telling. This has been told by other African groups and nations who had occasion to come in contact with these African peoples. However, like the indigenous people of Kimit, otherwise described as Herodotus stated in his Histories Book II, and quoted before in this volume, the Tutsi and Twa also came from the Great Lakes region around what is today Tanzania, Uganda, Burundi, Congo, Kenya, Sudan, Malawi, Zambia, Zimbebwe, and other regions which have had to adopt names which the European and European-American imperialists at the BERLIN CONFERENCE and BRUSSELS CONFERENCE of 1884 to 1896 C.E. forced upon the African peoples and land. All of this must relate back to the historic

---

*This term was designed to satisfy the racist stereotype projection of certain "Western professional educators" and "writers" as a vehicle by which the history of Africans (Blacks) "North of the Sahara" could be called "DARK-SKINNED CAUCASIANS, HAMITES, SEMITES," etc. and the others to the south could be called "NEGROES" and "NEGROIDS", and other such nomenclatures that were designed for them by their European and European-American slavemasters of the 16th century.

migrations of the Africans in their return from Upper Kimit (Egypt) to their original home from whence the beginning of the Nile commences.

394 - 378   THE XXIX DYNASTY   (Mendesian Origin): It was in the beginning of this dynasty that King Hager, whom the Greeks renamed "ACHORIS", repulsed the Persian invaders from Kimit after three (3) years of bitter resistance to protect their stolen empire and throne. This dynasty fell after twenty (20) short years of existence under Persian rule. In the sense of historical contributions toward the High-Culture the Africans had created in Kimit, this could be said to be one of the most un-eventful period in the glorious history of Kimit. The downfall of this empire must be attributed to Hager and Evagoras, both of whom had formed a partnership and aided Cyrus against the Persians.

378 - 341   THE XXXth DYNASTY   (Sebenytic Period): This dynasty was founded by Nectanebus I, last of the indigenous African (the so-called "NEGROES" and "BANTUS", etc.) dynasties of Kimit. He restored most of the ancient temples and monuments destroyed by the Assyrians and Persians, and also built many new ones, many of which have survived total destruction by later invasions by Greeks, Romans, and Arabs. He was intent on restoring Kimit's past glorious indigenous African stature, which was first besmirched by the invading Hyksos in 1675 B.C.E. He had also reorganized the government, and fortified the so-called "WHITE WALLS OF THE CITY OF MEMPHIS". He defeated Pharnabazus, the Persian Satrap

(Governor), who was being aided by the much feared General Iphicrates - the Greek. The local Persians, those who were able to commandeer certain minor vassal states within the Empire of Kimit, had hoped to defeat the people of Kimit and again seized control for Persia. Nectanebus' son and successor, DJED-HER, who the Greeks renamed TACHOS, had conspired with many Asian princes against the King of Persia because of his failure to join them in their useless plot to try and maintain Persian colonialism in Kimit. But, failure was his only reward as he too fell victim to his fellow co-conspirators' treachery.

341 - 332   <u>THE XXXIst DYNASTY</u> was founded by Artaxerxes III, Arses, and Darius (all of them Persians). This dynasty lasted until 332 B.C.E. The end came when Alexander "<u>the great</u>" defeated the Persian colonialist government of Kimit upon his return from Macedonia, which was following many of his other colonial exploits in what is today called the "MIDDLE EAST", formerly "ASIA-MINOR". Alexander's forces crushed the Persians under the command of the Persian Poser. But this defeat only introduced European (Caucasian, Greek) colonial rule for that of Asia (Persia). Alexander forgot very conveniently that it was the help of the Africans of Kimit that made it possible for the Greeks to be victorious over the Persians - their common enemy. The Africans had in fact changed an Asian colonial slavemaster for a European of the same type. This marked the first time in North African history, especially that of Kimit (Egypt), that Africans were to

be ruled by Europeans - otherwise called "CAUCASIANS", <u>light</u> or <u>dark-skinned</u>.*

332 - c47   <u>THE XXXIInd DYNASTY</u>: This dynasty ushered in the most barbarous period in the history of Kimit before the Christian and Arab eras. This period of infamy was later on to be called by European and European-American historians and other "<u>educators</u>",

THE GREEK EPOCH and PTOLEMAIC PERIOD,
both definitions falling short of the real and truthful classification of the periods.** Were these periods and the acts of barberism that took place in them by Europeans and European-African-Asian peoples (the result of the amalgamation that took place after the Greeks' conquest) the exploits of the Africans, they would become "CANNIBALISTIC, UNCIVILIZED, PRIMITIVE", and other such names generally reserved for indigenous Africans and things African.

c47 - 30   <u>THE POST DYNASTIC PERIODS</u>: These periods that preceded the Roman control of Northern Africa a few years before the

---

*It must be remembered that the indigenous Africans of Kimit, regardless of whether or not they are called "NEGROES, BANTUS, AFRICANS SOUTH OF THE SAHARA, PYGMIES," etc., or other racist stereotype names reserved for African Blacks, were never-the-less in total control of Kimit (Sais or Egypt) and all other lands of North Africa (Alkebu-lan) for more than forty-thousand years before the arrival of the first Europeans - the so-called "Caucasians" (Greeks) with the arrival of Alexander "the great" in 332 B.C.E. in search of the "ORACLE OF ANON".

**Note that the first of the Ptolemies was the Macedonian general - Soter - who declared himself PHAROAH PTOLEMY I after his boss Alexander II, "the great", conquered Kimit in 332 B.C.E. as shown before.

proclamation of the birth of the Christians' God - "JESUS CHRIST" - were divided into ROMAN (47 B.C.E. to 324 C.E.), and KOPTIC (or COPTIC 324 C.E. to 640 C.E.). The Koptic Period, in reality, ended at the arrival of the Asian Arab conquerors during the earliest periods of their jihads in their murderous sweep of northern Africa, beginning in the year 640 C.E. or 18 A.H. These periods were mostly marked by wars and destruction, as the foreigners carried out their "SCORCH EARTH" policy of prostilization of the indigenous African peoples of North and East Africa; of course palace intrigues went hand and glove with the genocide, as members of the conquering class fought to the death over the spoils of the African treasuries and artifacts, most of which are to be found in the museums and other places in Europe and the United States of America at present. The Beni Soleim Arabs, led by an African general of Islam who had adopted the name of the said tribe, was yet to be the master of North Africa in 640 B.C.E. Therefore, it can be wisely said that neither the North African Christians - the Koptics, nor the Moslems, did any good what-soever for the indigenous African peoples of North Africa, particularly those of Kimit (Sais, Egypt, presently renamed by the Arab-African-European amalgamation "THE UNITED ARAB REPUBLIC - U.A.R.).

SPECIAL DYNASTIC INFORMATION

During the XIIIth DYNASTY, Nehsira, also known as the "BLACKEST OF THE PHAROAHS", mounted the throne of Kimit. This occurred during the period when Kimit was supposed to have been divided into two seperate kingdoms - UPPER and LOWER or NORTH and SOUTH. It was the beginning of the end to the cohesion of the once greatest of all of the world's High-Culture ("civilization") ever devised by mankind anywhere. It is from these beginnings that the European - presently called "CAUCASIAN", got his first peep into what is today called "WESTERN CIVILIZATION". From these Africans who are today called "AFRICANS SOUTH OF THE SAHARA" (and other such names which colonist Europeans and European-Americans have labeled them) the first European historian - Herodotus, the first European physician - Hippocrates, the first European philosopher who was in fact an Ionian by birth but Greek by citizenship - Socrates, and all others that followed them received their education; and from these ancient indigenous Africans that which is today called "GREEK PHILOSOPHY" was stolen.

During the XVth DYNASTY Saltis, the first pharoah of this dynasty, ruled Kimit for the first time in 1675 B.C.E. He was the ruler of the many Hyksos tribes called "SHEPHERD KINGS", not Kamose, as it is erroneously stated sometimes in many so-called "authorities'" works. Kamose only came into power about 1580 B.C.E., which was more than ninety-four (94) long years after Saltis.

BIBLIOGRAPHY FOR CHAPTER IV

Wallis Budge, Sir E.A.	BOOK OF THE DEAD (translated papyri from their original Hieroglyphs to English).
Alexander, D.B.	HISTORY OF PHILOSOPHY.
Sandford, Eva M.	THE MEDITERRANEAN WORLD.
Vail, C.H.	ANCIENT MYSTERIES.
Kenrick, John	HISTORY OF ANCIENT EGYPT.
James, George G.M.	STOLEN LEGACY.
Besant, Annie	ESOTERIC CHRISTIANITY.
Herodotus	THE HISTORIES (translated from the original Greek to the English language by A. Selincourt).
Tyler and Sedgwick	HISTORY OF SCIENCE.
Muller, Max	EGYPTIAN MYTHOLOGY.
Reddick	HISTORY OF PHILOSOPHY.
Glanville, S.R.K. (ed.)	THE LEGACY OF EGYPT.
ben-Jochannan, Yosef	AFRICAN ORIGINS OF THE MAJOR "WESTERN RELIGIONS" (Judaism, Christianity, and Islam).
Huggins, W. & Jackson, J.	AN INTRODUCTION TO AFRICAN HISTORY.
Wells, H.G.	A SHORT HISTORY OF THE WORLD.
Adams, W. Marshan	BOOK OF THE MASTER.
Breasted, James H.	ANCIENT RECORDS OF EGYPT.
Volney, Count C.F.	RUINS OF EMPIRES.
deGraft-Johnson, J.C.	AFRICAN GLORY.

BIBLIOGRAPHY FOR CHAPTER IV (con't)

Churchward, Dr. Albert C.   THE ORIGIN OF FREEMASONRY.

- - - - -   SIGNS AND SYMBOLS OF PRIMORDIAL MAN.

- - - - -   ARCANA OF FREE MASONRY.

- - - - -   THE ORIGIN AND EVEOLUTION OF THE HUMAN RACE.

THE HOLY BIBLE, HOLY TORAH, HOLY KORAN.

NOTES ON EGYPTOLOGY

AN EXAMINATION INTO THE ORIGINAL TEACHINGS OF CREATION, DEATH, RESURRECTION, HEAVEN, HELL, ETC., FROM THE AFRICAN TEXTS OF KIMIT (Egypt)

Egyptologist, Sir Ernest A. Wallis Budge, late Keeper of the Egyptian and Assyrian Antiquities of the British Museum, in his book, EGYPTIAN LANGUAGE, etc, London, Routledge and Kegan Paul Ltd., 1910, stated in Chapter I, page 1, the following:

> It is hardly probable that the hieroglyphic system of writing was invented in Egypt, and the evidence on this point now accumulating indicates that it was brought there by invaders who came from north-east or central Asia;[1] they settled down in the valley of the Nile at some place between Memphis on the north and Thebes on the south, and gradually established their civilization and religion in their new home.

"...the evidence..., etc. to which Sir Wallis Budge referred was not specified or in any other way detailed in his work; neither can it be found in any of his other major works, which I must admit is very extensive. Even Professor Gaston Maspero, who wrote much more extensively than Budge, and whom Budge and most of the others associated with Budge have always quoted, on Egypt and other Nile Valley High-Cultures, did not attempt to prove the none-African origin of the language of ancient Kimit (Sais; the Hebrews' Egypt); to the contrary, as most egyptologists and paleontologists who wrote on Egypt,(prior to the period when Caucasianism and Negrophobism became of major importance in the world of history as written by most Europeans and European-Americans within the last two (2) centuries), agree to its Alkebu-lan ("Africa" according to the ancient Greeks and Romans) origin.

---

1. Words underscrored by your lecturer for emphasis in the quotation only; thus highlighting the distortion of history.

But, at what period did the alledged foreign invaders entered Egypt? Sir E. A. Wallis Budge, the instigator of the above hypothesis, which he expected we should accept as the gospel truth in his attempt to remove Egyptian origin entirely from the continent of Alkebu-lan, could not say. For the "invaders" to have had such influence on the Nile Valley African people - th. ROMITI (so-called "Egyptians")[1] they would have had to enter Egypt before the writing of the first texts that formed the BOOK OF THE DEAD about 6,00 - 4,000 B.C.E. at least; the same BOOK Sir E.A. Wallis Budge himself translated into English along with its accompanying work - the PAPYRUS OF ANI. However, the first record of any invasion of Egypt by any group of foreigners outside the continent of Alkebu-lan (Africa) was the so-called "HYKSOS" or "SHEPHERD KINGS" from Asia, all of whom arrived in Egypt by way of the Sinai Peninsula around c1675 B.C.E. (or B.C); and these "foreigners" were not known to have been proficient in any specific language-skill which they have left behind for mankind to learn from. Even the name "HYKSOS" was only speculatively given to these Asian invaders by anthropologists and historians of the discipline called "egyptology;" their place of origin having been assumed to have been "...somewhere along the Oxus River of Asia-Minor" (today's "Middle-East"). It must be also noted that the ancients, such as the Ionian that became a Greek citizen,- Herodotus, the first of the European historians (generally called by "Western" educators - "the father of history", European history

---

1. Romitu is singular, Romiti plural, Kimit the name of the nation. These indigenous people of nothern Alkebu-lan also called their nation "Sais," the same name which they also called one of their cities on the shores of the Kimit Sea - today's Mediterranean Sea. Egypt and Egyptians are foreign words.

that is of course, none other), in his most noted work, THE
HISTORIES, Book II, described the indigenous peoples of this area
during c450 B.C.E. in the following manner:

> The Colchians, Ethiopians and Egyptians have
> thick lips, broad nose, wooley hair, and they
> are burnt of skin.[1]

During, and before, the period Herodotus was writing (c457-450 B.C.E.), also highlighted by the writings of the vast majority of ancient writers who had experienced nothing like the "modern Negrophobism" of today, including those living in far off ELAM (the African kingdom of the Persian Empire that once captured and ruled Chaldea - even up to the time of the birth of the first Haribu or Hebrew[2] - AVRAM or ABRAHAM), the general population of this area of Alkebu-lan, Kimit or Egypt, was designated as being "ETHIOPIAN" - black (at least brown in color), and they were always dipicted in like manner on papyri and picture paintings. This does not, in any way whatsoever, attempt to imply that there were no people who are today called "CAUCASIANS, SEMITIES, HAMITES, ARYANS," even "WHITES," among these indigenous Africans - properly and appropriately, ROMITI,. They were thousands of the later groupings who came to learn from these Africans from ancient times of which there are no records to show just when they first arrived there. What is being said on the other hand is, that, the ancient Romiti of Kimit, who were the same as all other people of Alkebu-lan basically, as indicated by all of the presently available data of that era, did not find whatever physical

---
1. It is of major significance to note that most of the so-called "Western historians" and "educators" have edited-out all references to the "broad nose" and "thick lips."
2. The original name of the people of the Holy Torah, so-called "Chosen people" of the Book of Genesis - First Book of Moses.

differences they may have had sufficient to make it necessary to deal with each others in terms of the loathsome emotional word "modern man" (Europeans and European-Americans) have concocted for mankind as a whole, "RACE." This extraordinary emotionally-charged "WHITE-HEAT" that triggers "modern man's most bestial actions against those he (or she) considers below his own self-concerned omnipresence, because of some god-like endowment he assigned himself, has made him change certain indigenous Africans - "BLACKS" - to become "SEMITES, CAUCASIANS, CAUCASOIDS, HAMITES," and even special people for whom they are yet no known identification; all at the command of the "HOLY WHITE FATHERS" who control the education media of the vast majority of the inhabitants of this planet - EARTH.

There is still another point of view to be examined in the controversy over just who, in fact, were the ancestors of Kimit before the first none-African peoples invaded that nation in about c1675 B.C.E. That is (a); who decided what they were? (b); for what purpose? and (c); why was this plagerization of history allowed to continue unchallenged in any meaningful manner even up until this very day? One common answer can suffice the necessary inquiries; that is, the HOLY TRINITY conspiracy between so-called "Western Philosophy", also called - "JUDAEO-CHRISTIAN GREEK-CENTERED PHILOSOPHICAL EDUCATION," simply educational imperialism; formerly exemplified by the combination of the so-called "CHRISTIAN MISSIONARIES" (European-style) and their HOLY BIBLE (King James version and all others, Old and New Testament) side by side with the colonialist "entreprenuers" and plain old slavers under the banner of "...bringing civilization and Christianity to the uncivilized savages and heathen pagans of Darkest Africa;" of course the latter mission was extended to all areas of the world where Europeans and European-Americans colonized and enslaved.

The following statement by Sir Ernest A. Wallis Budge in his most noted work, BOOK OF THE DEAD, under the heading -"INTRODUCTION, page xi, is of great importance to the above remarks I have made. He wrote:

> <u>The home, origin, and early history of the collection of ancient religious texts which have descended to us</u> (Caucasians and Semites alike)[1] are, at present unknown, <u>and all working theories regarding them, however strongly supported by apparently well-ascertained facts, must be carefully distinguished as theories only, so long as a simple ancient necropolis in Egypt remains unexplored and its inscriptions are untranslated</u>.

At least Budge allowed one to say that he is consistent with respect to what he wrote in 1910 as being very similar to his former position of 1895. The statement was in effect dealing with the origin of Hieroglyphics. In the year 1895, however, he displayed uncertainty of the origin of what he preferred to call:

> "...immigrants from the Asiatic continent whence they came,..." etc.,

as he also added;"

> ...or whether they represent the religious books of the Egyptians incorporated with the funeral texts of some prehistoric dwellers on the banks of the Nile, are all questions which the possible discovery of inscription belonging to the first dynasties of the Early Empire can alone decide.

When Sir Ernest A. Wallis Budge wrote of "...the collection of ancient religious texts which have descended to us are...,"

---

1. Words in parentheses by your lecturer for clarity only.
2. Words underscored for particular emphasis on the point that Budge did not follow his own warning in the above remarks.

etc. he was obviously placing his finger on the crucial reason why "US" (his fellow Europeans and European-Americans, including "Caucasians" and "Semites") must prove the non-African origin of everything north African, muchless things of Egyptian origin in particular. The other major words to be carefully scrutinized are "...which have descended to us...." These words are representative of an intent to relieve the imperialist thieves from Europe, Britain and the United States of America, who have plundered and raped Africa of her most priceless treasures which are still found today in public and private "collections" under European names -such as "EBERS PAPYRUS, EDWIN C. SMITH PAPYRUS," etc.- from culpability as piratiers to that of legal owners by virtue of inheritance from their own racial Egyptian ancestors. Certainly, the extension of the prohibition against "stealing from one's neighbour," which the African-Haribus (Hebrews, misnomered "Jews") adopted and took with them from western Kimit (Egypt) before recording it in their HOLY TORAH (Four Books Of Moses, which later was expanded into Five) before the Christians and Muslims followed suit in their own bible - Qu'ran (or Koran), should have had its effects upon men such as Sir E.A.W. Budge, while they were preparing their manuscripts denying the African origin of things Egyptian. Obviously, however, "THOU SHALT NOT BEAR FALSE WITNESS" (tell lies), another of the so-called "TEN COMMANDMENTS" Moses supposedly received at Mount Sinai, which in fact he received from the BOOK OF THE DEAD, COFFIN TEXTS, and other Nile Valley religious and philosophical teachings, was the prohibition that was still in effect when the Budges, Breasteds, Jeffreys, Wiedners and other so-called "Western educators" and "egyptologists" and "paeleontologists" were perpetuating their myth of a "Negro-less" north Africa. Moreso, these two "Commandments" meant nothing to them, and most of the others of similar disciplines before them, and since; or the "US" in Sir Ernest A. Wallis Budge's statement above would have reflected the indigenous Africans described in Herodotus' THE HISTORIES, Book II; most of whom their descendants are today called such names as :

"NEGROES, NIGGERS, PYGMIES, CANNIBALS, HEATHENS, PRIMITIVES, BANTUS, AFRICANS SOUTH OF THE SAHARA,"

among other superlatives relating back to the colonialist slave period (1506-1865 C.E. or A.D.).[1]

The above facts had to be cited before it was logical to examine the BOOK OF THE DEAD or PAPYRUS OF ANI, COFFIN TEXTS, PYRAMID TEXTS, and other major African works which became the foundation (origin) of most of what is today called "Judaeo-Christianity, Islam, Greek Philosophy, Western Democracy," and even "Civilization." Were they left unexamined, then those who have made it their obsession to assure themselves that the "Caucasianism" and "Semitic origins of north Africa" they have been preaching about had become fact by virtue of default on the part of the present indigenous Africans and other peoples of African origin living in the so-called "Western" or "New World." Another baseless victory would hav been lossed to the African descendants who inherrited what have been passed down to them from their ancestors that established the Nile Valleys (Blue and White, including the Atbara River) and Great Lakes High-Cultures ("civilizations") of MOTHER-AFRICA, Alkebu-lan, the only true "GARDEN OF EDEN" - home of the oldest known fossil-

---

1. This period began with the Right Reverend Bishop Bartolome de LasCasas in Hispaniola (Hayte or Haiti) in 1506; and ended, theoratically) with President A. Lincoln of the U.S.A. in 1865.

man, ZINJANTHROPUS boisie, that preceded "Adam and Eve" of the Hebrew Holy Torah (Bible, Christian Old Testament) by more than one-million seven hundred and fifty thousand (1,750,000) years.

Speaking about the "Adam and Eve" myth of the "Creation of Man" drama in the BOOK OF GENESIS (First Book Of Moses), one sees the African origin of this myth in the following excerpt taken from the BOOK OF THE DEAD and the PAPYRUS OF ANI:

> In the primeval matter, or water, lived the God Tmu, and when he rose for the first time, in the form of the sun, he created the world.

The above extract is taken from the INTRODUCTION, page xvii of the BOOK OF THE DEAD. On pages xcvii and xcviii it is also shown that the pyramid of Pharoah Pepi I contains the following in one of the many inscriptions. That:

> ...there was neither heaven or earth, and when neither Gods had been born, nor men created, the God Tmu[1] was the father of human beings, even before death came into the world.

It is to be noted, however, that the actual text, which was taken word for word from the inscription without the above analysis, does state:

> (Rā) gave birth to Pepi his father Tmu[2] (when) not was created heaven, not was created earth, not were created men, not were born the Gods, not was created death.

The above point is further supported by another papyrus in the

---
1. God of the water and the world; joined by Ra; thus: TAMU-RA.
2. One of the origins the early Christians adopted for the Trinitarian myth.

British Museum under the following identification No. 10188 during the year 1889. See also ARCHAEOLOGIA, vol.lii, pp. 440-443, where it is written:

> I united myself to my shadow (spirit), and I sent forth Shu and Tefnut out from myself: thus from being one God I became three (the Trinitarian concept of the Christians of today),[1] and Shu and Tefnut gave birth to Nut and Seb, and Nut gave birth to Osiris, Horus-Khent-an-maa, Sut, Isis, and Nephthys, at one birth, one after the other, and their children multiply upon this earth.[2]

"I united myself to my shadow...," etc., is so obviously the origin from whence the Christians copied their Jesus Christ ghost-like characteristics that to deny it only causes one to dig deeper, only to find that this mythological theory, or concept, even existed for thousands of years before the God ANI or PEPI. Throughout the PAPYRUS OF ANI references to "virgin birth, resurrection, God (Ra) making man from other men, God (Ra) being superior to all other Gods," etc. have been shown to have preceded the Haribus (Hebrews, later "Jews") mythological "Creation" drama in the BOOK OF GENESIS and the Christians "VIRGIN MARY AND CHILD " (Jesus Christ of Nazareth) myth they adopted from the ISIS AND OSIRIS fertility image projected by the Africans of Kimit (Egypt) more than 4000 years before the birth of the first of the Haribus - Abraham.

At this juncture, one must be reminded that Moses was an African of Egypt, a Romitu; and that even Mount Sinai, which he allegedly climbed to receive the "Commandments," was, and still is, a part of Kimit, North Africa. History reveals that he

---
1. Words in parentheses by your lecturer for clarity only.
2. This is the origin of the method of dialogue adopted in the Hebrew and Christian bibles. The ancient writers not only plagerized the documents, they also adopted the exact style.

was never outside of Egyptian territory in his entire lifetime; and that all he learnt, from his birth until the day Jehovah mysteriously took him off the earth, came from the education he received among the African priests of the Kimit (Egyptian) Mysteries System along the banks of the Nile, and in particular at the Grand Lodge of Luxor. The Haribus tribes at that period in history were all Africans, as described by Herodotus; with...

> "...thick lips, broad nose, wooley hair, and burnt of skin...,"

like all of the other Africans that inhabited the entire continent as far south as Monomotapa. And before Moses the Haribus had not produced a solitary written document relating to "creation" or anything else similar. Moreover, Moses disappeared for hundreds of years before the first of the so-called "FOUR BOOKS OF MOSES" (later on expanded to FIVE) were written by men who allegedly remembered all that Moses taught. Of course those writers were all "...inspired men of God...," etc. But, strangely enough, the God RA, whom the Africans of Kimit and all of the other High-Cultures along the Nile and Great Lakes worshiped before the origin of the Haribus God - JEHOVAH - was created by Abraham's dream, said the same words following:

THOU SHALT HAVE NO OTHER GODS BEFORE ME,

which the God of the Haribus, Jehovah, adopted. Even the "JEALOUS" feature of the God RA was copied by Jehovah. This form of "Monotheism," which the Haribus were supposed to have originated, preceded the birth of the first Haribu (originally a Chaldean from the City of Ur) - Abraham (Avram, etc.) by more than 4000 years at minnimum.

In the PAPYRUS OF NU (also illegally held in the possession

of the British Museum), under Chapter III, Ani states:

> He hath performed the decree which hath been spoken to the mariners at eventide, and the Osiris Nu, whose word is truth, <u>shall live after his death</u>, even as doth Ra every day. Behold most certainly Ra was born yesterday, and the Osiris Nu was born yesterday.

The ressurection drama set forth in the above remarks is complementary to the following shown in Chapter IX, dealing with "THE STABBING OF SET."[1]

> I have opened every way in heaven and on earth. I am the son (Jesus Christ) who love his Fathers (Osiris or Jehovah).[2] I am a spirit-body. I am a spirit-soul.[3] I am equipped. Hail, every God and every spirit-soul. I have made the way to Osiris. I the Osiris the Scribe Ani, whose word is truth.

The above confession by Ani was made in the CHAMBER OF AMHET in the DOMAIN OF SEKER (the God of death). Osiris, who is "Father" in this case, represented also the "Son" - Jesus Christ. Thus, we have Osiris - the "Father;" Osiris - the "Son;" and Osiris - the "Soul" or Holy Ghost. This is one of the oldest example of the TRINITARIAN declaration, even older than that taught by Amen-ho-tep IV (Ikhanaten, Akhnaten, etc.), after whom modern Unitarianism patterened itself; and whose teachings formed the basis of Unitarian Christianisms and other philosophical customs evident in their worship.

I am compelled to divert attention, at this juncture, to a

---

1. This name was adopted by the Haribus as a name for Adam and Eve's third child - "SET."
2. Words in parentheses by the lecturer for clarity only.
3. Words underscored for specific emphasis and to highlight the extent to which the plagerism of the African-Americans heritage have been coopted by others and called "Semitic" and "Caucasoid" origins.

few citations on the "VIRGIN MARY" in order to support the contentions stated above. Thus, it is noted that in many countries of Europe, particularly those having statues of the "Virgin" on the streets shown holding the child, "JESUS CHRIST " (Osiris or Orus), on one arm, a branch of lilies (a European symbol of peace) - the lotus (an African or Egyptian symbol of peace) - in the hand of the other arm, standing with one foot upon the head of a serpent (the Snake Goddess), which has a spring of an apple-tree (the Tree of Life) with an apple on it in its mouth - its tail twisted about a globe partly enveloped in the clouds (the celestial globe). Mary's head is surrounded by the twelve (12) glorious stars (generally shown as the Seven (7) Pole Stars around the head of Isis - the Egyptian Goddess or Earth Mother of Fertility . Why the LOTUS, Egypt's most acred plant, as shown in all of the dramatical JUDGEMENT scenes in the BOOK OF THE DEAD and the PAPYRUS OF ANI, as used in the above remarks. (See R. Ker Porter, TRAVELS IN PERSIA, VI. p. 628, 4 to.; also, Sir Godfrey Higgins, ANACALYPSIS, Book IV, Chapter II, Section I, pp. 303-307). It is to be noted that Sir Geoffrey Higgins, as well as most of the other philosophical educators on comparative religions, religiously held to the position that Jesus Christ of Nazareth was, without a doubt,"BACCHUS" - the "Egyptians Sun diety" who was also called "ORUS." Furthermore, Jesus Christ was then called "IAW;" and he was shown to be a BLACK MAN FROM ETHIOPIA" or "INDIA." (See ANACALYPSIS, Vol. I, Book VI, Chapter II, Section 1, p. 303; also, OVID, FASTI, iii; in which "Libera" or "Ariadne" - Bacchus' pretended wife, whom Cicero's "de Nat. Deor" cites to be "Proserpina " Bacchus' mother).

It is certainly unfortunate that so many members of the clergy ("members of the cloth") do not read about the historical origin of their religion before assuming their declared "GOD'S CALL TO CONVERT THE HEATHENS." Of course anyone who is not a member of the religion of the person who is doing the particular conversion is a heathen. Even a Christian, Muslim or Jew of different sects is a "heathen" in this perspective. In this regards, I am reminded of a noted minister of the Gospel of Jesus who once told me, while sitting in the Chock Full O'Nuts restaurant at 125th Street, Harlem, New York City, New York:

> The only book on religion I believe, and will ever read, is the Holy Bible, the King James version.

Yet this man advises his parishoners, of which he controls more than 1,200 of them, and friends, on subjects ranging from religion to medicine and law; but, his formal education ceased to exist at the fourth grade , and his only subsequent reading experience amounted solely to the reading of the King James version of the Christian Holy Bible and the Daily News periodical. This man, nevertheless, is equally licensed by the State of New York to practice and advise countless numbers of people on almost anything imaginable. Behind this kind of background; is it any wonder that Karl Marx was obliged to dub religion "...the opiate of the people...," etc.?

The student of religion must, in all cases, be willing and ready to investigate all sort of information dealing with the historical origin and development of his or her religious belief, remembering all the time that a "belief" in itself expresses uncertainty. Also, as long as there was anything preceding that which one believes at any given time, the possibility exists that in the former teachings the true origin of the basic principle of said belief is inherent.

Returning to the main subject of our discussion, the BOOK OF THE DEAD and the PAPYRUS OF ANI, we find the pharoah, Ani, using the same design and shape "TABLET OF THE LAWS OF GOD - RA" as adopted by the Haribus (Hebrews) in their Mount Sinai's drama of Moses receiving "THE TEN COMMANDMENTS FROM GOD - JEHOVAH."[1] (See BOOK OF EXODUS - the First Book of Moses). In similar light we note that in the PAPYRUS OF ANI there are two (2) birds that represent the "soul of Ani - the "Kaa" and the "Baa" birds. The Kaa (Ka) bird is black; but, the Baa (Ba) bird is white. The Kaa bird symbolizes life; whereas, the Baa bird was always the opposite, death. We see the reversal of this with the Hebrews of Hellenic Greece, which was passed on to the Etruscans who changed the worship of the "Black Virgin and Child," Isis and Orus - to the "White Goddess Nurtia" or "Nortia," which Michaelangelo later copied and neutralized to appear as a northern Roman or Italian. (See F. Gorii Museum's print of the Etruscan VIRGIN AND CHILD, Tab. 4, Ant. Tram. Gorii, NORTIA TUSCORUM DEA; and Pliny, LIB. XXXVI. Cap. VII; Livy, LIB. VII; and Juvenalen, SAT. X. V. 74; Tertullian[1], APOLOGET, Cap. XXIV, must be included, also Marianus, LIB. de NUPTIIS PHILOLOG, Capt. IX.)

I suggest that the following extracts from Book II, Chapter II, Section 8, p. 311 of Sir Godfrey Higgins, ANACALYPSIS, needs to be investigated at this juncture. He wrote:

> No person who has considered well the character

---

1. Jehovah or Yaweh. Ywh is also called "Adoni" from a later development of the taboos of the Hebrew religion.
2. One of the African "Fathers of the Christian Church."

> of the temples of India and Egypt, can help being
> convinced of the identity of their character, and
> of their being the production of the same race of
> people; and this race evidently Ethiopian. The
> Sphinxes have all Ethiopian faces. The bust of
> Memmon in the British Museum is evidently Ethio-
> pian. The worship of the Mother and Child is
> seen in all parts of the Egyptian religion. It
> prevails everywhere. It is the worship of Isis
> and the infant Orus or Osiris.

In the same paragraph Sir Higgins continued:

> It (the Black Virgin and Child)[1] was the worship
> of the mother of the God Ixu, the Saviour ; Bacchus
> in Greece; Adonis[2] in Syria; Cristna in India;
> coming into Italy through the medium of the two
> Ethiopians, she was, as the Ethiopians were, <u>black</u>,[3]
> and such she still remains.

The above statements by Sir Godfrey Higgins, particularly the latter, should have been read by Frank M. Snowden, Jr. before he wrote his book, BLACKS OF ANTIQUITY,(etc.), Harvard University Press, Cambridge, Mass., 1970. For, though Mr. Snowden seemed to be well aware of the fact of just who the Greeks and Romans, of ancient times, meant when they said "Ethiopians;" he seems, never the less, to be quite uncertain or insecure of himself to cite that the term was synonymous of the soul brother or soul sister of today's African-American (black) communities. By being so reluctant to be specific, he apparently failed to notice that even the Greeks' Christ, CRISTOS - "the anointed one," was also said to have been an "Ethiopian" - Black, as mentioned above.

These citations certainly throw a different light on the teachings currently being perpetuated to the contrary by so-called

---

1. Words in parenthesis by the lecturer for clarity only.
2. Adonis is the Adonai of the Hebrews, or Jehovah (Ywh).
3. The underscored word , "black," is for special emphasis with regards to the present struggles being waged by Reverend Albert Cleage, Jr. of the Shrine (Church) of the Black Madonna for recognition of her African origin in the U.S.A.

"modern" historians, theologians, and "educators" in general, in our private and public educational institutions, religious and secular. For, the reverse is generally taught; this being especially true even in so-called "Negro Schools" and "Churches;" and by "Negro Clergymen."

> These words shalt thou declare, and these shalt thou hide. And when thou hast done, some things shalt thou publish, and some things shalt thou show secretly to the WISE.
> ...The Highest spake, saying, The first that thou had written publish openly, that the worthy and the unworthy may read it: but keep the seventy last, that thou mayest deliver them only to such as be WISE among the people. For in them is the spring of understanding, the fountain of WISDOM.

The above extract stems from the FOURTH BOOK of ESDRAS, Chapter XIV, pp. 6, 26, and 45. These were allegedly "told to Moses verbally at Mount Sinai (Kimit, Sais, or Egypt)[1] by Jehovah, as a secret." They were not included in the Pentateuch; nor were they written down. This was the basis upon which the Hebrew (Jewish) Kaballah was written, to record the concealed "TRUTH," about the Hebrew religion which was withheld from the general public or population of Israel (the people). Yet, Hebrew theologians and scholars dare to tell us that the WRITTEN LAWS, as they appear, came down to us unadulteratedly, without a solitary error. But before their own king, Josiah, the same set of "laws" were supposedly forgotten; as their priests, kings, and general population had turned to "idolatry," etc. thus the reason for the FOURTH BOOK OF EDRAS.

There is nothing to be found in the FOURTH BOOK OF EDRAS with respect to religious philosophy that the ancient Haribus did not learn in Kimit from the BOOK OF THE DEAD, PAPYRUS OF ANI,

---

[1]. Words in parenthesis by the lecturer for clarity only.

COFFIN TEXTS and PYRAMID TEXTS, before Moses allegedly "received the Ten Commandments from Jehovah on Mount Sinai." This also holds true for the QABBALAH (Khaballah) which most of the current Jewish scholars say is at least old or older than Moses; many of them point to the following teaching from oriental sources found in the SEPTUAGINT, of Deuteronomy XXXiii, 2, as supportive proof...

> ...he shined forth from Paran with thousands of
> saints, and having his angels on his right hand.[1]

The above translation can be seen in its total glory in the PAPYRUS OF ANI and the BOOK OF THE DEAD. Of course there is no doubt that the Kaa and Baa birds, the "souls of the dead," who flew in and out of the deceased to appeal for him (or her), were the angels being referred to; these two, not excluding the many others in the religion of the Nile River Valley High-Cultures (civilizations), are presently represented as "angels" in the Torah

If we are to accept the above quotation from the FOURTH BOOK OF EDRAS, however; how is it that the following two words in the BOOK OF GENESIS caused so many Jewish and Christian theologians of "authoritative" renown to differ sharply. Thus ראשית B-RASIT. The noted Rabbi Bachai and Rabbi Castali held that it meant "...IN ORDER BEFORE ALL;" the first of the greatest of the three "Christian Church Fathers" - an indigenous African himself (Black or Ethiopian), from Numidia, North Africa), Tertullian, held that it meant "...IN POWER;" Grotious, on the other hand said they stood for "...WHEN FIRST;" while Simeon "the great" held to "...BEFORE." But most of the modern scholars of Christian persuasion, including the noted theologians Jonathan ben Uzziel and Onkelos, held to the current translation "...IN THE BEGINNING."

---

1. Dr. Rees' ENCYCLOPEDIA, art. Cabala; Enfield's HISTORY OF PHILOSOPHY, Vol. II, Chapt. iii; Issac Myer's QABBALAH; etc.

The latter is the accepted holding in the SEPTUAGINT. "The first authoritative book of the Hebrew ("Jewish") religion," the JERUSALEM TARGUM, revealed that these two words mean,"...BY WISDOM." In the "ABODE OF THE BLESSED" we see the Africans of Kimit (Sais, Egypt) usage of the same two words in the following manner:

"Come forth from the waters, and bear up this God." But, the question is; which GOD? It is the God NUT, i.e., the Sky-Goddess...

"WHO RECEIVES RA,"

as described in the PAPYRUS OF ANI in the BOOK OF THE DEAD. In much more ancient times, long before the worship of RA, it was the Beettle Goddess - KHEPER-RA, for whom the following was said:

> Thou dost bring the Nile out from his cavern, thou makest the staff of life to flourish, thou makest the grian to come forth therefrom in thy name of Nu the Aged, thou makest the celestial deep to bring forth, thou makest water to appear on the mountains to give life to men and women.

In speaking about the "BEGINNING", we can also notice that in the PAPYRUS OF ANI the so-called "FORBIDDEN FRUIT TREE OF THE GARDEN OF EDEN," which the Haribus co-opted and attributed to their own God - YWH or JEHOVAH - was already mentioned in the following Africans of Egypt "SACRED SCRIPTURE:"

> ...he goeth to the great in the midst of the Field Of Offerings whereon the great Gods sit; and these great and never-failing Gods give unto him (to eat) of the tree of life of which they themselves do eat that he likewise may live.[1]

The constant co-optation by the ancient Haribus (Hebrews or Jews), who were in fact, simply, Africans of Egypt (Egyptians), if it is true that they remained in Kimit (Egypt) for more than

---

1. RECUEIL de TRAVAUX, t. VII, p. 154 (ll. 309, 310). Words in parenthesis by the lecturer for clarity only.

four hundred and thirty (430) years, according to EXODUS, XII, 40 (c1662-1232 B.C.E.), and were slaves to other fellow indigenous Africans that dominated the population of Kimit, is further shown in their adoption of ANU 🛆 of the BOOK OF THE DEAD - one of the "...many places where the spirit dwell on the way to Amenta."[1] But, the Haribus renamed it "ON," according to GENESIS xli, 45, 50; xlvi, 20; and "AVEN," according to EZEKIEL xxx, 17; also "BETH-SHEMESH," according to JEREMIAH xliii, 13. It is to be further noted, that Beth-Shemesh is an exact translation from the African Hieroglyph ⌐◯⌐ per Rā, which means in English "...HOUSE OF THE SUN;" also a designation for ANU. This same "HOME OF THE GODS" was also called "HELIOPOLIS" by the Greeks, which name still wrongfully appears on most maps of "modern" Egypt. (See also Strabo, XVII, 27ff; and Herodotus, II, 3,7,8,9, 59 and 93). Yet, the "modern" confessants (Europeans and European-Americans) of the Jewish religion, most of whom dwell in the United States of America and Israel,[2] refused to admit that they have adopted most of the so-called "MYTHOLOGICAL GODS" and "PLACES OF ABODE " of their ancient Black brothers - worshipers of RA and other Gods and Goddesses of Africa, Egypt particularly. They have conveniently forgotten that, even, their own Prophet, Moses, who was himself an African of Kimit, having been born, raised and disappeared into oblivion there at Mount Sinai, also received his education and all that he knew from the Priests of ANU, which was at the chief seat of the religion of the worship

---

1. Place where the SUN set; later on cemeteries in stony plateaus and mountains at the west bank of the Nile River.
2. Note that there are thousands of "Black Jews" still living in Ethiopia, East Africa. They are erroneously called "FALASHAS" and "FALASA;" however, the correct nomenclature the accept is "BET ISRAEL" or HOUSE OF ISRAEL and CHILDREN OF THE HOUSE OF ISRAEL. Their customs predate European-American Jews.

of the God RA. But, if they should investigate deeply into the religion of the Africans of Kimit, especially in the BOOK OF THE DEAD and the PAPYRUS OF ANI, they may discover, much to their displeasure, that their entire BOOK OF GENESIS, other labeled the "FIRST BOOK OF MOSES," is nothing more or less than an attempt to comuflage the philosophical teachings relative to "CREATION, LIFE. DEATH, RESURRECTION, HEAVEN, HELL, GOD" (Monotheism and Polytheism), etc. We must remember that the age of the Haribus extend only into antiquity as far as the birth of the first of their faith - AVRAM (Abraham, Abram, etc.), who was a Chaldean from the city of Ur; at the time Chaldea was a colony of Africans who had established the Kingdom of Elam within the Persian Empire. From Abrham to Moses the Haribus knew not what it was to have a set of works bearing the name "SCRIPTURES;" neither any "TEN COMMANDMENTS;" nor, even, an organized state or national grouping. Most of all EXODUS, otherwise called the "SECOND BOOK OF MOSES," states that the Haribus (Hebrews or Jews) that migrated from the southwestern part of Kimit (Egypt), Rameses to Succoth (Exodus xii, 37), to the northeastern part of said nation (Mount Sinai), were, in fact, "...A MIXED MULTITUDE..." (Exodus xii, 35, 36, 37, 38) of everything imaginable. What is even more significant, Moses did not arrive at Mount Sinai until "...forty (40) years..." after he fled to escape his fellow Africans of Kimit, having illegally killed Pharoah (his king) Rameses II soldier - a worshiper of the God RA. Therefore, it is obvious, that, the "mixed multitude" with Moses continued their worship in accordance with the teachings of God and religion they received from their fellow Africans, priests of the MYSTERIES

SYSTEM that existed in Kimit, all in (and to) the honour of RA. These Africans, including those who worshiped the God JEHOVAH, also worshiped the "GOLDEN CALF", one similar to that which they created after the disappearance of Moses on Mount Sinai; a figure that was totally a replica of the "HATHOR COW" worshiped in Kimit and other Nile and Great Lakes regions of north and east Africa at that period in history. (See EXODUS xxxii, 1,2,3 and 4).

For those of us who may become alarmed over the above revelations, please be not forgetful that it was the Roman Catholic Christian Bishops, members of the COUNCIL OF NICE, who in the 4th century C.E. (A.D.) presented Emperor Constantine "the great" with the decision to currupt the "HOLY BIBLE" by removing many of the basic books and other writings therein. Hopefully those who may have it in their mind that this book is sacrilegious would also realize that the HOLY BIBLE is merely a collection of writings that suffered various translations and transliterations by writers who copied from more ancient works which realized the same; and, that, the books therein are not written in any way, shape or form, by a single person, or a God, Jehovah included, Jesus Christ and Al'lah also. The conduct of the Bishops of the Council of Nice (or Nicene) should be sufficient proof to anyone whose brainwashing has not completely blocked their mind from thinking independently. For, if it was not to suppress information, which the "Bishops" thought were dangerous for the masses of people to know; what other purpose did it serve? Thus it became necessary, up until this very day, to have an "authorized version" of, even, the KING JAMES VERSION of the HOLY BIBLE. And in those BOOKS OF THE BIBLE, which were allegedly "lost," but never out of the possession of those who control and operate religious institutions for their own benefit and profit and that of the other members of the ruling class in secular society) the tales and myths of all sort still remain now for the masses to examine. From these so-called "LOST BOOKS OF THE BIBLE" and the "FORGOTTEN BOOKS OF EDEN" we can, and should, examine the humanity of both Jesus Christ and his mother, Mary. As such, we should be able to observe that the stories about their own GOD and GODDESS status are neither the "TRUTH", nor "WRITTEN BY INSPIRED MEN OF GOD" than all of the other writings that preceded and followed them. Thus; to say that...

       JESUS CHRIST HAS ENTERED INTO MORE PEOPLES' HEART
       BY WAY OF THE HOLY WORDS OF GOD,

his "Father," as so many European and European-American style Christian missionaries have proclaimed, is to ignore the fact that GUNPOWDER, COLONIALISM and SLAVERY (directed by so-called "entrepreneurs" and "explorers"), in fact, were the forces that made millions in Africa, Asia, Australia, the Americas and the islands of the Pacific, as elsewhere, exposed themselves to the brainwashing they were subjected to by said missionaries.

    To further support the above contentions, one sees in the so-called "MASONIC RITES" the following teaching most Freemasons will declare are "founded on the Masonic Square;" thus, they say:

       "...TO ACT ON THE SQUARE MASONICALLY."

But, the same teachings are given in the MYSTERIES SYSTEM of the Nile Valley Africans of Kimit (Sais or Egypt) more than 10,000 years before the origin of British (or "Western") Freemasonry that relates itself back to the TEMPLE OF KING SOLOMON OF ISRAEL. In the original source, the Africans of the Nile Valley Mysteries

System, as shown in the BOOK OF THE DEAD, PAPYRUS OF ANI, and, it is truly written:

...TO ACT RIGHTLY, TO ACT JUSTLY AND TRUTHFULLY, ON THE SQUARE, AND ACCORDING TO MAAT.[1]

Of course the "GREAT ARCHITECT OF THE UNIVERSE", which "Western" Freemasonry has adopted from the teachings of the Africans' BOOK OF THE DEAD, as shown in the PAPYRUS OF ANI, etc., that date back to at least 4,000 to 6,000 B.C.E. (Before the Christian Era), came from the "SQUARING OF THE HEAVENS BY PTAH" (one of the ancient Gods of Kimit). And the ⌐ right angle square, which the Freemasons also adopted "...TO SQUARE" their "...ACTIONS," is still the symbol of the "...SEAT OF GOD (OSIRIS) IN THE JUDGMENT HALL, FROM WHICH PLACE ALL ARE JUDGED" (with respect to their past activities) "...AND MUST BE FOUND PERFECT BEFORE PROCEEDING INTO AMENTA." (See Dr. Albert Churchward, SIGNS AND SYMBOLS OF PRIMORDIAL MAN, p. 303). Even the Apostle Paul spoke from the SQUARE with respect to Jesus Christ of Nazareth when he stated:

"CHRIST IS THE CHIEF CORNERSTONE...," etc.,

in the Temple that is built, according to EPISTLE ii, 20 - 22. There are many other examples which can be shown to support the position relating to the plagerization of the African worshipers of the God RA religious and philosophical teachings mentioned in the BOOK OF THE DEAD, COFFIN TEXTS, PYRAMID TEXTS, and other major written ("scripture") works. The last of these to be cited in this particular area is the farce being perpetuated over the so-called "ARK OF THE COVENANT." Hebrews (misnomered "Jews"), Christians and Muslims (Moslems) all over the world have for centuries

---

1. MAAT represented the so-called "Heaven" of today's Bibles; formerly "CREATION."

been told by their religious leaders that said "ARK" has no origin other than from (the African) Moses (a native of Kimit), whom they have designated a "SEMITE" and worshiper of a God they call "YWH" (Jehovah, etc.), instead of his own nation's God, RA, the SOLAR DIETY. Yet, we can see for ourselves (those of us who have been able to examine works such as BOOK OF THE DEAD, ANACALYPSIS, SIGNS AND SYMBOLS OF PRIMORDIAL MAN, ORIGIN AND EVOLUTION OF RELIGION, MAN AND HIS GODS, THE GOLDEN BOUGH, and thousand of others which have been hidden or suppressed from the general clergy, much less the parishoners of synagogues, churches, mosques, etc.) that Moses copied his "ARK" from the "STONE CHEST" described by his fellow African brothers of Kimit with respect to the "KING'S (Pharoah's) CHAMBER OF THE GREAT PYRAMID." For, it is within this same type of "CHAMBER" or "ARK" that the "RITUAL OF ANI" in the BOOK OF THE DEAD is cited. (See PAPYRUS OF ANI, Chapter I, p. 5; and Chapter xvii, p. 8). Accordingly, the "ARK" should have contained the "CONFINED ONE." However, it was only a minature symbol of the actual "CHAMBER" or "ARK" that the priests of Kimit carried around their temples in Memphis on very special occasions, during equally special religious rites. The "ARK OF THE COVENANT," which is mentioned in I KINGS, viii, 8, is described as having the same exterior regalias as the "STONE CHEST" of the "CHAMBER OF THE GREAT PYRAMID;" thus:

> The two winged Cherubin (angels)[1] on the covering, without hands; the wings meeting together in symbolic token of meeting hands, and a cloud above embraced by the wings.
> Bars on the side in criss-cross diagonal pattern.

---

1. The word in parenthesis by the lecturer for clarity only.

The above description of the "ARK" should be familiar to all Freemasons of the GRAND COUNCIL OF ROYAL SELECT AND SUPER-EXCELLENT MASTERS that its origin comes from the GRAND LODGE OF LUXOR. They are, or should have been, also familiar with the fact that Moses only used his "ARK" as a "COFFER" (Hebrew ארון or ARAN) or "CHEST" (Latin ARCA) to deposit the "TABLES" (Tablets) upon which the "WORDS OF THE COVENANTS" or the principal "COMMANDMENTS OF THE LAW" were allegedly written. Yet, on page 22, Chapter cxxxiii of the PAPYRUS OF ANI we can still see the same "TABLES" (Tablets) and "ARK" (Chest or Coffer) which once contained "ANI'S SOUL - THE CONFINED ONE."[1] Even the measurements and description of the "ARK'S" cube (size) and materials were taken from the "STONE CHEST of the Africans, countrymen of Moses, as described in the BOOK OF THE DEAD:

> Two cubits and a half in length;
> One cubit and a half wide;
> One cubit and a half high;
> made of Shifftin wood;
> Covered with the finest leaves of gold.

These were all adopted by Moses when he "BUILT" his "ARK IN THE WILDERNESS." Even the :

> ...four rings on the two sides, through
> which staves are placed for its
> lifting to take it through the wilderness

were also the same as the details given for the Africans "STONE CHEST" of the religion of RA Moses came in contact while receiving his own SECRET RITES and DEGREES in the GRAND LODGE OF LUXOR on the banks of the Nile River in Kimit, Africa, from fellow African (Ethiopians or "Negroes") priests of the Mysteries System.

---

1. A term used for "the entomb soul of the devine who watch over the Universe," according to the teachings of the Mysteries System of the Africans of Kimit (Sais or Egypt).

It is not strange that these facts, which have been withheld from the average Hebrew, Christian and Muslim, are also camouflage today to appear as if no African, especially those presently designated "NEGROES, BANTUS, HAMITES," etc., had absolutely nothing what-so-ever to do with the so-called HEBREW "ARK OF THE COVENANT." Unfortunately, however, the event that caused the following words to be uttered by the Prophet Jerimiah, we are able to witness for ourselves. He is supposed to have said:

> The Lord hath sworn that no man should know
> this place, nor discover it, till the Prophet
> Isaiah and myself return to the world; then
> we will lodge the Ark again in the Sanctuary
> under the Cherubin's wings.

Jerimiah's words followed the capture of the Israelites and Babylonians; and the attempt by the Haribus and others to loot the "ARK'S" holdings:

THE VEILS OF MOSES' TABERNACLE.

In this lecture, I have attempted to excite you, my students, purposefully, into some aggressive and most meaningful approach towards the historical and spiritual beginnings in the following works I am introducing for your perusal. Most of these works the vast majority of your elders are not even aware exist. Even most of the Rabbis, Priests, Ministers and Inmans are not familiar with them. You are, therefore, in a very select position to spread knowledge to your contemporaries; and to make the way possible that they could be had by your successors.

BIBLIOGRAPHY

1. SIGNS AND SYMBOLS OF PRIMORDIAL MAN, Dr. Albert Churchward, George Allen & Co., Ltd., London, 1910.
2. ORIGIN AND EVOLUTION OF RELIGION, Dr. Albert Churchward, Unvin Brothers, Ltd., London, 1924.
3. BLACK MAN OF THE NILE, Yosef ben-Jochannan, Alkebu-lan Books Assoc., New York, 1970.

4. BLACKS IN ANTIQUITY, etc., Frank M. Snowden, Jr., Harvard University Press, Cambridge, Mass., 1970.
5. BOOK OF THE DEAD, Sir Ernest A. Wallis Budge, Longmans & Co., et. al., London, England, 1894 (2nd. edition).
6. PAPYRUS OF ANI, " " " " " " " " "
7. ANACALYPSIS, Sir Godfrey Higgins, University Books, Inc., New York, 1965 (Originally published in 1836, London, England), Vol. I & II.
8. STOLEN LEGACY, Prof. George G. M. James, New York Philosophical Society, New York, 1954.
9. OSIRIS, Sir Ernest A. Wallis Budge, University Books Press, New York, 1961 (First published in London, 1911).
10. THE GOLDEN BOUGH, Sir James Frazier, The Macmillan Company, New York, 1922 (First publish in 13 Vols. in London, England).
11. MAN AND HIS GODS, Homer W. Smith, Little, Brown and Company, Boston, Mass., 1953.
12. THE LOST BOOKS OF THE BIBLE and the FORGOTTEN BOOKS OF EDEN, Forum Books, The World Publishing Co., Cleveland and New York, 1963.
13. THE HOLY BIBLE (King James, Rhames Duoy, Septuagint, American Revised Standard, Jerusalem, and all other versions).
14. HOLY TORAH.
15. HOLY QUR'AN.
16. THE BIBLE THROUGH THE AGES, Frank, Swain, Camby, World Publishing Co., Cleveland and New York, 1967.
20. FACING MOUNT KENYA, Jomo Kenyatta, Grove Press, New York.
21. BANTU PHILOSOPHIE, Rev. Fr. Placide Temples,
22. JOSEPHUS: Complete Works (translated by W. Whiston), Kregel Publications, Grand Rapids, Michigan, 1960.
23. THE QABBALAH, Isaac Myer, Philadelphia, Pa., 188.
24. THE DAWN OF CIVILIZATION, Prof. M. Maspero, Society For Promoting Christian Knowledge, London, 1901.
25. THE GODS OF THE EGYPTIANS, Sir Ernest A. Wallis Budge, University Press, Inc., New York, 1945.
26. THE MISHNAH, Herbert Danby, Oxford At the Clarendon Press, London, England, 1933.
27. FALASHA ANTHOLOGY, Wolf Leslau, Schocken Books, New York, 1961 (First published in 1951).
28. FROM BABYLON TO TIMBUKTU, Rudolph Windsor, Exposition Press, New York, 1969.
29. INTRODUCTION TO AFRICAN CIVILIZATION, John J. Jackson, University Press, New York, 1970.
30. AFRICAN ORIGINS OF THE MAJOR "WESTERN RELIGIONS," Yosef ben-Jochannan, Alkebu-lan Books Associates, New York, 1970.

>   Submitted by:
>   Adjunct Professor of History
>   Yosef ben-Jochannan
>   Manhattan Community College
>   City University of New York
>   November 18, 1970

CHAPTER V

AFRICAN ORIGINS OF "GREEK PHILOSOPHY"

"THE BASIC THEORY OF PHILOSOPHY IS SALVATION."[1] This was the foundation upon which the Africans' of Egypt "Mysteries System"[2] was founded. "GREEK PHILOSOPHY", which got its beginnings from the Egyptians and other indigenous Africans of the Nile Valleys and Great Lakes, follows the same fundamental teachings of "SALVATION". The indigenous Africans of Egypt Mysteries System's most important objective was the "DEIFICATION OF MAN". They taught that:

> THE SOUL OF MAN, IF LIBERATED FROM ITS BODILY ABODE, COULD ENABLE HIM TO BE IN REALITY GOD-LIKE.

According to this concept, they also held that:

> MAN WOULD BE AMONG THE GODS IN HIS LIFETIME ON EARTH AND ATTAIN THE BEATIFIC VISION* IN HOLY COMMUNION WITH THE IMMORTALS.

(See, C.H. Vail, ANCIENT MYSTERIES, p. 25; G.G.M. James, STOLEN LEGACY; and J.G. Jackson & W.N. Huggins, AN INTRODUCTION TO AFRICAN CIVILIZATIONS.)

It was Plutinus, the Greek, who stated that:

> ...THE LIBERATION OF THE MIND FROM ITS FINITE CONSCIOUNESS IS SALVATION.

But this concept was nothing new when Plutinus echoed it. The "highest step in the attainment of knowledge" in the Africans' Mysteries System was the "third step". This "last step" was

---
*Note that Christendom adopted the "BEATIFIC" theory of the indigenous Africans under the title of "SAINTS".

defined as the "CREATORS" or "SONS OF LIGHT". It only meant that the candidates had reached the point where they could "identify themselves with (or unite with) the light's (Wa's) true spiritual consciousness. (see, W. Marsham Adams, BOOK OF THE MASTER; and, Sir E.A. Wallis-Budge, BOOK OF THE DEAD.)[3]

According to Pietschmann, the Egyptian Mysteries System had three distinctly different grades of students, the THIRD (3rd) or highest STAGE having been already cited in the previous paragraph. They were as follows:

1st) THE MORTALS: i.e., students on probation under instruction, who had not yet achieved experience into the "inner vision".

2nd) THE INTELLIGENCES:
i.e., those students who had attained the "inner-vision", and received "mind" or "Nous".

3rd) THE CREATORS or SONS OF LIGHT:
i.e., those students who became a part of the "spiritual consciousness".

The three steps were also called: INITIATION, ILLUMINATION, and PERFECTION, all of which contained the 10 VIRTUES OF ETERNAL HAPPINESS taught in the 7 LIBERAL ARTS.[4]

It must be noted that a candidate (student) had to excell in the "7 LIBERAL ARTS",[5] which were intended to "LIBERATE HIS SOUL". This was necessary, for without that attainment on the part of the candidate there was not way in which he could have reached the rank (degree) of Priest or be entered into the priesthood to study the "Greater Mysteries" at the Grand Lodge of Luxor. Also, it was at the end of the 3rd stage that the candidate was introduced into the study of "ESOTERIC PHILOSOPHY",[6] which was only taught by the priests in the priesthood. This was truly necessary, because all of the 3rd stage students had to demonstrate a very strong sense of proficiency before they were allowed to matriculate into the "FINAL LEVEL OF WISDOM". (See, C.H. Vail, ANCIENT MYSTERIES, p.24-25.)[7]

The attainment of the witnessing of the DIVINE LOGOS was open to any student who could prove his* proficiency in grammar, logic, and rhetoric. These were the disciplines of "MORAL NATURE" by which the student's irrational tendencies of behavior were cleansed or otherwise purged - according to the teachings of the African Mysteries System along the Nile Valleys, particularly Egypt (Kimit).

All of the values so far cited were co-opted into another system which is today called "GREEK PHILOSOPHY". This newly created system by "modern historians and educators" uses for its authorities and creators most of the earliest known Ionians and Greeks who studies in Egypt or under Egyptian teachers outside of Egypt. Such students included personalities such as Herodotus, Socrates, Hypocrates, Anaxagores, Aristophanes, Plato, Aristotle, and others. In all fairness to the listed Greek students, it must be noted that they did not label the Africans' Mysteries System "GREEK PHILOSOPHY".[8] This term is of very recent origin, as it will be shown in the following pages of this chapter.

*No women were allowed in the Mysteries System of the Nile Valleys.

What, then, is the difference between Greek and Egyptian "PHILOSOPHY"? Or, at what point does "GREEK PHILOSOPHY" differ from "EGYPTIAN PHILOSOPHY" (The Mysteries)? When did each begin? Did any Greek reach the final stage of Perfection?* These are very few of the major questions to be answered in this chapter. They have exacted exhaustive research and documentation of the historical data, all of which support the following statement:

"THERE IS NO SUCH THING AS GREEK PHILOSOPHY."

Answers to the questions raised cannot be definitive enough to create a true separation between that which is being called "GREEK PHILOSOPHY" and its source of origin - the AFRICAN MYSTERIES SYSTEM of Egypt. Never-the-less, this investigation begins with the most celebrated of the so-called "Greek Philosophers" - Socrates. But, as one opens the pages of world history, it is very soon discovered that Socrates and many of the other Greeks (during, and after, his era) were persecuted and prosecuted by the Athenian (Greek) Government for teaching its own "GREEK PHILOSOPHY". This type of "world history" has been the basis upon which "Western man" (or as Professor Jeffreys calls him - "Modern Man") eradicated from the pages of history the indigenous Africans from the southern lands of Africa out of north and east Africa. The most common version of the charge against Socrates,

---

*The education and rites required to reach this stage are detailed on page   of this chapter. However, there are no records available that any of the Greeks or Ionians reached the stage of "Perfection".

as stated by his many fellow Greek citizens, was as follows:

> "...Socrates is an evildoer, who busies himself with investigating things beneath the earth and in the sky, and who makes the worse appear the better reason, and who teaches others these same things...," etc.*[9]

It must be noted, however, that Socrates was officially charged by the Athenian Government as follows:

> "...Socrates commits a crime by not believing in the Gods of the City (Athens),[10] and by introducing other new (Egyptian - African)[11] divinities. He also commits a crime by corrupting the youth...," etc.

Anaxagoras and Aristotle were similarly charged by the Government of Athens (Greece) during different periods.[12] Therefore, it is noteworthy to recall at this juncture that most of the Greeks and Ionians - the so-called "<u>Greek and Ionic Philosophers</u>" - received all of their basic education in Africa, (Egypt in particular) or from others who were educated there. Aristotle, for example, not only received his education in Egypt, he confiscated (stole) entire libraries of the works belonging to the Africans' of Egypt Mysteries System when he entered Egypt with Alexander "<u>the Great</u>" as conquerors in 332 B.C.E. Aristotle even went to the extent of placing his name on the works he confiscated, most of which he claimed authorship, especially those which he kept for his private collection. He sent other such works to

---

Note: Words in brackets by the author for clarity in this quotation.
*This charge was made by Aristophanes around 423 B.C.E. (See, Plato's, APOLOGY, C. 1-10; Aristophanes, FROG, 1071; APOLOGY, 18 B.C.; 19C APOLOGY, 24B).

many of the Greeks (his friends) who are now listed as "GREEK PHILOSOPHERS". They too placed their name on many of the works they received, and also claimed authorship. The works Aristotle did not claim for himself or send to his friends in Greece he allowed to remain in the <u>Library of Alexandria</u> - where he started a school with Greek students he had imported. These students were taught by African instructors of the <u>3rd stage</u>, many of whom had also reached priesthood - the most noted of them being the High-Priest <u>Manetho</u>. Aristotle also saw to it that those books which he did not like or understood were destroyed by fire - put to the torch.[13] But, most of the works that were not destroyed were beyond the comprehension of the remaining African teachers, most of whom had witnessed the mass extermination of their own African teachers and priests by the invading armies from Europe - Greece.

The acts which Socrates, Aristotle, Anaxagoras, and others were in fact guilty of committing were the teaching of (and furthering) the studies relating to philosophy, religion, metaphysics and of prompting investigations into astronomy, astrology, geometry, science and medicine, among other things and disciplines. All of these disciplines were introduced to them when they were students in Egypt, or when they were taught by teachers who studied in Egypt (Kimit).[14] These subjects were basic requirements in the curriculum of African students in the First (1st) Stage* of learning in the Africans' of Egypt and other areas of the Nile Valley Mysteries System. These disciplines were foreign to the Greeks and their government in Athens before their contact with the Africans and Asians; the Asians having learned a great deal, up to that time, from their African teachers. As such, they were most dangerous to the Greek city-states. And, each Greek City-State moved to protect itself by "arresting, prosecuting, and persecuting" those whom it felt were the enemies that were undermining its laws and religion.[15] The Greek government in Athens was no different than the governments of the Soviet Union, the Peoples Republic of China, and the United States of America in this respect. They all stamp out anti-governmental GODS, THOUGHTS, and PHILOSOPHIES, etc. especially when each is dedicated to a different economic system of government. These governments were used in this comparative analysis, but this in no way indicates that any other government will not so act if it had as much to lose as these giants did or do at present.

"SEAUTON GNOTHI" - MAN KNOW THYSELF - is an inscription which the indigenous Africans (Blacks, Negroes, or other names) of Egypt wrote on the inside and outside of their temples and pyramids for thousands of years before the birth of the Ionian -

---

*In the educational system of the United States of America this stage of learning would be equivalent to the "Bachelor's Degree". Note that there were no co-educational institutions among the ancients of Egypt, a prohibition which the Greeks also adopted.

Socrates and even before the birth of the first Hebrew - Abraham (Avram) about c1680 B.C.E. This historical fact has been supported by thousands of papyri, artifacts, and other documentary evidence that have been stolen and otherwise illegally removed from Alkebu-lan. The vast majority of this material evidence can be found in hundreds of museums, universities, libraries, and a host of other institutions of learning - including so-called "PRIVATE COLLECTIONS" - throughout the United States of America and Europe. It is to be noted, however, that quite a few still remain in many of the centers of learning in North Africa; primarily in Egypt. If this is true, then why is it that so many "Western" historians and other "educators" - called "authorities" - willingly attributed its origin to Socrates and others whom they have also labeled "GREEK PHILOSOPHERS", each knowing too well that Socrates and the others copied it from the Africans?* The answer is very simple. It is (consciously or sub-consciously) done in order to justify their long-established myth of the "SUPERIORITY OF THE WHITE RACE OVER ALL OTHER RACES".

At this juncture one needs to reflect somewhat on the teachings and writings of some of these "Western educators", the most noted of them are, or were, men such as Professor M.D.W.Jeffryes, Professor C.P. Groves, Dr. Henri Junod, and Sir Harry H. Johnston.

---

*See, F. Heller, HISTORY OF PHILOSOPHY, p.105; S. Clymer, FIRE PHILOSOPHY; and, Max Muller, EGYPTIAN MYTHOLOGY.

As one resumes this investigation into the life of the "GREEK PHILOSOPHERS" and "GREEK PHILOSOPHY" it is soon discovered that the same type of distortions on the part of most "Western" educators and historians are quite evident in the fact that the scientific theory of the FOUR ELEMENTS and FOUR QUALITIES - "THE PRINCIPLE OF OPPOSITES", along with its physical DIAGRAM, is attributed to the genius and authorship of Heracleitus and others called "IONIC PHILOSOPHERS". Yet, this principle, with no changes what-so-ever, appeared in various African inscriptions and writings on the walls of pyramids (tombs) and on papyri for many thousands of years before the birth of either of the so-called "IONIC PHILOSOPHERS", all of whom were colonial subjects of the Africans of Egypt. The origin of the discipline - the PRINCIPLE OF OPOSITES - was unknown to the Ionians before the birth of the first of the so-called "IONIC PHILOSOPHERS", much less known to those who taught the Greeks at a much later date in history. Its origin preceded the era of the Ionians' introduction into the world of literacy through the efforts of their African teachers from Egypt, Nubia, Kush, Punt, and other Nile Valleys and East African Great Lakes regions of ancient High-Cultures (civilizations.)

Saying that "the Ionic Philosophers were the first to introduce the PRINCIPLE OF OPPOSITES" is equal to saying that "Moses was the first to give the world the TEN LAWS in the" so-called "TEN COMMANDMENTS of the Hebrew Torah", or that "Jesus Christ was the first to be born of a VIRGIN BIRTH"; when in fact history shows that the NEGATIVE CONFESSIONS, from whence the TEN COMMANDMENTS originated, predated Moses, and that the VIRGIN BIRTH of Isis and Osiris - plus hundreds of other VIRGIN BIRTHS in Egypt and Greece - preceded Jesus Christ (a Jew or Hebrew) birth in Bethlehem, Palestine.[16] (See, Y. ben-Jochannan, AFRICAN ORIGINS OF THE MAJOR WESTERN RELIGIONS.)

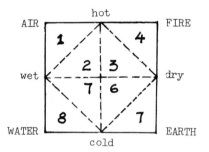

DIAGRAM OF THE PRINCIPLE OF OPPOSITES
The Four Elements: AIR, FIRE; WATER, EARTH.
The Four Qualities: Hot, Dry; Wet, Cold... & 8 Equal ▽ Pole Stars.

After the Africans of Egypt developed the fundamental PRINCIPLES OF OPPOSITES as "the underlying factor of life in the universe" and applied it to natural phenomena, Plato came forth with what he selected to call the "THEORY OF IDEAS", which was culminated in his "REPUBLIC: THE IDEAL STATE". However, this work, allegedly by Plato, has been, (and still is) challenged all the time by scholars of every era as to its authorship. One can readily understand why this is so, especially in the references Plato made to the Greeks using "CHARIOTEERS" and "WINGED STEEDS", all of which were already dramatized in the "JUDGMENT SCENES" of the COFFIN TEXTS - as shown in the BOOK OF THE DEAD,[17] where the proof of its African origin is clearly obvious. Thus, when one examines Plato's alleged "...ALLEGORY OF THE CHARIOTEER" and "WINGED STEED", and in the same instance reflect on the Egyptians' writings in the BOOK OF THE DEAD, one finds the necessary supportive documentary evidence to prove that Plato copied the fundamental basis of his work from African sources. Why is this so? Because, neither "<u>chariots</u>" nor "<u>winged steeds</u>" can be correctly attributed to Greek cultural development during Plato's lifetime, nor before his time. For nowhere in the history of Greece up to this period were the Greeks known to have these in their war machinery. And, it is without doubt or contradiction that they fought their wars with the Persians and Peloponnesians on the Mediterranean (Egyptian or Ionian) Sea. But, on the other hand, during this same period in <u>world history</u> the indigenous Africans of Egypt were known to be the main manufacturers of "<u>chariots</u>"; and also for their proficient breeding of horses - "<u>winged steeds</u>". (See, GENESIS, C. 45, V.27; C. 47, V. 17; DEUTERONOMY, C. 17, V. 16; I KINGS, C. 10, V. 28 - KING JAMES VERSION of the Christians "HOLY BIBLE". Also, see Hebrew TORAH.)[18]

Diogenes Laertius, Favotinus, and Aristoxenus (all of them Greeks) claimed that Plato's alleged discoveries in his "REPUBLIC" were all to be found in the controversies written by Protagoris who lived from 481 to 411 B.C.E. Therefore, at the time when Protagoris was a man, and writing his controversies, Plato was yet a very small boy indeed. (See, Diogenes Laertius, p. 311-327; Sir E.A. Wallis-Budge, BOOK OF THE DEAD, C. 17; Plato, REPUBLIC: THE IDEAL STATE, III, 415, V. 478, and VI, 490.)

The last example of the secrets the Greeks stole from the Africans, which modern "educators" prefer to call "GREEK PHILOSOPHY", appears in Aristotle's alleged work entitled - "DOCTRINE OF THE SOUL". Note that this philosophical goal is also found in the BOOK OF THE DEAD* (as translated into English from the Egyptians' COFFIN TEXTS) pages 29 trhough 64, where it is shown in all of its elaborate details; whereas, Aristotle used the information from the Coffin Texts very sparingly. This, of course, did not stop Aristotle's attempt to steal the authorship of Akhneton's DOCTRINE OF THE UNMOVED MOVER" - Proton Kinoun Akhneton, which came directly from the Memphite Theology's ATOM - the SUN GOD of Egypt (Kimit or Sais)**[19] consult "Memphite Theology" in Branfort's, HISTORY OF PHILOSOPHY, pp. 141-143; also George G.M. James, STOLEN LEGACY for further proof.

The preceding revelations are only a few of the dominant examples of how academic dishonesty is utilized in labeling one of the indigenous Africans' major contributions to mankind in the field of social studies - "GREEK PHILOSOPHY". Yet, there seems

---

*The Book Of The Dead is a compendium of Egyptian writings which have been translated from papyri dealing with the Africans' of Egypt transmigration to the Nether World as per the Coffin Texts.
**This philosophic principle is further detailed on page   of this volume. (See Dr. A.C. Churchward's ORIGIN AND EVOLUTION OF RELIGION).

to be no better source of exposure in this controversy than in the works of Sir. E.A. Wallis-Budge - BOOK OF THE DEAD, and OSIRIS. However, Professor George G.M. James' STOLEN LEGACY's critical analyses should be equally emphasized, especially since he was one of the first Black men in the Western Hemisphere willing to expose the notorious <u>myth</u> of a "GREEK PHILOSOPHY" that is supposed to be independent of its African origins. In regards to this contention Professor James wrote the following:

> THE GREEKS WERE NOT THE AUTHORS OF GREEK PHILOSOPHY, BUT THE PEOPLE OF NORTH AFRICA, COMMONLY CALLED THE "EGYPTIANS".*

It is understandable, though not at all acceptable, why most "<u>Western</u>" (European and European-American) historians and other "<u>educators</u>" have to deny that the origin of philosophy and other major disciplines were first introduced to the world by the ancestors of indigenous Africans which so many of them prefer to label "AFRICANS SOUTH OF THE SAHARA, BLACK AFRICANS, BANTUS, HOTTENTOTS, NEGROES, COLOURED PEOPLE, PYGMIES, NIGGERS", and a host of other such titles which are too numerous to list in this volume. This had to be done if the theory of the "INFERIORITY OF THE BLACKS" (indigenous Africans and their descendants throughout the world), with respect to Whites (Europeans and their descendants throughout the world), is to be forever perpetuated

---

*See title page of Professor George G.M. James' STOLEN LEGACY; Dr. A.C. Churchward, SIGNS AND SYMBOLS OF PRIMORDIAL MAN, and Sir Godfrey Higgins, ANACALYPSIS, 2 Vols; also Y. ben-Jochannan, AFRICAN ORIGINS OF THE MAJOR "WESTERN RELIGIONS" (Judaism, Christianity, Islam).

and maintained. To admit that the Egyptians, Kushites, Cartheginians, Ghanians, Moors or any other group of Africa's ancient indigenous peoples (who are today considered "inferior to Europeans and European-Americans") were the first teachers responsible for educating the ancient Greeks and Romans in civil living (social sciene "democracy") would in fact be admitting that all of the Europeans ("Caucasians") and their descendants were to a major extent "civilized" (cultured) by the same people who were supposedly their "inferiors". Upon such an admission, all of the major texts and trade books currently in use in European and European-American educational institutions dealing with the origin of science, law, pharmacology, religion, engineering, architecture, astronomy, philosophy, agriculture and every other discipline, would have to be totally revised, and in most cases discarded. The next step would have to be the re-education of the nations of Europe and European-America, including most of their "educators" who have willingly and knowingly distorted WORLD HISTORY, particularly that of Alkebu-lan (Africa), to suit their individual prejudice, bias, and religious bigotry about the "CHOSEN PEOPLE" status. Following these two steps, it will be necessary to re-establish the indigenous Africans (most of whom are called "Negroes" and "Bantus") and their descendants to their original role as contributors to the world's High-Culture - which has been also misnomered "CIVILIZATION"[21] by the same European and European-American "authorities" in the field of education. In light of these remarks further investigation into the African origins of "GREEK PHILOSOPHY" and the existence of "GREEK PHILOSOPHERS" continues.

The following chronological data is presented to show that most of the ancient Greeks and Ionians of note were taught and influenced by Africans.* This data is presented without regards as to whether or not the Africans were called by any of the other names already mentioned, or to be mentioned, throughout this volume. The Africans referred to in this perspective were the ancestors of the African-Americans and African-Caribbeans who are presently designated "NEGROES" and other names of inferiority by European and European-American slavemasters of Europe, the United States of America, the Caribbean Islands, and European-South America. (Wherever necessary, copies of duplicated documents, pictures, and other visual materials are also presented as supportive and added proof.)

A CHRONOLOGICAL LISTING OF THE MOST NOTED
SO-CALLED "Pre-Socratic GREEK PHILOSOPHERS"

Date BCE	Description
640	THALES received all of his basic education in Egypt along with his associates Anaximander and Anaximenes. They were natives of Ionia - an Egyptian colony in Asia-Minor. Ionia was at the time one of the strongholds of the

---

*Note that the indigenous Africans of Egypt originally came from East-Central Africa's Great Lakes region. Also, there were no natural barriers separating Africans from South, North, East or West Africa, as some "Western educators" have openly stated or implied. The countless documents and pictures are of African origins, and were very well known to "Western" scholars.

Africans' of Egypt and other Nile Valley High-Cultures' Mysteries System Schools (or Lodges) outside of Egypt. However they, as all others who entered such schools, had to study in Egypt for their advanced degrees leading to the Priesthood - the equivalent of the POST DOCTORATE DEGREE in PHILOSOPHY in any of the 20th Century C.E. universities throughout Europe and the United States of America. (See, E.M. Sandford, MEDITERRANEAN WORLD, pp. 195-205; G.G.M. James, STOLEN LEGACY; J.G. Jackson and Dr. W.N. Huggins, AN INTRODUCTION TO AFRICAN CIVILIZATION.)

576   XENOPHANES, PARMENIDES, ZENO, and MELISSUS (all four of them natives of Egypt's colony - Ionia) migrated to Elea, Italy, after receiving most of their education in Egypt under the tutelage of indigenous Nile Valley professors of the Priesthood in the Mysteries System. They established themselves while spreading the teachings of the African Mysteries. From Italy they journeyed into Greece where they continued their prostilization of the "<u>Egyptian Mysteries</u>" - of which PHILOSOPHY was only one of the major disciplines.[22]

540   PYTHAGORAS finished his education in Egypt and migrated to Croton, Southern Italy, shortly after returning to his native Island of Samos. From Elea he journeyed into West Greece where he established himself as a teacher in the fundamentals he learnt in the Mysteries System of Egypt.

530   HERACLITUS, EMPEDOCLES, ANAXAGORAS, and DEMOCRITUS were also natives of Ionia who became interested in physics. And, they too went to Greece after receiving their education in the Egyptian Mysteries System schools (Lodges) of their native homeland (at the time a colony of Egypt) and advanced studies in Egypt's "<u>Secret Temples</u>". In the <u>Temples</u> they were taught advanced disciplines and they were exposed to training and insights into the various SECRET SOCIETIES and DEGREES. Yet, not one of them completed the studies in the curriculum outline of the Mysteries [24] - which was necessary to obtain the degree or title of PRIEST, and of course HIGH PRIEST.

460?
457   HERODOTUS arrived in Egypt for the purpose of receiving his education from African teachers. His curriculum included studies in history, science, philosophy, religion, medicine, law, civics, etc.; the same having been required for all other ENTERED APPRENTICES, which included all of the other Greeks that preceded and followed him.

399 SOCRATES was sentenced to death for "THE TEACHING OF A PHILOSOPHY WHICH IS ALIEN TO OUR (Greek) DIVINITIES.[25] It was a philosophy which Socrates and all of the other Ionians and Greeks who preceded him learned of Egypt's colony of Ionia or in Egypt proper. (See, Zeller's HISTORY OF PHILOSOPHY, pp. 112, 127, 170-172.)[26] It must be remembered that Plato and Aristotle also had to flee Athens for their life, as they too were found guilty of teaching and spreading the same African (Egyptians) philosophy they received in Egypt among the indigenous Nile Valleys and Great Lakes African teachers and priests of the Mysteries System.[27] This analysis and explanation is expanded further on in this chapter.

In light of the above information it must be remembered that the period of ancient Greek and Ionian history, from Tales to Aristotle (640 - 332 B.C.E.), included the majority of the so-called IONIC PHILOSOPHERS, who were in fact not Greeks, but colonials of Egypt residing in Greece. Many of them were also Persian colonials after the Persians defeated and conquest of the Africans of LOWER EGYPT about 525 B.C.E. (See, Zeller's HISTORY OF PHILOSOPHY, pp. 37, 46, 58, 66-83, 112, 127, 170-172; William Turner, HISTORY OF PHILOSOPHY, pp. 34, 45, 53; Rogers' STUDENT HISTORY OF PHILOSOPHY, 15; D.B. Alexander, HISTORY OF PHILOSOPHY, pp. 13, 21; E.M. Sandford, THE MEDITER-RANEAN WORLD, pp. 157, 195 - 205.)

"GREEK PHILOSOPHY", one must remember, is in itself a mis-nomer. Also, it is merely the continuation of the Africans' (Egyptians') philosophic teachings which they first carried into Ionia (at the time an Egyptian colony), and from Ionia it entered Italy, then finally Greece (Athens).*28

For example DIODORUS (Greek scholar) and MANETHO (High-Priest during the Greeks' colonial rule of Egypt) recorded that the philosophic "teachings of the Africans of Egypt were written on columns..., etc. And, these columns were found as far off as Nyasa, Arabia. In the inscriptions of one of these columns were the images of the Goddess Isis and the God OSIRIS. On the column of the God OSIRIS the inscription revealed that he:

"...LED AN ARMY INTO INDIA, TO THE SOURCE OF THE GANGES, AND AS FAR AS THE INDUS OCEAN."

There could be no doubt that the Africans of the Egyptian (Kimit) empire and Mysteries System (at a very early date in history) included not only the islands off the Aegean Sea and Ionia (around today's Middle-East) but they also stretched to certain extremeties of the Asian FAR-EAST.

The historical account in the above paragraph was not the only one in wich the ancient indigenous Africans (labed "Negroes" and other such stereotyped terms) are shown to have conquered all the way to India, and probably much further east. In 1900 B.C.E., during the XIIth Dynasty (2000 - 1785 B.C.E.) Pharoah

---

*One must recall that during this period in Greek history Greece was not a homogeneous country with respect to its human population. To the contrary, it was heterogeneous. This is the reason that the majority of the Greeks of ancient history were in fact only citizens of Athens, but not Athenians by birth. Most of them came from Asia-Minor, the Island of Samos or Northern Africa. Included in this was Herodotus, the Greek citizen "Western Educators" call "THE FATHER OF HISTORY", when in fact he learned his history from the Africans of the Nile Valley High-Cultures. He was the FATHER OF EUROPEAN HISTORY only.

Senurset I conquered the coastline of India up to, and beyond, the Ganges River[30] and to the Eastern Ocean (Indus or Indian Ocean). There in India, he left thousands of indigenous African soldiers, just as General Ganges (the Ethiopian for whom this river was named) did. Those soldiers' offspring are only another segment of the present Indian population.[31] During this same period Pharoah Senurset I also captured and colonized Cyclades and a large area of southeastern Europe, leaving there thousands of indigenous African soldiers who, along with their offsprings, amalgamated with the indigenous European (Caucasian, White) population.[32]

The 1500 B.C.E. AMARNA LETTERS found in the government offices of Pharoah (King) Akhnaten (Ikhnaten, Amen-hotep IV - 1370 - 1352 B.C.E.) revealed that the African Empire of Egypt extended to western Asia - Syria and Palestine. It also indicated that for centuries Egyptian power had been supreme throughout ancient Africa, Europe, Asia, and their neighboring islands.[34] Therefore, it is also obvious that Egyptian High-Culture, with all of its indigenous African Nile Valley ramifications, became the religious belief, law and order of every colony within the empire. (See, J.H. Breasted, CONQUEST OF CIVILIZATION, p. 84; DIODORUS, p. 128; Manetho, HISTORY OF EGYPT; Strabo, Dicaerchus, and John Kendrik's, ANCIENT EGYPT.)

<u>LOOKING CLOSER INTO THE MISCONCEPTIONS OF THE EXISTENCE OF A BODY OF PHILOSOPHICAL THOUGHTS OF ANCIENT EGYPT misnomered "GREEK PHILOSOPHY."</u>

The book on nature commonly known as PERI PHYSEOS was allegedly written by Greek students who were interested in the study of nature. The earliest copies of this work are dated no further back into antiquity than the 16th Century B.C.E. Yet, PERI PHYSEOS was written in a manner that indicates an origin of at least c2000 B.C.E. or earlier, at which time the Greeks were not engaged in this height of High-Culture (civilization) or intellectual advancement. Within the said work most of the doctrinal basis is shown to be copies from the Egyptian Mysteries, all of which are commonly detailed in the BOOK OF THE DEAD and other works of its kind. This was part of the source of the original repository for the forerunners of "GREEK PHILOSOPHY". (See, William Turner, HISTORY OF PHILOSOPHY, p. 62)[35] The teachings in PERI PHYSEOS remained the exclusive domain of THE CENTER OF CULTURE OF THE ANCIENT WORLD.... It was exclusively of Egyptian origin until Egypt was conquered by Alexander "the Great" in 332 B.C.E.** This was true until the movements of Aristotle and his school of Greek students compiled the Africans' of Egypt works of the Mysteries System and claimed them to be his and other Greeks'. (See, C.H. Vail, ANCIENT MYSTERIES, p. 16).[36] Some of the other authors accredited with the origin of PERI PHYSEOS were Heraclitus, Anaximandes, Anaxagoras, and Parmenides. It is to be also noted that they were all students of African

---

*Before this period the Greeks in Egypt were of the "LOWER CLASS" of people. Very few of them were allowed in the Lodges.

(Egyptian) Philosophy, as well as other learnings (disciplines); and that, they were not in fact Greeks, but instead Ionians.

The SCHOOLS OF PHILOSOPHY of the ancient Chaldeans, Greeks, and Persians were extensions of the ancient Mysteries System and other Nile Valley High-Cultures systems of philosophical thoughts. This is the reason why in Greece, Chaldea, and Persia the students of these schools were repeatedly persecuted, prosecuted, and murdered. Why? Because of their "...ALIEN TEACHINGS."[37] It is not strange that in only one place were the teachings of the Africans of Egypt unchallenged by heads of government, and that was in Alkebu-lan (Africa).[38] One must remember that all of the instructions were given in secret according to the demands of OSIRIACA, whose teachings were common among all of the schools or lodges. The <u>Osirican laws</u> came down from the MOTHER LODGE centered in Sais (Egypt) - the GRAND LODGE OF LUXOR.*[40] Why? Because all colonial (subordinate) <u>Grand Lodges</u> were charted by the <u>Mother Lodge</u> - LUXOR.

The reliance upon Aristotle to establish the authorship of the Africans' works he stole, which when compiled is called "GREEK PHILOSOPHY", is by any stretch of the imagination incredulous. For nowhere in history is Aristotle accredited with one singular writing of any sort before he totally sacked the temples and lodges of the African Mysteries in Egypt upon his arrival in

---

*See map on page number 684 for location of the Grand Lodge of Luxor, Egypt - the Mother Lodge of the Egyptian Mysteries.

332 B.C.E. with Alexander "the Great" as conquerors of Egypt.[41] Subsequent to the conquest of Egypt by the Greeks, the African works Aristotle did not place under his own name he attributed to his fellow Greek colleagues, many of whom have no records of existence except for their alleged authorship of certain works that relate in too many ways to secrets of the Africans of Egypt which they could not have possibly known unless they too were part and parcel of the Egyptian Mysteries System.[42] (See, Alfred Weber, HISTORY OF PHILOSOPHY, p. 16; "Theophrastus, FRAGMENT 2 apud Diels", as shown in the introduction of Weber's work).

There is in existence a list of alleged GREEK PHILOSOPHERS who were "personae non gratis" (undesirables) within the Greek State in which they were citizens yet, they continued accepting their source of wisdom and knowledge from Egypt at the risk of physical injuries to themselves. They were men who kept their records in their head, and operated in deepest secrecy in fear of the State (Greece)* persecuting them for being:

"...TEACHERS OF AN ALIEN PHILOSOPHY...,"*

which was solely the teachings of the indigenous Africans of the Mysteries System commonly in use along the Nile Valleys and Great Lakes regions of Northern, Eastern, and Central Africa.

The following listings include some of the most noted men who were labeled GREEK and IONIAN "Philosophers", also Pre and Post

---

*Note that this charge was also lodged against Socrates, Aristotle; and other by the Athenian (Greek) Government.

Socratic "Philsophers". It will be noted that a few of them have been introduced earlier; however, not in the sense of their established existence recorded in the works of any noted historian. The following, therefore, is an accounting - chronologically - of these men's existence, if in fact they existed.

THE PRE-SOCRATIC PHILOSOPHERS

Date BCE	Description
640	THALES: Diogenes* said he was born in 640. Turner, HISTORY OF PHILOSOPHY, placed it at 620; A.K. Rogers, HISTORY OF PHILOSOPHY, at 624; and W.G. Tenneman, HISTORY OF PHILOSOPHY, at about 600.
570	XENOPHANES: Diogenes is very doubtful of his date of birth, but, he speculated that it was 570. Most "Western" historians speculate that it is totally unknown, but refuse to dismiss him from existence. Yet, Zeller sets it at 576.
546	ANAXIMENES: Diogenes accredited his birth to 546. Fuller, Rogers, and Thilly in their respective works, each entitled HISTORY OF PHILOSOPHY, refused setting any date what-so-ever. D.B. Alexander set it at 560; and Rogers at approximately 600.
580 570	PYTHAGORAS: Diogenes supposedly figured that he flourished during the dates between 580 and 570. Turner, Alexander, Rogers, and Tennenman established 582 to 500 as the approximate dates.
504 500	HERACLITUS: Diogenes believed that he flourished during the periods between 504 to 500. Zeller presupposes that he was born in 535; William Turner set it at 500; and Windelbrand at 536.
500	ANAXAGORAS: Diogenes' confidence was manifested in the date of 500. Turner, Rogers, and Alexander elected not to share Diogenes' enthusiasm and remained mute.
500	PARMENIDES: Diogenes established the date of his birth

*Diogenes Laentius was the first to establish a CHRONOLOGY on the so-called "GREEK PHILOSOPHERS".

at approximately 500. Rogers, Fuller, and Thilly said no date what-so-ever of this man's birth could be found in available records.

484   EMPEDOCLES: Diogenes placed his birth at 484. Rogers, Turner, Windelbrand, Fuller, and Alexander calculated that it was about 490.

464
460   XENO: Diogenes found it impossible to establish any date what-so-ever for this man's existence in history, much less his being a philosopher. However, he speculatively concluded that the date of his birth was 464 or 460. D.B. Alexander, Frank Thilly, and William Turner (in their respective works entitled HISTORY OF PHILOSOPHY) placed the date at 490; whereas, A.K. Rogers, Frank Fuller and W.G. Tenneman declared that the date is definitely unknown.*

The following list deals with the so-called POST-SOCRATIC PHILOSOPHERS. Yet, it is still unique that they had no historical data relative to their date of appearance into the world. There are no ancient records of their early youth, except for very few

---

*It is to be noted that although the guessing game about the existence, or date of birth, of these men (the so-called Greek Philosophers) continues from the time of the original Greek chronicleers, present day historians and educators still consider them "AUTHORITIES ON GREEK PHILOSOPHY", and even "AFRICAN HISTORY". It must be also noted, that none of the personalities so labeled - GREEK PHILOSOPHERS - were in existence within one thousand years after the Africans of Egypt published any of their works that appear in the BOOK OF THE DEAD, also in OSIRIS. Not one of them lived during the period of the IIIrd Dynasty (2789-2680 BCE), at which time Imhotep (the "God of Medicine" or Aescalapius according to Hypocrates) wrote philosophically; neither were they in existence when other Africans of Egypt, Kush (Ethiopia), Uganda, Kongo, Carthage, and other ancient African High-Cultures were preaching and teaching philosophy and other disciplines which are today co-opted into what is called "GREEK PHILOSOPHY". Yet, most of the so-called "Greek Philosophers" have allegedly written on the same subjects, and reached the exact conclusions, almost word for word as their African teachers and forerunners; all of which is called "GREEK PHILOSOPHY". But, most of them were persecuted for teaching their own Greek philosophical developments.

that are not mentioned here. It is also very strange that only SOCRATES, PLATO, and ARISTOTLE'S, of the so-called "GREEK PHILOSOPHERS", births are not truly subject to question. Most of them are only names; no other information about their birth and background is available anywhere, including in Greece.

THE POST-SOCRATIC PHILOSOPHERS

Date BCE	Discription and Documentation
325	ARISTOTLE: Except for his teaching in the gymnasium in Athens nothing is written about this personality. His fame begins with his entrance into Egypt (Kimit or Sais) with Alexander "the Great" (the son of Phillip of Macedonia) during the Greeks' invasion and conquest of the Africans in 332 B.C.E. The next time he is spoken of is when he led Greek soldiers in sacking the Lodges and Libraries of Egypt of everything movable. He is seen looting and destroying the most valuable works of the Africans' Mysteries System, these works predated his birth by thousands of years. The Africans' works which he did not claim or give to friends he destroyed in various ways - the most common method being by the torch - as stated before. He stole and plagiarized these works, many of them he placed his name as author; still others were accredited to him by so-called "authorities" of much later periods in history.
274	ERATOSTHENES: Called a "Stoic", compiled a chronology of his countrymen which he too called "GREEK PHILOSOPHERS" or other names to this effect. All of the men he listed were proven to have copied extensively from the works of the Africans of Nile Valleys and Great Lakes High-Cultures.
140	APOLLODORUS: He drew up another (the second) chronology of the sort arranged by Eratosthenes, upon whose original works during 274 to 194 B.C.E. he depended. He was equally as guilty as his predecessor for calling them "GREEK PHILOSOPHERS".
60 70	ADRONICUS: The so-called "Eleventh Head of the PERIPATIC SCHOOL" drew up another (the Third) chronology of the "Greek Philosophers". He dealt with those who supposedly lived during his lifetime. (See, "Introduction" to Zeller's HISTORY OF PHILOSOPHY.)

In cross referencing the alleged works by the so-called "GREEK PHILOSOPHERS" against the works of the Africans of the Nile Valleys and Great Lakes regions, as shown in the BOOK OF THE DEAD, and OSIRIS,* also many other major works in Egyptology, it is discovered that everything the Greeks have written stem from African Origins of thousands of years before the possibility of their own birth.

The Roman Emperor Justinian, whose EDICT closed the African's of Egypt <u>Mysteries System</u> and <u>Philosophical Schools</u> in Egypt and Greece, also plunged all of Europe into utter ignorance for more than ten centuries. At the same instance it allowed the Greeks to maintain total control over all of the data they seized (stole) from the Mysteries' repositories in UPPER and LOWER Egypt. It also gave them added opportunity to rewrite, and otherwise plagiarize, the Africans' works - which included among other disciplines - PHILOSOPHY. However, during this period, systemized education on the scale which the Africans had developed, and the Greeks overtook, disappeared, even in Egypt. But, the Greeks showed no creative genius in perpetuating the confiscated data under their control, as their African teachers were no longer available to them, and they were unable to improve upon what they

---

*The BOOK OF THE DEAD, also OSIRIS, are English translations of abstracts from the COFFIN TEXTS and other teachings by the ancient indigenous Africans of the more than 4,100 miles long Nile Valley (from Uganda to the Mediterranean Sea). The translator was Sir. E.A. Wallis Budge, formerly Keeper of the Egyptian and Assyrian Antiquities of the British Museum. There are countless other works that are comparative to Wallis Budge's.

remembered as a result of their tutelage under their African teachers in Egypt and Greece. (See, Sedgwick and Tyler, HISTORY OF SCIENCE, pp. 141 and 163; also, the *Introduction* to Zellers' HISTORY OF PHILOSOPHY, p. 31.)

In analyzing that which is called "GREEK PHILOSOPHY", one has to constantly remember that a later group of indigenous Africans of North Africa - called MOORS* - had preserved much of their ancestors' (the Africans of the Nile Valleys and Great Lakes High-Cultures) teachings about the Mysteries - of which PHILOSOPHY is one of the many disciplines. Unfortunately, most of the works by the Moors remain untranslated into the English language from the Arabic language which the African-Moors adopted after their conversion to Islam, thereby denying most of the information to the average English-reading public. This had allowed those who have control of such information to distort such information to appear that their ancestors were in fact the originators of the Africans' of Egypt and other Nile Valleys High-Cultures. The works in question included treatises and compendiums in science, medicine, pharmacology, astronomy, law, and other branches of the SEVEN LIBERAL ARTS. Yet, most of the works the Moors translated from Hieroglyiphics to Arabic were also used by men such as

---

*African peoples who originally moved up the coast from what is today called MAURITANIA (ancient Mauritus), all of whom came from points further south. These were not the Arab-Moors - who did not arrive in Africa until 640 C.E. or 18 A.H. during the Moslems' invasion of North Africa, they are the African-Moors, the ones who first entered Iberia in 711 C.E. with General Tarikh.

Leonardo Pisano for his mathematical thesis, and of course those which he did in philosophy and morals, natural science, and metaphisics. Other academically great works originating from the compilations of the Moors were translated by Guideo "the Monk of Arezzo" in his musical notations. Of course there are countless others worth mentioning here, but their listing will not change anything at this time. (See, Tyler and Sedgwick, HISTORY OF SCIENCE, Chapter IX).

The African-Moors' extensive knowledge of ancient Egypt was due to their constant cultural exchanges with their indigenous African brothers of Egypt through their Caliphates. (See, Ault's, EUROPE IN THE MIDDLE AGES, pp. 216-219). It should be also noted that members of medieval European science and other disciplines - such as Copernicus, Roger Bacon, and Johann Kepler, received their source of basic science from African-Moor (and of others who were of African-Arab-Berber Moorish stock) works. (See, C.H. Vail, ANCIENT MYSTERIES, pp. 59, 61, 75; Philo; P.K. Hitti, HISTORY OF THE ARABS, pp. 370, 629, 665, 572; and Annie Besant, ESOTERIC CHRISTIANITY, pp. 107, 128, 129; also Copernicus and Kepler's works in the GREAT BOOKS OF THE WESTERN WORLD published by Encyclopedia Britannica.)*

Herodotus' HISTORIES Book III; Pliny N.H., 36, 9; Diogenes VIII, 3; and Antipo (as recorded by Porphry), all recalled the fact that Pythagoras, a native son of Samos, secured and neces-

---
*See Volume 16 of these works for Copernicus and Kepler.

sary consent of the indigenous African High-Priests of Egypt. Accordingly, Diogenes Laentius stated that Amasis (the Pharoah -King- of Egypt) and Polycrates of Samos developed a friendship with Pythagoras, whom they introduced to the...

"PRIESTS FOR HIS INITIATION INTO THE MYSTERIES".

First he was presented to the Priests of Helipolis, then to the others in Memphis and Thebes. Each of them was presented with a gift of a silver goblet from Pythagoras. The goblets represented tokens of appreciation for his pending schooling by them, which included the discipline of "MEASUREMENTS". This discipline was to be later attributed to Pythagoras.

Pliny, Herodotus, and Jablonsk (all three of them) stated that Pythagoras was subsequently:

"...INITIATED AND RECEIVED ALL OF THE SECRETS"(Mys-steries)"INCLUDING PHILOSOPHY..., etc.,"

from the Egyptian priests. His lessons were received by him only after he had submitted to:

"...CIRCUMCISION AND OTHER SEVERE TRIALS..."

imposed upon him, along with the other INITIATES - also called "ENTERED APPRENTICES" and "NEOPHYTES". And, that among the disciplines he learnt were:

"...MEDICINE, THE DOCTRINE OF METEMPSYCHOSIS*
DIETETICS AND GEOMETRY...".

John Kendrick, in his HISTORY OF ANCIENT EGYPT, Volume I,

---

*There is no evidence available that would indicate that the Greeks were aware of this discipline before it was taught to Herodotus by the Nile Valleys Africans of Egypt.

p. 234, states that Pythagoras also "LEARNT MUSIC" in Egypt. Demetrius, Anthisthenes, and Plutarch wrote in their respective works that...

> PYTHAGORAS ESTABLISHED THE TEACHINGS OF SCIENCE AND MATHEMATICS...

among the Greeks. He also...

> SACRIFICED TO THE MUSES AFTER THE PRIESTS OF THE EGYPTIAN MYSTERIES EXPLAINED TO HIM THE PROPERTIES OF THE RIGHT TRIANGLE.

(See, Demetrius: Philarch, DE REPUGN STOIC, 2, p. 1089; Cicero's DE NATURA DEORUM, III, 36; and Anthisthenes' SUCCESSION.)

Democritus (a native of Abdera in Miletus) was also educated in Egypt - according to Demetrius' PEOPLE OF THE SAME NAME, and Anthisthenes' SUCCESSION. He received his education from the Egyptian Priests of the Mysteries. Diogenes and Herodotus verified the fact that Democritus spent five (5) years learning all phases of Egyptian disciplines after his submission to the same rites as Pythagoras. Origen (an Egyptian residing in Greece), in support of this contention, wrote:

> APUD AEGYPTIOS NULLUS AUT GEOMETRICA STUDEBAT, AUT ASTROMINE SECRETA REMABATUR, NISI CIRCUMCISIONE SUSCEPTA.

English translation:
> NO ONE AMONG THE EGYPTIANS EITHER STUDIED GEOMETRY, OR INVESTIGATED THE SECRETS OF ASTRONOMY, UNLESS CIRCUMCISION HAD BEEN UNDERTAKEN.*

---

*This aspect of African religiosity and philosophic thoughts, along with medical and scientific fundamentals, were adopted by all of the ancients from the Africans. The Hebrew Torah reveals its transformation to modern times through the Haribus (misnomered "Jews") who entered Sais (Egypt) in c1640 B.C.E.

History also reveals that Plato, another of the greatest of the so-called "GREEK PHILOSOPHERS", received his final education and insights into the Mysteries System and Secret Societies in Egypt (from African teachers) after visiting with Euclid at Metara along with other students of Socrates. He too was trained by the African priests of the Egyptian Mysteries System. But, it was Hermodorus who noted that...

> "PLATO WAS TWENTY-EIGHT YEARS OF AGE WHEN HE LEFT FOR SCHOOL IN EGYPT."

Although history does not specifically mention that Socrates and a few of the so-called "Pre-Socratic Philosophers" did, or did not, travel to Egypt for their respective education as did the others, their teachings were never-the-less wrought with the basic disciplines of the Egyptian Mysteries System which they learnt from others who went to Egypt for their schooling. The similarity of their propaganda, with regards to their being influenced by the Africans of Egypt, caused most of them to be arrested, tried, and convicted by the Athenian (Greek) Government on the charge of...

> "TEACHING A FOREIGN PHILOSOPHY AGAINST THE DIVINITIES AND LAWS OF THE" (Greek or Athenian) "STATE."

(See, William Turner, HISTORY OF PHILOSOPHY, pp. 62, 126; Zeller, HISTORY OF PHILOSOPHY, p. 84; Plato, PHAEDO; and W. Rogers, HISTORY OF PHILOSOPHY, p. 96.)

Max Muller's EGYPTIAN MYTHOLOGY, pp. 187-189; Bunsen I, p. 27; John Kendrick, ANCIENT EGYPT, Vol. II, pp. 56, 432; and

Diodorus 16 and 51 should have laid to rest the misnomer called "GREEK PHILOSOPHY" in its final resting place when they so adequately recalled, in the works already cited, that THE GREEKS RECEIVED MOST OF THEIR EARLIEST EDUCATION FROM LOOTING THE CENTRAL LIBRARIES of what is today called "ALEXANDRIA, THEBES," and "MENEPTHEION." The last of these libraries, the MENEPTHEION, was started by Pharoah Seti I - allegedly the Pharoah who was reigning when Moses (of the Hebrew Torah) was born in Africa - Kimit - which the Haribus perverted and called "EGYPT" in their religious mythology dealing with Noah and the Flood. (See Yosef ben-Jochannan, AFRICAN ORIGINS OF THE MAJOR WESTERN RELIGIONS.) It was completed by Pharoah Rameses II,*[44] the Pharoah who allegedly chased Moses and the multitudes out of North Africa (Egypt). Though it was rated "the finest of all libraries" of its period in history, nothing has been written about the works it contained after it was sacked by Aristotle and other Greeks during the colonial period of Greek rule in Egypt following the conquest of the Africans of the Mysteries System by Alexander "the Great" in 332 BCE.**

One should appreciate the fact that Aristotle had full run of all educational institutions in Egypt from 332 B.C.E. - the year Alexander "the Great" captured Kimit and established General Soter

---

*He reigned from 1298 to 1232 BCE. See page number 311 for other facts and pictures on Pharoah Rameses II.
**"Western" philosophers, historians, and other educators were saved the trouble of revealing who were the TRUE philosophers of that which is still being called "GREEK PHILOSOPHY".

(later Ptolemy I) as <u>Governor of Sais</u>.* Since Alexander, himself, was much more interested in meeting the ORACLE OF ANMON,[45] he obviously did not care what Aristotle or any other of his subordinates did to the Africans' libraries and lodges or the contents therein. Why? Because Alexander did not indicate any specific yearning for advance education through a systematized program of education. For, as king, he owned and controlled those who had obtained such learning from the Africans, including the so-called GREEK PHILOSOPHERS of his era.

The fact that the Greeks swarmed into Kimit (Sais) to be educated during the rule of Alexander "<u>the Great</u>" and Ptolemy Ist (Soter) reign is added proof that they were leaving their own inadequately developed schools in Greece for first-hand person to person learning of the teachings within the lodges (colleges and universities) of the Mysteries - where PHILOSOPHY was only one of the many disciplines being taught by the African Priests. This was long after the Africans' educational system had already become corrupted, having fallen into the hands of Aristotle and other Greek colonialist rulers of Sais. It is, therefore, very significant that the educational system of the Africans was a part of the loot the Greeks got from their conquest of Sais under the leadership of Alexander. From this loathsome beginning on the part of the Greeks with Alexander, Aristotle, and Soter, most <u>of what is today called "GREEK PHILOSOPHY"</u> had its origins, plagia-

*Sais was a city in ancient Kimit; sometimes used as the name of the nation; Egypt being not in existence as a term until the Haribus "Noah & Sons" myth.

rized as it is.

From all of the evidence so far cited, all of which history reveals had an African origin, one wonders how the name "GREEK PHILOSOPHY" can still justifiably stand. But, the evidence also show why it should be of no surprise to anyone that the African-Americans ("Negroes" or whatever) must be denied their ancient Nile Valleys and Great Lakes heritage; and why it will continue. Why must this remain so? Because such behavior among "Western" educators is the only method available to them in perpetuating the "GREAT MYTH" that...

"NORTH AFRICA'S HISTORY IS CAUCASIAN...," etc.^{46}

Yet, the records of world history will continue proving that...

AFRICA IS THE CRADLE OF MAN'S HIGH-CULTURES;^{47}

a sort of GARDEN OF EDEN, but not of the type mentioned in the Hebrew TORAH, Christian HOLY BIBLE, or Moslem KORAN. And, Sais,* which the Hebrews renamed "EGYPT", was the nation where the ancient indigenous people of KIMIT (the ROMITU)** (from the Great Lakes region of present day Uganda, Kenya, Ethiopia, Kongo, Tanzania, Malawi, Zambia, Zimbabwe (Rhodesia), Monomotapa (Mozambique), Burundi, Rwanda, Somaliland, and other areas of Central and East Africa) reached their zenith. From these areas the in-

<u>digenous African High-Cultures</u> (civilizations) travelled along in
*Sais is the name Egypt was called at the time the Haribus of Abraham's era entered that area of Africa (1640 B.C.E.). Note that the word JEW is a misnomer for the work JUDAH - one of the Haribu tribes.
**The term, or name, of Egypt, and of Egyptians, is not Egyptian. The Egyptians called themselves ROMITU or ROTU, and their country KIMIT, or KAM - THE BLACK LAND." (See Dr. Albert Churchward, ORIGIN AND EVOLUTION OF THE HUMAN RACE, p. 403.)

the same direction as the flow of the Blue and White Nile rivers - from Uganda to the Kimit Sea^{48} (renamed the Mediterranean Sea) in a south to north direction. From the shores of ALKEBU-LAN (<u>Africa, Olympia, Coryphe, Ortygia, Ethiopia,</u> and a host of other names by which this continent has been called) these High-Cultures crossed over into Greece and Italy; from thence into all of the other lands of Europe until it arrived in the AMERICAS (with the CARIBBEAN ISLANDS included.)* It is to be noted that Kimit is in the LOW LANDS of the Nile region, the DELTA - named after the lowest Greek letter of the alphabet which it appears to represent in shape.

The following map on page 682 entitled, "THE NILE VALLEYS," displays the various contours of the <u>three</u> (3) <u>main bodies of water</u> that comprise what is today called the NILE RIVER. However, one must always distinguish between the BLUE NILE, WHITE NILE, and ATBARA RIVER when dealing with the <u>bodies of water</u> that is usually meant by the term NILE. This map is based upon the present political and geographical boundaries established for this area of Alkebu-lan (Africa) by the colonialist nations of Europe and the United States of America at the BERLIN CONFERENCE of 1884-1885 C.E. (A.D.).** These boundaries were temporarily adopted by the countries whose borders they bound for the sake of expediency, and to prevent border wars. This display of Inter-

---

*Many historians claimed that Africans arrived in the Americas prior to the Christian Era.
**See Sir E. Hertslett, THE MAP OF AFRICA BY TREATY, 3 Vols. Also, Dr. J. Scott Keltie, THE PARTITION OF AFRICA.

national responsibility on the part of the African peoples and their leaders had been carefully ignored by "Western" educators and historians in their constant destructive criticisms of the Africans in their effort to build a powerful PAN-AFRICAN MOVEMENT.

It is to be noted that many of the names shown on this map, as well as others dealing with this area of Alkebu-lan, are of Greek, Roman, Persian, and Arab origin. This occurred as a result of Sais¹ being captured by the armed forces of the nations or peoples mentioned. These periods began about 1675 B.C.E., at which time the HYKSOS or SHEPHERD KINGS invaded and conquered the Romiti of Kimit. For example: The famous "SHEIKH EL-BELED" is the Arabic title for "MAYOR OF THE VILLAGE". The correct name of this African personality of world wide fame is KA-APER. (See Barbara Mertz, RED LAND, BLACK LAND, pp. 26-27.)

The following citations, or arguments, have been added to further clarify much of the existing confusion over the origin of the African disciplines adopted by the ancient Greeks and Romans (Europeans, "Light-skinned Caucasians") from their teachers of northeast and east Africa (Alkebu-lan), the most noted of whom were Egyptians, Nubians, Merowites, Ethiopians and other Africans of the Nile Valleys (Blue and White) and Great Lakes regions High-Cultures, who came from as far off south as the Monomotapa Empire's capital - ZIMBABWE, west as Ghana, northwest as Khart Haddas (Carthage); and also from Africa's dead center - the ManiKongo Empire and the Bonyoro Kingdoms. Re-examine all.

ARGUMENTS AND ANSWERS RELATIVE TO THE AFRICAN ORIGINS OF " GREEK PHILOSOPHY "

The proto map by Yosef ben-Jochannan shows the geo-political boundaries which were not in existence when the first of the Europeans - whom Professor Jeffreys called "MODERN MAN" and "LIGHT-SKINNED CAUCASIANS" - arrived in Alkebu-lan around the area designated as Egypt by the Haribus (people from Chaldea). Because of this reason it is appropriate at this juncture to familiarize one's self with the maps shown on pages 705, 706 -707, 708 - 709 of this volume. These maps contain many answers to the basic mis-conceptions about the peoples of Ethiopia and Egypt, as to which group was truly responsible for the creation of the High-Culture of the land presently called "EGYPT". This position, of course, includes the original creators of the discipline of "PHILOSOPHY". The maps also show how silly and racist it is to indicate in anyway what-so-ever the "CAUCASOID" origins of North, East, and Central Africa. South and West Africa are not being ignored in reference to this contention, for one has to remember that Professor M.D.W. Jeffreys pulled the famous "Hat Trick" and came up with Caucasian origins for people (Africans) called "GRIMALDIS" in the middle of Monomotapa (South Africa) who resided there for thousands of years before the arrival of the first Europeans (the Portuguese with Bartolome Dias) in approximately 1488 C.E. Although it is also quite obvious that European and European-American educators of all sorts have assigned these and other Africans special nomenclatures to suit their particular "RACIAL" and "ETHNIC" stereotype requirements, most of which are tied to geo-political considerations and not by any scientific examination or experimentation, the same is not true with respect to the MYTHICAL names that stemmed from the Hebrew TORAH. For example: The terms RACE and ETHNIC are as dangerous to the African peoples as the terms HAMITIC and SEMITIC. The latter two presuppose that there were no BLACK PEOPLE before the mythical character of the Hebrew Torah (Christian OLD TESTEMENT) called NOAH, and before the equally notorious tale about <u>the end of the world by flood.</u> The major assumption being that <u>the Black Man got his color from Noah's Nephew - HAM. HAM became black because</u> of a...

"CURSE GOD PLACE ON HIM FOR STARING AT HIS UNCLE'S NAKEDNESS, WHILE IN THE ARK, DURING THE FLOOD."

Note that some historians maintained that <u>Noah was Ham's father.</u> Yet, the Babylonian Talmudists (Jewish scholars)* of the 6th Century C.E. - maintained that <u>the Black Man's color came from a</u>...

"CURSE GOD PLACE UPON CAIN."** etc.

All of these terms and myths have no truthful bearing on Alkebulan (Africa) or her indigenous peoples. These terms were devised to meet the racist needs of the slavemasters, slave traders, co-

---

*The version of the TALMUD which these racist created is no longer used by any group today as the official text.
**See Graves and Patti, HEBREW MYTHS.

lonialists, and imperial expansionists' mentality. However, they have been a source of "ESTABLISHED FACTS" in the various institutions of learning controlled by Europeans and European-Americans and certain Blacks whom they have trained to do their bidding.* In using these terms of inferiority against the Africans, the racists have been able to remove Egypt and other parts of North Africa from the rest of the continent mentally. When this was not possible they established CAUCASOIDS, HAMITES, NIOLITES, SEMITES, BERBERS, and other "RACIAL" and "ETHNIC" groups in order to make the people they call "NEGROES", etc., only to have existed below the reaches of the SAHARA. It is impossible to overemphasize this point. Why? Because this is the basic mechanism used to destroy the Africans - similar to those one sees in the HARLEMS of the United States of America - as creators of that which is today called GREEK PHILOSOPHY, also EGYPTIAN HISTORY. In order to accomplish this end current references are always made to imply that the present majority of the population of Africanized and Europeanized Arabs, and Arabs were the direct descendants of the original Africans who produced the wonderous High-Culture that was ancient North Africa. Yet, the majority of these Western educators are (or should be) aware that these newcomers to North Africa did not arrive there until 640 C.E. Unfortunately many educators bearing the title "EGYPTOLOGIST,

---

*BLACK-owned or administered institutions of Higher Learning are carbon copies of WHITE-owned institutions. They follow every racist declaration about the Africans SOUTH OF THE SAHARA myth as do their White counterparts.

ANTHROPOLOGIST, PALEONTOLOGIST, ARCHAEOLOGIST", and many other nomenclatures of related and un-related disciplines have conceded to these racist terminologies and mythological proclamations in their hypotheses about the Africans and Africa. The saddest aspect of this academic dishonesty is that so many people of African origin, who have earned the highest degrees European and European-American institutions of higher learning can offer them, willingly and knowingly avoid writing about these areas of Alkebu-lan. Whenever they do summon enough courage to undertake this task they are generally willing to adopt the same racist poise of their teachers. However, the vast majority have been content with limiting their studies and other works to West Africa, and possibly Central Africa. They have even been willing to concede South Africa to "<u>Caucasian origin</u>". Although such profestations are by themselves obviously ridiculous, one must also admit that they are equally distorted to receive certain academic credibility and approval in order to maintain the image that suggests and very often declares the "CAUCASIAN ORIGIN OF EGYPTIAN HIGH-CULTURE". This is also obvious in the teachings of certain "<u>Western educators</u>" about the Africans' introduction to iron, which they have maintained Africans knew nothing of before the early 6th Century of the Christian Era (C.E.). One wonders what will they say now, being that the distortion of this truth has been proven to be just another lie with the uncovering of the African iron mine of deepest South Africa - in the nation called

Swaziland. The reader should review the report on this find on page 56 of this volume. It is controversies of this nature that caused this chapter to be so extensively detailed in its coverage of a few disciplines the Africans of Alkebu-lan created, developed and published while they were reaching their zenith in Kimit (Egypt). For this same reason it was necessary to continuously refer to the fact that the Africans of Egypt up to, and including, the building of the last of the major pyramids were similar to any AFRICAN-AMERICAN one sees all over the HARLEMS of the United States of America. This point cannot be over-emphasized, as a result this statement's appearance will be repetitious throughout.

Another aspect of North African and Nile Valley (Egyptian) Philosophy is called the SUMMUM BONUM. This too has been attributed to Pythagoras by most Western educators. On the other hand C.H. Vail, in his book, ANCIENT MYSTERIES, rightfully pointed to the fact that all FIVE (5) STATES are solely African (Egyptian). Another noted Egyptologist - Salust - supports C.H. Vails' findings. He stated that DIEFICATION - the act of becoming GODLIKE - was the main purpose of the Africans of Egypt's Mysteries System, which is in essence the whole meaning of the SUMMUN BONUM which translated into English means "DOCTRINE OF THE SUPREME GOOD". Pythagoras (one of the legendary Greek Philosophers) paraphrased this entire "Doctrine" in the following manner. He wrote that:

"MAN'S SUPREME GOOD IS TO BECOME GODLIKE..., etc."

He went on further and tried to describe this African principle by indicating the manner in which this state was to be achieved. This...

"THROUGH THE SUBORDINATION OF MAN'S LOWER SELF, TO THE HIGHER STAGE OF HIS BEING..., etc."

It should be obvious that Pythagoras' pronouncements were already described in the Africans' philosophical concepts and principles laid down in...

THE UNION OF OPPOSITES,

which were ferverently adhered to as major teachings of the Mysteries System. Zeller, in his HISTORY OF PHILOSOPHY, p. 43, very succinctly supported both Vail and Salust's positions. However, it must be noted that this obligation was not one of the higher aspects of the Mysteries which the NEOPHYTES had to pass through; it was just another step in the development of one's "LOWER STAGE" to that of a "HIGHER STAGE". This was in reality the Africans' way of describing the upward projection from the rank or degree of the "ENTERED APPRENTICE" to that of "MASTER". Is it strange that this upward movement is also prescibed in the stages required among the FREEMASONS of Europe and European-America, all of whom copied from the philosophical teachings of these indigenous Africans of the Grand Lodge of Luxor, and not from Pythagoras? (See Dr. Albert Churchward, ORIGIN OF FREEMASONRY; also his SIGNS AND SYMBOLS OF PRIMORDIAL MAN; G.G.M. James, STOLEN LEGACY; and E.A. Wallis Budge, OSIRIS, and BOOK OF THE

DEAD.) These same teachings were adopted by the Haribus in their temples long before the birth of King Solomon - who also studied in the Lodge established by the Africans at Mt. Carmel - the same Lodge in which Jesus Christ allegedly studied. These principles have been further moderated through the teachings of the British and their version of the Christian BIBLE (the KING JAMES VERSION) which they labeled SCOTTISH and YORK FREE MASONRY. One must understand that they could not pass down the total truth to the followers of Judaism or Christianity, as they too did not receive all of the works of the Africans Mysteries. Why? Of the 360 degrees required for the total learning processes of the Mysteries only 22 were passed on to the Westerners.

Some Free Masons have established 11 other <u>Honorary Degrees</u> that move the figure to 33; but these are also called "CHRISTIAN DEGREES". There is no such thing as a "CHRISTIAN DEGREE". The entire 360 Degrees of the Africans' Mysteries and Secrets of the Grand Lodge of Thebes and Luxor were already completed before the existense of the first Haribu (Jew) much less before Jesus Christ - the Jew who became the GOD OF THE CHRISTIANS.

All of the above teachings were copied from the PYRAMID and COFFIN TEXTS of the African Mysteries System by the Hebrews. They are found in the Hebrew Torah and all of the European VERSIONS of the Christian HOLY BIBLE. (See, Sir E.A. Wallis Budge, BOOK OF THE DEAD; Y. ben-Jochannan, AFRICAN ORIGINS OF THE MAJOR "WESTERN RELIGIONS"; G.G.M. James, STOLEN LEGACY; and Dr. A. Churchward,

ORIGIN OF FREEMASONRY; ARCANA OF FREE MASONRY; SIGNS AND SYMBOLS OF PRIMORDIAL MAN.)

It should be of no surprise that <u>Modern men</u>" as late as the 20th century C.E., should argue among themselves as to whether or not it was Socrates, Plato, Aristotle or Pythagoras who actually was responsible for the above mentioned philosophical concept originated by the Africans of the Nile Valleys' High-Cultures.

In attributing the same principle to Socrates, one finds that he held its attainment could only come...

"THROUGH SELF, AND THE ENHANCEMENT OF THE MIND."*

Plato held that it must be attained...

"BY HAPPINESS, THROUGH IDEA AND GOOD DEEDS, WHICH IS GOD."**

Aristotle, on the other hand, claimed that it must be obtained...

"BY HAPPINESS, THROUGH REASONING AND THE GIFTS OF FORTUNE."***

Of the three "GREEK PHILOSOPHERS" already mentioned, only Aristotle displayed a semblance of independence of thought on the subject, even though nothing original was really brought forth. Aristotle's divergence was due to his lateness of appearance on the scene (by comparison) to the other two, and because he was exposed to much later information in the works he stole from

---

*Xenophon, MEMORABALIA I, 5, 4.
**Plato, REPUBLIC; THE IDEAL STATE, IV, 441; Plato, THEAETUS, 176A; Plato, SYMPOSIUM 204E.
***Aristotle, ETHICS, Nic I, 9, 1099a, 31; Aristotle, Nic I, 6, 1097.

the Africans while he was in Egypt - most of which the others did not know existed; therefore, they were not able to deal with this principle in the same context.

Other than refering the reader to the general bibliography for this chapter, it is necessary that particular emphasis be placed on the following works with regards to the topic of issue at this juncture in the investigation of GREEK PHILOSOPHY and GREEK PHI- LOSOPHERS: Zeller, Rogers, Turner, Alexander, and Rudick, all of them wrote works entitled - HISTORY OF PHILOSOPHY. Rogers also wrote one entitled, STUDENT HISTORY OF PHILOSOPHY.

There are as many varied accounts of "GREEK PHILOSOPHY" and "GREEK PHILOSOPHERS" as there are writers and educators on these two subjects, most of whom are Europeans and European-Americans. The few who are not are never-the-less European and European-American oriented, and most find themselves being carbon copies of their models. Most of these historians and other educators of related disciplines are aware of the fact that very few of the alleged "Greek Philosophers" actually existed in reality, except for their names. Before the appearance of the Persian philosopher- ZORASTER - in Greece, with the theory of the Africans' "PHILOSOPHY OF FIRE", there were no accounts what-so-ever of the Greeks being involved with any form of philosophy, which included the so-called "IONIC PHILOSOPHERS" or "Pre-SOCRATIC PHILOSOPHERS". For a scholarly account of this period in Greek history Swinburne Clyner's work, PHILOSOPHY OF FIRE, particularly page 18, is recommended. According to Clyner:

> "THE STUDY OF THE MYSTERIES OF ISIS* AND OSIRIS**
> QUICKLY PROVES TO THE STUDENT THAT IT (the Africans' of Egypt teachings)*** WAS A PURE PHILOSOPHY."

Yet, it must be remembered that the teachings of FIRE PHILOSOPHY or the PHILOSOPHY OF FIRE was already common among all of the ancient peoples of Alkebu-lan, the Egyptians being only a small segment of said peoples. This teaching spread with the African conquerors of those lands and peoples of Europe and Asia who were later called "PHILOSOPHERS". In Europe, and in <u>Athens</u> (Greece) in particular, the Africans' teachings were projected through the person of the Gods - "CERES" and "PROSERPINE". In Asia, <u>Samothrace</u> in particular, its format did not change very much; as such it appeared as the "...MOTHER OF THE GODS". Even on the <u>Island of Crete,</u> located in the Egyptian (presently Mediterranean) Sea, it appeared as the "...GOD JUPITER". All of these were merely advanced variations and imitations of religions

---

*Isis was one of the major Goddesses of Egypt. In most cases she appears as the most powerful of them.

**Osiris was the greatest and most powerful of the Gods. He represented RA or PTAH and ONE (The Great I AM) just as Jesus Christ represents the Hebrews' JEHOVAH (YVH) for the Christians. It is from this and other such African philosophical teachings that the Christian version originated.

***These teachings originated around the East-Central areas of Alkebu-lan (Africa) by Africans who preceded the Egyptians by thousands of years. They were the ancestors of all Nile Valley peoples. The best report and historical analysis on this period to be found in the following works by Dr. Albert Churchward, M.D. - ORIGIN AND EVOLUTION OF THE HUMAN RACE, London, 1921; SIGNS AND SYMBOLS OF PRIMORDIAL MAN, London, 1910. There are many other works of this kind, such as Sir Godfrey Higgins, ANACALYPSIS, 2 Vols., London, 1840.

that came from Egypt by way of many other African lands. The fundamental teaching was the...

"CREATION OF THE UNIVERSE BY FIRE."

Thus, these Africans also maintained that...

"THE GOD ABOVE ALL GODS, IS THE FIRE GOD - RA."

It is to be noted that RA is also the GOD OF FIRE. He is otherwise called "THE FIRE GOD".

The type of FIRE PHILOSOPHY which the Africans created and developed also included the teachings of, and about, the NOUS (Mind); the THEORY OF IDEAS FROM THE NOUS; the LOGOS (Soul); the IMMORTALITY (Life after physical death); the UNMOVED MOVER; and the ATOM. Yet, one sees that the Ionic Philosophers, whom many Western educators implied were Greeks, are credited with the introduction of the above mentioned SEVEN (7) PHILOSOPHIC TRUTHS. They gave credit to Heraclitus for the creation of the LOGOS concept. To Democritus they gave the PRINCIPLES OF THE ATOM. And, to Anaxagoras they awarded the NOUS concept. But, for some unknown reason they failed to mention that all of these men were born during the period of the Africans' of Egypt colonization of Ionia. They, also, conveniently failed to mention that all three studied these disciplines in the Africans' Mysteries System under African teachers and priests from every area of the Nile Valleys and Great Lakes High-Cultures. The Africans taught them most of what they were teaching to the Greeks in Greece. Not only did they study in Ionia and Egypt, they also received degrees from the priesthood of the Mysteries and entered the various Secret Societies and Lodges that were required of them. But, not one of them received enough degrees to reach the rank of PRIEST.

If one is to examine the SEVEN (7) PHILOSOPHICAL CONCEPTS, as well as the life-history of the Greek or Ionian "PHILOSOPHERS" who allegedly brought them to the light of human knowledge, it would be easily discovered that Plato fled Athens (Greece) for fear of his own life, after Socrates was forced to commit suicide. Why was Socrates forced to commit suicide? Because he taught on "...ALIEN PHILOSOPHY..., etc." What country was the <u>alien philosophy</u> from? EGYPT. Who were the alien people? AFRICANS, otherwise called EGYPTIANS (originally ROMITI).

Another reason for Plato's dilemma was that he returned to Athens only after more than TWELVE (12) YEARS exile, most of which was spent in study in the African Mysteries System of Egypt. A lot of this time was also spent with the PYTHAGOREAN students and teachers of <u>African</u> (Egyptian) <u>Philosophy</u> in Italy. But, most of all, the Athenian (Greek) government resented the fact that Plato spent most of his time in absolute seclusion with the Priests of the Mysteries System studying philosophy and other disciplines which the Greeks felt were dangerous to their own survival. The Greek government was also suspicious of the fact that Plato arranged to meet Dionysius in Sicily, and with Euclid at Megara. Is it strange that the Greek Goverment should have felt this way? Not at all. Because all of these men Plato visited were in exile. Why? Because they too, as Socrates before them, were guilty of...

"TEACHING A FOREIGN PHILOSOPHY...," etc.

Due to all these contacts in Africa, the Island of Sicily, and in Europe (Italy) - Plato was able to establish his own ACADEMY where he too taught what he received from the Africans of Egypt, with AFRICAN PHILOSOPHY included.

In the case of Aristotle (who differed somewhat from the others, having had more of the Africans' secrets at his disposal after he sacked their libraries and Grand Lodge and stole all of the treasures in the archives) no one knows very much about his childhood, or even his early manhood. This was, of course, typical for most of the others mentioned. The earliest account of his education was that he spent an average of TWENTY (20) YEARS under the tutelege of Plato; and this is only by conjecture. Some historians even dared to suggest that...

"ARISTOTLE DID NOT VISIT EGYPT DURING ITS INVASION BY ALEXANDER the great IN 332 B.C. ...," etc.

Also, ...

"THE BOOKS AND OTHER DOCUMENTS (Which he stole and plagiarized) WERE GIVEN TO HIM; OTHERS HE BOUGHT WITH MONEY PROVIDED BY ALEXANDER."

The "authorities" who made these statements never took time to indicate from whom Alexander bought the treasures. They did not take into account that the Greeks were the colonial masters of the Africans of Egypt, and as such would not have paid for cap-

---
1. Words in parenthesis by the lecturer for the sake of clarity only.

tured bounty - something which they had not done in any other land they had captured up until that time. Such types of myths and downright lies must make one wonder if "WESTERN HISTORIANS" and other <u>educators</u> are not aware of the fact that the ancient conquerors of every nation in the history of the world looted and scoured the lands of conquered peoples everywhere.

As one examines the HOLY ORDERS of the Egyptian Mysteries System, it is soon discovered that the priests were subjected to an exact methodology of education that required at least FORTY (40) to FORTY-SEVEN (47) YEARS of seclusive studies of a curriculum which allowed nothing short of total DEVOTION within the LODGES of the PRIESTHOOD (Secret Societies). Such studies covered the entire scope of MEMPHYTE THEOLOGY - which included COSMOLOGY, PHILOSOPHY, SOCIAL SCIENCE and the SEVEN LIBERAL ARTS; APPLIED SCIENCE - which also included DISCIPLINES NECESSARY FOR CONDUCTING GEOGRAPHIC MEASUREMENTS, COMMERCE AND TRADE, THE SEVEN LIBERAL ARTS FOR THE ATTAINMENT AND ACCOMPLISHMENT OF THE SUMMUN BONUM AND THE THERAPUTIC CLEANSING OF THE SOUL FOR ITS ENTRANCE INTO THE NETHER WORLD (Hereafter, Heaven). These attributes were the minimum requirements in the field of education which the priests of the African(Egyptian) Mysteries System of the entire Nile Valleys and Great Lakes High-Cultures were required to display. They were the qualities which each and every so-called IONIC and GREEK philosopher was always trying to acquire for himself in Egypt or in other areas where the Egyptians had subordinate Lodges (colleges or universities).

The studies and duties already mentioned were exclusive of the FORTY-TWO (42) so-called "BOOKS OF HERNES" in which a priest had to prove his proficiency. Besides these works, a priest also had to be proficient in the "MAGICAL LANGUAGE" of the sciences - mathematics, magic, and astrology. This language is called "HIEROGLYPHICS" by <u>Western scholars.</u>

The above curriculum courses were only available to the LAST STAGE students of the PRIESTHOOD - in the various ORDERS and LODGES.* These students were of the rank of the SUMMUN BONUM. Their curriculum came directly from the OSIRICA (Grand Lodge in Luxor) to all of the SUBORDINATE LODGES in Egypt. All other Lodges - including those in Asia and Europe - received their instructions from the <u>Subordinate Lodges</u> in Egypt. Some of the most important Lodges of foreign note were: the Ionian Temple - DIDYMA; the Mergara Temple - EUCLID; the Crotona Temple - PYTHAGORAS; and the Delphi Temple - ORPHIC, including the later SCHOOLS of Plato and Aristotle. All of these <u>Subordinate Lodges</u> (Schools) existed in different forms and degrees until they were finally destroyed during the early beginnings of the Christian Era (C.E. or A.D.) as a direct result of the EDICTS of the Roman Emperors - THEODOIUS and JUSTINIAN - because of their fear that the <u>African Mysteries System</u> would have outlasted the "<u>New Religion</u>" - CHRISTIANITY. Yet, before the destruction of the Myster-

---
*Note that each ORDER or LODGE had its own assembly of Priests.

ies System's Lodges and the outlawing of their teachings both emperors, Justinian and Theodosius, made certain that their own soldiers and overseers made their scribes copy the ECCLESIASTICAL DOGMAS of the Mysteries System for adoption into the "New Religion" - CHRISTIANITY. Thus, the FIRST HOLY CATHOLIC CHURCH, the name which was adopted by the Romans for their own institution, later on to become, THE HOLY "ROMAN" CATHOLIC CHURCH. They corrupted the title with the word "ROMAN".

Even before the so-called GREEK and IONIC philosophers, during the construction of the GREAT PYRAMID OF KHUFU (Whom the Greeks misnamed "CHEOPS" or "KHEOPS"), the forerunners of the African Lodges attended by Moses of the Haribus, and Jesus Christ of the Christians - MOUNT CARMEL, were by Egyptians. Is it, then, strange that both of these sages of Judaism and Christianity, had to study under their Nile Valleys and Great Lakes African teachers and priests? No. Why not? Because it is shown that <u>Moses himself was an African</u> who lived among the priests of the Mysteries. He became a HIEROGRAMMAT, which was partly due to his royal upbringing. On the other hand, JESUS CHRIST, a fellow Haribu (Jew or Hebrew according to modern terminologies), never completed his final INITIATION. (There are no records that he did.)

The following works must be carefully read with respect to the above citations dealing with Moses and Jesus Christ - Annie Bessant, ESOTERIC CHRISTIANITY; C.H. Vail, ANCIENT MYSTERIES; H. S. Lewis, MYSTICAL LIFE OF JESUS CHRIST; Herodotus, HISTORIES;

Diogenes, BOOK IX; Max Muller, EGYPTIAN MYTHOLOGY; OVID FASTI III; Frankfort, CREATION STORY OF THE MEMHITE THEOLOGY; Sir G. Higgins, ANACALYPSIS, 2 Vols.; Sir J. Frazier, GOLDEN BOUGH; Count C. Volney, RUINS OF EMPIRES; Dr. A. Churchward, SIGNS AND SYMBOLS OF PRIMORDIAL MAN; G.G.M. James, STOLEN LEGACY; Patti and Graves, HEBREW MYTHS; and Y. ben-Jochannan, AFRICAN ORIGINS OF THE MAJOR "WESTERN RELIGIONS". Very special mention of Dr. Albert Churchward's ORIGIN OF FREEMASONRY is hereby given. One should also include among this list other ancient works on African origins of that which is called "GREEK PHILOSOPHY". All of these works should be compared with Socrates' "FAREWELL CONVERSATION" to his students and friends. In this work he is deeply involved in his African Mysteries, even referring to himself as a "BROTHER". He was a "Brother" in the sense that he was a subordinate of the <u>Secret Societies of the Nile</u>. (See, also, Zeller's HISTORY OF PHILOSOPHY; Max Muller, EGYPTIAN MYTHOLOGY; and S. Clynder, FIRE PHILOSOPHY.)

PROTON KINOUN AKHNATEN - THE UNMOVED MOVER. This classic philosophical concept was attributed to many of the teachings of Pharoah Akhnaten* (Amen-ho-tep IV) who lived and died more than one thousand and twenty (1,120) years (1,352) before the arrival of Aristotle with Alexander "<u>the Great</u>" in Egypt during 332 B.C.E. as conqueror of the Africans of Egypt. Yet, most of the "Western"

---

*The name of this Pharoah (King) is spelled in many ways. It all depends upon which author one is reading as to just what form his name will take. Either of the spellings is correct.

educators, many of whom are designated "AUTHORITIES OF AFRICAN HISTORY" and "EGYPTOLOGY", continue alluding to the origin of said principle as Aristotle's creation and genius. Note that the main figure in this philosophic concept is ATOM - the SUN GOD who sits on the knees of the God of all Gods - PTAH.* And, PTAH was never a God of Greece. (See, William Turner, HISTORY OF PHILOSOPHY, pp. 141, 143; Frankfurt's, ANCIENT EGYPTIAN RELIGION, c20; and D.B. Alexander, HISTORY OF PHILOSOPHY, pp. 102-103.) These concepts originated from the COSMOLOGY and RELIGION the Africans of the Nile Valleys, particularly those of Egypt, introduced to the world from their investigations of the INTERPLANETARY SYSTEM of the Universe and the NOMENCLATURE they established as the result of said studies. This they did, after painstaking scientific measurements and recordings of the development of everything they noticed around them. These things were only possible as a result of the great amount of attention they gave to the development of the NOUS (mind). Thus, one can understand why the Africans saw their RESURRECTION while they traveled through the NETHER WORLD. This belief caused them to write the following:

    MAN KNOW THYSELF (SEAUTON GNOTHI).

The English translation can be better detailed in the following

---

* Once this Gid held the same honor among the Gods as Ra or Re did earlier and later in Egyptian history. He too preceded the Haribu (Hebrew or Jewish) Yaweh (Jehovah or Adondi) by thousa of years before a African named Moses created Haribu mythology.

manner:

THE DOCTRINE OF SELF AWARENESS or SELF KNOWLEDGE.
(See, Zeller's, HISTORY OF PHILOSOPHY, p. 105; Max Muller, EGYPTIAN MYTHOLOGY; S. Clymer, FIRE PHILOSOPHY; C.H. Vail, ANCIENT MYSTERIES; F. Frankfurt, CREATION STORY OF MEMPHITE THEOLOGY; and Bruckner's, CRITICAL HISTORY OF PHILOSOPHY.)

One has to reflect on the fact that before the PELOPONNESIAN WARS (460-445 and 431-421 B.C.E.) the Greeks were not known for their astuteness or awareness in any philosophic discipline. It was because of their need to solve said deficiency in their own culture that they invaded neighboring Ionia and other peaceful nations. These wars were led by the military despotic rule of Pericles - who forced alliances upon the peoples he captured, thereby extending the Greek Empire from Thessaly to Argos in one direction, and from Euboea to Maupactus, Achaea, and the main islands of the Ionian (Mediterranean) Sea at the other end. These conquests gained for the Greeks major imperialist colonial treaty alliances with Phocis, Locris, and Boeotia by the year 460 B.C.E. But, these successes were to be followed by another one in 465 B.C.E. The Greeks' major frustation came in 447 B.C.E. when the formerly exiled Oligarchs of Thebes defeated the Athenians at Coronea and re-established the Boeotian League under Theban generalship. All of this were followed by the Euboean, Spartan, and Megaran revolts and invasions of Attica and Pericles; the latter two having finally to sue for peace. From this juncture in history onwards it was just a matter of one group of aliens or another who occupied Greece from time to time; each bringing into Greece its own cultural heritage, and influencing the Greeks who at this period in history had very little in the way of their own culture.

Of the various invaders who came into Greece during the periods in question, the most influential on them (the Greeks) were the Ionians. But the Ionians' culture was in fact African in origin; they were colonials of the Africans of Egypt before, and after, their own colonization and exploitation of the Greeks. So, whatever cultural disciplines the Ionians carried into Greek said disciplines they learned from the Africans who cultured and influenced them before they were able to develop their own High-Culture (civilization). These facts have moved such historians as the following to state in their works that the Greeks were not the originators of that which is still being called "GREEK PHILOSOPHY" and/or "GREEK PHILOSOPHERS"- Eva B. Sandford, MEDITERRANEAN WORLD; A. Couch, HISTORY OF GREECE, cXXII, W.J. Woodhouse, THE TUTORIAL HISTORY OF GREECE; Bostford and Robinson, HELLENIC HISTORY; G.G.M. James, STOLEN LEGACY; Sedgwick and Tyler, HISTORY OF SCIENCE cIX; and C.H. Vail, ANCIENT MYSTERIES.

However, the main thrust of Greek enlightenment began with the African, mainly the Egyptian and Ethiopian invasion and colonization of the Ionians. Prior to this the Greeks were almost totally ignorant of Africa's Nile Valleys High-Cultures and the developments in all of the major desciplines that were developed by said Africans before the birth of Greece (Pyrrh) itself as a City-State or nation. Yet, the Greeks' later contact with the Africans of Egypt, Nubia, and Ethiopia, in particular, brought on the DAWN OF GREEK ENLIGHTENMENT. (See, ERATOSTHENES AP STRABO 801-802; OVID FASTI III, 338; E.B. Sandford, MEDITERRANEAN WORLD; Herodotus, HISTORIES, Book II; Diogenes BOOK IX 49; G.G.M. James, STOLEN LEGACY; and PLUTARCH, p. 380. Added to these should be the following works: John Kendrick, ANCIENT EGYPT, Book II; Dr. Albert Churchward, SIGNS AND SYMBOLS OF PRIMORDIAL MAN; and many other works already listed on the subject of <u>African</u> (Egyptian) <u>Philosophy</u> and the Mysteries in general.)

The looting of the ROYAL LIBRARY OF THEBES, otherwise called the "MENEPHTHEION", by the imperial armies of Greece, also provided the military symbols adopted by the Greek armies, i.e., the SCIMITAR, SCOURGE, and PENDUM found in the Side Hall that stood 133 feet wide by 100 feet long, all of which were supported by a total of 48 columns - of which some were more than 32 feet tall, each having a circumference of at least 21 feet. It must be noted that this type of architectural splendor was copied by the Greeks in all the architectural structures they built following their exposure to the Africans'. In this GREAT HALL the Greeks also got their first glimpse at the GODDESS OF SAF, the APARTMENTS OF THOTH, and the SACRED LIBRARY which Diodorus called the "DISPENSARY OF THE MIND". (See, J. Kendrick, HISTORY OF ANCIENT EGYPT,

Book I; J. Kendrick, ANCIENT EGYPT; E.M. Sandford, MEDITERRANEAN WORLD; C.H. Vail, ANCIENT MYSTERIES; M. Muller, EGYPTIAN MYTHOLOGY ; J.H. Breasted, ANCIENT EGYPT; Sir E.A. Wallis Budge, ANCIENT EGYPT. The works of the following writers entitled "HISTORY OF PHILOSOPHY" should also be read in conjunction with this phase of the subject in question. They are: Rogers, Rudick, Fuller, Turner, and Zeller, all of whom are mentioned throughout this chapter.)

One can sum up EGYPTIAN (African) ORIGINS OF "GREEK PHILOSOPHY" with Xenophanes, a native of Colophon in Asia Minor. He was supposed to have existed from about 370 B.C.E. His date of departure from this world was not mentioned. He was one of the so-called "ELATIC PHILOSOPHERS". It was he who was accredited with the doctrine relating to THE UNITY OF GOD. This would mean that "THE UNITY OF GOD" concept pronounced by Akhnaten (Amen-ho-tep IV) more than 982 years before the birth of Xenophanes is to be ignored, and that the "I AM" spoken of by the Priests of the MYSTERIES SYSTEM with respect to the God RA, as cited in the various books of the origin of philosophy, did not exist. Both must, then, give preference to this character's plagiarisims. But, strange as it may seem, the source of it all is in the Africans' works recorded and noted in the English translation of what is called the "COFFIN TEXTS" by Sir E.A. Wallis-Budge in his BOOK OF THE DEAD; OSIRIS; and THE GODS OF EGYPT. Other works of this nature which need be consulted on this issue are by the following people and titles. Many of them are considered "AUTHORITIES" in their respective field. Thus - Sir James Frazier, GOLDEN BOUGH; Homer W. Smith, MAN AND HIS GODS; Professor James H. Breasted, THE DAWN OF CONSCIENCE; Count C.C. Volney, RUINS OF EMPIRES; Professor Yosef ben-Jochannan, AFRICAN ORIGINS OF MAJOR "WESTERN RELIGIONS". Added to these works, which are primarily historical or philosophical, should be the following: F.M. Barber, THE MECHANICAL TRIUMPHS OF THE ANCIENT EGYPTIANS; THE STROMATA OF CLEMENT OF ALEXANDRIA; F. Cajeri, HISTORY OF MATHEMATICS; W.W.R. Ball, HISTORY OF MATHEMATICS; Frankfurt's, ANCIENT EGYPTIAN RELIGION; Frankfurt's, INTELLECTUAL ADVENTURE OF MAN; and Frankfurt's KINGSHIP AND THE GODS.

The discrepancies related in the works, life, and dates of the so-called "GREEK PHILOSOPHERS" and their "GREEK PHILOSOPHY" are in themselves sufficient to cast doubt on said teachings and disciplines ever being of Greek origins. Moreover, was it at all possible for a hostile society, such as ancient Greece, to have produced a body (system) of teachings and disciplines dealing with the origin of life and everything within the universe? How did it provide its teachers and priests with the facilities needed for such academic growth, when in fact said system was contrary to the official sanctions and laws, also religion, of the hostile state in which it was supposedly developed? This was not possible by any stretch of the imagination in a hostile Greece, or for that matter in any society where said origins were not acceptable

to the ESTABLISHMENT (the powers that be). It is the same as
saying that COMMUNISM can thrive freely in the United States of
America; or, CAPITALISM has a free hand in the Soviet Union and
The Peoples Republic of China. Either of the last two statements
would be as equally ridiculous as the former in behalf of Greece.
Yet, certain "Western educators" of every discipline related to
this issue, project this type of irrational hypothesis year after
year in hundreds of thousands of publications under the title of
"GREEK PHILOSOPHY", when in fact they are very much aware that
the foundation of said disciplines was in reality African, and
the originators Africans. They equally know that "GREEK PHILOSO-
PHY" was derived from the Africans' of the Nile Valleys and Great
Lakes region MYSTERIES SYSTEM. It was developed along the more
than 4,100 mile long White and Blue Niles (from Uganda to Egypt,
and from Ethiopia to Egypt) thousands of years before the dawn
of Greek High-Culture ("civilization"). Yet, one cannot isolate
these developments to the very few areas of Alkebu-lan (the
Greeks and Romans' AFRICA), as there is no doubt that further
SOUTH in Zimbabwe (Rhodesia) and Zambia, as in Monomotapa (Union
of South Africa), very similar developments by the same group of
African people were taking place. Of course this position will
find very strong objections from those who are dead set on proving that "AFRICA SOUTH OF THE SAHARA" - their so-called "BLACK
AFRICA" - produced not a single High-Culture of greatness until
the arrival of the European (Professor Jeffreys' MODERN MAN and

LIGHT-SKINNED CAUCASIAN) colonialists in the 19th Century, C.E.*; all of which have been refuted by the overwhelming facts that are available to anyone who desires to do independent research apart from the usually racist presentation of the general stereotyped "HISTORY OF AFRICA" as shown in Henry Morton Stanley's book, DARKEST AFRICA, which millions of Europeans and European-Americans accept as TRUTH!** In fact, the basis of Stanley's work is the foundation of colonialism, imperialism, and neo-colonialism in the Africa of yesterday and today. It also formed the basis for the justification of genocide against the African peoples by Europeans and European-Americans for hundreds of years, including the present 1970's. For this reason the eight million (8,000,000) European Jews killed by Adolph Hitler in Europe are a major ca-tastrophe in all the publications in the United States of America's educational system, but the tens of millions killed by King Leopold II of Belgium, Henry Morton Stanley of the United States of America and England, Sir (and Lord) Lugard of England, Cecil Rhodes (of the infamous RHODES SCHOLARSHIP) of England, Il Duce Benito Mussolini of Italy, and the so-called "ENTREPRENUERS" of

---

*Although the Western Europeans arrived at West Africa around 1441 C.E., it was not until 1830 C.E. that France invaded Cueta, Morocco, to begin what is historically called "THE PARTITION OF AFRICA". (See, Sir E. Hertslett, THE MAP OF AFRICA BY TREATY.)
**See, Sir Edward Hertslett, MAP OF AFRICA BY TREATY, 3 Vols. London, 1889; Sir J. Scott-Keltie, PARTITION OF AFRICA, London, 1880-1900; Parker T. Moon, IMPERIALISM AND WORLD POLITICS, New York, 1934; Sir Edward Hertslett, THE BERLIN CONFERENCE, London, 1900; Henry Nevinson, A MODERN SLAVERY, London,   ; Eric Williams, CAPITALISM AND SLAVERY, New York, 1934.

the United States of American, are very seldom mentioned in the same light. Why is this so? Because of the same reason that makes AFRICAN (Egyptian) PHILOSOPHY "GREEK PHILOSOPHY", and AFRICAN PHILOSOPHERS "GREEK PHILOSOPHERS".

One must truly conclude that "GREEK PHILOSOPHY" is nothing more or less than the culmination of the development of bits and pieces of the teachings from African and Asian philosophical "TRUTHS" and "MYTHOLOGICAL CONCEPTS " that were first introduced to mankind along the Nile Valleys and Great Lakes of Alkebu-lan, and along the Tigris and Euphrates Valleys of Asia. At this point it would be worthwhile to review Chapter II, PREHISTORIC HOMO SAPIENS: ANCIENT AFRICAN MAN for supportive data. Also read Albert Churchward, M.D., ORIGIN AND EVOLUTION OF THE HUMAN RACE; Sonia Cole, THE PREHISTORY OF EAST AFRICA; H.A. Wieschoff, THE ZIMBABWE - MONOMOTAPA CULTURE OF S.E. AFRICA (In: Ugnada Journal, 14, 1950); and W.E. Clark LeGross and L.S.B. Leakey, THE NIOCENE HOMINOIDEA OF EAST AFRICA, London, 1951.

This chapter closes with a few citations on what is today called errornemously "FREEMASONRY", and equally distorted by "MODERN MAN" to appear as having been originated by the Palestinians or Israelites of King Solomon's temple; this being no different to the falsification of African and Asian PHILOSOPHY as the creation of European (Greek) genius. In the first instance it must be carefully remembered that King Solomon of Israel attended the subordinate Lodge of the Egyptian Mysteries System at Mount Carmel where he was received as an "ENTERED APPRENTICE" like all others before and after him who entered. This was the "FIRST STEP" out of the major mandatory "THREE STEPS"* necessary in the life of the INITIATE before he could have become a "MASTER OF THE MYSTERIES" (presently called "Master Mason"). Nevertheless, the original FIRST STEP in the African Mysteries System (Secret Society) required certain heights of attained knowledge from the ENTERED APPRENTICE through rigorous training surpassed all that is presently required of the "ROYAL ARCH" Freemason of the 20th century C.E., and very much more.

Although this analysis will not enter into a treatise on European and European-American versions of the African Mysteries System (so-called "Freemasonry") it will elaborate on at least three of the most commonly distorted of the basic "MASONIC RITUALS" and "SYMBOLS" used in the so-called "Western World" and its colonial empires. For example: The DOUBLE-TRIANGLE ⧖ symbol (sign), with each leg being equal to the other, is called by "Western" ROYAL ARCH FREEMASONS - the "SEAL OF KING SOLOMON." Yet, the origin of this composite TRIANGLE and its usage as a symbol in <u>religion</u> and <u>science</u> dates back to at least the beginning of the development of the worship of the God PTAH by the African priests at their capital cities in Memphis (Kimit) and Axum (Kush), the most noted of said priests being URA 𓃰 𓊽𓏤.** - KHERP HEM who was also known as the "ARCH CRAFTSMAN OF THE MYSTERIES SYSTEM" 𓂝𓏤.**

The Osirian ANKH ☥ which Europeans, primarily of ancient Greece and Rome, have distorted to form their "CHRISTIAN

---
* Note that the THREE STEPS have been detailed before in this chapter dealing with so-called "Greek Philosophy."
** The Hieroglyphic writings are presented to the student for further investigation and comparison between this African language and the English traslations and trasliterations available.

CROSS" and/or "CRUCIFIX" ⚵✝ also has been shown to have had a
DRUID-past in the same manner as the Nile Valley and Great Lakes
African "SWASTICA" (Western Swastika) ⛤ . The SWASTICA,
however, was distorted before its usage in Christendom, as
seen in archaeological artifacts found in England that date back
to an origin of approximately 3,000 B.C.E. It is also noted that
they indicated Haribu (Hebrew or Jewish) distortions - thus one
appears ⛤ . Is it not strange that the same SWASTICA was
used, minus the pyramid, as a symbol for the destruction of European Jews by Adolph Hitler and his Nazis and Fascist allies
in Europe and European-America. A tour of the AFRICAN WING of
the Museum of Natural History in New York City will reveal that
the Africans of central Africa commonly used the SWASTICA for religious and other ceremonial functions. One of the figures in a
display case is dressed in a religious robe with SWASTICAS printed all over its surface. This garment was used before there was
a German state, and before the birth of Baron von Bismarch, Kaiser
Wilhelm or Adolph Hitler. The ANKH ☥ on the otherhand is today
presented in every so-called "SCOTTISH RITE FREEMASON LODGE" as
the "CHRISTIAN CROSS" - ✝ ✚ ⚵ ☥.* But it must be noted that
Africans along the Niles (Blue and White, also the Atbara) and
Great Lakes also used the CROSS ✳ that was much more related to
the one in present use by the European and European-American
Christians. This latter CROSS is the one which Plato referred to
with respect to his "DIVINE MAN." The SWASTICA, or "GAMMADION"
(which it is also known as), can be found among the indigenous

---

* There are many other variations of the so-called "CHRISTIAN
CROSS" used today. Many others have been placed to rest in
peace during the colonial expansion of Christendom.

peoples of the continent nisnomered "SOUTH AMERICA" by European conquerors in honor of their fellow (Italian) colonialist explorer Amerigo Vespucci. The most noted of these so-called "AMERICANS" were the Zapotecs and Mayas whose major symbols resembled in most respect those of the Africans.

The three (3) equal legs of the triangle are not coinciden - tal they were designed in conjunction with the system of NUMEROLOGY that was common amongst the Priests of the MYSTERIES SYSTEM Lodges (Schools or colleges) along the Nile Valleys and Great Lakes. The numbers THREE (3), FIVE (5), SEVEN (7), Nine (9), and ELEVEN (11) played the most important roles. The SYSTEM OF NUMEROLOGICAL PHILOSOPHY was carried to other parts of the world by the Haribus from the days of the African - Moses, followed by the Druids, and lastly by the Greeks up until the time of Alexander II -"the great," Aristotle, and General Soter who later renamed himself "Ptolemy I." There is another dimension to this TRIANGLE, however. That is, its position in use. For, whereas the so-called FREEMASONS show it on its base , the Africans who created it first showed it on its apex as the SOLAR MYTHOS and called it the....

"SQUARE IN FOUR DIVISIONS" and /or "DIMENSIONS," also the...

"HEAVEN IN FOUR DIVISIONS."

The two (2) circles around the SQUARE and TRIANGLE represent the NINE DIVISIONS along with the SECTIONS formed by the SQUARE and TRIANGLE within the inner CIRCLE. This was also known as the STELLAR MYTHOS, the only difference being the insertion of the SIGN OF HORUS centered in the major equal-sided TRIANGLE ▲ as represented by a smaller TRIANGLE ▽ (the Heaven raised above man and earth), a small dot● as a STAR centered in the TRIANGLE (the God HORUS in Heaven), and SEVEN (7) RAYS – the SEVEN GLORIOUS ONES* (the other Gods who aided HORUS). Thus, one sees the DIVISION OF THE HEAVEN, North and South; the SACRED TRIANGLE; the FIRST TRINITY (Heaven in three – 3 – Divisions). All of these figures, symbols, and teachings are in the pre OSIRIAN RELIGION and entered the much later OSIRIAN and ATUM periods. These were all contained in the RITUALS showing the God ATUM as the...

"GREAT JUDGE UPON THE MOUNT OF AMENTA..."
during thousands of years before the introduction of the OSIRIAN DRAMA. How unfortunate it is that the vast majority of Freemasons and members that form the general Hebrew ("Jewish"), Christian, and Islamic clergy (the so-called "Men of the Cloth") are not made aware of these African beginnings in their education before they are allowed to become the "TEACHERS OF MEN." If this was done before, they would have known that the ancient Africans' Gods – HORUS, PATH, ATUM, AMEN, I;*and all others,"lift up the Heavens ▽ with WATER"∿∿∿ as stated in the following ritual by SEM 𓏃𓃀𓊃, the Prophet of Kimit (Sais or Egypt), as he a-nointed his followers with oils; saying:

> I** lustrate with water in TATU and with oil in ABYDOS, exalting HIM who is in the heights.***

---

*Students of religious courses dealing with "Comparative Religion" would recall that ONE is the name by which the oldest God of Kimit was known. Adopted by "Western " religions.
** The earliest name for today's Jehovah, Christ, Al'lah, etc.
*** See BOOK OF THE DEAD; OSIRIS; and GODS OF THE EGYPTIANS.

The JUDGMENT SCENES in the BOOK OF THE DEAD and also those in OSIRIS should prove to be of very great importance to the student who is using the following books as research materials: THE GOLDEN BOUGH (13 Vols.), by Sir James Frazier; MAN AND HIS GODS, by Homer W. Smith; and the two volume work, ANACALYPSIS, by Sir Godfrey Higgins. This suggestion refers particularly to any student in the field of study of AFRICAN RELIGIONS and their Asian and European off-shoots.

Because of the basic significance of the TRIANGLE (all forms of it) in everyone's life with respect to religion, science, medicine, astronomy and astrology, etc, it is necessary to further probe into its African origin. It existed before there was the first Haribu (Hebrew or "Jew") - ABRAHAM or ABRAM, muchless a Hebrew or Jewish Religion and its outgrowth - Christianity and Islam. The TRIANGLE of the God HORUS, I , which SHU "...<u>lifted up on the SEVEN STEPS to Heaven...</u>," should be noted as the forerunners of the Haribus MENORAH (candle holder with Seven,7, candles) that depicted the SEVEN STEPS dealing with an EXODUS or PASSOVER . They adopted this symbolic magical number, and not the SEVEN STEPS to the Freemasons' ROYAL ARCH DEGREE, the SEVEN (years) STEPS in agriculture in which the "<u>land must lay farrow</u>," and the SEVEN STEPS (years) which "...<u>no slave could be held beyond</u>...," etc. according the Haribu HOLY TORAH (Christians' OLD TESTAMENT).

The great architect Imhotep designed his SEVEN STEPS PYRAMID at Sakharah (Saqqara) during the year c3,000 BCE under the reign of Pharoah Djoser (whom the Greeks renamed "Zozer") - the third (3rd) pharoah of the first (1st) dynasty, before the creation of JEHOVAH, ADAM AND EVE, ABRAHAM and JUDAISM by Haribu mythologists.

The TRIANGLE was one of the most sacred of the symbols in the religious functions of the Nile Valley Africans of antiquity; thus they constructed their Pyramids - graves (last house of △ life's abode or earth) in the form of the TRIANGLE with three equal sides, or legs, and called it the...

"CONE OF THE GOD SET."

It is to be noted that it also symbolizes the...

"GOD OF THE SOUTH POLE STAR."

When it is placed on its APEX, as shown on most of the papyri and monuments, the ▽ represents the TRI-PARTITE DIVISION OF THE ECLIPTIC," and the "TRIPLE SEASON OF THE CALENDAR YEAR OF KIMIT" - thus the:

> Water Season (represented by the God HORUS), Wind and Equnoctical gales (represented by the God SHU); Dryness and Drought (represented by the God SUT).

Each season had FOUR (4) months; each year THREE (3) seasons; each month or moon had THREE (3) weeks of TEN (10) days each.*

This form of the TRIANGLE ▽ represents the highest degree - THIRTY-THIRD (33rd) when it is set on its APEX upon a CROSS** ⸸, which is set upon a royal CROWN. The CROWN rests on the DOUBLE-HEADED EAGLE 🦅 looking at where he was and where he is going, FROM WEST TO EAST IN SEARCH OF LIGHT. This CROWN, with its adornments, is known as the "ATET-CROWN OF THE ILLUMINATION " Third (3rd) Step, and stands over the "Two (2) PILLARS OF TAT" at the entrance of the "TEMPLES OF PTAH, AMENTA, and that of the later brother of the MYSTERIES SYSTEM - King Solomon of Israel. Yet it was first assigned to the God AMEN-RA.

---
* See page   for Solar Calendar of Kimit used from 4,100 BCE.
** Formerly and ANKH or ancient CROSS ✦.
*** One is expected to assume that this was originated by the King Solomon CULT and MYTHS, and ignore the suppressed facts relative to it in the BOOK OF THE DEAD and PAPYRUS OF ANI.

One may wonder why RELIGION is being stressed to such length in this latter part of the citations of the Greek-centric Anglo-Saxon Semitic MYTH. The reason is that RELIGION was in fact the beginning of man's total education with respect to all of the UNKNOWN qualities and quantities, and so it still remains in the 20th century C.E. RELIGION governed, and was responsible for every aspect of the MYSTERIES SYSTEM. The Haribus (Hebrews) carried it from Africa into Europe after it had entered Asia thousands of years before with other African worshipers of the SUN and FIRE. They were followed by the Greeks and Romans who took what the Haribus could not steal to the point where it was totally distorted to meet European needs and mentality. In this manner the Egyptians (Romiti) and other Nile Valleys and Great Lakes High-Culture allowed the STAR OF HORUS or STAR OF THE NORTH POLE ✡ to become the so-called ✶ "STAR OF DAVID" (Mogen David) or symbol of the "ROYAL ARCH DEGREE" of Freemasonry. Without entering into Freemasonry one will note, however, that the Africans had already bisected the TRIANGLE △ and produced their DOUBLE △ RIGHT TRIANGLE. These solutions preceded the birth of Pythagoras and his alleged "PYTHAGOREAN THEORUM" by thousands of years. The "THEORY" which he learnt while a student among the priests of the Niles (Blue and White) from Uganda to the Mediterranean Sea - 4100 miles from source to end.

The Greeks copied all of the above in their so-called "ZODIAC MYTHOS;" the Zodiac being no different than the MYTHOS employed by the Zapotecs and Mayas of "South America," and that of the Druids of northern and north-western Europe. (See Sir Godfrey Higgins, ANACALYPSIS, 2vols.; Dr. Albert C. Churchward, SIGNS AND

SYMBOLS OF PRIMORDIAL MAN; Prof. George G.M. James, STOLEN LEGACY; Sir E.A. Wallis Budge, BOOK OF THE DEAD; and Sir James Frazier, THE GOLDEN BOUGH). Each of these symbols and teachings are equally as common among the Yorubas, Edohs, Akans, and Mendes of West Africa who still use them even after what happened to them as a result of their suppression by the European-style Christianity imposed all over Africa during the infamous SLAVE-TRADING period and PARTITION of the entire continent from the middle of the 15th century to the late 19th century C.E. These are conditions whose effects are now felt even though the colonialist forces for the most part have returned to Europe.

The origin of the HORUS CIRCLE ⊙ , sometimes mistaken for the modern so-called "EVER SEEING EYE" 👁 , has been constantly attributed to the "COURT OF KING SOLOMON" when in fact it preceded the birth of King Solomon of Israel (Palestine) by more than 4100 years. The TRUTH of its origin stems from the Africans' first attempt to record the STELAR ECLIPSE OF THE MOON AND SUN (the God RA). RA - the SUN GOD - is the dot • centered in the disk ○ circle. This also represented the POLE STAR in the center of the UNIVERSE; it too has been referred to as the "EVER-SEEING-EYE" 👁 . But this symbol was always shown on African papyri and structures as ⊚ or ⚚ . Lastly, it was called the "MORNING STAR", as indicated in the following from the BOOK OF REVELATION 11:28 in the Haribu HOLY TORAH (Christian Old Testament):

"I WILL GIVE HIM THE MORNING STAR."

It is also shown in the BOOK OF THE DEAD's papyri from whence the Haribus (Hebrews) stole it.

From the Africans CREATION of the 𐌗 and the developments

associated with the ⬛ and ⊙, including the NUMEROLOGICAL SYSTEM (1,3,5,7,11 etc.) adopted by those who call themselves "ASTROLOGISTS" the Haribus corrupted; the "MAGICAL NUMBER SEVEN" (7) in the following manner:

"Thou shalt make the lamps thereof SEVEN"
See EXODUS XXV.

"There were SEVEN LAMPS of fire burning before the throne, which are the SEVEN SPIRITS OF GOD."
See REVELATIONS IV:5.

"And He had in His right hand SEVEN STARS."
See REVELATIONS I:16.

The latter is from the depiction of the God HORUS holding a TRIANGLE with a STAR at each tangent point ▷✶ while seated on the SEVEN STEPS to Heaven. Each STAR represented the measurement of the monthly LUNAR DAYS (3 x 10 = thirty, 30, days/month) of the God TAHT. From the Haribus it passed on to the Greeks who superimposed it in Christianity after their own ZODIAC MYTHOS. From these corrupted beginnings by the Haribus and Greeks they entered other parts of Europe and Britain, the latter having seen to it that it was brought into the United States of America when it was still a British colony. The MENORAH (the Seven Golden Candlesticks) was obviously no less a corruption by Moses and others who adopted the usage of the SEVEN (7) POLE STARS and the SEVEN GODS (Glorious Ones) that formed the constellation of the so-called "LESSER BEAR" that revolves around the GREAT JUDGE (the All Seeing Eye) - who appears as the figure of ANUP and the POLE in the PLANISPHERE OF DENDERAH. All of this Moses learned as a student in the Mysteries System's Lodges of Kimit (Egypt). Moses never-the-less failed to provide the Haribus with the information that it took the "CIRCLE OF RECESSION 25,827 YEARS TO MAKE EACH CYCLE" and that "EACH POLE STAR WAS VISIBLE AS A DIRECT RESULT OF THE BEAM OF LIGHT IT SHONE THROUGH THE LIGHT-PASSAGE ORIFICE LOCATED IN THE INTERIOR OF THE GREAT PYRAMID WHILE IN ITS REVOLUTION."*

What the student of Astrology will note from all of this is that the Greeks' alleged SYSTEM OF THE ZODICAL CIRCLE was taken from the Haribus' distortions of the true meaning of the DIVINE CIRCLE ⊙ , or SIGN OF THE GOD - RA (sometimes represented by the European-style Christians as they began their replacement of the Africans' Mysteries System's religion and substituted European-style Romanized-Christianity's version of Hebrewism, called "Judaism" at present), thus removing the ARK OF CONFESSIONS - which they called "ARK OF THE COVENANTS." By so doing this, the Haribus had also attempted to claim its origin from Moses as shown in the following excerpt from the BOOK OF EXODUS XXIV:4. Thus Moses...

> "builded an altar under the hill and TWELVE PILLARS, according to the TWELVE TRIBES of Israel...," etc.

The Christians, offspring of the Haribus, used this revised "MAGICAL NUMBER" - TWELVE (12) for most of their own undoing of the Haribus corrupted works they received intact from the Egyptian worshipers of the God RA and other Africans' MYSTERIES SYSTEM teachings. Thus we hear of the "TWELVE DISCIPLES, TWELVE DIVISIONS OF THE CELESTIAL CIRCLE, TWELVE PILLARS OF THE MASONIC GRAND LODGE," and the "TWELVE STATIONS OF JESUS CHRIST," etc. The MAGICAL NUMBER SEVEN (7) of the Africans NUMEROLOGY that the

---
* See MAGICAL MYSTERIES OF FREEMASONRY, and other secret societies books available in your college's library.

Haribus co-opted into their own system had been further co-opted by the European-style Christians (offshoots of the Haribus) and distorted to suit their own needs and mythos — thus TWELVE (12) for the so-called "TWELVE TRIBES OF ISRAEL."

Herodotus, in the year c450 BCE, reminded his fellow Greek citizens* that he was taught by Egyptian and other African priests of the Mysteries System. They had already plotted and calculated the course of the TRIANGLE and its SEVEN (7) POLE STAR; and besides this they had also recorded the moment of the sun's activity to the point where they noticed that it had...

> "SET WHERE IT NOW RISES, AND RISEN TWICE WHERE IT NOW SETS," etc.

Due to this disclosure by Herodotus, and as other Greek citizens before and after him received similar information in their studies under African priests (professors) in Africa and elsewhere, it became possible for men such as Drayson to figure out the Egyptian Priests' calculations revealing that ...

> "...the sun revolves around a centre just as the earth revolves around the sun, at the rate of travel equivalent to 40 miles per second, traveling through space 33,000,000,000,000,000 miles in performing its one year cycle.

This Stelar PHOTOGRAPHY, which the Africans of the Nile Valleys and Great Lakes had already developed before the dawn of the birth of the first Haribu — Abraham, much less before the birth of Jesus Christ of the Christians, provided further fundamentals for European (first the Greeks and then the Romans) and European-

---

* The student should keep in mind that Herodotus was a native son of Ionia, which was at the time of his birth a colony of Kimit (Sais or Egypt). Ionia was located in the area where sections of the present states of Jordan, Israel, and Syria now occupy.

American ASTRONOMY to the point where "modern" man can today project himself in "HEAVENLY-BOUND BODIES" which the Africans of the world of antiquity calculated would take place and noted in their works, as shown in the BOOK OF THE DEAD and other major English translatations of papyri and temple structures' inscriptions. All of these have added to the knowledge of so-called "MODERN MAN" in his reach for the OUTER WORLD (Nether World), which he could not have accomplish were it not for said Africans whose descendants are today still serving as slaves for Europeans and European-Americans (recipients of the SECRETS OF THE MYSTERIES of the Nile Valleys and Great Lakes indigenous peoples.)

The mere fact that European and European-American educators have separated learning into "SECULAR" and "RELIGIOUS," as if one is independent of the other, is no reason to believe such was ever the case with respect to the Africans' High-Cultures of antiquity (ancient) or contemporary times. For it is this very same attempt at departmentalizing and sectionalizing Nile Valley and Great Lakes African High-Cultures (civilizations) by European and European-American educators that caused Africans of the north and east to be labeled "CAUCASIANS, CAUCASOIDS, HAMITES" and "SEMITES," etc.; whereas those to the south of an imaginary geopolitical boundary at the southern reaches of the Sahara (Great Desert) are called "NEGROES, BANTUS, HOTTENTOTS, BUSHMEN," and a host of other names which these Africans have never authorized to be used in regards to themselves. Equally, it is because of the sectionalizing and departmentalizing that the Greeks were able to remove certain disciplines, especially the so-called "Greek Philosophy," and claim them as their own creative genius and development; but professor George G.M. James designated "GREEK PHILOSOPHY" as nothing more than a "STOLEN LEGACY"[1] in his book bearing the same name.

A greater in-depth study of other major "religious" and "secular" signs and symbols of the ancient Africans of the Niles and Great Lakes High-Cultures could have been entered into at this juncture. However, this was accomplished in another volume entitled THE ORIGIN OF RELIGION AS A WAY OF LIFE. Never-the-less the student should closely examine AFRICAN ORIGINS OF THE MAJOR "WESTERN RELIGIONS," by your own professor, and other works referred to therein, along with those cited in this volume, in order to grasp the full meaning of the theft of African origins and their eventual plagiarization and relabeling by European and European-American educators and others who call themselves "MEM - BERS OF THE CLERGY" and/or "THEOLOGIANS."

One need not worry about the so-called "SECRETS OF FREE- MASONRY" revealed herein, all of which are in fact detailed in the Hebrew HOLY TORAH and Christian Bible (New Testament) for anyone to read and observe. Yet, without works such as the BOOK OF THE DEAD, by Sir Ernest A. Wallis Budge; STOLEN LEGACY, by G. G.M. James; SIGNS AND SYMBOLS OF PRIMORDIAL MAN, by Dr. Albert C. Churchward; ANACALYPSIS (2 vols.), by Sir Godfrey Higgins; THE GOLDEN BOUGH, by Sir James Frazier; RUINS OF EMPIRES, by C. F. Volney, and a host of others to periodically consult and translate into 20th century C.E. understanding with respect to the teachings herein there would be more than enough reasons for the

---

1. Stolen Legacy has been quoted in many chapters and lecture-essays in this volume.

masses of people to remain ignorant of them.

The science of NUMEROLOGY, as practised by the Africans of Kimit before the arrival of the first European in central Africa to learn its rudiments, was fundamentally a religious development - but only in the sense of the usage of the word "RELIGION" in European-American context. Thus: The major factor which one has to overcome in order to truly comprehend the wealth of knowledge that is the African peoples' (everywhere) heritage is RELIGIOUS BIGOTRY, and more specifically the use of the term "HEATHEN" with regards to anything African which does not constitute what Judaeo-Christian or Muslim (Moslem) theologians (all of them conveniently forgetting that their own religious faith would not exist were it not for the fundamentals they stole from the same "Heathen" Africans) dictate to be GODLY or KOSHER and endorsed with their own SEAL OF GOOD RELIGION AND APPROVED THEOLOGY.

RELIGION that was not the Western-type (European and European-American) of organized capitalistic institutions serving as arms of national political entities, as observed by the student at this juncture, was responsible for all learning before the control of Rome over Christendom around 312 C.E. when Emperor Constantine "the great" became ruler of the Roman Empire of the East and West after having denuded himself of his own "DIVINE" significance. It is before this period that the STOLEN SECRETS were looted from the Grand Lodge of Luxor, other subordinate Lodges (universities) and libraries by Aristotle and company, and before them by Ionians and Persians who entered Greece (Pyrrhus) as teachers from their homelands (Egyptian colonies at the time).

If these basically fundamental factors revealed so far are constantly kept in mind, the students of AFRICAN, AFRICAN-AMERICAN and AFRICAN-CARIBBEAN history, or of any other AFRICAN PEOPLE THE WORLD OVER,* cannot fail but find in their further researches that MANDKIND AS A WHOLE ORIGINATED FROM A COMMON AFRICAN ANCESTOR and branched out from someplace around the African Great Lakes region of Central East and West Africa. And the High-Cultures of the White and Blue Nile Valleys, as well as the Atbara River Valley, only reached their zenith in Kush, Puanit, Nubia or Merowe, and Kimit to the north; and Zimbabwe, Swazi to the south; and Ghana, Melle (Mali), and Songhai (Songhay), etc., to the west because of the CREATIVE GENIUS AND RELIGIOUS DEVELOPMENT (both secular-material and spiritual) of people whom the so-called "Western man" or "modern man" (Light and Dark-Skinned Caucasian) of today still insultingly label "PYGMIES" while knowing too well that they are the TWA peoples; or "BUSHMEN" and "HOTTENTOTS," whom they know are KHOISAN peoples; and even "BANTUS" and "NEGROES " which they know are the same as all other African peoples regardless of which group has THIN or THICK LIPS, FRIZZLY or WOOLEN HAIR, POINTED or FLAT NOSE, BLACK or BROWN BURNT SKIN, or a combination of all of these physical traits which so-called "modern educators" have labled "RACES OF MANKIND" in their racism to establish their "LIGHT-SKINNED CAUCASIANS" as the choice selection of God, as a sort of "CHOOSEN PEOPLE OF JEHOVAH"* which the Haribus (Palestinians, Israelites, Jews, etc.) perpetuated in one of the earliest presentation of

---

* There are no such people as "NEGROES;"thus, no "NEGRO HISTORY" or "NEGRO STUDIES."

RACISM and RELIGIOUS BIGOTRY recorded in human history. (See Hebrew HOLY TORAH or Christian OLD TESTAMENT).*

The culmination of all that have been revealed in the previous chapters obviously relate directly to the research made in this chapter as to its origin. This is especially TRUE whether one is intellectualizing from an Anglo-Saxon, Anglo-Greek or Judaeo-Christian (European and European-American-style) foundation, as everyone of these nomenclatures had their origin in **ALKEBU-LAN** (which the Greeks and Romans renamed "Africa") by indigenous peoples whom the "FATHER OF EUROPEAN HISTORY - Herodotus described in his HISTORIES, Book II**, in the following manner:

> "THE COLCHIANS, EGYPTIANS AND ETHIOPIANS HAVE THICK LIPS, BROAD NOSES, WOOLY HAIR, AND THEY ARE BURNT OF SKIN."***

These ancient indigenous Africans ("Blacks, Negroes, Bantus" or whatever) from the dawn of the art of writing wrote on interior walls of their pyramids and on their papyri the famous words of this chapter's conclusion...

"MAN KNOW THYSELF"

Paraphrased: African peoples, know yourself and your glorious heritage from your "MOTHERLAND - ALKEBU-LAN.

---

*See Hebrew HOLY TORAH, also called Christian OLD TESTAMENT.
**Note that this quotation has been shown in other chapters of this volume.
***"BURNT OF SKIN" is an ancient expression for what is today called "BLACK SKIN", but not "DARK SKIN." The only people fitting such as description today are the so-called "BANTUS" and the "NEGROES" by European and European-American educators of varied disciplines.

WHO WERE THE ANCIENT INDIGENOUS AFRICANS OF KIMIT (Egypt or Sais)?

It is utterly impossible to understand why European and European-American "educators" would wonder about the physiognomy of the ancient Ethiopians and Egyptians[1] in view of the abundance of available data within their possession, most of which they illegally inherited from their ancestors who were pirates - called "discoverers" and "explorers," or slavers - called "entreprenuers". This fact is further accentuated when one considers that as early as the fifth (5th)-century before the Christian era (BCE or BC) Herodotus -- the Ionian (who became a Greek citizen after receiving his education in Kimit (Egypt)- made the people of Europe aware of the general indigenous population of north and northeast Africa's physical characteristics and colour of pigment. But, to expect everyone of the Africans on the continent of Africa to have "thick lips, broad nose," and "woolly hair," as Herodotus described them, one must equally expect that all Europeans (called "Caucasians") must have "thin lips, pointed nose, straight hair," and "blonde skin" with "blue eyes." The lack of 100% uniformity of facial characteristics among the so-called "Negroes" or "Negroids" is no less infrequent than that of the so-called "Caucasians" or "Caucasoids." If these truths can be properly observed without the general racist obsession that afflicted European and

---

1. "Egypt" and "Egyptians" are names given to this nation and its people by the ancient Haribus (Hebrews or Jews); just as "Africa" was given to them by the Romans and Greeks in place of the original Alkebu-lan the indigenous peoples called their continent. The correct name is Kimit or Sais; not even the current Misrair which the Arab conquerors call it today.

European-American thinking in their <u>Negrophobia</u> then, and only then, will it be possible to understand why the ancient Europeans (Greeks and Romans) of Herodotus' era called the indigenous Africans they encountered "ETHIOPIANS" -- literally "BLACKS."

Professor Gaston Maspero,[1] Albert Churchward M.D.,[2] and Sir Ernest A. Wallis Budge [3](called by many -- "<u>the most noted anthropologists and paleontologists of all times</u>") in their respective works have, without a shadow of doubt, articulated the above facts I have brought so far to your attention. Specifically Dr. Churchward in his ethnographical map shown on page 72 of this book, which has been supported by paleontologists from all over the world before colour prejudice became the established way-with-all it now is, has graphically demonstrated the unity and oneness of the people the ancient Romans and Greeks (European ancestors of the "modern Caucasians") identified and designated "ETHIOPIANS." It must be noted, however, that the word "ETHIOPIANS" (Blacks) came from the root -- "ETHIOPIA" (the nation) or the African "ITHIOP;" and that this word was originally used by the ancients of Europe to identify the entire continent now called "AFRICA," which the indigenous peoples had given the name "ALKEBU-LAN." Because of these facts, it is exceedingly strange that the United States of America's most distinguished Egyptologist of all times, Professor James Henry Breasted, Ph.D., equivocated over the same set of facts about the "Negroness" of certain

---
1. THE DAWN OF CIVILIZATION: EGYPT AND CHALDEA; STRUGGLE OF NATIONS; PASSING OF EMPIRES; and ART IN EGYPT; etc.
2. SIGNS AND SYMBOLS OF PRIMORDIAL MAN; THE ORIGIN AND EVOLUTION OF RELIGION; ARCANA OF FREEMASONRY; THE ORIGIN AND EVOLUTION OF THE HUMAN RACE; etc.
3. A HISTORY OF EGYPT; BOOK OF THE DEAD; THE FACIMILE OF ANI; THE GODS OF THE EGYPTIANS; OSIRIS; etc.

Africans which his forerunners found no reason to be protective of; this being inexcusable even when one takes into account the racist nature of the University of Chicago, Illinois (as most universities and other institutions of higher-learning), <u>Department of Oriental Studies</u> he established and developed.

Why is it necessary to specifically cite the late professor Breasted's works, especially his HISTORY OF EGYPT, and, THE DAWN OF CIVILIZATION. Because he, being <u>"the foremost"</u> of the European-American "Egyptologists," was most responsible for perpetuating the "Semitic"[1] and "Caucasian"[2] myth with respect to the indigenous "Ethiopians, Blacks, Negroes, Coloureds," or even "Niggers", of north Africa being of a different "race" than those of "Africa South of the Sahara." Of course professor Breasted astutely covered himself in the use of the quotation marks in most cases where he had occasion to mention the alleged differences between the "race" of the Egyptians, Nubians, Cushites (Ethiopians), Numidians, Carthagenians, Congolese, Puanits (Punts), Gandese, and other Africans. One can readily see the continued effects of the Breasted <u>Negromania</u> in the latest work by Frank M. Snowdon, Jr., Chairman of the Classics Department at Howard University, Washington, D.C., entitled, BLACKS IN ANTIQUITY, with the sub-title – <u>"Ethiopians in the Greco-Roman Experience</u>," published by the Belknap Press of Harvard University Press, Cambridge, Massachusetts, 1970.

---

1. A name from the mythical story of "Noah and the Flood" in the Hebrew Torah, the Book of Genesis. Allegedly the descendants of Shem, one of Noah's sons. Note that the Africans of Egypt existed thousands of years before this myth was concocted.
2. Allegedly the "superior race of mankind." Supposedly they have "the largest brain" found in all of mankind; etc.

In Mr. Snowden's work, which I wholeheartedly endorse with respect to historical information and exposure of certain truth hithertofore suppressed by European-American educators, there are to many references as to the allegedly different racial composition of the Ethiopians of Egypt and those of the other parts of the continent of Africa (Alkebu-lan). He, too, belatedly hedged and twisted in the very manner and fashion in order to avoid presenting a picture of the Egyptians (Ethiopians) being of the same "race" as all other so-called "Negroes" of today. He also failed to notice that he did not equally try to show that the Greeks and Romans were not uniformly "Caucasian" in their appearance either; yet, he had no problem in calling all of them "Caucasians." Mr. Snowden, even though trying to be impartial (whatever this is) in his great contribution to African, African-American and African-Caribbean Studies, so-called "Black Studies," nevertheless could not escape the taboos that permeated the national racist educational institutions and their teaching with respect to Caucasianism and Negroism in these United States of America from which we, everyone of us, developed our point of reference with regards to the emotional semantics of the verb -- "RACE." He, in my opinion, found it extraordinarily necessary to portray the measurements of nose, lips, and whatever else, to designate types of Ethiopians; when, in fact, the ancients made no such distinctions. The distinction the ancients made, he very adequately cited when he quoted their reference that precisely dealt with the "Ethiopians' color" in terms of they being that "much darker than Asians." Thus, he stated on page 109:

Further, if Diodorus' account of Ethiopians

who lived near the Nile is derived from Agatharchides, he may be recording a Ptolemaic description of the "<u>pure</u>" <u>Negro</u>.[1] The majority of Nile-dwelling Ethiopians, according to Diodorus, were black, flat-nosed, and ulotrichous.

But, what is a "pure Negro" or "pure Caucasian"? At what point did either begin? And, where did they originate?

It is impossible to expect that the same professors, who have for generations assisted in the suppression of African peoples' history and culture, especially with regards to the education of the earliest Europeans by Africans, would have changed their color like chameleons do. now that many of the Africans (Ethiopians or Black people) have uncovered much of the data in the timely work of Mr. Snowden. The United States of America's institutions of higher-learning, regardless if Black or White controlled, Anglo-Saxon Judaeo-Christian and Greek centric as they are, equally make it appear impossible for any approved works containing the endorsement of such institutions' trustees not to maintain the status quo of the "superiority" of the European or "Caucasian (White) race" over the African or "Negro (Black) race," and all other "races." It is because of the presentation of the Ethiopians' (Blacks) history in the manner, such as we find in professor Breasted's and Gerald Massey's works, which compel many Africans and African-Americans to maintain that European-Americans cannot teach "<u>Black Studies Courses</u>" to the satisfaction of people of African origin. Certainly anyone can remember dates and events, and then prattle them off before students who may be less aware of their occurence. But, it is the interpretation of

---

[1]. Words in brackets by the writer of this lecture for specific emphasis and clarity only. The word "race" is being used here

said data which makes the major difference between the African-American and the European-American instructors with respect to "Black Studies" or "White Studies", the latter of which we (Black people) must all submit ourself from the very first day of our educational experience, whether public or private, religious or secular.

When will it be that the Africans' contributions to the Europeans, and the world in general, would not have to be prefixed by the racist terms -- "SEMITIC" and "HAMITIC," or even "CAUCASIAN;" words that were created specifically to <u>minimize</u>, and in most cases <u>deny</u>, the Africans (Ethiopians) role in world history? Is it so damaging to European-Americans ego or cique that they cannot accept their African cultural heritage ever being controlled by people with "<u>thick lips, wide nose, woolly hair</u>" and <u>black skin;</u>" but can accept an "<u>ape-like ancestor</u>" instead? At least, they should be able to note that the Egyptian-type they are willing to accept as their ancestors only differs to the so-called "Negroes" and "Bantus" in variations of darkness and lightness; all of which are only <u>shades of black</u>. The other extremes are only with respect to language construction and religion; nevertheless generally having the same Nile Valleys and Great Lakes cultural root-base. It is unfortunate for the European-Americans that they were not satisfied with NEANDERTHAL MAN. If they were, and would have stopped at that point, then no problem of claim-

---

in context on the subject matter, and is not an acceptable value of this writer and lecturer. Equally, the word "Negro" is as repugnant to people of African origin who are aware of their very rich heritage and contributions to world civilizations, and in particular to the Europeans and European-Americans -- the so-called "Modern man."

ing BOSKOP MAN, ZIMBABWE (Rhodesia) MAN, BROKEN HILL MAN, ZINJANTHROPUS boisie, and other African fossil-man, in the center and southern parts of Alkebu-lan (Africa). But, in trying to establish their superiority, without leaving any trace or doubt of same, they have continuously unearthed truths that show themselves to be relatively recent in time of culture; the end result being their having to claim many of their so-called "Negro, Bantu, Pygmy, Bushman", and "Hottentot" brothers and sisters, and of course many of the "inferiors" of Asia also; especially the so-called "Indo-European Aryans." Even Adolph Hitler of Nazis Germany found it impossible to have his "pure Aryan race" without adopting some of the Asian "inferiors." These non-Caucasians, both of Africa and Asia, of yellow, brown, and black skin, have the historic background into antiquity that surpassed the Homeric and Greco-Roman experience of which Mr. Snowden wrote in his book, BLACKS IN ANTIQUITY...etc.

It is incumbent upon African-American scholars of Black Studies programs to do much more research; to write beyond the scope of the so-called "New Left Revolution;" and interpret their own history and experience in terms of their own values of "right" and "wrong;" and, of course, criticize all of the works relating to the African peoples and their descendants the world over. This would, definitely, require that such scholars place before their thrust for academic tenure in the various colleges, the quality of the data they desire to desiminate to their younger Black brothers and sisters, also those less fortunate in educational skills; and above all, publish their own works. So far I have been unable to observe in the so-called "Black Studies Courses" around at most campuses -- white or black -- material information beyond the rhetoric of instant revolution; no priority being given the historical achievements of the Africans and their descendants. Yet, those who have distracted young African-Americans from this latter course of their heritage have been busy doing extra-time work writing and teaching about the history of the so-called "Negro." However, would there have been any need for "cultural" or "political revolution" today if historical records of the Africans' experience over the world were not kept; records of events passed , but relevant to the African peoples who were brought to the "Western World" by force, and those who came as explorers before the arrival of the European to the shores of either North or South America?

Returning to professor Gaston Maspero's work, THE DAWN OF CIVILIZATION: EGYPT AND CHALDEA, published by the Society For Promoting Christian Knowledge, London, England, 1901 (as translated by M. L. McClure, member of the Committee of the Egypt Exploration Fund), Fourth Edition, page 398; he stated:

> "...the House of the Books" was doubtless, in the first place, a depository of official documents..., etc.

In the same paragraph he also stated that:

> ...it contain·ed also, however, literary works, many of which even at this early date were already old, prayers drawn up during the first dynasties, devout poetry belonging to times prior to the misty personage called mini-hymns to the gods of light, formulae of black magic, collections of mystical works, such as the Book of the Dead[1] and the "Ritual of the Tomb;" scientific treaties on medicine, geometry, mathe-

---
1. See Maspero, Etudes sur la Mythologie, etc., vol. i, pp. 367, 369; and Budge, Book of the Dead, and, Papyrus of Ani.

matics, and astronomy; manual of practical morals; and lastly, romance, or those marvellous stories which preceded the romance among Oriental Peoples.

To the average student today in BLACK STUDIES, equally to those in WHITE STUDIES, the above facts are confusing in many of the following respects:

a) The Egyptians were not known to have had "short stories" or " novels;"
b) "romance stories" were "only written by Orientals in ancient times;"
c) "magic is a heathen development" of the Africans south of the Sahara.

Both Black and White students were, and still are, taught these lies from elementary grades through their encounter with institutions of higher-learning. Never-the-less, even African-American (Black) professors of history, on the whole, do not challenge these age-old "WHITE LIES;" they, being too busy in their involvement with revolutionary rhetoric of the THIRD WORLD before they consentrate on revolutionizing their own mind and culture. These inconsistencies by "educators" forces one to query if the so-called "THIRD REVOLUTION" introduced to African-American students on campuses is not an attempt by the so-called "NEW LEFT," and their "OLD LEFT" financiers, to deter Blacks from their African heritage and independent political answer to meet their own particularized problems within the United States of America. I find it, also, a willful attempt to distract the Africans from a possible, natural and most desirable political affiliation with their brothers and sisters in the Caribbean and Africa towards an inter-continental brotherhood of African peoples. Strange as it is equally, that most of the latest of the so-called Black converts to the "New Left" found "cultural nationalism" offensive when young African-Americans show admiration for their own brother and hero -- Marcus Moziah Garvey, but ask them to revere Karl Marx Mao Tu Tsung and Che Guevera. However, it must be understood, I am not saying that it is inconsistent for an African-American to be a "New Left" supporter and at the same time giving some devotion towards his African heritage. What I am saying, is; everyone of their European-American and Asian-American co-leftist revolutionist, whether they were formerly attached to Judaism, Christianity, Islam, Bhuddism, or any other religious persuasion, have received their won indoctrination in their own cultural heritage and religion while they were still children in their home or religious institutions; and, of course the European-Americans and Asian-Americans were forced to study European and European-American history and culture -- "White Studies" or "White Power" -- the first day they entered public or private school, paroachial or secular, in everyone of the States of the United States of America.

In examining the map presented to you; what kind of superficial or material barrier can you discover which the ancient peoples of Alkebu-lan (Africa) did not know existed before the arrival of the European and European-American "educators" that discovered them thousands of years later? Does it indicate that there was any kind of racial, religious, or cultural barrier between the various Africans to prevent their amalgamation with each other; or that there were "Semites of Egypt, Negroes of Nubia," or "Hamites of Puanit" (Punt)?[1]

---

1. See page 133 of BLACK MAN OF THE NILE for map.

In BLACK MAN OF THE NILE, pages 4 and 5, I cited how one of European-America's chief exponent of Caucasianism (both "light" and "dark-skinned") entraped his ownself with his "Negro Enigma." At least this particular professor ("educator"), Dr. M. D. W. Jeffreys, did not find it necessary to hide behind quotation marks like those before him such as professor James Henry Breasted in his book, A HISTORY OF EGYPT, also in his, THE DAWN OF HISTORY.

Diodorus, Agatharchides and Artemidorus drew distinctions between types of Ethiopians, as stated by Mr. Snowden on page 109 of BLACKS ANTIQUITY ...., etc. He wrote:

> At any rate, Diodorus makes a clear distinction between savage, squalid Ethiopians and civilized Ethiopians not described in Agatharchides.

This does not in any way, manner or form, indicate different racial origin or stock on the part of either. Moreover, it was the Puanits (African peoples of Punt) whom the Africans of Egypt (Romiti) said were the:

> "..best diviners, pleasers of the Gods...,"etc.;

and next to them were the Ethiopians -- the same Africans Diodorus said were:

> "...black, flat-nosed, and ulotrichous...,"etc.;

and of whom Herodotus also said:

> "...have thick lips, broad nose, woolly hair, and they are burnt of skin."

Why is it conveniently forgotten that Herodotus also included the "Colchians" and "Egyptians" in the same description? The answer is, obviously, that the Europeans and European-Americans, whose desire it is to 'Caucasianize' and 'Semitize' all origins of the peoples of antiquity. did not know that the ancient Egyptians received their education from other indigenous Africans south of Egypt -- Nubia, Kush or Cush (Ethiopia), Bonyoro, Puanit, Zimbabwe, Congo, Monomotapa, etc. Because they did not have such information at the time when they were claiming "Egyptian ancestry" and "heritage," they were at the same instance claiming "Negro" and "Bantu heritage" which they must now make either "Caucasoid, Nilotic," or "Semitic." As such, they even resurrected their own term -- "Hamitic," which they had once used in describing Africans who are now called "Negro, Bantu, African South of the Sahara, Black African, Pygmy, Coloured," and even "Nigger" and a host of equally derogatory terms which they created for the continued perpetuation of chattel slavery and colonialism. How, despite all of the recent anthropological-archaeological discoveries being made throughout the African continent, can anyone in an African-American institution of professorship status continue perpetuating the same myth? The only reason for it is the fact that the African-American professors, most of us, have taken the path of least resistance and copied our master's voice, mannerisms and racism at their worse.

The late professor George G. M. James in his most outstanding work on the Africans of Egypt and their development of that which is still being called "Greek philosophy," which he entitled STOLEN LEGACY (published by the New York Philosophical Library, New York, 1954), on the title page, gave the answer to the Ethiopian-Negro fiasco still apparent in Mr. Snowden's otherwise timely book, BLACKS IN ANTIQUITY, etc. Professor James stated:

> "THE GREEKS WERE NOT THE AUTHORS OF GREEK PHILOSOPHY, BUT THE PEOPLE OF NORTH AFRICA, COMMONLY CALLED THE EGYPTIANS."

Professor James continued his citations on some of the tactics used by so-called "Western educators" to plagiarize and otherwise co-opt the indigenous Africans of Egypt and other Nile Valleys and Great Lakes African works; and even pointed out the earliest of the Greeks with whom the practice originated, such as Aristotle. For this reason professor James' historic and monumental achievement is not being reprinted; whereas thousands of other works of degrading contents, which still depict African peoples in terms of "Hamites" and "Semites , Negroids" and "Caucasoids," etc., are reproduced by the millions daily for use in Black Studies and African-Studies courses which, for the most part, are still controlled by European-Americans bearing the label "progressive" and/or "liberal."

Quoting professor James once more, from the INTRODUCTION on page 1; he wrote:

> "CHARACTERISTICS OF GREEK PHILOSOPHY
> The term Greek Philosophy, to begin with is a misnomer, for there is no such philosophy in existence. The ancient Egyptians had developed a very complex religious system, called the Mysteries, which was also the first system of salvation.

Like professor George G.M. James, professor James Henry Breasted also cited the origin of civilization and the beginning of philosophical thoughts on page 3 of his major work, A HISTORY OF EGYPT, Chapter I, under the sub-title : THE LAND. He wrote the following:

> The roots of modern civilization are planted deeply in highly elaborate life of theose nations which rose into power over six-thousand years ago, in the basin of the eastern Mediterranean, and the adjacent regions on the east of it. Had the Euphrates finally found its way into the Mediterranean, toward which, indeed, it seems to have started, both the early civilizations, to which we refer, might have been in-

cluded in the Mediterranean basin. As it is, the
scene of early oriental history does not fall
entirely within that basin, but must be designated as the eastern Mediterranean region."

Of course professor Breasted's dramatic proclamation was not intended to benifit the Africans of the Mediterranean limits of north Africa; to the contrary, he was only trying to establish the so-called "Indo-Europeans" link with antiquity and the origin of the people of "civilizations" beginning with the so-called "Garden of Eden." This, one must remember, was written at a period in history when the Euphrates and Tigris valleys were considered "the original home of the first man" which they gave the name "ADAM;" a theory long-since proven in total error with the unearthing of fossil-man in various parts of east-central Africa, Southern Africa, Northern Africa, Australia, Asia, and numerous islands of the world. It is for the same reason why works such as professor Breasted's have proven so timely in equating these later texts that tend to differ with the exper-

iences of men such as Herodotus, and other Greeks, who as early as c457-450 BCE described the indigenous people of Kimit or Egypt in a manner that could be only identical to Africans of today -- called derogatorily "Negroes, Bantus, Coloured Folks, Africans South of the Sahara," and even "Niggers" in the United States of America in particular.

One can cite the Hebrew (or Jewish) Holy Torah, the Christian Old Testament- for similar reasons. For if the Africans, "Ethiopians" according to the ancients, of Kimit are to be compared equally to the so-called "Negroes;" then Moses (or Moshe, also an African, and his Kushite or Cushite wife --"the daughter of the High-Priest of Cush"-- must be declared "Negroes", etc., as the other indigenous Africans "South of the Sahara". And, if Moses and his Cushite wife were "Ethiopians", "Negroes"; what were his brother--Aaron and sister--Miriam ? It would also mean that at least two of the most noted key leaders of the Hebrew, or Jewish, people--those called "Choosen People"--were "Negroes"; not "Caucasians" or "Semites", or even "Hamites". It would further tie the present Europeans and European-Americans, who prefer to call themselves "Semites" whenever it is convenient to so do, forgetting that the so-called "Hamites" also came from the same a ancestors as they did. Also, that the "HAMITES" were given the name "NEGROES" by White Jews because God-Jehovah, "...turned them black for staring at their "grandfather's nakedness". A myth that had its origin in the BOOK OF GENESIS' racism; this is, providing that the BOOK OF GENESIS' of First Book of Moses, and the BOOK OF EXODUS, or Second Book of Moses, are in fact "truth". And, if these two biblical books are truthful, as the rabbis declare they are; then the "children of Cush (Ethiopia of modern times) and those of "Ham" (once identified as "Negroes") are equally related to the present "SEMITES" in the United States of America, the State of Israel, Europe, South America, and elswhere, by virtue of the same ancestor, "NOAH".

As one penetrates deeper into the reason why European-Americans find it compulsory to separate "Ethiopians" from "Negroes" to suit the racist myth of an alleged "superior Caucasian" or "Indo-European Aryan race", it is equally proven that racism is

---

1. Allegedly indigenous Africans who are black and fit the same description given by Herodotus but not related to "Negroes".
2. This classification has been given already. There is not a single justification for its usage to African peoples.

not the only criteria of protection involved; therfore, they should be no reason why anyone should be astonished by the fact that more people bearing the name or label "Semite" are involved in the production and writing of what they believe to be the "Black man's history;" also establishing their own version of the "Black man's" TRUTH about his history and cultural heritage for <u>Black Studies Courses</u> of which, for the most part, they now control. Yet, they protest vehemently when "non-Semites" try to do likewise towards their cultural, religious, and historical past and present operation. It is, therefore, time for the African-Americans, the Black peoples of the United States of America, as elsewhere, to raise their voice in righteous indignation against this type of cultural and historical genocide they are being subjected to regardless of the charges of "anti-Semitism" which will naturally follow. Or, is it that "anti-Semitism" is worse than "anti-Blackism", or even "anti-Negroism"? The same holds true for those other European-Americans of the so-called "Indo-European Aryan (Caucasian) race," who otherwise call themselves "Gentiles, Christian Anglo-Saxons," etc., but find it compelling to attach themselves to African origins of North Africa, the Nile Valleys, and the African Great Lakes; all of which are African High-Cultures (civilizations) that are indigenous to the so-called "Negroes" (Ethiopians).

How can these guidelines be brought into workable operation? This is but one of the many questions African-American historians, sociologists, anthropologists, scholars of all sorts, and others in general, continue to ask. Most never stop to realize that they have to avoid being underwritten by the same people who are the ones that approve their manuscripts and publish their works. In cold hard facts, <u>to tell it like it is</u>, African-Americans in the field of "Black Studies" and "African Studies" have to <u>research, write, edit, finance and publish</u> their own works, also <u>distribute</u> it. Anything short of either of these controls negates the entire possibility of the "<u>truth</u>" about the African people **ever** reaching African-American students and the Black communities in general. Even very <u>well-meaning Whites</u>, the so-called "third world people, liberals," and "progressives, cannot be trusted with the responsibility of writing and making appraisal of the <u>true</u> history of the African peoples' past and present contributions to the world's High-Culture (civilization). Equally it must be observed that Africans, regardless of designations by Europeans and European-Americans, cannot expect to write the <u>true</u> history of European peoples and Asians, or any-other people , without having to withstand the same type of objective indignation on their part. For history is nothing more than a socio-political and philosophical interpretation of the makings of the past and present, and preparations for the future .

In order to fully comprehend my position, one must realize that all history were, and are, written to project the individual writer's bias or socio-political nationalism in terms of cultural contributions or the lack of it. Why then should the African people , whether they be in the "Western World,"Europe, or the "Eastern World," be expected in this area or discipline, as in all other areas, to act beyond the human capacity of all other peoples of the planet Earth and ignore their cultural genocide being perpetuated by others without righteous indignation on

their part? Why ask them to continually promise to obey the call
of the honored Reverend Doctor Martin Luther King, Jr.'s doctrine
that has been proven the not so good way-with-all end to any of
the African-American problems? Why ask African-Americans to obey
his call of:

"...IF ANY BLOOD IS TO BE SHED, LET IT BE OURS."
The African (or Ethiopian) peoples have already shed to many billions of gallons of physical and mental blood , not to mention
spiritual blood, for all other groups during their own enslavement under the Arabs (Asians) and "Westerners" (Europeans, European-Americans, and Britishers -- Irish, Scots, Welch, English),
from the early c640 C.E. or 18 A.H. - when the Arab Muslims invaded northern and eastern Africa from their homeland in the
Arabian Peninsula; and with the beginning of the Europeans degradation of the African-Moors (Maueritanians) by placing them
into slavery on the Island of Hispañiola (Hayte or Haiti) in
the year 1503 C.E.; followed by the enslavement of the Moors'
brothers and sisters from lower western Africa by the same Europeans during 1506 C.E.; and finally by the European-Americans in
the year 1619 or 1620 C.E. at Jamestown, Virginia, during British
colonial days, to the present 1970's in a state of mental slavery.

This type of appraisal of the Black man's experience may be
considered rather "militant" by some, "reverse racism" by others,
and even "stagnant cultural nationalism" by others yet. Never-the-less, Mr. Snowden appearently did not have in mind either
when this citation was but a mere thought; neither did his work
so become after its editorial completion and final publication.
What it does represent however, so far as this professor is con-

cern, is an open expression by an African-American (Ethiopian) in an attempt to appriase his fellow Ethiopians (brothers and sisters all), who may not have known of the age-old game that is still being perpetuated against African peoples origin in order to maintain the subtle alleged "superiority of the Caucasian race. (which includes "Semites, Hamites, Caucasoids," etc., over their own created "Negroes" and "Bantus" south of the Sahara.

African-American "educators", if such we are, should, and must be able and willing to be counted on this very stance. If not; upon what basis do we justify our continued outcry for what we erringly call "BLACK STUDIES COURSES," instead of 'AFRICAN, AFRICAN-AMERICAN, and AFRICAN-CARIBBEAN STUDIES,' in every level of institutionalized public and private education, secular or parochial, in these United States of America and its colonies in the Caribbean and the Pacific? Or, are we just fooling ourselves and following the latest educational fad that is similar to the sacredness of the so-called "integration of the races" we have become so acoustomed, and of which we once felt was the way-with-all to the solution of the problems of our master-slave relationship; this having been proven disasterously fatal before. Are we to continue as the disciples of "racial integration" still do, knowing to well that the society in which we still slave has no intent of recognizing us on par with the descendants of our former slavemasters? Maybe it is possible that we are not saying either. And probably all we are about is the begging into a system that has time and time again said it wants us not - on any term which we can be expected to enter under? Further still, it may be that the story in the African-American Spiritual, otherwise labeled "NEGRO SPIRITUAL," by European-Americans, and adopted by the so-called "Negroes;" requiring that...

> "...Moses" (an African Black man or Ethiopian) "go down in Egypt land and tell ole pharoah" (Rameses II, another black man) "let my people go,"...etc.,

is still to remain a biblical "<u>truth</u>" against one African people's enslavement of another that had no significant historical involvement with the Africans' enslavement in what is today called the West Indies and the <u>United States of America</u>. How could this be? How could European-American and European Jews be involved with this "<u>African Spiritual</u>" and their African Hebrew (Israelite) counterparts are excluded; and, in fact, it was supposed to have taken place in Africa - Alkebu-lan? How could this African, Moses, be related to European and European-American Jews, but not to African-American Israelites who are descended from the same Ethiopian source of origin from whence Moses sprung? How could Moses' Cushite wife, an Ethiopian in color, not produce Ethiopian ("Negro") offspring? These questions must be answered forthrightly by the so-called "Africanists" of European and European-American origin; and of course by Black professors who are assigned to <u>Black Studies</u> and <u>African Studies</u> courses. No amount of evading the issue will provide a safe hiding place for fence-stratling Blacks anymore on this biblical myth. For "young, black, and gifted," also "beautiful", African-America will not tolerate us in that light any longer. Therefore, it is incumbent upon those of us who are not willing to lead the struggle in that direction to hurriedly <u>get off the pot</u> and let those who are willing captain the helm, whether to sink or to swim.

This paper, or lecture-essay, like so many others I have

presented to several gatherings bearing the title "CONVENTION, CONFERENCE," etc., "OF BLACK SCHOLARS," etc., I suspect, will again be received and meet the same fate of all of the others; that is, <u>the waste paper basket</u>. Never-the-less, I must continue this fight for African (or Ethiopian) cultural redemption which others of noted greatness· such as Joel A. Rogers, Professor Leo Hansberry, Professor George, G. M. James, Dr. Carter G. Woodso , Dr. William E. B. DuBois, Professor Hubert H. Harrison, Dr. Wilmot E. Blyden, Author Olonzo Schomberg, and numerous others like them, have already started and distinguished themselves. All of these "<u>literary greats</u>" had trouble in one form or another in projecting their work to the African-American, African-Caribbean, and general African or Ethiopian population of the entire European and European-American dominated educational system of the colonial people's world. The course they have taken in order to accomplish this end may have to be diverted somewhat. Never-theless, we must follow religiously the ultimate result; that is, the "<u>Africans Right To Be Wrong</u>," even in the writing of his history and heritage - the same as all other peoples have done. For what is a people without their own interpretation of their history and experience?

Again, I must close this lecture with the age-old African (or Ethiopian, Black Man) maxim (or proverb) found in the pyramids, (or tombs) of our ancestors of Kimit (or Egypt) and others along the Lower Nile Valley, and on papyri held in the various museums, libraries and other private and public institutions in Europe, European-America, Great Britain (Ireland, Scotland, Wales, England), and elsewhere; which say to Alkebu-lan peoples:
"MAN...,KNOW THYSELF."

CHAPTER VI

REFLECTIONS ON ANCIENT KIMIT (SAIS OR EGYPT) HISTORY
(Upper and Lower Nile - Blue & White - and Atbara Valleys)

A Brief Chonological Review of Nile Valley Achievements:

10,000 BCE   Man's first calendar was introduced by the Africans along the Nile Valleys (Blue and White, also Atbara River). This major feat was only topped by the Africans' of Monomotapa's sculpture of a human figure carved about 30,000 B.C.E., and their iron mine of 43,000 B.C.E. The carving is presently misnamed "VENUS OF DUSSELDORF" by Europeans - and remains in the Museum of Vienna, Austria.[1]

5,000   The oldest and most noted statue of man and beast combined was worshipped as HORUS. This statue is still the greatest of <u>the wonders of the world</u> - The SPHINX OF GHIZEH. It was also worshipped as HARMACHIS - <u>The Sun God of Life and Light</u>.[2]

4,100   Introduction of the first SOLAR CALENDAR by the Africans of the empires of Kimit and Kush (Egypt and Ethiopia). It had $365\frac{1}{4}$ days to the year, 4 months to the season, 3 seasons to the year. See page 158 BLACK MAN OF THE NILE; compare it with the current Europeanized version.

3,200   The Paleolithic (Old Stone Age) Period; Neolithic (Old Stone Age) Period; The Prehistoric Epoch; The Tasian Period; The Badavian Period; and the PreDynastic Period. The PreDynastic Period introduced the first of the Pharoahs of Kimit - AHA, also called Narnmer, and changed to "MENES" by the Greeks . This was a period when the earliest of the European greats - HOMER - was still unborn, and Greek "<u>civilization</u>" was non-existent.

2,900   Africans from northern and eastern Africa (Alkebu-lan) invaded and established the Kingdom of ELAM in the Empire of Persia.[3] One of their first Kings was KUDAR NAKUNTAR who captured the Chaldeans and dominated them with his thousands of African troops. This was about 1,200 or more years before the birth of the first Haribu (Hebrew or "<u>Jew</u>") - ABRAHAM in the City of UR, Chaldea. It means that Africans by the thousands ruled Chaldea, amalgamated with the Chaldeans, before there was the first Haribu. Thus there was a "NEGRO, BANTU", etc., kingdom in Asia before the so-called "DARK-SKINNED CAUCASIANS" arrived in Kimit and other parts of North and East Africa. Is it possible this amalgamation in fact caused the origin of the "LIGHT" and "DARK-SKINNED" Caucasians one reads so much about in "Western educators" accounts of North and East African history?

2,780 The PYRAMID AGE. This period should have extended back a little earlier as there were many minor pyramids built all along the more than 4,100 mile White and Blue Nile extension of the Nile that continues from Atbara in Nubia all the way to the Kimit Sea (Mediterranean Sea). There are also smaller ones in the Kongo (Congo) and parts south of this area along the Great Lakes region, and at Monomotapa in the south. However, this title should only be representative of the age which brought the designing, planning, and building of the greatest ones; thus: The FIRST STEP PYRAMID AT SAKKARAH (also spelled "Saqqara" by Westerners) by the architect - Imhotep, under the reign of Pharoah Djoser[4] (Zoser or Zozer as renamed by the Greeks during their rule) between 2,780 - 2,680 B.C.E. (Ist pharoah of the IIIrd Dynasty); the PYRAMID OF KHUFU (the Greeks renamed him "Cheops" or "Kheops", pharoah during 2,680-2,658 (Old Kingdom - between the IInd and IVth Dynasties); the PYRAMID OF KHAFRA (the Greeks renamed him "Chephren") between the periods following Khufu; and the PYRAMID OF MYCERINUS, same period and dynasties as Khafra. The chief architect of the Step Pyramid - Imhotep[5] (The Step Pyramid at Sakkarah or Saqqara) supposedly built it with stones taken from quarries that were opened by Pharoah Semerkhet about 3,200 to 2,780 B.C.E. - 420 years before Pharoah Djoser's reign.

2,685 The GRAND LODGE OF LUXOR* was built at Danderah by Pharoah Khufu during the IIIrd Dynasty. This area is presently called Lower Egypt. It is also known as the TEMPLES OF THE ANCIENT CITY OF THEBES. The measurements of said structure were 2,000 feet long by 1,000 feet at its base, in an oblong shape (like a hen's egg) which all Masonic-type lodges copied. Here within these walls of the Grand Lodge of Luxor the fundamentals of the basic rituals of freemasonry and most 20th century "Western" secret societies were established.[6] The ancient Greeks, including Herodotus, visited this institution for their basic and advanced learning in philosophy, religion, engineering, history, medicine, etc. (See C.H. Vail, ANCIENT MYSTERIES; George G. McJames, STOLEN LEGACY; Max Muller, EGYPTIAN MYTHOLOGY; Plato, APOLOGY; Eva B. Standford, MEDITERRANEAN WORLD).[7]

---
*See footnotes for Luxor above on page 476 of this volume.

SOME OF THE SUBORDINATE LODGES OF THE GRAND LODGE OF LUXOR* IN ALKEBU-LAN, ASIA, EUROPE, AND ISLANDS

1) Mount Carmel (Palestine).[8]
2) Mount Lebanon (Syria).
3) Media (Near the Red Sea).
4) Babylon (Around the Tigris and Euphrates Valleys).
5) The Ganges (India).
6) Burma.
7) Athenian Lodge (Greece).
8) Rome.
9) Croton.
10) Rhodes.
11) Delphi.
12) Miletus.
13) Cyprus.
14) Corinth.
15) Crete.
16) Kush (in the City of Axum).
17) Zimbabwe (Monomotapa).
18) Punt (Somaliland).
19) Khart Haddas (Carthage).
20) Numidia.
21) Mauritis.
23) Kongo.

For the best information with relationship to the <u>Grand Lodge of Luxor</u> Eva M. Sandford's book, MEDITERRANEAN WORLD, pp. 135-139, is recommended. Other works in the footnote of this page should also prove most helpful, especially Churchward's and James'. However, the student must be very careful not to assume that the <u>Grand Lodge of Luxor</u> and the <u>anti-Grand Lodge of Delfi</u> are the same Lodge. There were times when both Lodges were used for the

---

*Note that all modern "secret lodges" (orders) in the so-called "Western World" are still patterned after these lodges, especially those of Palestinian origin after King Solomon's Grand Lodge. Yet, it must be carefully remembered that King Solomon, like Jesus Christ, attended the subordinate lodge called "MOUNT CARMEL", where each was "initiated" and served their "apprenticeship", etc. Luxor was the same Grand Lodge during the time when the other major Lodge of Delfi (Delphi) was burnt to the ground in 548 B.C.E. by foreigners who were jealous of the Africans' (the so-called "NEGROES, BANTUS," etc.) knowledge of the MYSTERIES - which included studies in the disciplines of science, religion, philosophy, mathematics, astronomy, astrology, triangulation, and others not mentioned here. (See James Hastings, ENCYCLOPEDIA OF RELIGION AND ETHICS; Thomas Stanley, HISTORY OF PHILOSOPHY; Diogenes Laertius, LIVES OF EMINENT PHILOSOPHERS; Dr. Albert C. Churchward, ORIGINS OF FREEMASONRY; A.C. Churchward, SIGNS AND SYMBOLS OF PRIMORDIAL MAN; G.G.M. James, STOLEN LEGACY.

same purpose and held in the same esteem when the MYSTERIES SYSTEM in Kimit was at its zenith. This was caused by the great amount of priests who did not have subordinate Lodges where they could be sent. John Kendrick's ANCIENT EGYPT, Book II, p. 363 should be examined with respect to this point in question.

2,400   The TEMPLE OF CARMAK, "<u>the most pompous of the Chapters of the Secret Societies of the Mysteries System</u>", was built at a distance of one-half (½) mile from the Grand Lodge of Luxor. Separated on both sides of its main entrance was an aisle with double rows of sphinxes twelve (12) feet apart. The width of the aisle was sixty (60) feet. In its perfection it was considered to be "...<u>the most magnificent architectural and landscape scene the world had ever witnessed</u>..."

2,340   Four different expeditions of Egyptian pharoahs left Egypt for visits to Nubia (Sudan) and Punt (Somaliland).[9] Their exploits were revealed as part of the African history found on the TOMB OF THE NOBLEMAN OF ASWAN. With regards to some of the journeys the following was written on a stelae:

      THE PHAROAH MERNERE MADE THREE VOYAGES.
             PEPI II MADE ONE.*

2,300   Imhotep of Kimit (Egypt or Sais), whom the Greeks and Romans of the ancient world called "AESCALAPIUS", was known to them as the GOD OF MEDICINE; he was so known to the rest of the ancient world. He was the first man in history recorded as a "PHYSICIAN" (2870-2680 B.C.E.). The Greeks and Romans, after other Africans and Asians, followed his era and learned from the works and writings he left mankind; these they learned from Africans in Kimit and Kush (Egypt and Ethiopia) as well as others who went to said nations for their education. Imhotep was also PRIME MINISTER under Pharoah Djoser (Zozer).[10] He was known to the Greeks and Romans as "THE PRINCE OF PEACE" over two-thousand and eighty-seven (2,087) years before the Christians' JESUS CHRIST was called "...THE PRINCE OF PEACE" (and the same before he was even born from his mother's Mary womb, whether through an "IMMACULATE CONCEPTION" or by simple "SEXUAL INTERCOURSE"

---

*See Dr. Arkell, HISTORY OF THE SUDAN.

by his father and mother - Joseph and Mary). Imhotep
was the foremost architect of the known world during
his lifetime, and designed the first STEP PYRAMID, also
many other modern structures of his era. (see page 317
of Chapter VI of this volume for pictures of Imhotep and
the first Step Pyramid of Sakkarah). It is Imhotep who
was credited with being the originator of the following
maxim:

EAT DRINK AND BE MERRY, FOR TOMORROW WE DIE.

Imhotep ("<u>Aescalapius</u>" according to the Greeks) lived
more then two-thousand three hundred (2,300) years before
the Europeans' "FATHER OF MEDICINE" - Hippocrates. Yet,
"<u>Western</u>" historians and other educators continue teaching that:

THE GREEKS WERE THE FIRST PHYSICIANS.

2,300   The oldest and first known records of a journey from
Aswan to Lower Kimit (Egypt) were written. It dealt
with Pharoah Mennere's ambassador's (the son of the
High-Priest of Ritual Ceremonies, named Iri) trip to
the KINGDOM OF YAM. The purpose was to commence the
building of a highway between Yam and Kimit, by way of
Mennere. The second journey of King (Pharoah) Mennere's
Ambassador on the Aswan Road (from Irthet to Mekher) to
Tereres and back to Irthet was a trip that totalled more
than eight (8) months' duration. (See J.H. Breasted,
ANCIENT RECORDS OF EGYPT, Chicago, Vol. I, pp. 333-336
and 353, 1906.)

1,555   Queen Hatshepsut (daughter of Pharoah Thotmes I) was
born.[11] She ruled as one of Egypt's most efficient monarchs. Her fame was known to the ancient world during
her own lifetime. She too made a trip to Punt (modern
Somaliland), Kush (modern Ethiopia), and Nubia (modern
Sudan) in c1490 B.C.E.[12]
During this same period the earliest known PRESCRIPTION
for FERTILITY CONTROL (Planned Parenthood or Birth Control) was developed. It could be seen in the British
Museum of London, England, under the title "EBERS PAPYRUS".
For a sample of this recipe see page 159, Chapter VI, BLACK
MAN OF THE NILE.

Amen-hotep IV, also known as Akhenaten (or Ikhnaten, and
other variations) was also born during this period.[13] He
was known to the ancients as the "RELIGIOUS KING". Way
back in the periods before the birth of the Christians'
JESUS CHRIST (God) Akhenaten spoke of a "TRINITARIAN

GOD". He called said God the "VIRTUES", or the "GOD IN THREE VIRTUES". He described the "VIRTUES" as:

LOVE, SOUL, AND BODY.*

He was not much of a politician or forceful man. This was at a time when Kimit needed a powerful leader to stem the tide of encroachments along her borders and the gnawing away of her foreign colonies. He made her weak militarily, and started her on a course of eventual downfall from "...THE MOST FEARED POWER OF HER TIME AND LEADER OF THE WORLD'S GREATEST HIGH-CULTURE".
The Africans' of the Nile Valley - Kimit, Nubia, Kush - <u>Fertility Control Recipe</u> was used widely in the areas named during the reign of this great pharoah, to the point where he made comments about it in his many writings.

1,490 Pharoah (Queen) Hat-shep-sut sent her expeditionary forces to the land of Punt (modern Somaliland and part of Kenya) after her own return to Kimit, and the Pharoah of Punt and his family went back to Punt. These voyages were made on the Red Sea with stops at Kush and Nubia. The Queen's journey is recorded on her temple at DEIR-EL-BAHRI. See story of trip to Punt and the funerary at Deir-el-Bahari on page 160, BLACK MAN OF THE NILE. The great queen also died in this year.

1,490 The Coeval of Queen Hat-shep-sut, Thotmosis (Tuthmosis) III, continued the trading expeditions she inaugurated with the country of Punt at the end of the Red Sea. (See James H. Breasted, ANCIENT RECORDS OF EGYPT, Vol. II, pp. 486-487, Chicago, 1906.)

1,405 Amenothis III founded the TEMPLE OF THE SECRET FIRE, a Chapter of the Grand Lodge of Luxor.[15] The latter was the "Mother of all Grand Chapters and Secret Lodges of the Ancient World". (See S. Clymer, FIRE PHILOSOPHY; G.G.M. James, STOLEN LEGACY; Dr. A. C. Churchward, SIGNS AND SYMBOLS OF PRIMORDIAL MAN; and, Max Muller, EGYPTIAN MYTHOLOGY.)

751 Pharoah Kashta died. He held dearly to the teachings by Pharoah Ori of Kush (Ethiopia):

THE POWER OF RIGHT IS GREATER THAN THE

---

*This word is sometimes substituted with "PURITY" by many authors. The translation to English from Hieroglyph is difficult.

GREATEST STRENGTH OF A MIGHTY WARRIOR.

This was said by that mighty Ethiopian ruler hundreds of years before the first day of the first king of the Dynastic and Pharonic period recorded by the High-Priest Manetho in his Chronological Listing of Kimit. Pharoah Piankhi, another Kushite, took it upon himself to carry forward the rule of Kashta. But before the end of Kashta's reign small feudal lords had commenced their own civil uprisings against the central government and formed their own capital at NAPATA. Taharqa took over from Piankhi and made Kush the world's leading power of his era. Of the solely indigenous African (so-called "NEGRO, BANTU", etc.) Pharonic Dynasties, Piankhi's was one of the most powerful.[16] It also included the first dynasty.

731   After approximately twenty-one (21) years of Piankhi's reign over Kimit and Kush, including Nubia, he erected a stelae or obelisk (tapered stone slab like a needle) at Jebel Barkal, a very short distance from the capital city of Kush, which he called NAPATA.

718   Shabaka (Sabacon), the Kushite, invaded Lower Kimit and brought it under captivity. He made his move from Nubia, presently called Sudan, originally "UPPER KIMIT" (also "Upper Egypt" by the Haribus, and Upper Sais by indigenous Africans). From this center of operation he also established the 25th Dynasty, however the exact year is not definitely known.

715   In this year the Nubians' rule was called the "NUBIAN DYNASTY OF UPPER EGYPT". Many "Western educators" have established this period as a separate dynastic period from that established by Pharoah Shabaka (Shabataka or Sabacon), which is an error, both men being of Nubian ancestry. The latter designation is solely political and geo-political, not "racial" in the sense used by "Westerners" with respect to their Negrophobia.

700   The world's "FIRST RELIGIOUS PRINCIPLE" was substantiated as having derived from the teachings of the Kushite, King Ori, more than 3758 B.C.E. It was uncovered when a basalt slab was unearthed from the debris of artifacts in an excavation. The inscriptions on the slab were in an ancient type of hieroglyphics that denoted a period preceding the first Dynasty c3000 B.C.E. This principle must not suffer confusion with the FIRST PRAYER. It is the FIRST PRINCIPLE dealing with "RIGHT AND WRONG" as absolutes without the need of physical force as authority

to make them so. Oris declaration made them the "WORDS OF GOD".[17] The "GOD" in question had to be either the SUN GOD or FIRE GOD who was worshipped by Nile Valley Africans during that period, which preceded the first so-called "WESTERN RELIGION" - Judaism or Hebrewism - by more than two-thousand one-hundred (2100) years.

670 Ionians and Carians were recruited for the first time to serve in the armies of Kimit. During this same period Greeks were also used as translators for the armies and other areas within the government of Kimit, these positions being the bases from whence they were able to secure most of the guarded secrets of Kimit that they were not exposed to previously. Much of what "Western educators" presently call "GREEK PHILOSOPHY" were obtained as a direct result of this incident in the history of Kimit. Yet hardly any of the projectionists of so-called "Greek Philosophy" mentioned any work on the subject existing in Greece before the Greeks began serving in the armed forces of Kimit, or because of their contact with African teachers of the Nile Valleys High-Cultures that descended through the Mysteries System Schools - the equivalent of today's "modern" universities and other institutions of higher learning.*

600 Pharoah Necho (Niku, Neku, etc.) II commissioned a fellow indigenous African to circumnavigate the entire continent of Alkebu-lan (Africa). The name of the African was Hanno (Hano), from Khart Haddas (also known as Carthage, a name given this area of Africa which is today called Tunisia as a result of the Arab invasion of North Africa). This fact certainly assails the claim by most "Western educators" that a Portuguese by the name of "VASCO deGAMA was the first person to sail around the tip of South Africa" (Monomotapa)", in the year 1489 A.D." This story is so silly as to ignore the thousands of years that the Africans of this area sailed around the Cape in their fishing expeditions, for no other reasons what-so-ever. It must be noted, however, that the Portuguese were the first of the EUROPEANS, rather than the first people, which would include Africans even before Admiral Hanno. For history shows quite clearly and dramatically that the first Europeans, the Portuguese, to arrive at

---

*It must be remembered that the "Father of European History", Herodotus, described the originators of the Mysteries System as being similar to any of the people called "NEGROES" in the United States of America, or "BANTUS" in the African continent; even those later on called "MOORS" fit this description.

Monomotapa depended upon information they had received
from African mariners to be able to arrive at "CABO de
TORNMENTO" with Bartolome Dias in 1486, and with turning
the Cabo with Vasco da Gama in 1496 C.E. on his way to
Kilwa, Malindi and other ports on Africa's east coast
before crossing the Indian Ocean to India. These facts
are available in countless documents recorded from the
log-books of everyone of the earliest of the European
mariners - the Portuguese, and later the Dutch. (see
Basil Davidson, AFRICAN PAST; George Padmore, AFRICA,
BRITAIN'S THIRD EMPIRE; H. Labourete, AFRICA BEFORE THE
WHITEMAN; A.B. Akintola, A HISTORY OF AFRICA BEFORE
EUROPEAN COLONIALISM.)

548   The Secret Temple of the Mysteries System, a Chapter of
the Grand Lodge of Luxor, Delfi, was burnt down to the
ground. This incident should not be confused with the
fire that burnt the entire anti-Grand Lodge before in
approximately 1000 B.C.E. In this fire the entire Lodge
was burnt to the ground, leaving only the main walls and
major pillars standing. It was rebuilt by its Grand-
master, the Most Worshipful Pharoah Amasis of Kimit, between the years 548 and 525 B.C.E. He personally donated
to its rebuilding fund the sum of 1,000 talents and about
50,000 pounds of alum. These donations were more than
three times the amount of the medium of exchange that
was needed by the bretherens. (See Eva M. Sandford,
MEDITERRANEAN WORLD, p. 135 and 139; also John Kendrick,
ANCIENT EGYPT, Book II, p. 363.)

525   Darius I, son of Emperor Hystopes of Persia (today's
Iran), became Pharoah of Kimit during the XXVIIth Dynasty
after the removal of Cambyses and his recall to Persia.
He was a very capable Pharoah, and saved Kimit from the
course of ruin set for it by Cambyses and his predecessors.
He also introduced the system of "MONEY EXCHANGE" to the
Africans of the Nile Valleys High-Cultures.
The genesis of Greek enlightenment came in Kimit from
the Africans of the Nile Valleys about this year - 525
B.C.E. At this time regulations or immigration barring
Greeks from entering Kimit in large numbers were lifted.
This also allowed them to settle in other areas than the
Delta, especially in Naucratis - where there was a center
of Secret Societies (Mysteries Systems). This was during
the reign of Pharoah Amasis, one of the Persian Pharoahs
who ruled during Persian colonialism over Kimit following the conquest of Lower Kimit* by Cambyses in approx-

*The Persians, as the Hyksos who preceded them, were militarily
incapable of capturing UPPER KIMIT (Upper Egypt, Nubia and Kush).

imately 663 B.C.E.; this period, however, was noted as the
SAITE PERIOD. Here at Naucratis the Greeks were first
introduced into the full secret of many of the Mystery
System's privacies which were not heretofore exposed to
Fraternal Brothers who were not Africans or Asians of
colonies under the Africans of Kimit's control. It is
after this entry that the Greeks commenced their first
studies and research in philosophy and other disciplines
to which they had some inclination by indirect exposure
due to the so-called Pre-Socratic and Socratic philosophers, most of whom were in fact Ionians - colonials of
Kimit at that time. From this beginning the Greeks began their major efforts in copying and otherwise plagiarizing Kimit's and other Nile Valley High-Cultures'
concepts; from here they carried their knowledge to their
home base in Greece where many of them had returned to
spread their newly acquired knowledge. (See Plutarch,
HISTORY, 380; Diogenes, BOOK IX, 49; OVID FASTI III, 338;
and Herodotus, THE HISTORIES.)

Pharoah Nectamebus I founded the last of the indigenous
African Dynasties of Upper and Lower Kimit (Egypt or Sais)
- the XXXth Dynasty, which also bore the name "SEBENYTIC
DYNASTY" according to "Western educators". This was in
fact the end of African control in Kimit, as the Africans
were never able to return to control until the emergence
of the present Arab dominated United Arab Republic (U.A.
R.) headed by Gamal Abdul Nasser and a few Arabized
Europeans and Africans (mostly Europeans). The Africans
have very little to say about the administration of what
was once their glorious High-Culture ("civilization").

525-332 Pharoah Artaxarexes III formed the last Kimit Dynasty
before the invasion by Alexander IInd of Greece, also
called "Alexander the Great"; the son of Philip of
Macedonia (Macedon). It was this dynasty that Alexander's
armies crushed, an event that started the first rule by
Europeans (so-called "Caucasians") in Kimit or any other
part of the more than 4,100 miles Nile Valleys (White and
Blue) High-Cultures. The victory which Alexander won in
332 B.C.E. gave the Greeks open run of their "STOLEN
LEGACY" - all that the Africans had created and developed
up until their arrival, which included law, science,
philosophy, medicine, pharmacology, astronomy, engineering, astrology, mathematics (all of its branches), and
a host of other disciplines which are today assigned to
the so-called "GREEK PHILOSOPHERS". The "STOLEN LEGACY",
(a name coined by Professor George G.M. James in his book
of a similar name) was initiated when General Soter (who
later declared himself "PHAROAH PTOLEMY I, RULER OF ALL

EGYPT) and Aristotle sacked all the Lodges and Libraries of the Mysteries System Schools and Secret Societies. (For further details on this phase of how the rape of Kimit (Egypt or Sais) was conducted, and the subsequent plagiarizing that took place; see Chapter IX - AFRICAN ORIGINS OF "GREEK PHILOSOPHY", in this volume.)

500   LOCHMAN (the African of Kimit), the "WORLD'S GREATEST FABLIST" (Story Teller), was born in Upper Egypt (today's Ethiopia) during the year 500 B.C.E. The Greeks, with whom he spent very few months of his life in Greece, renamed him "AESOP". (For a description of this great African see the only sketch* ever made of him during his lifetime on page   of this volume, Chapter VI, A PICTORIAL REVIEW OF ANCIENT AFRICAN PEOPLES, ARCHITECTURE, AND ART.)

500-450 Herodotus (Ionian with Greek citizenship), "FATHER OF EUROPEAN HISTORY", established through his writings that most of what the ancient Greeks culture ("<u>civilization</u>") had were only copies from the Egyptians, Nubians, Culchians, and Kushites. This revelation by Herodotus has caused most European and European-American historians and other educators to establish their color and racial distinction between the ancient indigenous Africans in contradiction of what he reported in his major works entitled - THE HISTORIES. Of course said educators have carefully avoided Herodotus' description of the physical appearance of the African peoples mentioned, from whom the Greeks and all other Europeans and European-Americans received their basic civilization. Because of these TRUTHS it became necessary for the separation of Africans into those "SOUTH OF THE SAHARA" and those "NORTH OF THE SAHARA" in order that the "SUPERIORITY OF THE CAUCASIANS" (Europeans and European-Americans, White people) MYTH could be maintained perpetually. They have also created new and "SEPARATE RACES" for Ethiopia (Kush) and other East African nations and peoples through the use of the Hebrew Torah (Christians' OLD TESTAMENT, any version) mythology dealing with the ridiculus story of how "NEGROES GOT THEIR BLACK COLOR". Of course the same work is mute on how HEBREWS (misnomered "<u>Jews</u>") GOT TO BE WHITE CAUCASIANS from SEMITES. Therefore, it also became necessary to introduce such characters as the terms "BANTUS, HAMITES,

---

*Note the comparative likeness of the three personalities of African birth and/or origin, and figure why only one is called a "NEGRO" by "Western standards" of RACISM or ETHNOLOGY. Can it be that no one designated "NEGRO, AFRICAN SOUTH OF THE SAHARA, BANTU", etc., fits this likeness? Who is lying?

SEMITES, NILITES, HOTTENTOTS, NEGROES", and others, (many of which have been already used in this volume) claiming each as a "SEPARATE RACE".[18] All of this they have done in order to escape being the recipient of early civilizing effects by the indigenous Africans Herodotus described - like the so-called "<u>Negroes</u>". It also indicates that the prejudices of European and European-American ("<u>Modern Man</u>"), of whom Professor Jeffreys so proudly boasted, are contaminated with an illness called "RACISM", of which the forerunners of Herodotus' era, and of Herodotus' era, did not suffer from. It obviously caused Herodotus no trouble what-so-ever when he stated that...,

THE COLCHIANS, EGYPTIANS, AND ETHIOPIANS HAVE
THICK LIPS, BROAD NOSES, WOOLY HAIR, AND THEY
ARE BURNT OF SKIN..., etc.

The fact that Herodotus described what is today called "NEGROES" is further evidence that the ancients were not preoccupied with racist concepts that cause "<u>Western</u>" (European and European-American) professors of history to color their interpretations of African history, and world history in general, to suit modern racist considerations, rather than accept historical TRUTHS as revealed in disciplinary academic research. But in their attempt at separating Africans into "RACES", they have utterly failed to recognize that the people of Punt (Somaliland, part of Kenya and Ethiopia) and Kush (Ethiopia), also Nubia (Sudan), were often ruled by various African groups along the more than 4,100 miles of Nile Valleys' (Blue and White, also Atbara River)* High-Cultures, which also included Kimit (Egypt or Sais). They have also overlooked, with careful intent, the fact that all of the

---

*Trace the Nile River from Central East Africa's Great Lakes and from the Ethiopian highlands on page 682.

peoples and nations at the upper end of the Nile Valley ruled supreme over those at the Lower end, and vise versa. By this latter fact - no more; could anyone, with any sense of certainty, still conclude that these nations and peoples, or any other along the Nile Valleys and Great Lakes Region of Alkebu-lan (Africa), originally were of "SEPARATE RACES" that were exterminated by events of mass genocide after being conquered by one or the other? Or should these revelations not support the fact that only indigenous African peoples, whatever they may be called, existed in Kimit[19] (Egypt) and all other lands bordering on the entire Nile River Valleys? It is equally ridiculous to speak of a "PURE WHITE EUROPEAN RACE OF CAUCASIANS" - the "MODERN MAN" and "LIGHT-SKINNED CAUCASIANS" of Professor Jeffreys, after the indigenous Africans of North Africa and Northeast Africa ran freely through the countries of Greece, Rome, Turkey, Spain, Portugal, and Southern France, a period beinnning before the birth of Abraham - c1640 B.C.E., and ending with the departure of the Moors from Granada, Spain, in 1485 C.E.; or even of a "PURE WHITE UNITED STATES OF AMERICA", when most of the slavemasters had themselves at least one African mistress ("Black" or "Negro"), most of whom bore many of today's whitest of blondes to be found in the southern states, and certainly all over the others, not to mention those whom the African-Americans call - "OUR PASSING BROTHERS AND SISTERS." At the same instance many of the Europeans who amalgamated with the indigenous Africans called "CARTHAGINIANS,

MOORS, ETHIOPIANS" and "EGYPTIANS" freely are the parents of millions of White Americans, most of whose ancestors being BLACK AS THE ACE OF SPADES and/or WHITE AS SOUR MILK; all as a result of a natural human function generally called "AMALGAMATION" or "MISCEGENATION".

One could conclude, or should, that the "<u>Light-skinned Modern Man</u>" of Professor Jeffreys (Greeks, Italians, French, Spaniards, Germans, and other Europeans) from Europe, south of Germany, or to its north, still remain "CAUCASIAN" or "PURE WHITE". Equally then, AFRICANS NORTH AND SOUTH OF THE SAHARA must remain <u>Africans</u>; not "NEGROES, BANTUS, HAMITES, SEMITES, NILITES" and other such names placed upon them by their European colonial and imperial slavemasters for over the past four-hundred (400) years.

Herodotus (himself) explained it with his comment on the appearance of the Colchians, Egyptians, and Ethiopians cited before in previous chapters, and in this one. He was speaking of the indigenous Africans under whom he too was a student studying history and philosophy, as well as other disciplines. The vast majority of the peoples of the Nile River Valleys and the Great Lakes region with whom he came in contact fitted his description; and it is most certainly befitting of the vast majority of the peoples in the United States of America who have been called "NEGROES, COLOURED FOLKS, NIGGERS", and other degrading stereotyped names who had their origin in the slave trading days of the 15th century C.E. (A.D.), all of which seems to have no apparent ending. (See Herodotus, THE HISTORIES, Book II).

It is to be noted that the Colchians, to whom Herodotus alluded, were Middle and Near-East peoples, many of whom descended from the Africans who built the Kingdom of Elam in Persia and conquered Chaldea - as mentioned before in this chapter. This area today called the "Middle-East" — it was previously called "ASIA-MINOR" by the same people who renamed it to suit their own geo-political and racist requirements. In speaking of the Africans, Herodotus also described them in his HISTORIES, by the following:

> AS THE BIRD BEING BLACK, THEY MERELY SIGNIFY THIS
> THAT THE WOMAN WAS AN EGYPTIAN...," etc.

He was, at this time, only describing why the ORACLE OF DODOMA, in Egypt, was being called "BLACK". In a similar manner he spoke of the Colchians' indigenous African ancestry when he wrote:

> ...my own idea on the subject was based first on
> the fact that they have black skin and wooly hair,
> and secondly, and more especially, on the fact that
> the Colchians, the Egyptians, and the Ethiopians
> are the only peoples which from ancient times have
> practiced circumcision..."*

What Herodotus had done was to lump all of the African people he saw into one category without regards as to whether or not they came from Northern Africa or Africa South of the Sahara; to him they all looked alike during his lifetime. This, of course, was before North Africa suffered the conquest of Greeks

---

*All of the peoples of Africa practiced this; many also practiced "excision"; all of which began before Abraham's of the Haribus circumcision in Chaldea, which came from the Elamites.

or Romans. His firsthand accounts of what he actually witnessed and recorded on the spot where the actions were taking place, were yet to be changed by "<u>Modern Man</u>" (the type which Professor Jeffreys and others like him prefer to call "LIGHT-SKINNED CAUCASIANS") to suit their own distortion of world history, in particular African history, with regards to their "NEGROES, AFRICANS SOUTH OF THE SAHARA, BANTUS, HAMITES, SEMITES," and their entire string of racist and stereotyped "ETHNOLOGICAL" semanticism. This is a disease many professors, who prefer to be called "LIBERAL", cannot divorce themselves from. Their Negrophobia prohibits them from seeing the indigenous Africans as contributors to the "<u>world's civilization</u>" before the Greeks and other Europeans who followed them on the world scale, including European-Americans, the last of the European-type "<u>civilizations</u>".

More than six-thousand (6,000) years after the historical recordings in the hundreds of tombs (pyramids) of the pharoahs (kings), more than three-thousand (3,000) years after the account of Queen Hatshep-sut's expedition to the land of Punt; and of course, over thousands of years before the birth of "<u>the first European historian</u>", Herodotus, the ancient Africans along the more than four-thousand and one-hundred (4,100) mile long White and Blue Niles Valleys, and elsewhere, recorded the history of their temples and other places of architectural greatness, many of which have survived the ravages of time to substantiate these facts. Yet the Africans of today must still present to themselves this part of their heritage which they know so little. Herodotus, whom the European and European-American "<u>educators</u>" erroneously call "THE FATHER OF HISTORY", instead of "THE FATHER OF EUROPEAN HISTORY", in honesty placed these "<u>educators</u>" in absolute HELL when he admitted in his own works, THE HISTORIES, that he learnt history from the African historians of Egypt and other areas of the Nile Valleys and the Great Lakes regions. But Herodotus could not, in reality, be the "FATHER OF EUROPEAN HISTORY".[20] It was the Africans who taught him; his only claim to any <u>first</u> in this respect should have been 'THE IONIAN FATHER OF GREEK HISTORY'. For much of what is today called "EUROPEAN HISTORY" just as in the case of "GREEK PHILOSOPHY", is only what Professor George G.M. James so adequately terms the..."

"STOLEN LEGACY."

Herodotus' recordings take one back to the chronological listings of major events in African history, particularly that of North and East Africa, and including areas all over the continent (from North to South, and East to West). But, before concentrating fully on the other revealtions to be unfolded, first look at what Africa seemed to be in the eyes of the Europeans during the lifetime of Herodotus and others. Yet, these were the earliest "EUROPEAN AUTHORITIES ON AFRICAN HISTORY". What is it Herodotus revealed that one must so carefully examine? His MAP OF AFRICA. (See page 206 for maps on Africa by Herodotus and Eratosthenes -

- 450 B.C.E. and 200 B.C.E. respectively in BLACK MAN OF THE NILE.

450   Herodotus arrived in Kimit for the purpose of receiving his education in history and all other disciplines being taught by the Africans in their Mysteries System Schools and Secret Societies. <u>Philosophy</u> was also included. It is questionable if the date of his arrival was 450 or 457 B.C.E. He was either 40 or 47 years old. He lived amongst the Priests of the Mysteries System (the intellectuals of their day)...,

"LEARNING AND COLLECTING CURIOUS INFORMATION"

on all that Egypt could offer him, which he recorded scrupulously. He consigned much to the Second Book of THE HISTORIES - which he called "EUTERPE". In his book, Herodotus stated much of that which the African High-Priest Manetho recorded in his own HISTORY OF EGYPT. Unfortunately Herodotus is still being called the "<u>Father of History</u>" in spite of all these facts. Those who have labeled him so have ignored his own works in which he quoted full pages of the historical data he learnt from the indigenous African historians of Egypt. These were the same sources used by Manetho hundreds of years later. Julius Africanus (Julius Afer, or Julius the African), Eusebius, and Josephus Flavius (all of them ancient historians of great repute) testify to the greatness of Manetho's works and to the copying of much of the information in Manetho's works by Greek students of history during the reign of the Ptolemies and Aristotle. It is obvious that Herodotus received his information from African sources in Egypt and all other areas along the Nile Valleys High-Cultures from whence his and Manetho's teachers - Priests - came.

430   Herodotus (the Greek citizen, and native of the former Egyptian colony of Ionia) traveled from Lower Egypt to Elephantine (Aswan). He detailed this journey in his book called EUTERPE. (See THE HISTORIES OF HERODOTUS, as translated by Aubrey de Selincourt, Penguin Books, 1954).

400   It is alleged that "<u>between 400 to 300 B.C.E., a Greek by the name of Euthyninus sailed to West Africa.</u>" Some "<u>Western</u>" historians claimed that "<u>he became the first European to find the Senegal River</u>", which he allegedly called "<u>Phremetes</u>".[21] This is quite probable, however, since the only other Europeans on record before the Christian Era (B.C.E.) to arrive in West Africa were

	Seutinus Flaccus and Julius Maternus in 50 and 30 B.C.E. respectively; and they wrote of "the Niger River", not the Senegal River.
345	Africans from Carthage (Khart Haddas) established an embassy in Rome. Many historians claimed it was set up at Fort Veii, a few miles from Rome; giving rise to the belief that the Etruscans were already expelled from Rome in 510 B.C.E. as stated in their works of much earlier periods when they also ruled the Mediterranean Sea.
332	Alexander II, also called Alexander "the great", of Greece (Macedonia) entered Egypt as a conqueror of the Africans, which began the Europeans" (Greeks) controlling influence and domination over Northern Africa's most eastern limits. Aristotle and his fellow Greek cohorts sacked the archives of Egypt, stealing what they understood, burning all they could not fathom. (See Professor George G.M. James, STOLEN LEGACY, New York Philosophical Library, New York 1954.)
323	Alexander "the great" died in Egypt. The vast empire he captured shattered into various divisions, each of his generals he had made governor over a particular nation took control of same and ignored the brother of Alexander, Philip IIIrd of Macedonia, whose authority they were usurping. Aristotle also joined with General Soter in the rebellion in Egypt.
306	General Soter, Alexander's greatest general and Governor of Egypt, declared himself "PHAROAH OF ALL EGYPT" and renamed himself "PTOLEMY I", immediately after the approval of said act by Aristotle and all of the other Greek rulers of Egypt during this period. He and Aristotle brought into Egypt (Kimit or Sais) the first of the Europeans to sit on the throne of "THE STAR OF THE NILE". All other rulers of Egypt who were aliens prior to this date were of Asian origin.* Manetho** (High Priest of Sebenmytos under the reign of Ptolemy Ist) became the world's first historian to codify Egyptian history based upon "DYNASTIC CLASSIFICATIONS". He also compiled Egypt's HISTORY OF ANTIQUITY, and divided it into the THIRTY - TWO ROYAL DYNASTIES which

*The Hyksos from c1675 to 1580 B.C.E.; the Persians from c341 to 332 B.C.E.
**An Egyptian of Greek (European or White) paternal ancestry and Egyptian (African or Black) maternal ancestry.

have just been shown and detailed. (See pages through Chapter IV, PREDYNASTIC and DYNASTIC KIMIT, NUBIA, KUSH and LIBYA in this volume for the consecutive chronological dates of the XXXII (32nd) Royal Dynasties and other information of the PreDynastic and PostDynastic eras and their ruling monarchs, etc.). Manetho's works have been translated by such noted historians as Josephus Flavius, Leo Africanus (Leo the African)*, and Eusebus - who was the creator of the best and most important translation to date.

It should be very much apparent by this juncture, from all of the evidence so far cited, that there is quite a lot in a NAME. And quite a lot of Africa's teachings have been labeled "GREEK PHILOSOPHY" because of a NAME or NAMES being changed during translation of the original African works into Greek and Latin, with the African authors NAMES being carefully and plagioristically removed and substituted with European NAMES. In this case the plagiorizer was none other than Aristotle, his NAME appearing on African works that predated his own birth by thousands of years. (See Professor George G.M.James, STOLEN LEGACY.) This practice reached its zenith when Alexander "<u>the great</u>" captured Egypt and set Aristotle loose in the Royal Libraries which he looted fully before renaming it the "LIBRARY OF ALEXANDRIA" in honor of his boss, Alexander II. The same fate fell on the Grand Lodge of Luxor's library. The majority of the indigenous African works therein were given Aristotle's and other Greeks labels.

---

*Note that Leo Africanus was an indigenous African, a so-called "NEGRO, BANTU", etc.; his name LEO having derived from his Godfather Pope Leo who was his slavemaster in Rome, he being sold to the Pope who saw to it that Leo was made a "CHRISTIAN CONVERT". Josephus Flavius was a Hebrew (misnomered "Jew").

Most of the works having been written hundreds of years, in many cases thousands of years, before the birth of either of the Greeks who placed their names on said African documents and other works of historical significance. It is these same works, many of which are today called "GREAT WORKS OF WESTERN CIVILIZATION, GREEK PHILOSOPHY, WESTERN HISTORY AND CULTURE", and a host of other NAMES bearing on European origin. However, the BLACK CULTURAL REVOLUTION is forcing much of the "TRUTH" about these historic events to the forefront daily. The age old maxim that...

THE TRUTH SHALL SET YE FREE...

now has come to haunt those who have taught this to the Africans whose ancestors were forced to parrot it in their slave churches, mosques, and synagogues. Today it is being called the "BLACK CONFRONTATION". Tomorrow it will be (again) called "AFRICAN PHILOSOPHY".

280   Merotic Script of Kimit (Egypt) introduced: An indigenous Nile Valley African form of communication through written words, in many ways very similar to Egyptian Demotic Script. Very little of this writing is understood or decoded to date. There are, however, many Ethiopian scripts now also considered dead languages, such as AGU, - are comparative to Merotic* Script.

260   The indigenous Africans of Carthage (Khart Haddas) were defeated in the Battle of Mylae. This was one of the major set backs that prepared the Africans of Carthage for final extermination by the Roman armies.

256   Africans of Carthage defeated at the Battle of Ecomus. The trend was permanently established in this battle;

---
*MEROWE was one of the African High-Cultures (state, nation, country, etc.) that occupied that part of the land which was later on called NUBIA, UPPER EGYPT, KUSH, and today's SUDAN.

the Carthagenians had allowed their armies to become untrained, and the strength of their navy had already been destroyed from the time of Admiral Hamaclair Barca's (General Hanibal Barca's father) naval disaster during the Mediterranean storm that sunk most of his ships.

200-190 Polybius, the Greek historian and colonialist explorer, allegedly visited the same ports in West Africa where Admiral Hanno of Carthage had already established trading posts more than three-hundred (300) years earlier (c600 B.C.E.). In Polybius' book, TRAVELOGUE, he described several West African rivers such as the GAMBIA - which he called "BAMBOTUS". One should take note that the present name the Mande (so-called Mandingoes) of THE GAMBIA called crocodile is still MAMBO, giving rise to the basis of the name Polybius called this river. This, of course, does not mean that Polybius went to West Africa. It does indicate, however, that he had some knowledge of the area, which could have come from the contacts he had with West Africans who visited Mediterranean seaport towns of southern Europe, including Greece.*

190-180 Another Greek, Eudoseus Of Cyzicus, also claimed to have sailed down the East Coast of Africa after leaving Arabia. It is written that...

>   HE SAILED AROUND THE CAPE OF MONOMOTAPA,
>   STOPPING AT NGOLA, EMPIRE OF KONGO....

One will note that "the Cape of Monomotapa" was in fact the same area at the southernmost tip of Alkebu-lan (Africa) which the Portuguese mariners called "CABO DE TORNMENTOS", in English - CAPE OF STORMS. Also, NGOLA was the original name the Africans used for the present Europeanized version of ANGOLA that the Portugese use. The recording also stated that...

>   HE RETURNED UP THE COAST OF WEST AFRICA, THEN
>   THROUGH THE PILLARS OF HERCULES,** AND ALONG

---

*There were countless visits by numerous West Africans of antiquity and ancient history who visited Greece. Many of them became Greek citizens, and appear in some of the earlier history books on Greece before "Modern Man's" racism became the foundation for writing world history. (See Snowden's BLACKS IN ANTIQUITY.)

**This was renamed the "STRAITS OF GIBRALTAR" after the conquest of the Iberian Peninsula by General Tarikh, the African-Moor, in 711 C.E. Thus: GIBRAL TARIKH, or ROCK OF GIBRALTAR.

THE MEDITERRANEAN SEA TO HIS NATIVE GREECE.*

50   Marc Antonio[10] (Mark Anthony) captured Egypt for his
     Emperor Julius Caesar and Rome. Caesar, through Antonio,
     forced Pharoah (Queen) Cleopatra VIIIth to surrender her
     throne and abdicate. Egypt was immediately after forced
     to accept Roman colonialism as she became a "PROVINCE
     OF THE ROMAN EMPIRE" by "DECREE OF EMPEROR JULIUS CAESAR".

47   Emperor Julius Caesar reinstated Cleopatra VIIIth as
     Pharoah of Egypt.**

30   Seutinus Flaccus crossed the Sahara to reach the Kingdom
     of Niger, West Africa, around the Lake Tchad (Chad) re-
     gion. He accompanied African caravans that were return-
     ing from North African seaports along the Mediterranean
     Sea.

1 B.C.E.
 + 0   This period marked the beginning of the dating process
1 C.E. called B.C.E. or B.C. and C.E. or A.D. Roman rule con-
       tinued in Egypt (Kimit) as the proclamation of...

   THE BIRTH OF JESUS CHRIST, KING OF THE JEWS,

was announced to the peoples of the world. Thirty-two
to thirty-three (32 to 33) years later the...

   DEATH OF THE MESSIAH, JESUS CHRIST, - THE
   FATHER, THE SON, AND THE HOLY GHOST,

was announced, from whence the division of the present
chronological dating process has been derived. For the
picture of Roman and Greek penetration in North, East,
and West Africa see the following map on page

---

*Note that there are no other records available indicating
further European voyages along East Africa and West Africa until 1,624 years later - 1,444 C.E. by Portugese mariners.
**Note that she was the daughter of Ptolemy XIIIth and an African
mother of the UPPER NILE. Ptolemy II-XV were African-Europeans.
Ptolemy I, General Soter, was a European, his wife an African
(Egyptian) princess.

BIBLIOGRAPHY FOR CHAPTER V

Wallis-Budge, Sir E.A.	BOOK OF THE DEAD
Arkel, Dr. A.	HISTORY OF THE SUDAN
James, George G. M.	STOLEN LEGACY
Muller, Max	EGYPTIAN MYTHOLOGY
Vail, C. H.	ANCIENT MYSTERIES
Clymer, S.	THE PHILOSOPHY OF EGYPT
Breasted, James H.	ANCIENT RECORDS OF EGYPT
Sandford, Eva M.	THE MEDITERRANEAN WORLD
Kendrick, John	ANCIENT EGYPT
Huggins and Jackson	AN INTRODUCTION TO AFRICAN CIVILIZATION
Herodotus	THE HISTORIES (as transl. by Aubrey de Selincourt)
Hastings, James	ENCYLCOPEDIA OF RELIGION AND ETHICS
Stanley, Thomas	HISTORY OF PHILOSOPHY
Laertius, Diogenes	BOOK IX
- - - --	LIVES OF EMINENT PHILOSOPHERS
Turner, William	HISTORY OF PHILOSOPHY
Frankfurt, F.	INTELLECTUAL ADVENTURE OF ANCIENT MAN
Alexander, D.B.	HISTORY OF PHILOSOPHY
Bakewell,	SOURCE BOOK OF PHILOSOPHY
Rogers, A.K.	HISTORY OF PHILOSOPHY
Botsford & Robinson	HELLENIC HISTORY

BIBLIOGRAPHY FOR CHAPTER V (con't)

Couch, R.	HISTORY OF GREECE
Woodhouse, W.J.	THE TUTORIAL HISTORY OF GREECE
Bury, T.B.	HISTORY OF GREECE
Thilly, Frank	HISTORY OF PHILOSOPHY
Weber, Alfred	HISTORY OF PHILOSOPHY
Tenneman, W.G.	HISTORY OF PHILOSOPHY

CHAPTER VII

CHRONOLOGY OF EGYPTIAN RULE OVER KUSH AND NUBIA (Upper Egypt).
(Merowe, Cush, Abyssinia, Ethiopia, etc.)

Introduction to Chapter:

The following chronology is presented for the student to observe the overlapping among monarchs (pharoahs, kings, queens, etc.) of Kimit, Nubia, and Kush with respect to the Nile Valley nations of the dynastic periods of Africa's history. This chronology should be compared with that of the Pharoahs of Egypt in order to see how the dates and pharoahs intermingle. It will be noted that there could be no clear-cut declaration as to just which nation among those mentioned above was in reality the creator of the High-Culture ("civilization") that is today called "ANCIENT EGYPT". Every bit of evidence points to the fact that there were too many times when the control of government passed from Upper to Lower and visa versa with respect to the Nile Valley High-Cultures.

There are many instances when Nubia, Merowe, and Kush will appear with respect to a particular monarch or monarchs during one or more periods. Such rulers would appear to have lived many times; however, the student will note that Kush, Nubia, and Merowe's history are overlapped through conquest and counter-conquest by monarchs of all of the various nations that existed along the banks of the two Niles during the periods being studied in the chronology.

The question marks are placed where dates should have appeared. The student should be aware that many historians have made assumptions and filled in such dates, which are only speculative. There is no data to substantiate them at present.

RULERS OF CUSH (KUSH) UNDER EGYPTIAN COLONIALISM

RULER OVER KUSH (Viceroy or Governor)	DATE B.C.E.	MONARCH (Pharoah)
Thure	1550 - 1528	Amenhotep I & Thutmose I
Seni	1528 - 1503	Thutmose I & II
Nehi	1503 - 1450	Hatshepsut & Thutmose III
Wesesersatet	1450 - 1417	Amenhotep II
Amenophis	1417 - 1402	Thutmose IX & Amenhotep III
Mermose	1402 - 1365	Amenhotep III
Thutmose	1373 - 1357	Amenhotep IV
Huy-Amenhotep	1357 - 1349	Tutankhamun
Paser I	1346 - 1315	Ay & Horemheb
Amenemopet	1320 - 1298	Seti I & Ramses I
Hekanakht	1298 - 1232	Ramses II
Passer II	1298 - 1232	Ramses II
Sethauw	1298 - 1232	Ramses II
Messuwy	1232 - 1224	Merneptah & Seti II
Seti	?	Siptah
Hori I	?	Siptah & Setinekht
Hori II	?	Ramses III & IV
Wetawuat	?	Ramses VI & VIII
Ramessenakht	?	Ramses IX
Pa-nehesi	?	Ramses XI
Herihor	?	Ramses XI
Piankhy (Pianki)	?	Herihor

Note:
? Accuracy of the exact date questionable. During these periods the reign of government was quite illusive.
Rameses is also written RAMESSES or RAMSESS. It all depends on the historian one is reading.

GREAT MONARCHS (Rulers) OF KUSH
(538-308 B.C.E.)

DATE B.C.E.

538 - 533	Analma'aye	483-418	Talakhamani
533 - 513	Amani-natake-lebte	418 - 398	Aman-nete-yerike
513 - 503	Korkamani	398 - 397	Baskakeren
503 - 478	Amani-astabarqa	397 - 362	Harisiotet
478 - 458	Sisaspiqa	362 - 342	(no record available)
458 - 453	Nasakhma	342 - 328	Akhratan
453 - 423	Malewiebamani	328 - 308	Nastasen

RULERS OF MERÖE
(Sudan and lower Ethiopia)

No.	Name	Date B.C.E.	No.	Name	Date B.C.E.
1.	Kashta	760-751	14.	Amani-nataki-lebte	538-519
2.	Piankhy (Piankhi)	751-716	15.	Karkamani	519-510
3.	Shabato	716-701	16.	Amaniqstabarqa	510-487
4.	Shebitku	701-690	17.	Siaspign	487-468
5.	Taharqa	690-664	18.	Malewiebamani	463-435
6.	Tanwetamani	664-653	19.	Tallakhamani	435-431
7.	Atlanersa	653-643	20.	Amani-nete-yerike	431-405
8.	Senkamanisken	643-623	21.	Baskakeren	405-404
9.	Antamani	623-593	22.	Harsiotef	404-369
10.	Aspelta	593-568	23.	(Unknown King)	369-350
11.	Malenaqen	568-555	24.	Akhnatan	350-335
12.	Amtalqa	555-542	25.	Nastasen	335-310
13.	Analmaye	542-538	26.	Amanibakhi	310-295

RULERS OF MEROE

No.

27.	Arakakami	295-275 B.C.E.
28.	Amanislo	275-260
29.	Queen Bartare	260-250
30.	Amani...takha	250-235
31.	Arnekhamani	235-218
32.	Arqamani	218-200
33.	Tabirqa	200-185
34.	...iwal (awal)	185-170
35.	Queen Shanakdakhete	170-160
36.	(Unknown King)	160-145
37.	Naqrinsan	145-120
38.	Tanyidamani	120-100
39.	....khale	100- 80
40.	....amani	80- 65
41.	Amanikhabale	65- 41 B.C.E.
42.	Queen Amanishabhete	41-(23 BCE Roman Invasion)-12
43.	Netakamani	12 B.C.E. - 12 C.E.
44.	Queen Amaritare	12 B.C.E. - 12 C.E.
45.	Sherkarer	C.E. 12 - 17
46.	Pisakar	17 - 35
47.	Amanitaraqide	35 - 45
48.	Amanitenmemide	45 - 62
49.	Queen Amanikhastashan	62 - 85
50.	Tarekeniwal	85 -103

RULERS OF MEROË

No.

51. Amanikhalika	103 - 108	(C.E. continued)
52. Aritenyesbekhe	108 - 132	
53. Aqrakamani	132 - 137	
54. Adeqetali	137 - 146	
55. Takideamani	146 - 165	
56. ...reqerem	165 - 184	
57. (Unknown)	184 - 194	
58. Teritedakhatey	194 - 209	
59. Aryesbekhe	209 - 228	
60. Teritnide	228 - 246	
61. Aretnide	246	
62. Teqerideamani	246 - 266	
63. Tamelerdpamani	266 - 283	
64. Yesbekheamani	283 - 300	
65. Lakhideamani	300 - 308	
66. Malegerebar	308 - 320	
	? - 350	(Fall of Meröe)

[See next page for other Major events]

MAJOR EVENTS IN SUDAN'S (Meröe)' HISTORY
(C.E. - Christian Era)
[See page 512 for end of B.C.E. and beginning of C.E.]

Date C.E.

? - 350	Fall of Meröe.
? - 550	Conversion of Nubia to Christianity, by force.
641 - ?	Moslems first invasion of the Sudan.
1484 - 1790 ?	Reign of the Fungs (Fung Kingdom).
1820 - 1821	Mohammad Ali of Egypt captured Sudan.
1982 - 1883	British forces occupied Egypt and Sudan.
Sept. 13, 1882	Battle of Tel-el-Keber.
1884 - 1898	Mahdi Rebellion [Mahdia Wars].
Jan. 12, 1885	Mahdi killed General "Chinese" Gordon of Britain.
Sept. 2, 1898	Battle of Omdurman was fought.
1899 - 1956	British Colonialism controlled Sudan under varied pretexes; including the Condominium [the forerunner of "neo-colonialism"].

Note: The dates shown above are for the student's cross-references with modern history. They are to be used with the more recent books on the geo-political history of the anti-colonial era.

BIBLIOGRAPHY FOR CHAPTER VII

Glanville, S.R.K.	THE LEGACY OF EGYPT
deGraft-Johnson, J.C.	AFRICAN GLORY
Leibovitch, J.	ANCIENT EGYPT
Rogers, J. A.	WORLD'S GREAT MEN OF COLOR
Arkell, Dr. R.	HISTORY OF THE SUDAN
Breasted, James H.	ANCIENT RECORDS OF EGYPT
Kendrick, J.	ANCIENT EGYPT

"CLEOPATRA'S NEEDLE"

A STOLEN AFRICAN TREASURE IN AMERICA

"Cleopatra's Needle" or "The Alexandrian Obelisk" are combinations of words which may represent very little, if anything at all, to most African-Americans in New York City, muchless throughout the United States of America. Yet, this ancient symbol of the Egyptian Mysteries System, which represents many of the secrets of today's Freemason's society, is a statue that once guarded the shrine where the African of the Hebrew Faith, Moses, received his "INITIATION" and other "DEGREES OF LEARNING." It looks over New York City's CENTRA PARK from January 22, 1881 C.E. (A.D.) until this very day while I sit and write this Lecture-Essay.

This historic masterpiece and constant reminder of the genius of the indigenous Africans (the so-called "Negroes") mind very seldom attracts the very feintest attention of young or old African-Americans - the descendants and legitimate inheritors of those indigenous Africans who created it. This obelisk, no different to the others ravaged of Egypt and carried off to London, Paris, even the Vatican City and other centers of Europe, was illegally transfered to the United States of America through the machinations of the Khedieve Ishmael (a ruler of Turkish and Albanian ancestry) of Egypt on May 18, 1879 C.E.

"Cleoptra's Needle" was cut from a stone of the quarry at Syent, and first was erected at the City of Heliopolis by Pharaoh Thotmes III in 1600 B.C.E. It was stolen from its original site by the Romans and re-erected at the City of Alexandria,

Egypt, under the reign of Emperor Agustus Caesar in 22 B.C.E. Finally it was removed from Alexandria and carried off to the United States of America by way of Paris, France, through the machinations of W. H. Vanderbilt and Ishmael — mentioned before, in 1881 C.E. The recepients for the United States of America were: Rutherford Burchard Hayes -- President of the United States of America, and William Maxwell Evart -- Hayes' Secretary of State. The removal and re-**erection** projects were under the sole supervision and direction of Lieutenant-Commander Henry H. Goringe of the United States Navy.

Is it at all strange that the laying of the "Cornerstone of Cleopatra's Needle" was done without a solitary person of African origin being invited to officiate in an official capacity, or even serve as an official guest? If you are amazed; just imagine that the so-called "Freemasons of the United States of America", then headed by the man who carried the title..."Most Worshipful Grand Master of the State of New York, " Jesse B. Anthony, with the full cooperation of the Commissioner of Public Parks of the City of New York -- who affixed the City's Seal to the Cornerstone on October 9, 1881 A.D., failed to have the oldest of the African-American Freemasons in the United States of America, the Prince Hall Masons that date back to America's War of Independence, as official honoured guests. Yet all of the so-called "<u>Three Letters Lodges</u>" of White Americans who wanted to join the official parade for the Cornerstone setting were entitled to so do by contacting the "Right Worshipful E.M.L. Ehlers, Grand Marshall of the Day" (of the New York Masonic Temple.) Thus you have seen that the inheritors, the only true ones, of the signs and symbols inscribed on "Cleopatra's Needle" (Masonically truth) were the ones barred by means of the type of racism that permeates the entire structure and fabric of European-American society; the White Brothers forgetting, conveniently, that the Grand Lodge of Luxor, the MOTHER LODGE of all Freemason Lodges, is still located in deepest north Africa along the banks of the Nile River.

The sadest spectacle of the entire affair was the parading of a group of Masons under the title of ...

"ANGLO-SAXON LODGE."

But, the worse of the many ironies came when the Grand Master addressed the "Craft" and reached the portion in his speech which states the following:

> ...Coming thus publicly before the world as members of an organization which commends itself to the favorable consideration of all candid and unprejudiced minds, it is creditable to you that as individual members, as lodges, and as commanderies you have responded so nobly...,"etc.

One must wonder how much of a racist a man or his organization must become before either will admit to "unprejudice minds!" The extremely lengthy speech of the Grand Master also cited the fact that:

> ...The Egyptians were the first to observe the course of the planets, and their observations led them to regulate the year from the course of the sun.

Of course the Grand Master failed to note why he and his subordinates barred the descendants of the Egyptians from participating in their own ancestors organization, their legitimate heritage; the laying of the Conerstone being in honour of said heritage. But to me, the highlight of the Grand Master's speech came when he confessed to his fellow Europeans and European-Americans greed, as he noted:

> Egypt abounded in obelisks, or monoliths, as they are termed, and they were errected to commemorate some particular event, perpetuate reputation, or down to posterity the glory, of some great monarch. They were errected in great numbers, and <u>many of them have been removed to Europe to add to the tropies of some city.</u>[1] That of which we have to-day laid the foundation-stone was one of the two originally located at Heliopolis some 3,400 years ago, and afterward, 23 years B.C., removed to Alexandria, where they..., etc., etc., etc....

Of course the United States of America added to its "<u>trophies</u>" one of the many obelisks illegally removed from Africa, Egypt in this case. It was removed by people who had no legitimate African heritage; and they did not gain it legally from the rightful and legal African owners, but from an invader -- the Khedieve Ishmael, a man who sold most of his empire to French and British interests in order to enhance his own personal financial wealth at the expence of the indigenous Africans of Egypt impoverishment.

The turn about face, and moment of maximum hipocracy, came when the Grand Master echoed the following remarks in order to maintain his Anglo-Saxon image and European-style Christianity as the origins of Freemasonry in racist European-America. He stated:

> It is questionable in my mind whether we are to confine ourselves to the historical rule -- that is, to limit our views to that which can only be proven by indisputable facts and consecutive links to be true. Should we not take a broader ground and look to the principles which antedate the time assumed for the origin of Masonry as at present constituted? There can be no question but that in the secret societies of Egypt are to be found

---

1. Words underscored by the lecturer for specific emphasis only.

some elements now embraced in the principles or symbolism of Masonry of the present, and yet, notwithstanding this, I am not prepared to state to state that we should consider that Freemasonry existed in those days.

It is quite sad to note that any head of a Freemason's body, especially a Grand Master, is not aware of the fact that the entire structure of Freemasonry is copied after the Grand Lodge of Luxor; and much more ancient still, back to the signs and symbols of primordial man -- the indigenous Twa people of central Africa (otherwise called "Pygmies" by European and European-American historians and other writers on Africa and her peoples.) I suggest that all Freemasons who are not aware of the history of their society's origin should read the following works on the subject relative to the meaning of their "I" or God-"<u>the Master of the East, RA, Giver of Light, Creator of the Mysteries, who resides in Amenta</u>:" George G. M. James, STOLEN LEGACY; Sir Geoffrey Higgins, ANACALYPSIS (2 vols.); Sir James Frazier, THE GOLDEN BOUGH (13 vols.); Count C. F. Volney, RUINS OF EMPIRES; Prof. Gaston Maspero, THE DAWN OF CIVILIZATION; Dr. Albert Churchward, ARCANA OF FREEMASONRY; Dr. Albert Churchward, SIGNS AND SYMBOLS OF PRIMORDIAL MAN; Dr. Albert Churchward, THE ORIGIN AND EVOLUTION OF RELIGION; Sir Ernest A Wallis Budge, BOOK OF THE DEAD; Sir E.A.W. Budge, PAPYRUS OF ANI; Sir E.A.W. Budge, OSIRIS; Sir E.A.W. Budge, THE GODS OF THE EGYPTIANS; John G. Jackson, INTRODUCTION TO AFRICAN CIVILIZATION; Homer W. Smith, MAN AND HIS GODS; and others.

Any of the above works should certainly reveal that even King Solomon of Israel had to attend the subordinate Lodge at Mount Carmel to receive his own initiation into the Egyptian Mysteries System. That the <u>System</u> was controlled by the Osirica of the Grand Lodge of Luxor. And that even the Christians' Jesus Christ of Nazzareth had to attend the Lodge at Carmel for his initiation under indigenous African Priests. Of course the Grand Master had not forgotten that the obelisk (for which he laid the Cornerstone) stood an the entrance of the Lodge where Moses received his education into the "Higher Mysteries."

Where are the pyramids <u>Ever-All-Seeing-Eye; Square of Lfe's Travails; Triangle of Heaven's Ladder; the 3,5, and 7; the Inner Sanctorium; Double Pyramids</u>" -- the so-called "Star of David "✡✡, et al? Are they not in the <u>Books of the Mysteries System</u>, and written in the Pyramid and Coffin Texts? Or, does the Grand Master not know these things? All of which modern Freemasonry cannot, or should not, do without; that is, if he is "<u>on the Square of the BOOK OF THE DEAD</u>," and follows the "<u>Commandments</u>" stated in the NEGATIVE CONFESSIONS (from which Moses co-opted his TEN COMMANDMENTS).

On page 145 of Henry H. Goringe's, EGYPTIAN OBELISKS, which I have already referred to repeatedly, under the heading -- "Record of all Egyptian Obelisks," there is a list of 43 obelisks of which more than half, 28, have been illegally removed from Egypt, Africa, and re-errected in places such as London, Rome, Paris, and other cities of Europe and the United States of America- including that which this lecture concerns itself with primarily. Goringe's historical account of these robberies must be very carefully studied by professors and students of African and African-American (Black) Studies programs. His work details all of the underhanded tactics employed publicly by the parties concerned with the illegal removal of the Alexanrian Monolith, so-called "<u>Cleopatra's Needle</u>," from Alexandria Egypt, North Africa, via Paris, France(Europe), to its present location in Central Park, New York, New York, U.S.A. The most comical of all the attempts at plagiarizing the history of this obelisk is the portrait of an Anglo-Saxon Caucasian woman on page 72a dipicting what is supposedly a likeness of Queen Cleopatra, allegedly taken from one of the coins used during her reign over Egypt. She is even shown dressed in the latest style of the year 1885 C.E., the same year Goringe published his book. See picture below.

THIS IS AN EXAMPLE OF THE "CAUCASIAN" and "SEMITIC" MYTH OF A CAUCASIAN AND SEMITIC NORTH AND EAST AFRICA. THE PERSON ABOVE IS SUPPOSED TO BE PHAROAH (Queen) CLEOPATRA VIII, DAUGHTER OF PHAROAH PTOLEMY XIII - WHO CALLED HIMSELF "The New Osiris." MANY OF THE PHAROAHS PRESENTED BY SO-CALLED "Modern educators" ARE FROM SIMILAR EUROPEANIZED CAUCASIAN AND SEMITIC MANUFACTURE.

The history of the obelisk of Central Park, "Cleopatra's Needle," had many other strange historical manipulations. It began with Emperor Napoleon, the very first European to consider removing one out of Africa. He was followed by the first to actually remove one -- King Louis XVIII. He had the French Consel-General in Alexandria, Egypt, bring pressure to bear on the Viceroy of Egypt for the Alexandrian Monolith -- "Cleopatra's Needle."

Of what major importance was <u>"Cleopatra's Needle"</u> that so much international intrigue was necessary to acquire it? Within its inscriptions are the keys to many signs and symbols, not only of the Egyptian Mysteries System, but of its own ancient history relative to the signs and symbols of the God of Puanit (Punt); the same Puanit which Queen Hat-shep-sut said:

> "Amon"(one of the major Gods of Egypt during her glorious reign) conceived the myrrh-terraces of Puanit, the original home of the Gods."

This queen, or pharaoh, also reproduced a "myrrh-terrace" of her own in Egypt according to the instructions on one of the "inspirations" she had "received from Amon." Thus, she said, with respect to her angelic calling:

> "Amon desired me to establish for him a Puanit in his house"(her temple at Dhari El Bahri).

Of course, since the queen did not receive her "calling" and "inspiration" from the same "God" the Hebrew and Christian prophets received theirs, "Western" theologians would have us reject hers and all others from such sources as not being God inspired revelations and writings like those in the Hebrew Holy Torah and the Christian Holy Bible, also the Moslem Holy Koran (Qu'ran), as if Moses, Jesus Christ, and Mohamet did not receive their "calling through the Africans of the Nile Valley, Egypt in particular, BOOK OF THE DEAD; and that from said eye-opener Moses took the foundation of Hebrewisn or Judaism -- the mother of Christianity, and grandmother of Islam; and from these things and the Coffin Texts' NEGATIVE CONFESSIONS of the Osirian Drama Moses copied his TEN COMMANDMENTS.

> It is a glorious region of God's-land, indeed it is my place of delight; I have made it myself in order to circumvent my inner-self (mind).[1]

The above quotation, the last from Queen Hat-shep-sut's report found in her temple, is not the only one of its kind in which a pharaoh of Egypt (Kimit) wrote of Puanit, its Gods, and its most beautiful "myrrh-terraces." Of course the story about "Noah and the flood" is not heathen rhetoric, being that it is the "inspired writings of the Holy scribes of God" -- the Hebrews, Christians and Moslems' God; whereas that of the queen is from a "pagan god;" at least this is the only impression one gets when reading the various remarks on this area in Goringe's work. This type of religious propaganda and mythological philosophy is daily instilled in the mind of the vast majority of African-Americans, many of whom pass it on as professors in Black Studies Courses in which the so-called "Western Religions" (Judaism, Christianity and Islam) are shown to be much the superior of <u>purely</u> west African religions. However, because to few African-American professors have tried to learn Hieroglyphs, they must accept second, third, and even fourth, class translations, transliterations, and interpretations of the most racist and religiously bigoted <u>Semiticized versions</u> of their African ancestors of Egypt, North Africa,

---

[1]. Words in parenthesis on this page and the previous are the lecturer's for clarity only.

history and contributions to world culture -- the origin upon which European (Greek and Roman) civilizations, and that of the so-called "Western world," rest.

The racial bigotry exhibited at the "Setting of the Cornerstone" for "Cleopatra's Needle" in Central Park, New York City, New York, a publicly supported place of recreation of which Blacks tax dollars also are also utilized for its upkeep; yet the image of this obelisk still remains stereotyped in all subsequent materials being written on an official basis from the Parks Department of the City of New York under whose care it remains. It is the same <u>Anglo-Saxon, Semite</u> and other European-Americans bearing the title,"Freemasons", who are still being said to be the inheritors of it; and it is still the same group who does not permit Blacks of United States of America's origin to enter their lodges under the pretext that the <u>"Freemason's law forbid the acceptance of ex-slaves for entrance into the craft."</u> If this is true, there should not be one European or European-American in the <u>craft.</u>

What is the primary cause for all of the confusion relative to the "setting of the Cornerstone" for one of Africa's sons and daughter's most precious jewels -- the so-called "Cleopatra's Needle"? It is birthed in the United States of America's Black man's almost complete ignorance of his historical and cultural heritage (through no fault of his) which his foreparents experienced in Africa long before the arrival of the Europeans in world history. And because of the African-American. lack of knowledge of his glorious and magnificent past which many European and European-American "liberal" and "conservative" mis-educators are able to deny him by co-opting his heritage under devious religious, racial, and philosophic semantical jargon; using words like "Caucasian" or "Caucasoid North Africa, Semitic peoples of Egypt, Nilotic Hamites of East Africa, Black Africans, Africans South of the Sahara, Negro Africa, Bantu Africa, Hottentots, Bushmen, Pygmies," and many other such racist and religously impregnated terms in a discipline they created and named "anthropology," and another called "palaeontology," both of them based upon the concept of the superiority of the so-called "Indo-European Aryan and Semitic-Caucasian race," whatever that is. Yet this 'God-perfected race' of men and women must reach deep down into the "Negro" quagmire of east and south Africa to claim the most ancient of fossil-men known to mankind -- Zijanthropus boisie, Boskop man, Zimbabwe (the so-called "Rhodesia") man, also others, and claim them as "Caucasians" and "Semites" in order to established their own antiquitus heritage to man's origin in Africa; thereby abandoning their own original "creation story" of an "Adam and Eve in the Garden of Eden" somewhere in Persia along the beginning of the Tigris and Euphrates valleys, all of which the Hebrew and Christian "Holy Scripture" have in the First Book of Moses (otherwise called the Book of Genesis) "written by God inspired men."

What is the answer? There are many answers to the general problem facing Black Studies and African Studies professors of African origin. However, the answer to this one is to be found in the lack of meaningful scholarship on the part of African-American and African educators in various fields and disciplines in which their African ancestors' contributions throughout north and east Africa are exploited by other people, due mostly to their own overt over-emphasis on west Africa, which they have been told is the only place from whence the Africans who were enslaved in the "New World" came. This type of stereotyping of the African-Americans, on the part of European-Americans, as well as some of their African underlings who have not studied on their own, but refering strictly to their former slavemasters racist concepts, cause them to surrender north African High-Culture and heritage to the Europeans and European-Americans by default. The slave mentality driven into most of us directs one to believe first:-- that <u>all of the African-Americans who were brought over to the Caribbeans and the Americas were "uncivilized;"</u> secondly: it leads one to believe that <u>there was some sort of "a natural barrier that seperated Africa south of the Sahara from the north;"</u> and that "<u>North Africa's history is seperate and Semitic;</u>" thirdly: that "<u>East Africa's history is Hamitic.</u>" All of these stereotype myths have remained basically unchallenged by the vast majority of African and African-American writers, historians, and general educators of all disciplines, most of us knowing very little better, and others only interested in west Africa alone -- from as far north as Tombut[1] to as far south as the Mani-Kongo River.[2] These educators and writers even tend to surrender the great heritage of the contributions of their ancestors at the University of Sankhore in Tombut, Melle,[3] and re-

---

1. The original name for the European's version called "Timbuktu, Timbuctoo, Timbuctu," and many other variations.
2. The original name of today's Congo and Ubhangi rivers.
3. Melle is the correct spelling of the Frenchized "Mali." Romans like Septimus Paulnius and Setunius Flaccus, as early as 50 and 30 BCE wrote about west African empires at the Niger.

late them solely to Arab influences from the southern Arabian
Peninsula by the way of Mecca and Medina; each conveniently forgetting that the Empire of Melle was itself an independent outgrowth of the High-Culture (civilization) that predated the great
West African Empire of Ghana[1] by thousands of years; yet we are
aware that they have been taught the <u>Arabic</u> and <u>Hamitic</u> slant in
West African history from European and European-American historians like Courland, H. M. Stanley, Erwin, and others of the <u>Semitic and Hamitic syndrome</u>. These conditions also relate to the
general lack of data Black Studies programs suffer because of
their professors and administrators refusal to engage in meaningful research and publication of materials which would remove the
type of racial stereotyping the European and European-American
mass-produced book companies are manufacturing from reharsh 18th
and 19th century colonial Tarzan and Jane carricature of the African peoples. They also happen because the control of research,
finance, publication, and distribution of African and African-American scholars, for the most part, are in the hands of people
who bear the title "<u>authority of African history</u> "due only to the
fact that they are in control of the areas of publication I have
just detailed; these being the same people who write their own
history in a lily-White perspective, thus taking for themselves
all of north Africa as "Caucasian" or "Caucasoid," and when this
is challenged somewhat they hide behind the biblical racism of
a "Semitic" and "Hamitic" north and east Africa. Blacks must control their own publication if they are to turn the teaching of

---

1. Most European and European-American historians set 300 A.D.
as the period in which the Empire of Ghana had its birth.
The Romans wrote of Ghana and her gold as early as 50 B.C.

the Black Experience in Africa and the world over into interpretations that have no place for the Stanley and Tarzan episodes in which present European and European-American educators continue to write about their "Negroes." The "authority" on African and African-American history and heritage must rest in the hands of people of African origin as with all other ethnic disciplines in institutions of higher-learning policies. For it is the Africans who are not alien to the Black Experience; and it is with them the truths of the Black Experience mut lie. Were these steps already taken, in defiance of the many anti this and anti that names which, naturally, will follow such action, then, and only then, other episodes like the "Cleopatra's Needle Cornerstone setting" racist spectacle will not re-occur. If not, then they will continue in excess like G. C. Seligman, RACES OF AFRICA, New York, 1938 (1967 and 1969). We, African and African-American educators and writers, must not be disillusioned into believing, anymore, that our history and heritage, glorious as they are to others, should be ignored by us as "cultural nationalism" and "chauvinism", as so frequently stated by the so-called "New" and "Old Left," and leave ours to study that of Karl Marx, Frederich Engles, Fidel Castro, Queen Victoria, Napoleon, Voltaire, unless they are studied in terms of our own Black Experience first. This does not, in any way whatsoever, mean that we do not study the works of each and every nation's people on the planet Earth, and of other planets there may be. What it does mean, however, is that we must first be verse in ours before we think of mastering someone else's, remembering all the time our indigenous ancestors age-old words of wisdom to us:

MAN, KNOW THYSELF.

We cannot ignore "Cleopatra's Needle," or any other aspect of our contributions to world civilization because of <u>leftist</u> or <u>rightist</u> rhetoric no more than we can ignore the multi-faceted philosophical life-style meaning our own religions of African vintage offer us. For in their religions our African forefathers based much of what we call today "secular history" and "religious education." The "separation of church and state, religious and secular, fane and the profane, are not concepts in African tradition anywhere on the continent of Alkebu-lan (Africa), they are strictly "Western" -- primarily European-American. Because this was done for centuries among the Europeans and European-Americans, whose culture and religions we were forced to take on, it is no reason why we, as African peoples with a distinctly different set of values, must follow. We were enslaved for a few hundred years by European and European-American imperialist and colonialist slavers, also by Arab Muslim slavemasters from the Arabian Peninsula, as well as Persians from the eastern side of said Peninsula, but this does not mean that we enjoyed any of our slavemasters, nor will we tolerate them now neither in the future.

The fact that such a monumental shrine of our African heritage, "Cleopatra's Needle," could be located just a stone's-throw from the world's largest Black Metropolis outside of Africa, Harlem, New York City, New York, and more than 99 percent of the entire population of African-Americans in it do not know that their own "Black and beautiful" sister's obelisk stands in Central Park, which connects to Harlem, is a catostrophic event in the African-American life which we may never live down. This shrine, equally that of Harriet Tubman at upstate New York; Frederick Douglass in Washington D.C.; Alexander Hamilton in Harlem, New York City; and all other related to the <u>Black Experience</u> in the United States of America, should be common-place names and historical biographies upon the tounge of each and every African-American man, woman, and child. It may even become necessary for rededicating all of our shrines according to standards and values establish by ourself. But, first of all, there must be a world-wide movement to force all European and European-American nations holding stolen African properties, or "tropies," such as "Cleopatra's Needle," to return them forthwith to their proper African nation from whence they were illegaly removed. For, is it not true that "the receiver of stolen property is equally as guilty as the thief" that stole it according to <u>Anglo-Saxon jurisprudence, morality, and law</u>? At least, this is what is written in legal books, the Hebrew or Jewish Holy Torah, the Christian Holy Bible (all versions of it), the Moslem or Muslim Koran or Qu'ran. Why not "Cleopatra's Needle" for a worthy beginning?

This lecture ends with the following translation from the original Hieroglyphic inscription on the Left Side of the Alexandrian Monolith, the so-called "Cleopatra's Needle," which has been extracted from EGYPTIAN OBELISKS by Henry H. Goringe.

        The Kingly HORUS,
The strong Bull, Son of Kheper-Ra,[1]
  the King of Upper and Lower Egypt,[2]
     RA-OUSOR-MA-SOTEP-EN-RA
        Golden Hawk,
      of abundant years,
       (very) victorious,
        Son of the Sun
     RAMESSOU MERIAMEN,
  who issued from the womb,[3]
 to take the corners of the Sun;
  whom the Sun generated to be

> (the) Sole Lord, Lord of the two lands,
> RA-OUSOR-MA-SOTEP-EN-RA,
> Son of the Sun,
> RAMESSON MERIAMEN
> the splendor of Osiris,
> like the Sun

One must assume that the Most Worshipful Grand Master was aware that the God -- RA -- was a God thousands of years before the birth of the first Hebrew or Jew, Abraham; and that the word "AMEN", as originally used, had nothing to do with "SO BE IT ". He was, in fact, one of the GODS of Egypt that Moses and all of the other Africans of Egypt worshipped when he attended the Lodge of the Mysteries System. I must say, however, had the Grand Master known what he was about, he could not have avoided making the inheritors of "Cleopatra's Needle" honoured guests at <u>their own signs and symbols.</u>

---

1. The creator of all things before Jehovah, Jesus Christ, Al'lah.

2. This word was originally "Kimit," later "Sais." The Haribus or Hebrews, today called "Jews" as a misnomer, Romans, and Greeks, renamed this Alkebu-lan nation "Egypt."

3. The issuance of "Virgin Gods" from "the womb" of other Gods and virgins were customary in the myths that existed thousands of years before it supposedly took place with the Christians' God's mother -- Mary.

CHAPTER VIII

THE RISE AND FALL OF THE AFRICANS OF KHART HADDAS
(The Africans of Carthage in History)

The present Republic of Tunisia, in Northern Africa, would to some indicate a nation that was for thousands of years occupied by the same type of <u>Arabs, Arabized-Africans,</u> and <u>Arabized-Europeans</u> that comprise the present population. But this would be as far from the truth about this nation's history as the statement that "NORTH AFRICA WAS ORIGINALLY SETTLED BY CAUCASIANS." It is because of this error, which at times is presented with intent to distort history in order to project the "CAUCASIAN NORTH AFRICA" myth, that this chapter begins with the founding of the nation that is today recorded in "<u>Western educators</u>" books as "CARTHAGE".

It will be noticed that the brief summation of the history of the Africans of Khart Haddas, which will be called Carthage for convenience henceforth, is presented in somewhat of a chronological order; yet, there are many instances where the dates shall shift from ancient to modern times (B.C.E. or B.C. to C.E. or A.D.). The reason for doing this is to make the history relavent to the present, and to provide cross-references for current reactions in the general area so far as the struggles for Pan-Africanism against Pan-Arabism are concerned. The student can then see much clearer why the so-called "NEGROID AFRICANS", while not opposed to Pan-Arabism, are never-the-less much more interested and related to Pan-Africanism historically, since they have never forgotten that the Arab population of North Africa is as colonialist in history as the Europeans population there.

1000 B.C.E. was the year Princess Elissar (Dido)* and a contingent of her Phoenician male subjects and a very small number of female attendants left from the City of Tyre** and set sail for refuge in North Africa among the ancient Africans who are today called "<u>Caucasoids</u>". They landed at the African nation called Khart Haddas after various other attempts to settle at more easterly shores of Northern Africa (Egypt, Libya, Numidia). It is this African nation of Khart Haddas, which will be hereafter called <u>Carthage</u>,[1] that the wandering Phoenicians found haven and hospitality, and as a result amalgamated with the Africans (the so-called "NEGROES, BANTUS", etc.) they met there; developing thus into the powerful nation that was later on to dominate the entire Mediterranean Sea and all the nations that bordered on all three sides of it. What had started out to be a fleeing and country-less Princess from the City-Kingdom of Tyre, because of the death of her father and the control of her greedy and ruthless brother, turned out to become one of the ancient

---

*The name Dido was given to this princess by Virgil in his writings about Carthage in the STORY OF AENEAS.
**Where "modern historians" call the MIDDLE EAST, which they earlier called ASIA-MINOR.
***A Carthagenian of Phoenician (Brown) and Khart Haddan (Black) parentage - of African-Asian origin, not "CAUCASOID". Note that Khart Haddas or Carthage means "THE NEW TOWN".

523

world's most powerful conglamorates of people assembled in one nation.

By the year 600 B.C.E. the <u>African-Asian,</u> predominantly <u>African,</u> peoples of Carthage established their first colony outside of Northern Africa on Iberia's southeastern coast; this was their first attempt at the conquest of southern Europe.

525 or 500 B.C.E. marked the period when the Carthagenian, Admiral Hanno, was commissioned by Pharoah Necho (Neku) IInd to circumnavigate (sail around) the continent of Alkebu-lan (Africa).[2] It will be noted that many historians have translated the date when this event took place in 600 B.C.E.; never-the-less it was around the periods between 600 to 500 B.C.E. The majority of historians dealing with this period are definite that it was during the year 522 B.C.E. that he did "<u>set sail with a Carthagenian fleet from Carthage and went through the PILLARS OF HERCULES, and thence to the coast of West Africa</u>" along the Atlantic and Ethiopian* oceans. History noted that his fleet consisted of 50 ships and over 2,000 sailors and officers, with a few colonists added in to settle the refueling depots they had to establish along their journey southwards before they arrived at the first major seaport at the Rio de Oro (River of Gold or Gold River). Here Hanno also established a small settlement, among his fellow Africans, which he called "KERNE". It became

---

*See map on page 680 of this volume showing Ethiopian Ocean. This Ocean became the "South Atlantic" as late as the 18th century C.E.

Carthage's most important West African trading post. Kerne was renamed "HERNE" by the present African population, which have themselves been renamed "MOORS" instead of the original "MAUERS" from the word MAUERITANIA[3]- the nation from whence they originated.

In 520 B.C.E. Admiral Hanno left for ports further south along the coast of what is today called Sierra Leone and Ghana until he arrived at WOURI (renamed "Kamerun" by German colonial imperialists and changed to Cameroun and Cameroon by French and English imperialists after they had confiscated the area from the Germans during the First World war - 1914-1918 C.E.).

518 B.C.E. was the year Admiral Hanno decided to return to Carthage by way of Kerne, with stops at other depots along the way which he had established from 522 to 518 B.C.E.[4]

In 509 B.C.E. Carthage and Rome signed their first TREATY OF FRIENDSHIP. The Etruscans (Tarquins or Romans as they were then also known) and the Carthagenians (Khart Haddans) were at this juncture in history on very friendly terms, even to the point of being allies in a plot to invade and conquer Greece (then called PYRRHUS, later Hellas, Argos, etc.).

500 B.C.E. was the year the Roman Republic was more-or-less established. In recognition, Carthage established an embassy in Rome.* Rome at this period in history occupied a minute enclave

---

*The Roman poet Livy gave a very good account of this diplomatic move on the part of the Africans of Carthage with respect to their Roman allies.

on the Italian Peninsula along the western Coast of the Etruscan Sea, just as Carthage was at that time only a city-state along what is today the Tunisian Peninsula of North Africa (along the Mediterranean Sea.) By 300 B.C.E. Rome, never-the-less, had expanded into a nation of at least four (4) times its original size.[5] It covered an area from the Etruscan Sea and across Italy to the eastern shores of the Adriatic Sea. This was her size up to the beginning of the Samite Wars. After the Samite Wars (up to the latter half of 290 B.C.E.) Rome occupied more than half of Italy. Rome's expansion was then leaping without any control what-so-ever. Her neighboring city-states were not able to contain her. And, by the end of the war with Pyrrhus (Greece) in 275 B.C.E., Rome had already engulfed all of the Italian Peninsula. In other words the city of Rome, in Italy, had become the nation and empire that was later to be called "THE ETERNAL ROMAN EMPIRE".

What did Rome's expansion mean to the North Africans during these periods, particularly to the Carthagenians? It meant that their eminent invasion from the Roman Empire was but a matter of time. This was obvious because <u>Sicily</u>, which is a natural geographic part of the Roman peninsula, was at the time under the colonial dommination of Carthage.[6] Carthage at this period had become the most feared nation in all of North Africa; just as Rome was equally feared in all of Europe. Of course Pyrrhus (Greece) also remained a natural challenge to young Rome. Yet the Carthagenians had sent their fleet to help Rome against

Greece,[7] which had held an enclave on Italy's east coast on the Adriatic Sea.

Why was the above TRUE? Because Rome, after the disastrous defeat of Pyrrhus (Greece), took on its victims' cultural, political, and commercial characteristics. The latter development forced Rome to challenge Carthage for mastery of the Mediterranean commerical trade around the Tryrrhenia Sea.* The area involved formed a triangular enclosure of the Mediterranean Sea that embraced both Rome and Carthage, the same triangle being the area that dominated Mediterranean trade.

With the fast growing commerical expansion of Carthage on the North African coast, from the frontiers of the Greek City of Cyrene westward to the Ethiopian Ocean,** Carthage had become the dominant power of the "<u>known world</u>". As a direct result of said power, Carthage began to expand her empire to satisfy her trade needs. The following chronology deals with the periods and events of Carthage's expansion, contraction, and defeat at the hands of the Romans and Numidians (fellow Africans of North Africa).

Carthage, in 600 B.C.E. had established, after annexing part of southern Spain, trading posts from the silver mines it con-

---

*See map on page 705 at the rear of this volume with respect to the 3rd century B.C.E. Roman and Carthagenian empires.
**Note that the present South Atlantic during said period in history (B.C.E.) was known to the ancients as "OCEANUS AETHI-OPICUS" (Ethiopian Ocean), even through the late 17th century C.E. (See page 680).

fiscated from the Spaniards.[8] It also took over British trading interests with Spain and commanded the strait of the Pillar of Hercules (Strait of Gibraltar).[9] The strait and the ports of southern Spain were closed by blockade to all shipping, except Carthaginian. All ships not having Carthaginian clearance were rammed by her warships and sunk. Carthage also maintained a panish zone control and "<u>sphere of influence</u>" until 500 B.C.E., at which time Rome signed a <u>treaty</u> with Carthage, which excluded Rome's trading rights in the Carthaginian area.* The <u>treaty</u> regulations finally infuriated the Roman Senate; for Roman merchant ships passing the Straits of Messing to the City of Messina were forced to receive Carthaginian clearance. The Mediterranean Sea had become, in fact, a kind of "CARTHAGINIAN LAKE". And Rome had also feared the Carthaginians'** closing of the "<u>Strait</u>".

Rome attacked Carthage in 264 B.C.E. This was the beginning of the Sicilian War; the attack had created an insurrection in in Carthaginian controlled Sicily. Sicily was a colony of Carthage at that time. The Carthaginian military garrison from Sicily followed the attack and invaded Rome in the latter part of 264 B.C.E. and occupied Messina (close to Rome). These indigenous Africans had, for the first time, invaded southwestern Europe and

---

*See Polybius, HISTORY, 400 to 370 B.C.
**It must be noted that the Carthagenians were not Phoenicians, as contended by many European and European-American historians. It would be implied by the term "Punic Wars" since "Punic" is the Latin word for "Phoenicia".

occupied European territory west of Greece as conquerors.[10] Rome had suffered her greatest defeat, to date, in history.

The first Roman army to cross over the Mediterranean Sea left Italy in November 264 B.C.E. to engage the Carthaginians, whom they had become to despise - for very obvious reasons.

The <u>Rome-Syracuse Alliance</u>, about 260 B.C.E., had given eastern Sicily to Rome because of the Roman invasion of that island in 264 B.C.E. - just four short years before the Alliance. It was the African colonizers' first real setback at the hands of the Europeans. However, just one year later, in 259 B.C.E., a Carthagenian military force battered the Roman fleet attempting to expand Rome's control over the entire island of Sicily. This defeat had virtually ended Rome's mastery of European naval powers. The Africans had once again become masters of all European nations along the Mediterranean seaboard.

In 242 B.C.E. the Romans' donations to their treasury in Rome was speeded up. Rome hurriedly built a new and much more modern navy than that which the Carthaginians had destroyed.[11] With a force of 200 warships, with 5 banks of oars each, its rebuilt navy met and defeated the Carthaginian navy in 242 B.C.E. This was to become the most significant turning point of the indigenous Africans' of Carthage mastery over the Europeans of Rome[12] and others all along the Mediterranean Sea.*

---

*The Mediterranean Sea was formerly called "Oceanus Aegypticus", Egyptian Sea or Ocean, also "Mare Aegypticus".

Between 242 and 241 B.C.E. somewhat of an uneasy peace ensued between Carthage and Rome. This was because the Romans had forced certain restrictions on Carthage after the Africans were defeated.[13] For example: The Romans compelled the Carthaginians to surrender the entire island of Sicily and neighboring islands to Rome, and to pay an almost impossible sum of 3,200 talents (over three and one/half million dollars - $3,500,000) within a period of ten (10) years (by 231 B.C.E.). Thus, after more than twenty-three (23) years of fighting (from 259 B.C.E. to 241 B.C.E.) the first battles of the struggle between Carthage and Rome were concluded. This victory gave Rome its first colony outside the Italian Peninsula. It was the beginning of a series of wars that were later called the "FIRST PUNIC WARS".*

The Romans invaded and annexed Corsica and Sardinia in 238 B.C.E., only a scant three (3) years after they had made a "peace treaty" with Carthage covering Mediterranean area limitations,

---

*Note: "Punic" is the Latin word for Phoenician, the name the Romans called the mixed African-Asian peoples of Khart Haddas - which they called Carthage. One has to remember that the original group of Asians in the area came from Phoenicia and amalgamated with the hundreds of thousands of indigenous Africans - the so-called "Negroes" and "Bantus", they met there. The Asians numbered less than 200 to 300 men, women, and children- the vast majority were sailors. However, in less than 100 years after their arrival, the Phoenicians and the Khart Haddans had all but developed one common African physical characteristic, as the Africans dominated the Asians. By any sense of United States of America's "RACIAL STANDARDS", and according to "Western anthropology", the indigenous Carthaginians[14] would have had to be classified as Blacks - African-Americans- who are called nefariously "NEGROES", and sometimes even "NIGGERS".

which did not include these two territories (island outposts). But, the Romans had also seized Gaul (France) and the Po Valley. Roman power then extended from the Alps Mountain range at the north and the entire Italian Peninsula down to the Mediterranean Sea at the south.

The Carthaginians, fearing Rome's expansion and her new power, invaded Spain anew under the leadership of General Hannibal Barca (who was the son of an equally famous father - the Commander of Carthaginian forces during the First Punic Wars - General Hamiclair Barca - in 238 B.C.E.). At this time in his life the younger Hannibal was only a mere twenty-four (24) years of age, having been born in the year 262 B.C.E. of both indigenous African parents. He was not of <u>African-Asian stock,</u> as shown on the Cartheginian coin on page 557 of this chapter.

General Hannibal Barca launched, in 220 or 218 B.C.E., the first battle of the <u>Second Punic Wars</u> when Roman and Carthaginian forces clashed along the Spanish-Roman borders. The young African general marched with a combined force of only seventy thousand (70,000)* men and a few hundred elephants against Rome's more than three hundred thousand (300,000) man army. He had started in a direction that ran along the east coast of Spain, from where he planned to cross Gaul (France) at the south, and invade Italy from the north.[15]

---

*Some "Western historians", in order to make the Romans appear superior to the Carthagenians, raised this figure to more than 300,000 men.

During the latter part of Autumn in 218 B.C.E. General Hannibal Barca reached Europe's magnificent and most frightful mountain range - the Alps. With his very small army having been forced to tackle vicious snow storms, avalanches, and with narrow pathways for the passing of the elephants (which required the soldiers to cut passages for them), he continued through the Alps. The savage fighting against the forces of nature, and the hostile Europeans who inhabited the mountain ranges, who were hardly removed from their cave-dwelling days, also became part of the general's problems he faced daily. The worse of these obstacles was the mountain dwellers' continuous hurling down of monsterous boulders (giant stones) along the mountain sides and precipices on the Carthaginian soldiers and elephants, forcing them to engage in bitter battles with the mountain peoples all along the way.

One solid year of wretched calamities sapped General Hannibal Barca's forces which had originally started out as seventy thousand (70,000) men. And by the time of his arrival in 217 B.C.E. out of the <u>Alpine Pass</u> and into the <u>Po Valley</u>, Italy, more than the astonishing figure of thirty-six thousand (36,000) of his best men were killed by one means or another, leaving a measly total striking force of thirty-four thousand (34,000) half-starving, frost-bitten, and weather-beaten African soldiers and no more than 100 of the elephants to face "<u>the world's most feared armies of mighty Rome</u>".[16]

After one year of exhaustive preparations (from 217 to 216 B.C.E.) the young general, Hannibal Barca, was ready for the big push into the heart of Rome after having pacified all of the Roman armies thrust against him while he was in the Po Valley preparing for the push. Amongst the defeated was the Roman's most honoured general, Consul Flaminius. The capture of his fortresses and the Apennines was a blessing that came to Hannibal. Hannibal followed the defeat of Falminius by systematically cutting the Roman legions to pieces at the shores of Lake Trasimeno. The Roman army suffered its most humiliating defeat in this battle. The Consul was himself killed in the battle. Hannibal was now only a few days from the "<u>gates of the Roman fortresses at Rome</u>". But the general's army was too weak to begin the seige of Rome. He, therefore, fought a few other battles to create some diversionary moves at inducing major desertions from the Romans to his side and at the same instance giving his men and animals (elephants) the much-needed chance to recuperate while expected supplies from Spain could arrive for the big push ahead.

Rome got its first real dictator in 217 B.C.E.[17] when the Roman Senate appointed Fabius "MARSHALL OF ALL FORCES" to stop the onslaught of the African invaders in northern Italy under the command of General Hannibal Barca. Fabius engaged Hannibal in a few small delaying skirmishes (battles). However, in the meantime, Rome was also rebuilding her army and extending her naval fleet. The people of Rome, angry with the tactics of Fabius who had been defeated battle after battle, began to call him "CUNTATOR" (the laggard).[18]

By the year 216 B.C.E. the Roman Consuls had organized a new and modern army of more than two-hundred thousand (200,000) men from all over their colonies, an army that was more than four (4) times the size of the remnant army of General Hannibal Barca that stood at the "GATES OF ROME". The Romans had taken advantage of the fact that Hannibal could not secure supplies or replacements for his soldiers. On the other hand, the Romans were able to secure as many men as they were capable of training, and needed ; this was the sole ace in the hold, but they were also fortunate in having the strategic advantage of being on their own home territory. Added to this was the fact that the African invaders were completely surrounded by hostile captives from the various battles Hannibal was forced to engage his army in on the way into northern Italy during his crossing of the Alps. Thus in 216 B.C.E. Rome was able to hurl her newly rebuilt and modernized army of the north, of seventy thousand (70,000) men, against the Africans who had by this time only thirty-thousand (30,000) men - many of whom were ill-trained Europeans captured in the Alps and along the Po Valley. This started the "BATTLE FOR CANNAE" at the gates of Rome.

During the Battle for Cannae in 216 B.C.E. General Hannibal Barca's cavalry chased the Roman horsemen into hasty retreat.

This caused the main divisions of the Roman army to be caught in the center of the two main columns of the Carthaginians on each side, with their murderous elephant-equipped cavalry at the rear. The general had held two units of the Carthaginian reserves, his crack sharpshooters, in the rear of the entire battle scene. These two African "FORCES OF DEATH", as they were called by the Romans who reported the battle events, closed in on approximately fifty-five thousand (55,000) Roman soldiers caught in the trap.* By nightfall of the same day the Africans closed in and every last Roman soldier in the trap was annihilated. Historians of this era in history have claimed that...

"ROMAN BLOOD FLOWED LIKE A RIVER..."[19]

during this battle, as the Africans slaughtered their trapped adversaries.

The Africans' humiliating defeat of the Roman army (considered the best in the world at that time) forced many nations along both sides of the Mediterranean Sea into treaty alliances with the Africans of Carthage. It was just this reaction that forced Macedonia in the same year 216 B.C.E. to sign a "TREATY OF ALLIANCE" with Carthage.

General Hannibal Barca (reputedly "the greatest general and military strategist of all times"), at the age of thirty (30),

---

*This same strategy was employed in the 18th century C.E. by the African general, Tchaka, of the Zulu nation of the Monomotapa Empire against the invading colonialist slavers of Europe.

had made Carthage the greatest single military power all over the Planet Earth - the "KNOWN WORLD". He had defeated "<u>the world's greatest military power</u>," Rome, and had taken the honor for the Africans of Carthage. He had destroyed the Roman armies within less than two (2) short years (216-214 B.C.E.). The Africans were "<u>masters of the Mediterranean world</u>", and now also "<u>masters of the northern Italy, all the areas of the Alpine Pass, all of the Iberian Peninsula, and all of the western islands of the Mediterranean Sea</u>."

General Hannibal Barca had established his mastery as a statesman over northern Italy by bringing in centralized authority over the area he controlled, something that area had not known before; and in his military genius and command, caused the allies of Rome to desert in panic during 213 B.C.E. The first to desert to Hannibal were the military leaders of northern Italy, followed by many Greek City-States. Even Syracuse, in Sicily, forsook Rome and joined the general. Only one Roman (Latin) State in southern Italy remained in <u>fact</u> and <u>truth</u> loyal to Rome. That was Central Italy, which became the core of Roman nationalism and resistance. But the Roman Senators, all of them, stood their ground after the humiliating defeat and the tail turning of their allies of long standing to the African invaders. But this was not the first time the Africans had defeated the Romans and other Europeans in battle. It was, however, the most humiliating of any of their defeats.

By 207 B.C.E., after ten (10) long years of African rule and amalgamation of the African soldiers with the European women of the Iberian Peninsula and northern Italy, General Barca's hard core of his best African (Carthaginian) soldiers started to dwindle from many causes. The most damaging reason being his inability to secure reinforcements from Africa.[20] As such, he was forced to use mainly deserters and other captured European soldiers to supplement his African "<u>crack-shot</u>" elite troops. But the Europeans could not take the rigorous training with the elephants and other military techniques that were totally foreign to them; and there were not sufficient African troops to spare for the sole purpose of training the Europeans, nor sufficient time in which to accomplish such a feat. The failure of the general to obtain sufficiently trained troops among the northern Italians forced him to dispatch his brother, Hasdrubal Barca, to Iberia (Spain) to gather Carthaginian troops holding that colony and Iberians whom they had time to train to relieve his men of the northern Italian frontier. Hasdrubal set forth to return to his brother the same year with the relief column to link up with the battle-weary Carthaginians, only to march directly between a Roman army twice the size of his relief column on both sides of a mountain pass in Iberia. The Romans swooped down upon the Spaniards and Africans and annihilated each and every man, including Hasdrubal. This defeat was the turning point of the African's rule over Roman territory in northern Italy. It was also the beginning of the end to African rule in all of Europe until 711 C.E., at which time the African-Moors* invaded and annexed Spain and parts of southern France under the command of General Tarikh (for whom the "ROCK OF GIBRALTAR" is named).

During the year 203 B.C.E. the Romans finally found a hero in a general who was born, raised and educated in Carthage. He was also trained as an officer in the Carthaginian military academy General Barca attended. This man was none other than the world-famous Scipio Nasica, the same general who had defeated the Carthaginians twice before, having been sent earlier by the Roman government to Spain to cut off the chief supply of money and men from Carthage passing through the Iberian Peninsula to Hannibal. This was possible only because General Scipio Nasica knew all of the strategic moves General Hannibal Barca had learnt in the military academy in which they were both trained in North Africa - Carthage. He was also very much aware of the fact that General Barca's supply line was disrupted to the point that his rear flank all the way back to Carthage was left unprotected.

Having convinced the Roman Senate in 203 B.C.E. not to attack General Hannibal Barca anymore in Northern Italy but in Carthage, General Scipio Nasica was allowed to invade Carthage, which he was to do with great success. This move forced General Hannibal Barca into hurried retreat as he returned to his native Carthage

---

*African people that invaded the Iberian Peninsula from Morocco, North Africa. They originally came from Mauretania (Mauritania), an African nation on the northwest coast of Alkebu-lan. These Africans were originally called "MAVERS".

where he would make his stand in defense against General Scipio Nasica. Hannibal's forces in Europe, both those he took from Africa and those he collected in Europe, were left at the "<u>Gates of Rome</u>". This had to be done, for it would have taken at least one (1) full year for them to retreat with their general back to Carthage by way of the Alpine Pass and the Iberian Peninsula, cross the Straits of Hercules, and then along northwest Africa to Carthage. This would have been the only way in which to retreat his forces unless he had journeyed to the Mediterranean Sea and tried to cross from this point, which would have been utterly impossible since the Carthaginian navy was already destroyed.

In 202 B.C.E. the big showdown came. But General Hannibal Barca had returned to a Carthaginian army that was allowed to carouse and grow fat and lazy, while he was still in Europe fighting with haggard troops in northern Italy. His only experienced and battle-ready troops had been left striking "<u>at the gates of Rome</u>".

General Hannibal Barca, determined as ever to defeat the Romans, met General Scipio Nasica and a Roman command of the most powerful striking force ever assembled in history up to that day. This historic beginning of the BATTLE OF ZAMA was to be in fact the beginning of the end of Carthage. It was also to be the final battle between the Carthaginians and Romans, even to the point that it was labeled by many "<u>Western historians</u>" as...

    THE BATTLE FOR SUPREMACY OF THE MEDITERRANEAN SEA.

It was the most bitter battle so far fought by either Rome or Carthage to date; it was a battle in which the African-trained Nasica defeated the African and African-trained Barca. Over one hundred thousand (100,000) men died in this engagement, most of them unseasoned Carthaginian enlistees. The seasoned soldiers had become aged, overstuffed, and unable to give any leadership what-so-ever to the recruits.

Just before the final surrender of the Carthaginians, General Hannibal Barca escaped a trap set for him by General Scipio Nasica. The old "<u>foxy</u>" African was set on regrouping his forces for another final try at Rome. But, by 201 B.C.E., all of Carthage's ability to defend itself was depleted. Carthage was forced to the peace table once again due to Roman power, where it was forced to sign a "TREATY OF SURRENDER". Carthage was compelled to pay Rome "<u>ten thousand talents</u>" (a little better than $11,000,000) in a period of fifty (50) years (by the year 151 B.C.E.). It was forced to surrender all of its warships, except for ten (10) <u>triremes</u>.[21]

The worse part of Carthage's humiliation was that it could not wage war against any nation without consent from Rome. Neither was it allowed to conduct any foreign trade without Rome's sanction. In other words, Carthage had lost its independence and became, for all practical purposes, a colony of Rome. North Africa had become the victim of another foreign invader. And thousands of her most valiant sons were left stranded at the gates of Rome in middle Italy.[22]

During the year 201 B.C.E. the Romans demanded that their African colony, Carthage, expel General Hannibal Barca from the country. The general, who was at this juncture fifty (50) years old, was deported to the east beyond Numidia* - around Libya and Egypt. From his exile, however, he continued his eternal fight against Rome by stirring up the successors of Alexander "the great" - the Ptolemies, the rulers of Egypt (Kimit, Sais), in a plan for a combined invasion of Rome with Greek and Egyptian (African) forces.[23]

"CARTHAGE MUST BE DESTROYED" was the constant cry of Senator Cato at the end of every speech he made in the Rome Senate during 146 B.C.E., some fifty-five (55) years after Carthage's surrender to Roman forces under General Nasica. This was in answer to Carthage's phenomenal prosperity in her return as a powerful nation despite of the almost impossible colonial bondage which it had to accept in its peace treaty after its surrender to Rome. Senator Cato and other Roman senators who joined in with him (business entreprenuers, etc.), were afraid of the Africans of Carthage recapturing their control over the Mediterranean Sea trade. At the same time the Carthaginians were also in fear of the Numidians** whom they hated for joining with the Romans

---

*The Numidians were indigenous Africans from an adjacent nation of Carthage. Numidia was located in an area where presently stands Algeria and Libya. It joined with Italy to crush Carthage during Hannibal Barca's defense of Carthage.
**They were ancient colonialists like their later imitators of the 19th through 20th century C.E. cartelists in the Congo and other parts of present day Africa-such as Henry Morton Stanley, etc.

against them; also for their constant attacks against Carthaginian merchant ships, a condition which Rome supported all along. But Carthage was forced to invade Numidia, which was in direct violation of its treaty with Rome after its defeat in the Battle of Zana. The provision of the "treaty" being that...

> "CARTHAGE SHALL MAKE NO WAR AGAINST ANY OF ITS NEIGHBORS WITHOUT THE SANCTION OF ROME...," etc.

The Carthaginians had failed to live by this clause in their treaty obligation, as they could no longer survive with the constant attacks on their merchant ships by the Numidians - fellow Africans who had the blessings and encouragement of the Romans.

In the year 149 B.C.E., when Carthage attacked Numidia, the Roman Senators (many of whom had encouraged Numidia's attacks against Carthaginian vessels) decided to once and for all to destroy Carthage. This cry was again led by Senator Cato, the arch exponent of the "CARTHAGE MUST BE DESTROYED" theory. It is behind this type of agitation that Rome finally called Carthage to task for its "TREATY VIOLATION". Carthage refused to allow its own destruction at the hands of European Rome or African Numidia and decided that it was better to be destroyed fighting to the death than by strangulation by either nation. The Carthaginians' defiance was met with an attack on Carthage by the Romans who were joined by their African allies - the Numidians - in 146 B.C.E.

The beginning of the "THIRD PUNIC WAR" was now launched in

full force. This war raged on in its most vicious form of man's hatred for his fellowman for three most horrible years (149-146 B.C.E.). It was equalled in its atrocities on both sides. For the Carthaginians it was a war of genocide. For the Romans it was a war of integrity and commercial dominance of the Mediterranean Sea. For the Numidians* it was a war to get rid of their fellow Africans whom they feared even more than the Romans or any other people on the face of the earth at that juncture in their very short history as an African nation.

By the end of 146 B.C.E., Rome and Numidia had sufficiently destroyed Carthage's man-power and cut off its trading routes to the extent that the Carthaginians could not secure needed supplies from the outside world. Cut off from the outside world, the Carthaginians made their final stand against their common enemies - Numidia and Rome. Reduced to a mere police force, these brave African soldiers of Carthage fought the Europeans and their fellow Africans (Romans and Numidians) until the battle entered each and every last street of the city of Carthage, where they also fought from house to house. But the gravely ill-armed and under-supplied Carthaginians could not stop the combined forces and military hardware of both Rome and Numidia.

In 146 B.C.E. the Romans and Numidians finally set fire to the "PEARL OF NORTH AFRICA" - Carthage, destroying all that

---

*The Numidians and the Carthaginians were bitter enemies for centuries before the Roman-Carthaginian (Punic) Wars.

physically remained after the house to house fighting. So intense was the loyalty and patriotism of the Africans of this metropolis physically, educationally, emotionally, scientifically, and commercially, that thousands upon thousands of them elected to die in a religious compact in the fire which was consuming their city, rather than submit to Roman and Numidian mercy and live under captivity as slaves for foreign and domestic imperialism, colonialism, and/or neo-colonialism.

During 146 B.C.E., after Carthage was already burnt down to the ground and its death ashes were blown to the four corners of the earth, the Europeans (Romans) annexed what was left of this nation, thereby officially reducing it to a...

"ROMAN PROVINCE IN AFRICA."

So ended the only rival Rome had in the west Mediterranean world. It was a struggle which lasted for approximately one hundred (100) to one hundred and twenty-six (126) years (266-146 B.C.E.). Senator Cato had seen his fanatical cries of ...

CARTHAGE MUST BE DESTROYED...,

become a historic reality. Carthage was in fact "...DESTROYED." Senator Cato had been satisfied. The beginning of the end to indigenous African rule in North Africa had begun and foreign colonialism was set in motion. It also proved to be the beginning of the end to indigenous African rule over the entire continent of ALKEBU-LAN* - Mother Africa.

*The people of Khart Haddas called their continent "ALKEBU-LAN" before the arrival of the Phoenicians to Africa, and before it was renamed "AFRICA" by the Greeks and Romans of Europe.

If one is to read other works such as the author's seven volume manuscript entitled, AFRICA (Alkebu-lan); HER PEOPLES AND EVER CHANGING MAP, 1,750,000 B.C.E. - 1966 C.E., currently being prepared for publication, it will chronologically show that from the destruction of Carthage in the year 146 B.C.E. the end to the indigenous Africans' (the so-called "BANTUS, NEGROES", etc.) rule in Africa began. It is not to be construed that the Greeks' prior invasion and conquest of Kimit (Egypt or Sais) in 332 B.C.E. should be overlooked with regards to this point, however. The Greeks had already demonstrated in their conquest of the Africans of Kimit that they had exhausted their own capability to expand their war machinery beyond that point in northern Africa, and certainly they could not penetrate UPPER EGYPT (Upper Kimit) - NUBIA or KUSH (Sudan or Ethiopia).[24] On the other hand, Roman power at the end of the THIRD PUNIC WAR* was a growing monster, destined to devour anything within its path. And from this juncture (146 B.C.E.) onwards, it was all Europeans over Africans until the year 640 C.E. (or 18 A.H.) when the Arabs from Arabia - called Muslims or Moslems - and other points east (Asia) invaded and conquered most of North Africa to become the new slave-masters and imperialist rulers of the indigenous Africans of North Africa. The Arabs not only turned the tide of European

---

*Roman (European) and Numidian (African) against Carthaginian (African) - ROME-NUBIA-CARTHAGE WARS. The first two (2) PUNIC WARS were between Rome (Europeans) and Carthage (African) alone.

rule in North Africa, but weakened the Europeans to the point where they could join the indigenous African Moors as slavemasters over Europeans of the Iberian Peninsula (Spain, Portugal, and parts of southern France) from the year 711 C.E. or 89 A.H. until 1485 C.E. or 863 A.H. Yet, just as it was the Moors* of African origin who first entered the Iberian Peninsula as conquerors in 711 C.E., it was also they who were the last to be forced out by the Spaniards (the "Christians") in 1485 C.E. from Granada. The expulsion of the African-Moors came just seven (7) short years before Cristobal Colon (Christopher Columbus) and his African-Moorish Chief Navigator and Captain of the Flagship SANTA MARIA - Pietro Olonzo Niño (a native of Morocco, North Africa) set sail for a shorter route to the Far East and ended up in what is today called the "WEST INDIES", but which is reality the CARIBBEAN. The final expulsion of the Africans, Arabs, and African-Arabs** from Granada, Spain (southwestern Europe), in 1485 C.E., initiated another chain of victories by the Europeans over the Africans until they were partially checked in 1957 C.E.; at which time Dr. Kwame Nkrumah ("Osagyefo" - Savior or Redeemer) led the Africans of the former so-called "GOLD COAST CROWN COLONY OF GREAT BRITAIN" to a semblance of political free-

---

*"Western" historians continually try to impress everyone that the Moors were an Arab people, carefully forgetting that they were two types of Moors, the African-Moors - the first to enter Iberia in 711 C.E. with Tarikh.

** There were amalgamated African-Asian Moors, the offsprings of African and Asian Muslims. The Asians, originally from Arabia and other areas around the Fertile Crescent, entered Iberia 12 years (723 C.E.) later.

dom under the name of the "COMMONWEALTH OF GHANA", which was later on changed to the "REPUBLIC OF GHANA" in 1958 C.E.

The "PEARL OF NORTH AFRICA", a name which the ancients called the glorious nation of the Africans called "CARTHAGINIANS" who were in fact KHART HADDANS, is best seen in its reconstruction when it was once also known as "...

THE GREATEST METROPOLIS EVER CREATED BY MAN...,"
as shown below on this page. This was the CITY-STATE OF CARTHAGE during the period from 600 to 350 B.C.E.*

A reconstruction of Carthage at the height of its power

---

*Note that the likeness of General Hannibal Barca, shown above, was photographed from one side of a coin used in Carthage during his lifetime. The elephant shown is on the opposite side of the coin. Why is he projected as a "CAUCASIAN" by European and European-American "educators"? Are they not aware of the existance of these coins? It is data such as this that makes one wonder why Africans who are today called "BANTUS" and "NEGROES" are not shown in pictures with respect to North Africa.

BIBLIOGRAPHY FOR CHAPTER VIII *

Sandford, E.M.	THE MEDITERRANEAN WORLD
Virgil	STORY OF AENEAS
Wells, H.G.	A SHORT STORY OF THE WORLD
deGraft-Johnson, J.C.	AFRICAN GLORY
Rogers, J.A.	WORLD'S GREAT MEN OF COLOR, Vol. I.
Huggins and Jackson	AN INTRODUCTION TO AFRICAN HISTORY
ben-Jochannan, Y.	AFRICA (Alkebu-lan); HER PEOPLES AND EVER CHANGING MAP, 1,750,000 B.C.E. - 1966 C.E. (unpublished manuscript).
----------	AFRICAN ORIGINS OF THE MAJOR "WESTERN RELIGIONS"
----------	AFRICA: The Land, The People, The Culture (co-authors: Kempton Webb, Ph.D. and Hugh Brooks, Ph.D.)
Lane-Poole, S.	THE MOORS IN SPAIN
Erskin, Mrs. Steuart	VANISHED CITIES OF NORTH AFRICA
Soames, Jane	COAST OF THE BARBARY

---

*The student will note that many of the books in the bibliography for Chapter VII and Chapter IX can be used with great advantage for information pertaining to this chapter also. There are many overlapping facts relating to Kimit (Egypt or Sais) that are common to the history of Khart Haddas (Carthage).

THE BLACK MAN OF ANTIQUITY

(THE ANCIENT AFRICANS AND THEIR DESCENDANTS CASTIGATED)

"Such was in brief the scene in which developed the people of the Nile, whose culture dominated of the eastern Mediterranean in the age when Europe was emerging into the second stages of civilization, and becoming into contact with the culture of the early east. Nowhere on earth have the witness of a great, but now extinct civilization, been so plentifully preserved as long as the banks of the Nile. Even in the Delta(the Mediterranean shores),[1] where the storms of war beat more fiercely than in the valley above (near Nubia -- the so-called "Negro" or "Black Belt")[1], and where the slow accumulations from the early flood have gradually entombed them, the splendid cities of the Pharoahs have left great stretches, cumbered with enormous blocks of granite, limestone and sandstone, sheltered obelisks, and massive pylon base, to proclaim the wealth and power of forgotten ages; while an ever growing multitude of modern visitors are drawn to the Upper Valley (Nubia)[1] by the colossal ruins that greet the wondering traveller at every bend in the stream. Nowhere else in the ancient world were such massive stone buildings erected, and nowhere else has a dry atmosphere, coupled with an almost absence of rain, permitted the survival of such wealth of the best and highest in the life of an ancient people, in so far as that life found expression in material form. In the plentitude of its splendour, mush of it thus survive into the classic age of European civilization, and hence it was, that as Egypt was gradually overpowered and absorbed by the Western World,[2] the currents of life for west and east(Africa and Asia)comingled here, as they have never done elsewhere. Both in the Nile Valley (Uganda in central Africa to the shores of the Mediterranean) and beyond it, the west (Europe and European-America) thus felt the full impact of Egyptian civilization for many centuries, and gained from it all that is manifold culture had to

---

1. Words in parenthesis by the lecturer for clarity only.
2. Europeans and European-Americans. Underscored by the lecturer.

549

> contribute. The career which made Egypt (the land of the Ethiopians or Blacks according to Herodotus and others of Greece and Rome) so rich a heritage of alien peoples, and a legacy so valuable to all later ages (including the present 1970's), we shall endeavour to trade in the ensuing chapters."

The above extract is taken from professor James H. Breasted's (now deceased) outstanding book, A HISTORY OF EGYPT, Charles Scribner's Sons, New York, 1937, Chapter I, pages 12 and 13. The professor (of whom I have mentioned in Part I of this lecture, was "founder of the Oriental Institute at the University of Chicago, Illinois;" published his work originally in 1905. It was the first of its kind in the history of the United States of America, no other European or African-American having reached such academic qualification as an "Egyptologist" before. But let us examine more closely the above remarks by professor Breasted; paricularly the highlights of his astounding declarations and confessions with respect to these indigenous Ethiopians' ("Negroes" or "Blacks", beginnings of all of mankind's civilizations (or High-Cultures) he implied.

> a) That "nowhere else on earth" was there in history another civilization as which the indigenous Africans of Egypt created equalled;
>
> b) the height of greatness that was Egypt and her African inhabitants have never been reached by others, including European-Americans;
>
> c) nowhere else in the entire world were the structures built by the Egyptians equalled, which included Greece and Rome;
>
> d) the zenith of Egypt's magnificent splendor was not isolated, but plentiful among the Africans all along the Nile Valley;
>
> e) Europeans and European-Americans ("Caucasians, Semites," etc.), the "Western World," including the ancient Greeks and Romans, absorbed their beginnings from these original

indigenous Ethiopians, Africans of Egypt — the so-called "Negroes;"

f) and, that the "legacy" of Egypt is an African heritage which Europeans and European-Americans must try to capture, which they have done, or trying to accomplish, by means of injecting the terms "<u>Semitic, and Hamitic" Caucasian</u>" where Black or Ethiopian should have appeared.

Professor Breasted's profound confession should have been sufficient proof of the African-Americans logical right to their claim of Egyptian heritage without the need for any further verification. But, there had to be others that followed him, and even himself at a later date, who had to satisfy and justify their own <u>racial, ethnic</u> and <u>religious superiority</u> over the African-Americans in order to fulfill the unquenchable thirst and gluttonous behavioural demands of the <u>racist ego</u> -- the ID -- so common to European-American society. One such person, a professor M.D.W. Jeffreys, author of an article entitled "<u>The Negro Enigma</u>" in the WEST AFRICAN REVIEW, September 1951 issue (as cited in my own book, BLACK MAN OF THE NILE, pages 4 through 10, which is before this august body), even dared to suggest that the so-called "<u>Negro</u>" had "<u>no history dating back to the Stone Age</u>." And, like many of his own disciples, he further stated that there was no trace of "<u>Negroes" in Africa</u>"before 6000 B.C." But professor Gaston Maspero, whose works Sir Ernest A. Wallis Budge, Dr. Albert Churchward, Gerald Massey, professor James H. Breasted, and many hundreds since them, have depended upon for historical data pertaining to the indigenous Africans of Egypt of the pre and post-Hyksos period, showed the Egyptian Empire extending all the way from the Uazit Orit (Mediterranean Sea) inland to points beyond the sixth Cataract (where the Blue and White Niles meet) and all along the highlands of Cush (Ethiopia) on the coast of the Qim Orit (Red Sea) on his map entitled <u>THE EASTERN WORLD in the XIV<u>th</u> Century B.C.</u> (republished in London, England, by the Society for Promoting Christian Knowledge). This presentation is cited in professor Maspero's book, THE STRUGGLE OF THE NATIONS — EGYPT, SYRIA & ASSYRIA (edited by A. H. Sayce, professor of Assyriology, Oxford; translated into English from its original French by M. L. McClure, Member of the Committee of the Egypt Exploration Fund, London, 1896); a follow-up work of his, THE DAWN OF CIVILIZATION:-- <u>Egypt and Chaldea</u>, was published later.

Unlike professor Maspero, Professor Breasted got into the <u>Negrophobia</u> syndrome common to European-American historians and educators of other related disciplines and introduced his own <u>Negrophobic</u> dialouge on page 134 of his, A HISTORY OF EGYPT. He wrote:

> "The foreign policy of"(Pharoah) "Pepi I was more vigorous than that of any Pharoah of earlier times. To Nubia"(once Upper Egypt)"he gained such control over the Negro tribes that they were obliged to contribute quotas to his army in case of war, and when such war was in the north"(Lower Egypt),"where safety permitted, the Negro levies were freely employed."

There are two primary objects of direct <u>unadulterated racism</u> expressed in professor Breasted's statement; (a) the mythological distinction between his so-called "Nubian" and "Egyptians" as separate peoples; (b) the usage of the word "<u>tribes</u>" with respect to the Africans of Nubia and not those of Egypt; (c) the use of the word "<u>negro</u>" as a thing, rather than (at least) a human being; and (d) the lack of citing in what document by the Egyptians or Nubians he found any mention of a word that would suggest any semantical similarity to "<u>Negro.</u>" Yet, on page 137 he is praising the works of the pharoah whom most racist historians agree was a "<u>Negro Pharoah</u>" -- Mernere, and whose mummy (head) he displayed on Plate -- Fig. 77 marked -- "<u>Head of King Mernere</u> (Cairo Museum)", with its broad nose and other so-called "<u>Negroid features</u>." Thus, he stated on page 137:

> Doubtless utilizing his new canal, Mernere devoted special attention to the exploitation of these regions. His power was so respected by the chiefs of Wawat, Irthet, Mazoi and Yam that they furnished the timber for the heavy cargo-boats built by Uni for the granite blocks which he took out at the first Cataract.

In the last paragraph on page 137 and the beginning of page 138 we find professor Breasted also stating:

> Mernere now utilized the services of the elephantine nobles in tightening his hold upon the southern chiefs. Harkhuf, who was then lord of Elephantine, was also appointed governor of the south, prehaps as the sucessor of Uni, who was now too old for active service, or had meantime possibly died; although the title had now become an honourable wourn by more than one deserving noble at this time.

The problem professor Breasted **had was** no different than those facing his followers and disciples of the 1970s, whose attempts are being equally frustrated in their obsessive desire to remake the Nubians "<u>Negroes,</u>" and of an "<u>uncivilized tribal origin,</u>" while at the same time admitting that it was in reality "<u>in Nubia</u>" that the greatest of the "<u>Egyptian civilization actually reached its zenith.</u>"

European and European-American professors, such as Breasted and M.D.W. Jeffreys, must not have been aware of Dr. Albert

---

1. Words in parenthesis by the lecturer and writer of this paper for the sake of clarity only.

Churchward's palaeontological map of "PREHISTORIC AFRICA" shown in his major work, ORIGIN AND EVOLUTION OF FREEMASONRY, in which he showed that mankind -- including "Caucasians, Semites, Hamites, Indo-European Aryans " etc. descended from the so-called "Pygmies" (Twa peoples, very small but proportionally built human beings), "True Negro, Mastaba Negro" and "Nilotic Negro;" as shown on page 6b or 11 of my book, BLACK MAN OF THE NILE, before you.

On page 76 of his outstanding work, SIGNS AND SYMBOLS OF PRIMORDIAL MAN, Dr. Churchward states:

> Mr. Hall, in his work, "Great Zimbabwe," draws a page of customs (100 - 101) of the Makalanga and the Jews, showing that they were the same, and evidently arrives at the conclusion that they derived all these from the Jews of ancient times," and are descendants of the same. We cannot agree with Mr. Hall and others who have come to this conclusion. No doubt many of the customs are the same, because we know that the Jews borrowed nearly all the laws and customs from the ancient Egyptians, and therefore they would be identical with them;"..., etc.

Going back still further, professor Churchward, M.D. even pointed out the fact that what we do not see "Cleopatra's Needle" (now in Central Park, New York City, New York) in its true perspecti

> ...likewise show that many of the symbols pertaining to the rites of modern Freemasonry were used in Egypt 3500 years ago. This obelisk was for" (Queen) Hapshepsut, who lived 1600 B.C. -- i.e. 3500 years ago.

Professor Churchward's statement is corroborated in the following from the official records of the Freemasons report on the OBELISK; thus:

> What remains of the hieroglyphs in this square (on the obelisk)[1] has been literally translated by Mr. deMorgan as follows:***giver, Ra-men-Kheper, gracious God, lord of the world, giver of life, beloved by Tum, master of the world. The word Ra-men-Kheper is enclosed in an oval with a line tangent (tow line)[1] to the lower end, that

is known as a cartouch. It is the prenomen of
the king (pharoah)[1], Thotmes III. On the upper
right square the god is Ra."

The above statement was extracted from page 62 of the book, EGYPTIAN OBELISKS, by Henry H. Corringe (Lt. Commander, USN), John C. Nimmo, London, 1885. Certain Freemasons, those who can observe this much <u>light</u> would or should, understand the Masonic mystery inherent in this Egyptian notation from Egypt's Mysteries System created in central Africa by the Twa people, and developed to its zenith by the Africans of the Blue and White Nile valleys. This also proves that it is all a part of the great lie to make King Solomon of Israel's Temple in Jerusalem "...<u>the original place where Freemasonry began</u>." This is the same as saying that the <u>double-pyramid</u> ⏳✡ or <u>double-triangle</u> was originally called the "<u>Star of David</u>" or "<u>Mogen David</u>;" when in fact, it predated the first of the Hebrew (or Jewish) people — Abraham-by more than three-thousand (3000) years; even Adam, the so-called "<u>first man</u>," of Hebrew mythology, was not yet created when the <u>double-triangle</u> symbol was first used by the Twa (also called derogatorily "Pygmies" by Europeans and European-Americans).

We can observe the same behavioral pattern expressed by professor Breasted with respect to his own <u>Negrophobia</u> on page 184 in A HISTORY OF EGYPT, where he denied the indigenous so-called "Negro" origin of certain African basics which many Europeans and European-Americans, including the so-called "Semites," have attempted to co-opt for centuries. With respect to Nubia, the land beginning at the second Cataract, sometimes also called

---

1. Words in parenthesis by the lecturer and author for clarity.
   Note that "Cleopatra's Needle" is in fact a misnomer. It is
   the obelisk of Queen (Paroah) Hatshepsut who preceded Cleopatra by at least 1553 years (c1600-47 BCE).

"part of Upper Egypt," Breasted wrote:

> He (Sesotris III or Khekure)[1] errected on each side of the river (the Nile) a stele marking the boundary-line, and one of these two important landmarks has survived; it bears the following significant inscription: "Southern boundary made in the year eight, under the majesty of the king of Upper and Lower Egypt, Sesostris III, who is given life for ever and eyer: - in order to prevent that any negro[2] should cross it by wat water or by land, with a ship, or any herds of the negro who shall cross it to do trading...or with a commission."

I suppose that racism is an accepted essence of academic scholarship. For, not only did professor Breasted refused to translate what he saw by making the word "Nubian" or "Nubians" appear to be the equivalent of the degrading term "Negro " He also repeatedly use the term as if it was a pronoun; thus, "the negro" this, and "the negro" that. Even the capitalization of the word he, obviously, found to contemptuous for his type of scholarship. Moreover professor Breasted, an educator and administrator of very long standing in American higher-education, must have been familiar with the fact that the word "NEGRO" did not exist in any language prior to its 16th or 17th century C.E. introduction by the imperialist Portuguese slavemasters as a name of contempt for their west African captives; similarly for the word "NEGROLAND." It is quite unfortunate that this type of ranked racism and rancid Negrophobia can still go unchallenged by most "Black Studies" professors of African heritage.

The irony of professor Breasted's own Negrophobia, which is

---

1. Words in parenthesis by the lecturer for clarity only.
2. Words underscored for specific emphasis in the comments to be made by the lecturer. See map, BLACK MAN OF THE NILE.

in some respects similar to professor M.D.W. Jeffreys' proclamations in his THE NEGRO ENIGMA, is best displayed on the same page, 184. He wrote:

> Sesostris III had therefore errected a strong fortress on each side of the river at this point. The stranger and larger of the two, at Semneh, on the west side, was called "Mighty is Khekure" (Sesostris III)[1] and within its fortified enclosure he built a temple to Dedwen, a <u>native</u> god of Nubia.

Is it not strange that the above did not end with <u>a" Negro "god of Nubia</u>? Why "<u>native</u>" at this point instead of the "negro" he so well spoke of in all cases related to Nubia? If the Pharoah, Khehure, held the type of contempt for the so-called "<u>negroes</u>;" why would he build"<u>a temple to</u> " a 'Negro' god? Secondly: The Gods of Nubia were, for the most part, according to all of the ancient documents of this land and others related thereto, the same as those of Egypt; as many times the two nations shared the same pharoah (king) and common culture. Sometimes the control was in the hands of the Africans of Egypt, other times in the hands of those of Nubia; and of course, there were other times when it was in the hands of the Cushites (Ethiopians) -- also called "<u>true Negroes, Mastaba Negroes, Nilotic Negroes,</u>" etc. by Dr. Churchward and hundreds more before <u>racism</u> became the dominant criteria for judging the ancient peoples of antiquity contributions to world civilization. The indigenous Africans that made up the population of all of these countries also came from other nations along the Nile Valleys, which included those at the end of the White Nile (Uganda or the Bonyoro Kingdom), and those all the way south to the Monomotapa Em-

---

1. Words in parenthesis by the lecturer for clarity only.

pire where the capital city, Zimbabwe, stood.

Professor Breasted was not only a racist, as shown by his own works dealing with the so-called "negroes;" he also indicated his utter ignorance and confusion between what were the nations of "Cush" and "Nubia." And by adding the word "Sudan," the Arabic name for the former NUBIA, he even became much more confused than he was before. Thus, he wrote on page 184, the following:

> Four years later disturbances among the turbulent Nubian tribes[1] south of the frontier again called the king (Pharoah Khekure or Sesostris III)[2] into Nubia. Although Egypt did not claim soverignty in Kush (The land of modern Ethiopia), the country above the second Cataract, it was nevertheless necessary for the Pharoah to protect the trade-routes leading though it to his new frontier, from the extreme south-routes along which the products of the Sudan were now constantly passing into Egypt.

First of all, just as professor Breasted was able (at this juncture) to correctly translate from the original Hieroglyphs to English the words "Nubian tribes," which should have read "Nubians". only, he could have avoided using the word "negro" (with or without a capital N) at any point. Secondly: Cush could not have occupied the same area Nubia stood at the same period in history, unless both names represented the same nation, which was not the case in history. Thirdly: Cush was geographically located at the highlands to the southeast of the second Cataract, not directly south of it. Directly south was Nubia, today's Sudan. Slightly northwest of it was the nation called "Meroe" (Meröwe). Both Nubia and Meroe's former territories are today located, for

---

1. Words underscored by this for specific emphasis.
2. Words in parenthesis are by the lecturer for clarity only.

the most part, totally within the geo-political compact of today's Sudan, formerly "<u>el Sud</u>" or "<u>marshland</u>" -- according to the Arab Muslim invaders that captured this area of Africa.

One must wonder whether or not professor Breasted depended on other translations of this part of the Africans of north and east Africa's history, or that these misquotations and racist infractions were only his own concoctions, caused by an accute case of <u>Negrophobia</u>. I cannot understand how he could have read the same sources in the original Hieroglyphics and end in such a sharply different English translation than that which I gather, or that which hundreds more dealing with the same data found. And, I must need say that <u>some of the "most famous and highly rated Egyptologists of all times</u>"-such as Sir E. A. Wallis Budge, Sir James Frazier, Professor G. Maspero, Albert Churchward, M.D., George G. M. James, Count C. F. Volney, Baron Viviant Denon, and even Gerald Massey, do not support the extent of such racism and translations by "<u>the United States of America's most noted Egyptologist of all times</u>"- Professor James Henry Breasted, Ph.D.

Certainly this forthright appraisal of a man of the standing of Professor Breasted in the United States of America's academic society, which image he aided in creating, shall be met with object vengance. But, this too is the price those of us who are of African origin, and involved in the teaching of the history, culture and heritage of the African peoples and their descendants must be ready to pay for the correction of African history as presently taught by racists and religious bigots.

On the next page, 187, Professor Breasted wrote of another of Pharaoh Khekure's sucessful invasions and conquests; this time of Syria. But, he carefully avoided using the name of the Syrians as a pro-noun. Thus, he wrote:

> The Asiatics were defeated in battle, and Sebekhu (the same military commander who fought against the Nubians)[1] took a prisoner.

The good professor failed to insinuate that Syria was made up of many different "tribes," as in the case of his "Nubian tribes." And, of course he could not translate the spelling of the word Syrians with a lower case, or common, "s", syrians, as he did with the word "negroes." Neither did he make them 'syrian herds' like his "negro herds." The Syrians were, during his lifetime, as they are today, considered by his colleagues and educators of the present (all of whom are Europeans and European-Americans) "...one of the Indo-European Aryan peoples," etc., just as European and European-American educators have considered themselves to be over the past two-hundred years; that is, since they became the conquerors of the known world around the early part of the 19th century C.E., beginning with the division of the world between Spain and Portugal by the Pope of the Roman Catholic Church in the middle of the 15th century C.E.

Leaving professor Breasted, for a while at least, one sees the same kind of sophisticated racist Negrophobia in the HANDBOOK OF WORLD HISTORY:CONCEPTS AND ISSUES (Joseph Dunner, Editor), published by the Philosophical Library, Inc., New York, 1967. On page 4, under the meaning of the word "ABOLITIONISM," in the last paragraph by one H. L. Trefousse, the following appears:

> Abolitionism in America played an important role in focusing attention upon the do-

---

1. Words in parenthesis by the lecturer for clarity only.

> mestic evils of slavery. Even though its proponents were often extreme, they succeeded in preparing the way for less radical antislavery leaders.[1] Their skill in propaganda, untiring efforts in the cause, and personal dedication to freedom made them a force for progress in the United States.

It is obvious that the good "liberal", H. L. Trefousse, would have considered Nat Turner and Denmark Vesey (both of them late African Christian members of the clergy, and trained in the Gospel of Jesus Christ according to the King James Version of the Christians' "Holy Bible," and by White Folks) "extremists" for burning down their slavemasters' homes and plantations, or their stud farms where black men and women were studded like wild beasts, or even because their masters were beheaded by them. One would wonder if he would have seen Moses, the redeemer of the African Jews in the Holy Torah; or the Christian George Washington, the first President of the United States of America; in their respective role against the Pharoah Rameses II, and King George II of England, in the same light as "extremists"?

On pages 45 to 46 of the same book one Tibor Payzs wrote the following:

> The notable contributions of the ancient world to Western Civilization were the development of the Greek city-state (polis) particularly the manners and institutions of the Athenian democracy; Hellenic philosophy, particularly that of Socrates,[1] Plato and Aristotle; and the jurisprudence of classical Rome. In theology, the religion of the Hebrews centering around God as a person, and the life and teachings of Jesus Christ had shaped the history of Western man most significantly.

Obviously Tibor Payzs had the opportunity of reading pro-

---

1. Words underscored by the lecturer for special emphasis.

fessor George G. M. James' book, STOLEN LEGACY, New York, 1954, with respect to where the so-called "Greek philosophers" (who were allegedly what Payzs prefered to call "Hellenic philosophers ") received their philosophical training and experience. He also failed to recall that "Socrates," and later on "Aristotle," both were persecuted and prosecuted by the same "Athenian" government's officials for teaching what they learnt from the indigenous Africans of the Nile Valley living in Egypt -- the so-called "Negroes" of today's ancestors. With respect to the "Hebrews," one must wonder if he ever heard of the KABALLAH, and works beyond its scope in importance of the origin of the Hebrew or Jewish religion, such as the NEGATIVE CONFESSIONS from the Osirian Drama of the Coffin Texts where "Moses" co-opted his so-called "TEN COMMANDMENTS" before reaching Mount Sinai for the Lord Jehovah to have handed him another set. In the case of Aristotle, maybe he is unaware how this Greek sacked the Lodges and Libraries of the Africans of Egypt and plagiarized their great works to which he and his cohorts thereafter attached their name.

Tibor Payzs was moved to end his entry in the following manner:

> Born among the Jews, <u>the people of God</u>,[1] received their code of law in the Ten Commandments through the hands of Moses (the Egyptian, and Ethiopian or "Negro")[2], the words of Jesus Christ were to become the norm and measure at the dawn of a era.

Of course "the people of God," or otherwise the so-called "Choosen People" of the Hebrew (Jewish) Torah, are to be accepted

---

1. Words underscored by the lecturer for special emphasis.
2. Words in parenthesis by the lecturer for clarity only.

as such by everyone wherever the "Christian missionaries" of European-American style Christianity dominate jointly with "Western" imperialism and colonialism through usurpers bearing the name "settlers." Other peoples' God or Gods are merely 'heathen false idols' to be relegated to the devil -- His Satanic Majesty. One must wonder if Payzs ever heard of the history of the beginning of the Christian religion and Church in north Africa, Egypt to be exact. Or, of the "three Fathers of the Church"-- Tertullian, St. Augustine and St. Cyprian, all of whom were indigenous Africans like those we call "Negroes, Bantus," and "Africans South of the Sahara." Also, that it was three indigenous Africans who were the first to become martyrs of Christendom -- Felicita, Nymphamo and Perpetua, all three of them having made sainthood later by European Popes of the Christian Church of Europe that succeeded the North African Church. Were it not for men and women such as these great so-called "Negroes", who were most responsible for the popularization of "the Gospel of Jesus Christ" -- Payzs' "norm," there may have been no Christian religion today amounting to much.

Closing with Abraham G. Duker's installment, under the word "anti-Semitism," from page 47 through 64, he deals with all kinds of "anti-Semites", beginning with one "Wilhelm Marr (1873?)", and ending with many who were of "Jewish descent." However, nowhere in his comments has he dealt with the type of 'anti-Semitism' existing among European and European-American (White) Jews with respect to their Black brother and sister Jews of Africa -- the so-called "Falashas," who are properly named BETA ISRAEL (The House of Israel); of the Cochin Jews, many of whom once had to return to their native India due to ranked racism on the part of their fellow Jews from Europe and the United States of America, all because of their brown skin; yet many of those "Chosen people" had suffered the sting of the worse form of racism under the heels of genocide by Adolph Hitler and his Nazis. How strange it is the way we (mankind) behave to each other when we are a part of the oppressor class! How different we behave when our own God (or Gods) is the one who dishes out the punishment to others we do not like! How noble it is to say <u>"we are less racist than the White Anglo-Saxon Protestants"</u> to our so-called "Negro" brothers and sisters because of our financial contributions to "worthy responsible Negro Organization" whose national officers outside of the African-American (Black) communities we control by holding their pursestrings, or by dominating their board of directors! How we too cry "law and order" when in fact we realy and truly mean 'peace and tranquility with the Nigger in his place; just as we say "Urban renewal", when in fact we mean 'Nigger removal'.

The patterns we have witnessed in the major works examined are not specifically isolated incidents, to the contrary, they are the "norm" in European-America (White, Caucasian or Semitic, Christian and Jewish) institutions of learning, private or public, parochial or secular. Sadly enough, these images have been adopted by most of the major "Negro" istitutions dealing with "education for the benifit of African-Americans."This they have done without question, as those who dare to differ in the slightest, and question the racist content of 'anti-Black propaganda,' are themselves immediately charged with 'anti-Semitism' or "anti-

Caucasianism' and soon find their economic livelihood in danger.

The African-American (Black man or woman), having no real economic base in the so-called "American Dream," finds it utterly frustrating and meaningless to act in their proper role in the presence of their spouse in the face of what they have to undergo for their European-American counterparts. This nothingness reverts to the degradation, humiliation, and destruction of the Black man's person to the point where he must sometimes even abandon his most precious heritage -- his family. The responsibility for providing the cultural image that would change this leturgic tradegy rests squarely upon those most involved with the shaping of the Black man's mind - the "BLACK STUDIES INSTRUCTORS" and "WRITERS OF HISTORY" and "BLACK LITERATURE." It is these, who must provide such leadership that would challenge the type of racism displayed in the works of the Breasteds, Budges, Jeffreys, Junods, Hebrew Torah, Christian Bible, and anyother person's works that degrade the image of the African peoples and their descendants anywhere in the world. It is these, who must also provide the facts necessary to show people of African origin everywhere the great and precious heritage that is theirs. It is these, who must record the true history of Black forefathers, so that the black man and his woman and children can have the image necessary for the upliftment of their children unborn to come. It is these, who must make the age-old African proverb that recites,

"MAN KNOW THYSELF",

have usefull meaning to the descendants of those lofty Africans of the Nile Valleys and Great Lakes High-Cultures (civilizations). It is these, who must be the beacon light and the catylistic dynamo for African peoples through their history of the present, having dealt with their past, and make way for their future. And, it is these most sacred responsibilities we, those of us who accept the title of <u>teacher</u>, cannot desicrate; for these are our most sacred TRUST.

>PART I & PART II: Submitted to the African Peoples Congress, Atlanta Georgia, History Workshop Professor John Henrike Clarke, Dr. Harding and Skinner, and Yosef ben-Jochannan, Co-Chr'mn. September 3-6, 1970 C.E.

WHAT "Black Is Beautiful" IS NOT YET READY TO HEAR

Lecture-Essay by yosef ben-jochannan
Instructor in History and Religious Philosophy Africana

Marymount College, Tarrytown, New York

The Assumption: "Black is Beautiful." The fact is that this most common phrase of the late 1960s and beginning of the 1970s is nothing new. "Black" have always been "BEAUTIFUL" from the day the first Black person was born unto a woman and a man in central Africa or Alkebu-lan. But this phrase, the most commonly popular rhetoric being used in the United States of America today, has much more to it. Along with this fad or phrase, however, is the basically underlying force which prevent "Black" from being totally "Beautiful" mentally and spiritually. This phenomena is called "RELIGION," broken down into three main branches -- Judaism, Christianity and Islam. The departmentalization does not ignore the many other religions and their offshoots that are also prevalent among the Blacks; but these are only representative of the barest of minority religious institutions among the so-called "ghetto" or "inner-City" religious adherents, which includes fanatics as well as casual participants.

The major premises of these religions is that "God's" (depending upon which one you believe) "words are written in the scriptures" (Bibles, all of them -- Torah and Quran included) "by His holy inspired men." Anything, and everything, which does not subscribed to this basic dogma can be as "Black" and as "Beautiful" as it desire; yet, it will be austracized by those "Blacks" for whom this declaration, mythological and dogmatical as it is, means everything. Therefore, "Black is Beautiful" only when one is informed of the historical facts, mythological beliefs, and biblical plagerization of more ancient teachings which were responsible for the creation of the various so-called -- "Holy Scriptures " (the Christian Holy Bible, Hebrew or Jewish Holy Torah, and Moslem Holy Qu'ran).

In dealing with religious teachings relative to the three most powerful religions in the "Western World" (Judaism, Christianity and Islam) it is impossible to bypass the foundation upon which all three lies -- THE BOOK OF THE DEAD; the "Book" that records the most ancient written religious and philosophical thoughts known to mankind, all of which were originated and developed by indigenous Africans more than three-thousand (3000) years before the creation of the Holy Torah's "Jehovah, World," and "Adam and Eve " (as related in the First Book of Moses -- Genesis).

Bringing into examination and to the attention of the major Black Community,(to most of them for the first time) will be the following works and many of their writings as extracted themes:

1. Papyrus of Ani
2. Book of the Dead
3. Negative Confessions
4. Coffin Texts
5. Pyramid Texts
6. The Gods of the Egyptians
7. The Golden Bough,(13 vol's.)
8. The Lost Books of the Bible
9. Anacalypsis (2 vols.)
10. Ruins of Empires
11. The Complete Works of Josephus
12. Kaballah
13. Bible Myths and Their Parallels in Other Religions
14. Man and His Gods
15. The Mishna
16. The Tenach
17. The Holy Quran: Text Translation and Community
18. The Bible Handbook

19. The Dawn of Civilization
20. Stolen Legacy
21. The Origin and Evolution of Religion
22. Signs and Symbols of Primordial Man
23. The Bhaghitah
24. Teachings of Amen-e-eope
25. Black Man of the Nile
26. Religion and Mythology
27. The Sixteen Crucified Christs
28. African Origin of the Major "Western Religions"

There will be a host of other offerings as the course continues many of which, like most of these already listed, cannot be purchased at this time due to the fact that they have been out of print for many generations. The fact that most of our professors in the majority of our seminaries are not aware of these works or their contents surely makes it that more important for us to examine them. For it is with the basic information which is unknown to the seminaries, primarily, that this course deals.

Since there will be a significant amount of references to the Africans of Ethiopia; it must be stated, at this juncture, that the indigenous Ethiopians in this context does not in anyway shape or form suggest that the so-called "Sabeans," one is so often told, were the original settlers of that area of Africa; and that they originally came from "Arabia Felix" -- The Arabian Peninsula. The Ethiopia, otherwise called "Kush, Cush, Habeshestan, Abyssinia," etc., being referred to is that area of Africa that was inhabited by Africans indigenous to the continent that was originally called "ALKEBU-LAN" before the Greeks and Romans gave it its present nomenclature --"Africa." It is the same land which was once called "Upper Egypt" and "Axum," Gheeze and Ag'-iate, among many other names by foreigners from Asia and Europe before and since the Christian Era --(birth of Jesus Christ of Nazareth" the last of the "sixteen crucified Christs").

The statement by King Solomon of the Hebrews, or Jews, in which he is supposed to have stated:

"I AM BLACK AND COMELY,"

should serve Black America in ways never yet understood by ordained seminarians or "jack-leg storefront preachers" who received their "calling in a cotton patch" and other such places. But, to deal with the message from Solomon in the context of its Blacknes will draw from the "Negro" ministers and their "Caucasian" (also Semites) teachers the ridiculus cry of "Black" or "Negro racism." However, the blue-eyed blonde Jesus Christ and the Holy Family presented to Blacks remain the God and family that have no color. As such, it should be no wonder that "Negro" educators find it necessary to remove from their library-shelves materials such as this; but they still keep their Holy Bibles that speak of "chosen people" and "inferior people" who Jehovah designated to be blasted into oblivion by various methods of barbarism to obtain the result of genocide. If the Black communities throughout the United States of America and elsewhere can intelligently accept the type of genocide committed by the Hebrews against the Amalakites, Hittites, Jebusites, and countless other nations of people, and the enslavement of others still, on the sole basis that their conduct was "the command of God "-- Jehovah; then they must equally accept that their own enslavement and attempted liquidation by the descendants of the same element of the Bible people was the "command" of the same "God"-- Jehovah. Herein lies the fundamental challenge to the Black Christian, Jew, and Moslem. This is moreso true, especially when one remembers that the "Commandment" that recites:

THOU SHALT NOT KILL

was already "delivered to Moses on Mount Sinai" by the same Jehovah. This bit of Hebrew mythology, loaded as it's with plagiarized particles of information co-opted from the Papyrus of Ani and the Coffin Texts' Negative Confessions, nevertheless, should have guided the moral sensitivity of the Black community against the biblical genocide. Why is the opposite in fact true? Because Blacks, similarly their White counterparts, have been told that the only book they need to read about their religious belief and religion's history is the "Holy Scriptures;" of course the only "true scriptures" depend upon which one of the so-called "Western Religions" -- Judaism, Christianity and Islam -- one subcribe to.

But, what happens to the "Black Is Beautiful" desenters or the curious? What happens when they cite the following descrepancies in the so-called "Holy Scriptures inspired by God"? Especially in the First Book of Moses, Genesis, of the Holy Torah (Christian "Old Testament"), ii: 17, which states:

> But of the tree of knowledge of good and evil, thou shalt not eat of it: for in the day that thou eatest thereof thou shalt surely die.

Genesis v : 5 states:

> And all the days that Adam lived were nine hundred and thirty years; and he died.

Something is radically wrong between the above two statements. Adam "ate of the forbidden fruit" hundreds of years before he was to "...surely die." The day that he actually "died" from the effects of eating the "fruit" was so remotely connected to the penalty for doing same that it appears to be profitable to take a chance in violating prohibitions of said nature. But, in the

571

same Genesis i : 25, 26, one finds God, the Hebrew, Christian and Moslem -- Jehovah, Jesus Christ, Al'lah, doing the following:

> And God made the beast of the earth after his kind, and cattle after their kind, and everything that creepeth upon the earth after his kind: and God saw that it was good.
> And God said, Let us make man in our image, after our likeness.

However, Genesis ii : 18 - 20, contradicts the above. It states:
> And the Lord God said, it is not good that the man should be alone; I will make him an help meet for him. And out of the ground the Lord God formed every beast of the field, and every fowl of the air; and brought them unto Adam... but for Adam there was not found an help meet for him.

In the first statement "man" was made after the "beasts;" and in the latter he was made before the "beasts." Which one of these is correct?

We note that "Keturah" was "Abraham's wife, as stated in Genesis xxvi : 1; yet, Chronicles i : 32, mention that the same "Keturah" was in fact:

Abraham's concubine.

The above discrepancies in the "God inspired" written Book of Genesis, the First Book of Moses, are no better than those in the so-called "Lost Books of the Bible" -- otherwise known as the "Apocrypha." These are the volumes of the "Holy Bible" which deal with the life of Jesus Christ coming and doings, all of which were treated as the esoteric possession of certain wealthy and learned scholars, particularly those of the Upper-Class in the clergy. For this reason they were only availabe in their original Greek and Latin versions for centuries. Now that they have been reduced to every-day English, they have been ignored by the masses of the parishoners who once clamoured to know about them. Why? Because of the same type of propaganda which keeps them believing that "the only true Books of the Holy Bible are those selected by the Council of Bishops at Nicene." They should examine them, even though the "Lost Books" are in most instances no less mythological than the others; this being true, as in the following from the the BOOK OF MARY, Chapter II, Verse 6:

> For the first mother of your nation Sarah, was she not barren even till her eightieth year: And yet even in the end of her old age brought forth Isaac, in whom the promise was made a blessing to all nations.

The above story was also mentioned in Genesis xvi : 2, etc. and xviii : 10 etc. What would happen in 1970 C.E. if an eighty year old woman said that she was pregnant? Which doctor, priest, rabbi, minister or iman would beleive her? Yet, we are to believe that this was not so very strange a happening in ancient biblical times; because Mary's mother, Anna, the grandmother of Jesus Christ of Nazareth, also became pregnant by an angel when she conceived her; the only difference between both conceptions being that Mary was only thirteen (13) years old at the time of her pregnancy. Note, also, that Joachin, Anna's husband and Mary's father, had nothing to do with Anna's pregnancy, she too being a virgin at Mary's birth; the angel had struck before; and all of this appeared in THE BOOK OF MARY, Chapter iii, Verses 1 - 5; see also Luke i : 28; Mathew xiv : 26; and Luke ii : 37. What is stranger yet; Joseph, Mary's husband and Jesus Christ's father, had two (2) fathers, according to the following account in Luke iii :23:

> Jesus... the son of Joseph, which was the son of Heli,"...etc.;

and according to Mathew i : 6:

> And Jacob begat Joseph, the husband of Mary,

of whom was born Jesus;"...etc.

The entire episode between Joseph and Mary was heightened when Joseph found out that Mary was pregnant for someone else besides himself (see BOOK OF MARY, Chapter viii, Verses 1 - 8). It took some very careful pleading by "...and angel of God..." to convince Joseph against his "suspecion of (Mary) being a whore " (See BOOK OF MARY, Chapter viii, Verse 6). Joseph was asleep and dreaming when he was convinced that Mary was pregnant for God and not for another mortal man (See Matthew i : 19).

All of the above myths deal with the birth and origin of Jesus Christ of Nazzareth. His death also created just as many myths. But, in Acts xxvi : 23 the following appears:

> "Christ...the first that should rise from the dead...,"etc.

Yet, in REVELATION i : 5 it is said that Jesus Christ was...:

> "The first begotten of the dead.

However, JOHN xi : 43 - 44; also 2 KINGS iv : 32, 35; and LUKE vii : 12 - 15 recite the following about his death:

> And when he thus had spoken, he cried with a loud voice, Lazarus, come forth. And he that was dead came forth, bound hand and foot with grave-clothes.

It should be obvious to anyone that the chroniclers, if at all acting from God's "inspiration," were not checking their own, or each other, manuscript for errors and contradictions. Because certain individuals may not be able to accept these facts as being historically biblical, the following source materials are listed: THE BIBLE HANDBOOK, edited by G.W. Foote and W.P. Ball, The Pioneer Press, London, 1888; also, THE LOST BOOKS OF THE BIBLE and the FORGOTTEN BOOKS OF EDEN,(Forum Books), The World

Publishing Company, Cleveland and New York, 1963.

    Among the Yorubas of west Africa's God, Olodumare, His Orishas (minor-Gods or Angels) were equally birthed by both male and female "virgins" who had no sexual intercourse; also in many hundreds of cases this happened with the ancient Africans of Egypt, Europeans of Greece, Asians of Persia, etc. But, before Jesus Christ of Nazzareth and the Orishas of Olodumare the God Ra of Kimit (Sais or Egypt) was known to be the first to cause "virgin births to occur"(more than 4000 years before the beginning of Adam and Eve's creation by the Hebrew and Christian God, Jehovah) This one can be best observed in the PAPYRUS OF ANI or BOOK OF THE DEAD. Even the "resurrection of the dead, reincarnation, releasing of the spirit and soul, entrance into heaven," are all known to have been taught and experienced by the indigenous Africans of the Nile Valleys (Blue and White, also Atbara) and Great Lakes region High-Cultures (civilizations). In the PAPYRUS OF ANI the God Horus and the God Osiris are involved with the Goddess Isis in the reproduction of each other, and in the capacity of their mother, through "virgin births." Among the Asian religions and their teaching the God Bacchus, who is sometimes called "Jesus Christ," was also said to be born of a "virgin birth" before the same trick was accomplished by the "virgin Mary,"Jesus Christ of Nazzareth's mother, thousands of years later. The same parallels are also appearent in the Hindu and Shintu religions of the "Far East." In Ethiopia there were also countless minor Gods that came about from the Sun God by way of "virgin births" without the benifit of sexual intercourse or artificial insemination; the latter scientific procedure not being known to the ancients, nor to anyone else until the late 19th and 20th century C.E.

In MAN AND HIS GODS the author, Homer W. Smith, set the entire scene straight when he wrote the following:

> So important was the holy traffic of the temple that at the opening of Mesopotanian history the priests virtually controlled the country. They acted as intermediaries in all business transactions, they lent grain and precious metals at high rates of interest, they dictated the laws of marriage, slavery and real estate, and otherwise by their sasred trusteeship invaded all economic life. It was the essential tragedy of the Land of of the Two Rivers, the prototype of the Garden of Eden, that it never gained freedom from the dominance of the priestly mind

Mr. Smith's observations are typically what happened at the dawn of all High-Cultures both in Africa and Asia; the same held true for Europe later on when the Greeks and Romans came into contact with the Africans and Asians (just before Homer) and copied civilized living from them, thus establishing the same type of priestly dominated way-with-all system of living. It was the priestly cast who also influenced and controlled the ancient Hebrews, including Moses, and Abraham (the first Hebrew or "Jew") before him, also the Greeks and Romans -- the so-called "philosophers -- through the Mysteries System philosophic teachings they had developed in Kimit (Egypt) after receiving it from Puanit and other High-Cultures further south. These institutions of learning, "LODGES," had their main center -- "GRAND LODGE" or "MOTHER LODGE" -- located on the banks of the Nile River at a place in Kimit called "LUXOR." The main center was where all priests, the title more-or-less equivalent to Ph.D. in modern times, received their final degrees in all of the major disciplines , including philosophy, religion, medicine, science, mathematics, etc., all of which have been attributed to the so-called "Greek Philosophers," most of whom were educated in Kimit under African Priests of the Mysteries System; those who were not were educated by teachers who were themselves educated by said Africans.

The priests, as later on the "disciples of Jesus Christ," were the very ones who shaped the thinking of their followers, which included the king and his subjects, thus the entire nation. In so doing they made certain that their teaching also perpetuated their own personal economic holdings as being "sacred." And, in order to maintain their own personal wealth and upper-class status in each government they also steered their religion's teachings and writings, "sacred" and "Inspired" of course, towards myths that made their holding typical to that of their God. This was the role of the priests of all of the ancient religions before the Christian era. It is a role that has seen very little meaningful changes in the last 6000 to 8000 years. For, at no time in the history of organized society has religion and religious community within any state gone against the prevailing rulers that be, the so-called "Power Structure," for the benefit of its parishioners so long as said "power" guaranteed its special privilege status for the priests that is on par with rulers of the peoples' "secular life." Church and state have always shared in the exploitation of the masses of people; this marriage having existed even in the United States of America to a great degree; and as long as the state remains as is it shall not be severed. The national religion of the United States of America is in fact Christianity, the sect otherwise known as "Protestantism, an extension of Hebrewism -- "Judaism" as its misnomer; but Roman Catholicism, from its home base in the Vatican City (Rome) remains a potent factor in America's Christendom. Judaism, on the otherhand, must encourage said establishment in order for its own survival, being that it is in fact the mother" of all forms of Christianity; its mother, the religion of the God Ra (the Sun God of the indigenous Gods of Alkebu-lan which the Greeks and Romans renamed "Africa"), is nevertheless purposefully suppressed as if it was not responsible for them all, including Islam; even the type of Islam practise by the Honourable Elijah Mohammed's "NATION OF ISLAM" -- "Black Muslims" according to professor Eric C. Lincoln's book of said name.

After examining the indigenous Mexicans "FIRST WOMAN," also Called by their Spanish colonizers and enslavers "the Woman of Our Flesh," which is appearently older than Jesus Christ's mother, Mary; and even Adam's Eve; we find that she too was accompanied by a great male "snake" that appeared to be tempting her. On this point Franklin was obliged to write in his historic work, BUDDHISTS AND JEYNES, the following:

> A striking instance is recorded by the very intelligent traveler (Wilson), regarding a representation of the Fall of our first parents, sculptured in the magnificent temple of Ipsambul, in Nubia. He says that a very exact representation of Adam and Eve in the Garden of Eden is to be seen in the cave, and that the serpent climbing round the tree is especially delineated, and the whole subject of the tempting of our first parents most accurately exhibited.

The above extract was taken from Sir Godfrey Higgins two volumes work, ANACALYPSIS, page 403. This type of reporting was not in any sense of the imagination an isolated incident; for in addressing his audience with regards to the "...inspiration of the scriptures...," the "fall of man,""incarnation, atonement," and "...the Devil with his Hell-fire..," Sir William Jones, first president of the Royal Asiatic Society, wrote:

> Either the first eleven chapters of Genesis, all due allowance being made for a figurative Eastern style, are true, or the whole fabric of our religion is false.

The above was extracted from the ASIATIC RESEARCHES, vol. i, page 225.

Quoting from Sir Godfrey Higgins' ANACALYPSIS, vol. I, page 104, once more, one finds that a Colonel Tod, in his work, HISTORY RAJAPOUTANA, page 581, states:

> A drawing, brought by Colonel Combs from a scuptured column in a cave-temple in the South of India, represents the first pair at the foot of the ambrosial tree, and a serpent entwined among the heavily-laden boughs, presenting to them some of the fruit from his mouth. The tempter appears to be at that part of his discourse, when '--his words, replete with guile, into her heart too easy entrance won: Fixed on the fruit she gazed.

This is quite a curious subject to have been engraved on an ancient 'pagan temple' and at the same time appear in the 'holy scripture' of the Holy Torah, Holy Bible (all versions), and the Holy Qur'an.

Even realizing that their Judaeo-Christian religion came from an African-Asian mythological foundation that spreaded all over the entire world, including the so-called "Western World" and "New World" -- before Cristobal Colon (Christopehr Columbus) reached the Caribbean Islands in 1492 C.E., not discovered them, the "greats" of England could not accept this truth; neither can the "greats" of the United States of America theological adherents of the 20th century C.E. In this same regards one finds the

Bishop of Manchester, England, Church of England, writing the following in the MANCHESTER EXAMINER AND TIMES:

> The very foundation of our faith, the very basis, the very nearnest and dearest of our consolations are taken from us, when one line of that sacred volume, on which we base everything, is declared to be untruthful and untrustworthy.

Lastly, the principal of St Aiden's College, Dr. Baylee, a theological university at Birkenhead, England, and also author of the "Manual" entitled, VERBAL INSPIRATION, which was directed specifically to the students of his institution, wrote:

> ...if the account of Creation in Genesis falls, Christ and the apostles follows if the book of Genesis is erroneous , so also are the Gospels.

Ironically, it is this basic fear among modern-day theologians, members of the Hebrew, Christian and Islamic clergy, also their lay workers, which makes it impossible for even professors in their seminaries to tell the TRUTH that the story of "Adam and Eve in the Garden of Eden" is a common-place myth that has its corallory all over the inhabited world; and that most of the variances are older than the adopted version of the Hebrews as written in their First Book of Moses -- Genesis. They fear that their church, synagogue, temple, or mosque, will be emptied the first day they reveal to their parishioners that the "Creation" story was not in fact "written by God" and "handed down to Moses on Mount Sinai;" but, that it is a common folklore in many places all over the planet Earth. That the errors, inconsistencies and contradictions in their "Holy scriptures" or "Holy Bible" (Old Testament and New, Torah and Qur'an, etc.) are the same type of confusion generally suffered by ordinary men throughout their attempts at trying to write about the beginning, destiny, and the end of man's life as it seemed; death being the basis for most of the so-called "Holy scriptures" or Holy writings." Also, that in the BOOK OF THE DEAD or PAPYRUS OF ANI, 6000 years before Jesus Christ of Nazzareth was born, the ancient indigenous Africans had already undertaken to decipher the beginning and the ending to human life and their meaning. And, that before them, the Romiti -- otherwise called "Egyptians," other Africans from central-east Africa had already reached their own zenith in these pursuits to the point of establishing most of the signs and symbols, also numerological system, mankind still use in Judaism, Christianity and Islam, the so-called "Western Religions." For further readings into this area the following works of Albert Churchward, M.D., should be used: THE ORIGIN AND EVOLUTION OF RELIGION: SIGNS AND SYMBOLS OF PRIMORDIAL MAN; THE ORIGIN AND EVOLUTION OF MANKIND. To these should be added Homer W. Smith's, MAN AND HIS GODS.

Certainly most of those who correctly beleive that "Black is Beautiful" will be astounded by the revelations in the works I have so far suggested for research and analysis; that is, providing they have not already read my two works, BLACK MAN OF THE NILE, and, AFRICAN ORIGINS OF THE MAJOR "WESTERN RELIGIONS." Yet, the following works must be added to your reading list with respect to the same reason given before, and for reasons which you will draw by your own conclusion after reading them: Count C.F. Volney's, RUINS OF EMPIRES; Sir James Frazier's, THE GOLDEN BOUGH, 13 vols.; George C. M. James,' STOLEN LEGACY; all of them reveal much of the hidden truth about the so-called "Western Religions" which most religious leaders suppress and try to keep secretly in their own possession; of course this does not apply to the average "men of the cloth" who received they "calling" without having the feintest of idea about the history of any religion except for the particular version of the bible given to them from birth or during their conversion to whatever faith they belong, which of course includes Judaism, Christianity and Islam.

This lecture, as all of the others I have so far given you, is certainly provocative, and it is meant to be; but, in the last analysis it is you, the student, who must conclude your own position from the data presented to you in the works you have had the privilege of examining, which very few of your predecessors or contemporaries even know existed. It is you, who must scrutinize each and every word of truth or lie therein. It is you, who must be willing to examine every word and let the truth, as you understand it, fall wherever it may. It is upon you that the burden of conscience as to just what is truth or lie, morality or myth, in the so-called "Sacred Scriptures" which we have become so accustomed to believe we cannot live without is infallable or fallable.

The most ironic aspect of it all is that it is in fact you who will be judged the "heritic" if you find that the "Holy Scriptures" are in error; and it is also you who shall be equally crucified if you do not. For, at both extremes of this issue, man and his religion, stand the watch-dogs who must protect their respective and particular political, economic, social, and financial interests in what is otherwise called "RELIGION" and "RELIGIOUS INSTITUTIONS." These religiously bigoted men and women, and sometimes their children are added in, can hear no other "TRUTH" than that which they have established or adopted to protect their own personal interests, which of course become synonymous with "God's interests." For these reasons, and many more not mentioned in this or any other lecture I have given you, you too may learn what it means to be "NAILED TO THE CROSS."

As your instructor, I only ask of you to consider that it is not necessary to change ones religious belief, neither to be tolerant of others, nor even to recognize that others exist; for to do any of these would be to act in object selfishness. What if you should follow my advise; you would only notice that that is what is being demanded of us by our so-called "religious leaders" in all of the so-called "Western Religions." However it is in my own opinion, no one else do I speak for in this regard, wrong. Therefore, what I ask in reality is that you, look for "TRUTH;" and when you find that you have discovered "TRUTH," act with the deepest sense of your own conviction, but remembering always these simple little words from THE KASIDAH OF HAJI ABU el-YEZDI (as translated into English from the original Arabic by Sir Richard F. Burton):

> ALL FAITH IS FALSE, ALL FAITH IS TRUE
> TRUTH IS THE SHATTERED MIRRORS STREWN
> IN MYRIAD BITS; WHILE EACH BELIEVES
> HIS LITTLE BIT THE WHOLE TO OWN.

But always also taking into mind:

> RELIGIOUS MISERY REPRESENTS AT ONCE THE EXPRESSION OF AND THE PROTEST AGAINST ACTUAL MISERY. RELIGION IS THE MOAN OF THE OPPRESSED CREATURES, THE HEART OF A HEARTLESS WORLD, THE SENSE OF SENSELESS CONDITIONS. IT IS THE OPIUM OF THE PEOPLE.[1]

---

1. Zur Kritik der Hegelschen Rechtsphilosophie, Aus dem literischen Nachlass von Karl Marx, Berlin, 1928, vol. I, pp 384f.

JUDAISM, THE BLACK JEW or ISRAELITE?

and

AFRICAN-AMERICAN or BLACK NATIONALISM

Twenty-two (22) years ago (1949 C.E.) when I wrote and published (in Spain) a pamphlet entitled "NOSOTRO LOS JUDEOS NEGRO," WE THE BLACK JEWS, I was still an ardent adherent of the Hebrew faith (Jewish religion); a son of GAD - one of the "TRIBES OF ISRAEL" which is no longer represented among European and European-American (White) Jews; European-American Jewry only having among its community - KAHENS (Cohens), LEVITES, JUDAHS (misnomered "Jews") and ISRAELITES (the common people).

My disillusionment with Western Judaism came a very short time after I arrived in the United States of America and witnessed that the WHITE JEWS, the so-called "SEMITES," had no official association with the BLACK JEWS; and, that, the behaviour of the WHITE JEWS to their BLACK co-religionists was no different to that of the WHITE CHRISTIANS with respect to their BLACK CHRISTIAN brothers and sisters. Yet, wherever there existed a variance to this observed patern of behaviour, the WHITE Christian Church had opened its doors officially ; a few even had one or more ordained BLACK ministers; but, not a single WHITE Synagogue had the first BLACK rabbi or cantor on its staff, the same in reverse for the BLACK SYNAGOGUES.

Having been involved with what was officially a 99.9999 etc. percent predominantly WHITE <u>Inter-collegiate Zionist Federation Of America</u> (IZFA) at one of the colleges where I studied and lectured, and also attended a few of said organization's area-group sessions of which I was the only BLACK Hebrew (Jew); here too I was constantly greeted with examinations and challenges to my "JEWISHNESS;" something which no WHITE student who joined IZFA was ever subjected. I also visited the Hilel Foundation meetings at various colleges in the New York metropolitan area; but, I found no fellowship and brotherhood, except at the Uptown City College Hilel Foundation Center under the rabbinical supervision of one Rabbi Zuckerman - a very fine man; and particularly from a fellow student who was planning to enter the rabbinate - Victor (Vic) Cohen, also his girlfriend or fiancee - Minnie. All three of them I have unfortunately failed to keep in contact over the past years. They were the only fellow Hebrews, or Jews, of the WHITE Jewish student body of European-American origin that treated me as a fellow human being, much less a fellow Hebrew. From this point onwards I decided to re-examine my own involvement and relationship to Judaism; particularly with non-Falasha Isiah oriented forms of Hebrewism. Because I could not accept my Beta Israel - House of Israel (Falasa) upbringing as being typical to the European-American Talmudic oriented Judaism and its race prejudice. There was more to my re-examination of course. The first was my inability to compromise not "...EATING MEAT AND MILK TOGETHER...," a prohibition not mentioned in any part of the HOLY TORAH, but certainly in the European-American Jewish TALMUD. Falashas accept the HOLY TORAH'S <u>"Thou shalt not boil the meat in its mother's milk</u>...," etc. This is just a sample of what was later to cause my complete break with "Western man's Talmudic Judaism.

 Not being able to have ANIMAL SACRIFICE on Yum Kippur, Rosh Hashanah and Pesach (Day of Atonement, New Year and Pass Over), among other religious customs, taboos, etc. practiced by the Hebrews of Ethiopia, but in variance or non-existent among European and European-American Judaism; as such, life as a BLACK Hebrew or Jew in the City of New York began to become unbearable.

My break with <u>Talmudic Judaism</u>, as the only way of life, did not begin as a result of my intolerable understanding of its "Westernized" customs and practices; such as having tombstone to mark the grave of the deceased; or the association of Judaism and its teachings in the HOLY TORAH with capitalistic democracy, etc. It began as a direct result of the willIful mis-interpretations of the "CHOOSEN PEOPLE" proclamation in the HOLY TORAH (Christian OLD TESTAMENT) by European-American (White) Jewish leaders as a criteria for some sort of a "..SPECIAL RACE OF PEOPLE" called "SEMITES" rather than a religious explanation or classification. For, with the "CHOOSEN PEOPLE" myth came the equally bigoted "SEMITIC RACE" syndrome, which, of course, excluded me from KOSHER status with the SEMITES, being that my colour - BLACK - allegedly made me one of the "CURSED" descendants of "CANAAN" - the "SON OF HAM," the "GRANDSON OF NOAH." This latter biblical "CURSE" I have detailed in AFRICAN ORIGINS OF THE MAJOR "WESTERN RELIGIONS" before you - one of your required readings. And, it is at this very point in my religious life that I was first enticed to examining my own religious belief in the "CHOSEN PEOPLE" propaganda honestly. In so doing, I was supprised to discover that the one book I considered to be THE ONLY SACRED POSITION one could have that is not material in value was just a compilation of facts and fiction, myths and taboos; some of original Hebrew vintage, the vast majority primarily of rehashed African and Asian peoples' creative development and mythological concepts about their own fear of the unknown; very few, if any, European in origin. For the first time I also began looking at the various taboos in my own religion which prevented my total **involvement with the African-American struggles** within the United States of America and other parts of the "Western Hemisphere," seeing myself only as an Ethiopian (Black) Hebrew whose sole fight against European and European-American imperial colonialism and neo-colonialism resting solely in the continent of Alkebu-lan (Africa); but at the same instance being totally involved in assisting projects designed exclusively for the enhancement of the sales of ISRAEL BONDS; not remembering that Kimit (Sais or Egypt) is still Alkebu-lan territory, though the current leadership is not pro-African nationalist in the sense of a Nkrumah or Nyeree, but instead pro-Pan-Arabic in its nationalism - solely religious (Muslim or Moslem) as the Israelis. I had to examine this aspect of my involvement with international politics from the point of where I fit into the total scheme of things should either side of the European-American Jew or Asian-Arab Muslim contestants win their never-ending war of <u>genocide, racism and religious bigotry</u>. It is at this juncture that the racist interpretation of the "CHOSEN PEOPLE" myth slapped me directly in the eyes of TRUTH and REALITY, which made me seek further clarification among BLACK JEWS (who prefer to be called "ISRAELITES") born and raised in the United States of America and the Caribbean Islands. But, there was no depth of feeling on this question amongst them. They too were caught-up in a state of vacillation, a state of non-committedness, on the part of the Arab Muslims or the European

Jews on the Egyptian-Israelis war and land question; even worse than this on the "AFRICAN NATIONALIST" vs "NEGRO INTEGRATIONIST" committment. They were, and so far as I can observe at present, still are, FENCE STRATTLERS as I have pointed out in AFRICAN ORIGINS OF THE "WESTERN RELIGIONS,"Alkebeu-lan Books Associates, New York, 1970.

Having no real base to rest my African Nationalist orientation in the United States of America, except for the very weak pro-Marcus Moziah Garvey-type movements that struggled almost helplessly to exist, being the BLACK BOOGEYMAN organization during the period before Malcom X became African or BLACK NATIONALIST conscious (at the time being still of the Nation Of Islam that teaches the "ASIATIC BLACK MAN" theory), I considered, and consented, to assist the local Harlem African Nationalist movements that were "BACK TO AFRICA" oriented. The group which I felt was doing the most in this direction, at that time, was the one that was actively engaged in rendering aid and comfort to the "AFRICAN FREEDOM FIGTHERS who came to the United Nations Organization in search of "JUSTICE" against the same people who actually dominated this so-called "PEACE-KEEPING ORGANIZATION," the so-called "FREE WORLD NATIONS AND THEIR REPRESENTATIVES." The Africans,the African Nationalists of Harlem were aiding came from such colonies as Ghana (formerly called "Gold Coast Crown Colony" by the British), Congo (both French and Belgium controlled), Ngola (Portugese Angola), Monomotapa (Portugese Mozambique), Zambia and Zimbabwe (British Northern and Southern Rhodesia), Guinea (French controlled), and other groups like those of the Monomotapa Empire (today's citadel of "White Supremacy," otherwise called "REPUBLIC OF SOUTH AFRICA "- a member of the so-called "FREE WORLD", also a member of the "UNITED NATIONS ORGANIZATION"). There were countless others from islands of the British Caribbeans. The organization which I am alluding to was the AFRICAN NATIONALS IN AMERICA, Inc., founded and led by its then President, Louis Michaux, proprietor of one of the only two (2) bookstores in Harlem at the time dealing primarily with the history and culture of BLACK PEOPLES of the world; the other being the FREDERICK DOUGLAS BOOK CENTER under the ownership of the historian, Richard B. Moore, author of THE WORD NEGRO, ITS ORIGIN AND EVIL USE. The organization's <u>African Assistance Program</u> was under the direction of Alex Prempeh - its Vice-President.

My selection of the Michaux-led group did not in any way or form underplayed the major significance of the AFRICAN NATIONALIST PIONEER MOVEMENT founded and led by the late Carlos Cooks, its Administrator. But, whereas Cooks' group was solely domestic in its politics and operations, and quite anti-African heads-of-state; Michaux's group was the complete opposite, to the point of overtness in its dedication towards Pan-Africanism. Yet, it was Carlos Cooks' group that was most instrumental in propagandizing the "BUY BLACK, LOOK BLACK, THINK BLACK, LIVE BLACK, BLACK IS BEAUTIFUL" image and psychology which is today most dominant in the mind of " YOUNG BLACK AND BEAUTIFUL" African-Americans with their "NATURAL" hair-do, misnomered "Afro-Style" by European-Americans. It was also the Cooks-oriented Garveyite people, the GRANDIOSA MODELS" - headed by the Bratwaithe brothers - who actually spearheaded the drive in "NATURAL LOOK" among Black female and male at a time when they were subjected to all sorts of "anti-Black

Nationalists" cat-calls from European-American dominated integrationist "Negroes" of "RESPONSIBLE-TYPE CIVIL RIGHTS ORGANIZATIONS" having the <u>good seal of approval</u> from "WELL-MEANING" paternalistic "WHITE LIBERALS" who still control the purse-strings of said "NEGRO MOVEMENTS." These points, plus many others too numerous to mention here, finally caused my total engagement with the African Nationals In America, Inc., and my eventual election as its President in 1963 C.E.; a position I held until my resignation in 1966 C.E. My election followed the resignation of President Michaux. At this period I was quite involved with the United Nations Educational, Scientific and Cultural Organization, a quasi-agency of the U.N., otherwise known as UNESCO; also with the independence struggle of the Africans of Zanzibar against the British appointed Arabs who were given control of that African nation after Britain could no longer drain the land and people of their natural resources and life-blood; this obligation I discharged with full devotion even through the revolution in December 1963 to January 1964, and up to its unification with the Republic of Tanganyika under the name of the REPUBLIC OF TANZANIA in 1964, a few short months after the Africans victory over the inheritors of an Arab-British colonial empire.

Having taught on the college level in various local and out-of-town institutions during this same period, mostly in the capacity of "VISITING LECTURER IN AFRICAN AND CARIBBEAN HISTORY AND CULTURE" (cultural or social anthropology and history departments) - at the time not yet designated AFRICAN or BLACK STUDIES, I was obliged to return to my writing in these two (2) disciplines; being that I was constantly subjected to not having my contract renewed at the colleges I lectured. Why? Because I dared to teach, at that time before "Black Power" became popular, or was even proposed, what you find in my two (2) latest books - BLACK MAN OF THE NILE, and , AFRICAN ORIGINS OF THE MAJOR "WESTERN RELIGIONS," all of which I am now still teaching on a full-time basis; and, all of which I am again saying in many of the colleges that previously refused me renewal of my contract. This type of acceptance also made me take time-out to further re-examine my own position and involvement in my hold on BLACK JUDAISM and my HEBREWISM; having been convinced at that juncture that it could no longer serve my needs nationalistically, or even "RACIALLY;" since in these United States of America and the nation called ISRAEL it is in fact operating on a RACIAL level as well as RELIGIOUSLY; my BLACK SKIN therefore making me PERSONAE NON-GRATIS in either scope amongst its European and European-American controllers in the United States of America and Israel.

Where was the best place to start my re-examination? The BOOK OF GENESIS (First Book Of Moses), of course. This was the book Moses personally wrote, including the BOOK OF EXODUS (Second Book Of Moses), according to Jewish mythology, which states that:

"..MOSES WROTE FROM THE DICTATION BY JEHOVAH;"
at least this is the way it was spoon-fed to me as a youngster. From this juncture I was on my way to write a treatise on the meaning of the ISRAELITE WAY-OF-LIFE and the RELIGIOUS TEACHINGS OF EUROPEAN-AMERICAN JUDAISM as seen by an African Nationalist. But, where did I found I could not any longer support my religion or its religious teachings as being the "SOLE TRUTH"? The same BOOK OF GENESIS, which was allegedly "...WTITTEN BY GOD-INSPIRED

PROPHETS AND SCRIBES, HOLY MEN;" of course no INSPIRED HOLY WOMEN was capable of Jehovah's (God's) message passing down to them. If "GOD-INSPIRED SCRIBE" wrote the BOOK OF GENESIS and all of the other FIVE BOOKS OF MOSES in the Holy Torah I re-examined, He must have also had His "...HOLY SCRIBES" write the Africans of Kimit's (Romiti of Kimit - Egypt) BOOK OF THE DEAD, PAPYRUS OF ANI, PYRAMID TEXTS, COFFIN TEXTS, NEGATIVE CONFESSIONS, and many of the other Africans' works plagiarized by His "HOLY SCRIBES" that wrote the Haribu (Hebrew or "Jewish") HOLY TORAH, MISHNAH, AFT-TORAH, KABALLAH, and other works of Judaica - including those allegedly "...WRITTEN BY MOSES" himself.

Let us examine together a few of my findings which Jewish theologians and rabbis charged to God - JEHOVAH or ADONOI (ADNOI) and His "...INSPIRED HOLY MEN." We have Abraham, the first of the Haribus (today misnomered " Jews "), living among the "NEGROES" or "CANAANITES" - the descendants of HAM, the SON OF NOAH, upon whom a "CURSE " was placed by Jehovah - himself. Abraham is with them because Jehovah allowed a famine to take place, the same FAMINE Abraham and his family encountered in the Asian desert. This was during the period when the Haribu-speaking, not Yiddish-speaking, tribes were being pushed out of Asia towards Africa - Kimit - by the Hittite , Palestinian and Mitanian peoples from Harran, also by the Assyrians that later joined them. The rulers of this conglamorate of all kinds of mankind were called "HYKSOS KINGS;" the same people that invaded Kimit (Egypt according to "Jewish" mythology in the Holy Torah) later on in c1675 and was driven out in c1750 BCE. This period is aptly referred to in GENESIS XII; also in my book, BLACK MAN OF THE NILE.

We must note that the ancient Haribus wanted their own glory when they became literate in Kimit; therefore Abraham is shown entering Kimit around c1730 BCE with his teenage wife - SARA (Sarah), whom the Hyksos Pharoah (King) of Kimit tried to seduce but was unable to so do <u>because of the intercession of by Jehovah</u> - the Haribus' God. But this myth was not a Haribu original. The story is taken from the "TALE OF TWO BROTHERS" in the Africans of Kimit's work from which the entire "JOSEPH AND HIS BROTHERS" myth also had its origin. Abraham's distrust of the pharoah raping his teenage wife, and trying to conceal her in his chest (box), also came from the warped interpretations by the European Jews following the Sixth (6th) century Babylonian Talmudist scholars "westernized" version on the HAM and the END OF THE WORLD myth in GENESIS X:6; since Kimit (Egypt) - the biblical MIZRAIN - was supposed to have been one of Ham's sons; Ham having been subjected to the same "CURSE" Jehovah allegedly placed upon his son - CANAAN because his father - HAM - "STARED AT HIS" grandfather's - NOAH - "NAKEDNESS" while he was laying drunk in the ARK which Jehovah made him build to save his family and two of each living thing before the FLOOD that ended the Haribus' WORLD. From here on we commence to see a series of plagiarizms on the part of the ancient Haribu, or "Jewish," scribes and prophets. One must wonder what other acts of similar magnitude there were in the MISSING BOOKS OF THE HOLY TORAH" - such as the BOOK OF YASHER and the BOOK OF THE WARS OF YWH dealing with the assemblage of the Haribus as they wandered in the most destitute condition in the Asian desert before being saved among the indigenous Africans (Blacks or "Negroes") of Kimit they so much came to despise much later on. Yet, only little bits of information from these two ("lost") books are shown in the BOOK OF JOSHUA X:13; NUMBERS XXI:14; and 2 SAMUEL I:18. But the earliest of the "MISSING BOOKS," the BOOK OF THE STORY OF ADAM mentioned in GENESIS V:1, was suppressed to avoid anyone actually tracing the common genealogy of the Haribus from "CRATION" to "NOAH AND THE FLOOD," according to the Hebrew myth about how "JEHOVAH CREATED THE UNIVERSE." There was, also, a BOOK OF GENEALOGY that suffered suppression for the same reason as the latter. Of course the BOOK OF YWH (another way of saying Jehovah) had to be suppressed because of its infantile description of a mythological "GOD" which not even the most devoutly religious fanatic of the late twentieth-century C.E. could accept as TRUTH. In this latter work Ywh also appeared in different animal forms, similar to the teachings of the VOODOO religion of West Africa, and as later adopted in the PASSOVER story of EXODUS XIV:23 when Ywh appeared as a "MERE (female) HORSE" according to the MIDRASH of Mekhilta di R. Shimon 51, 54; and MIDRACH WAYOSHA 52. For further details on these facts refer to Robert Graves and Raphael Pati, HEBREW MYTHS: THE BOOK OF GENESIS, McGraw-Hill Book Company, New York, 1966, p. 11 (first published by Doubleday Company, Garden City, New York, 1963).

Entering further into Hebrew mythology in this lecture-essay serves no useful purpose at this time, because I have treated it much more extensively in other lectures in this course and in works before you. However, I do hope that you, as students, will gather why (at this zenith) I decided that if I had to remain a religious person (according to common usage in its "Western" sense), I would have had to become much more informed in the sources from whence the BOOK OF GENESIS - the First Book Of Moses- received its information. As such, I began my own collection of books and other materials presently in my library, which you have had at your use, of comparative works on religious philosophical thoughts and basic writers of each. In so doing, I also discovered that it is a wilfull lie to say that "PHILOSOPHY" is absent in certain "PAGAN RELIGIONS;" and that the term "GREEK PHILOSOPHY" is a bigger lie yet.

These findings, as many more, shook my faith in my former professors and members of the clergy, all of whom taught me these lies which I hold they should have known better. And because of these misgivings I seeked-out and got my first copies of the Egyptian BOOK OF THE DEAD and the FACIMILE OF ANI, both translated from the original Hieroglyphic texts into English by Sir Ernest A. Wallis Budge, and published for the last time by the LONDON MUSEUM in 1885 C.E.; the first copies I had were loaned to me and destroyed in a fire that reduced my entire library to ashes sometime around 1960. These two (2) books I have found to be the basis for most of the so-called "CREATION STORY" of Judaeo-Christianity and Islam - the so-called "WESTERN RELIGIONS."

One of the major failures I first encountered when I began special research into biblical mythology was my own inefficiency in languages, particularly those of Africa and Asia. I thereupon extended my language comprehension to Hieroglyphics, Hieratics, Hebrew, Aramaic, Arabic and a bit of Sanskrit, also in many related "dialects" of Europe, Asia and Africa, to supplement my Latin and poor knowledge of classical Greek. I cannot express sufficiently to young African-American aspirants who are serious about AFRICAN, AFRICAN-AMERICAN and AFRICAN-CARIBBEAN history and culture, so-called "BLACK STUDIES" or "BLACK EXPERIENCE," the need to acquire as much as an extensive repetoire of languages possible along with your training in history, anthropology and archaeology; for without a very good language background one's research, in too many areas, become's subjected solely to second-handed translations and transliterations, also interpretations; the latter being the one area in which most of the RACISM and RELIGIOUS BIGOTRY crept into ancient documentaries which did not have them in terms of the "modern" anxieties we, today, call "RACE" and/or "CIVILIZATION."

My reappraisal of European-American "TALMUDIC JUDAISM" and "AFRICAN NATIONALISM," not "Black Nationalism,"[1] made me take my stand on the side of the struggle by African peoples everywhere for their "SACRED RIGHT TO BE WRONG" (as stated in the late 1800s by one of Africa's most distinguished sons - Dr. Edward Wilmot Blyden, one of the first of the Pan-Africanists; formerly President of the College Of Liberia, West Africa; Ambassador to the Court of St. James, Great Britain, for the Republic of Liberia; Advisor to Muslim and Christian governments on Africa; "authority on the Holy Qu'ran;" author of many books on West Africa, the most noted of which is CHRISTIANITY, ISLAM AND THE NEGRO), and remain a loyal follower of the teachings of the PHILOSOPHY AND

---

[1]. Nationalism in its classic sense deals with land, people, culture and politics. Such affiliations may be based upon a common bond which color can play a significant role. However, color is not the sole purpose or ingredient of nationalism. There is a distinct difference between a "Black Nationalist" and an "African Nationalist;" both terms have their meaning inherent in the words used to describe itself.

OPINIONS of the late Honourable Marcus Moziah Garvey as presented in his auto-biography bearing the same title, edited by his second wife - Amy Jacques Garvey. This I do, bearing in mind at all times the following watch-words by Dr. E.W. Blyden in 1885 C.E.

"AFRICA FOR THE AFRICANS;"

which was extended and amended by Mr. Garvey in the early 1900's in the following manner:

"THOSE AT HOME, AND THOSE ABROAD."

AFRICA FOR THE AFRICANS, THOSE AT HOME AND THOSE ABROAD." THE AFRICANS' RIGHT TO BE WRONG IS SACRED." With these words I say, once more:

> Submitted by Yosef ben-Jochannan
> Chairman: AFRICAN, AFRICAN-AMERICAN,
> AFRICAN-CARIBBEAN STUDIES; Harlem
> Preparatory School of New York,
> February 1969. (Re-edited and prepared for publication in 1971).

This lecture was presented to a class of students who had to take notes as it was given. The method of teaching history and other cultural subjects at this school was on a level equivalent to any freshman-year college work; yet these African-American brothers and sisters were once deemed "UNTEACHABLE." The entire faculty and staff, more the student body, disproved this myth.

ROOTS OF "BIBLICAL ANTI-NEGROISM," ETC.

A Cause For

BLACK "ANTI- SEMITISM"
_____

The issue of "BLACK ANTI-SEMITISM" reached its zenith in the year 1970 C.E.; long before the Black Panthers proclaimed their "...SUPPORT FOR THE UNITED ARAB REPUBLIC" (Egypt) and its leader, now deceased, President Abdul Gamal Nasser (Nassir); yet it must be admitted that said declaration augmented whatever degree there was of "NEGRO" or "BLACK ANTI-SEMITIC BIGOTRY."

When did it all begin? Some historians, mostly the so-called "Jewish (Semite) historians," traced anti-Semitism back to the Hebrew Holy Torah (Christian Old Testament) days; Christian and Muslim theologians and historians to the same source, but mostly to the specific mythical drama of "NOAH AND THE FLOOD." I prefer to direct its origin to the Sixth (6th) century C.E. (A.D.) Babylonian Talmudist[1] scholars and rabbis of "anti-Semitic" Europe. I must, therefore, call your attention to remarks made on page 5 of T.F. Gossett, RACE - THE HISTORY OF AN IDEA IN AMERICA, 1963, in which he attributed the first mention of HAM - one of NOAH'S sons - and his descendants as being "CURSED BY GOD;[2] and as a result of said "CURSE," CANAAN TURNED BLACK. The joke of the matter is that CANAAN, HAM'S son, was not the one who committed the offence against NOAH, his grandfather; it was HAM, his father. From this ridiculous myth, rabbinical scholars that followed in Europe during the Middle Ages, using it as their reference, drew the following interpretation from their TALMUD'S racism:

_____
1. Collected works of oral traditions of Jews relative to the Torah.
2. Jehovah or Yawh. There numerous derivations of this word.

> Now I cannot beget the fourth son whose children I would have ordered to serve you and your brothers! Therefore it must be Canaan, your first born, whom they enslave. And since you have disabled me...doing ugly things in blackness of night, Canaan's children shall be born ugly and black! Moreover, because you twisted your head around to see my nakedness, your grandchildren's hair shall be twisted into kinks, and their eyes red; again because your lips jested at my misfortune, theirs shall swell; and because you neglected my nakedness, they shall go naked, and <u>their male members shall be shamefully elongated! Men of this race are called Negroes,</u>[1] <u>their forefather Canaan commanded them to love theft and fornication, to be banded together in hatred of their masters and never to tell the truth.</u>

The above extract is taken from page 121 of Robert Graves and Raphael Pati, HEBREW MYTHS, Doubbleday and Co., New York, 1964. But Canaan, according to the original story in the BOOK OF GENESIS, the so-called "First Book of Moses," in the HOLY TORAH, mention nothing about "NEGROES" or the COLOR of anyone. Why? Because the Haribus (Hebrews, later on misnomered "Jews"), at the time of the writing of the FIRST BOOK OF MOSES, were themselves of all color of which mankind is made-up. The TORAH'S account of the NOAH"S incident, or drama, which allegedly took place, is as follows:

> Cursed be Canaan,
> A servant of servants shall he be unto his brethren.
> And he said,
> Blessed be Jehovah, the God of Shem;
> And let Canaan be his servant.
> God enlarge Japhet,
> And let him dwell in the tent of Shem;
> And let Canaan be his servant.

Obviously the God of the Jews, JEHOVAH, must have been speaking to the brother of Shem, who came from the same father, NOAH, and mother - thus Shem's full brother. Secondly: They, Shem

---
1. Words underscored are for specific emphasis and further comments by your lecturer.

and HAM, were not "CAUCASIANS, like modern day Jews that register as such in the United States of America's CENSUS, while at the same instance claim to be of the "SEMITIC RACE" - "DESCENDANTS OF SHEM." But Jehovah did not mention any racial difference between SHEM and his nephew, CANAAN; neither of his brother, HAM. Here is where the RACIST theories began; and, it is at this juncture that the biblical COLOR-LINE interpretation that established the MORAL BASIS for "NEGRO" slavery for the Jews of Europe and European-America, Christians in both continents, and the Arab Muslims of Arabia (Asia); this being, also, the basis for later counter-action today called "NEGRO ANTI-SEMITISM." Prior to this interpretation slavery was an object synonymous with conquered victims of any society, regardless of RACE, CREED, COLOR, SEX, NATIONAL ORIGIN, etc. It was in this latter vein that the Haribus of ancient times suffered slavery under other national groupings; and it was the same reason when they also subjected others to their own slave system; this being evident in the order by Jehovah against CANAAN, and as further detailed in its entirety in the SECOND BOOK OF MOSES (Exodus).

In pursuit of the SHEMITIC or SEMITIC NEGROPHOBIA demonstrated by the Middle Ages European (or Caucasian) rabbinical scholars, one sees the same type of "modern" Jewish scholars still operating in the twentieth century C.E. The best demonstration of "modern" Jewish "ANTI-NEGROISM" is seen on page 96 of C. G. Seligman, RACES OF AFRICA, New York, 1966 (which he first published in 1930 and republished in 1957, without any changes with repect to this area, what-so-ever). He wrote:

> Apart from relatively late Semitic influence...the civilizations of the Hamites, its history the re-

> cord of these peoples and of their interaction
> with the two other African stocks, the Negro
> and the Bushman, whether this influence was
> exerted by highly civilized Egyptians or by
> such wider pastoralists as are represented
> at the present day by the Beja and Somali...
> The incoming Hamites[1] were pastoral 'Euro-
> peans' - arriving wave after wave - better
> armed as well as quicker witted than the
> "dark agricultural Negroes."

Before making further equations with respect to the development of reverse racism on the part of "Negroes" toward JEWS in the United States of America (and its colonies and other spheres of political and economic influence) one must analyze between Seligman and his racist and religiously bigoted predecessors of the Middle Ages. Thus - they establish that the Hamite, Seligman's ..."...dark agricultural Negroes...," were the people "CURSED" by Jehovah. Yet, Seligman stated that, in fact, the CURSED people were the Caucasians (Whites) who he referred to as "...incoming Hamites were pastoral Europeans...." Of course anyone familiar with the SEMITIC-HAMITIC syndrome knows that Seligman was not the first of the so-called (modern)"authority on Africa" to project this theory or hypothesis; the works of Dr. Donald Wiedner, presently professor in African studies at Temple University, Philadelphia, Pa., ranks with such racist Negrophobia, not to mention those of Jeffreys, Junod, Groves and others cited before. Not only does Wiedner hold to the SEMITIC-CAUCASIAN myth of of his predecessors of the Middle Ages; this being obvious in the map he created for his paleontological hypothesis that all of North Africa, north-east Africa, and much of south-east Africa, was originally inhabited by "CAUCASIAN" and "Semitic" peoples. Said map appears on page 19 of his book, A HISTORY OF AFRICA SOUTH OF THE SAHARA..., etc., Vintage Books, New York, 1962; it also appears in extract on page 10 of my own book, BLACK MAN OF THE NILE, Alkebu-lan Books Associates, New York, 1970. These men's resurrection and projection of the SEMITIC-HAMITIC myth must have had its effect upon many of the active racist historians of the past and present; and their works will certainly guide the pathological racist yet to come on the same pathway.

The very suggestion by Seligman that the Egyptians were of a "...different race..." than the "...Negroes...", of course a race created by himself - the mythical CAUCASIAN-HAMITES who entered Egypt "WAVE AFTER WAVE," highlights the frustration "modern" Jews suffer over having been slaves (their ancestors) to an African slavemaster (Egyptians, Ethiopians, or "Negroes," etc.). In this fact alone, it is therefore understandable why the rabbis of the Middle Ages and their stooges that followed them had to maintain their own NEGROMANIA and "ANTI-NEGROISM" that filtered down to their descendants here in the United States of America and in Israel. But the end result, so far, has been the so-called "NEGRO ANTI-SEMITISM." What else did the European and European-American Jews, who are in fact European in ethnic and cultural origin, and not Asian as they would like to be whenever convenient, expect their "NEGROES" would have become when they got knowledge of such writings examined? The "NEGRO" related the entire "HAM" and "CANAAN" enslavement myth to their own economic envolvement in the garment industry as the porters and other functionaries of the same to the European and European-American (White) Jews.[1] They see this role also transfered to the do-

---

1. There are thousands of Black Jews, correctly "ISRAELITES", in the United States of America; a few are in Israel today.

minantly Jewish TEACHERS' UNION under the control of Albert Shanka; even to the predominance of Jewish landlords and retail store owners in the hundreds of Harlems of the United States of America. These images are not easily removed by an occasional wealthy Jew's financial contribution to a few of the so-called "NEGRO" or "COLORED ORGANIZATION" which board of directors is dominated by Jews and Gentiles of European-American origin. Even the Judaeo-Christian envolvement of the "NEGRO" has become questionable, with respect to its teachings, and specifically with regards to the BOOK OF GENESIS and the BOOK OF EXODUS, relative to the moral acceptance of the Jewish God, JEHOVAH, and the current, and past, enslavement of the "NEGRO;" all of which said God condoned in the writings of his "...HOLY SCRIPTURES " by his "...INSPIRED MEN."

There is another vitally important factor to be considered in "NEGRO ANTI-SEMITISM;" that is, the European-American Jews avoidance of "NEGROES" as much as their Christian brothers and sisters of the same European "ETHNIC" background, while at the same instance citing their own equal minority status as their "NEGRO" victims of WHITE AMERICAN RACISM.

The racist interpretations of the TORAH and TALMUD'S prohibitions and penalties by Jews, both of the United States of America and Europe, are in themselves inexcusable; for no one in his right mind could show any legitimate justification in transfering the story of NOAH and his sons, equally his grandchildren, to the "NEGROES." This type of warped interpretaion of biblical mythology only adds to show how deprave the Jews concience had become after their confiscation of the Canaanites' land, and their subsequent enslavement of said people. This state of depravity being later on also transfered to their own situation as the slaves of their fellow Europeans during the Middle Ages in Europe's progroms and other forms of Jewish ghetto life, all of which took place in "Christian Europe." Even the Frenchman, Voltaire, whom so many have quoted as a "LIBERTARIAN," was embued by the type of Hamitic Negrophobia established by the warped interpretaions given the biblical myths on Canaan - the so-called "FATHER OF THE NE-GROES." Yet, he maintained aetheistic adherance; while at the same instance professing that the "NEGRO" is not the equivalent of a man, a sort of "SUB-HUMAN." These beliefs on the part of Voltaire are best demonstrated in W.J. Fleming's version of Voltaire in his own book entitled, THE WORKS OF VOLTAIRE: <u>A Contemporany View,</u> New York, 1901. Unfortunately the "NEGRO" was not only made the scorn of the Europeans of the Christian faith, as the Jews and Moslems also subjected him to live "...JEHOVAH'S COMMAND..." that allegedly recites:

"A SERVANT OF SERVANTS SHALL YE BE;"

meaning that the "NEGRO" would be a slave until the end of the world; and, that, even his prayers God, JEHOVAH, AL'LAH, JESUS CHRIST, would not hear and change his "CURSE." Robert Graves and Raphael Pati placed it in its proper perspective when they cited the full meaning of the "CANAAN" myth established by the Jewish scholars of the Middle Ages. They wrote:

> ...Negroes are doomed to serve men of lighter color was a view gratefully borrowed by Christians in the Middle Ages; a severe shortage of cheap manual labor caused by the plague made the reinstitution of slavery attractive.

On the other hand Eric Williams in his book, CAPITALISM AND SLAVERY, Carolina, 1944, established that the Christian Europeans, along with some Jews, made certain that Graves and Patai's citation was effective when they held that "Negro slaves" moral value detoriated in proportion to their economic value; and that said value included his image as "...A SERVANT..." for "SHEM" and "JAPHET" all the days of his life. But, the inhuman enslavement of the Africans, the so-called "NEGROES," in the Americas was to take on its own moral perspective from a standpoint other than the racist stereotype established by the Talmudist scholars and rabbinical sages myth of Europe's Middle Ages. Yet, European-American slave holders found in the physical condemnation of the African the same sexual and grotesque qualities cited by the Talmudist scholars; thus, the "...elongated" penis of the male, liers, thieves (in both sexes), and "...ugly black..." and "...thick lips..." features of all "Negroes;" the only feature truly omitted being the "CURSE." The European Christian had become much more sophisticated in their racism than their erstwhile European Jewish counterpart with respect to their "NEGROES," and did not want to make their own God - JESUS CHRIST OF NAZZARETH - a racist like his predecessor - JEHOVAH - he had replaced as the "...ONLY TRUE GOD."

The Jewish traveler and merchant of the twelfth-century C.E., Benjamin of Tudela, moved "JEWISH ANTI-NEGROISM", or "ANTI-BLACKISM," from the sixth-century to a period much closer to our own era. With respect to the Africans of Kimit (Egypt) and Nubia (Sudan), south of Aswan, he wrote:

> There is a people...who, like animals, eat of the herbs that grow on the banks of the Nile and in their fields. They go about naked and have not the intelligence of ordinary men. They cohabit with their sisters and anyone they can find...

they are taken as slaves and sold in Egypt and
neighbouring countries. These sons of Ham are
black slaves.

R. Hess, TRAVELS OF BENJAMIN OF TUDELA, Journal of African History, VI, I (1965), page 17, give further details of the racism that was prominent among European Jewry. But, here again, we see the "HAMITES" of the twelfth-century C.E. (A.D.) were the "NEGROES" of today; not the European "herds of Hamites" of Seligman's Negromania. Benjamin's reference to the "...SONS OF HAM ARE BLACK SLAVES" clearly shows that Jewish thoughts on the African, at least during his lifetime, was still obsessed with the HAMITIC SYNDROME of their biblical origin and the Talmudic interpretations rendered, much of which are still present among twentieth-century C.E. European and European-American Jews who still perpetuate the "SEMITIC" and "HAMITIC" hypothesis of their ancestors of Europe's Middle Ages. This is being done conciously by some, but quite unconsciously by the vast majority. Where is the concious application of the myth most dominant; in our synagouges, temples, and yishivas, all of which are prostelized by so-called "men of the cloth;" men who swear to their God - JEHOVAH - that they are free of "ANTI NEGRO FEELINGS;" and, that they too are victims of the racism which began among the European Christians; forgetting that the Christians only continued what the Jews had already invented in their most holy books - THE FIVE BOOKS OF MOSES, or HOLY TORAH, (originally FOUR - Christians' OLD TESTAMENT). Of course the Jews mentioned in Moses' marriage to the Ethiopian (Cushite) woman, the "DAUGHTER OF THE HIGH PRIEST," a relative of the modern-day so-called "FALASHAS" or "BLACK JEWS", properly called "BETA ISRAEL" or "CHILDREN OF THE HOUSE OF ISRAEL (House of Israel), are not to be included in the "CURSE" on the Canaanites or Hamites by God - JEHOVAH.

The "Negro Hamites" were written of as late as the seventeenth-century C.E. by European authors in the same derogatory manner as their predecessors. But, the "Negro" was still considered a "HAMITE," no European having been labeled such, not even the sable-skinned Greeks, Italians or Iberians (Portuguese, Spaniards and some of the southern French). Europeans that visited the African continent for various reasons within said period wrote in the same vein; men, such as Richard Jobson in his book, THE GOLDEN TRADE, 1623, and Sir Thomas Herbert in ,SOME YEARS OF TRAVELS INTO DIVERS PARTS OF AFRICA, 1677; but, not one of them spoke of a <u>Semitic African people</u> in their works. Historians of modern vintage tried to change the African-Arab, Leo Africanus (Leo the African , who was adopted and named by Pope Leo X of the Roman Catholic Church after receiving him as a slave) of having written about his African ancestors as "HAMITES" during the turn of the 1600's. This misinterpretation of Leo Africanus' work was made by the Englishman John Pory, in a work he entitled TRANSLATION OF LEO AFRICANUS, published by the Hakluyt Society, XCII-XCIV, London, 1896. But John Pory's work included his own commentary on the Africans, of whom he did not recognized Leo Africanus as being a part. Pory, like thousands more Europeans and European-American writers, could not distinguish the difference between an Arab and a Moslem; thus, every Moslem, African or Asian, in or from the Iberian Peninsula during the Moors occupation of said land (711-1485 C.E.) were Arabs, accordingly.

The modern twentieth-century C.E. European-American Jewish

racism is seen in professor Wolf Leslau, FALASHA ANTHOLOGY: <u>The Black Jews Of Ethiopia</u>, Schocken Books, New York, 1969 (first published in 1951 by Yale University Press as Volume I of the Yale Judaica Series), page ix. Professor Leslau wrote:

> In some REGIONS north of Lake Tana in Ethiopia lives a population of Jewish faith called Fallashas. <u>Their historical origin and racial affinities present many difficult problems.</u>[1]

To whom does the Falashas "...present many difficult problems?" And who in Europe, America, or Asia, Israel in particular, can prove his or her JEWISH ANCESTRY moreso than the African Jews, FALASHAS, of Ethiopia? Leslau wanted to know if they were "<u>converted</u>;" and, if so, <u>who converted them to Judaism</u>? He wrote:

> These questions have occupied all who have dealt with the Falashas.

The only people who are wondering, and suffer from the "...racial affinities..." or "...historical origin..." of the "Falashas," are the racists and religious bigots from Europe and European-America of the Christian and Hebrew ("Jewish") religions. As Leslau continued his own Jewish "anti-Negroism," as I see it; he pondered:

> The sources of our knowledge of the Falashas are of various kinds. Among the oldest testimonies to the existence of Jews in Ethiopia are the reports of Jewish travelers like Eldad Haddani (ninth century), Benjamin of Tudela (twelfth-century), Elijah of Ferrara (fifteenth century), and others. Most of these accounts report things of legendary character that lack historical basis, and are presumably based on hearsay.

What writing "...lack historical basis..." more than the Jewish TORAH and other so-called "...<u>inspired works by Holy men of God</u>...," etc.? What ever happened to the professor's memory with respect to the Falasha High Priest's daughter Moses married, according to the SECOND BOOK OF MOSES (Exodus)? Maybe this is one of the many cases in which the HOLY TORAH (Christian OLD TESTAMENT) "...<u>lack historical basis</u>...." Or is one of the places in which the Hamitic, Semitic, and "Negro" syndrome dealing with the "...CURSE OF CANAAN..." myth in the FIRST BOOK OF MOSES, Genesis, becomes most confusing in its racist proclamation.

I could go on for hours on the good professor's "anti-Negro" stance; but, I shall end with the following from page x that follows the professor's citation of many European Jews that were dispatched to prove the kosher status of the "BLACK JEWS OF ETHIOPIA" but not the "WHITE JEWS OF SWEDEN, GERMANY, ENGLAND, EUROPEAN-AMERICA, ISRAEL," etc. One of the people he cited was "...<u>the noted Semitist Joseph Halevy</u>." What is a <u>"Semitist"</u> other than a racist term? But, even Halevy's findings that there were in fact Jews in Ethiopia, "BLACK JEWS "(who Halevy was certain met the standards of kosher Jews anywhere), were rejected by European Jews; who, according to the professor,..."received" the report:

> ...with incredulity in some Jewish quarters, and a counter-mission headed by a Rabbi Nahoun was dispatched.

After noting other actions on the part of the European Jewish community, and the entrance of the European-American Jews of the United States of America in the TRUE JEWS proving of the Falashas, the professor concluded in the next paragraph on the same page:

> Most of the reports that have so far been made about the Falsahas have been incomplete and characterized by a Christian or Jewish missionary tendency which appreciably diminishes their usefulness and objectivity.

Who besides Professor Wolf Leslau, and others of his own ilk, needs to prove the authenticity of the Falashas' JEWISHNESS as reported by outstanding Jews- such as Professor Jacques Faitlovitch, Joseph Halévy, Flad, Rabbi Nahoun, and others? Who is to pass on them, as if they were checking Kosher meat? Who set the criteria for "SEMITIC" RELIABILITY he applied? Who established them for all of the European and European-American (White) Jews in the world today and yesterday? Did the professor passed the same BOARD OF TRUE JEW CERTIFIERS? Is he a registered "WHITE CAUCASIAN" or an "ASIAN SEMITE" on the United States of America's Census report? Lastly, is the professor not suffering from the same BLACK CURSE which his God, JEHOVAH, placed upon his fellow Jews, the CANAANITES, which he sees, appearently, in the Falashas of Ethiopia, East Africa. And, would the recognition of the BLACK JEWS in Ethiopia not force recognition of BLACK or "NEGRO JEWS" throughout the Harlems of the United States of America as being kosher as their fellow JEWS of white skin, much to the latter's dismay of possible RACIAL SUICIDE? In light of the last observation, we find one Professor Howard M. Brotz (a fellow European-American Jew, appearently) in his book, THE BLACK JEWS OF HARLEM, etc., Schocken Books, New York, 1970 (firt published in 1964), page 7, saying the following:

> The parallelism that he (Brotz' Negro Jews)[1] was able to draw between his own bondage and that of the ancient Hebrews who had once before been rescued from bondage has had, as is readily familiar, a powerful part in the content of his song. As we shall see, the inward dignity that he was able to acquire by conceiving of himself as a descendant of patriarchs is a central theme of the Black Jews.

---

1. Words in parenthesis by the lecturer for clarity only.

Obviously, Brotz failed to remember that there were thousands of Hebrews (Jews) that were forced down to the interior of the west coast of Africa from Cyrene (Cyrenica) during the Roman invasion of northern Africa; also during the jihads[1] by the Muslim Arab invaders from the Arabian Peninsula in 640 C.E. or 18A.H. If Brotz was not familiar with this very important aspect of the subject he selected to tackle, JEWISH HISTORY, particularly that of the African-American Hebrew (Israelite) community, he could have, and should have, read Professor J.C. deGraft-Johnson, AFRICAN GLORY, London, 1954; J. A. Rogers, WORLD'S GREAT MEN OF COLOR, New York, 1947; C.K. Meek, HEBREWISM IN WEST AFRICA, London, 1934; and my own work, WE THE BLACK JEWS, Madrid, 1949 (pamphlet). If he is still interested he should read my other works, specifically BLACK MAN OF THE NILE, and AFRICAN ORIGINS OF THE MAJOR "WESTERN RELIGIONS." This is, providing Brotz is unaware of the fact that the Hebrew peoples, or Jewish peoples, either way he prefers to speak of them, Black or White, technicolor also, from the earliest time of their history and beginning as a united force, were also enslaved by African people whom many Jewish historians of European and European-American birth called "NEGROES;" others having called them "HAMITES" and "CANAANITES," etc., etc., etc. almost endlessly. Brotz also failed to note that Moses, the most noted and revered of the ancient Haribus (Hebrews, today called by the misnomer "JEWS"), was himself of the same African stock of the "NEGRO JEWS" he selected to trace from origins which date back to...

> "As early as 1900, Negro preachers were traveling
> through the Carolinas preaching a doctrine that

---

[1]. Muslims holy wars following the founding of Islan in 622 C.E.

the so-called Negroes were really the lost sheep of the House of Israel."

The above extract was taken from page v of Brotz' book. But, like so many other Jewish writers who have established themselves as "AUTHORITY ON NEGRO HISTORY AND CULTURE," Brotz has on the cover of the same book the following:

"SOURCEBOOKS IN NEGRO HISTORY."

What kind of an AUTHORITATIVE "SOURCEBOOKS IN NEGRO HISTORY" that is unaware of the fact that many of the so-called "Negroes" saw themselves as the children of the Hebrews long before the turn of the twentieth century C.E. I suggest that this AUTHORITY also read Wilson Armistad, A TRIBUTE TO THE NEGRO, London, 1848; and J.A. Rogers, AFRICA'S GIFT TO AMERICA, New York, 1961. In the first place, just what caused Brotz to investigate the basis of "NEGRO JUDAISM"? Is the basis for his "NEGRO JUDAISM" any different for "CAUCASIAN JUDAISM"? Is Judaism a RACE-CULTURE or RACE-RELIGION of a compact that only take in "SEMITES". Who ever heard of a "CAUCASIAN SEMITE"? If the former is true, them European and European-American Jews have been committing a fraud each time they have registered in the United States of America's CENSUS. Secondly: How can European-American Judaism prove that it did not spring from the "MIX-MULTITUDE" spoken of in the SECOND BOOK OF MOSES (Exodus) in the HOLY TORAH? And, how can it be said that the JEWISH MOTHER from whom all Jews took their JEWISHNESS was not the same one raped by the Africans of Kimit (Egypt), the Roman soldiers in Palestine, Persians in Israel, or the Christians all over Europe? She is the same "MOTHER" who was raped by Christians, Muslims; and moreso by Christians within the last four hundred (400) years in Africa, Europe, Asia, European-America, and the islands of the Caribbeans. She was not necessarily BLACK, WHITE, RED, BROWN, YELLOW, or even TECHNICOLOR. She bore every color imaginable in human pigmentation. And, She was also the "MOTHER" who had her sons exterminate the Hittites, Amalakites, Moabites, Jebusites, Pezarites and a host of others when She took the land of the peoples of CANAAN ("CURSED" land) through genocide, allegedly on "the command of Jehovah."

Brotz not only attacked "NEGRO JUDAISM," which he failed to respect in any manner whatsoever; not even trying to findout how those of us who are attached thereto call ourselves, by lumping all branches of "BLACK ISRAELITES" (Jews) into one ; which is as ridiculous as lumping Reform, Reconstruction, Orthodox, Conservative, and Jewish Scientist, as one. But, Brotz also included in his book a warped appraisal of what he believed to be an insight into "NEGRO NATIONALISM AND THE DILEMMA OF NEGRO LEADERSHIP." Like all of the others, the so-called "LIBERALS" and "AUTHORITIES ON NEGRO HISTORY AND CULTURE," who remain outside of Black communities and listen to certain "RESPONSIBLE NEGRO LEADERS" talk about "NEGROES" who they seldom meet in their suburban sorroundings, Brotz also reached his alleged AUTHORITATIVE SOCIAL STUDY OF THE "NEGRO JEWS OF HARLEM !" If this type of conduct is not the equivalent of "anti-Negroism," what is it? For example: On page 11 of his work, Brotz wrote:

> Garveyism did not coincide with his (Arnold Ford)[1] own outlook, for Garvey rejected his counsel to adopt Judaism as the Negro's religion.

---
1. Words in parenthesis by the lecturer for the sake of clarity only. Ford was a Black Rabbi of one of the Israelite communities that was more interested in integrating with White Jews than being envolved with the struggle for African peoples liberation from White colonialism (Christians and Jews alike). Brotz did not interview Garvey on this point.

Brotz appearent contempt for "NEGRO JUDAISM" is best seen on page 10, as he stated:

> During the period 1919-1931 there are records of at least eight Black Jewish cults that originated in Harlem, the leaders of whom were all asquainted and in several cases associated with each other from time to time as congregation would rise, split, collapse, and reorganize. Several of the "rabbis" took "Jewish" names: Mordecai Herman, Ishi Kaufman, Israel ben Yomen, Simon Schurz, and they differentiated themselves from each other in their interpretations or simple knowledge of orthodox Jewish law and custom.

If Brotz was not aware of practically everyone of his points above taking place in the European-American (White) Jewish communities, he must have been very much color-blind. There is nothing in Brotz' complaint against the BLACK JEWS that the WHITE JEWS are not guilty of, even those WHITE RABBIS which he does not mention in quotation marks, or the splinter groups among them which he does not call "sects." As for non-Jewish names, the leaders of the modern state of Israel did not have Hebrew names, which includes the present Prime Minister - Golda Muir; all of them had to change from European Christian names to Hebrew names. Most Jews all over the world do not have Hebrew names for public designation; even those who have accepted one for the purpose of being called to "<u>the reading of the LAW</u>" in the Holy Torah. The vast majority of Jews in the "NEW WORLD" and Europe had to accept Christian names forced upon them in similar circumstances as the African-Americans under European and European-American (White) Christian slavemasters; thus we have the name GINSBERG for the White Jew, and Jones for the Black Jew; and so we have Mordecai Kaplan and his RECONSTRUCTION MOVEMENT, as Wentworth Matthews and his COMMANDMENT KEEPERS ETHIOPIAN HEBREW CONGREGATION (both men of equal rabbinical status in the eyes of their respective congregation); neither congregation a "cult." Is it not a fact that the Black Jews during the same period Brotz refered to were trying very hard to have a reunion with their White brethren, who they felt were different to the White Christians but found out were no different when it came to the color question, very much to their dismay? Instead of castigating the Black Jews of Harlem, or anywhere else, for acting brotherly as Jews to their White fellow Jews, who had become CAUCASIANS in their more than one-thousand (1,000) years sojourn in Europe, most of which was spent in the SLAVIC STATES and TZARIST RUSSIA, and no longer "SEMITES" at that period, they should have welcomed the Black Jews attempt to consolidate all of the "JEWISH" peoples of the "NEW WORLD - the United States of America in particular. Certainly the only rejection they suffered from their White Jewish brothers and sisters was "ANTI-NEGROISM," today called "ANTI-BLACKISM," solely due to their BLACK POSTURE Herodotus described as "THICK LIPS, BROAD NOSE, WOOLLY HAIR, AND BURNT SKIN." The Hasidic Jews who have recently arrived in these United States of America, like the Black Jews who have been here for over seventy years as an incoming group with a cohesive congregation (not to mention those who have claimed Hebrew origin from Biblical teachings in Africa), also do not have many university-trained rabbis on the educational level of most European-American rabbis who have been here for a greater amount of time - those coming from an Anglo-Saxon background (national origin); yet, the Hasidic (Jewish) rabbis are accepted in general within White Jewish communities of this country. Why? Simply this; they too equally have WHITE SKIN and qualify as "CAUCASIANS" and

"SEMITES" under the racist GENTLEMEN'S AGREEMENT among the JEW-MAKERS and KOSHER JEW CERTIFIERS.

Lastly: Brotz, on page 15 of the same book in review, in an attack on the oldest Black Jewish congregation in existence in the United States of America - THE COMMANDMENT KEEPERS. wrote:

> The Black Jews contend that the so-called Negroes Negroes in Maerica are really Ethiopian Hebrews or Falashas who had been stripped of their knowledge of their name and religion during slavery. The term Negro, they further contend, is a word invented by the slavemasters and imposed upon the slaves together with the white man's religion in order to demoralize them;...etc.

If Brotz does not know that the name "NEGRO" originated from the mythical nation the Portuguses slavers created for an area of west Africa they also named "NEGROLAND," he should certainly register for some courses in "BLACK STUDIES," if not "AFRICAN STUDIES." I suggest that he read BLACK MAN OF THE NILE and examine the map on page 267; also, Richard B. Moore's THE WORD NEGRO, ITS ORIGIN AND EVIL USE, New York,(1960?). The same area the Portuguse willfully misnamed "NEGROLAND" was still at that period properly called "SONGHAI" or "SONGHAY" by the indigenous Ethiopians (Africans according to the Greeks and Romans; Alkebulan according to the earliest inhabitants of this continent) who originally named it. The word "NEGRO", unlike the word "JEW," has no basis for credibility with respect to the history and heritage of any African or African-American other than that which his or her slavemaster from Europe and European-America (White - Christians, Jews, or Muslims) attached to said slaves. Truly it is a fact, the BLACKS in the United States of America used similar tactics to prove their Hebrew or Jewish heritage as did many WHITES in Europe tried to prove heritage with the "CHOOSEN PEOPLE" of the

Hebrew HOLY TORAH, dating back to Abraham (Avram or Abram) in the Asian desert more than three-thousand six-hundred and ten (3,610) years ago (c1640 B.C.E. - 1971 C.E.); they even claim a heritage dating back to Moses and the EXODUS or PASSOVER, when Moses had to flee his fellow African of Kimit (Egypt) - Pharoah Rameses II -about c1298-1232 B.C.E.; some even closer to our era; yet these Europeans and European-Americans, all of whom claimed to be "CAUCASIANS" as well as "SEMITES," consider themselves to be more "JEWISH" than BLACKS who used the same basis for their claim to the "CHOOSEN PEOPLE" myth.

When did the "SEMITIC LANGUAGE" become a RACE? If it did; who established it as such? There are millions of African people, Asians as well, who speak so-called "SEMITIC LANGUAGES," including the vast majority of the Arab population of the Arabian Peninsula; Yet, they are not considered "SEMITES" today, but, instead "HAMITES." "SEMITISM" today, as used in the United States of America, is synonymous with "CAUCASIANISM;" and has adopted all of the racist and bigoted inheritance of its predecessor's history. This reminds me of the following maxim (or proverbs):

"HE WHO LAYS WITH THE DOG, ARISE WITH ITS FLEAS."

"BLACK" or "NEGRO ANTI-SEMITISM'S" growth does not only relate back to Hebrew biblical teachings; but, also to the Calvinist doctrines and other orthodox Christian racist bigotry, all of which can be traced back to the earliest teachings of the "JEWS KILLED CHRIST (meaning in fact GOD); each forgetting that the same God was a fellow JEW. Such "ANTI-SEMITIC" bigotry is taught each and every Sunday of the year; and especially during the PASSION PERIOD (Lent to Easter Sunday), and again during the Christmas season. The BLACK JEWS do not totally escape this venomous characterization of their fellow Jews solely on the basis that they do not have WHITE SKIN. They too suffer from this type of "ANTI-SEMITISM" from "BLACK CHRISTIANS" who are taught by those who also taught them their European-style version of Christianity. They knew nothing about European-style Christianity, Copticism, neither North African Christianity nor East African Christianity that preceded the Roman Catholic Church of Rome established officially under the reign of Emperor Constantine ("the great") in the fourth (4th) century C.E. Their teachers did not even tell them that many of the "FATHERS OF THE CHRISTIAN CHURCH" - such as St. Cyprian, St. Augustine and Tertullian, also others, were indigenous (Ethiopian, Black, or even "Negro") Africans as they are, or were. They were only fed, brainwashed, into the same bigoted hatred for the WHITE JEWS, not knowing there are those of other colors the vast majority of their slavemasters brought over from Europe with regards to the Jewish ghetto and progrom dwellers all over Europe. In other words, "ANTI-SEMITISM" on the part of the African-American, the so-called "NEGROES," was taught to them by Europeans of the Christian faith against their fellow Europeans of the Hebrew or Jewish faith. Most of them had no other point of reference they could have referred to for validating the bigoted information presented to them as "...THE WORDS OF GOD-INSPIRED HOLY SCRIBES." As far as they were concerned, <u>GOD</u> - meaning JESUS CHRIST OF NAZZARETH, <u>ordered the persecution of the Jews as retribution for their having killed him</u>. At one time, for over two-hundred (200) years, this was the only type of literature they were permitted to read, and had forced down their throat by some of the world's most avid racists and religious bigots, most of whom even got their "NEGROES" to accept their own enslavement as "...THE WILL OF GOD" - Jesus Christ that is - "...FOR SINS COMMITTED" - when their "NEGROES" first parent (HAM) "...STARED AT HIS FATHER'S (NOAH) NAKEDNESS IN THE ARK" during the "FLOOD." This type of "ANTI-NEGROISM" can be still heard in many so-called "NEGRO CHURCHES" (up until this very date) being echoed by JACK-LEG PREACHERS who "...RECEIVED" their "...CALL FROM GOD" (Jesus Christ) "IN THE COTTON PATCH" and other such places.

True, there is a lot of "BLACK ANTI-SEMITISM," or "NEGRO ANTI-SEMITISM," either one you choose to use. But such "ANTI-SEMITIC" expressions, racism or religious bigotry, is not the kind which the African-Americans have developed; but, that which they have found convenient to use as a weapon against those Jews with whom they must come in conflict as their bosses, school teachers, shop owners, landlords, judges, and in other areas of authority or control in which they must always pay reverence, and none return to them.

"NEGRO ANTI-SEMITISM, overtly expressed as it was in the late 1960's against JEWISH CONTROL OF THE NEW YORK CITY BOARD OF EDUCATION and LOCAL SCHOOLS in the Harlems of New York City, was no more than "JEWISH ANTI-CATHOLICISM" displayed against the Irish when they dominated and controlled the same BOARD OF EDUCATION at 110 Livingstone Street, Brooklyn, New York; or "IRISH ANTI-GERMANIC PEOPLES" when the German-Dutch were in control; nor "JEWISH ANTI-NEGROISM", now that the African-Americans are trying to uproot some of the Jews from their previleged positions on the same BOARD. This also happened with the dominantly Jewish-controlled

United Federation of Teachers and schools in the Harlems (so-called "Ghetto areas") of the City of New York.

By virtue of the fact that the vast majority of the most important retail-store merchants are Jews in these so-called "Negro ghettos;" and, that they control the economic life of said communities through said control; and, whereas the African-Americans cannot break the barrier to establish similar economic enterprises in "Jewish ghettos " and other "European-American ghettos" throughout the City of New York, as well as other cities throughout the United States of America, the tensions heighten constantly. But, there is no reason to believe that similar types of contact between African-Americans (Blacks or "Negroes") would have been different with European-Americans (Whites or "Honkies") of the Christian or any other faith. Yet, this is not the present situation. The fact is, that, the confrontation is basically one between White Jews and Blacks (of all faiths, Jewish included) for the same status in a relatively-set White ANGLO-SAXON PROTESTANT CHRISTIAN GREEK-CENTRIC society called a "DEMOCRACY." However, the conflict is not because the Jews are "KILLERS OF CHRIST;" to the contrary, the vast majority of African-Americans really do not seggregate or show hatred for the Jews on this biblical myth so pronounced in White Christian communities. The African-Americans first consideration about the Jews is one of them being fellow WHITES; most being completely unaware, or skeptical of the term "WASP." They see the Jew as the "WHITE MAN" who they come in contact constantly in their so-called "ghettos", which I prefer to call as is - BLACK COMMUNITIES. They see Jews in the banks, department stores, supermarkets, theatres, even in the police and fire departments; always in a commanding role. And, because the Jews find themselves, for the most part, biblically driven to guide the "NEGRO" (similar to the White European-style Christians) towards what they believe is the "Negroes" social goal in "CIVIL RIGHTS" (beginning with the creation of the NIAGARA MOVEMENT by the SPINGARM brothers in the early 1900's), from which the Jews equally benifit beyond the dream of the "Negroes;" the "Negros" thus find themselves unable to make their own mistakes in mastering the so-called "AMERICAN DREAM;" a "DREAM" that is solely based upon the amount of money and material things one can control or own; a "DREAM" the "NEGRO" has been made to believe is in SOCIAL ACCEPTANCE BY THOSE WHO HAVE MASTERED THE ECONOMIC GOAL OF AMERICA.

"Negro anti-Semitism" will never cease as long as Jews are seen in the top role of so-called "CIVIL RIGHTS ORGANIZATIONS" directed towards the freedom of "Negroes;" whereas, no BLACK man is seen in a similar position in any White Jewish organization designated to bring about the same DREAM for Jews - such as B'NAI B'RITH, HADDASAH, THE JEWISH CONGRESS, and the likes of them; even a little BLACK JEW at the top would have made a difference.

One of the sore spots of "anti-Semitism" among African-Americans is the parading of "Negroes " "the respectable and responsible" kind to challenge everything and anything African-Americans do against the interest of White Jews who have gained the endorsement of some "Negro" organizations. The use of certain "Negro leaders" to decry the teaching of KiSWAHILI as an African language for credit in the city's public schools, while other languages of many ethnic group from Europe are taught on said basis, including Hebrew in some cases. The injection of Jewish causes in <u>Black Studies Courses</u>, such as one finds in the United Federation of Teachers' book they have published for such use under the title - LESSON PLANS ON AFRICAN-AMERICAN HISTORY, continues to heighten the areas of confrontation. As an example: On page 41 of the above mentioned book is a very neat little trick under the caption -"<u>Procedure and Points to Emphasize</u>"-that proves the point being made. The <u>work-study project</u> requires that the students:

> "1. Tell story of Jews in Egypt and of the custom of slavery in the ancient world as described in Background Information."

Items #2 and #3 are no better than #1. But item #4 tops them all. It orders the students to:

> "4. Discus meaning of the words Egyptian, Israel, oppressed and Pharoah.

What a sly way of implying and guiding the students into bigoted conclusions by teachers that the EGYPTIANS OPPRESSED THE ISRAELIS of today, when in fact there was no ISRAEL during the period when the Haribus (Hebrews, later called "Jews") were allegedly "SLAVES IN EGYPT." Secondly: The word "EGYPTIAN" should have been equated to the word JEW, not ISRAEL. This type of subtle racism, as I see it, is used in this book, which is supposedly to be the model for elementary school children in both Black and White <u>ghettos</u> (Christian as well as Jewish.) But, in which book written exclusively to deal with Jewish history and heritage, especially dealing with the Jews as slaves under the Africans of Kimit (Egypt), written primarily by Jewish authorities for Jewish children of such tender age, is the teacher reminded and asked to mention that THE NEGROES WERE SLAVES TO THE PRE-

SIDENT OF THE UNITED STATES OF AMERICA - GEORGE WASHINGTON; or that JEWS OPPRESSED THE HITTITES, AMALAKITES, MOABITES, ZEBUSITES, etc., such as one finds in this book ; allegedly designed to teach American children of the BLACK EXPERIENCE - the history and culture of the African-American people? In practically every page of this book something, or some aspect or the other of Jewish life, religion, culture, and/or oppression have been carefully and shrudely inserted into the areas that should have solely projected the history and cultural heritage of the African-American children in the classroom. The assumption being that the JEWS OPPRESSED in Egypt, if such they were, were not also Africans like those found in the Harlems of the United States of America; and that Jews were not also guilty of oppressing other peoples in biblical times. Those of us who are of similar background, also of Black color, cannot tolerate this type of projection to African-American children; at least those of us who are aware of our Hebrew heritage in a BLACK (Ethiopian) KIMIT (Egypt).

Of course the vast majority of the AUTHORITATIVE SOURCES and REFERENCES are by Jewish (White) writers and publishing houses. These are not accidental occurances, as far as I can observe; they are obviously very well thought-out and executed by people who masquerade as "<u>liberals</u>" and "<u>well-meaning friends of the Negro children</u>." This technique would have succeded without notice, at least once the people who directed this operation would have included another group of people who also suffered oppression through their enslavement by others; and this would have envolved every group on the American scene; but this is not a book geared to deal with the history of slavery of all Americans.

I suggest that the UNITED FEDERATION OF TEACHERS, AFL-CIO, Local #2, headed by Albert Shanka, also had a hard time in finding adequate materials written by people of African origin before "BLACK POWER" and "BLACK STUDIES" became nasty words and phrases. Why? Because I am not familiar with any such literature ever being published by this, or any other teachers group, before said book (which would have served a better purpose not published.) Are we to understand that teachers holding history degree, those who have no "SOUTHERNISMS " in their speech, eastern EUROPEANISM not important, could not find any written materials of the "NEGROES" until some African-Americans set fire to private properties and exerted a little violence here and there around the United States of America, New York City in particular?

As long as these subtifuge continue, regardless of how many Bayard Rustin and Roy Wilkins are brought forward to defend those applying them, the African-American who is concious of his (or her) proud heritage(which includes the BLACK EXPERIENCE IN EGYPT with PHAROAH RAMESES II and MOSES DURING THE EXODUS PassOver , about c1298-1232 B.C.E.), there will continue to be "BLACK" or "NEGRO anti-Semitism." This does not, in any way, mean that any form of "ANTI" anyone on the sole basis of color, religion, sex, national origin, etc. is proper or tolerable; it does mean, on the other hand, that African-Americans, like all other peoples of the world, will use whatever means at their disposal to fight when freightened to the point of believing that their "RACE" is at stake. The expectancy of African-Americans not being as racist or as bigotted as anyother group in the United States of America is inconsistent with their historic past in the "NEW WORLD" as the slaves to everyone except the true owners of this land - those people Cristobal Colon (Christopher Colombus) wrongfully renamed "INDIANS." Never-the-less, this is what is expected of each and every African-American; and this is what will never be. The African-American, or BLACK person, is a byproduct of the same society with its racist dimensions that create all forms of bigotry. He, or she, has adopted most, if not all, of the taboos of their European-American (Christians, as well as Jews and Muslims) teachers; and, will certainly respond in kind whenever necessary. By-in-large, it is safe to say that no form of racism or bigotry in the "AMERICAN EXPERIENCE" or "DREAM" is any less or greater than the other. <u>They are all based upon unproven fallacies, truths and half-truths, but mostly myths and lies</u>. And worse of all, as long as the WHITE JEWS, anyone at all, regardless of how well-meaning, try to determing the course of the African-Americans in their quest for ascendency to the zenith of the "AMERICAN DREAM," they too will find the same bitter experiences his or her fellow European-American Christians encounter from the African-Americans (Jewish, Christian, Muslim or others).

How can one expect that the enslavement of the Jews more than three-thousand (3,000) years ago could be much more important to the African-Americans than the present mental and cultural enslavement, and the effects of their past physcial enslavement they must suffer daily to the tune of a memory of horror that dates back to 1503 in Hispaniola (Hayte) at their first domicile in the WESTERN WORLD under the torture of Roman Ctholicism with Bishop Bartolome de LasCasas; 1619 or 1620 with their transfer from the Caribbeans to the British colonies of North America;

1776 as "three-fifths of a man" under the "FATHER OF THE UNITED STATES OF AMERICA" - George Washington; 1865 with the doubble-cross by Abraham Lincoln; and all that happened between said periods of their BLACK EXPERIENCE in THE LAND OF THE FREE AND THE HOME OF THE "EUROPEAN-AMERICANS.

The "ROOTS OF NEGRO ANTI-SEMITISM" or "BLACK ANTI-SEMITISM," as used by many in its modern semantics, was not manufactured by the African-American; it was, and still is, the end result of centuries of racism and bigotry like "JEWISH ANTI-NEGROISM" or "JEWISH ANTI-EGYPTIANISM," CHRISTIAN ANTI-SEMITISM," "JEWISH ANTI-CHRISTIANISM," etc., etc., etc., almost never ending. From Europe it was transfered to these United States of America and all other parts of the entire world where European and European-American colonialism, imperialism, and tourism reached.

This lecture-essay is sure to be misunderstood. Yes; but, who will misunderstand it? Not those who are aware of "WORLD HISTORY." Not those who are in-charge of educational institutions relegated to teach religion and/or history, or even philosophy. Not those who are realy and truly interested in examining the facts of the BLACK-WHITE CONFRONTATION current in these United States of America and its colonies and territories, including some now renamed "COMMONWEALTH" in the Caribbeans.

In his book, THE RISING TIDE OF COLOR, by Lothrop Stoddard (Charles Scribner's Sons, New York, 1921) page 165, the following appears:

> "Our country (the United States of America),[1] originally settled almost exclusively by Nordics, was toward the close of the nine-

---

1. Words in parenthesis by the lecturer for clarity only.

teenth century invaded by hordes of immigrant Alpines and Mediterraneans, not to mention Asiatic elements like Levantines and Jews. As a result, the Nordic native American has crowded out with amazing rapidity by these swarming, prolific aliens, and after two short generations he has in many of our urban areas become almost extinct.

There could be no better way in which to end this lecture-essay than with the sick statement of Dr. Stoddard, who earned his Ph.D. at Harvard University; a typical <u>educator</u> of the type that created all kinds of "ANTI" feelings of a racial and religious nature that still plague the "AMERICAN DREAM." Men such as the good doctor have planted their seeds that grow into "NEGRO ANTI-SEMITISM" and "JEWISH ANTI-NEGROISM," and all other "ANTI-ISMS" which bring about only NEGATIVISM.

Submitted by:

Professor yosef ben-Jochannan to YALE BLACK SEMINARIANS at Union Theological Seminary, New York City, New York, November 1970. Training Program Auspices of the COMMISSION FOR RACIAL JUSTICE of the United Church of Christ, Park Avenue South, New York, N.Y. Reverend George Bell-Project Director.

A LECTURE ON THE BEGINNING OF THE CHRISTIAN CHURCH IN
NORTH AND EAST AFRICA

by

Instructor Yosef ben-Jochannan
Marymount College, Tarrytown, New York

In the ABODE OF THE BLESSED it is shown that there was a major treatise called "BOOK OF THE KNOWING THE EVOLUTIONS OF RA." In this work that existed for at least more than six thousand (6,000) years before the Hebrew Torah (Old Testament of the Christians or FIVE BOOKS OF MOSES), there, it is also shown where Moses got his idea of the "Creation of heaven and earth," etc. in his First Book or Book of Genesis. Thus we see in the Abode of the Blessed the God Neb-er-tcher, the "Lord of the Company of the Gods," recording the story of "Creation" and the "birth of the Gods." He wrote:

> I am he who evolved himself, under the form of the God - Khepera; I, the evolver of the evolutions evolved myself, the evolver of all evolutions, after many evolutions and developments which came forth from my mouth. No heaven existed, and no earth, and no terrestrial animals or reptiles had come into being. I formed them out of the inert mass of watery matter, I found no place upon which to stand,..., I was alone, and the Gods Shu and Tefnut[1] had gone forth from me;..." etc.

The "**CREATION**" story continued very much in the same manner as its later adopted Hebrew, Christian and Islamic versions. However, the plagerisms did not change the basic teaching very much. Thus we find Khepera having further declared:

> "...there existed none other who labored with me. I set the foundations of all things by my will, and everything evolved themselves therefrom.[2]

---

1. God - Jehovah, in the Book of Genesis, copied the Egyptian script in the following:..."Let us make man...," etc. Some

> I united myself to my shadow, and I sent forth
> Shu and Tefnut out from myself; thus from being
> one God I became three,[3] and Shu and Tefnut out
> from birth to Nut and Seb, and Nut gave birth
> to Osiris, Horus-Khent-an-maa, Sut, Isis, and
> Nephtys, at one birth, one after the other, and
> their children multiply upon this earth.

For further details in this area of concern, with respect to the "Creation Drama" copied by the Hebrews or Jews, Moses particularly, see the Hieroglyphic transcripts and English translations dealing with same in the ARCHAEOLOGIA, Vol. lii., pp. 440-443. The exact pages from which the above extracted texts were taken are the following: Col. 26, l. 22; Col. 27, 15; and Col. 28, l. 20; Col. 29, l.6. The truly original papyrus from whence it derived is housed in the British Museum, London, England, like so many other of the thousands of treasures British colonialists stole from the Africans and carried off to Britain, hundreds of which are today part of many European and European-American "COLLECTIONS " both private and public; the largest of said "Collections" being in Europe.

If any Rabbi, Minister, Priest, Iman, or whatever else there is in religious titles, cannot see the basic African foundation in that which they continue to call "Western Religions" having its origins in the above extract; then either can be said to be actually blinded by his or her religious bigotry, and cannot accept facts of a historical nature. For what makes the "Story of

---

Christians interpret this to mean "Jehovah and Jesus Christ" instead of Shu and Tefnut.
2. Sir E.A. Wallis Budge translated this sentence: "I laid the foundations of all things by my will, and all things evolved themselves therefrom."
3. It is from this that the so-called "Trinity" in the Christian religious theory is taken.

Creation" in the Hebrew Holy Torah or Christian Old Testament so detestable to some? The fact that its author or authors knowingly and purposefully failed to mention that their theory of God - Jehovah and all that followed said "Supreme Being" were not original when they first wrote of them; and as they were very much aware of the fact that all Moses knew about any God, whatsoever the extent of his information, he learnt among his fellow Africans of Kimit (Sais or Egypt); and that the Hebrews ("Jews' as a misnomer) had no written "scriptures" of a "God - Jehovah" or "Creation" before Moses, muchless a BOOK OF GENESIS which they have otherwise called the "FIRST BOOK OF MOSES." That Judaism is in fact an African-based religion which has been "Westernized" thousands of years after its original creation and development in Africa and Asia had taken place hundreds of years after the "disappearance of Moses on Mount Sinai" - in Kimit (northeast Africa.)

The "Heaven" to which the Africans of Kimit referred was originally called by them PET -- written in Hieroglyph ⌐⌐⌐ , which later on was changed to ⌐⌐⌐ , and stood for the Goddess NUT. The latter is also shown in some of the papyrus as a woman stretched out with her hands and arms down in a free fall and her feet on the ground with her body forming an arch while her head remain suspended in a turn towards her upright legs ⌐⌐⌐ . The Goddess two hands and arms, along with her feet and legs formed the "four pillars" that "held up the heavens." Her hanging breasts are always shown accentuated as a part of the "fertility symbolism" that fits into the following "...their children multiply upon the earth..." teaching already mentioned in the "Creation Drama" above, which has been extracted from the BOOK OF THE KNOW-

ING THE EVOLUTIONS OF RA, another of the major works of the Africans of Kimit from whence their fellow African, Moses, received much of his teachings in the so-called "FIVE BOOKS OF MOSES."

There were many features and characteristics which the Goddess NUT had, all of which the Hebrews (ancient Haribus) copied and moderated to suit their own cultural needs in the desert of Asia after they were allegedly forced out of Kimit, northeast Africa, by Pharoah Rameses II sometime between 1298 and 1232 BCE. Her feet were always shown pointing east, while her hands extended to the west. Sometimes her hands even formed a ladder. This "ladder" was symbolic of the rituals that spoke of the "...soul climbing up into heaven...," the origin of the so-called "Jacob Ladder" of the Hebrew and Christian mythology. Thus one finds the following in the TEXT OF UNAS on the walls of a pyramid:

> Hail to thee, O daughter of Amenta, mistress of Peteru of heaven, thou gift of Thoth, thou mistress of the two sides ladder, open a way to Unas, let Unas pass.

Through what was Unas to pass? The soul of Unas, as the soul of all who died, made its way up the "two sides ladder" to the "Abode Of The Gods" in the "Nether World" (or Other World). Many other texts indicate that:

> ...the Gods soul entered Amenta through a gap in the mountains of Abydos of Peka,

shown as the following ▱𓄿𓅭𓊖 But the final destination from Abydos of Peka "was still a place established in the Sekhet-Hetep," according to the pyramid TEXTS OF SEKHET-AARU, "where the God Horus and the God Set dwell" in the northern part of Kimit" in the FIELD OF THE REED PLANTS."

Though the indigenous Africans of Kimit (Sais or Egypt) thought of entering the sky at the "eastern mountain peak," which they called "Bakhatet," and wrote [hieroglyphs], and the western mountain peak" or "Manu," which they also wrote [hieroglyphs]; they nevertheless also believed in the "Circuit of Osiris" they called the TUAT, and wrote [hieroglyphs]. This place, TUAT, was the UNDER WORLD, also known as "the place of departed souls." In the Hebrew Torah's plagerization of this aspect of African philosophy and mythology, equally as that in the Christian and Muslim "Holy Scriptures" taken from the Hebrew texts, the "Underworld" would also represent "the place of the body of the departed soul," but not of the "soul" itself; the Hebrew, Christian and Muslim "soul" go instead to "Heaven" or Amenta. The best description of this Christian myth is given by Dr. Brugsch in his major work on the "Egyptian Religion" entitled, RELIGION und MYTHOLOGIE; particularly pages 211 through 216. On page 211 the latter points have been cited; whereas on page 216 the description of "Heaven" is detailed.

Hopefully so-called "modern" or "Western man," who believes that Judaism, Christianity or Islam was the religion upon which the "Creation Story" in the BOOK OF GENESIS (First Book Of Moses) was originated, would examine other noted works on their own religion that preceded the Hebrew Holy Torah or Christian Old Testament, Christian New Testament (including those books removed in order to keep Christians ignorant on order of the Roman Pope through the findings of his Bishops at the Conference of Nicene - the so-called "LOST BOOKS OF THE BIBLE"), and Muslim Qu'ran; this only if we are truly and honestly seeking TRUTH. Unfortunately most Hebrews, Christians and Muslims believe without question or reservation whatever their religious leaders tell them about their respective God-head; even if what they are told is to their own personal detriment. Why is this TRUE? Because religion is basically the historical recordings of a peoples heritage with a preponderance of mythology surrounding their national heroes who were most instrumental in creating their political compact (nation); it being the height of ancestral worship (this being a term generally reserved for "pagan peoples" - primarily Africans.) The reincarnate myth with all of its taboos looses its belief-reality and becomes a fact-reality as soon as it is transformed into "sacred texts" and "Holy writings" of institutionalized religion; as a direct result certain of its members become dependent upon it for their livelihood or economic salvation (such as ministers, rabbis, priests, imans, readers, etc., including many of their auxilliary aides). As long as this latter objective remains one of the basic reasons for the perpetuation of any religion, irrespective of its sectual or denominational name or Godhead, then there will never be a point in which mankind can come together to examine in honesty the minimun and maximum of the "TRUTHS" in each, or be able to seperate TRUTH from the accompanying MYTHS. Until this is accomplished, however, mankind can only hope against the day when science, missused as it is by men and women who cannot hear no one outside of their own discipline, engulfs the planet Earth and everything thereon by way of atomic fission or the likes of it.

Nevertheless are we to accept most of the current histo-philosophers and histo-theologians who hold similar views as the following expressed by Mircea Eliade in his book, COSMOS AND HISTORY: THE MYTH OF THE ETERNAL RETURN (translated from French to English by Willard R. Trask), Harper Torchbooks - Harper & Row, New York, 1959, p. 52.[1] He wrote:

> In the particulars of his concious behavior, the "primitive," the archaic man, acknowledges no act which has not been previously poisted and lived by someone else, some other being who was not a man. What he does has been done before. His life is the ceaseless repitition of gestures initiated by others.

Certainly we cannot accept the above presumption as fact. Why? Because the so-called "primitive" was the originator of most of what we are still holding as GOD - Jehovah, Jesus Christ or Al'lah. Yet this extract is typical of the findings of thousands of so-called "modern" or "Western man" of the past three to four hundred years; the best example of this being the findings by the Reverend Placide Temples in his book, BANTU PHILOSOPHIE,[2] in which he holds that:

> ...the primitive Bantu religion had no philosophie equivalent to Judaeo-Christianity.

Both Eliade's and Temples' obsession with their own importance and religion made them fail to observe that their histo-philosophic theories rest squarely upon the creative genius of the same so-called "primitives" they have attempted to berate and degrade. For it is upon the "primitive Bantus" of the entire Nile Valley and Great Lakes High-Cultures, and others at points much further south - all the way to Monomotapa (Zimbabwe), religions - Judaism, Christianity and Islam rest; their origin having taken root in the Mysteries System of Kimit (Sais or Egypt), Nubia (Sudan), Meröwe (Sudan), Axum (Cush, Ethiopia or Abyssinia) and

---

1. Originally; LeMythe de l'eternel retour: archetypes et repetition (Paris, Librairie Gallimard, 1949).

2. Originally; La Philosphie Bantoue, by Dr. Rubbens of Fr. Temples original work (The Revd. Collin King, M.A. translator).

Puanit (Punt or Somaliland area); not even to mention the major contributions made by the numerous other "primitive" High-Cultures all over the continent of Alkebu-lan (the Romans and Greeks "Africa, Ethiopia, Libya, Hesperia," etc.), particularly the Twa people, whom so-called "modern man" labeled "pygmies," of central Alkebulan - where it all began.

What is basically obvious, or should be, in the writings of "modern man," "Caucasian" as he prefer to be called, is the racism and religious bigotry he constantly introduce into every aspect of the Africans heritage, especially their religions, as "TRUTH." He begins his work with the basic presumption that he has reached a stage in life that is "superior to the primitives." Of course Europeans and European-Americans (Jews or Gentiles) are never depicted as ever being "primitive" or "uncivilized"; these two terms being primarily reserved for most Asian people, all of those of the Pacific Islands, the Caribbean Islands, the indigenous of the Americas and the Australians, but most precisely those of Alkebulan (Africa). Yet it was the Africans of Kimit and the Nile Valley High-Cultures who were the ones that first educated the "primitive Greeks, Romans," and all other Europeans that followed in their footsteps - British and European-Americans included; all of which became the foundation for what is today being called "WESTERN CIVILIZATION" and "WESTERN RELIGION."

R.C. Collingwood in his book, THE IDEA OF HISTORY, Oxford University Press, New York, etc., 1956 (first published by the Clarendon Press, 1946), Part I, p. 14, under the heading -"Greco-Roman Historiography;" § I: Theocratic history and myth; wrote:

> By what steps and stages did the modern European idea of history come into existence? Since I do not

> think that any of these stages occurred outside the Mediterranean to Mesopotania, and the northern African coastlands, I am precluded from saying anything about historical thought in China or in any other part of the world except the region I have mentioned.

If Collingwood, as most of his fellow histographers before and since him, attempted to clarify what he felt is truly history; was it not incumbent upon him, as all of the others, to examine all known works designated "history" by their author or national custodian before he made his conclusions? Certainly. But he went on in the very next paragraph:

> I have quited one example of early Mesopotanian history from a document of about 2500 B.C. I say history, but I ought rather to say quasi-history, because, as I have pointed out, the thought expressed in this document resembles what we call history in the making statements about the past, but differs from it, first, in that these statements are not answers to questions, not the fruits of research, but mere assertions of what the writer already knows; and secondly, that the deeds recorded are not human actions but, in the first instance at any rate, divine actions.

What Collingwood, as most of his contemporaries and those of today, failed to observe is that the ancestors of the African and Asian peoples, the ancients, did not seperate that which is today called "secular history" from "religious history" as so-called "modern man" - like himself; all of which educators of today believe they have accomplished, but in reality failed to do miserably so. It is, therefore, difficult to understand how an appearently educated historian as himself could not invison this when he read the BOOK OF THE DEAD or the PAPYRUS OF ANI; assuming that he was aware of these works existence. Since he has assumed the responsiblity of an authority in histography, he could not have shrugged off the equal responsibility of being familiar with these two works. Therefore, he should have recognized that the life of many of the Gods (who were for the most part actually deceased kings - pharoahs) had to do with much of their performance while they were still alive on this planet - Earth, in Kimit (Egypt), North Africa. Another cardinal point must certainly be in the form of a question, thus; Why did Collingwood (as most of the others who still restrict their researhes to this area of the entire planet Earth, as if all knowledge originated there) ignore all other areas of the antiquitous world for his study? Is it not true that the answer in this case is the same as it is in most cases dealing with the origin of European and European-American history and heritage - otherwise called "Caucasian" or "modern man's civilization and religion " (High-Culture); and especially that which they have selected to misname "Greek Philosophy?" Certainly this is the case in this situation also. However, what is most significant in Collingwood's work, unlike those of many of his disciples and others of his discipline, is that he challenged "Mesopotanian history" as not being true "history" in the sense as that of the Ionian, a Greek citizen - Herodotus - the so-called "father of history." Of course the fact that Herodotus, who is always projected as a Greek by birth, when in fact he was an Ionian (a colonly of Kimit at the time of his birth), recorded much of the events in his own book, THE HISTORIES, from hearsay evidence, most of which were from secondhand sources, appearently had no fundamental significance to Collingwood, as shown in his work.

Examining another of the so-called "modern scholars," who commenced his world of everything from the point of a Greek-centric Anglo-Saxon Judaeo-Christian orientation, one finds the following in Wilhelm Windelband's book, A HISTORY OF PHILOSOPHY, vol. II, Harper & Row (Harper Torchbooks), New York, 1958, Chapt. 2, 37, under the heading, The Problem of Civilization: Compact Theory, page 518. He wrote:

> The fundamental thought, which the philosophy of the Enlightenment would hold as to the great institutions of human society and its historical monument, was prescribed for it in advance, partly by its dependence upon natural-science metaphisic, and partly by its own psychological tendency.

What is there in Windelband's statement that was not common in the teachings in the PYRAMID TEXTS, BOOK OF THE DEAD, OSIRIAN DRAMA and other Nile Valley Mysteries System writings of the indigenous Africans of Kimit and other nations all the way south to Monomotapa? Nothing. Is it not a fact that the entire basis of what we have called "Greek Philosophy" for the past few hundred years is nothing more than the embodiment of "natural-science" in an arrangement of the "metaphisics" established by the Africans and Asians of antiquity? All of which even so-called "modern" or "Western man," including European-Americans, derived their "Western Philosophy." Is it not equally true that the United States of America's own system of justice rests upon the foundation of the symbolism inherent in the totems, signs and metaphysical science of "primordial" or "primitive" Africans who are also called, degradingly, "pygmies"? Certainly the Goddess of Justice shown holding the scale with the "...heart of Ani..." ballanced by the "feather," while blindfolded (teachings which did not only pass from Kimit to Greece before they arrived in other parts of Europe and to the Island of Great Britain, but also to these

United States of America and all other parts of North and South America, the Caribbeans included) also had its origin in Puanit (Punt or modern somalilands), Axum (Cush, Ethiopia or Abyssinia), Nubia (modern Sudan) and other nations of Alkebu-lan (Africa of the Romans and Greeks) further south before it reached Kimit (Egypt of the Hebrews). These totems or sign-symbols are best detailed in the PAPYRUS OF ANI and the BOOK OF THE DEAD, particularly in the Facimile Text on plates 3 and 4 of the PAPYRUS OF ANI - which dates back to more than 6000 years before there was a "Hebrew people" or "Adam and Eve," muchless a "Greek Philosophy."

In the scenes shown in both of the major African works mentioned above, even the "plumb-bob" and other most important symbols which "Western Freemasory" cannot do without are in display; the same "plumb-bob" which members of the craft (Worthy Brothers) continue attributing to the Hebrew and Christian "Sacred Scriptures" with relationship "King Solomon's Temple," when in fact it was in use all along the Nile Valleys (Blue and White, also Atbara River) and other points south (as shown in the BOOK OF THE DEAD) for thousands of years before and African of Kimit, Moses, adopted it into his own version of the African-based religion we today call "Judaism" - in the past "Hebrewism." From Judaism it entered Christianity, the daughter of Judaism; and from Christianity to Islam, the grandchild of Judaism and child of Christianity.

In the PAPYRUS OF ANI, where it is showing "Ani's heart" and the "feather of justice," there appears the "Twelve Gods" or "Judges" from whence the system of Twelve Juries and Twelve

Apostles in modern Judaeo-Christian Jurisprudence originated. The "feather", symbolic of the the "weighing of right against wrong," is the element of "natural-science metaphisics" spoken of by Windelband above. The jackal-headed God - ANUBIS - takes the place of the blinded-woman with the sword of vengance in her one hand while she holds the "scale" that weighs the "feather" in the other, all of which European-Americans have adopted from their Greek antecendants who learned of them while they were students under African priests of the Mysteries System of the Nile Valley High-Cultures in Kimit (Egypt). The God THOTH; also represented as the "...scribe of the Gods" (court reporter) in many of the "Judgement" scenes in the PAPYRUS OF ANI, is shown noting the procedings of the "trial of Ani;" behind Toth the monster-God AMEN-IT (the court guard or marshall), the "DEVOWER," stands. If these scenes were not sufficient to tell "modern man" ("Western man," European or European-American, even "Caucasians" and "Semites") that the ancient indigenous Africans, the so-called "primitives," were the ones who made the natural appear in the super-natural, then "modern man" is certainly void of the necessary phenomenum and understanding that created the philosophical presentation of religion among the "primitives" who did not seperate the "secular" from the "spiritual" (or "religious") within their culture. Obviously this is the basically fundamental conflict between African and Asian metaphisical and philosophical experiences and thought to that of European and European-American materialistic version of "science-metaphisics" or exestentialism. European and European-American thought process cannot visualize "material" as being no different than the "spirit" or the "soul" that "material" embodies; the Africans and Asians in general, on the other hand expounding its reality. Thus the African "ancestral spirits" in constant communication with their living relatives without the need of transendental invocation by mediums for a fee as it is in Europe, England and the Americas. But European and European-American "ancestral spirits" exist only in the person of the departed; only to be called "Saint" sometime in the distant future by the authorities in-charge of sainthood. The point is; who makes "saints" and "angels'? Is it not the same human being that makes "ancestral spirits;" the same person that created the "Gods, God-heads," or "Supreme Being" with the stokes of his pen?

The Gods or Orishas of the Yoruba religion of West Africa, headed by the Supreme Being - OLUDUMARE (or Oledamare), aided by His ancestral spirits; and of course VODUM - the Supreme Being or God of the Voodoo religion; also teach the same "TRUTH" as do the Gods - Jehovah of the Hebrews (misnomered "Jews"), Jesus Christ of Nazzareth (the "Nazzarine") of the Christians, and Al'lah of the Muslims (or Moslems) religion. Yet "metaphisics" and "philosophy" have been taught in a manner suggestive of their non-existence in the two African religions of West Africa mentioned above, but not of the other three they have labeled "Western Religions" - forgetting that the fundamental base of all three originated at the same source the other two also took root; such, however, being typical of professors who are oriented to the type of Anglo-Saxon Protestant Judaeo-Christian Greek-centric racism and religious bigotry that permeated "Western" education. Nevertheless they cannot escape history; the BOOK OF THE DEAD, PAPYRUS OF ANI, NEGATIVE CONFESSIONS, and other major works by the ancient indigenous Africans constantly remain as the ghosts that haunt them in their memory of how the Hebrews entered north Africa, Kimit (Egypt), and learnt much of what we today prefer to misnomer "Judaism." And if "Judaism" was so influenced, Judaism's child, "Christianity," could not escape said African experience; neither could its grandchild,"Islam."

In his book, A STUDY OF HISTORY, the English historian, Arnold J. Toynbee, wrote the following:

> We have already found that <u>our own Western Society</u> (or civilization) <u>is affiliated to a predecessor</u>.[1] The obvious method of pursuing <u>our search</u> for further societies of the same species will be to take the other existing examples, the Orthodox Christian, the Islamic, the Hindu and the Far Eastern, and see if we can discover 'parents' for them also. <u>But before we set out on the search we must be clear what we are looking for</u>: in other words, <u>what are the tokens of apparentation - and - affiliation which we are to accept as valid evidence. What tokens of such relationship</u> did we, in fact, find in the case of our own society's affiliation to the Hellenic Society?

The above extract was taken from the two volume abridged edition of Toymbee's six volume work. The editor of this edition is D.C. Somervill (who claimed endorsement of Toynbee himself), published his work through Dell Publishing Company Co., Inc., New York, 1965. (See Chapter II - The Comparative Study of Civilizations, page 28.)

Toynbee's own words set the stage for further examination of the prejudicial basis upon which he illiminated many High-Cultures (civlizations). But, what is in reality "Western Society" other than a conglomeration of collected little bits of High-

---

1. Words underscored in the above extract for the purpose of emphacizing particular points, only, by your lecturer.

Cultures from Asia and Africa nurtured in Europe; and from Asia, Africa and indigenous America among the European-Americans. Even the term "Indo-European Aryan" suggests a non-Western (European or European-American) origin. Of course this term would not have been expanded if Zinjanthropus boisie had been already unearthed in central east Africa when it was first used as a means of indicating the "superiority of the Caucasian over the "so-called "Negroes" or "Bantus" (even "Africans South of the Sahara" and "Black Africans)". For during that period of its origin the Tigris and Euphrates were still considered to be the "...original home of mankind " or "Garden of Eden" according to the Hebrew Holy Torah. Now that the original "Garden of Eden" has been relocated in Africa's central lands the inheritors of the Greek-centric Anglo-Saxon Indo-European Aryanisms, who once called said indigenous Africans of east central Africa "Hamites" instead of "Negroes" and "Bantus," have followed the same line specified in Toynbee's comments I have extracted above; a line which hundreds of Europeans and European-Americans that preceded him established for him to ape. It is very much necessary to state that this abridged two volume work has not, in anyway, failed to capture the six volume work by Toynbee - himself. The original only detailed the general information that much more; nevertheless, the reader should be able to observe the implicit racism that is typical in both editions.

As it is with all of my other works, specifically those related to critical analysis of writings on Africa, or of things African, so is this one; the purpose of which is to enlighten my African brethren of that which others have done to Africa's heritage, and continue doing, without proper reproach from those of us who claim to be "Black" and "African Studies professors" etc. And as Toynbee stated:

> ...before we set out on the search we must be clear what we are looking for..., etc., etc.

In otherwords; what is the priority of the African-American with respect to Toynbee's statement? In it I see a chalenge to the very cultural and historical survival of the African as one of the basic contributors of what Toynbee and others notoriously call "Western Society" and "Western civilization." But,is our struggle one of CLASS AGAINST CLASS? All of which occupies the overwhelming amount of our time in "Black" and "African Studies Courses." Or is it not one of RACE AGAINST RACE? If it is neither; then, what is it? We must be "...very clear..." what it is and what "we set out to prove." Toynbee and other Europeans and European-Americans are "very clear" on what theirs are, and were. He cited it quite sucinctly when he noted:

> We have already found that our own Western Society (or civlization) is affiliated to a predeeessor...

which is in no way whatsoever connected to the African or African-American as we know and respect him. And in his work, all six (6) volumes of it, he set out to "search" for proof of a common and similar Anglo-Saxon or Greco-Roman Christian beginning in the predecessors he needed to establish or re-establish, which ever it is. It was obvious that whatever society he discovered in his "search" would not have had to bear the lable of "Negro" or anyother such name of disrepute in "Western Society," but instead one of an Anglo-Saxon Christian Indo-European Aryan, or simply Caucasian and White, origin.

Although Toynbee, Collingwood, Eliade, and others like them, have not actually said that the Africans of ancient times (their so-called "primitives"), were inferior; they, nevertheless, inferred as much when they took the position that Africa below the Mediterranean shores had nothing whatsoever to do with the origin of so-called "Western Society" or Orthodox Christianity. Nothing could be further from the TRUTH; for we find C. P. Groves in volume I of his four volume work, THE PLANTING OF CHRISTIANITY IN AFRICA, page 22, saying the following:

> (3) The Social Pattern.
> For the most part the peoples of Africa live in communities characterized by a definite social pattern. Individuals are securely woven into it, so that any response to a religious message that involves new forms of behaviour will be correspondingly difficult to secure with sincerity. While each group must be studied seperately for its own detailed social pattern, yet there are certain features found in common that may be usefully set down here.

Obviously professor Grove (who depended largely upon the racist conclusions in C.G. Seligman's, RACES OF AFRICA, New York, 1930, like Toynbee and other European and European-American historians, "Christian missionaries"—European-style — theologians, etc.) considered Christianity the equivalent and synonymous to "Western civlization" or "society;" and of course, the same correspondingly to "Caucasianism" and "capitalism" for over the last two to three hundred years. For this very reason it is necessary to ignore the reference to the Africans of Ethiopia in the BOOK OF ACTS of the Christian Holy Bible (any version). It is also necessary to convert the Africans - Tertullian, St. Cyprian and St. Augustine, "FATHERS OF THE CHRISTIAN CHURCH," into "Caucasian Europeans," thereby perpetuating the myth that "Christianity had its origin in Rome as an organized religious institution, as well as in Africa;" a myth that is as far from the TRUTH as night is to day, which each of them is aware actually began in Kimit or Egypt (North Africa) But what are they going to do with Jesus Christ -- their God? He was neither an African or Indo-European Aryan with Greco-Roman orientation; nor was He "Caucasian" of "Western Society," according to the "Sacred Scriptures written by God-inspired Holy men." Accordingly the present day Jews said He was a "Semite," one of their own who fell afoul of the Jewish moral laws found in their Holy Torah. He was an Asian; thus -- brown or yellow-skinned at the least. Of course this is not so according to Michaelangelo's PIETRA, JESUS ON THE CROSS, LAST SUPPER, etc. Even the LAST SUPPER (Passover), from whence the Hebrew copied the "twelve (12) Judges" or Gods that sat in judgement of Ani (as shown in the BOOK OF THE DEAD and the PAPYRUS OF ANI), a copy of the "SEDER" of the Africans of Kimit, did not show any BLACK desciple.

BLACK STUDIES, which this lecture-essay shall be called by many, is nevertheless a term which cannot apply to this work; for this is not a study of BLACKS alone, but of how BLACKS have been robbed of their heritage by WHITES masquerading through the disguise of religious teachers of biblical truth, historians with "authority" on African peoples and Africa, anthropologists, paeleontologists, etc. It is, therefore, incumbent upon all educators in the area so designated,"BLACK STUDIES," to demand that all manner of study related to the "BLACK EXPERIENCE," beginning in Africa and at present in the so-called "Western World," be immediately placed under the direct control of BLACK STUDIES DE-

PARTMENTS," first of which must naturally be "AFRICAN STUDIES" - this being the most essential and basic ingredient to any study dealing with people of African origin. The purpose for this appearently tacid digression is to set the foundation of the following revelations with respect to the origin of Christianity in northern Africa (Egypt) and not in Asia (Palestine, where Jesus Christ was born) as it has been proclaimed to have been for the past few hundred years, and that "the north African Church was of Caucasian origin."

The earliest form of Christianity on an institutional basis had its origin in Egypt, northern or north-eastern Africa; this being over two hundred (200) years before Emperor Constantine ("the great") of the Roman Empire made Rome a "Christian nation." The early "Christians," in fact, formerly Jews and members of religions indigenous to the Nile Valley High-Cultures, were not so called at the time of the workings of their God - Jesus Christ of Nazzareth, "The Nazzarine." Even Jesus Christ himself was a Jew or Hebrew that worshiped in the synagouge. The noted Christian historian, Harnach, in his work, THE MISSION AND EXPANSION OF CHRISTIANITY (2nd. Edition, 1908), vol. II, p. 162, stated that a larger number of Jews became converts to Christianity along the banks of the Nile River in Egypt than anywhere else. But European-Christian Church history conveniently does not project in details the North African Church of Egypt before the period of the episcopate of Demetrius of Alexandria (C.E. or A.D. 189-232), this also being noted by Harnach on pages 160-162 of the same work and chapter; yet he attempted to give the impression that a chronological summary of said period only involved incidents which he listed under eight (8) solitary items with no details whatsoever. Nevertheless, it was Demetrius who appointed the first bishops, three (3) of them, which had increased to more than twenty-seven (27) at the time of another African "great," Augustine (later on "Saint"), the Bishop of Hippo Regius (A.D. 385-430). On the otherhand, Harnach declared that there were only twenty-three (23); equally Lightfoot in his work, PHILIPPIANS, p. 230; but others, such as Count C.F. Volney in his work, RUINS OF EMPIRES; and Professor J.C.deGraft-Johnson in his, AFRICAN GLORY; held that the figure was at least twenty-seven (27).

There were in fact two (2) branches or sects of the "...followers of the Master, Jesus Christ," that became the nucleus of today's Christianity and Christendom. The oldest of the two was composed of indigenous Africans of Egypt who spoke a local African language and also a mixed African-European (Egyptian-Greek) language called "COPTIC" - the language of the present predominantly Europeanized population bearing the name "COPTS."[1] The other group was Egyptian-born Europeans of Greek ancestry who were primarily the descendants of the Greek and Macedonian invaders of Egypt with Alexander ("the great") II in 332 B.C.E., and others that were imported later on by Aristotle when he and General Soter (who declared himself "Ptolemy I" in 324 B.C.E.) had already sacked Egypt's treasures, including the Library of the Grand Lodge at Luxor on the banks of the Upper Nile (Nubia at times) Egypt at others. These people used Greek as their language, and mostly occupied cities along the Mediterranean shore --- which

---

1. This word is taken from the Latin "coptus," which had its origin the Arabic "quft" or "qubt." There is a word in Coptic called "gyptios," which the Greeks made "aigyptios" from which the anglocized "Egypt" had its origin. See also Hebrew Torah.

they gave the name "DELTA." Among these were also Greek-speaking Hebrews (or "Jews", a misnomer for all other Hebrews than those of the tribe of Judah); the same people who translated the so-called "SACRED (Hebrew) SCRIPTURES" into the Greek language -- the SEPTUAGINT (BIBLE) according to cf. H. G. Meecham's, OLDEST VERSION OF THE BIBLE (1932). Even the PENTATEUCH they had translated into Greek before the middle of the 3rd. century before the Christian era (B.C.E.); also all of the other works of the HOLY TORAH -- the FOUR BOOKS OF MOSES (later expanded into FIVE the Christian OLD TESTAMENT by c130 B.C.). It is at this juncture that the philosophic idealism Plato adopted from the Ethiopians of Kimit (Egypt or Sais) was introduced into the Hebrew "Sacred Scriptures" by Hellenic oriented Jews. From these Jewish works Greek mythology also entered into early Christian teachings of the bishops - Pantaenus, Origen and Clement; all of them contemporaries of Demetrius - the founder of the noted CATECHETICAL SCHOOL OF ALEXANDRIA - where all of them were schooled by other Africans of earlier religious philosophical thoughts, and where they too taught. It was also this school that was proclaimed "the finest centre of Christian scholarship without rival throughout Christendom" for centuries following. But,it was impossible for the earliest Christian and Hebrew "Sacred Scriptures" not to be equally influenced by the purely African religion of the worship of the God - OSIRIS, the representative of "the God above all other Gods -" RA - the most popular religion and God throughout Egypt and other Nile Valley High-Cultures at this period when Christianity was still a very small cultist movement. The sole difference of the cultist Christians, at that time, to that of their Osirian hosts, was their teaching of a God - "JESUS CHRIST OF NAZZARETH" (formerly patterned after the Middle-Eastern God - BACCHUS), their "SAVIOUR," who had "conquered death." This was the general background of the earliest Christians in Egypt, at the time there being none in Rome, and other areas of north and east Africa (Alkebu-lan); they later on crossed over into Greece and Rome by way of the Mediterranean Sea. There was no Pope Peter of the Roman Catholic Church as yet in Christian Church History; there were no Christians in Jerusalem - where Jesus Christ was supposed to have been born, around the period of at least seventeen (17) years after the Romans pushed the Greeks out of Kimit (Egypt) in their attempt to conquer the known world of antiquity, otherwise called "30 B.C." These are just a few of the basic facts Eusebius of Caesarea (c260-339 C.E. or A.D.) needed to mention in his major work he called, CHURCH HISTORY. They are some of the basics which very few Christians, including most of those who call themselves "MEMBERS OF THE CLERGY," know about their own religion's history and traditional belief they inherrited from their African and Asian forebears.

Is it not strange that some so-called "Christian historians" even dared to suggest that "none of the apostles evangelized on African soil during the Apostolic Age"? Even Eusebius in his CHURCH HISTORY, II, 1§13, was obliged to admit that John Mark, the evangelist, "missioned in Egypt and established churches there. But Dr. J.N. Farquhar, centuries later, wrote in his work, THE APOSTLE THOMAS IN NORTH INDIA (in: THE BULLETIN OF THE JOHN RYLANDS LIBRARY, X (1929), 29-30):

We may think it possible that Thomas was one of

> the men who proclaimed Christ in Egypt, Cyrene and further West.

On the otherhand Harnach in his work, THE MISSION AND EXPANSION OF CHRISTIANITY (2nd. Edition, 1908), tried to degrade Eusebius' declaration about John Mark. He wrote:

> We have no means of checking this statement.

What Dr. Farquhar failed to observe is that - "We" - also "have no means of checking" the proclamation that Mary, Jesus Christ of Nazzareth's mother, was a "virgin when she conceived him" from "an angel of God." Which is harder to check? But M.R. James was quite emphatic in his work, THE APOCRYPHAL NEW TESTAMENT (1942), p. 204, about John Mark's apostolic mission in Africa, inspite of men such as Harnack and other Europeans and European-Americans who are still manipulating to remove Christianity's origin from the pages of history relative to north Africa, just as they have tried to remove philosophy from the African teachings that originated along the Nile Valley and Great Lakes High-Cultures before it was adopted and expanded by European students from Greece and called "GREEK PHILOSOPHY."

One finds in the BOOK OF ACTS 8 : 26-40 the biblical reference to the African from Ethiopia who became a Christian before any European did. But Professor C. P. Groves could not allow this African to be what his own Christian "Holy Scripture" or "New Testament" said he was. Thus on page 34 of his work, THE PLANTING OF CHRISTIANITY IN AFRICA, Vol. I: To 1840, he wrote:

> The Ethiopian in the story came, not from Abyssinia, but the region of the Nile between Aswan and Khartoum.

One must assume that Professor Grove must have also conceived that Balthazer, one of the "THREE WISE MEN," also did not come from the land the bible writers described as "Ethiopia" or "Cush." Or is it that "Ethiopia," his "Abyssinia," is to far south of the Sahara and too "negroid" to have been mentioned in his Christian Bible. If the biblical recorders were in error here, they were equally in error with the sole basis of the "Christian Holy Scripture" - the "birth of Jesus Christ of Nazzareth" and the "Holy Trinity" concept which the Christians copied from the BOOK OF THE DEAD and taught by Pharoah Amen-hotep IV - who was also known as Ikhnaten and Akhnaten ("the God Aten is light).

The perpetrators of the non-Apostolic Africans theory forget, quite conveniently so, that Luke 23:26 stated that "Simon of Cyrene," who "bore Jesus' cross" as a display of concern for his leader, was a north African. The Africans of north Africa, many of whom were at the time Hebrews (or "Jews"), were also mentioned in Acts 2:20; 6:9; 11:20; and 13:1. Even Jesus Christ, shortly after leaving his mother - Mary's - womb, entered Africa with his father - Joseph during their flight from Roman and Hebrew prosecution and persecution, as stated in Matthew 2:13-15. Last, but not least, even a citizen of Alexandria, Egypt, of African-European parentage, Apollos, appeared in Ephesus and Corinth as a missionary teaching the words of the "Saviour and Redeemer, the only son of Jehovah, Jesus of Nazzareth." This man is also mentioned in the BOOK OF ACTS 18:24-19 : 1.

"The eunach, Judich, the son of the Candace" (queen) of the African nation then known as Meröwe or Meröe, "went to Jerusalem bearing gifts for the feasts of the child - Jesus Christ." A most literate man, Judich, he was able to translate the Greek version of the SEPTUAGINT (Christian Old Testament or Hebrew Five Books

Of Moses, the HOLY TORAH) into his own language, a sort of Merotic script spoken of by modern anthropologists and linguists. (See Jackson and Lake, THE BEGINNING OF CHRISTIANITY, III (1933), pp. 89-90; also, Henry J. Cadbury, V (1933), pp. 66-67.)

And "...Judich went rejoicing into Africa...," etc., according to Philip. He also referred to this African as "the Suffering Servant" as he did with respect to the passage in the SEPTUAGINT refering to Jesus Christ, his own Saviour. Even Irenaeus recognized Judich's missionary skills; equally did Eusebius, who also called him "...a missionary to his people." (See Esebius, CHURCH HISTORY, III, 1 § 13; Irenaeus, AGAINST HERESIES, III, xii, 8; also, Jackson and Lake, THE BEGINNINGS OF CHRISTIANITY, IV, 95-99).

Count C.F. Volney's, RUINS OF EMPIRES, p. 122, states, with respect to Egypt:

> Thus the Ethiopian of Thebes named stars of inundation, or Aguarius, those stars under which the Nile began overflow;* stars of the ox or bull, those under which they began to plow; stars of the lion, those under which that animal, driven for the sheaf, or of the harvest virgin, those of the reaping season; stars of the lamb, stars of the two kids, those under which these precious animals were brought forth: and thus was resolved the first part of the difficulty.

The asterix* represented the following footnote by Volney: "This must have been June." In another paragraph, on the same page, Volney also wrote:

> Thus the same Ethiopian having observed that the return of the inundation always corresponded with the rising of a beautiful star which appeared towards the source of the Nile, and seemed to warn the husbandman against the coming waters, he compared this action to that of the animal who, by his barking, gives notice of danger, and he called this star the dog, the barker (Sirius). In the same manner he named the stars of the crab,

> those where the sun, having arrived at the tropic, retreated by a slow retrograde motion like the crab or cancer. He named stars of the wild goat, or Capricorn, those where the sun, having reached the highest point in his annuary tract, rests at the summit of the horary gnomon, and imitates the goat, who delights to climb the summit of the rocks.

Volney pursued this course of reporting on the greatness of the Ethiopians - Blacks of Africa. But on pages 16 and 17 he described the "Ethiopians" (the ancient word for all Africans) of Egypt in the following manner:

> There a people, now forgotten, discovered, while others were yet barbarians, the elements of the arts sciences. A race of men now rejected from society for their sable skin and frizzled hair, founded on the study of the laws of nature, those civil and religious systems which still govern the universe.

Count Volney[1] left no doubt for anyone's mind that he meant the Judaeo-Christian religion and its Moslem offspring were "Ethiopian" in origin, as he traced the roots of the "sable skin and frizzled hair" men of Tyre, Sidon, Ascalon, Gaza and Berytus, even to the lands of the "River Jordan." He also included the "desert of Hored" and "Mount Sinai; where by means beyond vulgar reach, a genius, profound and bold, established institutions which have weighed on the whole human race." Count Volney lived with the descendants of the "Ethiopians," the so-called "Negroes," he was writing of while he was in Egypt during the late part of the 18th century C.E. (A.D.), along with Baron Viviant Denon - who

---

1. See Count C. F. Volney, RUINS OF EMPIRE (Truth Seeker Company, 1950). It was first published in French in Paris, France, in 1821 A.D. by Bossange one year following Volney's death. His widow and nephew had the manuscript and printing done with their final approval; whereas, the first English translation was by Levrault, QUAI MALAQUAIS, 1802, under the direction and supervison of Volney - himself.

drew the picture of the Ethiopian-faced SPHINX OF GHIZEH (Akhet Khufu, the Greeks "Horizon of Cheops") shown on page 156 of my BLACK MAN OF THE NILE, and in countless other works.

This lecture-essay, one of many submitted for your critical analysis, ends on the above note by Count C.F. Volney. But what about your own ending? Is it one that is completed before your own physical and spiritual (mental) death? Is it one that terminated when your parents, priests, rabbis, inmans, ministers, and others in-charge of your religious institution told you that "GOD MADE MAN IN HIS OWN IMAGE;" and that said "GOD" is only the one you are to worship? Should it not be that your death, mentally or spiritually, never comes until your total self ceases to exist no more? And, if the latter is the case; then, should you not examine all religious materials, regardless of censors, to find the ultimate or absolute "TRUTH," if at all possible? For, is it not equally "TRUE" that the only "TRUTH" you know is life itself? Thus; is it not better that we die, if that we must, seeking "TRUTH" in the age-old Ethiopian teachings that say:

"MAN KNOW THYSELF."

November 1970

> Submitted to the Yale University BLACK SEMENARIANS at the Union Theological Semenary, New York, New York. Course under the auspicies of the COMMISSION FOR RACIAL JUSTICE of the United Church of Christ, Inc.

THE AFRICANS RIGHT TO BE WRONG IS SACRED
Lecture-Essay by "Master"
Yosef ben-Jochannan
Harlem Preparatory School of N.Y.
December 1969

One of the major question plaging so-called "Black Studies Courses" professors and administrators in these United States of America institutions of higher-learning is: How long will African-Americans continue letting people of non-African origin or heritage dominate and control <u>African Studies</u> and <u>Black Studies</u> departments in European-American owned, as well as "Negro" owned, schools without some sort or righteous indignation on their part? For, where do we find the Irish, French, White Jew, German, or anyother European-American people's history totally controlled by Africans and African-Americans under any circumstance without open protest on the part of such "Caucasians"? Nowhere on this planet Earth.

Yes, it is true, the Black man needs a "New religion." He is in need of a <u>New Christianity</u>, a <u>New Judaism</u>, a <u>New Islam</u>; certainly it must be a "<u>New religion</u>" in which his God is "created in his own image" as all other people's God is "created in" their "own image," which is not only understandable, but reasonable. But the argument always forced into the African-Americans' mind against having a Black God is:

"GOD HAS NO COLOR."

To this we must concur; but, we must also ask: How was the other people's God seen by them? And, who was it that saw a colorless

God--Jehovah, Jesus Christ, or Al'lah? Why do these people always say that their God is a "Semite" in the case of Jehovah among the European-American (White) Jews; "Caucasian" in the case of Jesus Christ among the Roman Catholic and Protestant Europeans and European-Americans; a Brown-skinned "Hamite" among the Arabian Moslems? Why, then, should the people of African origin, Black as they are, not have a God in their own color as well as in their own image"? A God from Africa. The answer lies in the fact that "Black Studies Courses" professors, most of us, have not yet dealt with "THE AFRICANS RIGHT TO BE WRONG" as a "SACRED TRUST" which we are obliged to perpetuate as all other people perpetuate their own culture, religion and economic way of life. Why? Because we are barraged with the hypotectical theory that it is <u>right</u> and <u>non-racist</u> for a Michaelangelo's blonde Jesus Christ of Nazzareth or "Aryan" and "Semitic" Moses with "Semitic characteristics" to be displayed in churches and synagouges, even in so-called "Negro churches;" but not a solitary half-black, or even "mullato," Jesus Christ or Moses. Again; why? Because those who are in control of <u>African Studies</u> and <u>Black Studies</u> courses and/or departments, almost everywhere, also dominate all manufacturing of "Holy Bibles," "Holy Torahs," and 'most <u>Black Studies</u> books' they have made "Holy"; this being also true for the Black writers and historians materials written on the history of the Black Experience all over the world, which is being edited, financed, published and distributed by the same non-African people who are in control of what we read and think about ourself; and of course they also control what we are to know about their own history and cultural heritage--European history that is.

"African Studies" is the foundation of "Black Studies", and <u>must</u> be brought within the fold and control of Black Studies Departments. This control must be under African or African-American personnel everywhere. Furthermore, Black Studies Courses and Departmets must decide what is the direction the mind of the Black man is to go; as the Black personnel in-charge of the data to be taught in them should be capable of making rational judgement of the "authority" of the information they contain. Unfortunately this area is still under the control of those who are most unfriendly to the interest of the African, African-American and their descendants today in these United States of America. Is this the manner in which all other ethnic courses are conducted and operated in this nation's educational institutions. No.

Just as we cannot have a Christian Pope being the "authority" over Judaism for the Jews, especially the European and European-American Jews that operate under the name of "Semites;" just so we cannot have a Grand Rabbi as the "authority" for what Christianity realy is to European and European-American Christians. Following the same type of reasoning that is common in this European-American society we cannot have European-American, be he or she Jew or Gentile, Christian or Moslem, blonde or brunette, rich or poor, "New Left, Old Left," or plain old "Conservative." In short, the African or African-American must be in the position to interpret his own experience and history, or cultural heritage, in terms he see fitting his African Experiences, and not in terms of how European and European-American writers and educators see him -- as the case presently is; and this does not in anyway or form exclude anyone bearing the tag "liberal" or "well-meaning

White."

In this perspective the Africans' GODS will not remain "heathen" or "pagan idols" so-long as African Studies Courses and Departments become Africanized and placed under the control of Blacks who are proud of their African heritage. For, this type of religious bigotry can only happen when those in control of Black or African Studies God or Gods are non-African as they are, even though the Gods --(Jehovah, Jesus Christ, and Al'lah) developed from African philosophic teachings, as well as Asian, that preceded the origin of Europeans(called "Caucasian" or "Semite ") most ancient history, which includes Greece and Rome -- the oldest of Europe's High-Cultures or civilizations. Because of this fact Jehovah remains superior to Ra -- the African God from whence Jehovah got a "Ten Commandments;" Al'lah remains supperior to Oledumare -- the African God of all Gods of the Yoruba-speaking people of West Africa and all descendants in the Caribbeans and the Americas; and, Jesus Christ remains superior to Ngai -- the African God of the Agikuyu (or Kikuyus) of east Africa, Kenya. Yet all of them stemmed from the original teachings that were created and developed by the so-called "lowly Pygmies" of central Africa along the African Great Lakes and the beginning of the head-waters of the Nile River Valley -- the Twas. This does not in any way mean that the Gods of West and South Africa and their teachings of philosophical thoughts did not have overriding influence on the others -now called "Gods of the Western Religions;" "Western Religions" being Judaism, Christianity and Islam; the latter as practiced by the international body of orthodox Moslems or Muslims, and not according to the edicts of the Nation Of Islam, the so-called "Black Muslims." Of course I wholeheartedly indorse the attitude of the Honourable Elijah Mohammed to make the religion of his followers, for whom he is the sole "Prophet," fit their image and needs.

Africa, correctly ALKEBU-LAN, is the motherland of all Black people in the world, our world, the planet Earth; and this is regardless of where they may have been born. As such, African Studies is the mother of all "Studies" dealing with the indigenous peoples of all over Africa and their descendants wherever they are to be found today.

How can the slavemaster write a complimentary history of his or her slaves and the relationship of master and slaves between them remain static? Who expects the slave master's pen to move in such a direction? Is it not inconsistent to have a slavemaster interpret morality for his slaves on the basis of the teachings of his own God, when in fact the slavemaster also set all values of "right" and "wrong" for himself (or herself) and the slaves? In such a relationship, is it not also true that it is perfectly "right" for the slavemaster to legally rape any of his physically virgin female slaves? But, is it also not equally true that it is "legally, morally, and spiritually "wrong" for the slave to even harbour the thought of asking the slavemaster's daughter (whether prostitute or virgin) hand in holy wedlock; and even worse yet, if he dares to harbour the thought of physically having intercourse sexually with her? Then why expect the former physical slaves' ancestors to allow their former slavemasters' children to continue control of their every way-with-all.

"Thou Shalt Not Steal" is one of the famous laws the Hebrew

Africans of ancient Egypt co-opted from their fellow Egyptians of the worship of the God --AMEN-RA, or RA; a law that is taken from the "<u>Negative Confessions</u>" of the <u>Osirian Drama</u> in the <u>COFFIN TEXTS</u>) of the Egyptian Mysteries System. Yet, we are taught that the <u>Ten Commandments were ...handed down to Moses by God</u>"--Jehovah" <u>at Mount Sinai</u>." To whom did God "...<u>handed down</u>.." the laws that allegedly govern the moral way of life of so-called "Jews, Christians and Moslems" of today? Moses, or Moshe; an indigenous African born in the land of Kimit, the land the ancient Haribus (or Hebrews) renamed "<u>Egypt</u>" to keep in focus of their own mythology they developed from the teachings they received while in Kimit. Yet, when the Africans and African-Americans try to retake what was stolen or co-opted from their ancestors, their forebearers, and from themselves while they were enslaved by European and European-American slavemasters in Africa, Europe, and the Americas -- which include the Caribbean Islands, the Ten Commandments suddenly become inoperative; thus, "<u>Thou Shalt Not Steal</u>" only having meaning for the slaves honesty and morality, but not for the slavemaster. Maybe in the case of the so-called "Negro," who is allegedly the people God of the Christian, Hebrew (called Jews) and Moslem (Jehovah, Jesus Christ and Al'lah) "CURSED BE CANAAN" drama in the First Book of Moses (Genesis) the "Commandments" are to be disavowed. Could it be that the "CURSE" on Canaan is the color "<u>Black</u>," which we have been taught by our slavemasters clergy (which includes many "Negroes of the cloth"?) The latter I have dealt with in other CHAPTERS and LECTURES; also in my book, AFRICAN ORIGINS OF THE MAJOR "WESTERN RELIGIONS."

    The African cannot accept any "<u>Commandment</u>," irrespective of whose God it is that ordered it, whenever his "RIGHT" is being abrogated. He, or she, will have to be able to feel free of any moral or spiritual obligation to any "law" or "Commandment" which is designed specifically, or by intent, towards his or her detriment, or works against their natural, social, political or religious interest; whatever, or whenever, that may be. If the moral laws demand reparations for one ethnic group against another in Europe because of wrongful confication of property, and genocide, then the same morality in "Anglo-Saxon Caucasian Semitic" law must also hold true for the wrongful confiscation and expropriation of the Africans property, and genocide against them, here in these United States of America and the so-called "New World" in general, by Europeans and European-Americans -- Gentiles in the main, and a few Jews along with them. This point, however, will ony hold merit when Black Studies and African Studies courses and departments are merged under the control of African peoples who are aware of their historical "RIGHT;" particularly by those who must interpret this phase of the "Black Experience" in terms of the interest of the Africans and their descendants, and not in terms of how Europeans and European-Americans feel it should be.

How can anyother people, especially those whose ancestors were the perpetuators of slavery and genocide, also high-theft, against the African peoples, teach the truth in the light of the African peoples' values in Black Studies or African Studies courses? They cannot. If they try, which they are currently doing inspite of certain protest reaction in limited quarters, it must, and will, be nothing more than watered-down "Negro history" of some sort of a "GOD DOES NOT LIKE REVENGE" or "TWO WRONGS DO NOT

MAKE ONE RIGHT" kind of "White liberal" analysis which did not apply in the case of the Nazis Germans against the European Jews; the British against the Irish republicans; the Russians against the Hungarians; the Japanese against the European-Americans; and even, the British against the European-American colonists in the thirteen colonies of King George IIIrd of Great Britain. "TWO WRONGS" did make "ONE RIGHT" in all of the cases mentioned; but not in the case of the European-Americans (both Christians and Jews) against the Africans and African-Americas in the Americas, the United States of America in particular; not even to the point of our collecting on the " FIFTY ACRES AND A MULE " promised us by "honest Abe Lincoln" after the "big war" between the slavemasters of northern and southern United States of America. The reason for this is without doubt the fact that <u>African-Americans do not set their own "moral standards."</u> The reason they <u>do not set their own "moral standards"</u> squarely centers in the area of their mental orientation; <u>they do not have "...a God of" their "OWN"</u> as all of the other people who have been successful in turning tragedy into success. A God that suffers when they do; cry when they do; smythe their enemies when they are in battle; or even help them to slave when they must. Why is this so? Because <u>the African-Americans' God is the same "God" and "image" created by their enemies.</u> Such a God, their enemies "image," is to be found errected in almost everyone of their churches and temples, and of course in their living and bed rooms. He is the "Caucasian Semite" of "Indo-European" and "Aryan" characteristics Michalangelo created for his fellow Europeans; and He is "superior to all other Gods" of each and every "inferior race" which did not have the good fortune of being created "Caucasian" or "Semitic." But; How did our God get this way, we ask in Black Studies Courses, while we continue reading from our picture-studded Holy Bible "written by God inspired men," neither of whom, we are told, was an African, muchless an African-American? He got this way because those who are presently, and of the past three to four-hundred (300-400) years, writing our "authroritative experiences" are still Europeans and European-Americans who teach that <u>we were cannibals in Africa and sold our own brothers into slavery before European and European-American Christian missionaries civilized us and planted their religion in Africa."</u> G. C, Seligman in his book on African peoples, which he entitled "RACES OF AFRICA, said we were uncivilized until "...hordes of Hamitic Europeans...," whatever that is, swarm down into Egypt and other parts of north Africa to save us from ourselves. Of course he could not resist reminding us that it was the "<u>Semites</u>" who actually built the great High-Culture in Egypt; not the "<u>Negroes.</u>" Thus all who want to be save from themselves must come by way of the Europeans and European-Americans; an echo which we are acoustomed to hear in the following manner:

" ALL WHO WANT TO BE SAVE MUST COME BY WAY OF HIM."
Of course "<u>Him</u>" is the Europeanized version of the Asian Jesus Christ, who is not even allowed to be the <u>son of Jews.</u>

When African Studies courses are controlled by African and African-American people, then, and only then, <u>African values shall be interpreted according to African needs.</u> Polygamy will not be inferior to monogamy --which has been spoken of in countless volumes and from just as many pulpits, but never practised.

Beauty (which is a nagative value that cannot be measured scientifically) would, never-the-less, be from a Black perspective, thus, allowing a coal-black woman with kinky hair, thick lips, broad nose, burnt skin, pierced nose, and robust breasts and behind, to win beauty contests; thereby illiminating the need for African and African-American women and their daughters to use skin-lightening creams, hair straighteners, lip pressers, and nose pointers and squeezers -- BLACK WILL BE SURELY BEAUTIFUL.

How can one have Jewish Studies, but the "Semitic Studies Department" is headed by an ex-Nazis or German national who cannot see Adolph Hitler's misgivings with repect to his Jewish victims; or Irish Studies, but the Department of Gaelic Studies is headed by British Commissioner for English nationalism and colonial affairs; a communist school of Marxist-Leninist Doctrine, but the Department of Communist Studies is headed by the Chairman of the Board of the Wall Street Journal? Just as ridiculous as these combinations are, equally is the suggestion or fact that African Studies or Black Studies and African and African-American professors and administrators, for the most part, are still under the control of European and European-American administrators and professors in most of the schools of higher-learning in these United States of America. But stanger yet, the teaching of African history and culture in many, or most, so-called "Negro" educational institutions is headed by Europeans or European-Americans.

When Dr. Edward Wilmot Blyden coined the historic phrase:--
"THE AFRICANS RIGHT TO WRONG
IS SACRED,"
he not only opened the flood-gate òf educational innundation for

the Black or African (Ethiopian) peoples of the world, he also re-established, that very instance, the basic moral and spiritual position upon which "BLACK REVOLUTIONARY PRICIPLES," be they "right" or "Wrong," must again be based. For what is "Right" or "Wrong" beyond the values and deffinitions given them by those whose interest these terms are to serve?

Is "<u>right</u>" or "<u>wrong</u>" a universal truth? Yes, both words are; but the "<u>truth</u>" within either is as varied as night is to day, or man to woman, yet maintaining the necessity for each other. "<u>Right</u>" in one culture could be "<u>wrong</u>"in another, as is so often the case. What is "<u>right</u>" for the slavemasters and their descendants is seldom, if ever, not "<u>wrong</u>" for the slaves and their descendants.

An African Studies Department headed by a capable African or African-American would be equipt with historical materials showing how Africa and her children were raped by the Arab Moslems and western European Christians and Jews. It would be records that demonstrate it was not "<u>the planting of Christianity in Africa</u>" as cited by C. P. Groves in his four volumes work of like name, nor the "<u>bringing of Christianity and civilization</u>" as claimed by other imperialist Christian missionaries, that brought the Europeans for the first time to west Africa in the early part of the 15th century. That it was hunger and the need for trade, at first; and by the 19th century it had already changed to greed and jealousy over the wealth of Africa and her children. This type of presentation would, of course, find no comfort in the present <u>White-dominated</u> Black Studies departments, because they upset the Stanley and Livingstone, Tarzan and Jane, image of the

African peoples as seen through the eyes of Europeans and European-Americans. It would also show that the Boers and Hugenots claim that when they "...<u>arrived in South Africa</u>"(the Monomotapa Empire)"<u>there were no Bantus there</u>, is a lie. And, that the Boers arrived during the latter part of the 16th century; whereas the Portuguese, the first of the Europeans in the area, arrived there in 1486 C.E. with Bartolome Dias, captain of their ship, and were hospitably received and outfitted by the "<u>Bantus</u>" whom they then called "<u>Khaffir</u>" or "<u>Caffir</u>." The south African Whites, who have for centuries conducted the worse system of genocide ever, will be shown to have surpassed anything done by Adolph Hitler and his Nazis empire; even surpassing King Leopold II of Belgium and Henry Morton Stanley and their American cohorts in the so-called "Congo Free State." <u>Natives</u> would become, once more that is, people such as Nigerians, Ethiopians, Liberians, etc.; <u>fierce warriors</u> will return to generals and soldiers; <u>chiefs</u> will be governors, and paramount-chiefs regional prime ministers; and of course "<u>Negroes</u>" must return to indigenous Africans, thus no more "<u>N</u>egroland" for them to had originated from. Yes, my students of Africa and her peoples, the Africans would not have "<u>voluntarily enslaved themselves</u>" and "<u>climb up on the slaveship Jesus Christ deLobic</u>" of the Right Reverend Captain John Hawkins of the Church of England (Anglican Church) to cross the treacherous Middle Passage to the Island of Hispaniola (Hayte or Haiti), where the Right Reverend Bishop Bartolome de LasCasas of the Roman Catholic Church began the infamous slave trade to the "Western World" in the year 1503 C.E. with the aid of Pope Clement V and the king and queen of Spain. Even Queen Victoria of Great

Britain would be shown to have been a greater murderer than Adolph Hitler of Nazis Germany and Benito Musolini of Fascist Italy (both of them together); she too surpassing even the despotism of King Leopold II. The "Rape of Africa" would not be the fault of the victims -- the Africans, but of those Europeans and European-Americans who came to Africa as "Christian missionaries" and "entepreneurs" and blasted the Africans into oblivion in the process of giving their "talking pipes" -- guns and cannons -- target practise while they confiscated their African victims real and personal properties. These points, even though they have been some very feeble attempts made to address them are, never-the-less, given interpretations suggestive of "the Africans own fault" why they happened.

Last, but by no means or stretch of the imagination the least, north and east African history would be reunited with that of the rest of Africa's -- Carthage, Numidia, Legbu (Libya), Kimit (Egypt) and Mauretania (Morocco or Mauritania) included. The history of Africa will have the names of her nations restored and the slave era nomenclature deposited in the trash basket where it has always belong. Rhodesia will return to Zimbabwe, South Africa to Monomotapa, Angola to Ngola, Portuguese Guinea to Nbia, etc. These African nations sons and daughters would no longer be listed as "Great Thinkers of the Western World," and their works --"Great Books of the Western World" as in the case of the volumes published by the University of Chicago under said terminologies. Saint Cyprian and Saint Augustine, as well as Tertullian, would return to their native birthplace in Numidia and Carthage respectively, but remain as ever the "Fathers of the (Christian) Church" now dominated in Rome and Canterbury. Stranger yet, Christendom would be shown to have existed first all over north, northeast and east Africa before its arrival in southern Europe by way of Greece and Rome; and that it all got its institutionalized beginnings in Kimit (Egypt) among the African bishops of the early Church, when Jesus Christ was still the "fallen Leader" and not yet declared "God," and his Church was still the "Brethren."

Maybe what I have cited above is just the reason European and European-American educators and historians prefer that African Studies courses and departments be kept seperate from the Black Studies professors and administrators. Maybe this is only an infinitisimal sample of a mere peep into that which an open examination of an African-controlled African Studies combined with Black Studies department will expose, all of which those who are presently in control prefer to remain under cover.

The control of African Studies departments will provide access to Black people those documents that reveal the "X's" the African "chiefs" allegedly made when they were supposed to have "voluntarily transfered their land " to the European overlords and imperialist colonialist settlers who later on called themselves "entrprenuers." These "contracts, treatise, concessions" etc. granted the European and European-American pirates that came to Africa in the name of "explorers" untold riches which can be seen in the capitals of Europe and the Americas in every avenue of life and business. Such farcical documents would be made public for all to see that the Africans were in fact swindled; their personal properties illegally confiscated by men whose fortunes we can still identify, all of which having been built upon the Africans bodies and floated in their blood. In this regard we may not cherish the role the United States of America's government played in the colonization of the Liberia and Maryland colonies on the west coast of Africa jointly with the European-American dominated American Colonization Society, all of whom exploited the ex-slaves who were trying desperately to remove themselves as far from American "democracy" as they could have gotten. We will also observe that the entire operation between the quasi-religious politically oriented American Colonisation Society that claimed "Christian brotherhood" with the ex-slaves they exploited was only what the United States of America hoped would have been to it as the Roman Catholic Church was to Spain and Portugal, and the Church of England to Great Britain, in terms of pacifying the Africans through the use of the Holy Bible, the King James Bible Version, after the holy gunpowder had taken its toll of African men, women and children.

Speaking of the United States of America in the colonization of Africa, which it was not to have had any hands into; we would, on the contrary, observed that the United States of America played one of the vilest role in the 1864-65 C.E. or A.D. Berlin Conference called by Kaiser Wilhelm and Otto von Bismarck in the discussions leading to the partition of Africa; also in the talks at Brussels, or Brussels Conference called by Leopold II over the stolen African land which the United States of America, Great Britain, and twelve colonialist nations of Europe gave him at the Berlin Conference and registered in a document called the "Berlin Act." This is necessary to know at this time, even though African Studies still rest in the hands of European-Americans, because most European-Americans are of the opinion that their government had nothing to do with the actual partition of Africa, which is as far from the truth as it could possibly be. The United-States of America had colonial interest in Africa then, and have much more than it had then now, especially in the so-called "Republic of South Africa."

We, as Africans and peoples of African origin and descent, may also find out that the fate of the Africans and their natural resources caused the founding of the first so-called "international conference of the nations of the world," the "world" at that time being only White people and their nations, which finally led to what was later on called the "League of Nations" in 1918 C.E. following the end of the first worldiwide conflict between European and European-American nations over the African and Asian peoples land and riches; and out of that came the present United Nations Organization following another hollocaust by the same nations, along with Japan, that ended in 1945 C.E.

African Studies controlled by African peoples is a must. Anything short of this is intollerable. The peoples of Africa and their descendants must control, interpret, and decide for themselves their own past, present, and determine the course of the future. It is each and every African and African-American professor and administrator of educational institutions sacred duty and first priority in the Black peoples struggle for nationhood and cultural survival. We, professors, Black people all, should no longer tolerate anyone who stands in our way to deter our "African Right to be Wrong." In order to accomplish this, our goal; as such, we are force to take immediate and positive action on the campus where we work. We must (1); at every opportunity make it extremely clear at each faculty meeting we have the opportunity of being at that we demand the consolidation of both Black Studies and African Studies courses and departments (2); make it compulsory that the dean or chairman of said departments be an African or person of African ancestry (3); and that all professors and materials used in said departments must meet standards establish by a committee of Black scholars, students and staff (4); also that a standing committee of black scholars in the necessary field and discipline related to both Black Studies and African Studies be established and comprised of such functionaries throughout the United States of America, their duty to provide recomendations of materials and scholars and other related matters for the education of the peoples of African origin and descent here in these United States of America.

It is a sad state of affair each year when almost lily-White councils of men and women assemble in some European or European-American capital under the name of "authorities on African" history or society or "International Society of " etc., etc. In such organizations Africans or peoples of African ancestry make up an infinitisimal part of the membership; but in most there are no Africans at all. And in the few that we may find one or two, not one of them leads it. These Europeans and European-Americans, Canadians and Britishers included (even this period when the African peoples are in their cultural and political revolutionary transformation from an enslaved people to people of free nations) expect that they should be allowed to continue masquerading as the interpretors and proginators of African history, culture, religion, science, law, and all other aspects of African life; and that they should continue having the last word of "authority" over the Africans and themselves also, as if they were still the sole rulers of the entire world. Any suggestion to the contrary always meet with crocodile chants of "Negro racism," yet there is not one organization anywhere on the planet Earth established as the "authority" of European or European-American history that is dominated by Africans. There is not one African society established to formulate policies of "authority" over European or European-American history or culture, whether such society be Irish, German, Greek, American, or anyother. Why, then, should the African peoples anywhere around the world accept the self-styled "authority" of European and European-American people over anything of African origin, and especially history and culture, two of the most basic controling factors that affect the peoples of Africa's destiny? There is no logical answer, religious or secular, to justify its continuation, either. And there is no precedent whereby Europeans and European-Americans can show that they can be impartial in their interpretation of the Africans experience in world history and culture. In the first place, it is impossible for anyone to be impartial with the history and cultural heritage of another whom he or she must write about as the <u>inferior race</u>.' It is in this latter light that each and every European and European-American controlled organization and society, academic or otherwise, operate against the interest of the African continent and its indigenous sons and daughters, along with their descendants everywhere.

There can be no exception to the rule that requires all heads of Black Studies departments, which must include all African

Studies departments and courses, must be of African origin and indigenous to the people of that land. African peoples in this sense would mean, those whose ancestors were indigenous to the African continent prior to the arrival of the Greeks and Romans in north Africa, the Persians and Arabs in east Africa, and the Portuguese and Spanish in west Africa. These are the people who are commonly designated "Negroes, Bantus, Africans South of the Sahara, Bantus, Pygmies, Hottentots, Bushmen," and other such names of contempt place upon the indigenous Africans by their European and European-American slavemasters and colonialist exploiters over the last four centuries.

Africans and their African-American brothers and sisters must boycott any and all African Studies Courses failing to comply with the re-Africanization and de-Europeanization processies outlined herein, or as specified by other groups or individuals meeting for purposes of control by African peoples of educational operations designated for the benifit of African peoples. In this regards, it must be made very clear that the Europeans and their descendants in places such as the so-called "Republic of South Africa" and "Republic of Rhodesia," along with those in French Somaliland, the Portuguese and Spanish colonies, are not "African peoples and their descendants" according to the description of this term used in this work or any of my lectures at anytime during this course. These European peoples, "Caucasians" as they still prefer to be classified, had every opportunity from the mid-fifteenth century C.E. to prove their desire to become "African peoples" and have held any such consideration in contempt, and did nothing else but try to exterminate the indigenous Africans in their insane desire to rule and control all of Africa's natural resources for their own exclusive use.

Africans must be practical. They must understand international politics and gutter diplomacy as practise by the so-called "Free World Nations of the Western World." this does not mean that they should not keep up their guard when dealing with the "Eastern World." For just as a handful of European Jews could claim in the halls of "International Law and Justice" their right to a land they had not occupied for over two thousand years, basing claim to it through biblical mythology that said "...land was given them by Jehovah...," etc., equally the African people whose Gods gave them Africa -- Alkebu-lan -- and have never left any section of it have the same rights in the same "Hall of International Justice." Not only the Jews of Europe and European-America claimed this right and prevailed; the Irish and others of Europe during the Nazis and Fascist invasions of their fellow European nations did the same; the Cypriots followed the same against the British. The only reason Africans and African-Americans cannot act on this level in the international arena is due to the fact that we do not control Black studies and African-Studies departments that would teach us how to deal with our European and European-American enemies. If we do not have control in this area, then we also do not have influence over our present experience, thus we cannot actively influence the course of our future, no can we actually say that we know where we have been, where we are, nor where we are going. All of the sucessful people control the areas of discipline dealing with the way their followers think, as such they were able to see one goal and one destiny.

The European and European-American Jews in Isreal are sucessful because the head of their organizations are European and European-American Jews; yet, there are millions of Black and Brown Jews from Africa and Asia, also many thousands more in the United States of America, not one of them in control of a White owned Jewish anything. The Irish, like the Jews, did not have anyone else head their organizations but sons of Erin -- the Old Sod, not even the wife of one of their leaders was from any other ethnic group or religious affilliation than Roman Catholic, the religion of the vast majority of the people to which their pledge alligance. When Africans and African-Americans begin to think along these selfish lines the same people who have gained their success by this method hollers loudly, to the tip of their voice, "NEGRO REVERSE RACISM, NEGRO ANTI-SEMITISM, CRIME IN THE STREET," and even,"HELP - RAPE."

There must be a deadline established in each case. This must be a reasonable one. In no case the turn-over should require more than one (1) semester-year to accomplish. The sole objective being the control of Black and African Studies in the hands of people of African origin and ancestry.

Of course one constantly hear about whether or not "White people can or cannot teach Black studies cources." I say to this, Yes, they can under Black "authority" and Black leadership and total control; just as Black people teach White Studies Courses under total White controls and "authority." When a Black professor fails to teach White Studies Courses according to White "authority", which we must all learn in every school or other institution of education or religious training (private, public, parochial or others), as prescribed by White "authority," even in so-called "Negro institutions of higher-learning," he or she is immediately dismissed. Maybe I should say, 'ASKED TO RESIGN'. This same "authority" must exist in the hands of the Black administrators of Black Studies Departments, which must include African Studies.

Gentlemen or brothers, ladies or sisters, students all of you, we are in a death-struggle. The first step out of this devilish quagmire is our mind. Our mind cannot think in terms of freedom from our slavemasters or his children as long as either of them does our training, tells us who we were, what we are, and what we should hope to be; leaving said teacher to think for the victor and the victim at the same time when such interests are in conflict.

Students, brothers and sisters, a slave and his master can never have mutual interest in the operation of the slave's property; that is, irrespective of what said property entails. How can we know ourself when someone else tells us who we are, and who they are, and we do not check to find out for our self. Who do we tell who they are? Let me end with what you shall find is my most prejudice point of reference taken from my ancestors of the Nile Valleys, your ancestors also, the indigenous Africans of Kimit, Nubia, Meröe, Cush, Puanit, and others. They said to all of us, and wrote these words in, and on, their tombs -- less we forget:

"MAN"(Black Man)"KNOW THYSELF."

CONCLUSION

One should not expect "educators" of Europe and European-America (Modern man) to produce works of a nature that would give credit to the indigenous Africans - the so-called "NEGROES, BANTUS, AFRICANS SOUTH OF THE SAHARA, HOTTENTOTS, PYGMIES, BUSHMEN, NIGGERS", and others whom they have labeled with such stereotyped nomenclature of inferior status, for having been the originators of anything which Europeans and European-Americans built upon in order to create their own past and present High-Cultures ("civilizations"). Regarding this fact, note the ending of Thomas Hodgkin's article in THE HIGHWAY, under the title - "National Movements In West Africa":*

> "WE SHALL PROBABLY HAVE TO WAIT A LITTLE WHILE FOR THE REAL HISTORY OF AFRICA TO BE WRITTEN BY AFRICAN SCHOLARS FOR AN AFRICAN READING PUBLIC."

*See pages 58 and 59 of this volume for the full tex of Mr. Thomas Hodgkin's statement.

Map Of AFRICA.
1688 C.E.

AFRICA, by the Ancients, was called *Olympia, Hesperia, Oceania, Coryphe, Ammonis, Oriygia*, and *Æthiopia*. By the Greeks and Romans, *Lybia* and *Africa*. By the *Æthiopians* and *Moors, Alkebu-lan*.

Note: European and European-American imperialists, colonialists, neo-colonialists, settler groups and Christian missionaries, from the 15th through 19th century C.E., including many of today in the 20th century C.E., refused to accept their ignorance of Africa's interior and made all sorts of map with waterways, mountains, nations and peoples which did and do not exist on the continent of ALKEBU-LAN (Africa), except in their mind. To fully understand the distortions one needs to compare this map with those on pages 680 and 681, also with maps of 1815, 1874-75, 1900-12, and 1971. Pay particular attention to "NEGROLAND" on page 680, the mythological land invented by Europeans for ALKEBU-LAN around the 16th century.

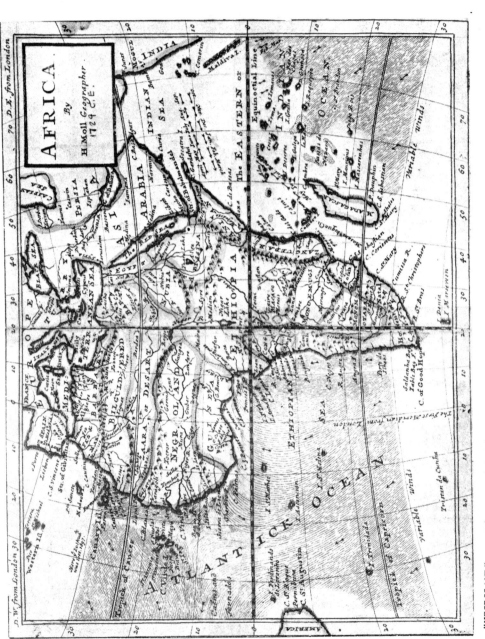

"NEGROLAND" on this map hightlights the usual distortion of Africa's geography. This map is representative of the Europeans attempt to be "AUTHORITIES" on Africa and its people, though they were not knowledgeable of most of the continent's landmass or cultural groupings.

Note: The student must observe that the SOUTH ATLANTIC, as late as the year 1878 C.E. (A.D.), was still called "OCEANUS AETHI-OPICUS" (Ethiopian Ocean). That the rivers, lakes, and moun-tains have changed very little from the map on page 680. The Nile River is still shown crossing the Sahara from East to West.

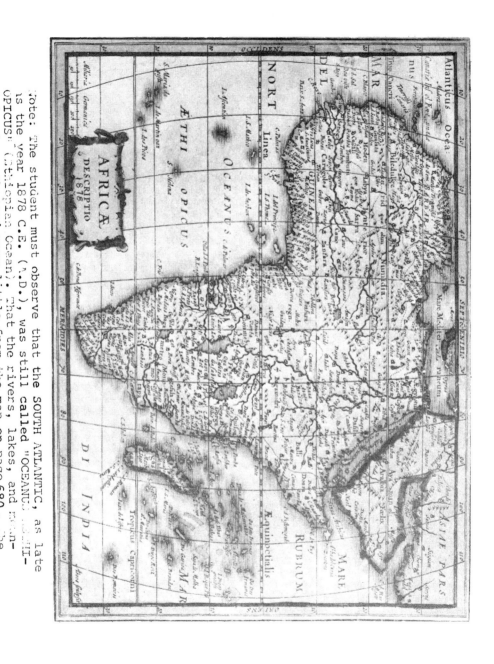

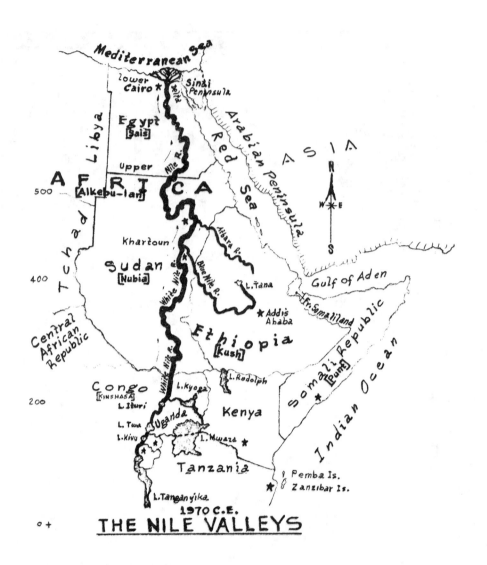

THE NILE VALLEYS
1970 C.E.

Note: The boundary lines dividing each nation shown in this map were established by the colonialist and imperialist nations (12 of Europe, Great Britain and the United States of America) at the BERLIN CONFERENCE in 1884-1885 C.E. How was it possible for the indigenous Africans of Kimit to have been "CAUCASIAN" or "SEMITE" and those of Punanit and Kush "HAMITES", while the others were "NEGROES"?

ORIGIN OF THE NILE
THE
MAJOR LAKES and FALLS
Scale: 1" = Statute Miles

Note: Buganda is Cross-hatched in Green-Colored Uganda. Dotted
Line across Lake Nyanza is border line Limits; same
through other lakes.

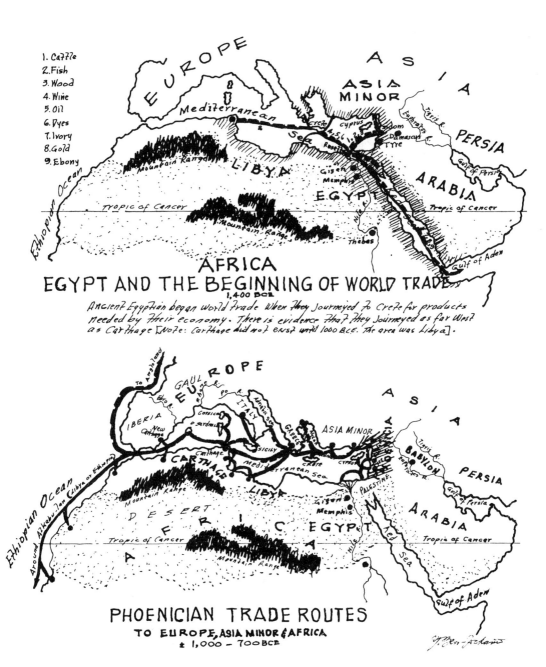

Note: Indigenous Africans and Asians influence in Europe through trade routes established before the creation of the Greek nation.

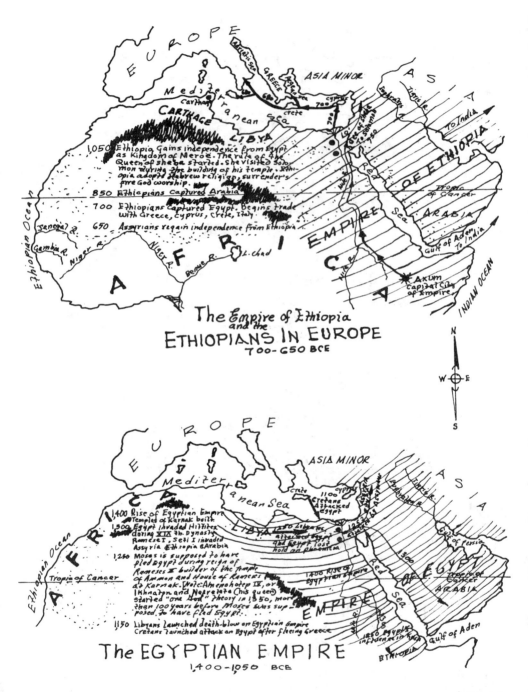

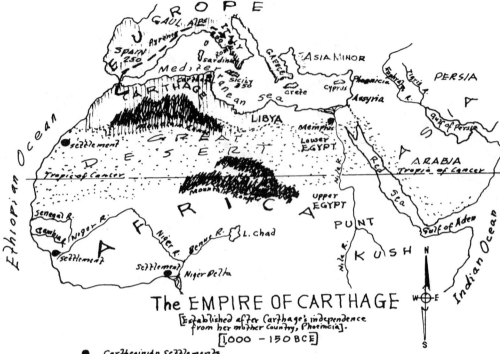

The EMPIRE OF CARTHAGE
[Established after Carthage's independence from her mother country, Phoenicia].
[1,000 - 150 BCE]

● Carthaginian settlements

1. Carthage founded in 1,000 B.C.E. by Phoenician mariners.
2. Carthage became independent operating power in 850 B.C.E. by African-Phoenicians.
3. Carthage officially considered a Phoenician "tributary", Sidom and Tyre were also made tributaries; But all were to be ruled by the Assyrians and Chaldeans. Carthage refused, and was never ruled by them. 700-650 BCE.
4. Carthaginian fleet defeated by Greek fleet. Subsequent wars followed (450-400).
5. Carthaginians conquered Sicily in 350. Phoenicia was captured by by the Greeks and became a Province of Greece fifty years later.
6. Spain became a Province of Carthage (Phoenicia) under Hamilcar. The beginning of the first Punic War (250 B.C.E.).
7. General Hanibal and his African troops (along with his Elephants) entered Europe through Spain, and crossed the Alps in an attempt to capture Rome. Hanibal defeated all of Europe's Roman legions sent against him. 200 BCE. Hanibal's brother, Hasdrubal, defeated in Spain while attempting to raise a military force to aid the army of Hanibal (who was fighting to enter Rome).
8. Carthaginians expelled by the Spaniards from Spain after Hasdrubal's defeat. Carthaginians annexed Sardinia after treaty with Rome, thereby causing the beginning of the Second Punic War. 200 BCE.
9. Scipio defeated Hanibal's army in Carthage after joining with Greek forces against the Carthaginians in 150 BCE at the Battle of Zama.
10. Carthage captured and destroyed during Third Punic War in 100 B.C.E. Carthage became one of Rome's 8 Provinces. End of the Empire of Carthage.

by: J. Ben-Jochannan
5/10/68

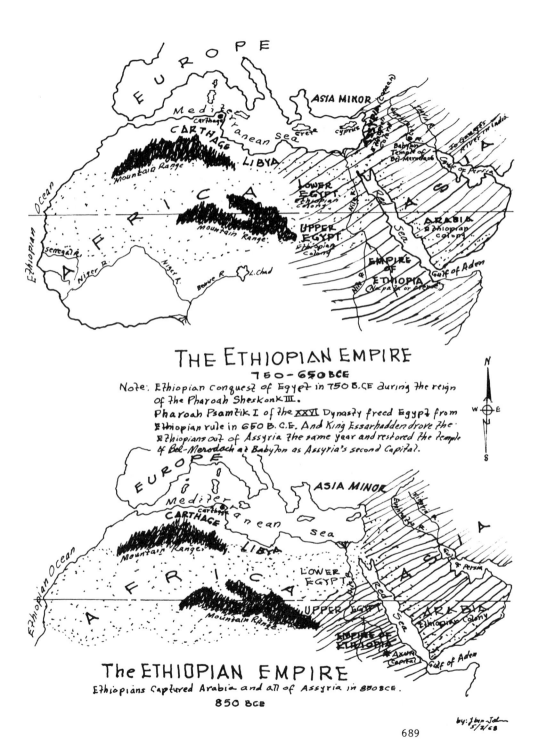

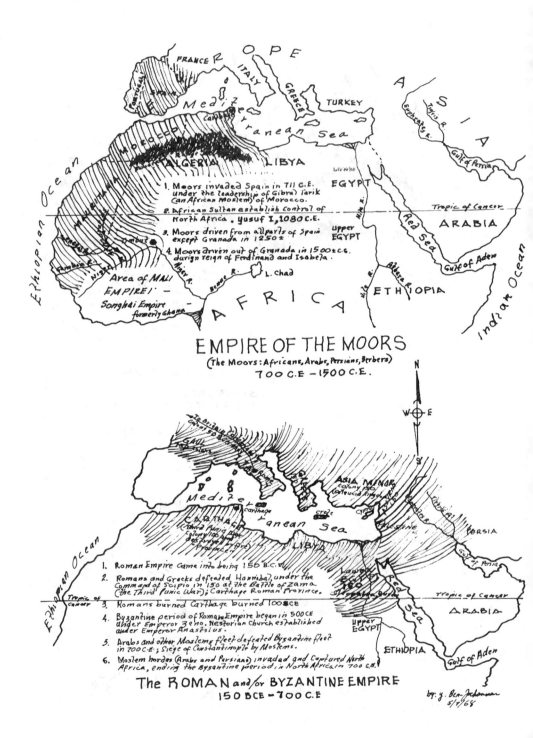

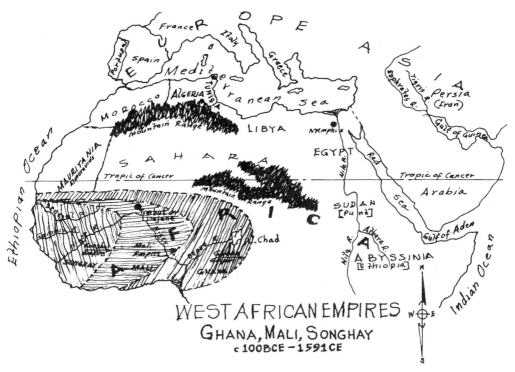

WEST AFRICAN EMPIRES
GHANA, MALI, SONGHAY
c 100 BCE – 1591 CE

1. Ghana Empire established between BCE 50 and 100 C.E. The exact year is debatable, however there are sufficient fossils and artifacts unearthed in the area to established that Ghana was established before the turn of the Christian Era. Note: The Romans who visited the northern reaches of the Niger River and around Lake Chad about 50 BCE gave data which describe other visitors at the area findings centuries later.

2. Ancient Ghana was destroyed by Almoravids (Africans and Berbers) around 1076 C.E. The had destroyed Ghana (Dejene), the capital city before, in 10__.

3. The Mali Kingdom, which was under the Ghana Empire, was established by Sundiata (Mari Jata) in 1230 C.E.

4. The Mali Kingdom became an Empire under Sundiata in 1238 C.E.

5. The Mali Empire ended in 1890 C.E. when attacked by the Tuaregs from the North. Mansa Musa II was king at the time of the destruction.

6. The Songhai Kingdom was established in 1464 C.E. by Sonni Ali.

7. In 1488 C.E. the Songhai Kingdom became an Empire under Sonni Ali.

8. In 1591 C.E. the Songhai Empire was destroyed by moors from the North. The invasion from Morocco started in 1582, at the end of King Askia Ishak II reign.

Note: Timbut (Timbuctoo, Timbuktu, Timbuctu) was the capital City of the Mali Kingdom and Empire. At the area where Timbut stood the capital City of Ghana, Dejene, stood.

----- The dotted lines indicate the distance from the Ethiopian Ocean each empire extended Eastwards into the interior of the continent. [The Ethiopian Ocean has been renamed "Atlantic Ocean about the 17th Century]

The period between Ghana's destruction and Mali's prominence is marked by a lack of information, due the almost total destruction of the records of Ghana.

by: Y Ben-Jochanan
5/8/68

CHAPTER I NOTES

1. .All sorts of attempts are being made to reconstruct ancient man, which is in itself laudable. However, the attempt to reconstruct the African fossils along European (Caucasian) standards indicate the extent to which "racism" interfers with scientific research. It is as unlikely for Neanderthal man to have been an African - with white skin, thin lips, blue eyes, etc., as Zinjanthropus boisie being a European - with black skin, thick lips, brown eyes, etc.

2. There are literally thousands of Africa's art treasures and other artifacts in Musems and private collections throughout Europe, Britain and the Americas. Most of them have been taken out of Africa without the permission of the Africans to whom they belong. They were confiscated or stolen.

3. These hypothectical maps indicate how much the "authorities" differ on ancient man's history. Note the "racial" conflict within the authors' mind on who settled Central Africa in prehistroic times. Of course, ancient man had to be an Anglo-Saxon Caucasian of Indo-European Aryan background, with a dash of Semiticism (for good measure) thrown in.

4. Because of this usage of the word "primates", and other similar connotations, the author of this work has refused to use the word "primitive" to living people.

5. This was true in the United States of America until the Fourteenth Amendment of the Federal Constitution changed the "Negro" status from "slave" to "citizen"; "three-fifths of a man" originally.

6. Some historians relate the origin of the indigenous Australians-the so-called "Aboriginees", to East Africa and Southeast Africa; others refute it. The indigenous peoples' representatives at the "African peoples Congress", Atlanta, Georgia, U.S.A.guaranteed its veracity.(See speech by Mrs.Pat Kruger,at the Congress, and United Nations Organization- where genocide was charged against the White Australians).

6a. "Huxley - Wilbeforce debates of 1861", presided over by John Steven Henslow.

7. Theologians willfully distort Darwin's pronouncement on earliest man in order to prejudice their followers against any attempt to prove any origin of mankind other than the Jewish myth about "Adam and Eve in the Garden of Eden." (See the "First Book of Moses" or "Genesis" in the Hebrew Holy Torah - Christian Old Testament).

8. The Christian Church was the prosecutor and persecutor of many leading palaeontologists and other scientists of the 19th Century C.E.

CHAPTER I NOTES
(cont'd)

9. The Hyksos were the first non-African invaders of Egypt (Kimit). They captured Lower Egypt in 1675 B.C.E.

10. <u>Monomotapa</u> was the name the indigenous Africans gave to this area of their continent before it was called "<u>Union of South Africa</u>", and "<u>Republic of South Africa</u>", by European imperialist slave runners, colonialist invaders and settlers. See reports by Captain Bartoleme Dias (a Portuguese - the first European to visit the area, in 1488 C.B. This was later corroborated by Captain Vasco daGama's subsequent trip in 1496 on his way to India).

11. Most books on Africa's <u>prehistoric fossils</u> will reveal others not listed here. Unfortunately no book (to date) published lists all of the fossils or artifacts. This is because of the frequency of the finds, also the hardship of dating them and making certain other classifications are met.

12. Dr. Louis B. Leakey is the husband of Dr. Mary Leakey. They work as a team in most excavations and other work.

13. There are much more modern methods of dating prehistoric materials at present than were available when <u>Zinjanthropus boisie</u> was dated. He was updated from the original figure of 600,000 years old to the current 1,750,000 (1.8 million).

14. Tanganyika joined with Zanzibar in 1964 to form the "Republic of Tanzania." The Island of Zanzibar and the Island of Pemba were called the "Republic of Zanzibar." The "Republic of Tanganyika" was on mainland Africa. The two islands are approximately forty miles off the east coast of Tanganyika in the Indian Ocean.

15. This conclusion is, of course, quite speculative. There is no hard-fast fact that every animal with smaller brain than man have to be less intellegent. Since there is no prehistoric man's brain to be examined at present one can only speculate.

16. The question of what color the prehistoric men of Africa were is only fulfilling to those who need such support. To intellegent humans the import is that there could be a link found between man as he is today and he was in yester-years. Would it make a difference if the people on the Moon were technicolored? If they are <u>Black</u>, should all effort to make contact with them cease? One has to remember that the same Africa that was rejected proved to be the best possibility of the true "<u>Garden of Eden</u>" (Original Home of Man); thus the "<u>Caucasian</u>" and "<u>Semitic</u>" North and East Africa mythology so prevalent of late among European and European-American educators.

CHAPTER II NOTES

1. This area of Africa was invaded in the late 19th century and conquered by British imperialist military forces of the colonial office in the early 20th century C.E. Britain was forced out in 1957. Ghana was the first of the indigenous African-controlled country in Africa to win its political freedom after World War II. Ghana's "Father of Independence," first Prime Minister and President, was Dr. Kwame Nkrumah-otherwise known as "OSAGYEFO" (the Redeemer or Savior of his peoples).

2. The TWI people, for centuries, had their own written language and alphabet. Wars with the various European colonial powers destroyed their culture, including their educators and educational system. This is typical of what happened to the indigenous Africans of Egypt by the Arab invaders in 640 C.E. It is to be noted that the Arabs also aided in the destruction of many West African cultures, including the TWI'S.

3. The Nile is comprised of the "WHITE" and "BLUE" bodies of water, also the ATBARA RIVER. The Blue Nile starts at Lake Tana in the Ethiopian High-lands, and ends at Khartoun, Sudan. The White-Nile starts at Mwanza Nyanza (also called "Lake Victoria" by the British colonialists), Uganda, and ends at Khartoun. Above this tangent point the Nile continues northwards to Atbara, Sudan where it is joined by the Atbara River. It then flows through Sudan and Egypt into the Mediterranean Sea. Note that the Nile River flows from south to north; not east to west as Herodotus and other early Europeans believed. (See BLACK MAN OF THE NILE page 206 for map by Herodotus).

4. Monomotapa was the name of the entire southern tip of Africa according to the logs of the first Europeans to arrive there and meet the Africans - Captain Bartolome Dias (a Portuguese), 1488 C.E., and Captain Vasco daGama (another Portuguese), 1499. This vast empire extended as far north as Zimbabwe (Zimboae according to the Portuguese), presently called "Rhodesia" by the European colonialists that control it, in honor of Cecil Rhodes - one of the world's master at genocide during the 19th century C.E. It ended as far south as the Cape of Storms (Cabo de Tormentos, according to the Portuguese).

5. Herodotus' description of the indigenous Africans of Egypt in 450 B.C.E. is shown on pages 200-203, BLACK MAN OF THE NILE. See Herodotus', HISTORIES, Book II, Chapter 57.

6. Practically every European and European historian starts European and European-American history from the earliest Greeks (Pyrrhus) and Romans (Etruscans); the assumption being that "...from the Greeks all knowledge originated."

7. See G.G.M. James, STOLEN LEGACY; Sir E.A. Wallis Budge, BOOK OF THE DEAD; J. Kendrick, THE HISTORY OF PHILOSOPHY; and Pliny, HISTORY.

CHAPTER II NOTES
(cont'd)

8. This is a common theory among European and European-American historians and others of related desciplines. No proof to justify this conclusion has ever been submitted. It is all conjecture.

9. This revelation completely refutes Professor Jeffreys' statement on page 7 of this volume. (See Professor Jeffreys, "The Negro Enigma", in the September, 1951, issue of the WEST AFRICAN REVIEW).

10. Note that the usage of the word "primitive" by H. G. Wells is no longer tolerated when applied to people of Caucasian origin. Such reference is generally used, currently, to Africans, Asians and indigenous Americans, almost exclusively; the assumption being the same for the word "tribe."

11. See J. A. Rogers, SEX AND RACE, Vol. I, II & III; and WORLD'S GREAT MEN OF COLOR, Vol. I & II.

12. The Africans of the Kingdom of Elam, in Persia, were also described in the same manner that Herodotus described the indigenous Africans of Egypt, Ethiopia and Colchis. The Ethiopians that invaded India and settled there were described equally.

13. This struggle had its zenith in the successful revolution in Haiti against the French; and the frustrating defeat of "Queen Mary, Bottom Belly" and "Ellen Fire-bun" in their attempt to seize the Danish Virgin Islands during the 19th century C.E. These three African women led an independence struggle that almost topple Danish colonialism in the Caribbean.

14. Sabacom, Piankhi and others from Nubia (Sudan) and Kush (Ethiopia) ruled Egypt as Pharoahs (Kings). See page 160 of BLACK MAN OF THE NILE. Note that the Nubians (Sudanese) ruled Egypt from approximately 775 B.C.E. until 653 B.C.E.

15. The Moors introduced the "common bath" to the Europeans of southern France, Spain and Portugal. They also introduced the use of "undergarment" and "linen wear" from 711 C.E. (See Jane Soames, THE COAST OF THE BARBARY; J.C. deGraft-Johnson, AFRICAN GLORY; and Stanley Lane-Poole, THE MOORS IN SPAIN).

16. Note Herodotus' description of the Egyptians he saw and met when he attended school in Egypt (See, Sir E.A. Wallis Budge, BOOK OF THE DEAD; Count C. Volney, RUINS OF EMPIRE; G.G.M. James, STOLEN LEGACY; H.G. Wells, A SHORT HISTORY OF THE WORLD; J. A. Rogers, WORLD'S GREAT MEN OF COLOR, Vol. I; J. Dorsey, CIVILIZATION MAN'S OWN SHOW).

17. Ibid. Also J. Frazier, THE GOLDEN BOUGH; H.W. Smith, MAN AND HIS GODS; and Eva M. Sandford, THE MEDITERRANEAN WORLD.

CHAPTER II NOTES
(cont'd)

18. The Hyksos invaded Egypt in c1675 B.C.E.; the Persians in c616 B.C.E.; the Greeks in c332 B.C.E.; and the Romans in c47 B.C.E. (See pages 154 and 155 of BLACK MAN OF THE NILE).

19. The Nile River in this case starts at the Second CATARACT and ends at the Mediterranean Sea.

20. The Arabs came to North Africa as invaders in 640 C.E. Their zeal, under the sword of Islam, raised as much havoc against the indigenous Africans as did the Europeans with their guns and Christianity. Both of them brought their own God, in their own likeness, and imposed them upon the indigenous Africans through Holy Wars (Jihads).

21. "AFRICAN GLORY" was once universally considered as one of the major books on African High-Cultures; especially West and North African history.

22. The word "Negro" came from the Portuguese. It was also placed on maps of the 17th century C.E. by other colonialist-minded Europeans in West Africa to coinside with the mythical "Negroland" they had already established. (See the following maps on pages 679 and 680).

23. See note No. 22 of this chapter.

24. See note No. 5 of this chapter.

24a. Note that he is also known as Orsokon II. (See pages 42 and 160 BLACK MAN OF THE NILE. He reigned from c870 to 847 B.C.E.

25. The U.S.A.'s "racial" scale is the best example. A person can be blonde with golden hair and still be a "Negro" according to the U.S.A.'s census standard. "Negro", like "Caucasian", is not a definite measurement; neither is it scientific.

26. This type of propaganda is still being preached inside and outside of Africa by Christian missionaries from Europe, Britain and the United States of America.

27. See, "Liber Pontificals" (Book of the Popes), p. 17, for Pope Victor's birth; for Melchiades' (also known as Miltiades) p. 40; for Galasius', p. 110. (As translated by L.R. Loomis, New York, 1916). See also: J.C. deGraft-Johnson, AFRICAN GLORY; A. Weisberger, LES BLANCS d'AFRIQUE (The Whites of Africa), p. 83, Paris, 1910. He detailed the peoples of the area from whence these popes came.

28. Count C. Volney's, RUINS OF EMPIRES, described the indigenous Africans he met in Egypt back in the 18th century C.E. as being similar to the "Negroes" of the United States of America. Baron Denom made the same observations in describing the Sphinx of Ghizeh in his works and painting of this monument. (See pages 149 and 243, BLACK MAN OF THE NILE, 1971.)

CHAPTER II NOTES
(cont'd)

29. Some historians have tried to claim that the Hyksos were from Europe. In their hypothesis they have failed to show any proof of the Hyksos civilization in Europe. The most accurate location of their civilization before entering Egypt is to date (currently) called the "Middle-East" (olden Asia-Minor).

30. See Manetho's, "History of Egypt" (A chronological history of dynastic Egypt).

31. The current reckless usage of the term "RACE" is much worse than it was in H.G. Wells' lifetime. Today's usage makes every national grouping a "race of people", etc.

32. See Adolph Hitler's "Mein Kampf", or South Africa's "apartheid." In the case of the latter "God made the Bantu Negroes to serve the white man", etc. The former placed anyone who was not an "Aryan" as a slave, thus making millions of Europeans similar to the "Negroes" they considered to their inferior.

33. See H. Nevinson's, "A Modern Slavery"; H.M. Stanley's, "The Dark Continent"; C. P. Groves', "The Planting of Christianity in Africa"; Eric Williams, "Capitalism and Slavery"; and L. S. Stoddard's, "The Rising Tide of Color".

34. Herein lies the basis for most of the lynchings of "Negro" males in the United States of America for the mere "staring at "Caucasian" females.

35. The reaction to the "brutish sexual potentials" which the "Negro" males are supposed to have in "abundance" brings forward the usual White American query..."Would you like your daughter to marry a Nigger"? The word "Nigger" would be "Negro, depending upon which section of the United States of America the question is asked; or type of a gathering in each area of the nation geographically.

36. The word "Jews" stems from the word "Judah", one of the Haribu (Jewish) tribes mentioned in the Hebrew Torah (Bible, Five Books of Moses, Old Testament). Thus; the Jewish People, or the Tribe of Judah.

36a. See statements by both men in other pages of BLACK MAN OF THE NILE.

37. He has been credited with many other racist remarks in his alleged works, much of which predates him.

38. "American Negroes" were property (chattel slaves) at the time of the framing and adoption of the United States of America's Federal Constitution. Most of the signators of this document were slave holders, including America's first President-George Washington. The Fourteenth Amendment of said document made

CHAPTER II NOTES
(cont'd)

the "Negro" human; at least this is what the amenders implied.

39. This statement completely refutes the positions of Professor Jeffreys, Dr. L. Stoddard and others who claimed "no Negro" (African) "lived in the Stone Age Era".

40. Sir Wallis Budge's conclusion has been stated for hundreds of years by African writers and oral traditionalists. Current archaeological findings and other existing artifacts and structures along the 4,100 miles (plus) Nile River Valley have proven this point. These facts are common knowledge to "educators" in this field; but politics and prejudice cause many of these truths to be smothered. Puanit, or Punt, was located where the Somalis, parts of South-eastern Ethiopia and north-eastern Kenya now occupy.

41. Those who claim that "Caucasians" and "Semites" occupied the Nile Valley before the present Negroes" (Africans, not the Arabized Africans) have submitted only theories, no facts whatsoever.

42. To what degree can the Europeans and European-Americans prove that there are no Moors, Carthaginians or Egyptians in their ancestral lineage after having been subjugated by these Africans. Obviously no more so than the African-Americans can now prove the absence of European lineage in their families.

43. He professed "Christianity."

44. See Sir E. A. Wallis Budge's,"Osiris"; J.A. Rogers', "World's Great Men of Color";vol. I; also statues of the same in Rome, Madrid and other capital cities in Europe.

45. See J.C. deGraft-Johnson's, "African Glory;" J.A. Rogers', "Africa's Gift To America"; B. Davidson's, "The African Past;" and Y. ben-Jochannan's, "Africa (Alkebu-lan): Her Peoples and Ever Changing Map"; "Africa: Land, People, Culture."

46 Ibid.

47. The concentration camps,for indigenous Africans only, are called "Native Reserves" by the Afrikaaners and other "Whites" of the world. They reflect certain vivid similarities to the "Indian Reservations" in the United States of America.

48. Typical orthodox Christian Missionaries (a-la-European style) teaching and practice.

49. Sir Harry must not have read Herodotus' description of the Africans of Nort Africa. In order to call any African "Hamitic," he or she must have followed "Ham's" (Noah's son) lineage. What color or physical characteristics does he claim for Ham? Where does the line between "Negro" and "Negroid" begins and ends. Who desides the criteria to be used for determining who is of what "PURE RACE" or not?

CHAPTER II NOTES
(con'td)

49a. See J.C. deGraft-Johnson's, "African Glory;" J.A. Rogers', World's Great Men of Color."

50. Septimus Servus and his son - Caracalla. (See J.C. deGraft-Johnson's, "African Glory:" Jane Soaanes', "The Coast of the Coast of the Barbary;" J.A. Rogers', "World's Great Men of Color").

51. He was born in Lipsus Magna, North Africa.

51a. Swarthy color, thick lips, broad nose, etc., usually assigned to the Africans - so-called "Negroes, Bantus," etc.

52. See: J.C. deGraft-Johnson's, "African Glory"; Jane Soames, "The Coast of Barbary"; J.A. Roger's "World's Great Men of Color"; Raymond Lull's "Lull Reports; Mrs. Stewart Erskine's "Vanished Cities of Northern Africa".

53. Augustine was born in Numidia; Cyprian and Tertullian in Carthage (all in North Africa). These names were the so-called "Christian" (European) "names" given them when they became converts to European-Style (Roman) Christianity; they are in fact European names which have nothing to do with Jesus Christ.

54. The current teaching in Christian Churches credits the Romans for this accomplishment.

55. Who can tell what color or facial characteristics all of their ancestors had?

56. The Vatican in Rome, Italy; the Church of England (Anglican) in England; the Methodist, Baptist and other White Protestant groups in the United States of America.

57. The reference to "Jesus Christ" does not endorse his existence, nor deny it. It is only used in this manner as a frame of reference in history.

58. These wars are detailed in Chapter VIII, including the 3rd Punic War.

59. Coptic (Koptic) Christians from Egypt and Ethiopia carried Christianity to these parts of Africa before the arrival of the first European (the Portuguese) in West Africa during the mid-Fifteenth Century C.E.

60. Pope Martin V was given the first Africans enslaved by the pirates employed by Prince Henry (the so-called "Navigator"), also some of the gold they stole from their victims. The Church in Rome sanctioned the import of slaves from Africa into the Caribbeans upon request of the Right Reverend Bishop Bartolome de LasCasas on the Island of Hispaniola (Hayte or Haiti and Santo Domingo) from the early 16th century (c503-1506) C.E.

CHAPTER II NOTES
(cont'd)

61. Leopold was awarded the entire Congo nation as his personal estate at the Berlin Conference in 1884-1885. The United States of America took part in this "Act" even though it refused to sign the final document called....."The Berlin Act." The lack of the signature was only a formality, as the United States of America took part in bringing about all of the repressive measures within this infamous document that later became the nucleus of what is today called "International Law", which is in fact a body of laws by European and European-American (White) nations only.

62. China, Viet Nam, Congo, Sudan, etc.

63. Before Dr. Gertrude Caton-Thompson's work, the Africans who spoke of Zimbabwe's existence were scorned by their European conquerors as being "all hearsay nonsense." This was also true after some European prospectors visited Zimbabwe's holy places. (See page 229 BLACK MAN OF THE NILE).

64. "The Moors" (Africans) "wore baggy pants" that were "wide at the knees and narrow at the ankles;" of course "picturesque in color."

65. J. A. Rogers', "Nature Knows No Color Line"; J. C. deGraft-Johnson's, "African Glory"; B. Davidson's, "The African Past"; Stanley Lane-Poole, "The Moors in Spain"; Jane Soames', "The Coast of Barbary."

66. See: J.C. deGraft-Johnson's, "African Glory"; J.A. Rogers', "World's Great Men of Color."

67. J. C. deGraft-Johnson"s, "African Glory"; Jane Soames', "The Coast of Barbary."

68. Ibid.

69. Jane Soames', "The Coast of Barbary"; J. C. deGraft-Johnson, "African Glory"; J. A. Rogers', "World's Great Men of Color"; B. Davidson's, "The African Past."

70. The term "Negroid" has no definite scientific basis; the same for "Caucasoid" and "Mongoloid". One can see any of these alleged "racial traits" in any group of people.

Chief among those who continue to perpetuate certain ethnic slurs against Blacks("Negroes"), yet claiming leadership of the same people, are the National Association for the Advancement of Colored People (NAACP), Urban League, National Association of Colored Women, etc. For example: Can anyone see anything which does not have a color? What then is meant by "Colored Women?" Continued usage does not by itself make anything right; proof by facts, through evidence, does.

CHAPTER II NOTES
(cont'd)

71. See page 245 of this work.

72. Professor Breasted wisely hid his own classification of the indigenous Africans of Egypt and those "<u>South of the Sahara</u>" by means of the quotation signs. The result is the same if he had not placed this common connotation in quotes. He too attempted to prove that the Africans <u>North of the Sahara</u> were of a different "<u>RACE</u>" than those <u>South of the Sahara.</u> What was there among the ancient Egyptians (North Africans) one could not find among those of Central and South African except for a much more extensive development of common cultures; all of which is evidenced around the African Great Lakes near the Congo, Uganda, Ethiopia, Tanzania, Tchad (Chad) etc.(See pages 679-682 for geographic location of this area).

73. Common Orthodox Christian teachings on the "<u>first martyrs of Christendom.</u>"

74. Those who agree with the "<u>martyrdoms</u>", but differ between father and son's responsibility for the acts.

75. "<u>Modern Man</u>"(whatever this is) claims to have become wiser than his more ancient brother. Maybe the fact that the ancients avoided the heat of <u>color prejudice</u> is the reason for"Modern Man" to call it a sign of their so-called "<u>primitive mentality.</u>" So it remains, if the prevailing <u>racism</u> of modern educators is to prevail.

76. All Roman Catholic Church history known to the author have established this date.

77. He mounted the throne of the Roman Empire in 167 C.E.(See: Jane Soames', "<u>The Coast of Barbary</u>"; J.C. deGraft-Johnson's "<u>African Glory</u>"; J.A. Rogers', "<u>World's Great Men of Color</u>").

78. The Roman Catholic church was involved with dividing the world between Spain and Portugal during the 15th century. It was involved with the first Africans enslaved in Europe; when Pope Martin V accepted a present of 5 Africans- as slaves-from Prince Henry of Portugal. The church was once the biggest slave owners in the world. One of its Bishops-the Right Reverend Bartolome de LasCasas - introduced Africans from Spain,called "Moors", into slavery on the Island of Hayte(or Hispaniola) in the Western Hemisphere (Caribbean Islands). This does not exclude the Protestants who followed the lead of the Roman Church.

78a. This does not mean that today's Roman Catholics are to be persecuted for the wrongs of their forerunners. It does mean, however, that they must make reparations to the victims.

79. General pulpit lectures by the clergy against all who

CHAPTER II NOTES
(cont'd)

had to fight the early Christians. Their defeat was said to have been the works of "<u>Jesus Christ</u>" (or "God"). They see professing Christianity tantamount to "<u>righteousness</u>" and "<u>Godliness</u>". That they are the "<u>representatives of God</u> <u>(Jesus Christ) "on earth</u>". Yet, they do not see that the same "<u>God</u>" crushed the <u>Crusaders</u>. Of course, the latter is not considered <u>a failure of God to help his "onward Christian Soldiers" defeat the "pagan Muslims"</u> and other "<u>heathens</u>".

80. Some "<u>Negro preachers</u>" still claim, in their pulpit, that their own Black people are paying a price because of "<u>God's</u> <u>curse against Ham</u>". They have accepted the mythical story of "Ham" in the Hebrew Torah (Bible) as being..."<u>the source</u> <u>from whence Black people originated</u>". Fortunately most Black clergymen from seminaries have refused to prattle this stereotype racist gospel; but the so-called "<u>Store Front</u> <u>Preachers</u> continue its perpetuation.

81. There are thousands of clergymen whose only knowledge of their religion is through one version of the Christian "<u>Holy Bible</u>" or another. They have never received any form of secular teachings of the history within the same book. Some actually believe that...."<u>God wrote the Bible</u>". Some even claim that...."<u>the Christian Religion was the first religion known to man</u>", and other such beliefs; yet these "<u>Men of God</u>" are responsible for most of the religious bigotry and racial prejudice amongst mankind today, just as they were in yester-years.

82. These questions prepresent truly existing conditions. Shrugging them off, as was the case for the last four-hundred years, will not make them go away. They are basic to world peace. Certainly they are direct, and maybe prickle some puritans; that is good. Maybe someone who can change these things may move in such direction due to this open and frank dialogue.

CHAPTER III NOTES

1. DuBois was himself of African and European origin, the same as many members of the royal houses of England and Sweden today.

2. See Note No. 22 of <u>Chapter II</u> Notes.

3. The old English translation is from the original work.

3a. The "<u>f</u>" was used as "<u>s</u>" in old English.

4. Translations into English by Griffith, Ranke (in Gressmann, Lange, <u>Das Weisberthsbuch des Amen-em-ope</u>, 1925).

4a. See Story of Moses' birth, upbringing, charge of crime, etc. in Hebrew Torah.

5. Although Sir John Harris is supposedly critcizing his fellow colonialist, slave master Cecil Rhodes; he too shows racial contempt for the African peoples when he refers to them as "<u>backward peoples</u>." In what ways are they "<u>backward</u>" more so than certain "Europeans"? Who is to determine what is "<u>forward</u>" in an African culture besides the Africans?

6. "<u>Rhodesia</u>" is a colonialist name. It honors the <u>Hitler of South Africa-an Englishman named Cecil Rhodes</u>. The correct name for this land is "<u>Zimbabwe</u>". The northern half is "Zambia".

7. It is strange how some formerly persecuted people find no hardship in persecuting others less fortunate than themselves at present.

8. What is meant by the "<u>Dark Continent</u>"? There is no precisely established meaning for this phrase. For each writer this term means something different. In general it is degrading in every aspect it is applied. It is the basis for many of the most racist stereotype books written about indigenous African people.

9. Volney spoke from first hand experiences; yet those who followed him by over 100 years give the impression that the opposite is fact.

10. One marvels how "modern" historians make the Sphinx of Ghizeh (Giza) and other major African structures European ("Caucasian"). It is obvious that these facts have been known to "western" educators from the late 18th Century C.E. Why, then, were these and other facts held in secret from Black and White alike by certain "educators"? To perpetuate the "Caucasian" and "Semitic" myth that is so prevalent today.

CHAPTER IV NOTES

1. "High-Culture" is used in place of "Civilization." The latter has no set or detailed standard other than the racist theory that any society which does not ape European and European-American values of culture and economics is not "CIVILIZED;" otherwise said to be "UNCIVILIZED." Yet, experience has shown that where more than two people live together for the common good of each other a CIVIL COMPACT exists. This is regardless of what their values may be; even if they decided to EAT EACH OTHER.

2. The foundation for the most part of what every EGYPROLOGIST KNOWS ABOUT THE AFRICANS OF KIMIT (Egypt) CAME FROM THE HIGH PRIEST, Manetho, MASTERFULL WORKS, History of Egypt.

Note: This chapter must be studied many times in order to digest the great amount of material information presented. The student must realize that the information presented to them for the first time in their educational experience goes counter to most of the information they received previously in the United States of America's school systems, both secular and religious. That the old theory of a CAUCASIAN and/or SEMITIC North and East Africa is but a mere DREAM in the eyes of most European and European-American writers and educators, most of whom settled for a NEGRO AFRICA, all over the continent, before it was discovered that the ancient indigenous Africans of the North and East were responsible for MOST OF WHAT THE GREEKS AND HEBREWS PROJECTED AS BEING OF THEIR OWN CREATION OR DEVELOPMENT. Also, from the time the OLDEST OF FOSSIL-MEN were discovered to have ORIGINATED IN ALKEBU-LAN (Africa); not in the TIGRIS or EUPHRATES valleys, as was believed in the Hebrew myth about ADAM AND EVE IN THE GARDEN OF EDEN found in the First Book of Moses - also called GENESIS. All of the SOURCE BOOKS must be consulted for further details, particularly those used in the preparation of this volume.

CHAPTER V NOTES

1. The making of <u>Jesus Christ</u> a <u>God-Head</u> figure was done by man in the First Century of the Christian Era, and reconfirmed in the 4th Century (c 320 C.E.) at the <u>Conference of Nicene</u> ordered by Emperor Constantine "the great". Similarly, it is man who said that <u>"God inspired"</u> those they called <u>"prophets"</u> to speak about each particular religious philosophy; and of course the same applied to those who wrote the <u>"Christian New Testament Bible,"</u> Hebrew Torah, <u>Muslim Quoran (Koran) and all other religious rule books</u>. All of them based upon the same theory of the Africans view of <u>"Salvation."</u>

2. "<u>Mysteries System</u>" is a name established by Egyptologist for the system of order that existed in ancient Kimit (Egypt) with regards to religion and education in all disciplines

3. See also G.G.M. James', "<u>Stolen Legacy</u>".

4. Note that these <u>three</u> (3) <u>Stations</u> in man's experiences are also fundamental principles in practically all religious and secret societies (such as the Free Masons, Knights of Colombus, Ekls, Druids, Odd Fellows, etc.) in Europe and the Americas.

5. All western higher <u>institution of learning</u> still cling to the African values.

6. "<u>Esoteric Philosophy</u>" is claimed to be part of the development of "<u>Greek Philosophy</u>" in most universities in Europe and the Americas; yet the ancient Africans used it long before the first European (the Greek) "<u>philosophers</u>" had schools of learning.

7. Professor G.G.M. James in his book, "<u>Stolen Legacy</u>", also made extensive researches and drew definite conclusions on these points.

8. The Greeks themselves did not call their development "<u>Greek Philosophy</u>", as they did not claim to have had anything new or different in <u>philosophic ideals</u> to that which they had learned from their African teachers in Kimit (Egypt).

9. It is strange that Greek officials would have challenged the teachings of Socrates in this manner if it was <u>the official philosophy of Greece</u> (Pyrrhus) he was spreading.

10. Word in brackets by the author.

11. Ibid.

12. If Aristotle and the Greek students he had migrated to Egypt

705

CHAPTER V NOTES
(cont'd)

    to be taught by indigenous African teachers (such as the High Priest Manetho) did in fact develop a <u>Greek-based philosophy</u>, as most "Western" educators claimed; why did he also suffer rejection by his fellow Greeks because of said teachings? Because the new "<u>philosophy</u>" he taught, he learned from his African professors of (and in) Egypt. Professors who came from the length and breadth of the Nile Valley High-Cultures, Great Lakes region, and elsewhere in Alkebu-lan. Some came to Kimit from as far south as Zimbabwe. (See Dr. Churchward's, "<u>The Origin of Free Masonry</u>" and "<u>Signs and Symbols of Primordial Man</u>; G.G.M. James', "<u>Stolen Legacy</u>".

13. See G.G.M. James', "<u>Stolen Legacy</u>"; S. Clymer's, "<u>Fire Philosophy</u>"; Kendrick's, "<u>History of Philosophy</u>"; William Turner's, "<u>History of Philosphy</u>".

14. There are no records of these men ever being engaged in these pursuits prior to their education in them while studying in Egypt. And there are no justifiable reasons to assume that such was the case.

15. Refer back to the charges brought against Socrates on page 379 of this work for observation of the depth to which the state felt it was being undermined by the introduction of the Africans philosophic concepts brought back by its nationals who had studied in Kimit's "<u>Mysteries System</u>".

16. These two concepts (the last paragraph on page 383 and this), like the others, are teachings that preceded the birth of all of the so-called "<u>Greek Philosophers</u>"-from Thales to Aristotle.

17. Religious recordings and beliefs of the Africans of Egypt as translated into English from its original Hieroglyph by Sir Ernest A. Wallis Budge.

18. It is not strange that one can still hear "Western" educators claim that...."<u>the Africans knew nothing of the wheel before the Europeans introduced it to them</u> ..." Yet one finds that the Africans were the "<u>master chariot builders</u>" of ancient days. The question is:....<u>Was this fact unknown to the educators in "Western" institutions of higher learning?</u> If yes; <u>Why was the opposite taught?</u>

19. Note that Akhnaten wrote his philosophical works more than one thousand (1,000) years before the birth of Aristotle.

20. To date these three works are the most descriptive on the subject matter in discussion.

21. This negative term, like the word "<u>RACE</u>", is used to degrade those who do not meet certain standards established by the

CHAPTER V NOTES
(cont'd)

user. Of course, the user is "<u>civilize</u>". The one to whom its addressed is naturally the "<u>un-civilized</u>".

22. Note that the period involved is more than <u>one-hundred</u> years before any knowledge of Socrates is recorded, and more than <u>two-hundred</u> years before Aristotle.

23. Here in Egypt amongst the Africans Pythagoras learnt the fundamentals for what is now called the...."<u>Pythgorum Theorum</u>".

24. Used bibliography on Socrates following.

25. These references are also applicable to Heraclitus and others in note 24; and Herodotus in the preceding paragraph.

26. See page 379 for review on the official charge and its analysis.

27. Ibid.

28. It was also carried eastward into Asia. Thus; in Babylonia, Asyria, Persia and other parts along the Tigris and Euphrates Valleys.

29. See ancient maps on the Egyptian Empire on pages in this work.

30. Note that the name "<u>Ganges</u>" itself came from the famous Kushite (Ethiopian) general Ganges, who led Ethiopian and other Africa forces into this area of Asia.

31. This historical fact should answer much of Professor Jeffreys' dilemma shown on pages 61-64.

32. With this background in mind; how is it possible to claim this area of Europe as "<u>pure white</u>" or "<u>pure Caucasian</u>" today, if at all? These facts are widely known to academicians in the various institutions of "<u>higher learning</u>"; yet they are constantly suppress andkept from students of social subjects, much less the general reading public.

33. Also Ikhnaton, Akhnaten, Akhenaten, Amem-hotep IV, etc.

34. "<u>Black power</u>, <u>Negro power</u>, <u>Bantu power</u>" etc., either name. It all means that at one time in history the indigenous African ancestors of the African peoples in Africa, Europe and the Caribbeans were powerful enough to have been rulers over the Europeans and Asians (Professor Jeffreys' "<u>light-skinned</u>" and "<u>dark skinned</u>" Caucasians). It also shows that man, be he <u>black, white, yellow, red, brown,</u> or even <u>technicolor</u>, has ruled others as he is, or was, ruled by them.

CHAPTER V NOTES
(cont'd)

35. See G.G.M. James', "Stolen Legacy"; and John Kendrick's, "Ancient Egypt", for more critical analysis of a detailed discipline. (Although the former is very hard to be had, there are existing copies available. This book is particularly recommended for students wanting to examine these facts further).

36. Other works should be equally consulted. The specific reference to this work is due to the exact wording on that page.

37. The suicide of Socrates and the exile of Aristotle, and others, are marked examples.

38. Because of its Egyptian origin, it is only logical that Egypt would be the last place to expect persecutions and prosecutions.

39. None.

40. This Lodge is the "Mother Lodge" of all existing Masonic Orders in the world. Also "Luxor".

41. 323 or 325 B.C.E. "Western" historians vary on these two dates.

42. Some of the indigenous Africans of Kimit works attributed to Aristotle he did not claim for himself. They were claimed for him by other European and European-American "scholars" and "educators" who followed him almost two-thousand years later.

43. Most of these men's history began after their own education in Egypt. The average one was more than forty years old when history first referred to them. Many of them were not even Greek nationals.

44. From approximately 1318-1232 B.C.E. These figures represent the beginning of Seti I reign to the end of Rameses II reign. (See page 311 of this work for chronological review).

45. The ORACLE was a man"..... who could tell the future...." During this period the Oracle of Anmon, in Egypt, was considered "the greatest in the world".

46. The prevailing teaching in all "Western" institutions of higher learning follow this concept.

47. See materials on Dr. L.S.B. Leakey's find Zinjanthropus boisie." A 1,750,000 year old fossil-man of Africa's middle-eastern region. Also known as "Nutcracker Man". This fossil was discovered on July 17, 1959 in the

CHAPTER V NOTES
(cont'd)

47. Olduvai Gorge, Tanganyika (Tanzania), East Africa. Its age was determined by the process called..."Krypton-argon method". (A scientific process of dating matter through measuring its carbon contents. It is popularly known as the "carbon-test").

48. See maps on Egyptian Sea and Libyan Sea.

CHAPTER VI NOTES

1. There is no record of this statute ever being sold by any African. It was taken out of Africa illegally, 1the same as the overwhelming majority of other African properties in private art collections and public museums throughout Europe, Britain and the United States of America.

2. See page 92 middle and bottom pictures, BLACK MAN OF THE NILE.

3. See: J.A. Rogers', "World's Great Men of Color", Vol. I; J.C. deGraft-Johnson's, "African Glory".

4. See page 317.

5. Ibid.

6. Richards', "Freemansonry"; Dr. Albert Churchwards', "Origin and Evolution of Free Masonry"; J.A. Rogers', "World's Great Men of Color".

7. All of these authors attested to the African origin of Free Masonry (See: A. Churchward's, "Arcana of Free Masonry", 1915).

8. G.G.M. James', "Stolen Legacy", claimed that Jesus Christ and King Solomon visited and took instructions from the Lodge at Mt. Carmel. This is supported by most researchers on secret societies.

9. The most publicized trip to Puanit (Punt) by Egyptian royalty was the trip of Queen Hatshepsut. (See page 160 for story, in Egyptian script, BLACK MAN OF THE NILE.

10. Djoser was renamed "Zozer" by the early Greeks who found it difficult to pronounce   African name

11. See page 311.

12. See page 160. BLACK MAN OF THE NILE.

13. Ibid. page 165. Unitarianism, as a religious force, is built upon the philosophical concepts of Akh-naten.

14. Note that the Africans had developed this science beyond the current methods; since the average housewife could have made her own compound from the ingredients.

15. See also G.G.M. James', "Stolen Legacy"; Frankfurt's, "History of Philosophy"; John Kendrick's, "History of Philosophy."

16. See "The Legacy of Egypt", (ed by S.R.K. Glanville); J.A. Rogers', "World's Great Men of Color"; G.G.M. James', "Stolen Legacy".

CHAPTER VI NOTES
(cont'd)

17. This occured before there was a **Moses** of the Hebrew Holy Torah. Everyone of the laws in the Hebrew "**Ten Commandments**" God-JEHOVAH (Yawh) was supposed to have given Moses at Mt. Sinai were in effect in **Ithiopi** (Ethiopia or Kush) under King Ori, and in Kimit (Egypt or Sais) for over three-thousand years before **Moses** was born in Kimit.

18. This is the old "**divide and conquer**" technique mastered by Napoleon and other European and European-American colonialists.

19. See writings of Herodotus in his own book, "**The Histories**".

20. All of these facts were available to European-America's educational institutions of higher learning for centuries.

21. Like the **Columbus - Lief Ericson** fiasco, the Portuguese got credit above the Greeks as being the first Europeans to sail along the West African coast because the Greeks failed to record their voyage as well as the Portuguese did. And because of the small area of communication during B.C.E. as against C.E.

CHAPTER VII NOTES

1. The present political boundaries of Egypt, Ethiopia, Sudan, Libya and all other African nations and colonies were not in fact established by the Africans. Most of them were established at the <u>Berlin Conference</u> of 1884-1885 C.E. in a document entitled the <u>"Berlin Act"</u>. A subsequent gathering, equally and exclusively for Europeans and European-Americans (whites), in 1896, called the <u>"Brussels Conference"</u>, made some <u>adjustments</u>. The last <u>adjustments</u> being made during the periods when the European colonialist and imperialist powers were being politically forced out from their former African colonies, beginning in 1957 C.E. at the so-called <u>"British Gold Coast Crown Colony"</u> - today's <u>Ghana</u>, under the astute leadership of the Ghanians <u>"father of their country"</u> - Dr. Kwame Nkrumah.

CHAPTER VIII NOTES

1. Carthage was once a City-State, Nation, and an Empire. It was originally called "KHART HADDAD", or NEW TOWN, by the indigenous Africans thousands of years before the arrival of Princess Elisar (Dido) with her Phoenician countrymen.

2. See Jane Soaames', The Coast of the Barbary"; J.A. Rogers', "World's Great Men of Color", Vol. I; J.C. deGraft-Johnson's, "African Glory."

3. Arabs (Asian 640 C.E.); Berbers (European 150-146 B.C.E.); Africans (indigenous peoples). The dates indicate the arrival of the various foreign groups to the area. The so-called "BERBERS" are the remnants of the Vandals and Etruscans (Romans, etc.) who conquered Carthage and traded with the North African peoples, also those of the southern limits. The Arabs came to North Africa spreading the gospel of Islam, Al'lah, in two (2) JIHADS (waves of religious wars similar to the Christian Six - 6 - Crusades).

4. See Jane Soaames', " The Coast of the Barbary"; J.C. deGraft-Johnson's, "African Glory"; J.A. Rogers', "World's Great Men Of Color".

5. Rome's expansion was due to her conquest over less powerful states of the Italian Peninsula.

6. Carthage was using Sicily as a military outpost.

7. Pyrrhus was the Greek name for today's GREECE. The latter is an English.

8. Carthage at this period in history had established settlements along Africa's West coast for trading purposes.

9. GIBRALTAR (Gibral Tarikh, or Rock of Tarikh) is named in honor of the indigenous African who invaded and conquered southern Spain in 711 C.E. - General Tarikh. (See J.A. Rogers', "World's Great Men of Color"; J.C. deGraft-Johnson's, "African Glory"; Jane Soaames', "The Coast of Barbary"; C.P. Groves', "The Planting of Christianity in Africa"; H. Leclercq's, "L' Afrique Christiene"; Stanley Lane-Poole's, "THE MOORS IN SPAIN.

10. General Hamilcar Barca, Hanibal's and Hastrubal's father, was commander of the Carthaginian military forces.

11. During this period the Carthaginians were enjoying their defeat of the Romans, and failed to rebuild their damaged naval vessels.

12. This was the beginning of Carthage's downfall.

13. None of these restrictions had anything to do with the Africans COLOR or RACE, as som "Western" (European-American) historians and other educators have implied. Jane Soaames in her noted work, COAST OF THE BARBARY, made certain to mention that Rome was not a homogeneous society of one ethnic (White or Caucasian) group.

CHAPTER VIII NOTES
(cont'd)

14. Most historians carefully ignore the indigenous African peoples of Carthage, and give the impression that the Carthaginians were "<u>Caucasians</u>." There was no difference between the Africans of Carthage experience with the Phoenecian imperialists and what the West Africans experienced with the colonialist Europeans from 1830 C.E. to the present. For regardless of the role of the conqueror and the conquered, carnal intercourse between both groups will enevitably take place. The conqueror always raped the women of the conquered.

15. Hannibal was forced to make this decision, as the Carthaginian naval fleet was all but destroyed in the latter part of the 1st <u>Rome-Carthage</u> War. (Punic War).

16. Hannibal did try to recruit Europeans along the way, but most of them were not trainable in a short space of time to meet the standards set for his army. They were only suitable for labor details. It would have taken months to get them acquainted with the elephants that terrified them, much less commanding them in military formation.

17. Rome had appointed many dictators for periods of a few months during crisis, but this was the first time that no time limit was established by the Senate for the end of Fabius' dictatorial rule.

18. Fabius was obviously only holding Hannibal's forces until the new Roman army could complete its training; and until the navy could be rebuilt.

19. S. Selicourt's, "<u>The Carthaginians in Europe</u>".

20. His supply line could not meet his war demands without a full-size sea power which was at this time impossible, being that the fleet had been destroyed.

21. A <u>trireme</u> (tri-rem) is a vessel with three benches or banks of oars on a side; or a galley.

22. These Africans were eventually forced into the Roman army and became <u>Roman citizens</u>.

23. This plan was **never tried.** Hannibal tried many other places, but was always turned down.

24. Upon Alexander "<u>the great</u>" untimely death the Greeks fought among themselves over who was going to rule what captured land and people. Soter I (or Ptolemy I), Alexander's Macedonian general, took Egypt.

ACKNOWLEDGEMENT

This work would not have been possible by myself alone. I am seriously indebted to the following people for their wholehearted cooperation extended to me in the preparation of the manuscript. My special thanks to Mrs. Cheryl Calnek for editing the final manuscript; Miss Doris Mosley for editing the original draft of the manuscript; Mr. Carl Calnek for checking the historical notes; Mr. George Simmonds for checking the historical documentation; Miss Bess Ruth Terry for sentence structure and reading ease; my daughter, Collette (Makeda), for checking the ease of reading style between the college level and the genergl public ability to digest the material; and to Mrs. Sandra Troyanos and Miss Carol Howard who brought the final draft into working form for camera and printing of the finished product.

I am also indebted in a special way to the many students who criticized the original lectures and essays as they were given; all of whom I would have liked to list individually, but space forced me to thank them collectively.

Without funds none of the above would have been possible. In this regards, I am most obligated to Mr. Roger Pryor, and to Mr. Clarence Harris and his Committee For Students Rights of Detroit, Michigan.

There were countless other people who were instrumental in one way or another over the last four years while I wrote and otherwise developed the manuscript. To all of them I extend my sincerest appreciation.

Note: All of the artwork have been sketched by myself in order to reproduced the facsimile of their antiquus appearence; bearing in mind the ancients were without sophisticated tools of today.

(Photo by Al Burliegh Studio, 1/12/70; at Harlem Prep.)
The author, Yosef ben-Jochannan, declared that...THE ONLY CREDENTIALS NECESAARY IN THE PRESENTATION OF AFRICAN HISTORY, OTHERWISE MISNOMERED "The Black Experience" and "Black Studies," ARE THE DOCUMENTED FACTS AND THE SOURCES FROM WHENCE THEY ARE TAKEN. Also,...TITLES AND/OR DEGREES, ALTHOUGH HAVING THEIR MERITS, DO NOT MAKE HISTORY CORRECT. That in this respect, the records show, THE VAST MAJORITY OF THE PEOPLE MOST INVOLVED WITH "Black Studies" BEFORE THE LAST FIVE (5) YEARS WERE THE SO-CALLED "Street Corner Speakers;" NOT ONE OF WHOM WAS NOT LABELED A RACIST, IRRESPONSIBLE, PREACHER OF HATE, ETC. YET, TODAY, THESE UNSUNG HEROES ROLE HAS BEEN CAREFULLY IGNORED BY MOST OF OUR PROFESSORS AND WRITERS WHO SPECIALIZE ON AFRICAN PEOPLES' HISTORY AND CULTURE.

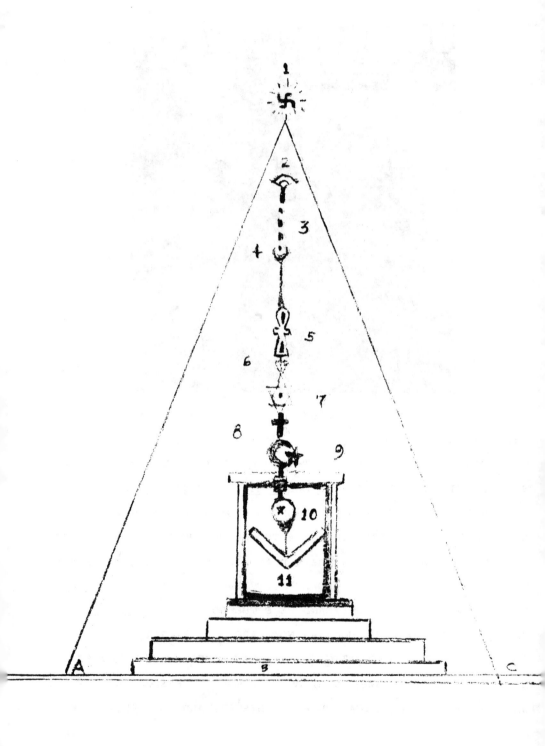

COVER DESIGN DESCRIPTION

1. **Swatzthika** (Swastika adopted by Adolph Hitler et al of the Nazis Party of Germany) imposed upon the SUN-BURST (Rā or Rē) at the top of the Pyramid.

2. **The Ever-Seeing Eye of Horus** (adopted by the United States of America on its legal tender).

3. **Tears** from the Eyes of Horus.

4. **The Sephulcup** receiving Tears from the Eyes of Horus (adopted by the Christians as the Chalis).

5. **The Ankh** (Key of Life, the original Cross, corrupted by the Christians of Rome).

6. **Lotus Plant - Flower of LOWER KIMIT** (Plant in the Book of the Dead's JUDGEMENT SCENE).

7. **Rā (●) in His Pole Star** (the Doubble Pyramid adopted by the Hebrews, or Jews, as the Star of David).

8. **The Cross - symbol of death** (adopted by European Christians and of North Africa for Jesus of Nazzareth).

9. **Star of Amenta** (adopted by the Muslims as the Fertile Crescent of Al'lah).

10. **Pointer of Rē with imposed Pole Star** (adopted by the Freemasons and other "Secret Societies" as the Plumb-bob that symbolizes mankind's "UPRIGHT POSITION").

11. **Doubble-Right Angle Pyramid or Square** (adopted by the above mentioned organizations as the symbol of the "SQUARING OF MAN'S DEEDS;" also on the United States of America's legal tender).

A. **Doubble-Right Angle Pyramid** - House of Fire, House of the Nether World, House of Amenta, House of Heaven (adopted by every civilization of the so-called "Western World" as a symbol of "STRENGTH" and the "REACHING OUT INTO THE HEAVENS" to the God JEHOBAH - an offspring of the God RA or RE, etc.).

B. **Seven-Steps Sephulcur-Chest** (adopted by the Haribus, so-called "Jews," as the "ARK OF THE COVENANT JEHOVAH GAVE TO MOSES").

C. **Earth's Dead-Level** (adopted by Freemasonry and other Secret Societies as the "DEAD-LEVEL FROM WHENCE MAN COMETH INTO LIFE").

Note: Numbers 2 through 11, and letter B, are all inside the Pyramid; number 10 is inside number 11. Cover Design by the author - Yosef ben-Jochannan - to symbolize the most commonly used signs and symbols in the "WESTERN WORLD," Europe and European-America, adopted from ALKEBU-LAN'S ("Mother Africa's") sons and daughters. Each symbol is at least 4000 years older than Judaeo-Christianity.

Select Bibliography

Adams, Walter M., *the Book of the Master Of the Hidden Places*. London: The Search Publishing Co., 1933.

Aristotle, *Ethics, Book I. Politics, Book I*. Translated by W. D. Ross. Chicago: H. Regnery, 1954.

Arkell, Anthony, J. *A History of the Sudan: From the Earliest Times to 1821*. London: Athlone Press, 1955.

Armistead, Wilson. *A Tribute for the Negro*. Manchester: W. Irwin, 1848.

Augustine, Aurelius. *On Christian Doctrine*. Edinburgh: T and T. Clark, 1892.

_____ *The Confessions of St. Augustine*. London: Chatto and Windus, 1909.

_____ *The City of God*. New York: Modern Library, 1950.

Ault, Warren, O. *Europe in the Middle Ages*. Boston: D.C. Heath and Co., 1932.

Baker, Samuel W. *The Albert N'yanza, Great Basin of the Nile, and Explorations of the Nile Sources*. Vols. 1-2. London: MacMillan and Co., 1866.

Bakewell, Charles M. *Source Book in Ancient Philosophy*. New York: C. Scribner's Sons, 1907.

Barber, Francis M. *The Mechanical Triumphs of the Ancient Egyptians*. London: K. Paul, Trench, Trubner and Co., 1900.

Ben-Jochannan, Yosef, Hugh Brooks, and Kempton Webb, *Africa: Lands, Peoples, and Cultures of the World*. New York: W. H. Sadlier, 1970.

Ben-Jochannan, Yosef. African Origins of the Major Western Religions. New York: Alkebu-lan Books Associates, 1970.

_____ *Black Man of the Nile*. New York: Alkebu-lan Books Associates, 1970.

_____ *We the Black Jews*. Spain: N.P., 1949.

Bent, James T. *The Ruined Cities of Mashonaland*. London: Longmans, Green and Co., 1892.

Besant, Annie W. *Esoteric Christianity; or, the Lesser Mysteries*. New York: J. Lane, 1902.

Bovill, E.W. *The Golden Trade of the Moors*. London: Oxford University Press, 1958.

_____ *Caravans of the Old Sahara*. London: Oxford University Press, 1933.

Breasted, James H. *Ancient Records of Egypt; Historical Documents From the Earliest Times to the Persian Conquest*. Vols. 1-5. Chicago: The University of Chicago Press, 1906-1907.

_____ *The Dawn of Conscience*. New York: C. Scribner's Sons, 1933.

Brown, Robert. *The Story of Africa and its Explorers*. Vols. 1-4. London: Cassell and Co., Limited, 1892-1895.

Browne, William G. *Travels in Africa, Egypt, and Syria*. London: T. Cadell and W. Davies, 1806.

Budge, Ernest A. *The Book of the Dead: The Hieroglyphic Transcript of the Papyrus of Ani*. New York: Bell Publishing Co., 1960.

_____ *The Book of the Dead: The Papyrus of Ani in the British Museum*. London: British Museum, Longmans and Co., 1895. ed. and trans.

_____ *Osiris and the Egyptian Resurrection*. Vols. 1-2. London: P. L. Warner, 1911.

_____ *The Negative Confession*. New York: Bell Publishing Co., 1960.

_____ *The Papyrus of Ani*. Vols. 1-3. New York: G. P. Putnam's Sons, 1913.

_____ *Egypt*. New York: H. Holt and Co., 1925.

_____ *The Gods of the Egyptians*. Vols. 1-2. London: Methuen and Co., 1904.

_____ *A History of Egypt From the End of the Neolithic Period to the Death of Cleopatra VII B.C. 30*. Vols. 1-8. London: K. Paul, Trench, Trubner and Co., 1902.

_____ *A History of Ethiopia, Nubia and Ablyssinia*. Vols. 1-2. London: Methuen and Co. Ltd., 1928.

_____ *The Egyptian Sudan; Its History and Monuments*. Vols. 1-2. London: K. Paul, Trench, Trubner and Co., 1907.

Bullock, Charles. *The Mashona.* Cape Town: Juta and Co., Ltd., 1928.

Bunbury, Edward H. *The History of Ancient Geography Among the Greeks and Romans, From the Earliest Ages Till the Fall of the Roman Empire.* Vols. 1-2. London: J. Murray, 1879.

Burckhardt, John L. *Travels in Nubia.* London: J. Murray, 1819.

Burkitt, Miles C. *South Africa's Past in Stone and Paint.* Cambridge, England: Cambridge University Press, 1928.

Burton, Richard F. *The Lake Regions of Central Africa.* Vols. 1-2. London: Longman, Green, Longman, and Roberts, 1860.

Cajori, Florian. *A History of Mathematics.* New York: Macmillan and Co., 1894.

Caton-Thompson, Gertrude. *The Zimbabwe Culture.* Oxford, England: Clarendon Press, 1931.

Childe, Vere G., *Man Makes Himself.* London: Watts, 1965.

Churchward, Albert, *The Arcana of Freemasonry.* New York: Macoy Publishing and Masonic Supply Co., 1915.

_____ *The Origin and Evolution of Freemasonry Connected With the Origin and Evolution of the Human Race.* London: G. Allen and Unwin, 1920.

_____ *The Origin and Evolution of Religion.* London: G. Allen and Unwin, Ltd., 1924.

_____ *The Signs and Symbols of Primordial Man:* New York: E.P. Dutton and Co., 1910.

_____ *Origin and Evolution of the Human Race.* London: G. Allen and Unwin, Ltd., 1921.

Clark, John D. *The Stone Age Cultures of Northern Rhodesia.* Claremont: South African Archaeological Society, 1950.

Clark, Wilfrid E. and Louis S. Leakey, *The Miocene Hominoidea of East Africa.* London: The Trustees of the British Museum, 1951.

Clymer, Reuben S. *The Philosophy of Fire.* Quakertown, Pa.: The Philosophical Publishing Co., 1920.

Cole, Sonia M. *The Prehistory of East Africa.* New York: Macmillan, 1963.

Collingwood, Robin G. *The Idea of History.* New York: Oxford University Press, 1956.

Cook, Stanley A. *The Religion of Ancient Palestine in the Light of Archaeology.* London: Oxford University Press, 1930.

Danby, Herbert. *The Mishnah.* London: Oxford University Press, 1938.

Darwin, Charles R. *The Origin of Species.* New York: Appleton, 1904.

_____ *The Next Million Years.* London: R. Hart-Davis, 1952.

Davidson, Basil. *The Lost Cities of Africa.* Boston: Little, Brown, 1959.

_____ *The African Past.* Boston: Little, Brown, 1964.

Dawson, Christopher H. *The Making of Europe,* New York: Meridian Books, 1956.

De Buck, Adriaan and Alan H. Gardiner, editors, *The Egyptian Coffin Texts.* Vols. 1-7. Chicago: University of Chicago Press, 1935-1961.

DeGraft-Johnson, John C. *African Glory.* New York: Frederick A. Praeger, Inc., 1955.

Denon, Dominique V. *Travels in Upper and Lower Egypt.* Vols. 1-2. London: B. Crosby and Co., 1802.

Diogenes Laertius. *Lives of Eminent Philosophers.* Vols. 1-2. New York: G. P. Putnam's Sons, 1925.

Doane, Thomas W. *Bible Myths and Their Parallels in Other Religions.* New Hyde Park, N.Y.: University Books, 1971.

Doresse, Jean. *Ethiopia.* New York: Putnam, 1959.

Dorsey, George A. *The Story of Civilization; Man's Own Show.* New York: Halcyon House, 1931.

Dubois, Felix. *Timbuctoo the Mysterious.* New York: Longmans, Green and Co., 1896.

Erskine, Beatrice, Steuart, *Vanished Cities of Northern Africa.* London: Hutchinson and Company, Ltd., 1927.

Foote, George W. and W.P. Ball, eds., *The Bible Handbook For Freethinkers and Inquiring Christians.* London: The Pioneer Press, 1921.

Frank, Harry T. et al., *The Bible Through The Ages*. Cleveland: World Pub. Co., 1967.

Frankfort, Henri, *Kinship and the Gods*. Chicago: University of Chicago Press, 1958.

_____ *The Intellectual Adventure of Ancient Man*. Chicago: University of Chicago Press, 1957.

_____ *Ancient Egyptian Religion, An Interpretation*. New York: Columbia University Press, 1948.

Frazer, James G., *The Golden Bough; A Study in Magic and Religion*. Vols. 1-13. London: Macmillan, 1911-1936.

Frobenius, Leo, *The Voice of Africa*. Vols. 1-2. London: Hutchinson and Company, 1913.

Glanville, Stephen R., ed., *The Legacy of Egypt*. Oxford: The Clarendon Press, 1942.

Gorringe, Henry H., *Egyptian Obelisks*. New York: the author, 1882.

Graves, Kersey, *The World's Sixteen Crucified Saviors, or, Christianity Before Christ*. Boston: Colby and Rich, 1875.

Graves, Robert and Raphael Patai, *Hebrew Myths: The Book of Genesis*. New York: Doubleday and Company, Inc., 1964.

Groves, Charles P., *The Planting of Christianity In Africa*. Vols. 1-4. London: Lutterworth Press, 1948-1958.

Harris, John H., *Slavery or "Sacred Trust."* New York: Negro Universities Press, 1969.

Hastings, James, editor, *Encyclopedia of Religion and Ethics*. Vols. 1-13. New York: C. Scribner's Sons, 1908-1926.

Hall, Richard N., *Prehistoric Rhodesia*. London: T. F. Unwin, 1909.

Herodotus, *The Histories*. Aubrey de Selincourt Trans. Baltimore, MD: Penguin Books, 1955.

Hertslet, Edward, *The Map of Africa by Treaty*. Vols. 1-3. London: Harrison and Sons, 1909.

Higgins, Godfrey, *Anacalypsis*. Vols. 1-2. London: Longman, 1836.

Hitti, Philip K., *History of the Arabs*. New York: Macmillan, 1951.

The Holy Qur'an. Commentary and Translation by Maulana Muhammad Ali. Lahore, Pakistan: The Ahmadiyyah Anjuman Isha' at Islam, 1963.

Huggins, Willis N., and John G. Jackson, *An Introduction to African Civilizations, with Main Currents in Ethiopian History*. New York: Negro Universities Press, 1969.

Hutchins, Robert M., editor. *Great Books of The Western World*. Vols. 1-54. Chicago: Encyclopedia Britannica, 1955.

Hurry, Jamieson B., *Imhotep*. London: Oxford University Press, 1926.

Jackson, John G., *Introduction to African Civilizations*. New York: University Books, 1970.

John, Janheinz, *Muntu; An Outline of the New African Culture*. New York: Grove Press, 1961.

James, George G.M., *Stolen Legacy*. New York: Philosophical Library, 1954.

Johnston, Harry H., *The Nile Quest: A Record of the Exploration of the Nile and its Basin*. New York: Frederick A. Stokes Co., 1903.

_____ *A History of the Colonization of Africa by Alien Races*. Cambridge, England: University Press, 1899.

Josephus, Flavius, *The Complete Works of Flavius-Josephus*. Chicago: Thompson and Thomas, 1900.

Keltie, John Scott, *The Partition of Africa*. London: E. Stanford, 1893.

Kenrick, John, *Ancient Egypt Under the Pharaohs*. Vols. 1-2. London: B. Fellowes, 1850.

Kenyatta, Jomo, *Facing Mount Kenya*. New York: Vintage Books, 1962.

Labouret, Henri, *Africa Before the White Man*. New York: Walker, 1963.

Lane-Poole, Stanley, *The Moors in Spain*. London: T. Fisher Unwin, 1887.

Leakey, Louis S.B., *The Stone Age Culture of Kenya Colony*. Cambridge, England: The University Press, 1931.

_____ *The Stone Age Races of Kenya*. London: Oxford University Press, 1935.

Leo Africanus, Joannes, *The History and Description of Africa*. Vols. 1-3. London: Hakluyt Society, 1896.

Leslau, Wolf, *Falasha Anthology: The Black Jews of Ethiopia*. New York: Schocken Books, 1969.

Lewis, Harve S., *The Mystical Life of Jesus*. San Jose, Calif.: Rosicrucian Press, AMORC College, 1929.

The Lost Books of the Bible and the Forgotten Books of Eden. New York: The World Publishing Co., 1963.

Lugard, Flora L., *A Tropical Dependency*. London: J. Nisbet and Co., 1905.

Maspero, Gaston C., *The Dawn of Civilization, Egypt and Chaldea*. London: Society for Promoting Christian Knowledge, 1901.

_____ *The Passing of Empires, 850 B.C. to 330 B.C.* New York: D. Appleton and Co., 1900.

_____ *The Struggle of The Nations, Egypt, Syria and Assyria*. New York: D. Appleton and Co., 1897.

Massey, Gerald. *Ancient Egypt, The Light of the World*. Vols. 1-2. New York: S. Weiser, 1970.

_____ *A Book of the Beginnings*. Vols. 1-2. London: Williams and Norgate, 1881.

Moon, Parker T., *Imperialism and World Politics*. New York: The Macmillan Co., 1936.

Moore, Richard B., *The Name "Negro," Its Origin and Evil Use*. New York: Afroamerican Publishers, 1960.

Myer, Isaac., trans. *Qabbalah*. Philadelphia, Pa: The author, 1888.

Nevinson, Henry W., *A Modern Slavery*. London: Harper and Brothers, 1906.

Padmore, George, *Africa: Britain's Third Empire*. London: D. Dobson, 1949.

Parkyns, Mansfield, *Life In Abyssinia*. London: Cass, 1966.

The Pentateuch. London: J. Harris, 1818.

Petrie, William M., *A History of Egypt*. Vols. 1-6. London: Methuen and Co., 1898-1905.

Plato, *The Apology of Plato*. Oxford: The University Press, 1877.

_____ *The Phaedo*. London: Macmillan and Co., 1933.

_____ *The Republic*. Vols. 1-2. London: W. Heinemann, 1930-35.

Pyramid Texts. Vols. 1-4. New York: Longmans, Green, 1952.

Randall-MacIver, David, *Medieval Rhodesia*. London: Macmillan and Co., 1906.

Robinson, Theodore H. and Oesterley, William O., *A History of Israel*. Vols. 1-2. Oxford: The Clarendon Press, 1932.

Rogers, Joel A., *Africa's Gift To America; The Afro-American in the Making and Saving of the United States*. New York: J.A. Rogers Publications, 1959.

_____ *Nature Knows No Color Line*. New York: J. A. Rogers Publications, 1952.

_____ *Sex and Race*. Vols. 1-3 New York, N.Y.: J.A. Rogers Publications, 1940-1944.

_____ *World's Great Men of Color*. Vols. 1-2. New York: J.A. Rogers Publications, 1946-1947.

St. Jerome's Latin Vulgate New Testament. Edited with a vocabulary by L.R. Lind. Lawrence, Kansas: N.P., 1960. see 16.76.

Sanford, Eva M., *The Mediterranean World in Ancient Times*. New York: The Ronald Press Co., 1938.

Sedgwick, William T. and Harry W. Tyler, *A Short History of Science*. New York: Macmillan Co., 1917.

Seligman, Charles G., *Races of Africa*. London: T. Butterworth, 1930.

The Septuagint Version of the Old Testament with an English Translation. 2 vols. in 1. London: S. Bagster and Sons, 1896.

Smith, Homer W., *Man and His Gods*. Boston: Little, Brown, 1952.

Snowden, Jr., Frank M., *Blacks in Antiquity: Ethiopians in the Greco-Roman Experience*. Cambridge, Mass.: The Belknap Press of Harvard University Press, 1970.

Soames, Jane, *The Coast of Barbary*. London: J. Cape, 1938.

Speke, John H., *What Led to the Discovery of the Source of the Nile.* London: Cass, 1967.
Stanley, Henry M., *In Darkest Africa.* Vols. 1-2, New York: C. Scribner's Sons, 1890.
Stanley, Thomas, *History of Philosophy.* Vols. 1-3. London: H. Moseley and T. Dring, 1655-1660.
Stoddard, Theodore L., *The Rising Tide of Color Against White World Supremacy.* New York: Scribner, 1920.
Tempels, Placide, *Bantu Philosophy.* Paris, France: Presence Africaine, 1969.
Tennemann, Wilhelm G., *A Manual of the History of Philosophy.* London: H.G. Bohn, 1852.
Theal, George M., *Records of Southeastern Africa Collected in Various Libraries and Archive Departments In Europe.* Vols. 1-9. London: The Government of the Cape Colony, 1898-1903.
Thilly, Frank, *A History of Philosophy.* New York: H. Holt and Co., 1914.
The Torah: The Five Books of Moses. Philadelphia: The Jewish Publication Society of America, 1962.
Turner, William, *History of Philosophy.* Boston: Ginn and Co., 1929.
Vail, Charles H., *Ancient Mysteries and Modern Masonry.* New York: Macoy Publishing and Masonic Supply Co., 1909.
Volney, Constantin F., *The Ruins: Or a Survey of the Revolutions of Empires.* London: J. Johnson, 1795.
Weber, Alfred, *History of Philosophy.* New York: C. Scribner's Sons, 1896.
Wells, Herbert G., *A Short History of the World.* New York: Macmillan Co., 1922.
Wiedner, Donald L., *A History of Africa South of the Sahara.* New York: Random House, 1962.
Williams, Eric E., *Capitalism and Slavery.* Chapel Hill, N.C.: University of North Carolina Press, 1944.
Willoughby, John C., *A Narrative of Further Excavations at Zimbabwe (Mashonaland).* London: G. Philip and Son, 1893.
Woodhouse, William J., *The Tutorial History of Greece.* London: W. B. Clive, 1907.
Windsor, Rudolph R., *From Babylon To Timbuktu; A History of the Ancient Black Races Including the Black Hebrews.* New York: Exposition Press, 1969.
Zeller, Eduard, *A History of Greek Philosophy From the Earliest Period to the Time of Socrates.* Vols. 1-2. London: Longmans, Green, and Co., 1881.
Zeller, Eduard, *Outlines of the History of Greek Philosophy.* London: Longman's, Green, and Co., 1914.
Posnansky *The Greek Commonwealth, Politics and Economics in Fifth Century Athens.* Oxford: The Clarendon Press, 1911.

Periodicals, Journals and Newspapers.

"43,000 year Old Mine Discovered in Swaziland." *The New York Times,* February 8, 1970, p. 6.
"Fossils Trace Man Back 600,000 Years in Gorge in Africa." *The New York Times,* August 24, 1959, p. 23.
Bishop, W.W., and Posnansky, M. Pleiotocene Environments and Early Man in Uganda." *The Uganda Journals,* Vol. 24, No. 1, March 1960, pp. 44-61.
Danquah, J.B., "The Culture of Akan." Africa, Vol. 22, No. 4, October 1952, pp. 360-366.
Hess, Robert L., "The Itinerary of Benjamin of Tudela: A Twelfth Century Jewish Description of North-East Africa." *Journal of African History,* Vol. 6, No. 1, 1965, pp. 15-24.
Hodgkin, Thomas, "National Movements In West Africa." *The Highway,* Vol. 43, February 1950, pp. 169-174.
Randall-MacIver, David, "The Rhodesia Ruins: Their Probable Origin and Significance." *The Geographical Journal.* Vol. 27, No. 4, April 1906, pp. 325-347.
Schofield, J.F., "Zimbabwe: A Critical Examination of the Building Methods Employed" *South African Journal of Science.* Vol. 33, December 1926, pp. 971-986.
Weiner, J.S., "The Pattern of Evolutionary Development of the Genus Homo." *The South African Journal of Medical Sciences.* Vol. 23, Nos. 3 and 4, December 1958, pp. 111-120.

NAME INDEX

A

Aaron, 467
Abel, 69
Abraham, 95, 130, 189, 260, 315, 357, 367, 382, 474, 521, 576, 592, 593, 617
Adam, xviii, 31, 95, 189, 266, 571, 578, 580, 594
Adronicus, 399
Aeschylus, 241
Africanus, Julius, 491
Africanus, Leo, 171, 271, 493, 607
Aha, Pharoah, 263, 264, 269, 270, 278, 474
Ahmes I, Pharoah, 108
Alexander, the Great, 6, 109-111, 156, 239, 241, 257-259, 342-343, 379, 396, 405-407, 427, 439, 483, 492-493, 648
Amasis, Pharoah, 403, 482
Amenemhat I, Pharoah, 319
Amenemhat III, Pharoah, 321
Amen-em-ope, Pharoah, xix, 180
Amenhotep I, Pharoah, 326
Amenhotep II, Pharoah, 310
Amenhotep III, Pharoah, 325
Amenhotep IV, Pharoah, (Akhnaten) 358, 393, 427, 478, 652
Amenothis III, Pharoah, 479
Amyrtaeos, Pharoah, 339
Anaxagores, 377, 379-380, 397
Antonio, Marc, 112-113, 496
Apollo, 315-316
Aristotle, vii, viii, 9, 110-111, 204, 257-258, 377, 379-380, 386, 391, 396, 399, 405-407, 423, 427, 484, 491-493, 561-562
Aristoxenus, 385
Ashmes, Pharoah, 325-326
Ashurbanipal, Pharoah, 337
Aspelta, Pharoah, 293-294
Authmosis, 155

B

Baker, Samuel W., 217-218, 222
Barca, Hamiclair, 531
Barca, Hannibal (Hannibal the Great), 531-541, 547, 688
Barca, Hasdrubal, 537

Bismarch, Otto von, 438, 670
Blyden, Wilmot E., 473
Bonaparte, Napolean, 6-7, 194-195, 254-256, 293, 512, 518
Breasted, James H., 153-154, 276, 454-455, 457, 465-466, 550-556, 558-560
Brotz, Howard M., 610-614, 617
Budge, Ernest W. A., 28-29, 92-94, 107, 121, 179, 244, 246, 247, 276, 348-349, 353-354, 387, 454, 551

C

Caesar, Julius, 111-112, 496
Cain, 69
Cannan, 598-599, 604, 661
Caracalla, Emperor, 119, 133, 135, 158-159
Carmichael, Stokely, 2
Castro, Fidel, 518
Caton-Thomas, Gertrude, 148, 282, 284, 286
Champollion, Jean F., 6, 18, 256-257, 260-261
Churchward, Albert, 17, 72, 74, 454, 554
Clarke, John Henrike, 226
Cleopatra VIII, Queen, xx, 111-112, 496, 511
Clifford, Hugh, Sir, 59-60
Columbus, Christopher, 546, 579, 623
Constantine, Emperor, 368, 450

D

da Gama, Vasco, 280, 482
D'Anville, Jean Baptiste Bourguignon, xix, 214-215
Davidson, Basil, 173, 228-231
Darwin, Charles, Sir, 39-40, 48-49, 74-78
deGraft-Johnson, J. C., 97, 99, 100
Demetrius, 404, 647
Democritus, 390, 404
Denon, Baron Viviant, 7-8, 194-195
Dias, Bartolome, 61, 280, 482

NAME INDEX

Diogenes, 385, 397, 403-404
Djoser, Pharoah, 265, 271, 317, 475, 477
Douglass, Frederick, 520
DuBois, William E. B., 247-248, 473

E

Elissar, Princess (Dido), 523
Eusebius, 207, 271, 493, 650
Eve, xviii, 95, 189, 266, 578, 580
Ezekiel, 146

F

Fabius, 533-534
Felicita, 89, 160, 563
Flaccus, Seutinus, 31, 492, 496
Flaminius, Consul, 533

G

Ganges, General, 393
Garvey, Marcus, 462, 597, 613
George III, King, xxi-xxii
George IV, King, 186
Ghana, King, 176
Ghandi, Mohandas K., 212
Goringe, Henry H., 506, 510, 513, 520
Guevera, Che, 462

H

Hadra, 111
Hager, King, 341
Ham, 70, 95, 187, 202, 208, 265, 412, 467, 593, 598
Hamilton, Alexander, 520
Hansberry, Leo, 473
Harrison, Hubert H., 3, 473
Hatchett, John F., 244-247
Hatshep-sat, Queen, 154-155, 237, 478-479, 512-513, 554-555
Heracleitus, 383, 390, 397
Herodotus, 67(fn), 106, 155-157, 204, 229, 238, 255, 259, 270, 273, 277-279, 311, 340, 345, 350, 377, 390, 402-404, 447, 452, 484-485, 488-491, 615, 637
Higgins, Godfrey, Sir, 184-186, 359, 361-362, 578-579
Hippocrates, 271(fn), 315, 345, 377, 478
Hitler, Adolf, 104, 209, 222, 435, 438
Hodgkin, Thomas, 58-59, 85
Homer, 241

I

Imhotep, 271, 315, 317, 441, 475, 477, 478
Innis, Roy, 2
Isis, 126, 356, 361, 392, 420(fn), 575
Ismael, Khedive, 505, 508

J

James, George G. M., 387, 449, 464-465, 473, 581
Jeffreys, M. D. W., 61-64, 66, 74, 76-77, 79-82, 103, 156, 231, 262, 382, 486-487, 551
Jesus, xviii, 126, 133, 159, 162-165, 220, 359, 370, 383-384, 426, 496, 512, 563, 574-575, 578
Jones, Leroi (Immamu Baraka), 2
Joseph (Father of Jesus), 573-574, 652
Josephus, Favius, 107, 271-272
Junod, Henri, 144
Justinian, Emperor, 400, 425-426

K

Kamose, Pharoah, 345
Kashta, Pharoah, 240, 479
Khafra, Pharoah, 265, 271, 475
Khuru, Pharoah, 265
King, Martin Luther, Jr., 470

L

Lane-Poole, Stanley, 149-151
Las Casas, Bartholome de, Bishop,

NAME INDEX

91, 143, 623, 667
Leakey, Louis, 42-49, 50, 52
Leakey, Mary, 42-49, 50, 52
Leo X, Pope, 607
Leopold II, King, 26, 127, 169, 435, 667, 670
Lincoln, Abraham, 624
Lincoln, C. Eric, 578
Lugard, Lord (Captain), 169, 210, 435

M

Mac Iver, D. Randall, 282, 285
Makeda, Queen (Queen of Sheba), 232, 235, 329
Malcolm X, 2, 588
Manetho (High Priest), 207, 264, 274, 392, 491, 492, 493
Marx, Karl, 360, 462, 518
Mary (Mother of Jesus), 573-574, 578
Maspero, Gaston, 7-9, 25, 29, 206, 276, 454, 551-552
Maternus, Julius, 130-131, 492
Melenik I, Emperor, 232-235, 329
Melle, King, 176
Menkaure, Pharoah, 265
Michaelangelo, 125-126, 166, 220, 646, 663
Michaux, Lewis H., 3, 589
Miriam, 467
Mohammed, Elijah, 578, 660
Moore, Richard B., 5, 226, 581
Moses, 130, 190, 238, 266, 311, 357, 366-368, 372, 426, 439, 445-446, 562, 576, 606, 617, 631, 661
Mussolini, Benito, 169, 435

N

Namphamo, 136, 160, 563
Nascio, Scipio General, 538-541
Nasser, Gamal Abdul, 83, 598
Neb-Maat-Ra, xxii
Necho II, Pharoah, 481, 524
Nectanebus I, 313, 341-342, 483
Nehsira, Pharoah, 344
Nekhem, Pharoah, 269
Nero, Emperor, 223

Nino, Pietro Olonzo, 151
Nkrumah, Kwame, 59(fn), 546
Noah, 16, 70, 95

O

Ori, Pharoah, 479-480
Osiris, 126, 356, 358, 392, 400, 420(fn), 575
Osorkon I (Priest King), 334
Osorkon II, (Priest King), 334

P

Parmenides, 390, 397-398
Peaker, Charles, 3
Pedro I, Emperor, xxi
Pepi I, Pharoah, 355
Pepi II, Pharoah, 237, 263-264
Perpetua, 89, 160, 563
Phillips, Bessie, 3
Piankhi, Pharoah, 239, 292, 295-297, 334-335, 480
Plato, 377, 384-385, 391, 399, 405, 422-423, 561
Plutarch, 404
Plutinus, 375
Polybius, 495
Polycrates, 403
Powell, Adam Clayton, 2
Psemthek I, Pharoah, 337
Ptolemy I, Pharoah, xix, 110-111, 241, 257-258, 343, 405, 407, 439, 492, 496, 648
Ptolemy V, Pharoah, 257, 313
Ptolemy IX, Pharoah, 112, 313
Ptolemy X, Pharoah, 112, 313
Ptolemy XII, Pharoah, 112, 313
Ptolemy XIII, Pharoah, xxii, 112, 496, 511
Ptolemy XIV, Pharoah, 111, 313
Punk, Chief, 154
Pushkin, Alexander, xxii

R

Ra, Seqenen I, King, 311, 324
Ra, Seqenen II, King, 324
Ra, Seqenen III, King, 324-325
Ramses I, Pharoah, 311, 328

NAME INDEX

Ramses II, Pharoah, 238, 311, 315(fn), 329-330, 405
Ramses III, Pharoah, 20, 238, 311, 332
Rhodes, Cecil, 2(fn), 47(fn), 169, 182-183, 210, 435
Rockwell, George L., 127
Rogers, J. A., 33, 85, 473, 611, 612
Rustin, Bayard, 624

S

Salitis, Pharoah, 272, 345
Salvanius (Monk), 146
Schumburg, Olonzo, (Arthur), 226, 473
Selassie, Haile I, xix, xxi, 250 (il)
Seligman, C. G., 186-187, 189, 231, 251, 518, 601-602, 606, 664
Semerkhet, Pharoah, 475
Seneferu, Pharoah, 296
Seqenenra III, Prince, 108
Seti, Pharoah, 238, 311, 328-329
Severus, Septimus, 119, 133, 135, 152, 158-160
Shabaka, Pharoah, 239, 312, 336, 480
Shakespeare, William, 191
Shanka, Albert, 622
Shashanq, Pharoah, 333-334
Shem, 208, 235, 265, 599
Siculus, Diodorus, 278, 392-393
Simeon, 364
Simoes, Diogo, 175
Skemiophries, Pharoah, 321
Smith, Homer W., 576
Snow, C.P., 80
Soames, Jane, 136, 162-162
Socrates, 345, 377-379, 399, 405, 423, 561
Soloman, King, 179-180, 232, 333, 417, 436, 551
Sophia, Queen, xxi, xxii
Soter, See Ptolemy I
St. Augustine, 89, 136, 563
St. Cyprian, 89, 136, 563
Stanley, Henry M., 26, 127, 191-192, 196-197, 222, 249, 435
Stoddard, Lothrop, 116-119, 139-140, 142-144, 625
Syncellus, 207

T

Taharqa, 239, 480
Tanutemun, Pharoah, 240, 312
Tarikh, General, 126, 151-152, 538, 690
Tarzan, 86, 666
Tertullian, 89, 136-137, 563
Thales, 389, 397
Theodosius, Emperor, 425-426
Ti, 318
Toynbee, Arnold J., 642-645
Trajan, Pharoah, 18
Tsung, Mao Tu, 462
Tubman, Harriet, 520
Turner, Nat, 561
Tutankhamen, Pharoah, 263, 311, 327

U

Usertsen II, Pharoah, 102-103, 105, 312(fn)
Usertsen III, Pharoah, 105

V

Vanderbilt, W. H., 506
Vesey, Denmark, 561
Victoria, Queen, xxi, 44(fn), 210, 518, 667-668
Voerword, Heinrick, 127, 140

W

Washington, George, xxi, 120
Wiedner, Donald, 32, 71-74, 79-80, 85, 88, 114, 127
Wilberforce, Bishop, 39-40
Wilhelm, Kaiser, 438, 670
Wilkins, Roy, 622
Williams, Eric, 604
Woodson, Carter G., 473

X, Y, Z

Xeno, 398
Xenophanes, 432

Yassu, Lidy, xxi

Zeno, 390

SUBJECT INDEX

A

Africa
   birthplace of man, 31-56
   ethnography, 71 (map)
   names of, 679 (map)
   prehistoric, 72 (map), 73 (map)

African
   ancient, 31-56, 57 (il)
   Arab rule, 307
   art, 33 (il)
   European theocratic rule, 313
   fossil fields, 34-35 (maps)
   fossils, 32-50
   Great Lakes, 304
   historic quotations, 168-198
   legacy, 549-551
   origin of man, 31-56
   origin of Western religion, 567-583
   peoples, xxi-xxiv (il), 218 (il), 451
   prehistoric, 33 (il)
   studies, 145-146, 658-677
   texts, ancient 348-373

African-American nationalism, 584-597

Alkebu-lan
   ancient, 57-167
   Book of the Dead, 249
   definition, xviii, 5, 9, 569
   origin of word, 544
   origins of Egyptian language, 348
   prehistoric homo sapien, 31-56

Amratian period, 308

Ankh
   Christian cross based on, 437-438
   earliest use of, 294

Antiquity, Black man of, 549-566

Anti-semitism, 598-627

Arab-African rule, 307

Australopithecus
   classification, 36
   discovery of, 38, 48
   racism and, 33

B

Bible
   African origins, 178-180, 510-513
   anti-Negroism, 598-619

Birthplace of man, 31-56

Black
   anti-Semiticism, 598-627
   inferiority of, 144-146
   is beautiful, 567-583
   Jew, 584-597, 600-618
   man of antiquity, 549-566
   nationalism, 584-597
   studies, 628-655, 656-678

Book of the Dead
   Definition, 400
   Ethiopia, 249
   excerpts from, 355-373, 444
   first books of, 349
   origins of Greek philosophy, 385-386, 638-641
   origins of Judaica, 592
   origins of "western religions," 513, 568
   plagiarized by Holy Scribes, 592, 638-641
   valuable resource, 10

Boskop man, 41

British conquest, 307

Bubastite period, 307

Byzantine
   empire, 690 (map)
   epoch, 307

C

Caucasian, Semitic, Hamite syndrome, xi-xiv, 228-252

Calendar, first, 474

Carthage
   defeated in battles, 494-495
   definition, 523
   embassy in Rome, 492

SUBJECT INDEX

map, 688
rise and fall of, 522-548

Chattel slavery, 300

Christian
  Church beginnings, 628-655
  cross, xviii, 438
  Holy Bible, 178-180
  missionaries, 136-148
  rule, 313

Christianity
  Book of the Dead and, 513, 568
  Ethiopian origins of, 249
  European style, 26, 125
  first martyrs, 136

Cleopatra's needle
  Freemasonry rites and, 554
  history, 505-521

Council of Nice, 368

Creation story
  African origins of, 628-632
  original teachings on, 348-373

D, E

Dynasties, 304-347

Egypt
  archaeology, 684 (map)
  Hyksos invasion, 310, 349, 687 (map)
  Kimit, 253-291, 304-345
  lower, 267-269
  United Arab Republic, 307
  upper, 267-269
  world trade, 685 (map)

Egyptian
  ankh, 294, 437
  dynasties, 304-347
  empire, 686 (map)
  hieroglyph, 348, 355 (il)
  history (ancient), 474-475
  history (chronology), 306-313 (charts)
  history (predynastic), 263-264, 269
  language, 348
  literature, 293-298
  monarchs, 308-313
  original teachings, 348-371
  rule over Kush and Nubia, 499-504

Egyptians, indigenous, 453-473

Egyptology, 348-374

Ethiopia
  map, 686
  origins of Christianity, 249
  predynastic and dynastic periods, 304-345

Ethiopian
  empire, 689 (map)
  Ocean, 681 (map)
  Saite period, 307

European history, father of 484-491

F

Family of man, 12

Fire God, 481

Fire, philosophy of, 419-421

Florisbad, 37

Fossil
  field sites, 34-35
  man, 21, 38-50

Fossils, 32-50

Freemasonry
  African mysteries system, 417, 436-437, 443-447
  African origins of, 508-510
  forbids acceptance of ex-slaves, 514
  rites, 554-555
  secrets of, 449

G

Garden of Eden
  African inhabitants, 33

SUBJECT INDEX

date of, 266
location, 1, 23, 354, 515
map, ix
predated by African civilization, xviii
prehistoric ancestors, 48

Gebel Barka, ruins of, 295

Gerzean period, 308

Ghana
ancient kingdom of, xiii
map, 691
political freedom, 546-547

Ghizeh, See Sphinx of Ghizeh

Grand Lodge at Luxor, 475, 576-577, 648

Great Lakes, African, 304

Greek
"blood baths," 111-113
dynasty, 313, 343
history, 481-484
philosophy, African origins, vii, xvii, 375-410, 411-473
slavery, viii

H

Haribus (Hebrews or Jews)
African mysteries system, 443-447
Black Jew, 584-597, 606-618
chosen people, ix, 451-452
co-option of sacred scripture, 365-368
definition, 411
history, 474, 481
map, 687

Heathen, 450

Hebrew, See Haribus

Helivan period, 308

Hieroglyphics
deciphering, 260
definition, 304
illustration, 355
Nubians, 102
obelisk, 554-555
origins, 348
secrets, 255
stele, 292-293

Hippocratic Oath, 316

Historians, racism, 228-252

History, father of European, 484-491

Homo Capenses, 41

Homo Neanderthalensis, 36

Homo sapiens, prehistoric, 31-56

Horus
African origins, 444-445
Egyptian obelisks, 520-521
Sphinx of Ghizeh, 474

Hyksos
definition, 272
Egyptian occupation, 273-275
invasion into Africa, 310, 349, 687 (map)

I, J

Islam
African origins, xviii
conversions of Christians, 152
impact on Blacks, 567-577

Judaism, See Haribus

Judeo Christian religion
African origins, xviii
bias, 302

K

Khart Haddas, See Carthage

Kimit

SUBJECT INDEX

captured by Alexander the Great, 406
Egyptologists, 6
history, 253-291, 474-498
illustration, 317
language, 348
Napata, 293
people, 453-473
predynastic and dynastic periods, 304-345

Kiswahili, xvi, 304

Kush, See Ethiopia

L

Libraries
Grand Lodge at Luxor, 648
looting by Alexander, 406-407, 493
Maneptheion, 406
renaming of, 493
sacking by Aristotle, 423

Libya, 687 (map)

Libyan dynasty, 312

Lodges
Delfi, 482
description, 425
Grand Lodge at Luxor, 475, 576-577, 648
initiations, 509-510
Prince Hall Masons, 506
racism, 506-508, 514
Subordinate, 476-477

Luxor, See Grand Lodge at Luxor

M

Mali, 691 (map)

Memphites, 312

Mendesian period
late epoch, 307
Persian invaders, 341
reconstruction of temples, 338, 307, 338, 341

Meneptheion, 406

Meroe (Sudan)
high culture, 494
history, 504
location, 558-559

Middle Kingdom
dates, 306
monarchs, 310

Missing link, 37

Monarchs, Egyptian, 308-313

Moors
empire (map), 690
history, 150-152
Negroes, xiv, 481
originators of African high culture, 401-402
types, 546

N

Napata, 293, 480
Name, value of, 1-30
Neanderthal, 38, 41
Negro, definition, 4-30
Negroland, 680 (map)

Negrophobia
Historians and, 246-247, 555-556
in academia, 153
Negro as less than human, 116-117
racism and religion, 142

Neolithic period
dates, 306
chronology, 474

New Kingdom
dates, 306
monarchs, 311

Niah, 37

Niceon, 368

Nile River
Atbara River, 409
Blue Nile, 18, 409

SUBJECT INDEX

description, 409
"discoveries of," 199-223
Hymn of, 18
maps, 215-217, 683
quest, x, 199-223
White Nile, 18, 409

Nile Valleys
chronology, 474-475
civilization, 549-550
early man, 51
map, ix, 682
people, 199-227

Nubia
and Negro, 555-558
chronology, 480
history and culture, 292-303
illustration, 263

Numidians
battles with Carthage, 543
description, 541

O

Old Kingdom
dates, 306
monarchs, 309

Opposites, principles of
illustration, 384
origins, 383

Ottoman Turks, 307

P

Palaentology
focus on Africa, 41
history, 37-55

Paleolithic periods
chronology, 474
dates, 306
indigenous African during, 267
monarchs, 308

Papyrus of Ani
Egyptian origins, 349
excerpts, 355-373
Hymn of the Nile, 18-21

origins of Judeo-Christian
jurisprudence, 638-641
plagiarized by Holy Scribes, 592
writers of, 10

Peloponnesian wars, 429

Persian period
dates, 307
monarchs, 313
reconstruction of temples, 337-338

Phoenicians
expedition to Carthage, 523
trade route map, 685

Pithecanthropus, 36

Post dynasties
description, 343-344
monarchs, 313-314

Post-Socratic philosophers, 399-410

Predynastic period
dates, 306-308
history, 474

Prehistoric epoch
dates, 306
history, 31-56, 474

Pre-Socratic philosophers, 397-398

Ptolemic period
dates, 307
description, 343
monarchs, 313

Pyramid
age, 19, 306, 474
builders, 265, 309
illustration, 317
major, 8
seven step, 441

Pythagorean theorum, origins, 443

Q, R

Quotations, about Africans, 168-198

Racism
and name giving, 4-30
and religion, ix, 142-153

SUBJECT INDEX

Biblical anti-Negroism, 598-619
Caucasian, Semetic, Hamite
   syndrome, xi-xiv, 228-252
chosen people myth, ix, 451-452
heathen, 450
inferiority of Blacks, 144-146

Religions
   African origins of, 567-583
   and racism, 142-153
   anti-Negroism, 598-619
   in early Africa, 136-167
   mysteries system, 443
   new religion, 656-678
   non-Western type, 450
   Western, 567-583

Religious
   first principle, 480-481
   first writings, 348-378
   symbols, 437-449, 554-555
   teachings, 567-583

Roman
   colonialism, 307, 496
   empire, 690 (map)
   period, 313, 525-544

Rosetta Stone
   Egyptian origins, 6
   history, 256-257

Ruins of Gebel Barka, 295

S

Saite period, 313

Slave trade
   effects of, 444
   introduction of, 171-173

Slavery
   and abolition, 560-561
   beginnings of, 300
   chattel, 300
   effect on image of African-
     American, vii

   philosophical origins of, viii

Solar calendar
   history, 474
   introduction of, 306

Songhay empire, 691 (map)

Sphinx of Ghizeh
   durability of, 9
   French destruction to, 7-8
   Horus, 474
   illustrations, 195

Stele (obelisk)
   Cleopatra's needle, 505-521, 554
   history, 293-299
   Gebel Barka, 480

Sun God, 481

Swastica, 438

Swaziland, 56 (il)

Symbols, 437-449

T

Tanite period
   dates, 306
   monarch, 312

Tasian period
   dates, 306, 308
   history, 474

Temple of Amen-Ra, 293

Ten Commandments
   African origins of, 364, 383
   Negative Confessions, 510-513, 562

Thebian period
   dates, 306
   monarch, 312

Triangle, 437-447

V, W, Z

Venus (sculpture), 474

Western
   religions, 567-583
   world (beginnings of), 549-550

Zimbabnoids, 37

Zinjanthropus Boisie
   claimed as Caucasian, 21, 515
   description, 10
   discovery, 43
   illustration, 49-50

Zodiac, 443